Praise for *The Fall of the Roman Empire*

"Like a late Roman emperor, Heather is determined to impose order on a fabric that is always threatening to fragment and collapse into confusion; unlike most late Roman emperors, he succeeds triumphantly." —*The Times of London*

"A rich and dramatic synthesis of the latest research on Gibbon's old story. . . . The drama of Mr. Heather's book lies not just in the world-changing story he has to tell, but in his behind-the-scenes view of how historians work. Like a master detective, Mr. Heather employs the most various techniques—everything from pollen sampling to archaeology to literary criticism—to wring the truth from the reticent past. . . . What Mr. Heather offers is not easy analogies but a realization of the complex strangeness of the past—the achievement of a great historian." —Adam Kirsch, *New York Sun*

"Gibbon's 'awful revolution'—the decline and fall of the Roman Empire in the West—still casts a pall. Yet, as Peter Heather's brilliant mixture of rapid flowing narrative and deeply thought analysis fully brings out, it still exerts a pull too. 'Lepcisgate,' Alaric's Goths, and Attila's Huns are all thrown into Heather's melting pot along with Roman imperial aims and mismanagement. The outcome is a conclusion Heather finds pleasing—and Gibbon would not have despised—that Roman imperialism was ultimately responsible for its own demise." —Paul Cartledge, University of Cambridge

"To a period that has often appeared as impenetrable as it is momentous, Peter Heather brings a rare combination of scholarship and flair for narrative. With this book, a powerful searchlight has been shone upon the shadow-dimmed end of Rome's western empire." —Tom Holland, author of *Rubicon: The Last Years of the Roman Republic*

"Deftly covering the necessary economic and political realities of decline and fall, Heather also presents the stories and the characters of this tumultuous epoch, in a colorful and enthralling narrative." —*The Independent*

The Fall of the Roman Empire

A New History of Rome and the Barbarians

PETER HEATHER

OXFORD
UNIVERSITY PRESS

OXFORD
UNIVERSITY PRESS

Oxford University Press, Inc., publishes works that further
Oxford University's objective of excellence
in research, scholarship, and education.

Oxford New York
Auckland Cape Town Dar es Salaam Hong Kong Karachi
Kuala Lumpur Madrid Melbourne Mexico City Nairobi
New Delhi Shanghai Taipei Toronto

With offices in
Argentina Austria Brazil Chile Czech Republic France Greece
Guatemala Hungary Italy Japan Poland Portugal Singapore
South Korea Switzerland Thailand Turkey Ukraine Vietnam

Published by Oxford University Press, Inc., 2006
198 Madison Avenue, New York, New York 10016
www.oup.com

First issued as an Oxford University Press paperback, 2007
ISBN 978-0-19-532541-6

The Library of Congress has cataloged the hardcover edition as follows:
Heather, P. J. (Peter J.)
The fall of the Roman Empire : a new history of Rome and the barbarians / Peter Heather.
p. cm.
Includes bibliographical references and index.
ISBN-13: 978-0-19-515954-7
1. Rome—History—Empire, 284–476.
2. Rome—History—Germanic Invasions, 3rd–6th centuries.
I. Title.

DG311.H43 2005
937'.09—dc22

2005047345

Photographic Acknowledgments
AKG Images: 7, 15, 23, 24, 26, 27; Ancient Art & Architecture Collection: 1, 3, 5, 6, 8, 11,
17, 18, 20, 21, 22, 25; The Art Archive: 2, 10 top; Bridgeman Art Library: 4, 10 left and right,
13, 14, 19; Corbis: 16 (Robert Estall); Scala Archives: 9.

22 23
Printed in the United States of America
on acid-free paper

CONTENTS

Maps

Acknowledgements

The contract for this project was signed only about four years ago, but there is a very real sense in which I have been writing this book for much of the nearly twenty-five years I have been engaged in research on matters Roman and barbarian. In that sense, there really are too many people for me to thank and acknowledge from everyone who has taught me, especially my DPhil supervisors James Howard-Johnston and John Matthews, to all the friends and colleagues from whom I have learned so much, both in London and Oxford, to all the long-suffering students who have put up so cheerfully both with different versions of the various arguments on which this book rests and my delight in really dreadful puns. And although I would lay intellectual claim to some of the key observations and connections which knit this book together, the narrative also reflects my understanding of the general (and sometimes more particular) significance of the entire historical tradition in which I work. My debt to the scholarship and intellect of others is enormous and I would like to make this point explicit here, as the constraints of writing this book for a more general audience mean that the notes do not always fully acknowledge my intellectual debts. I am strongly aware, however, that they exist, and would like in particular to thank all the colleagues and friends who proved such stimulating company in the first half of the 1990s, when I was lucky enough to learn a huge amount from participating in the European Science Foundation's Transformation of the Roman World project. More specifically, I would like to thank Jason Cooper, my editor at Macmillan, whose wise advice has sustained me throughout, Sue Phillpott, my copy-editor, who put in a huge amount of work on my behalf, and all the friends who have listened to, read, and offered advice on all or part of what follows. Not least, I owe more than I can begin to calculate to my family who always cheer me up when I'm too miserable to carry on writing, and to the dog and cats – the need to pay their food bills keeps me at my desk when I would long since have been out enjoying myself.

INTRODUCTION

THE ROMAN EMPIRE was the largest state western Eurasia has ever known. For over four hundred years it stretched from Hadrian's Wall to the River Euphrates, transforming the lives of all the inhabitants within its frontiers and dominating landscapes and peoples for hundreds of kilometres beyond. Interconnected fortress systems, strategic road networks and professional, highly trained armies both symbolized and ensured this domination, and Roman forces were not averse to massacring any neighbour who stepped out of line. The opening scenes of the 2000 blockbuster *Gladiator* are based on the victories of Marcus Aurelius over the Marcomanni, a Germanic tribe of south-central Europe, in the third quarter of the second century. Two hundred years later, the Romans were still at it. In 357, 12,000 of the emperor Julian's Romans routed an army of 30,000 Alamanni at the battle of Strasbourg.

But within a generation, the Roman order was shaken to its core and Roman armies, as one contemporary put it, 'vanished like shadows'. In 376, a large band of Gothic refugees arrived at the Empire's Danube frontier, asking for asylum. In a complete break with established Roman policy, they were allowed in, unsubdued. They revolted, and within two years had defeated and killed the emperor Valens – the one who had received them – along with two-thirds of his army, at the battle of Hadrianople. On 4 September 476, one hundred years after the Goths crossed the Danube, the last Roman emperor in the west, Romulus Augustulus, was deposed, and it was the descendants of those Gothic refugees who provided the military core of one of the main successor states to the Empire: the Visigothic kingdom. This kingdom of south-western France and Spain was only one of several, all based on the military power of immigrant outsiders, that emerges from the ruins of Roman Europe. The fall of Rome, and with it the western half of the Empire, constitutes one of the formative revolutions of European history, and has traditionally been seen as heralding the end of the ancient world and the start of the Middle

Ages. Like the Renaissance, the Reformation and the Industrial Revolution, it changed the world for ever.

Starting with Gibbon's multivolume epic published during 1776–88, there have been the odd hundred or two studies devoted to the subject, or to particular aspects of it, with as yet no sign of let-up. In the 1990s, the European Science Foundation funded a five-year project to investigate 'The Transformation of the Roman World', and its volumes continue to appear. As has always been the case, historians fall a long way short of general agreement, either on the big issues or – where you might more expect it – on matters of detail. Argument has always focused on what it was, exactly, that caused Rome to fall. Since they provided the military muscle behind the new kingdoms, armed outsiders – 'barbarians' – obviously had something to do with it. But historians both before and after Gibbon have felt that a power as great as Rome could not have been brought low by illiterates whose culture – political, social, economic, artistic – did not even begin to rival the sometimes astonishingly precocious levels of the Roman world. The Romans had central heating, a form of banking based on capitalist principles, weapons factories, even spin-doctors, whereas the barbarians were simple agriculturalists with a penchant for decorative safety-pins.[1] So while the barbarians had something to do with it, they couldn't really have caused the fall of the Empire. Surely the barbarians merely took advantage of more fundamental problems rife within the Roman world.

But did they? This book will reopen one of history's greatest mysteries: the strange death of Roman Europe.

My justifications for doing so are both general and specific. Generally, the period from about AD 300–600, covering the fall of the western Empire and the creation of its early medieval successor kingdoms, has been the subject of some of the most innovative historical scholarship of the last forty years. Traditionally, the era was a black hole, a no man's land between ancient and medieval history, studied properly in neither. Since the 1960s, huge leaps have been made in our understanding of the many facets of this period, rechristened 'late antiquity'. Many of these discoveries are now common knowledge among specialists, but have yet to feed through to the general public, whose expectations (judging, at least, by the prejudices with which some of my students still come to the subject) are still conditioned by older traditions stretching back to Gibbon. In the last forty years, teachers and students have for the first time made the acquaintance of a later Roman Empire that was not on the brink of social, economic and moral collapse, and a world beyond its frontiers that was not characterized by simple, unchanging barbarism. Two generations of scholarship since the Second World War have revolutionized our understanding both of the Roman Empire and of the wider world that the Romans knew as *barbaricum*, 'the land of the barbarians'. This book draws heavily upon that scholarship.

MORE SPECIFICALLY, THE enthusiastic 'discovery' of late antiquity occurred in an intellectual environment in which historians of all periods were realizing that there was much more to history than the economics, high politics, war and diplomacy that had been its traditional stock-in-trade. Late antiquity, with its wealth of written and archaeological sources, generated not least by the highly sophisticated literary culture typical of educated Roman elites, has proved a fruitful area for research in many disciplines: gender and cultural history, and the history of popular belief, for instance. It has also provided a rich vein for study in tune with recent trends in historical writing which have sought to challenge the unspoken prejudices which inform the 'great narratives' of traditional history. The image of the 'civilized' but ever declining Romans implacably at war with 'barbarian' outsiders is a prime example of one such narrative at work. Recent thinking has rightly tried to escape the clutches of this tradition, pinpointing the many instances that our sources provide of barbarian–Roman cooperation and nonviolent interaction. An emphasis on reading individual texts with a view to understanding the ideological visions of the world that underlie them has also had a dramatic impact. This type of interpretation requires historians to treat ancient authors, not as sources of fact, but rather like second-hand-car salesmen whom they would do well to approach with a healthy caution.

The intellectual impact of these trends on the study of late antiquity has been electric, but has tended towards fragmentation, leading scholars away from synthesis and into detailed studies of particular aspects. They have also tended to turn away from attempts to reconstruct a narrative of what actually happened, to concentrate on how individuals and sources perceived and represented what happened. In the last decade or so pioneering monographs have appeared on many relevant topics and on individual authors, but there has been no attempt at a general overview of Roman collapse.[2] I have no doubt that this kind of more intense study of the constituent parts of the subject was, and remains, absolutely necessary.[3] But detailed reinterpretations of particular aspects of a period can have implications for the understanding of the whole, and it is time, in my view, to start putting the much-better-understood fragments back together and focusing on what they tell us about the fall of Rome itself.[4] Readers will judge for themselves whether this approach is well founded.

I will also be arguing that it is vitally important not to lose sight of narrative in the midst of the current emphasis on ideology and perception, much of it inspired by recent trends in literary criticism. Some scholars have even been led to doubt whether it is possible, given the nature of our sources, to get past these sources' representations of reality to 'actual events'. Sometimes, it quite clearly isn't. I would argue, however, that the kinds of intellectual process suitable for literary criticism are not always adequate for historical studies. The tools of literary analysis are hugely valuable when applied to individual sources, but a legal analogy, it seems to me, is more appropriate to the overall enterprise of history. All of our sources are witnesses, many trying to advocate, for their own reasons, a particular view of events, but what they are describing are not, or not all the time, constructs of their authors' imaginations, in the way that literary texts are. History, like the legal system, does have measurably burgled property and actual dead bodies to deal with, even if an understanding of these phenomena has to be built from ideologically constructed sources. The Roman Empire encompassed many ideologies, as will emerge, and promoted a highly particular way of looking at the world. But it also employed bureaucracies, passed laws, collected taxes and trained armies. And in the course of the fifth century, the western half of the Roman Empire, along with all the structures and procedures it had maintained over centuries, ceased to exist, leaving behind the corpse that lies at the heart of this book.

What follows is an attempt, through narrative reconstruction, to understand this huge revolution in European history in a way that does justice to the wealth of sophisticated scholarship generated in recent years. My expertise is as much late Roman as it is 'barbarian'. My teaching and specialist publications have dealt pretty much equally with both sides of the frontier, and focus on the later fourth and fifth centuries. And while I draw on other people's work, the particular

synthesis that characterizes this book is of course my own, as are some
of the key ideas and observations upon which it is based.

BEYOND RECONSTRUCTING as best I can the history of Rome's fall, and
presenting the particular interpretation of it that I find convincing, I
have one further aim for this book. Understanding the past is always
a detective story. To get to grips with what was actually going on, the
reader is invited to become a member of the jury – to extend the legal
analogy – to become involved in the process of evaluating and
synthesizing the different kinds of evidence that will be presented. The
structure of the book encourages this approach. It is not simply a
narrative of the collapse of the western Empire in the fifth century,
but also an analytical exploration. Part One, therefore, is devoted to
building up a picture of the state of the Empire and its European
neighbours in the later fourth century. Without thus setting the scene,
a real understanding of the subsequent collapse would be impossible.
Analysis is also part and parcel of the more narrative chapters of Parts
Two and Three; and throughout the book I have tried to involve the
reader fully in the detective work, not simply casting him or her as
the recipient of oracular answers. In the same spirit, where there are
loose ends, where the trail disappears, as occasionally happens, I do
not attempt to disguise it. One of the main reasons I have chosen to
work on the middle years of the first millennium – apart from a
fascination for ancient remains engendered in me by my mother
during many childhood visits to Roman villas, baths and fortresses – is
the type of intellectual challenge it poses. I love puzzles, and so much
of the evidence is either missing, or comes enciphered in the com-
licated codes of Roman literary genres (one of the reasons why
postmodernist lines of critique are so helpful in this field), that very
little is ever straightforward. For some, this is simply annoying and
detracts from what would otherwise be a very interesting period. For
others, myself included, it is part of the thrill, and I can always tell
from their instinctive response to shortage of evidence whether or not
my students belong among nature's first-millennialists.

While telling the story – and it *is* quite a story – I also want to
introduce the reader to the processes involved in its generation,
therefore, and to open up the main bodies of available evidence. With
this end firmly in mind, I tell as much of the story as possible, directly
and indirectly, in the words of eyewitnesses, the individuals caught up

in the maelstrom of events that would transform European history for ever. There are many more of these, and of a wider variety, than you might expect. Decoded, their writings make the collapse of the western Empire one of the most vividly documented eras in ancient history.

PART ONE

PAX ROMANA

1

ROMANS

Early winter in 54 bc: a typically wet, grey November day in eastern Belgium. In a Roman military camp on the site of modern-day Tongres, close to where the borders of Belgium, Holland and Germany now meet, a council of war was under way. One full legion – ten cohorts notionally of 500 men apiece – and five additional cohorts had been brigaded together in winter quarters here, just to the west of the Rhine in the territory of a small Germanic-speaking tribe called the Eburones. At the end of each campaigning season, Julius Caesar's standard practice was to disperse his legions to fortified encampments. The legionaries constructed these themselves, according to a standard pattern: ditch, mound, rampart and defensive towers on the outside, barrack blocks within. The length of the walls was dictated by an ancient formula: two hundred times the square root of the number of cohorts to be accommodated. Subdued tribes in the immediate neighbourhood were responsible for supplying the troops through the winter, until the grass grew again to support the pack animals, and campaigning could begin anew.

At first, all had gone well. The Roman force was led to its encampment by the two kings of the Eburones, Ambiorix and the rather older Catuvoleus. The fort was built on time, and the Eburones brought in the first food supplies. But about three weeks later, things started to go wrong. Encouraged by stirrings of revolt elsewhere, and roused by Indutiomarus, leader of the much more numerous Treveri, a neighbouring tribe from the Moselle valley, some Eburones ambushed and wiped out a small Roman foraging party. They then rushed the Roman ramparts, but quickly withdrew under a hail of missiles. The atmosphere in the Roman camp was suddenly uneasy, and it quickly intensified. Ambiorix and Catuvoleus set up a parley, both claiming that a bunch of hotheads was responsible for the attack, while Ambiorix in particular was keen to portray himself as a committed Roman ally. He said that a major revolt was certainly in the offing, with huge numbers of hired Germani about to descend on Gaul from east of the Rhine. It was not for him to tell the Roman commanders what to do, he pointed out, but if they wanted to concentrate their forces against the attack, he would guarantee the brigade a safe passage to either of two other legionary encampments situated about fifty miles away, one to the south-east, the other to the south-west.

Matters could not have gone better had Ambiorix written the script himself. The Roman force was commanded by a pair of legates, Quintus Titurius Sabinus and Lucius Aurunculeius Cotta. Their council of war was long and rancorous. Cotta and some of his senior subordinates were determined to stay put. They had food, and the camp was fully entrenched; Caesar would send reinforcements as soon as he heard of the revolt – and Gaul was famous for the speed with which rumour could travel. Sabinus, however, argued that the natives would not have dared to revolt if Caesar had not already left for Italy. Goodness only knew when news of the revolt would reach him, and the legions, dispersed as they were in their separate winter quarters, faced the prospect of being wiped out piecemeal. For Sabinus, therefore, the offer of safe passage had to be accepted. There was no time to lose. He was also influenced by the fact that the fort contained the least experienced of Caesar's legions, enrolled only the previous spring, and used as baggage guards in the major battles of the last campaigning season. The council continued, with tempers frayed and voices raised, Sabinus deliberately letting on to the soldiers that a plan that would lead them quickly to safety was being ignored. Around midnight, Cotta gave way. The most important thing for morale was to maintain a united front among the officers. Hurriedly the legionaries prepared to leave, and at dawn they were off. Believing that Ambiorix had spoken as a friend, the Roman force left in marching, not battle, order, an extended column carrying most of its heavy baggage.

Two miles outside the camp, the route passed through thick woods and down into a deep valley. Before the advance guard had climbed up the other side, and while the bulk of the column was strung out along the valley floor, the trap was sprung. Eburones appear above them on either side and deluge the Romans with missiles. The fighting is drawn out, but the victory of the Eburones total. By dawn the next day, only a few Roman stragglers who went to ground in the chaos are left alive. The vast majority of the seven thousand-plus men who built their camp just weeks before are dead. A brutal sequence of events, and startling in their unexpectedness. Not the fate you'd expect to be meted out to any of the army of Julius Caesar, famous for that most grandiose of boasts: *veni vidi vici* – 'I came, I saw, I conquered.'

The action, however, bears closer inspection. While this particular Roman force was overwhelmed, the details of the engagement graphically demonstrate the astonishing fighting capacities of the legionary soldier on which the Roman Empire itself was built. Sabinus lost his head as the ambush began: not surprising in a commander who must have realized immediately that he'd led his men into a death-trap. Cotta fared better. He'd smelt a rat all along and taken what precautions he could. When the missiles started flying, he and his senior centurions quickly pulled the drawn-out column into a square, abandoning the baggage. Now orders could be given and the cohorts manoeuvred as a unit, even though the tactical position was entirely against them. Ambiorix had the height advantage and sufficient control of his followers to use it. The Eburones avoided hand-to-hand fighting for several hours, simply pouring down missiles from above: spears, arrows, sling bullets. The Roman casualties rapidly mounted; every time a cohort made an ordered sortie to left or right in an attempt to get to grips with their tormentors, they exposed themselves to raking fire from the rear. Trapped, their strength ebbing away, the Roman force held on for an extraordinary eight hours. At this point Sabinus tried to parley with Ambiorix, but Romans did not discuss terms with an armed enemy, growled Cotta, despite having been hit full in the face by a sling bullet. Sabinus was struck down while still talking, and this was the signal for the Eburones to charge down for the kill. Many legionaries fought and died with Cotta in the valley bottom, but some still kept formation and made their way back to the camp two miles away. There the survivors kept the Eburones out until nightfall, and then, to a man, committed suicide rather than fall into the hands of the enemy. If the baggage guard would fight all day with no hope of success and commit mass suicide rather than surrender, Rome's enemies were going to be in serious trouble.[1]

The Rise of Imperial Rome

IF THE ROOTS OF Roman imperial power lay firmly in the military might of its legions, the cornerstone of their astonishing fighting spirit can be attributed to their training. As with all elite military formations – ancient and modern – discipline was ferocious. With no courts of human rights to worry about, instructors were at liberty to beat the disobedient – to death if necessary. And if a whole cohort disobeyed orders, the punishment was decimation: every tenth man flogged to death in front of his comrades. But you can never base morale on fear exclusively, and group cohesion was also generated by more positive methods. Recruits trained together, fought together and played together in groups of eight: a *contubernium* (literally, a group sharing a tent). And they were taken young: all armies prefer young men with plenty of testosterone. Legionaries were also denied regular sexual contact: wives and children might make them think twice about the risks of battle. Basic training was gruelling. You had to learn to march 36 kilometres in five hours, weighed down with 25 kilos or more of armour and equipment. All the time you were being told how special you were, how special your friends were, what an elite force you belonged to. Just like the Marines, but much nastier.

The result of all this was groups of super-fit young men, partly brutalized and therefore brutal themselves, closely bonded with one another though denied other strong emotional ties, and taking a triumphant pride in the unit to which they belonged. This was symbolized in the religious oaths sworn to the unit standards, the legendary eagles. On successful graduation, the legionary vowed on his life and honour to follow the eagles and never desert them, even in death. Such was the determination not to let the standards fall into enemy hands that one of Cotta's standard bearers, Lucius Petrosidius, hurled his eagle over the rampart at Tongres as he himself was struck down, rather than let it be captured. The honour of the unit, and the bond with fellow soldiers, became the most important element in a legionary's life, sustaining a fighting spirit and willingness to obey orders which few opponents could match.

To this psychological and physical conditioning, Roman training added first-rate practical skills. Roman legionaries were well armed by the standards of the day, but possessed no secret weapons. Much of their equipment was copied from their neighbours: the legionary's distinctive and massive shield – the *scutum* – for instance, from the Celts. But they were carefully trained to make the best use of it. Individually, they were taught to despise wild swinging blows with the sword. These were to be parried with the shield, and the legionary's characteristic short sword – the *gladius* – brought up in a short stabbing motion into the side of an opponent exposed by his own swing. Legionaries were also equipped with defensive armour, and this, plus the weapons training, gave them a huge advantage in hand-to-hand combat.

Throughout Caesar's wars in Gaul, therefore, his troops were able to defeat much larger opposition forces; Ambiorix was well advised to keep his Eburones from rushing down from the heights until eight hours' worth of missiles had greatly reduced Roman numbers. On a larger scale, legions were trained to manoeuvre as units, receiving their orders by bugle call and maintaining their cohesion even in the chaos of battle. As a result, any Roman commander worth his salt could deliver maximum force when opportunity presented itself, and retreat in good order if necessary. Disciplined, coherent forces have a massive advantage over even very large numbers of ferocious opponents acting as individuals, and it was only the ultimate tactical disadvantage of being trapped in a valley that prevented Cotta from bringing his cohorts to bear with telling effect. On more even ground, on another occasion, just 300 legionaries who had been cut off were able to defend themselves for hours against 6,000 opponents at the cost of only a few wounded.[2]

A Roman legion also had other skills. Learning to build, and build quickly, was a standard element of training: roads, fortified camps and siege engines were but a few of the tasks undertaken. On one occasion, Caesar put a pontoon bridge across the Rhine in just ten days, and quite small contingents of Roman troops regularly controlled large territories from their own defensive ramparts. Cotta's advice to stay put that November day might well have proved successful. Three years before, another Roman force, comprising just eight cohorts, had been sent to overwinter in an Alpine valley at the headwaters of the River Rhône above Lake Geneva, because Caesar was looking to secure the St Bernard Pass. Confronted with an enemy that massively outnumbered them, they used their fortifications and tactical nous to inflict such a defeat on their attackers that they were subsequently able to effect an unharassed withdrawal.

The legions' building skills could be just as effectively employed in offensive siege warfare – most famously in subduing Alesia, hill-fort and headquarters of the great Gallic leader Vercingetorix. Here, over a circuit of 14 miles, Caesar's legions dug three concentric sets of ditches facing inwards – one 20 feet wide and deep, the other two 15 feet – full of booby-traps of various lethal kinds, backed by the standard ramp and palisade 12 feet high, topped with battlements and studded with towers at 80-foot intervals. When a Gallic relief force came to raise the siege, a similar set of barricades was added facing outwards. As a result, the Romans were able to prevent many attempts by their more numerous opponents to break in or out, fighting always with tactical advantage, the fortifications giving them sufficient time to rush reserves to the threatened spots. At another siege, that of the seemingly impregnable Gallic fort at Uxellodunum, Caesar used a ten-storey tower on a massive ramp, together with underground mines, to deny the defenders access to the mountain spring which was their only source of water, and so compelled their surrender.

If the Roman legion in combat was a professional killing-machine, it was also much more. Its building capacity could turn immediate military victory into the long-term domination of territories and regions: a strategic weapon on which an empire could be built.[3]

Caesar's campaigns in Gaul belong to a relatively late phase in Rome's rise to imperial domination. It had started life as one city-state among many, struggling first for survival and then for local hegemony in central and southern Italy. The city's origins are shrouded in myth, as are the details of many of its early local wars. Something is known of these struggles from the late sixth century BC, however, and they continued periodically down to the early third century, when Rome's dominance over its home sphere was established by the capitulation of the Etruscans in 283, and the defeat of the Greek city-states of south-ern Italy in 275. As winner of its local qualifiers, Rome graduated to regional matches against Carthage, the other major power of the western Mediterranean. The first of the so-called Punic wars lasted from 264 to 241 BC, and ended with the Romans turning Sicily into their first province. It took two further wars, spanning 218–202 and 149–146, for Carthaginian power finally to be crushed, but victory left Rome unchallenged in the western Mediterranean, and added North Africa and Spain to its existing power-base. At the same time, Roman power also began to spread more widely. Macedonia was conquered in 167 BC and direct rule over Greece was established from the 140s. This presaged the assertion of Roman hegemony over all the rich hinterlands of the eastern Mediterranean. By about 100 BC, Cilicia, Phrygia, Lydia, Caria and many of the other provinces of Asia Minor were in Roman hands. Others quickly followed. The circle of Mediterranean domination was completed by Pompey's annexation of Seleucid Syria in 64 BC, and Octavian's of Egypt in 30 BC.

The Mediterranean and its coastlands were always the main focus of Rome's imperial ambitions, but to secure them, it soon proved necessary to move the legions north of the Alps into non-Mediterranean Europe. The assertion of Roman dominion over the Celts of northern Italy was followed in short order by the creation in the 120s BC of the province of Gallia Narbonensis, essentially Mediterranean France. This new territory was required to defend northern Italy, since mountain ranges – even high ones – do not by themselves a frontier make, as Hannibal had proved. In the late republican and early imperial periods, roughly the fifty years either side of the birth of Christ, the Empire also continued to grow because of the desire of individual leaders for self-glorification. By this date, conquest overseas had become a recognized route to power in Rome, so that conquests continued into areas that were neither so profitable, nor strategically vital. Thanks to Julius Caesar, all of Gaul fell under Roman sway between 58 and 50 BC. Further conquests followed under his nephew and adopted successor Octavian, better known as Augustus, the first of the Roman emperors. By 15 BC, the legionaries' hob-nailed sandals were moving into the Upper and Middle Danube regions – roughly modern Bavaria, Austria and Hungary. Some of these lands had long belonged to Roman client kings, but now they were turned into provinces and brought under direct control. By 9 BC all the territory as far as the River Danube had been annexed, and an arc of territory around the Alpine passes into Italy added to the Empire. For the next thirty years or so, its north European boundary moved back and forth towards the River Elbe, before the difficulty of conquering the forests of Germany led to the abandonment of ambitions east of the Rhine. In AD 43, under Claudius, the conquest of Britain was begun, and the old Thracian kingdom (the territory of modern Bulgaria and beyond) was formally incorporated into the Empire as a province some three years later. The northern frontiers finally came to rest on the lines of two great rivers – the Rhine and the Danube – and there they broadly remained for the rest of the Empire's history.[4]

The Roman military system and Rome's acquisitions were thus the product of centuries of warfare; military force alone, however, was not enough to build an empire. Throughout, it had also been combined

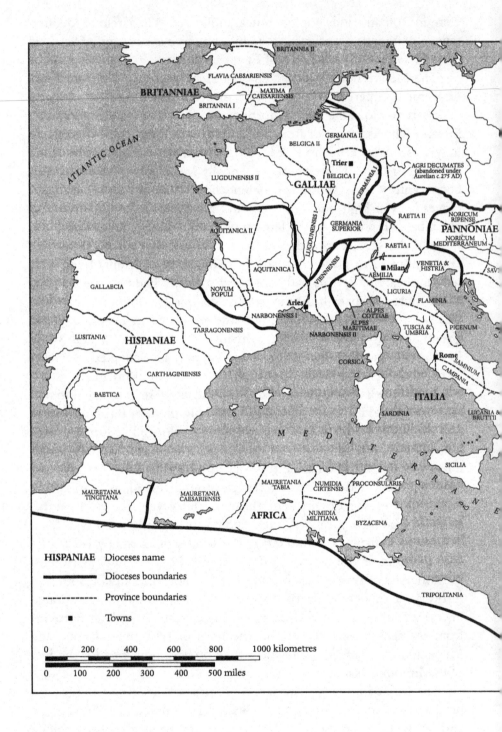

BRITANNIA II

FLAVIA CAESARIENSIS

BRITANNIAE   MAXIMA
                        CAESARIENSIS

BRITANNIA I

ATLANTIC OCEAN

GERMANIA II

BELGICA II

Trier ■

LUGDUNENSIS II   BELGICA I

AGRI DECUMATES
(abandoned under
Aurelian c.275 AD)

GALLIAE

AQUITANICA II

GERMANIA
SUPERIOR

RAETIA II   NORICUM
                   RIPENSE

PANNONIAE

NORICUM
MEDITERRANEUM

AQUITANICA I

RAETIA I

VIENNENSIS

VENETIA &
HISTRIA   SAV

■ Milan

AEMILIA

GALLAECIA

NOVUM
POPULI

Arles ■

NARBONENSIS I

LIGURIA   FLAMINIA

LUSITANIA   **HISPANIAE**

TARRAGONENSIS

ALPES
COTTIAE

ALPES
MARITIMAE
NARBONENSIS II

TUSCIA &
UMBRIA   PICENUM

■ Rome

CORSICA   SAMNIUM

CAMPANIA

CARTHAGINIENSIS

BAETICA

ITALIA

SARDINIA   LUCANIA &
                  BRUTTII

M E D I T E R R A N E

SICILIA

MAURETANIA
TINGITANA   MAURETANIA
                   CAESARIENSIS

MAURETANIA
TABIA   NUMIDIA
               CIRTENSIS   PROCONSULARIS

AFRICA   NUMIDIA
                    MILITIANA   BYZACENA

HISPANIAE   Dioceses name

───────   Dioceses boundaries

----------   Province boundaries

■   Towns

TRIPOLITANIA

0   200   400   600   800   1000 kilometres

0   100   200   300   400   500 miles

1. The Roman Empire in the fourth century

with targeted diplomacy and, where necessary, total ruthlessness. On several occasions Caesar treated his Gallic captives with great clemency, sending them home if he thought it was in Rome's interests. He was likewise always careful not to overstretch the loyalty of Gallic groups who had surrendered to him, imposing only moderate demands for auxiliaries and food supplies. He would also happily deploy his legions to protect new allies from the aggression of any third party. Given this relatively moderate stance, many Gallic groups were quick to take the point that cooperation was likely to prove more profitable than confrontation. Such tactics had long been employed, so that the military business of Roman empire-building was repeatedly punctuated by moments of diplomatic success. In 133 BC, for instance, Attalus III, the last independent ruler of the rich Hellenistic kingdom of Pergamum in modern north-west Turkey, bequeathed his state to Rome in his will.

Conciliatory diplomacy only achieved such successes, though, because it was offered in selected cases against a backdrop of well controlled and ruthless brutality. After the Third Punic War, which finally humbled the power of Carthage, the Roman Senate decreed that the entire city should be eradicated from the map. The site was ploughed symbolically with salt to prevent its future occupation. Further east, Rome's greatest enemy was Mithradates VI Eupator Dionysus, king of Pontus, who at one point ruled most of modern Turkey and the northern Black Sea coast. He was responsible for the atrocity known as the Asian Vespers, when thousands of resident Romans and Italians were killed in the territories under his rule. It took a while, but three separate campaigns – the Mithradatic Wars – finally, by 63 BC, saw the once proud king reduced to a last redoubt in the Crimea. There he decided to take his own life: but since years of preventive practice had inured him to poison, he had to ask one of his guardsmen to run him through.

Caesar's approach to the Gallic problem could be equally implacable. Opposition leaders held responsible for fomenting trouble were flogged to death – the punishment meted out to Acco, leader of the Gallic Senones and Cornuti at the end of the campaigning season of 53 BC. Whole opposition groups who failed to surrender as the legions approached might be sold into slavery or even, on occasion, simply slaughtered. In 52 BC, Caesar was held up for a while by a sustained defence of the hill-fort at Avaricum, an action following on from a massacre of Roman traders and their families. When the defences were finally breached, the legions were set loose to massacre and pillage: reportedly only 800 people survived from a total population of 40,000 men, women and children. Here, as always, there is no way of knowing by how much Caesar exaggerated his figures, but there is also no doubting the ferocity with which the Romans cowed their opponents.[5]

ALSO, THEY NEVER forgave or forgot. The same ruthlessness was duly deployed to avenge the deaths of Cotta and his men. Later spotted leading some siege operations, Indutiomarus of the Treveri was singled out for a cavalry sortie, which cut him down. As for the Eburones, they were forced to scatter in the face of a sustained assault on their homelands in the next campaigning season. Rather than wasting the lives of his own troopers in flushing them out of the woods, Caesar magnanimously issued a general invitation to neighbouring tribes to come and join in the pillaging. All of their villages were burned, and many of them died in the numerous skirmishes. The Eburones' king, Catuvoleus, had soon had enough. As Caesar reports it, 'Finding that he could not endure the effort of war or flight, [he] cursed Ambiorix by all his gods for suggesting such a project, and hanged himself from a yew tree.' It's quite possible that if he hadn't hanged himself, someone else would have done it for him. As for Ambiorix, he survived on the run for several years and his fate is not recorded in Caesar's *Gallic War*. Our last glimpse of him comes in 51 BC, when a further Roman force pillaged and burned the territory of the Eburones, with the specific object of making Ambiorix so hated that his own countrymen would deal with him themselves.[6]

Such stick-and-carrot policy combinations were hardly the work of genius, but they didn't need to be. When combined with the legions at this juncture in western Eurasian history, they were a sufficient tool for building an empire.

Rome thus created a vast state which, on the longest diagonal, ran from Hadrian's Wall on the border between England and Scotland to Mesopotamia where the Rivers Tigris and Euphrates flowed: a distance of about 4,000 kilometres. On the other, a relatively trifling 2,000 kilometres separated Roman installations at the mouth of the Rhine from guard posts in the Atlas Mountains of North Africa. The Roman Empire was also long-lived. Not counting a brief Transylvanian adventure (which lasted a mere 150 years), Rome ran this territory in pretty much its entirety for a staggering 450 years, from the age of Augustus to the fifth century AD. With events so far in the past, any real sense of time can get lost. It is worth pausing for just a moment to contemplate that counting back 450 years from today takes you to 1555, in British history just before Elizabeth I came to the throne; and, on a broader front, to a Europe seething with the religious turmoil of the Reformation. The Roman Empire lasted, in other words, for an immense period of time. And in both its size and its longevity, the military might of Rome's legions created the most successful state that this corner of the globe has ever known. It is, of course, the sheer extent of this success that has always made the study of its collapse so compelling.

The Empire's longevity leads us to another point of crucial importance. When you stop to think about it, it becomes immediately obvious that over so many centuries the Empire could not have remained unchanged. England has been a kingdom more or less continuously since the time of Elizabeth I, but has changed out of all recognition. So too the Roman Empire: 400-plus years of history turned the later Roman Empire of the fourth century AD into an animal that Julius Caesar would scarcely have recognized. These two factors have traditionally been linked, producing a school of thought that sees the major transformations worked out over these long imperial centuries as the root cause of the Empire's final collapse. Different historians have chosen to emphasize different transformations. For Edward Gibbon, famously, the Christianization of the Empire was a crucial moment, its pacifist ideologies sapping the fighting spirit of the Roman army and its theology spreading a superstition which undermined the rationality of classical culture. In the twentieth century, there was a stronger tendency to concentrate on economic factors: A. H. M. Jones, for instance, argued in 1964 that the burden of taxation became so heavy in the fourth-century Empire that peasants were left with too little of their produce to ensure their families' survival.[7]

There is no doubt that in order to say anything sensible about Rome's fall, it is necessary to understand the internal changes that made the late Empire so different from its early counterpart. On the other hand, this book will argue that the view that Rome's own internal transformations had so weakened it by the fourth century that it was ready to collapse under its own weight in the fifth, has become unsustainable. The roots of fifth-century collapse must be sought elsewhere. To establish this fundamental starting-point, it is necessary to explore in some depth the workings of the later Roman Empire and the changes that created it. The place to begin is Rome itself.

'The Better Part of Humankind'

THE CITY REMAINED in the fourth century AD, as it had been in the time of Caesar, a sprawling imperial mass. Visitors came, as they do now, to admire its monuments: the forum, the Colosseum, the Senate and a string of imperial and private palaces. Roman rulers had endowed it with monuments to their glory: for instance, the carved column of Marcus Aurelius celebrating his victorious foreign wars in the second century, and, more recently, the arch of Constantine I, erected in the 310s to mark that emperor's victories over internal enemies. Its population, likewise, was in a strong sense still an imperial one, artificially swollen by a flow of revenues from the rest of the Empire. Rome numbered perhaps a million in the fourth century, whereas no more than a handful of other cities had more than 100,000 inhabitants, and most had under 10,000. Feeding this population was a constant headache, especially as large numbers still qualified for free daily donations of bread, olive oil and wine assigned to the city as the perquisites of conquest. The most striking reflection of the resulting supply problem is the still stunning remains of Rome's two port cities: Ostia and Tibur. One lot of docks was not enough to generate a sufficient through-put of food, so they built a second. The huge UNESCO-sponsored excavations at Carthage, capital of Roman North Africa, have illuminated the problem from the other end, unearthing the massive harbour installations constructed there for loading the ships with the grain destined to supply the heart of the Empire.[8]

At the heart of the city, in every sense, stood the Senate, the political hub that had produced Caesar himself, together with most of his allies and opponents. In his day, the Senate numbered about nine hundred men, all of them rich landowners, ex-magistrates and their cronies from the immediate hinterland of the city. These were the patrician families who dominated the politics, culture and economics of republican Rome.[9] The fourth-century Senate numbered few, if any, direct descendants of these old families. There was a simple reason for this. Monogamous marriage tends to produce a male heir for no more than three generations at a time. In natural circumstances, about 20 per cent of monogamous relationships will produce no children at all, and another 20 per cent all girls. Exceptions occur (most notably the Capetian royal family of medieval France, which produced male heirs in the direct line for over 600 years), but it's a fair bet that no fourth-century senatorial families led back directly through the male line to contemporaries of Julius Caesar. Indirectly, however, many were descended from the grandees of old – a number certainly claimed as much – and the patterns of their wealth indicate the same.

Of all late Roman senators, the best known to us, from his own writings, is a certain Quintus Aurelius Symmachus, whose adult life spanned the second half of the fourth century. The writings consist of seven speeches and about 900 letters, composed between 364 and his death in 402. Partly edited by the author himself, they were published posthumously by his son, and widely copied by monks in the Middle Ages as an exemplar of Latin style. The speeches have their own points of interest, some of which will concern us later in the chapter, but the letter collection is fascinating for the sheer number of its correspondents and for the light it sheds on different aspects of the lifestyles of the late Romans of Rome. Symmachus himself was hugely wealthy and entirely typical of his class in having a portfolio of landed estates dotted across central and southern Italy, Sicily and North Africa; others of his peers owned estates in Spain and southern Gaul as well.[10] The Sicilian and North African elements of this portfolio reflect the gains made in these areas by old Roman grandees from victories in the Punic wars over Carthage, and the subsequent shuffling around of these lands amongst their descendants over centuries of inheritance and marriage settlements. Each imperial reign had seen the rise of some 'new men' who married into its existing ranks, but the Senate had, through the centuries, remained the apogee of imperial society, the standard of excellence towards which all Roman wannabees had consistently aimed. The geographical spread of senatorial landed fortunes, even after many centuries, thus continued to reflect Rome's original rise to greatness.

Symmachus and his peers were acutely conscious of the weight of history accumulated in themselves and in their institution, and this too is clearly registered in the letters. In a couple of them, Symmachus refers to the Senate of Rome as 'the better part of humankind', *pars melior humani generis*.[11] And by this he didn't just mean that he and his peers were richer than anyone else, rather that they were 'better' human beings in a moral sense as well: greater in virtue. In the past, it was much more usual to claim that one had more because one's greater moral worth entitled one to it. Only since the Second World War has the cult of wealth for its own sake become so prevalent that no further justification for privileged ownership seems to be required. The letters give us unique insight into the self-image of personal superiority with which the Romans of Rome justified their wealth. About one quarter of the nine hundred letters are recommendations, introducing younger peers to Symmachus' grander acquaintances. Virtues of one kind or another are bandied about: 'integrity', 'rectitude', 'honesty' and 'purity of manners' all recur at regular intervals. This is no random collection of attributes: for Symmachus and his peers, their possession was explicitly linked to a particular type of education.

The bedrock of the system was the intense study of a small number of literary texts under the guidance of an expert in language and literary interpretation, the grammarian. This occupied the individual for seven or more years from about the age of eight, and concentrated on just four authors: Vergil, Cicero, Sallust and Terence. You then graduated to a rhetor, with whom a wider range of texts was studied, but the methods employed were broadly the same. Texts were read line by line, and every twist of language dutifully identified and discussed. A typical school exercise would consist of having to express some everyday happening in the style of one of the chosen authors ('Chariot race as it might be told by Vergil: Go'). Essentially, these texts were held to contain within them a canon of 'correct' language, and children were to learn that language – both the particular vocabulary and a complex grammar within which to employ it. One thing this did was to hold educated Latin in a kind of cultural vice, preventing or at least significantly slowing down the normal processes of linguistic change. It also had the effect of allowing instant identification. As soon as a member of the Roman elite opened his mouth, it was obvious that he had learned 'correct' Latin. It is as though a modern education system concentrated on the works of Shakespeare with the object of distinguishing the educated by their ability to speak Shakespearean English to one another. To indicate how different, by the fourth century, elite Latin may have been from popular speech, the graffiti found at Pompeii – buried in the eruption of AD 79 – suggest that in everyday usage Latin was already evolving into less grammatically structured Romance.

But talking the talk was only part of the story. Aside from the language of these texts, Symmachus and his friends also claimed that absorbing their contents made them human beings of a calibre quite unmatched by anyone else. Latin grammar, they argued, was a tool for developing a logical, precise mind. If you didn't have a mastery of moods and tenses, you couldn't say precisely what you meant, or accurately express the exact relationship between things.[12] Grammar, in other words, was an introduction to formal logic. They also saw their literary texts as a kind of accumulated moral database of human behaviour – both good and bad – from which, with guidance, one could learn what to do and what not to do. On a simple level, from the fate of Alexander the Great you could learn not to get drunk at dinner and throw spears at your best friend. But there were also more subtle lessons to be learned, about pride, endurance, love and so forth, and their consequences: all exemplified in particular individuals' actions and fates. Still more profoundly – and here they were echoing an educational philosophy developed originally in classical Greece – Symmachus and his peers argued that it was only by pondering on a wide recorded range of men behaving well and badly that it was possible to develop a full intellectual and emotional range in oneself, to bring one to the highest state achievable. True pity, true love, true hate and true admiration were not things that occurred naturally in uneducated humans; enlightenment and true humanity had to be refined in the forge of the Latin schoolroom. As Symmachus put it in the case of one Palladius: '[His] eloquence moved his Latin audience by the skill with which the speech was organized, the richness of his imagination, the weight of his thoughts, the brilliance of his style. I will give you my own opinion: the gifts of his oratory are as exemplary as his character.'[13] Not only did educated Romans speak a superior language, but, in the view of Symmachus and his fellows, they had things to discuss in that language which were inaccessible to the uneducated.

To the modern eye, much of this is very unappealing. Although the grammarian did also use his texts to raise historical, geographical, scientific and other matters, as appropriate, the curriculum was extraordinarily narrow. The focus on language also had the effect of turning written Latin into a profoundly formal medium. In his letters, Symmachus tends to address everyone – as Queen Victoria complained of Gladstone – like a public meeting: 'So that no one should accuse me of the crime of interrupting our correspondence, I would rather hurry to fulfil my duties than to await, in long inaction, your reply.'[14] This is the opening of the first letter of the collection, written to his father in 375. Such formality between father and son wasn't seen as untoward in the fourth century. Indeed, as far as the ancients were concerned, the fruits of this precious education were held to manifest themselves first and foremost in the art of skilled public speaking. Symmachus was known in his own time, and wished to be known, as 'the Orator', and had the habit of sending his friends copies of his speeches.[15]

Not all late Romans were quite so focused on education and its importance as Symmachus, but all agreed that it not only equipped the individual to identify virtue for himself, but gave him the necessary tools to persuade others of his (correct) opinion. In other words, what it did was to equip its beneficiaries to lead the rest of mankind.

As might be expected, various responsibilities were held to follow from possession of this hugely coveted advantage. Having been prepared for leadership, one had to lead. This could take the form of helping to frame just laws, of holding high office with exemplary rectitude, or, less formally, of simply setting a public example of proper behaviour. Ancient Roman society held that you should not attempt to control others until you could control yourself. The educated also owed a duty of service to the literary tradition in which they had been taught. Study of the ancient texts, sometimes manifesting itself in new editions and commentaries, was a lifelong duty, and one which Symmachus and his friends were happy to continue. The letters mention his own work on Pliny's *Natural History* and one of his closest friends, Vettius Agorius Praetextatus, was an expert on the philosophy of Aristotle. The manuscript traditions of most classical texts preserve the marginal comments of different Roman grandees copied out again and again over the centuries by medieval scribes.[16]

Perhaps most important of all, a member of the educated elite was obliged to maintain good relations with his peers. In many ways, Symmachus' letters are highly frustrating. He lived in interesting times, knew everyone who was anyone, and wrote to most of them. But his letters comment on current affairs extremely rarely. As a result, exasperated historians have often dismissed them: 'never has any man written so much to say so little'.[17] In fact Symmachus did have opinions, and strong ones, but that isn't really the issue. The main historical importance of the letters lies in their collective mass, and in what they tell us about late Roman elite values, not in what they do or don't say about specific events. Their message is that the Roman elite share a distinct and privileged culture and need to stick together through thick and thin. They communicate the idea that both sender and recipient belong to the club – that both, in Margaret Thatcher's inimitable phrase, are 'one of us'. There was a well defined etiquette. A first letter to someone was like making a first visit in person; and failure to write without reasonable excuse might arouse suspicion or dislike. Acceptable excuses for silence, once communication had been established, included personal or familial illness, and the burden of office. Rather strangely, a person leaving Rome had to write first; only then could his correspondent reply. Once established, a relationship could serve many different purposes – as Symmachus' 200-odd letters of recommendation attest – but the most important thing was the relationship itself.[18]

Much of this world and its cultural assumptions would have been familiar to Julius Caesar. It was through contact with Greece, where intellectuals had been spinning sophisticated social and political theories from the middle of the first millennium BC, that most of Symmachus' educational ideology entered Roman culture. Much of it had already done so by the time of Caesar. Caesar was himself a man of letters and of oratory, living in a society where such skills were highly valued. Cicero, the greatest of all Latin orators and one of the canonical gang of four studied by Symmachus and his friends with such enthusiasm in the fourth century, was Caesar's contemporary. As one might expect after four hundred years of further study of a limited body of material, the rules of composition in the different genres of Latin literature had become more complicated than in Caesar's day, but the basic idea was the same. Equally familiar to both eras would have been the vision of an elite marked out by an exclusive education and by the destiny to lead humankind.[19]

Caesar would also have recognized, more or less, the thronging non-elite who still made up most of the population of Rome in the fourth century. They figure only in asides in Symmachus' letters, but we glimpse the same basic need for *panem et circenses* – bread and circuses – to keep them happy and prevent social unrest. When, on one occasion, food failed to arrive from North Africa in Symmachus' time, the non-landowning plebeians turned nasty, as they had once done in his father's day – and with good reason – when there was a wine shortage. The Romans had a recipe for underwater concrete which involved wine, and the elder Symmachus was overseeing some building work using this mixture when the commons got wind of it. Using wine to make concrete when *they* were running short was certainly a rioting matter.[20] Symmachus *père* was forced to leave the city.

A concern to keep the people happy also shows in the younger Symmachus' elaborate preparations for the games that his son had to give to mark his own ascent into the senatorial order. Caesar had given such games himself centuries before. Amongst other attractions, Symmachus obtained seven Scottish hunting dogs – presumably wolf-hounds of some kind – and, from contacts on the frontier, twenty slaves, five each to be given to the four chariot-racing factions of the Hippodrome. The whole thing was a huge theatrical production, but it reads from the letters like a chapter of accidents, even if some were only minor irritations. A rather peeved Symmachus complains in one letter about having to pay customs duty on bears he was importing from North Africa.[21] More annoyingly, a troop of actors and circus professionals hired from Sicily got 'lost' on the beaches of the bay of Naples, where they were presumably doing a little impromptu moon-lighting, before Symmachus' agent managed to track them down and bundle them on to Rome.[22] Spanish horses had gone down particularly well in his own consular games a decade earlier, so Symmachus badgered an Iberian contact into procuring some for his son. Unfortu-nately, only eleven out of the sixteen survived the journey, which ruined the plan. (You needed four sets of four – one for each faction – for chariot-racing.[23]) Our last glimpse of Symmachus the circus master is a fairly desperate one. There had been delays, the letters tell us, and since the only surviving crocodiles were refusing to eat, he was anxiously urging that the games be staged before the poor animals expired from starvation.[24] Still, the reality behind all good theatre is total chaos, and this must certainly have been so in Caesar's time.

Restricting our gaze to the city of Rome, the extent of the Empire's transformation between the eras of Caesar and Symmachus is not immediately apparent. Rome was still, in the fourth century, a bloated imperial power-base, its population and grandeur swollen by the revenues of Empire. Still dominated, likewise, by a self-regarding and determinedly blue-blooded elite, confidently assertive of its superiority, it cast only the occasional glance over its shoulder at the urban masses. But, however grand, Rome was only one corner of the Empire, and, even in its continuing grandeur, absence of change was more apparent than real.

The Imperial Crown

IN EARLY WINTER 368/9, Symmachus left Rome and headed north. This was no sightseeing tour. He was leading a senatorial embassy north of the Alps, to the city of Trier in the Moselle valley (where Germany now borders France and Luxembourg) – the old stamping-ground of Indutiomarus, the leader of the Treveri, who had pushed the Eburones into attacking Sabinus and Cotta some 421 years before. Typically, none of Symmachus' letters gives any details of the trip, either its route or its circumstances. As an official senatorial mission, however, its members were entitled to use the *cursus publicus*, the officially maintained network of stopping-points where changes of horses could be had and/or lodging for the night. The main road north led through the Alps over the St Bernard Pass to the headwaters of the Rhône, then on beside the River Saône to the headwaters of the Moselle and so down the river to the city of Trier. Had Caesar's deified ghost journeyed with these ambassadors, any comforting sense of familiarity that the city of Rome might still have generated would quickly have disappeared as it surveyed the magnitude of the transformation wrought in these territories during the intervening four centuries.

One profound if obvious change was encompassed in the object of the mission. Symmachus and his friends were bringing crown gold (*aurum coronarium*) to the reigning emperor, Valentinian I. Crown gold was a theoretically voluntary cash payment, which the cities of the Empire handed over to emperors on their accession and on every fifth anniversary (*quinquennalia*) subsequently. Valentinian had been elevated to the purple in 364, so Symmachus' embassy marked his fifth year in power. It was a touch early, but the ambassadors were giving themselves plenty of time to get to Valentinian by 26 February, the actual anniversary. In Caesar's day, of course, there had been no emperor at the head of the Roman Empire, but a series of quarrelling oligarchs whose rivalries and contentions generated civil wars aplenty. In 45 BC Caesar had been made *imperator* (commander of the army) for life and was offered the crown a year later, just before his murder. Nonetheless, the imperial title was a novelty when it was claimed and defined by Caesar's nephew Octavian under the name Augustus. Since then the office had been transformed out of all recognition.

For one thing, all pretence of republicanism had vanished. Augustus had worked hard at pretending that the power structures he had created around himself did not represent the overthrow of the old Republic, and that, in a mixed constitution, the Senate continued to have important functions. But even in his lifetime the veneer had looked pretty thin, and by the fourth century no one thought of the emperor as anything other than an autocratic monarch. Hellenistic concepts of rulership, developed across the successor kingdoms which emerged from Alexander the Great's short-lived Empire, had transformed the ideologies and ceremonial life that defined the imperial image. These ideologies argued that legitimate rulers were divinely inspired and divinely chosen. The first among equals became a sacred ruler, communing with the Divinity, and ordinary human beings had to act with due deference. By the fourth century, standard protocols included *proskynesis* – throwing yourself down on the ground when introduced into the sacred imperial presence – and, for the privileged few, being allowed to kiss the hem of the emperor's robe. And emperors, of course, were expected to play their part in the drama. One memorable ceremonial moment described by the fourth-century historian Ammianus Marcellinus is the entry of the Emperor Constantius II into Rome in 357. Although Ammianus did not altogether approve of Constantius, he did think him the ideal ceremonial emperor: 'As if his neck were in a vice, he kept the gaze of his eyes straight ahead, and turned his face neither to the right nor left, nor . . . did he nod when the wheel jolted, nor was he ever seen to spit, or to wipe or rub his face or nose, or move his hands about.' Thus, when the occasion demanded it – and on the big days, as was only fitting in a divinely chosen ruler – Constantius could behave in superhuman fashion, showing no signs whatsoever of normal human frailty.[25]

Nor did fourth-century emperors merely look more powerful than their first-century counterparts. From Augustus onwards, emperors had enjoyed enormous authority, but the job description widened still further over the centuries. Take, for instance, law-making. Up to the middle of the third century, the Roman legal system developed via a variety of channels. The Senate could make laws, and so could the emperor. However, the group primarily responsible for legal innovation had been specialist academic lawyers called 'jurisconsults'. These were licensed by the emperor to deal with questions of interpretation, and with new issues to which they applied established legal principles. From the first to the mid-third century Roman law had developed primarily on the back of their learned opinions. By the fourth, though, the jurisconsults had been eclipsed by the emperor; doubtful legal matters were now referred to him. As a result, the emperor completely dominated the process of law-making. A similar story could be told in a number of other areas, not least in the fiscal structure, where by the fourth century the emperor's officials played a much more direct role in the taxing of the Empire than they had in the first. Emperors had always had the potential authority to expand their range of function. By the fourth century much of that potential had become reality, in both ceremonial presentation and function.[26]

Equally fundamental, it was now well-established custom for the office to be divided – for more than one emperor to rule at the same time. In the fourth century, this never quite formalized into a system of distinct eastern and western halves of Empire, each with its own ruler, and there were times when one man did try to rule the entire Empire on his own. The emperor Constantius II (337–61) ruled alone for part of his reign, his immediate successors Julian and Jovian did so again during 361–4, and Theodosius I once more in the early 390s. But none of these experiments in sole rule lasted very long, and for most of the fourth century the job of governing the Empire was split. Power-sharing was organized in a variety of ways. Some emperors used younger relations – sons if they had them, nephews if they didn't – as junior but nonetheless imperial colleagues with their own courts. Constantine I utilized this model from the 310s down to his death in 337, Constantius II did the same with his nephews Gallus and Julian for most of the 350s, and Theodosius I was moving towards it with his two sons in the 390s. They had been promoted to the rank of Augustus, but were too young at the time of their father's death to exercise real authority. Other emperors shared sovereignty on an equal basis with other relatives, usually brothers. The sons of Constantine I operated in this fashion from 337 to 351, as did Valentinian I and

Valens for a decade after 364. In addition, at the end of the third and start of the fourth centuries, there had been a long period when power was shared on a broadly equal basis by non-relatives. The emperor Diocletian established the so-called Tetrarchy ('rule of four') in the 290s, sharing power, as Augustus, with one other fellow Augustus and two Caesars,[27] all four having defined geographical zones of operation. Different individuals came and went, but the tetrarchic model continued to operate in some sense down to the early 320s. The late Empire thus saw many different models of power-sharing, but for much of the fourth century there were two emperors, one usually based in the west and the other in the east, and by the fifth this had crystallized more or less into a formal system.

Not only was there now an emperor, and usually more than one, but a further key transformation is implicit in the fact that Symmachus' embassy had to travel north to find Valentinian on such a momentous occasion as the fifth anniversary of his accession. There is a somewhat bemusing scholarly argument in the field of late Roman studies about whether a reigning emperor visited Rome on five occasions in the fourth century (for perhaps up to a month at a time), or just four.[28] This is a startling *kind* of argument. Whether it was four or five times doesn't actually matter: the point is that, by the fourth century, emperors hardly visited Rome at all. While the city remained the Empire's symbolic capital, and still received a disproportionate percentage of imperial revenues in the form of free food and other subsidies, it was no longer a political or administrative centre of importance. Especially in the later third and earlier fourth centuries, new centres of power had developed much closer to the main imperial frontiers. Within Italy, Milan, several days' journey north of Rome, had emerged as the main seat of active imperial government. Elsewhere, at different times, Trier on the Moselle, Sirmium by the confluence of the Save and the Danube, Nicomedia in Asia Minor, and Antioch close to the Persian front, had all become important, particularly under Diocletian's Tetrarchy when the four active emperors had had separate geographical spheres. In the fourth century, things stabilized a little: Milan and Trier in the west, together with Antioch and a new capital, Constantinople, in the east, emerged as the dominant administrative and political centres of the Empire.

In a speech to Valentinian's brother Valens in 364, the philosopher and orator Themistius implies, to devastating effect, a comparison between Constantinople and Rome that highlights the latter's drawbacks as an imperial capital:

> Constantinople links the two continents [Europe and Asia], is an anchorage for maritime needs, a market for trade by land and sea, an effective adornment of Roman rule. For it has not been built, like some sacred precinct, far from the highway nor does it keep the emperors from attending to public affairs if they are engaged in business there, but is a place through which all must pass who arrive from and set out in all directions, so that whenever it keeps them closest to home, it puts them at the very centre of the whole empire.[29]

'A sacred precinct' – full of temples to the gods who had presided over the ancient victories – 'far from the highway' more or less sums up fourth-century Rome. As Themistius identified so accurately, one reason for emperors abandoning their original home was administrative necessity. The pressing external threats that commanded their attention were to be found east of the River Rhine, north of the River Danube, and on the Persian front between the Tigris and the Euphrates. This meant that the strategic axis of the Empire ran on a rough diagonal from the North Sea along the Rhine and Danube as far as the Iron Gates where the Danube is crossed by the Carpathian Mountains, then overland across the Balkans and Asia Minor to the city of Antioch, from which point the eastern front could be supervised. All the fourth-century capitals were situated on or close to this line of power (map 1). Rome was just too far away from it to function effectively; information flowed in too slowly, and commands sent out took too long to take effect.[30]

But administrative necessity alone does not get to the crux of how it was that Rome could now be so thoroughly ignored. The same kind of logistic and strategic necessity had drawn Julius Caesar north of the Alps, west into Spain, or out into the eastern Mediterranean every summer, but he nevertheless returned to Rome most winters to secure his political position, handing out presents to his friends and intimidating his opponents. He had to do this because, in his time, the Senate of Rome had provided the one and only participatory audience for the political power struggles that consumed both his energies and those of his fellow oligarchs (when they weren't too busy conquering other bits of the Mediterranean). All of Caesar's important political supporters and opponents were members of the Senate, most senior legionary officers and certainly the commanders were of senatorial standing, and it was in front of the Senate that the big power contests were played out. It was on the steps of the Senate too, symbolically, on the Ides of March in 44 BC that Caesar was assassinated. Fourth-century emperors, by contrast, didn't need to spend time in Rome because, in addition to the administrative pressures that drew them out of Italy, they were also playing to a different political audience. Emperors didn't go to Rome very much in the fourth century because, for political reasons, they needed to operate elsewhere. The starting-point for understanding this critical development in the evolution of the Empire is the fact that the imperial court – wherever it might be – was the distribution centre for everything that aspirational Romans desired. Wealth, dignities, favours, promotions: all flowed from the imperial presence, the point at which the tax revenues of western Eurasia were redistributed.

Contemporaries were well aware of this. In 310 a speaker before the emperor Constantine put it succinctly: 'For in whatever places your divinity distinguishes most frequently with his visits, everything is increased – men, walls and favours; nor more abundantly did the earth send forth fresh flowers for Jupiter and Juno to lie on than do cities and temples spring up in your footsteps.'[31] In Caesar's time, all of this wealth had been redistributed within the confines of the city of Rome in order to win friends and influence people in that crucial arena. But to follow such a strategy in the fourth century would have been political suicide. Four hundred years on from the Ides of March, patronage had to be distributed much more widely.

Rather than in the Roman Senate, the critical political audience of the fourth-century Empire was to be found in two other quarters. One of these was a long-standing player of the game of imperial politics: the army, or, rather, its officer corps. It is traditional to talk of 'the Roman army' as a political player, but in normal circumstances the rank and file didn't have opinions of their own, and wherever we have more detailed narrative accounts it is always groups of senior officers that are involved in deciding who should succeed to the purple or organizing coups. The fact that the battle order of the army had changed since the time of Julius Caesar naturally affected which of its officers played a leading political role. In Caesar's time, the army came in the form of legions of over 5,000 men, each in itself a major military formation. Individual legionary commanders – legates (who were also usually of senatorial background) – thus tended to be significant in their own right. By the fourth century, the key figures in the military hierarchy were the senior general officers and staffs of mobile regional field armies, called *comitatenses*. Broadly speaking, there was always one important mobile force covering each of the three key frontiers: one in the west (grouped on the Rhine frontier and – often – in northern Italy as well), another in the Balkans covering the Danube, and a third in northern Mesopotamia covering the east.[32]

The other key political force in the late Empire was the imperial bureaucracy (often called *palatini*: from *palatium*, Latin for 'palace'). Although bureaucrats did not possess the military clout available to a senior general, they controlled both finance and the processes of law-making and enforcement, and no imperial regime could function without their active participation. There always had been bureaucratic functionaries around the emperor, and they had always been powerful. In the early Empire, the emperor's freedmen were particularly feared. What was new in the late Empire was the size of the central bureaucratic machine. As late as AD 249 there were still only 250 senior bureaucratic functionaries in the entire Empire. By the year 400, just 150 years later, there were 6,000. Most operated at the major imperial headquarters from which the key frontiers were supervised: not in Rome, therefore, but, depending on the emperor, at Trier and/or Milan for the Rhine, Sirmium or increasingly Constantinople for the Danube, and Antioch for the east. It was no longer the Senate of Rome, but the comitatensian commanders, concentrated on key frontiers, and the senior bureaucrats, gathered in the capitals from which these frontiers were administered, who settled the political fate of the Empire.[33]

The imperial throne was generally passed on by dynastic succession, but only if there was a suitable candidate who could command a reasonable degree of consensus among the generals and bureaucrats. The emperor Jovian, for example, left an infant son on his death in 364, who was passed over, and in 378 the unrelated Theodosius I was elevated to the purple because, although two sons of Valentinian I had already been made emperor, the second, Valentinian II, was still too young to rule effectively in the east. There were also times of dynastic discontinuity. In 363/4 the Constantinian dynasty ran out of appointable heirs, prompting a cabal of senior generals and bureaucrats to discuss a range of possible candidates. In practice, army officers tended to get the nod at such moments (first Jovian in 363 and then, after his early death, Valentinian in 364), but the higher bureaucracy was involved in the process, and it was not impossible for its members to contemplate bidding for power. On the promotion of Jovian in 363, a bureaucrat of the same name was lobbed down a well because he posed a potential threat, and in 371 a senior pen-pusher by the name of Theodorus was executed for plotting against Valentinian's brother Valens. This plot involved a seance where Theodorus and his friends asked for the name of the next emperor. The ouija board spelled out Th-e-o-d – at which point they stopped to open a bottle of Falernian, one of the most expensive wines of antiquity. If they'd only carried on, they could have saved themselves both false hopes and nasty deaths, since Valens' successor was called Theodosius.[34]

A potent combination of logistics and politics had thus worked a fundamental change in the geography of power. Because of this, armies, emperors and bureaucrats had all emigrated out of Italy. This process also explains why, more than ever before, more than one emperor was needed. Administratively, Antioch or Constantinople was too far from the Rhine, and Trier or Milan too far from the east, for one emperor to exercise effective control over all three key frontiers. Politically, too, one centre of patronage distribution was not sufficient to keep all the senior army officers and bureaucrats happy enough to prevent usurpations. Each of the three major army groups required a fair share of the spoils, paid to them in gold in relatively small annual amounts, and much larger ones on major imperial anniversaries (such as the *quinquennalia* which brought Symmachus northwards). Their officers also liked all the promotions and distinctions – not to mention invitations to dinner – which flowed from the imperial presence. The same was true on the civilian side. No regime could afford to concentrate all its patronage in just one capital, or too many bigwigs would be left out of the loop. In the fourth century this political necessity was generally appreciated, and where an emperor did try to rule alone for any extended period there was usually trouble. Late in the century, Theodosius I was based in Constantinople, and for his own dynastic reasons (he wanted his two sons each eventually to inherit half of the Empire) refused to appoint a recognized counterpart in the west. As a result, he was faced with rumbling discontent there, as well as dangerous usurpers, who found plentiful support among the bureaucrats and military officers who felt they were not getting a fair share of the imperial cake.

THIS ECLIPSE OF Rome's importance in both politics and administration was no sudden development. As far back as the first and second centuries AD emperors had become increasingly peripatetic, already sometimes operating with an imperial colleague to help them deal with problems as they arose.[35] Between 161 and 169, Lucius Verus was co-Augustus alongside Marcus Aurelius. By the fourth century, the glory days of the Republic, when it was home to every faction and conspiracy of importance and when the Senate's resolutions played a major role in the running of the state, had gone for ever. The Senate's role within the Empire was now essentially ceremonial, its actions and members playing only a marginal role in the acquisition and exercise of power. Individual senators remained rich and might have significant political careers.[36] But even here, there was an important limitation. The late Roman senatorial career ladder – the *cursus honorem* – was an entirely civilian one, involving no military commands. This militated against a senator taking the ultimate step towards imperial power, which tended, as we have seen, to be the preserve of generals. Senatorial minutes were forwarded to the emperor for his perusal (of course he read them ...), imperial despatches kept the Senate informed about important matters (it was a mark of honour, and one sometimes enjoyed by Symmachus, to be picked to read them out) and the Senate could make representations by embassy to the emperor on matters of particular significance to its own members. But it was not much involved in active policy making, and little courting of its opinion took place, except when it came to deciding the size of its annual 'voluntary' contribution to the imperial finances. The Senate was full of wealthy men who paid a useful amount of tax and might enjoy important careers, but it was no longer – as a body – a major player in struggles over power and policy.

Not surprisingly, therefore, membership was gradually downgraded. Before the fourth century, the senators of Rome (titled *clarissimi*, 'most distinguished') enjoyed a unique status. They were immune from obligations to serve on other city councils, and enjoyed various financial and legal privileges. In the course of the fourth century, a number of developments altered this situation. First, emperors slowly but surely advanced large numbers of their new bureaucrats up the social scale towards senatorial status. Initially, this happened piecemeal, but in AD 367 the emperor Valentinian introduced a major reform of the honours system which aligned and combined all the possible marks of social status that could be acquired in both the civilian and military branches of imperial service into one system, where *clarissimus* became everyone's aim. From then until the end of the century, there was a marked inflation which saw huge numbers of bureaucratic jobs acquire the *clarissimus* grade. The 6,000 top imperial functionaries of AD 400 were all occupying jobs that involved senatorial status either in post or upon retirement. The traditional senatorial families of Rome thus ceased to occupy their unique social niche. Even worse, the large numbers of new *clarissimi* made it necessary for emperors (in order still to have something to bestow) to subdivide the senatorial class and create two higher grades – *spectabiles* and *illustres* – which by and large could only be obtained by active bureaucratic service rather than by birth. At broadly the same time, between the 330s and the end of the century, a succession of emperors passed measures that created a second and equal imperial Senate in the new capital of the east, largely by promoting new men but also by transferring some old Roman senators already resident in the east.

Between AD 250 and 400, then, the blue-blooded senators of Rome saw their cherished position eaten away by the emergence of a vast senatorial class, as well as the slow but steady rise of a sister body in Constantinople.[37]

All these developments created a political world that Julius Caesar would not have recognized. The first among equals had become a divinely appointed ruler of what some historians have christened the 'inside out' Empire from the geography of its active capitals, generally operating with at least one colleague of equal status and exercising wide-ranging authority over every aspect of life. The imperial bureaucracy had emerged as the new Roman aristocracy, replacing the demilitarized and marginalized Senate of Rome. These developments also explain, of course, why, when they went bearing gold in search of the emperor Valentinian, Symmachus and his embassy had to make the trek to Trier. Between them, these transformations raise another, still more fundamental issue. The Roman world in Caesar's day had been physically just as large, but there had been no need for two emperors or for such a wide distribution of patronage to prevent usurpation and revolt. What, then, had changed between 50 BC and

AD 369? To find the answer to this question, we must take a closer look at the destination of Symmachus' embassy: the city of Trier, command centre for the Rhine frontier.

Rome Is Where the Heart Is

ROMAN TRIER started out as a small military installation, set on a strategic ford across the River Moselle in the old heartlands of the hostile Treveri. The city that greeted Symmachus and his fellow ambassadors in winter 368/9, however, was no military camp, but the populous and prosperous bastion of *Romanitas* – 'Romanness' – of the Rhine frontier region. If the ambassadors had approached the city from the west, they would have entered by the Porta Nigra – the Black Gates – the finest example of a Roman city gateway still standing in any part of the former Empire. Surrounded by modern buildings, it still impresses. In the fourth century, its impact was much stronger. You were first faced with a massive iron portcullis; if admitted, you were led into a courtyard, then through to the gate proper. On either side were four-storey arcaded towers, bristling with guards ready to pour down missiles on any hostile force trapped between the portcullis and the gate. This particular gateway owes its survival to a tenth-century Holy Man who made it his cell. Hence it eventually became a church, whereas the rest of the Roman city walls and gates have long since been quarried for building stone. In Symmachus' day, the gate punctuated a 6-kilometre wall, 3 metres thick and 6 high, which enclosed a city area of 285 hectares. Another massive gateway dominated the bridge over the Moselle, which had long since replaced the original ford and is pictured in a fourth-century gold medallion struck at Trier.

Inside, the city was no less impressive. In the early fourth century, the whole north-east quarter was rebuilt as the functional and ceremonial centre of imperial rule in the region. From the 310s, the work was carried forward by different members of the Constantinian dynasty, then, after the death of its last representative, continued by their non-dynastic successors. Palace, cathedral and circus – together with a set of perhaps private imperial baths – the 'Kaiserthermen' – now dominated this part of the city. Many late Roman imperial ceremonies were orchestrated in the circus, and underground passages led from the palace to the imperial box there. The ground-plan of the cathedral, which, literary sources indicate, was complete by the late 360s, was recovered in excavations after the Second World War. Above ground, you can still see remains of the bath complex and, more or less intact, the basilica – the emperors' great audience chamber. Like the Porta Nigra, this also survived into the medieval period by dint of becoming a church and now stands stark and isolated in the middle of a one-way traffic system.[38]

Back in the fourth century, the basilica was flanked by porticoes and the more private areas of the palace, but would still have stood out as impressive: 67 metres long, 27.5 wide and 30 from floor to ceiling, it could virtually hold the Porta Nigra twice. The basilica is of particular interest to us because it was here that Symmachus and his embassy presented the emperor Valentinian with the gift of gold they had brought from Rome. The building's exterior was originally finished in white plaster. In its current state, the inside is as plain as the outside, but this was not its fourth-century form. The floor then consisted of black and white tiles arranged in geometric patterns, marble veneering stretched from floor to the windows, and niches indicate that the walls were decorated with many statues. The ambassadors would have entered this splendid edifice through its main doors to the south, to discover the emperor sitting opposite them in the apse at the far end. Normally, the imperial presence was veiled from the rest of the audience hall by curtains, through which the outlines of the great and the good could just be made out. On a great ceremonial occasion such as the presentation of crown gold, however, they were drawn back. The civilian and military dignitaries of court would have stood along the sides of the hall, sporting their gorgeous robes and arranged in rows strictly reflecting the order of precedence that Valentinian had established so clearly just a couple of years before. The impression was of splendour and order, and the eye was led irresistibly to the imperial personage. Then, one short speech and the job was done.[39] The ambassadors were free to go.

But Symmachus didn't leave. He stayed in and around Trier for the rest of the year. This gave him plenty of time to contemplate the city, its countryside and its inhabitants. What would have struck him immediately was that Trier was Roman to the core, and had been for a long time. The new imperial buildings had been grafted on to what was already a fully Roman city. Set just inside the gateway to the bridge over the Moselle, on the eastern side, was one of the two largest bath complexes in the western Empire outside of Rome, the so-called 'Barbarathermen' (the other was the 'Kaiserthermen'). This huge public amenity, comprising porticoed courtyard, cold, tepid and hot baths and a gymnasium, had been constructed in the second quarter of the second century and was still going strong when Symmachus arrived. Close by stood municipal buildings comprising the forum, the law courts and the meeting house of the city's ruling council. This, the political heart of the city, had been reworked many times over the years, but the first Roman public building had been erected as long ago as the first century. About the same time, the city had also acquired an amphitheatre; set in the hillside to the east, opposite the baths, it was larger than the surviving Roman amphitheatres of Arles and Nîmes in modern France. Just south-west of the amphitheatre, in the so-called Altbachtal, were some fifty temple shrines, forming the largest shrine complex in the western Empire. In addition, although it has not been found, we know there was a temple somewhere in the city dedicated to Rome's governing deity: Jupiter Optimus Maximus. Trier later acquired a theatre and, in the third century, an improved water supply: an aqueduct 12 kilometres long was built, running down from the Ruwer valley in the hills behind the city to service its fountains and its sewers. From the beginning of the second century AD the city had been a properly Roman urban space, and it had continued to evolve.

This transformation wasn't just true of Trier. Throughout northern Gaul, Roman cities dotted the map. You could also find them in Britain, Spain, North Africa, the Balkans, Asia Minor and the Fertile Crescent. Based on Greek antecedents, many such cities were already to be found in the Mediterranean area at the time of the Roman conquest. Elsewhere some were erected in the first century AD; in more backward places like Britain, perhaps the second. Their number varied from region to region, and once you left the Mediterranean hinterland they became comparatively sparse. The extent of the transformation should not, however, be underestimated. Caesar's ghost, had it made its way as far north as Symmachus' embassy, would have been astonished. In his day, northern Europe had been marked only by odd native hill-forts, numerous rustic villages and the odd Roman military encampment. Now it was an almost entirely Roman landscape, its towns the administrative bedrock of the Empire. For a

Roman town was more than its urban core: it also possessed, and administered, a dependent rural territory. By the fourth century, barring very few exceptions, the Empire in administrative terms consisted of a mosaic of city territories, each city governed by a city council (*curia*) of decurions (also known as *curiales*).[40]

In the course of his year at Valentinian's court, Symmachus was entertained by many grandees. Some lived in fine Roman town houses; odd fragments of one or two of these, usually in the form of beautiful mosaic floors, have been unearthed within the modern city. Many also owned luxurious dwellings in the surrounding countryside, which, because they do not lie beneath a modern town, are much better known. The grandest so far excavated – at Konz – was situated about eighty kilometres upstream at the confluence of the Moselle and the Saar. It stood high up on a steep river bank with magnificent views, and its buildings spread over a rectangle of about 100 by 35 metres, the whole edifice focused on a central audience hall complete with apse. There is good reason to think that this might have been the imperial summer retreat of Contoniacum. If he was lucky enough to get an invitation here, Symmachus will have been royally entertained.

In fact, Trier and its environs have thrown up a whole host of villas, many only marginally less grand (the majority were of private, not imperial, construction), strung out in desirable locations along the river banks. All combined, in addition to the barns and storage facilities appropriate to working estates, the classic mixture of public and private rooms held to be necessary for living a civilized Roman life in the countryside: bath suite, audience hall, mosaics and central heating, plus shady porticoed courtyards, elegant gardens and fountains. And, again, there is nothing exceptional in the fact that such gems of Roman elegance should be found this far outside Italy. The proximity of Trier and the spending power of the imperial court undoubtedly made the fourth-century villas of the Moselle region larger and more magnificent than they might otherwise have been. But villas weren't a new phenomenon here. They had begun to appear by AD 100, and had been a constant feature ever since. The only standard Italo-Roman practice that the northern ones didn't emulate, because of disparities in rainfall and temperature, was the installation of an open roof in the middle the house to feed a pool of cooling water. And, just as outside Trier, Roman villas dotted the countryside around all the other new Roman towns, in areas that had fallen under imperial control. There were variations in their density, in the speed with which they appeared, and in grandeur. In Britain – the mid-first-century palace of Fishbourne apart – villas began a little later and developed more slowly. In the fourth century, after 200 years during which black and white geometric patterns had been the norm, full-colour picture mosaics finally reached the provinces north of the Channel. Countryside and town alike had evolved to conform with standard Roman patterns in the four centuries separating Caesar from Symmachus.[41]

The transformation extended to people as well as to buildings. Symmachus made, and exploited, many contacts during his year at court in Trier, and the most important among them was a fellow specialist in Latin language and literature, Decimius Magnus Ausonius, perhaps as much as thirty years older than Symmachus. After a distinguished academic career, he was engaged by the emperor Valentinian to act as tutor for his son, the future emperor Gratian. Symmachus' initial letter of approach to Ausonius, couched in highly flattering terms, has recently been identified among the anonymous letters in the collection.[42] Two points of particular interest emerge. First, a perceived superiority in Latin could override social inferiority. Ausonius, though numbered among the educated Roman elite, came from nothing like so distinguished a background as Symmachus. Second, and for present purposes much more important, Ausonius had made his name as a self-employed teacher of Latin rhetoric operating under the auspices of the university of Bordeaux, near the Atlantic coast of Gaul. By the fourth century, Bordeaux had emerged as one of the major centres of Latin excellence in the Empire. Not only does this show us expertise in Latin flourishing well beyond the confines of Italy, but Ausonius himself was not from Rome, nor even from Italy, but of Gallic background.[43] Yet here we have one of the blue-blooded Romans of Rome approaching him with deference, and seeking his good graces in matters to do with Latin literature. Furthermore, in his opening epistolary gambit, Symmachus had been able to use the fact that he himself had been taught Latin rhetoric in Rome by a tutor from Gaul.

The case of Ausonius demonstrates, again, how far the Roman world had changed. Like the town and the villas of Trier, he is representative of broad patterns of transformation. In Caesar's day there were certainly Gauls who had a good knowledge of Latin, especially in the towns of Gallia Narbonensis, the Roman province of

Mediterranean Gaul. But the idea that a Rome-trained Latin expert of senatorial status might approach a Gaul as his superior in the Latin tradition could only have struck Caesar as preposterous.

Shortly after the establishment of the Empire, the two imperial languages – Latin in the west supplemented to some extent by Greek in the east – began to be acquired in addition to their native tongues by Rome's new subjects, and particularly by those from wealthier backgrounds. This happened at first on a fairly ad hoc basis, but, remarkably quickly, Latin grammarians started to operate in many of the towns of the Empire. Schools had already been set up in Autun in central France – the original hometown of Ausonius' family – by AD 23. And once such schools were in operation, the same kind of intensive training in language and literature was being offered throughout the Empire. By the fourth century, a good Latin education at the hands of a grammarian could be had anywhere. The language of the surviving letters of St Patrick, from a fairly minor landowning family in north-west Britain, shows that you could still get such an education at that extreme point of the Empire as late as AD 400, while North Africa, at another, was famous for its educational tradition, producing in St Augustine of Hippo one of the best-educated late Romans of all. Vergil had triumphed over all his non-Latin, pre-Roman cultural rivals.

This brings us face to face with the most fundamental change of all, the dimension of imperial evolution that underlies all the others: the creation of Roman rural and urban landscapes outside of Italy, and the widening of political community that sidelined Rome and her Senate. Latin language and literature spread across the Roman world because people who had originally been conquered by Caesar's legions came to buy into the Roman ethos and adopt it as their own. This was far more than learning a little Latin for pragmatic reasons, like selling the odd cow or pig to a conquering Roman soldier (though this certainly also happened). Accepting the grammarian and the kind of education he offered meant accepting the whole value system which, as we have seen, reckoned that only this kind of education could create properly developed – and therefore superior – human beings.

It was the same process of buying into Roman values that created Roman towns and villas in those parts of the Empire where such phenomena had been completely unknown before the arrival of the legions. All the models for Trier's urban life originated in the Mediter-ranean, and in a number of newly conquered territories settlements of

Roman veterans were established, to give the natives a close-up view of Roman urban life as led by 'proper' Romans. Roman Trier, however, had different origins. The official title of the city (whose modern French name is Trèves) gives the game away: *Augusta Treverorum*, 'Augusta of the Treveri'. This indicates that the city had been legally constituted under the emperor Augustus for the tribesmen of the Treveri – the group, of course, that had produced Indutiomarus, ultimately responsible for the deaths of Cotta and his legionaries. First- and second-century Trier was built by members of the Treveri who wanted their own Roman city. Its extensive corpus of dedicatory inscriptions confirms the point, as for so many other Roman cities of the type. The majority of such cities' public buildings were financed by local donations and subscriptions. Such was their enthusiasm for showing how Roman they were that former (Gallic, British, Iberian, whatever) tribesmen would borrow heavily from Italian moneylenders to fund their projects, and occasionally got themselves into severe financial trouble. The first Roman settlement at Trier may have been a military fort, but the Roman city of Trier, like the other towns of the Empire, was built not by immigrants from Italy but by the indigenous people. From the second century onwards, likewise it is impossible to tell a villa built by an Italian Roman from a villa built by a provincial.

The buildings characteristic of a Roman town – the baths, the temples, the council house, the amphitheatre – were all purpose-built spaces for particular functions and events, and you didn't bother to build them unless you intended to hold those events. Roman bathing was public, the religious cults involved ceremonies in which the entire urban population participated, the council house and its courtyard was the place to debate local issues, the forum in every sense for local self-government. And in the Roman ideology of civilization, descended directly from that of the classical Greeks, local self-government was seen to be an important vehicle for generating civilized human beings. In the act of debating local issues in front of one's discerning peers, it was held, rational faculties were developed to a level that would otherwise have been impossible.[44] Thus, the founding of a Roman town did not just consist in putting up an identikit collection of Roman buildings, but also in reforming local political life after a very particular, Roman pattern.

The exact nature of these reforms has been illustrated by a series of stunning finds from the southern coastal hinterland of Mediterranean Spain. After the Roman conquest of this region, a number of local communities here too reconstituted themselves over time as Roman towns, but, for some reason, they chose to inscribe their new constitutions on bronze tablets. The most complete set of these was found in the spring of 1981 on an obscure hill called Molino del Postero in the province of Seville. The finds originally comprised ten bronze tablets about 58 centimetres high by 90 wide, on which was inscribed – in three columns per tablet – the *Lex Irnitana*: the constitution of the Roman town of Irni. Comparing this set of tablets with extant fragments from other places has shown that there was one basic constitution, composed in Rome, which all these towns adopted, changing just a few of the details to suit their own circumstances. The laws are massively detailed; one composite text created by combining fragments from different settlements runs to eighteen dense pages in its English translation.[45] Amongst other things, the laws laid down who should qualify for the local council, and how the magistrates (executive officers, normally *duumviri*, 'two men') should be chosen from it; which legal cases could be handled locally, and how financial affairs were to be managed and audited. It was only such details as the number of councillors appointed that varied from place to place, according to the size and wealth of the community. Likewise with that very particular form of country dwelling, the villa: the design reflected canonical Graeco-Roman notions of how to live a civilized life out of town.[46]

Mediterranean values crept into life in the provinces in many other ways too. Roman religious cults insisted on separating the living from the dead, for instance, so that cemeteries for the new towns were never established inside urban boundaries. This custom quickly became part and parcel of the new model of urban living. Much more mundanely, the habit of turning staple grains into bread rather than porridge, with all the changes in cooking equipment and techniques that this required, likewise spread northwards with the adoption of Roman patterns of living.

The transformation of life in the conquered provinces thus led provincials everywhere to remake their lives after Roman patterns and value systems. Within a century or two of conquest, the whole of the Empire had become properly Roman. The old *Ladybird Book of British History* had a vivid picture of Roman Britain coming to an abrupt end in the fifth century with the legions marching off and the Roman names for places being superseded (a composite image of departing soldiers and broken signposts, as I recall it). But this is a mistaken view of what happened. By the late Empire, the Romans of Roman Britain were not immigrants from Italy but locals who had adopted the Roman lifestyle and everything that came with it. A bunch of legionaries departing the island would not bring Roman life to an end. Britain, as everywhere else between Hadrian's Wall and the Euphrates, was no longer Roman merely by 'occupation'.

Count Third-Class

SYMMACHUS EVENTUALLY turned homewards early in the year 369. He had seen the flourishing Romanness of the Moselle valley at first hand. The senatorial mission had completed its purpose, and he had been extensively entertained by the emperor and many of his notables. Carrying out successful embassies for your city was recorded as a distinction on your CV, and so it was with Symmachus, who also returned to Rome with a court title: at some point during the visit, Valentinian made him *comes ordinis tertii* – literally 'count third-class'. The counts (*comites*) were an order of imperial companions created by the emperor Constantine primarily as an honorific mark of personal favour, although some real posts carried the title as well. All in all, it was a job well done, and Symmachus' letters show how well he exploited in subsequent years the connections he had made at Valentinian's court. Knowing so many of the great and the good meant that he was especially sought after by young men just finishing their higher education in Rome and seeking letters of introduction. The senator made a career out of obliging them.

Not the least important of his court contacts was the Gallic rhetor Ausonius. But preserved in their otherwise amicable correspondence is one discordant letter. Shortly after returning to Rome, Symmachus wrote to his friend:

Your *Mosella* – that poem which has immortalized a river in heavenly verse – flits from hand to hand [in Rome] and from bosom to bosom of many: I can only watch it gliding past. Please tell me, why did you choose to deny me part or share in that little book? You thought me either too uncultivated to be able to appreciate it, or at all events too grudging to praise it, and thereby have offered the greatest possible affront to my head or my heart.[47]

The *Mosella* survives and is generally reckoned Ausonius' greatest work. It follows an established poetic tradition in using a major river as a vehicle on which to hang praise for an entire region. So, while the river itself comes in for extensive treatment, it is scarcely a poem about *natural* beauty at all, but about the deeper beauty that man's interaction with the natural environment has created there: an appropriate vision for a society which, as we've seen, regarded all truly civilized qualities as the products of careful cultivation rather than of natural talent. After dwelling in a famous passage on all the fish in the river, Ausonius then pictures the valley as a whole:[48]

From the topmost ridge to the foot of the slope, the river-side is thickly planted with green vines. The people, happy in their toil, and the restless husbandmen are busy, now on the hill-top, now on the slope exchanging shouts in boisterous rivalry. Here the wayfarer tramping along the low-lying bank, and there the barge-man floating by, shout their rude jokes at the loitering vine-dressers.

Amongst the Roman sculpture of Trier survives a beautifully carved wine barge on the Moselle, complete with rowers and casks.

Ausonius then moves on to the elegant villas that lined the river's banks:

What need to mention their courtyards set beside lush meadows, or their neat roofs resting upon countless pillars? What of their baths, built low down on the edge of the bank? ... But if a stranger were to arrive here from the shores of Cumae, he would believe that Euboean Baiae had bestowed on this region a miniature copy of its own delights: so great is the charm of its refinement and distinction, while its pleasures breed no excess.

Cumae and Baiae, the latter a renowned spa, were watering-holes of the Roman rich and famous on the Bay of Naples (both founded by Greek colonists from Euboea in the eighth century BC), so Ausonius was stressing that the Moselle could match the best that the rest of the Empire had to offer in terms of civilized Roman country life. Note too that, according to him, rural life around Trier had not slipped into the characteristic – from the Roman point of view – Greek vice of self-indulgence.

After our trip through the countryside, we reach the city of Trier itself:

> I shall mention your peaceful peasantry, your skilful lawyers, and your powerful barristers, the great defence of the accused; those in whom the Council of the townsmen has seen its chief leaders and a Senate of its own, those whose famed eloquence in the schools of youth has raised them to the height of old Quintilian's renown.

Quintilian (who was active about AD 35–95) was a famous lawyer who systematized many of the rules of rhetoric by which the educated Latin of Symmachus and Ausonius was defined.[49] What Ausonius is telling us, of course, is that Trier was rich in those essential Roman virtues whose widespread adoption lay at the heart of the revolution we have been surveying: educated speech and morals, the rule of law, and local self-government by peers. In short, in its agriculture, in its country seats and in its capital city, the Moselle region was completely civilized in the proper Roman manner.

We don't know for certain why Ausonius didn't send Symmachus a copy of the *Mosella*, but I can hazard a guess. During his stay in the Rhine frontier region, Symmachus gave a number of set-piece orations in front of the emperor and his court, of which fragments of three are preserved in the one surviving (damaged) manuscript of his speeches. The fragments present an interesting picture of Symmachus' notion of how the city of Rome perceived the Rhine frontier. In Oration 1, he sums it up: 'If you're interested in letters, said Cicero, for Greek you go to Athens not Libya, and for Latin you go to Rome and not Sicily.' Or, more generally: 'Leaving the East to your undefeated brother [Valens], you [Valentinian] swiftly took the path to the semi-barbarian banks of the unsubdued Rhine . . . you revert to the old model of an Empire created for military endeavours.'

For Symmachus, Rome was the hub of Roman civilization as encapsulated in the Latin language, and it was the job of the 'semi-barbarian' frontier provinces to protect it at all costs. One can well imagine what Valentinian's court made of the stuck-up young senator who'd come north to lecture them on what a good job they were doing for Roman Romanness. I strongly suspect, therefore, that Ausonius didn't send Symmachus a copy of the *Mosella* because it was a deliberate rebuttal of the attitude Symmachus had adopted in his year at the 'front'. Trier and its environs were not, as Symmachus would have it, semi-barbarian, but the domain of real Roman civilization. It is also particularly striking that Ausonius compared the villas on the banks of the Moselle with those of the resort of Baiae – Symmachus' letters regularly dwell on the particular pleasures of one of his own houses there.[50] He must have driven the locals of Trier to distraction with his praise of the beauties of Baiae. If Ausonius did decide to have some fun at his expense, once he had safely departed for Rome, then the passage may also be accusing Symmachus himself, and all the other Roman bigwigs whose names no doubt peppered his conversation, of Greek self-indulgence.

No wonder Ausonius didn't send Symmachus the poem. He had him hook, line and sinker, and all Symmachus could manage in response, when he did finally reel in a copy, was a little sarcasm about the number of fish:

> I should certainly not believe all the great things you say of the source of the Moselle, did I not know that you never tell a lie: even in poetry ... And yet, though I have often found myself at your table and there have marvelled at most other articles of food ... I have never found there fish such as you describe.[51]

Leaving aside the question of fish, Ausonius' *Mosella* caught the prevailing mood of its Treveran audience and due rewards quickly followed. Symmachus' countship had made him – briefly – Ausonius' superior (fifteen–love). But 'count third-class' has a rather dismally dismissive ring to it anyway, which is not just to do with literal translation,[52] and shortly after composing the *Mosella* Ausonius was promoted to *comes et quaestor*, count and quaestor. The quaestor was the emperor's legal officer and ranked as count first-class (thirty–fifteen Ausonius). Then, on Valentinian's death in November 375, Ausonius' old pupil Gratian became emperor instead, and Ausonius' family was launched on a round of nepotism that beggars the imagination. Ausonius himself became Praetorian Prefect (first minister) for Gaul and then for Gaul, Italy and Africa (an unusual combination). In the meantime, his son operated as joint first minister in Gaul, and then first minister in Italy; his father – now about ninety years old – became first minister in the western Balkans (Illyricum); his son-in-law became deputy first minister in Macedonia, and his nephew head of the imperial treasury (game, set, match and championship Ausonius). Such a spectacular gathering of the reins of power into the hands of Ausonius' family could not have been predicted in 371, but the deft aim of the *Mosella* was enough to convince Symmachus that any sarcasm he might be tempted to vent needed to be tempered. His letter of complaint ended with praise of the verse, and was followed by many friendlier ones; Ausonius was too useful and important a contact at court for Symmachus to cut off his nose and spite his face over a few fish.[53]

Symmachus' senatorial embassy, and the literary exchange with which it ended, open up for us, therefore, the root-and-branch transformations that had remade the Roman world in the 400 years since Julius Caesar. Everywhere, the enthusiastic adoption of Roman values had made proper Romans of provincials. This was the true genius of the Empire as a historical phenomenon. Originally conquered and subdued by the legions, the indigenous people had gone on to build Roman towns and villas and to live Roman lives in their own communities. This did not happen overnight but nonetheless relatively early on – within two to four generations – in the history of an Empire that spanned 450 years. That the new subjects also swallowed wholesale the proclaimed virtues of the Latin language needs to be underlined. Not only did a few of the very wealthiest in the dominated areas attend metropolitan educational institutions – prompting modern parallels of Indian princes going to Eton, or the elites of Asia and South America to Harvard or MIT – but exact copies were set up in the provinces. Eventually, the teachers there became so expert that, as in the case of Ausonius, the provincials were able to instruct the metropolitans.

These astonishing developments changed what it meant to be Roman. Once the same political culture, lifestyle and value system had established themselves more or less evenly from Hadrian's Wall to the Euphrates, then all inhabitants of this huge area were legitimately Roman. 'Roman', no longer a geographic epithet, was now an entirely cultural identity accessible, potentially, to all. From this followed the most significant consequence of imperial success: having acquired Romanness, the new Romans were bound to assert their right to participate in the political process, to some share in the power and benefits that a stake in such a vast state brought with it. As early as

AD 69 there was a major revolt in Gaul, partly motivated by this rising sense of a new identity. The revolt was defeated, but by the fourth century the balance of power had changed. Symmachus, in Trier, was shown in no uncertain terms that 'the better part of humankind' comprised not just the Senate of Rome, but civilized Romans throughout the Roman world.

2

BARBARIANS

IN AD 15, THE ROMAN ARMY of Germanicus Caesar, nephew of the reigning Augustus Tiberius, approached the Teutobergiensis Saltus (the Teutoburg Forest, 300 kilometres north-east of Trier). Six years before, three entire Roman legions commanded by P. Quinctilius Varus, totalling with their attendant auxiliary troops maybe twenty thousand men, had been massacred there in one of the most famous battles of antiquity.

> The scene lived up to its horrible associations. Varus' extensive first camp, with its broad extent and headquarters marked out, testified to the whole army's labours. Then a half-ruined breast-work and shallow ditch showed where the last pathetic remnant had gathered. On the open ground were whitening bones, scattered where men had fled, heaped up where they had stood and fought back. Fragments of spears and of horses' limbs lay there, also human heads fastened to tree trunks. In groves nearby were the outlandish altars at which the Germans had massacred the Roman 'colonels' and 'senior company-commanders'. Survivors of the catastrophe, who had escaped from the battle or from captivity, pointed out where the generals had fallen, and where the Eagles were captured. They showed where Varus had received his first wound, and where he died by his own unhappy hand. And they told of . . . all the gibbets and pits for the prisoners.[1]

The massacre was the work of a coalition of Germanic warriors marshalled by one Arminius, a chieftain of the Cherusci, a small tribe living between the River Ems and the River Weser in what is now northern Germany. The ancient Roman sources describing the defeat were rediscovered and passed into broader circulation among Latin scholars in the fifteenth and sixteenth centuries, and from that point on Arminius, generally known as Hermann ('the German') – the delatinized version of his name – became a symbol of German nationhood.

Between 1676 and 1910 an extraordinary seventy-six operas were composed to celebrate his exploits, and in the nineteenth century a huge monument was constructed in his honour near the small city of Detmold in the middle of what is today called the Teutoburger Wald. The foundation stone was laid in 1841, and the monument was finally dedicated in 1875, four years after Bismarck's defeat of France had united much of the German-speaking world of north-central Europe behind the Prussian monarchy. The 28-metre copper statue of Hermann is mounted on top of a stone base of similar height, which itself sits on top of a 400-metre hill. The edifice was a reminder that the triumph of modern German unification had its counterpart in the Roman era.

The Hermann monument is actually in the wrong place. The name Teutoburger Wald was first coined for the forested area around Detmold in the seventeenth century, as people began to conjecture where the ancient battle might have taken place. Thanks to some extraordinary finds, part of the actual battlefield has now been identified about 70 kilometres to the north. Just outside Osnabrück, the north German coastal plain is fringed by uplands known as the Wiehengebirge. Since 1987, a large number of Roman coins and various items of military equipment have been recovered from an area about 6 by 4.5 kilometres on the northern fringes of this range, known as the Kalkriese-Niewedde depression. The southern boundary is marked by the Kalkriese Berg, a 100-metre hill, which was heavily wooded in antiquity. At the foot of its northern slope was a strip of sandy soil, part of it so narrow that only four men could have marched abreast. On the other side was a huge peat bog. In AD 9, the Roman army had been moving east–west along the narrow strip led by native guides provided by Arminius – he had convinced Varus that he had Rome's interests at heart – when it was caught in an ambush between the wooded slopes to its south and the peat bog to the north. As told by our best source, a four-day running battle ensued, during the first part of which the Romans, despite substantial losses, held formation and continued to advance towards safety. By the fourth day, however, it had become clear that the army was cornered and doomed. At this point Varus, having given permission to his surviving troops to do whatever seemed best in the circumstances, committed suicide rather than fall into the hands of his attackers. Few survived to tell the tale.[2]

The catastrophe reads like a larger-scale version of that suffered by

Cotta and his men, betrayed on to similarly impossible ground sixty-three years earlier. The long-term outcome, however, was different. Whereas the Eburones and the Treveri were eventually conquered, and propelled towards learning Latin, wearing togas and building self-governing towns, Arminius' Cherusci were not. In the late Roman period, the area between the Rhine and the Elbe still remained beyond the imperial frontier, its material culture betraying none of the characteristic marks of Roman civilization. This ancient line in the European sand is still discernible in the modern divide between Romance languages descended from Latin, and Germanic languages. On the face of it, this would explain why the western Roman Empire was to give way, in the fifth century, to a series of successor kingdoms with, at their core, groups of armed Germanic-speakers. Germania east of the Rhine was not swallowed up by Rome's legions in the conquest period because its inhabitants fought tooth and nail against them, and eventually had their full revenge more than four centuries later in the destruction of the Empire. This was certainly the explanation given by nineteenth-century German nationalists; argued in scholarly circles, it was also brought home to a much wider audience. Felix Dahn, whose great work on Germanic kingship remains a classic, also wrote a famous novel, *Ein Kampf um Rom* (*War against Rome*), which went through multiple editions in the late nineteenth and early twentieth centuries.[3]

The odd thing about all this, though, is that if you had asked any fourth-century Roman where the main threat to imperial security lay, he would undoubtedly have said with Persia in the east. This was only sensible, because in about AD 300 Persia posed an incomparably greater threat to Roman order than did Germania, and no other frontier offered any real threat whatsoever.[4] A closer reading of the sources, especially in the light of archaeological evidence that was unavailable to Dahn, suggests a rather different reason for the halting of the legions on the Rhine and Danube in the early first century from stirrings of German nationalism. It also explains why late Romans were much more concerned about Persia than about Germanic tribesmen.

Germania and the Limits of Roman Expansion

IN THE FIRST CENTURY AD, Germanic-speaking groups dominated most of central and northern Europe beyond Rome's riverine frontiers. The Germani, as the Romans called them, spread all the way from the Rhine in the west (which, before the Roman conquest, had marked an approximate boundary between Europe's Germanic and Celtic speakers) to beyond the River Vistula in the east, and from the Danube in the south to the North and Baltic Seas. Apart from some Iranian-speaking Sarmatian nomads on the Great Hungarian Plain, and Dacian-speakers in and around the arc of the Carpathians, Rome's immediate neighbours were all Germanic-speakers: from Arminius' Cherusci and their allies at the mouth of the Rhine, to the Bastarnae who dominated substantial tracts of territory at the mouth of the Danube (map 2). First-century Germania was thus much bigger than modern Germany.

Trying to reconstruct the way of life and social institutions, not to mention the political and ideological structures of this vast territory, is a hugely difficult task. The main problem is that the societies of Germanic Europe, in the Roman period, were essentially illiterate. There is a fair amount of information of various kinds to be gleaned from Greek and Latin authors, but this has two major drawbacks. First, Roman writers were chiefly interested in Germanic societies for the threat – potential or actual – that they might pose to frontier security. What you find for the most part, therefore, are isolated pieces of narrative information concerning relations between the Empire and one or more of its immediate Germanic neighbours. Groups living away from the frontier hardly ever figure, and the inner workings of Germanic society are never explored. Second, what information there is is deeply coloured by the fact that, to Roman eyes, all Germani were barbarians. Barbarians were expected to behave in certain ways and embody a particular range of negative characteristics, and Roman commentators went out of their way to prove that this was so.

Little survives from inside the Germanic world to correct the misapprehensions, omissions and slanted perspectives of our Roman authors. The Germani did use runes for divinatory purposes for much of the Roman period, and there are other, limited, exceptions to the illiteracy rule, but no detailed first-hand account of life has come down to us from inside Germania. So there is much that we do not know,

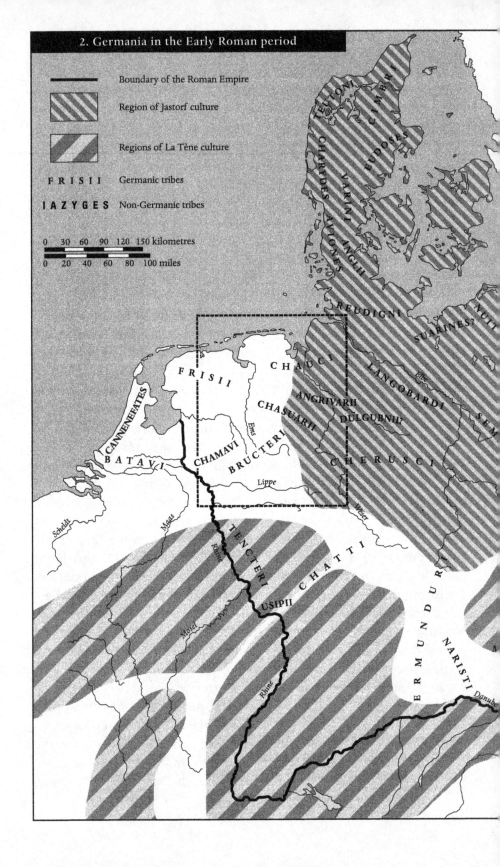

2. Germania in the Early Roman period

Boundary of the Roman Empire

Region of Jastorf culture

Regions of La Tène culture

FRISII   Germanic tribes

IAZYGES   Non-Germanic tribes

0   30 60 90 120 150 kilometres

0   20 40 60 80 100 miles

TEUTONI

CIMBRI

CHARUDES

VARINI

AVIONES

ANGLII

EUDOSES

REUDIGNI

SUARINES?

NUIT

LANGOBARDI

SEM

FRISII

CHAUCI

ANGRIVARII

DULGUBNII?

CHASUARII

CHERUSCI

CANNENEFATES

BATAVI

CHAMAVI

BRUCTERI

Ems

Elbe

Weser

Lippe

Scheldt

Maas

TENCTERI

Rhine

USIPII

CHATTI

ERMUNDURI

NARISTI

Mosel

Rhine

Danube

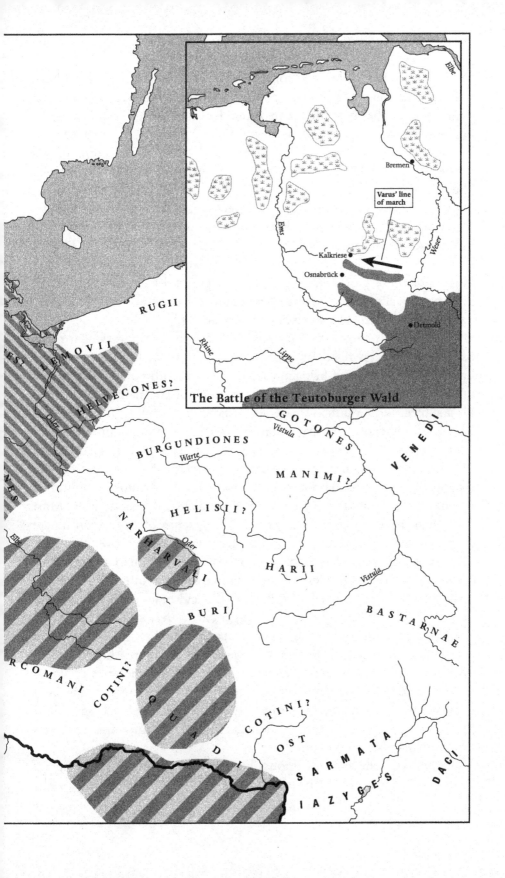

The Battle of the Teutoburger Wald

RUGII

LEMOVII

HELVECONES?

GOTONES

VENEDI

BURGUNDIONES

Warte

MANIMI?

HELISII?

NARHARVALI

HARII

Oder

BURI

BASTARNAE

Vistula

RCOMANI

COTINI?

QUADI

COTINI?

OST

SARMATA

IAZYGES

DACI

Elbe

Rhine

Lippe

Ems

Weser

Vistula

Kalkriese

Osnabrück

Bremen

Detmold

Varus' line of march

and cannot ever know, and for most areas of life we have to fall back on information from Roman sources and on more or less informed guesswork. The best that can often be done when attempting to reconstruct social institutions, for instance, is to look at literary sources – especially legal ones – from Germanic-dominated kingdoms of the later fifth and sixth centuries, then try to extrapolate what might also be relevant to earlier eras. Stretching from the Rhine to the Crimea, Germania encompassed many different geographical and economic landscapes, and it is always necessary to consider whether something reported of one group might also be true of another. The literary evidence thus offers us a not entirely palatable choice between the biased testimony of Roman sources and material of a later date. Both can be revealing, but they must be handled honestly and with explicit acknowledgement of their inherent limitations.

To some extent, the lack of first-hand contemporary Germanic sources has been filled by archaeological investigation. This has the priceless advantage of bringing us face to face with contemporary and genuinely Germanic artefacts and contexts, but Germanic archaeology is a subject with a difficult past. As a scientific discipline, it emerged in the late nineteenth century when the Hermann monument was under construction and when nationalism was sweeping through most of Europe. It was generally assumed at this date that the 'nation', or 'people', was the fundamental unit in which large groupings of human beings had operated in the distant past, and should operate now. Most nationalisms were also fuelled by a strong sense of their own innate superiority. The German nation may have been split up over time into lots of small political entities, but the efforts of Bismarck and others were now, through German unification, successfully restoring the natural and ancient order of things. In this cultural context, Germanic archaeology could have only one agenda: to research the historical origins and homeland of the German people. The first great proponent of such studies, Gustav Kossinna, noticed that the increasing quantities of artefacts then coming to light from excavated cemeteries could be grouped together by similarity of design and burial custom. He built his reputation on the argument that the geographical spread of particular groupings of artefacts and customs represented the territories of particular ancient peoples.[5]

Such was the quasi-religious fervour surrounding the concept of the nation that politicians were ready to use identifications of the ancient spread of 'peoples' as evidence for claims about the present. At Versailles in 1919, Kossinna and one of his Polish disciples, Vladimir Kostrewszki, made rival cases for the positioning of the new German-Polish border on the basis of different identifications of the same set of ancient remains. Things got nastier still in the Nazi period, when high-flown claims about ancient Germania became a basis-cum-justification for territorial demands in Poland and the Ukraine, and an associated sense of ancient Germanic racial superiority led directly to the atro-cious treatment of Slavic prisoners-of-war. In the last two generations, however, Germanic archaeology has successfully reinvented itself, and from this have resulted huge advances in our understanding of the long-term social and economic development of the Germani. With the excision of nationalistic assumptions from the interpretation of literary sources, the history of Germanic-speaking Europe in the Roman period can be rewritten in new and exciting ways.

A first gain stems directly from new understandings of the pat-terns of similar remains which Kossinna was sure could identify the territories of ancient 'peoples'. While the territory of ancient Germa-nia was clearly dominated in a political sense by Germanic-speaking groups, it has emerged that the population of this vast territory was far from entirely Germanic. In the great era of nationalism, any-where that threw up plausibly ancient Germanic remains was claimed as part of an ancient and greater German homeland. Analysis of river names has shown, however, that there was once in northern Europe a third population group with its own Indo-European language, located between the Celts and the Germani. These people were under the domination of the other two long before Roman commen-tators reached the area, and we know nothing about them. Much of ancient Germania was also the product of periodic Germanic expansion, west, south and east from a first, traceable, heartland beside the Baltic. Some early land-grabbing episodes made enough of a stir to register in ancient Greek sources, while others occurred after the rise of Rome and are better known. But this kind of expansion did not annihilate the indigenous, non-Germanic population of the areas concerned, so it is important to perceive Germania as meaning *Germanic-dominated* Europe. The more one moved south and east through the region during the Roman period, the more likely it is that Germanic-speakers constituted a politically dominant force in very mixed societies.

The other salient fact about Germania in the Roman period was its complete lack of political unity. As map 2 (based on Tacitus' gazetteer) makes clear, it was a highly fragmented world, comprising over fifty small sociopolitical units. There was a variety of ways in which, for brief periods, some of them might be brought together for particular purposes. As we have seen, Arminius mobilized a mixed force of tribesmen in AD 9 to defeat Varus. Half a century earlier, Julius Caesar had encountered another Germanic leader of extraordinary and slightly longer-lived power: Ariovistus, King of the Suebi, who by 71 BC had built up a substantial power-base on the eastern fringes of Gaul and for a time was even recognized as 'friend' by the Romans. Caesar eventually picked a fight with him in 58 BC, routing his army in Alsace. One major defeat was enough to break up the coalition. In Arminius' day there was one other pre-eminent Germanic leader, Maroboduus, who ruled a coalition of various groupings based in Bohemia. Tacitus also records that some Germanic tribes belonged to cult leagues, and pinpoints a moment when one particular prophetess, Veleda, acquired huge influence. But neither cult leagues, nor prophetesses, nor temporarily pre-eminent leaders represented major steps towards Germanic unification.[6]

As Roman power moved east of the Rhine, different Germanic groups were quite as likely to fight each other as to fight the Romans, and the results could be as brutal as the Teutoburger Wald. There is little discernible cultural difference between these groups, and it was essentially different political identities that divided them, and through which struggles for control of the best lands and other economic assets were fought out. Late in the first century, for instance, a coalition of their neighbours turned on the Bructeri, and invited Roman observers to enjoy the spectacle, reportedly, of 60,000 people being massacred. Tacitus' *Annals* also record a fight to the death between the Hermenduri and the Chatti, and the eventual destruction of the landless, and hence troublesome, Ampsivarii: 'In their protracted wanderings, the exiles were treated as guests, then as beggars, then as enemies. Finally, their fighting-men were exterminated, their young and old distributed as booty.'[7]

It could hardly be clearer that nineteenth-century visions of an ancient German nation were way off-target. Temporary alliances and unusually powerful kings might for a time knit together a couple or more of its many small tribes, but the inhabitants of first-century

Germania had no capacity to formulate and put into practice sustained and unifying political agendas.

Why did Roman expansion fail to swallow this highly fragmented world whole, as it had done Celtic Europe? The halting of the legions' progress through northern Europe has often been attributed to Arminius' great victory, but like the destruction of the legion commanded by Sabinus and Cotta in 54 BC, the massacre of Varus' command was a one-off event for which the Romans duly extracted revenge. Germanicus' visit to the Teutoburger Wald in AD 15 was part of another major campaign against Arminius' Cherusci. In the course of it, a second Roman force was ambushed by Arminius' warriors, but this time the outcome was different. Although hard pressed for a time, the Romans eventually lured their opponents into a trap, with a predictable outcome: 'The *Germani* went down, as defenceless in defeat as success had made them impetuous. Arminius got away unhurt [but] the massacre of the rank and file went on as long as fury and daylight lasted.'[8] The Romans were assisted by Segestes, a second leader of the Cherusci, who, like many Gallic Celtic chiefs in the time of Julius Caesar, saw considerable advantages in his territory becoming part of the Roman Empire. Not even the Cherusci, let alone the Germani as a whole, were united in their resistance to Rome, and the Teutoburger Wald did not stop the advance of the legions in its tracks. More Roman victories followed in AD 16, and about three years later Arminius was murdered by a faction of his own tribesmen. His son was brought up in Ravenna. Arminus had won one huge, fluke victory, but the underlying reasons for the halting of the legions on the fringes of first-century Germania were altogether different.

LOGISTICS MADE IT likely enough that Rome's European frontiers would end up on river lines somewhere. Rivers made supplying the many troops stationed on the frontier a much more practical proposition. An early imperial Roman legion of about 5,000 men required about 7,500 kilos of grain and 450 kilos of fodder per day, or 225 and 13.5 tonnes, respectively, per month.[9] Most Roman troops at this date were placed on or close to the frontier, and conditions in most border regions, before economic development had set in, meant that it was impossible to satisfy their needs from purely local sources. Halting the western frontier at the Rhine, rather than on any of the other north–south rivers of western or central Europe – of which there are many, notably the Elbe – had another advantage too. Using the Rhône and (via a brief portage) the Moselle, supplies could be moved by water directly from the Mediterranean to the Rhine without having to brave wilder waters.

The real reason why the Rhine eventually emerged as the frontier lay in the interaction of the motives underlying Roman expansion and comparative levels of social and economic development within pre-Roman Europe. Roman expansion was driven by the internal power struggles of republican oligarchs such as Julius Caesar and by early emperors' desires for glory. Expansion as the route to political power at Rome had built up momentum at a point when there were still numerous unconquered wealthy communities around the Mediterranean waiting to be picked off. Once annexed, they became a new source of tribute flowing into Rome, as well as making the name of the general who had organized their conquest. Over time, however, the richest prizes were scooped up until, in the early imperial era, expansion was sucking in territories that did not really produce sufficient income to justify the costs of conquest. Britain in particular, the ancient sources stress, was taken only because the emperor Claudius wanted the glory.[10] With this in mind, the limits of Rome's northern expansion take on a particular significance when charted against levels of economic development in non-Roman Europe.

Expansion eventually ground to a halt in an intermediate zone between two major material cultures: the so-called La Tène and Jastorf cultures (map 2). Some key differences in the general character of life distinguished the two. As well as villages, La Tène Europe had also generated, before the Roman conquest, much larger settlements, sometimes identified as towns (in Latin, *oppida* – hence its other common name, 'the Oppida culture'). In some La Tène areas coins were in use, and some of its populations were literate. Caesar's *Gallic War* describes the complex political and religious institutions that prevailed among at least some of the La Tène groups he conquered, particularly the Aedui of south-western Gaul. All of this rested upon an economy that could produce sufficient food surpluses to support warrior, priestly and artisan classes not engaged in primary agricultural production. Jastorf Europe, by contrast, operated at a much starker level of subsistence, with a greater emphasis on pastoral agriculture and much less of a food surplus. Its population had no coinage or literacy, and, by the birth of Christ, had produced no substantial settlements – not even villages. Also, its remains have produced almost no evidence for any kind of specialized economic activity.

In the days when Kossinna's assumptions ruled, and cultural zones were associated with 'peoples', it was traditional to equate the La Tène and Jastorf cultures respectively with Celts and Germani, but such simple equations don't work. Zones of archaeological similarity reflect patterns of material culture, and material culture can be acquired; people aren't just born with one set of weapons, pots and ornaments that they retain through thick and thin. While La Tène cultural patterns did originally emerge among some of Europe's Celtic-speakers, and their Jastorf equivalents among certain Germanic groups, there was no golden rule that made it impossible for Germanic groups to adopt elements of La Tène material culture. And by the time Roman power advanced north of the Alps, some Germanic groups on the fringes of the Celtic world, particularly those around the mouth of the Rhine, had evolved a culture that was much more in line with La Tène than with Jastorf norms.

The Roman advance ground to a halt not on an ethnic divide, therefore, but around a major fault-line in European socio-economic organization. What happened was that most of more advanced La Tène Europe was taken into the Empire, while most of Jastorf Europe was excluded.

This fits a much broader pattern. As has also been observed in the case of China, there is a general tendency for the frontiers of an empire based on arable agriculture to stabilize in an intermediate, part-arable part-pastoral zone, where the productive capacity of the local economy is not by itself sufficient to support the empire's armies. Expansionary ideologies and individual rulers' desires for glory will carry those armies some way beyond the gain line; but, eventually, the difficulties involved in incorporating the next patch of territory, combined with the relative lack of wealth that can be extracted from it, make further conquest unattractive. A two-speed Europe is not a new phenomenon, and the Romans drew the logical conclusion. Augustus' successor Tiberius saw that Germania just wasn't worth conquering. The more widely dispersed populations of these still heavily forested corners of Europe could be defeated in individual engagements, but the Jastorf regions proved much more difficult to dominate strategically than the concentrated and ordered populations occupying the La Tène towns. It was the logistic convenience of the Rhine–Moselle axis and cost-

benefit calculations concerning the limited economy of Jastorf Europe
that combined to stop the legions in their tracks. Germania as a whole
was also far too disunited politically to pose a major threat to the
richer lands already conquered. It was thus entirely appropriate that
nineteenth-century German nationalists put the Hermann monument
in the wrong place, since they also mistook his real significance. It was
not the military prowess of the Germani that kept them outside the
Empire, but their poverty.[11]

As a result, the defended Roman frontier came by the mid-first
century AD to be established broadly along a line marked by the Rivers
Rhine and Danube. Some minor adjustments apart, it was still there
three hundred years later. The consequences were profound. West and
south of these riverine frontiers, European populations, whether Jastorf
or La Tène, found themselves sucked into a trajectory towards Latin,
togas, towns and, eventually, Christianity. Watching from the side-
lines as neighbouring populations were transformed by Romanization,
Germanic-dominated Europe north and east of this line never became
part of the Roman world. In Roman terms, Germania remained the
home of unreconstructed barbarians. The same label was used of the
Persians in the east. However, this second major group of barbarians
posed an altogether different level of threat.

Persia and the Third-Century Crisis

AT NAQS-I RUSTAM, seven kilometres north of Persepolis, lies the
burial place of the famous Achaemenid Persian kings of antiquity,
Darius and his son Xerxes, whose unwelcome attentions the Athenians
and their allies fought off at the battles of Marathon and Salamis in
490 and 480 BC. Here, too, were discovered in 1936, inscribed in three
languages on the side of a Zoroastrian fire temple, the proud boasts of
a much later Persian king:

> I am the Mazda-worshipping divine Shapur, King of Kings . . . of
> the race of the Gods, son of the Mazda-worshipping divine
> Ardashir, King of Kings . . . When I was first established over the
> dominion of the nations, the Caesar Gordian [emperor, 238–44]
> from the whole of the Roman Empire . . . raised an army and
> marched . . . against us. A great battle took place between the two

sides on the frontiers of Assyria at Meshike. Caesar Gordian was destroyed and the Roman army was annihilated. The Romans proclaimed Philip Caesar. And Caesar Philip came to sue for peace, and for their lives he paid a ransom of 500,000 denarii and became tributary to us ... And the Caesar lied again and did injustice to Armenia. We marched against the Roman Empire and annihilated a Roman army of 60,000 men at Barbalissos. The nation of Syria and whatever nations and plains that were above it, we set on fire and devastated and laid waste. And in the campaign [we took] ... thirty-seven cities with their surrounding territories. In the third contest ... Caesar Valerian came upon us. There was with him a force of 70,000 men ... A great battle took place beyond Carrhae and Edessa between us and Caesar Valerian and we took him prisoner with our own hands, as well as all the other commanders of the army ... On this campaign, we also conquered ... thirty-six cities with their surrounding territories.

This is from the *Res Gestae Divi Saporis* (*The Acts of the Divine Shapur*); it encapsulates a strategic revolution, beginning in the third century AD, which transformed the Roman Empire.[12]

Hitherto, resistance to Rome in the east had been led by the Parthian Arsacid dynasty, which had first established itself about 250 BC. The Arsacids ruled a world that could not have been more different from the forested homes of the north European Germani. The dynasty originated in Parthia and began to spread its dominion more widely over the Near East in the third century BC, quickly bringing under its sway territory from the Euphrates to the Indus. It thus encompassed a huge range of populations and habitats, but the dynasty's heartland was soon to be Mesopotamia. Again unlike Germania, the history of this region had been punctuated by the rise and fall of great empires, not least the Achaemenid Empire of Cyrus, Darius and Xerxes. They had ruled not only the Near East, but also Egypt, western Turkey and the Fertile Crescent, and had even come within a whisker of swallowing Greece.

The Parthian Arsacids had scored some early victories over the Empire in the late republican period, when Roman power had first penetrated so far east, most famously in the destruction of the army of Crassus, father and son, in 53 BC. But by the second century AD the dynasty's capacity to mount serious resistance to Rome had diminished, and a succession of emperors won major victories on the Persian front. The latest came in the 190s, when Septimius Severus created two new provinces, Osrhoene and Mesopotamia, thereby advancing the frontier south and east. His victories threw the world ruled by the Parthians into crisis. Various members of the dynasty struggled for control, and some outlying regions threw off its suzerainty. As early as 205/6, rebellion began in the province of Fars beside the Indian Ocean. It was led by Sasan, the most important of the regional magnates, and was continued after his death by Shapur's father, Ardashir I (reigned AD 224–40), the real founder of the Sasanian dynasty. In 224 and 225, he defeated two rival Arsacid rulers and established his control over the other regional magnates who had also broken away from Arsacid domination, before having himself crowned King of Kings in Persepolis in September 226.[13]

As the *Res Gestae Divi Saporis* makes clear, the rise to prominence of the Sasanian dynasty was not just a major episode in the internal history of modern Iraq and Iran. Defeat at the hands of a succession of Roman emperors in the second century was a fundamental reason behind the collapse of Arsacid hegemony, and the Sasanians were able rapidly and effectively to reverse the prevailing balance of power. Ardashir I began the process. Invading Roman Mesopotamia for the first time between 237 and 240, he captured the major cities of Carrhae, Nisibis and Hatra (map 3). Rome responded to the challenge by launching three major counterattacks during the first twenty years of the reign of Ardashir's son Shapur I (reigned 240–72). The results were as Shapur's inscription records. Three huge defeats were inflicted on the Romans, two emperors were dead, and a third, Valerian, captured. Shapur proceeded to drag Valerian around with him, in chains, as a symbol of his own greatness – an image preserved for posterity in the great carved relief of Bishapur. After his death, Shapur had him skinned and tanned as a permanent trophy. Later in the century, a second Roman emperor, Numerianus, was also captured, but killed immediately: 'They flayed him and made his skin into a sack. And they treated it with myrh [to preserve it] and kept it as an object of exceptional splendour.'[14] Whether this was also Valerian's fate, or whether he was kept on the floor or the wall, the sources don't say.

Nothing could better symbolize the new world order. The rise of the Sasanians destroyed what was by then more or less a century of Roman hegemony in the east. Rome's overall strategic situation had suddenly and decisively deteriorated, for the Sasanian superpower, this new Persian dynasty, despite Rome's best efforts in the middle of the third century, would not quickly disappear. The Sasanians marshalled the resources of Mesopotamia and the Iranian plateau much more efficiently than their Arsacid predecessors had done. Outlying principalities were welded more fully into a single political structure, while the labour of Roman prisoners was used for massive irrigation projects that would eventually generate a 50 per cent rise in the settlement and

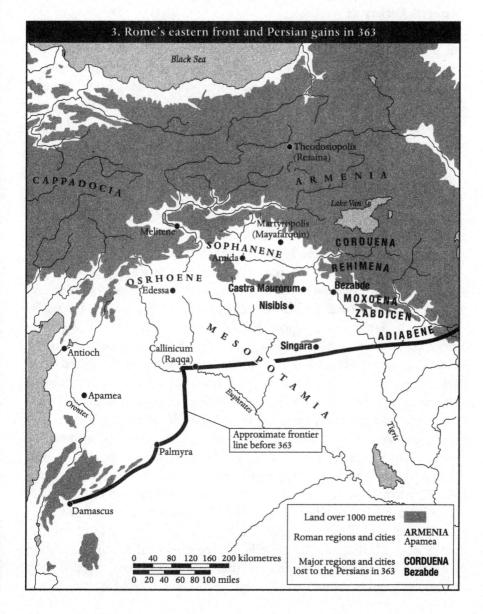

3. Rome's eastern front and Persian gains in 363

Land over 1000 metres

Roman regions and cities **ARMENIA** Apamea

Major regions and cities lost to the Persians in 363 **CORDUENA** **Bezabde** cultivation of the lands between the Tigris and Euphrates. This certainly began under Shapur, if not his father, and the resulting increase in tax revenues was coordinated by a burgeoning bureaucracy and directed to the maintenance of an at least partly professional army. Not for nothing did Shapur revive, in his diplomatic posturing towards the Romans, a claim to the old Achaemenid Empire in its entirety: he wanted not only Iran and Iraq, but Egypt, the Fertile Crescent and western Turkey as well.[15]

Previously, Rome had operated in a context of dominance across all its frontier zones. Opponents might achieve local successes, but defeats could easily be reversed by mobilizing the Empire's existing resources. Now, the rise of a rival superpower was a huge strategic shock. It had reverberations not just for the eastern frontier regions, as Shapur's record of sackings and captures recounts, but for the Empire as a whole. Not only did a much more powerful enemy have to be confronted on its eastern frontier, but the defence of all the other frontiers still had to be maintained. For this to be possible, a major increase in the power of the Roman military was necessary. By the fourth century, this had produced both larger and substantially reorganized armed forces.

As we saw in Chapter 1, the Roman army of the early imperial era was divided into legions, each a small expeditionary army of 5,000-plus men, recruited exclusively from existing Roman citizens, with auxiliary units (infantry *cohortes* and cavalry *alae*) recruited from non-citizens. By the fourth century, the legions had been broken down into a greater array of smaller units. In some ways this formalized actual Roman practice, for individual cohorts of 500 men had often operated separately from the main body of their legion. In addition, the different classes of unit had been reorganized. Instead of legions and auxiliaries, the late Roman army was composed of frontier garrison troops (*limitanei*) and mobile field forces (*comitatenses*) gathered behind the three main frontiers: the Rhine, the Danube and the east. The field forces were more heavily equipped and a touch better paid, but the garrison troops were formidable too, not part-time soldier-farmers as they have sometimes been portrayed. For particular campaigns, they were often mobilized alongside the field forces. There was also much more specialization at the unit level: regiments of mounted archers (*sagitarii*), heavy artillerymen (*ballistiarii*) and plate-armoured cavalry (*clibanarii*, 'boiler boys') were employed. Overall, where Caesar had relied almost exclusively on the legionary footsoldier, there was now a greater emphasis on cavalry. Some of the heavy cavalry units were developed in direct imitation of their Persian counterparts, who had played a major role in the defeats of Gordian, Philip and Valerian. Nonetheless, in terms of numbers the late Roman army continued to be dominated by infantry, especially the mobile field forces; infantry-men, not dependent on the availability of animal fodder and able to move long distances while still fighting effectively, were actually more mobile in strategic terms.

The size of the late Roman army remains a hotly debated topic. We have a pretty good idea of the paper strength of the army under the Severan emperors of the early third century, immediately before the rise of the Sasanians. It consisted of thirty legions of 5,000-plus men each, and a similar number of auxiliaries, making a grand total of around 300,000 troops. But attempts to calculate total army size for the late Empire on a similar basis, even though we have a pretty complete listing of its units dating from about AD 400 in a source called the *Notitia Dignitatum* (see pp. 246–8), founder on the fact that the theoretical strength of the various types of unit generated by the reorganization clearly varied, and we are not sure how big some of them were. Argument has turned, therefore, on two reported global figures: one of 645,000; the other, referring specifically to the time of the eastern emperor Diocletian (reigned AD 284–305), of 389,704 plus 45,562 in the fleets, making a total of 435,266 men. Both estimates are problematic. The first figure is given by the historian Agathias, writing in the early 570s, in a passage which favourably contrasts the 645,000 with a military establishment in his own day of 150,000 as a means of criticizing contemporary emperors. It was entirely to his point to exaggerate the past figure. The figure of 435,266 commands, a priori, greater credibility both because of its precision and the fact that the context is non-polemical. But it, too, is given by a sixth- rather than a fourth-century writer, in a text composed over two hundred years after Diocletian's death, which is hardly ideal. We also know that substantial military reorganization continued after Diocletian's reign, with the distinction between *comitatenses* and *limitanei* becoming fully formalized under Constantine. Even if we accept the figure as accur-ate, then, there is every reason to suppose that the army continued to expand subsequently; historians' estimates have therefore ranged between 400,000 and 600,000. Even a lower estimate would suggest that between the early third and mid-fourth centuries the 300,000-strong Roman army increased in size by at least one-third, and quite possibly by substantially more.[16]

That there was such a large increase is placed beyond doubt, to my mind, not only by the evolving strategic situation – the fact that Rome now faced a rival superpower in the east – but also by the fact that the late third and early fourth centuries saw a major financial restructuring of the Empire. The largest item of expenditure had always been the army: even an increase in size of one-third, a conservative estimate, represented a huge increase in the total amount of revenue that needed to be raised by the Roman state. Ask a modern state to fund an increase of 33 per cent or more in its largest budgetary item, and you would soon see bureaucratic hair turning grey. It is entirely consistent with both the size of the new Persian threat, and of even the lowest estimates for late Roman military expansion, that the fiscal patterns of the Empire had to be radically transformed as part of its response to the rise of the Sasanians. Much of the Roman response to third-century crisis has often been attributed to the emperor Diocletian. But while his reign saw many reforms brought to completion or substantially advanced, most of these changes were long-term processes rather than the product of a single mind. This was certainly the case with the reorganization and expansion of the army, and equally true of the financial reforms required to fund it.

The first fiscal response of third-century emperors to the onset of crisis was to lay claim to all existing sources of revenue. Sometime in the 240s–60s, first of all, long-established city revenues – the proceeds of endowments, local tolls and taxes – were confiscated by the state. City officials continued to have to raise the monies and administer the endowments, but the proceeds could no longer be spent locally. This change has often been blamed on Diocletian, but none of our sources for his reign, many of them hostile to his financial reforms, mentions it. It was one of the easiest possible, and hence probably one of the first, responses to financial crisis. These new funds were not inconsiderable, and in the fourth century a portion was sometimes returned to the cities by emperors who wished to curry local favour.[17]

This income was not enough, however, to cover the entire cost of the new army, and in the late third century emperors also pursued two further strategies. First, they debased the coinage, reducing the silver content of the *denarii* with which the army was customarily paid.

Those of Gallienus (reigned 253–68), for example, were essentially copper coins, containing less than 5 per cent silver. This strategy produced more coins, but the inevitable result was massive price inflation. Diocletian's Prices Edict of AD 301 fixed the price of a measure of wheat, which in the second century had cost about half a *denarius*, at no less than a hundred of the new, debased *denarii*. Comparative evidence suggests that you have about a month before merchants realize that the new coins are even worse than the old ones and put the prices up, so each debasement bought hard-pressed emperors a brief breathing space. Debasement and price-fixing were no long-term solution, since merchants just took their goods off the shelves and operated a black market instead. In the longer term, the only remedy was to extract a greater proportion of the Empire's wealth – its Gross Imperial Product – via taxation. This too was instigated in the depths of the third-century crisis, when, at particular moments of stress, emperors would raise extraordinary taxes, in the form of foodstuffs. This bypassed problems with the coinage, but, by the nature of its unpredictability, was very unpopular. Finally, under Diocletian, a new regular tax on economic production, the *annona militaris*, was fully systematized.[18]

The sudden appearance of a Persian superpower in the east in the third century thus generated a massive restructuring of the Roman Empire. The effects of the measures it took to counter the threat were not instant, but the restructuring eventually achieved the desired outcome. By the end of the third century, Rome had the strategic situation broadly under control: enough extra troops had been paid for to stabilize the eastern front. In AD 298 the emperor Galerius, Diocletian's co-ruler, won a major victory over the Persians, and from that point on Persian power was more or less effectively parried. There were some further, occasionally dramatic, Roman losses in the next century, but also some victories, and generally speaking the new military establishment was doing its job. Roman–Persian warfare now centred on periodic sieges of massively defended fortifications rather than seriously damaging campaigns of manoeuvre such as Shapur's invasions of Syria. Fortresses might occasionally be lost, such as Amida in 359, but this kind of defeat bore no resemblance in scale to the disasters of the third century. The strategic clock could not be put back, but both military and fiscal structures had expanded appropriately to cope with the greater Persian threat.[19]

It is important to recognize, however, just how much of an effort the Romans had to make in order to achieve this state of affairs. Confiscating city revenues and reforming general taxation were not easy matters. It took over fifty years from the first appearance of the aggressive Sasanian dynasty for Rome to put its financial house in order, and all this required a massive expansion of the central government machine to supervise the process. As we saw in Chapter 1, from AD 250 onwards there was a substantial increase in the number of higher-level imperial bureaucratic posts. Military and financial restructuring, therefore, had profound political consequences. The geographical shift of power away from Rome and Italy, already apparent in embryo in the second century, was greatly accelerated by the Empire's response to the rise of Persia. And while multiple emperors co-reigning had not been unknown in the second century, in the third it was the political as well as administrative need for more than one emperor that cemented the phenomenon as a general feature of late Roman public life.

As a string of emperors was forced eastwards from the 230s onwards to deal with the Persians, this left the west, and particularly the Rhine frontier region, denuded of an official imperial presence. As a result, too many soldiers and officials dropped out of the loop of patronage distribution, generating severe and long-lasting political turmoil at the top. In what has sometimes been called the 'military anarchy', the fifty years following the murder of emperor Alexander Severus in AD 235 saw the reins of Roman power pass through the hands of no fewer than twenty legitimate emperors and a host of usurpers, between them each averaging no more than two and a half years in office. Such a flurry of emperors is a telling indicator of an underlying structural problem. Whenever emperors concentrated, at this time, on just one part of the Empire, it generated enough disgruntled army commanders and bureaucrats elsewhere to inspire thoughts of usurpation. Particularly interesting in this respect is the so-called 'Gallic Empire'. When Valerian was captured by the Persians in 259, civilian functionaries and military commanders on the Rhine frontier put together their own regime under the leadership of a series of generals, who ran Gaul for the best part of three decades. It was an entirely non-separatist, properly Roman regime: quite simply a way of making sure that a satisfactory slice of the imperial cake was distributed in their own corner of the Empire.[20]

★

IN THEIR DIFFERENT WAYS, then, both of the Empire's most dangerous neighbours profoundly influenced its development. The relatively low level of economic achievement prevalent among the warmongering and politically fragmented Germani imposed a barrier to imperial expansion beyond which it was too unprofitable to continue. As a result, Rome's European frontiers came broadly to rest along the Rhine and Danube. The Near East, home to an equally martial population, had a stronger history of political cooperation and an economy capable of supporting a larger population in a wider variety of activities. The catalyst provided by the Sasanian dynasty turned the region into a rival superpower, whose appearance on the scene forced the Roman state to take stock. Army, taxation, bureaucracy and politics: all had to adapt in order to meet the Persian challenge. The one aspect of the Empire that did not adapt was its ideological world view, and, within that, the position it allocated to all these 'barbarians'.

Barbarians and the Roman Order

IN THE SUMMER OF AD 370, a group of shipborne Saxon raiders slipped out of the River Elbe, and headed west along the north coast of continental Europe. Avoiding the defended Roman frontier, they eventually disembarked in northern France, probably somewhere west of the Seine. The Romans quickly brought up enough troops to force them to negotiate. As Ammianus Marcellinus, our best fourth-century Roman historian, reports it:[21]

> After a long and varied discussion, since it seemed to be in the interest of the state, a truce was agreed upon, and in accordance with the conditions that were proposed the Saxons gave as hostages many young men fit for military service, and then were allowed to depart and return home without hindrance to the place from which they had come.

But things were not what they seemed. While negotiating, the Romans secretly placed heavy cavalry, together with some infantry, between the Saxons and their ships:

> The Romans with strengthened courage pressed upon the Saxons from all sides, surrounded them, and slew them with their drawn

swords; not one of them could again return to his native home, not a single one was allowed to survive the slaughter of his comrades.

Ammianus continues:

> Although some just judge might condemn this act as treacherous and hateful, yet on careful consideration of the matter he will not think it improper that a destructive band of brigands was destroyed when the opportunity at last presented itself.

As far as Ammianus was concerned, when it came to despatching barbarians, double-dealing wasn't a problem.

Killing barbarians still went down extremely well with the average Roman audience. Roman amphitheatres saw many different acts of violence, of course, from gladiatorial combat to highly inventive forms of judicial execution. A staggering 200,000 people, it has been calculated, met a violent death in the Colosseum alone, and there were similar, smaller, arenas in every major city of the Empire. Watching barbarians die was a standard part of the fun. In 306, to celebrate his pacification of the Rhine frontier, the emperor Constantine had two captured Germanic Frankish kings, Ascaricus and Merogaisus, fed to wild beasts in the arena at Trier. He also made very sure that a wider audience around the Empire heard of his triumph.[22] If no barbarian kings were available, there were always alternatives. In 383 our old friend Symmachus, then Urban Prefect of Rome, wrote to the emperor Valentinian II to say how much the Roman audience had enjoyed feasting their eyes on the spectacle of some rank-and-file Iranian-speaking Sarmatian being slaughtered by gladiators. What's striking is Symmachus' commentary:

> Rumour does not conceal the splendid outcome of your wars, but a victory gains greater credence if it is confirmed by sight . . . We have now seen things that surprised us when they were read out to us: a column of chained prisoners . . . led in procession, and faces once so fierce now changed to pitiable pallor. A name which was once terrifying to us [is] now the object of our delight, and hands trained to wield outlandish weapons afraid to meet the equipment of gladiators. May you enjoy the laurels of victory often and easily . . . let our brave soldiers take [the barbarians] prisoner and the arena in the city finish them off.[23]

For him these deaths symbolized that civilized Roman order would continue to prevail over the barbarian forces of chaos.

The antipathy towards barbarians so uninhibitedly expressed in the arena rested, for articulate Romans, on much more than mere hatred. At more or less the same moment as the Saxons were being ambushed on Rome's north-west frontier, the orator and philosopher Themistius, employed as an imperial spin-doctor, was standing in front of the Senate of Constantinople to justify the policies of his employer, the emperor Valens. The speech contains one particularly telling remark: 'There is in each of us a barbarian tribe extremely overbearing and intractable – I mean temper and those insatiable desires which stand opposed to rationality as Scythians and Germans do to the Romans.'[24]

Barbarians had their own well defined place in this Roman universe, based on a specific vision of the cosmos. Human beings, Romans argued, consist of two elements: an intelligent, rational spirit, and a physical body. Above humankind in the cosmos there exist other beings who, although endowed with greater and lesser powers, all share the characteristic of being formed purely of spirit. Below humankind are animals, encompassing pure physicality. Humanity is unique in combining both spirit and body, and from this flowed the Roman vision of rationality. In fully rational people – such as elite Romans, of course – the rational spirit controlled the physical body. But in lesser human beings – barbarians – body ruled mind. Barbarians, in short, were the reverse image of Romans loving alcohol, sex and worldly wealth.

Barbarian irrationality showed up in other ways too. As far as a Roman was concerned, you could easily tell a barbarian by how he reacted to fortune. Give him one little stroke of luck, and he would think he had conquered the world. But, equally, the slightest setback would find him in deepest despair, lamenting his fate. Where Romans would calculate probabilities, formulate sensible plans and stick to them through thick and thin, hapless barbarians were always being blown all over the place by chance events. Barbarian society was also collectively inferior: a world where might equalled right, and where those with the largest biceps triumphed. Barbarians thus provided the crucial 'other' in the Roman self-image: the inferior society whose failings underlined and legitimized the superiorities of the dominant imperial power. Indeed, the Roman state saw itself not as just marginally better than those beyond its frontiers – but massively and absolutely superior, because its social order was divinely ordained. This ideology not only made upper-class Romans feel good about themselves, but was part and parcel of the functioning of Empire. In the fourth century, regular references to the barbarian menace made its population broadly willing to pay their taxes, despite the particular increases necessitated by the third-century crisis.[25]

Although the strategy worked well enough, casting their neighbours beyond the frontiers as the antithesis of Roman order while using them as a peg on which to hang the burden of taxation was not without its own costs. The image of the barbarian made anyone from outside the Empire seem a threat, and also, by definition, a lesser human being belonging to a benighted society. The overwhelming implications of this attitude were, first, that conflict should be the normal state of relations between Roman and non-Roman; and second, that the Roman Empire should be victorious in whatever it aspired to. What did divine favour mean, if not security against defeat at the hands of those lacking that divine favour? The supreme imperial virtue – again often represented pictorially on coinage as a deity awarding a crown of laurel leaves as this suggests, was one of victory. And any failure to deliver it could be taken as a sign that the current incumbent of the purple was not the right man for the job.[26]

Imperial spokesmen faced the task, therefore, of angling their accounts of events on the frontier to maintain the required image of imperial invincibility. In early 363, for instance, the emperor Julian took a huge military gamble, leading his army 500 kilometres on to Persian soil right up to the outskirts of the capital, Ctesiphon. The Persian King of Kings, Chosroes, had let him advance, then sprung a trap. The Romans were forced into a fighting retreat all the way back to home territory. By the end of June, when Julian was killed in a skirmish, the situation was hopeless. The Roman army still had 250 kilometres to go, had more or less run out of supplies, and was managing to retreat only about five kilometres a day because of Persian harassment. Julian's successor Jovian – elected on the campaign – had no choice but to negotiate a humiliating peace. The Roman army was allowed to depart, but surrendered to the Persians two major cities, Nisibis and Sangara, a host of strongpoints and five border provinces (map 3). But so pressing was the expectation of victory, especially at the start of a reign when the seal of divine approval needed to be particularly evident, that Jovian could not afford to acknowledge defeat. His coinage proclaimed the Persian peace a victory and Themistius was trundled out to reinforce the point. The spin-doctor's discomfort is only too evident. The best he could come up with was this: 'The Persians showed that they were voting for [Jovian as emperor] no less than the Romans by throwing aside their weapons as soon as they became aware of the proclamation, and shortly after were wary of the same men of whom before they had had no fear.' He followed up with the quip, based on a famous story about the election of the Achaemenid King of Kings Darius in 522 BC, that the – obviously irrational – Persians chose their rulers according to the neighing of horses.

Not a bad effort at a brave front, perhaps, but this was one spin that no one was buying. By January 364, Jovian had already faced protests from eastern cities complaining about the surrender and, tellingly, in a speech to the Senate that lasted at least three-quarters of an hour Themistius devoted only about a minute to the Persian question before moving on smartly to more promising matters.[27] In this case, policy could not be made to square with expectations of victory, and Themistius, shortly after, was on much safer ground when he could admit it. Jovian died in February 364, and, at the end of the year in a first speech for his successor Valens, Themistius seized upon Jovian's early death, after only eight months in power, as a clear sign that his rule had not been divinely sanctioned. In this way, the loss to the Persians could be satisfactorily explained, and a nasty dent in the Roman self-image removed.[28]

But such catastrophic losses even to the Persians were now rare, as we have seen, and Rome held an overall military advantage on its European frontiers. With just the odd white lie, expectations of victory could usually be satisfied and inconvenient reality prevented from scrambling the key message: the barbarian on the other side of the frontier had no place in the Roman order, and was being duly and regularly destroyed. Indeed, violent confrontation was a significant element in Roman foreign policy on all its frontiers, but reality – as much on the Rhine and Danube as in the east – was much more complicated than was implied by the simple 'them and us' view.

To explore this reality in more detail, we can narrow the focus to one corner of Rome's European frontier, the lower reaches of the River Danube separating the Roman diocese of Thrace from the

Germanic-speaking Goths who, in the fourth century, dominated lands between the Carpathians and the Black Sea.

Thrace: The Final Frontier

IN 369, THE SAME YEAR that Symmachus' embassy presented the emperor Valentinian with crown gold (p. 22), a summit meeting took place in the middle of the River Danube, close to the fortress of Noviodunum. Valentinian's brother, the emperor Valens, ruler of the eastern Empire, pushed off from the south bank in a magnificent imperial barge. From the north bank he was joined by Athanaric, leader of the Tervingi, the Germanic Goths settled closest to the frontier. Athanaric had been at war with Valens for the best part of three years. For once, we have an eyewitness account of the event, penned by Themistius for the Senate of Constantinople. He had attended the meeting as the head of a senatorial embassy to the emperor. As Themistius tells it, Valens managed thoroughly to perplex his enemy:[29]

> Valens was so much cleverer than the man who spoke for the barbarians that he undermined their confidence in him and rendered the verbal contest [on the boat] even more hazardous than the armed [contest of the previous three years]. All the same, having thrown his opponent he then set him on his feet once more, stretched out his hand to him in his confusion and made him a friend before witnesses . . . And so [Athanaric] went away highly contented, in the grip of contrary emotions: at once confident and fearful, both contemptuous and wary of his subjects, cast down in spirit by those aspects of the treaty in which he had lost his case but exulting in those in which success had fallen to him.

Athanaric's followers were in pretty poor shape too:

> [They] were dispersed in groups along the bank in docile and amenable mood, a horde defying enumeration . . . Looking at both banks of the river, [I saw] the [Roman one] glittering with soldiers who in good order looked on with tranquil pride at what was being done, the other burdened with a disordered rabble of suppliants cast down upon the earth.

Athanaric and his Goths thus played their parts perfectly, according to the traditional Roman script. The details of the peace agreement mentioned by Themistius only confirmed Valens' domination. The emperor now discontinued the annual gifts that the Goths had been accustomed to receive, confined cross-border trade to only two designated centres, and inaugurated a programme of defensive building to ensure that Gothic raiders would have no opportunity for causing further trouble. Expectations of Roman dominance over pathetically inferior barbarians had been magnificently fulfilled.

But looked at more closely, the story as told by Themistius doesn't quite add up. Hostilities had not been opened by Valens, but by Athanaric. In 364/5, Roman intelligence reports were already indicating that the Goths were becoming restive, and Valens had sent reinforcements to the Danube front. When, in 365, those reinforcements were bribed by Procopius, the uncle of the former emperor Julian, to kick-start his usurpation, Athanaric sent the would-be usurper a contingent of three thousand Goths. If the Goths had been happy being paid to keep the peace, as Themistius reports, why had Athanaric behaved so aggressively? Valens also failed, despite three years of campaigning, actually to defeat the Goths in battle. In 367 and 369 his armies ranged at will in Gothic territories, looting as they went. And they were only kept at bay in 368 by a premature melting of the Alpine and Carpathian snows. The flooding Danube made it impossible for the Romans to string up the pontoon bridges by which they customarily moved their heavy equipment across the river. Through strategic manoeuvre – running away – Athanaric managed to avoid being cornered. By the time peace was made, the Goths were massively inconvenienced and suffering major food shortages, but they were never trapped into total submission in the way that they had been some thirty years earlier, in the time of the emperor Constantine, who had forced their unconditional surrender. Since the Romans had not so decisively defeated them as Themistius would have us believe, it seems odd that the treaty of 369 enforced harsher terms upon them than that of 332.

In his speech, Themistius 'forgot' to mention, however, one crucial extra detail. Halfway through Valens' Gothic campaign, all hell had broken loose on a corner of the Persian front. Having made major gains in Mesopotamia through the treaty with Jovian, the Persian King of Kings Chosroes now turned his attention to Caucasia. In 367/8 he ousted the rulers of Armenia and eastern Georgia, who had been

Roman allies, and replaced them with his own nominees. Safeguarding the Persian front was much more important to Valens than reducing the Goths to total submission, so that this new threat exerted huge pressure on him to extract his forces from the Balkans and redirect them eastwards. But Valens had already mobilized on the Danube and his taxpayers were expecting victory. He also had the Goths' support of Procopius to avenge. He thus kept the war going into 369, but when total victory again proved elusive, he needed to make a compromise peace. That the meeting between Valens and Athanaric did generate a compromise is clear. Themistius notes that the Goth was 'exulting in those [aspects of the treaty] in which success had fallen to him'. The same point is made, interestingly, by the *location* of the summit meeting. Roman emperors normally paraded their standards triumphantly on barbarian soil, and forced barbarian kings to submit to them there. Only one other waterborne summit is recorded in fourth-century sources, this time on the Rhine – again, a Roman emperor (Valentinian) needed to secure one frontier to tackle a problem on another. That peace was also a compromise.[30]

The real task facing Themistius in selling the Gothic peace to the Senate now comes into focus. He presented the discontinuation of annual gifts to the Goths as a great gain to the Roman state. In fact, it was a rather small one. The state had used gifts for centuries to build up the position of client kings. We would call it 'foreign aid'. The great loss to the Romans – which Themistius *doesn't* mention – was the right, now rescinded, to call on Gothic military assistance against Persia. What emerges particularly clearly is the slickness of Themistius. A vivid scene of Gothic submission was conjured up for his audience, with Valens all-powerful at the peace-making. And the orator's bravado performance seems to have done the trick, since two contemporary sources describe the peace as a reasonable end to the war. Valens' face had been successfully saved.[31]

For our purposes, however, there is a shadowy but much more important point lurking behind Themistius' smoke-screen. It is impossible to know everything that Athanaric had in mind, since his precise aims are not recorded by our Roman sources, but he was clearly no mere stock barbarian of the Roman ideological 'other'. He and his fellow Tervingi had been in receipt of Roman gifts for thirty years but were willing to put them at risk to avoid having to fight for the Empire. The same went for the trading privileges inherent in the open frontier established by their earlier treaty with Constantine. That these privileges were real and enjoyed by the Goths is visible in the archaeological record. Fourth-century Gothic sites are littered with the pottery sherds of Roman amphorae, most of them broken wine containers (by the sixth century *biberunt ut Gothi* – 'drinking like Goths' – had become proverbial). Despite this, Athanaric had a determined agenda to extract the Tervingi from the least acceptable constraints of Roman domination. He was able to rally support for this stance from among his Goths, and then used sophisticated strategies to achieve his ends. At first he had been ready to fight the Empire outright, but when Procopius' plans for usurpation offered him the opportunity to fiddle in internal Roman politics instead, he took this route – hoping, presumably, that a successful Procopius would grant willingly what the Goths would otherwise have had to extract from Valens by force.

Here, reality contradicts Roman ideology in substantial ways. The usurpation of Procopius saw one Roman allying with a barbarian against another Roman, although, admittedly, Athanaric was no more than a junior ally. Nor was he an aimless barbarian intent only on the nearest bit of plunder. He had, rather, pursued a variety of means to renegotiate the bundle of obligations and privileges that Constantine had imposed on the Tervingi after his great victory of the 330s. Constantine had also tried – in a stock Roman diplomatic manoeuvre – to impress upon the ruling house of the Tervingi the benefits of Roman civilization. One of the hostages sent to Constantinople as part of his treaty was the son of the then ruler. Such hostages could be, and were, executed if the terms of peace were broken. But, more generally, they were used to convince the next generation of barbarian movers and shakers that hostility to Rome was pointless, and that they would be much better off embracing it. Sometimes the strategy worked; in this case it didn't. The prince of the Tervingi sent to Constantinople was Athanaric's father, and even though they put up a statue to him behind the Senate house, he was not won over (maybe they should have tried putting it in front). When handing on power in due course to his son, he forbade Athanaric ever to set foot on Roman soil, and Athanaric continued to press for as much separation as possible.[32] The shipborne setting of his summit meeting with Valens implicitly acknowledged the Goth's sovereignty over lands beyond the Danube, and, in the aftermath of the new agreement, Athanaric found himself free to persecute Gothic Christians. Christianization had been promoted among the Goths by previous emperors, as we shall see in a moment, so here was another deliberate rejection of Roman ideologies. No low-level barbarian, Athanaric was a client king with a coherent agenda for renegotiating his relationship with the Roman Empire.

Little Wolf

IF THE REAL PROFILE of Athanaric can be partially recovered from the distorting mirror of Themistius' speech, two astonishing manuscripts give us much more direct access to the Gothic world of the fourth century. The first is one of the greatest treasures to survive from antiquity: the *Codex Argenteus*. Now housed in the Uppsala University Library in Sweden, it is a luxury copy of a translation of the four Gospels into the Gothic language. Transcribed in Italy in the sixth century, the book originally comprised 336 pages. Only 187 survived at Uppsala, but much excitement accompanied the discovery of one more, in 1970, in a long-forgotten hiding-place for relics in the cathedral at Speyer in south-west Germany. The text is written in gold and silver ink on purple-dyed parchment of an exceptional fineness – it was made from the skin of newborn (or even unborn) calves. Ink, dye and parchment all mark this out as a colossally expensive book commissioned by an individual of the highest standing, quite likely Theoderic the Amal, Ostrogothic king of Italy in the sixth century. The second manuscript is more modest but, in its own way, equally extraordinary: a plain and quite badly damaged fifth-century text prosaically known as *Parisinus Latinus* 8907. Most of it is devoted to an account of the Council of Aquileia in 381, when Bishop Ambrose of Milan, a stalwart of what was just about to become Christian ortho-doxy, defeated his opponents, and to the first two books of Ambrose's most famous work, the *De Fide* (*On the Faith*). Written into the margins of the *De Fide* is another work, known only from this battered manuscript: a commentary on Aquileia by Bishop Palladius of Ratiaria, one of Ambrose's opponents there. This commentary includes a letter written by Auxentius of Durostorum, which, together with the *Codex Argenteus*, illuminates the extraordinary achievements of one of Athan-aric's humblest subjects: Ulfilas, the Little Wolf of the Goths.[33]

Born at the beginning of the fourth century, Ulfilas was the offspring of Roman prisoners living among the Tervingi. They were part of a substantial community of captives taken by Goths during the late third century. At this point, Goths were launching seaborne attacks across the Black Sea from southern Russia into Roman Asia Minor. Ulfilas's family was taken from a small village called Sadagolthina near the city of Parnassus in Cappadocia, located on the northern shores of what is now Lake Tattu in central Turkey. His name, meaning 'Little Wolf', is unequivocally Gothic, showing that the captives adapted linguistically to their new situation; but they continued to use their own languages too. In addition to Gothic, Ulfilas grew up literate in both Latin and Greek, and Greek was probably his language of preference. That he had these accomplishments implies a great deal about the captives' living conditions. They probably formed a largely autonomous body of farmers, required to hand over a substantial portion of their produce to their Gothic masters but otherwise left more or less to their own devices. Quite a lot of them were firm Christians. Ulfilas, we are told, grew up and matured in his faith in this decidedly polyglot setting, becoming a junior clergyman with the rank of lector in the exiles' church. This kind of subject community is known to have existed in other barbarian kingdoms in late antiquity, and some were able to preserve a sense of difference over several generations. In the case of Ulfilas, the relatively obscure life of a second-generation involuntary immigrant was about to be transformed by the fact that the Tervingi happened to be the group of Goths settled closest to the Roman frontier at a moment when the Empire was busy converting itself to Christianity.

In the early 340s the emperor Constantius II decided to raise the stakes in the hostage situation in which Athanaric's father was currently ensnared. Flexing his political muscles in the way he was about to do was only possible, of course, because of the military dominance that Constantius' father Constantine had established over the Tervingi in the 330s. As one of several initiatives designed to show off his Christian piety, Constantius attempted to boost the fortunes of his fellow Christians living under non-Christian rule. He thus arranged for Ulfilas, already prominent among the prisoner community, to be ordained bishop 'for the Christians in Gothia', bringing him to Constantinople for the purpose in 341 as part of an embassy. Ulfilas then went back north of the Danube and for the next seven years ministered happily to his flock. But something went wrong and, in the winter of 347/8, when he found himself at the centre of a diplomatic crisis in Gotho-

Roman relations, he was expelled from Gothia by his Tervingian masters, along with a large number of his fellow Gothic Christians. Historians have guessed that he may have spread his message beyond the prisoner community to other Goths, but there was also a wider context. By 348, Constantius wanted to draw another military contingent from the Tervingi for the latest bout of Roman–Persian warfare, and accepting that his Christianizing initiative should stop was perhaps the price he had to pay for it. Nonetheless, Constantius went to the Danube and greeted Ulfilas 'as if he were Moses himself'.[34]

It might have seemed like the end, but it was only the beginning. Ulfilas and his followers were settled around the city of Nicopolis ad Istrum, close to the Danube frontier and still in contact with what must have been the many Christians who remained in Gothic territories. It was here that Ulfilas produced the Gothic Bible translation preserved in the *Codex Argenteus*. His method was simple – he gives a word-for-word rendering of a standard fourth-century Greek Bible text – and his translation owes more to Greek grammar and syntax than to that of the Goths. It was a prodigious feat. According to tradition, Ulfilas translated everything except the Old Testament Book of Kings, which he thought would only have encouraged the Goths to become even more warlike than they already were. A low-status subject member of the Gothic Tervingi had produced the first literary work in any Germanic language.[35]

This was one part of the Ulfilas story. The other is told in Auxentius' letter so uniquely preserved in *Parisinus Latinus* 8907. Constantine's conversion brought about extraordinary transformations within Christianity. Amongst other things, it became imperative for Christians, who no longer lived in communities mainly isolated from one another by the hostility of the Roman state, to define a set of doctrines. The process began at the Council of Nicaea in 325, where the relationship of God the Son to God the Father was defined as *homousios*: 'of the *same* substance/essence'. But this was just the start of the argument. The Nicene definition of the Christian faith only became fully accepted, after much argument, following the Council of Constantinople in 381, and for much of the intervening fifty-six years official Roman Christianity held to a much more traditional position, describing Christ as 'like' (*omoios*) or '*similar* in substance/essence to' (*homoeusios*) God the Father.

Much effort in the interim had gone into constructing coalitions between different Churchmen, many of whom had hitherto simply assumed that they believed the same things. They were now being forced to decide which of a range of theological positions best expressed their understanding of the faith. Into this arena, sometime after 348, strode Ulfilas. Auxentius' letter contains the statement of belief that Ulfilas left as his last will and testament, and succinctly explains the reasoning behind it. Ulfilas was one of the more traditional Christians: he found the Nicene definition unacceptable because it contradicted the scriptural evidence and seemed to leave little room for distinguishing God the Father from God the Son. In Auxentius' account:

> In accordance with tradition and the authority of the Divine Scriptures, [Ulfilas] never concealed that this God [the Son] is in second place and the originator of all things from the Father and after the Father and on account of the Father and for the glory of the Father ... holding as greater [than himself] God his own Father [John 14:28] – this he always made clear according to the Holy Gospel.

What's more, people listened. Again, in Auxentius' words:

> Flourishing gloriously for forty years in the bishopric, [Ulfilas] preached unceasingly with apostolic grace in the Greek, Latin, and Gothic languages ... bearing witness that there is but one flock of Christ our Lord and God ... And all that he said, and all I have set down, is from the divine Scriptures: 'let him that readeth understand' [Matthew 24:15]. He left behind him several tractates and many commentaries in these three languages for the benefit of all those willing to accept it, and as his own eternal memorial and recompense.

Unfortunately, the tractates and commentaries haven't survived. Ulfilas ended up on the losing side of doctrinal debate and his works, like those of so many of his party, were not preserved. But we do know from Auxentius and other sources that he was heavily courted not only by Constantius but also by the eastern emperor Valens, and did eventually sign up to the doctrinal settlements they put forward in, respectively, 359 and 370. He also built around himself an influential group of non-Nicene Balkan bishops, who were a major force within the Church. Auxentius was one of these, and Palladius of Ratiaria another. The last image we have is of Ulfilas riding into doctrinal battle yet again, at the age of seventy, at the Council of Constantinople in 381. This was his last hurrah, and the Council's decisions effectively consigned him and his followers to the footnotes of history. But that was not how it was in his own lifetime. This Gothic subject of humble origins was a major player in the doctrinal debates of the mid-fourth century.[36]

AGAIN, REALITY confounds image. Viewed through a Roman lens, barbarians were utterly incapable of rational thought or planning; sensualists, they lacked motive, apart from an overwhelming desire for the next fix. But our two fourth-century barbarians were neither stupid nor irrational. At the pinnacle of Gothic society, Athanaric and his councillors were faced with the brute reality of devising ways of coping with overwhelming Roman power. They could hope neither to defeat it in open conflict nor to insulate themselves from it. They could, however, formulate and pursue agendas designed to shape their relations with the Empire in the way that best suited them, while minimizing those aspects of Roman domination they found most oppressive. They could also be desirable allies in wartime and in civil conflict, and could sometimes manipulate matters for their own benefit. Lower down the social scale were communities literate in Greek and Latin who transmitted enough of current Christian culture to generate a man like Ulfilas.

The reality of Roman-Gothic relations was not, therefore, the unremitting conflict between absolute superior and inferior that Roman ideology required. The Romans still held themselves aloof, the dominant party, but Goths could be useful. The periodic conflict between them was part of a diplomatic dance that saw both sides taking steps to maximize their advantage. Barbarians weren't what they used to be. Even if cast firmly as junior members, the Goths were part of the Roman world.

Client Kingdoms

THIS DIDN'T APPLY exclusively to the Goths on the Danube, even if most fourth-century Germanic societies are not so well documented as the Tervingi. Small-scale raiding into imperial territory was endemic.

The Saxon raid of 370 was perhaps more serious than some, but it wasn't just spin on Themistius' part that he ends his account of the Gothic war of 367–9 with a vignette of Valens fortifying those parts of the Lower Danube frontier that other emperors hadn't reached. He and his brother were active in both building fortifications and providing garrisons. But in the fourth century, major conflicts occurred only about once in a generation on Rome's European frontiers. One of the first acts of the emperor Constantine, in the 310s, was to undertake a major pacification of the Rhine frontier – the lands of the Franks and Alamanni (map 4). We know of no further serious conflict in this region until the early 350s. The trouble that broke out again in 364/5 was to do with a change in Roman policy (a unilateral cut in the foreign aid budget); otherwise, nothing of note occurred here before the end of the 370s. Further east, the Middle Danube frontier facing the Sarmatians, Quadi and Marcomanni saw a major Roman military intervention under the emperor Constantine, but much later in his reign, in the 330s. The next outbreak of violence there came in 357, and another in 374/5. On the Lower Danube, home to the Goths, the

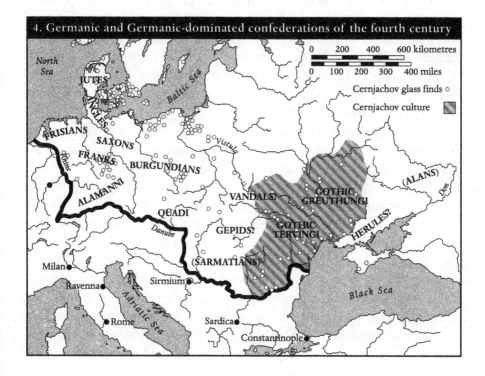

4. Germanic and Germanic-dominated confederations of the fourth century

settlement of the 330s gave, as we have seen, more or less thirty years of peace.

In each of these campaigns, the Romans – with greater or lesser difficulty – established their military dominance, sometimes just by pillaging widely enough to force submission, sometimes by victory in a set-piece battle. In 357, for instance, the emperor Julian led a Roman force of 13,000 men into action near the city of Strasbourg on the Roman side of the Rhine, against the assembled kings of the Alamanni. He won a stunning victory. Of the 35,000 opponents led by their pre-eminent overking, Chnodomarius, some 6,000 were left dead on the battlefield and countless others drowned trying to flee across the river, while the Romans lost a grand total of 243 soldiers and four high-ranking officers.[37] The battle is an excellent example of the continued effectiveness of the remodelled Roman army of the late imperial era. From the massacring of Saxon raiders in northern France to Constantine's subjugation of the Tervingi, this type of military dominance was the norm at all levels on Rome's European frontiers.

In one respect, such victories were an end in themselves. They punished and intimidated, and certainly the historian Ammianus considered that it was necessary to hit barbarians regularly to make them keep the peace. On another level entirely, however, military victory was the first act in constructing broader diplomatic settlements. After Strasbourg, Julian spent the next two years on the other side of the Rhine making separate peace treaties with various Alamannic kings, just as his co-emperor Constantius II was doing with other groups on the Middle Danube.

As we have seen, to the Roman public these treaties were all presented as following essentially the same pattern: the barbarians surrendered themselves completely (called in Latin an act of *deditio*) and were then graciously granted terms in a treaty (Latin, *foedus*), which made them imperial subjects. In reality, however, the details varied dramatically, both in the degree of subjection enforced and in the practical arrangements. Where the Romans were fully in control of the situation, as Constantius was on the Middle Danube in 357, they might well interfere in their opponents' political structures, dismantling confederations that appeared overly dangerous and promoting pliant sub-kings to independent authority as seemed to best suit Rome's long-term interests. The Romans also extracted recruits for their army as part of most agreements, sometimes stipulating as well that larger bodies of men should be provided for particular campaigns. In 357/8 the emperor Julian also made the Alamanni pay reparations for the damage they had caused. These often took the form of grain supplies, as in this instance, but, where this was impossible, labour, wood for construction and cartage were demanded. Giving hostages, as happened with Athanaric's father, was also quite standard, and sometimes brought greater success. One Alamannic prince was so impressed with the Mediterranean religions he encountered on Roman soil that on his return he renamed his son Serapio in honour of the Egyptian god Serapis. Where the Romans were less in control, labour, raw materials and manpower might have to be paid for, and political structures that had evolved independently given the stamp of approval. Either way, beyond the defended frontier itself lay a belt of largely Germanic client kingdoms that were firmly part of the Roman world.[38]

This is not to say that these states were entirely under Roman control, or necessarily happy about being junior members of the Roman world order, as we have seen in the case of Athanaric. If other priorities got in the way, then barbarians could find themselves prospering, sometimes temporarily, sometimes more permanently. The early 350s, for instance, saw a rash of usurpations in the western half of the Empire, beginning with the murder of Constans, brother of the then eastern emperor Constantius. Constantius made it his priority to suppress the usurpers, and it was this which allowed Chnodomarius to build up the Alamannic army that would face Julian at Strasbourg. Once the usurpers had been put down, however, the Romans reined in, then utterly defeated, the Alamanni in two years of campaigning. Chnodomarius had been too aggressive, even seizing territory on the Roman bank of the Rhine, for the Romans to contemplate doing a deal. About a decade later, however, a new, pre-eminent leader of the Alamanni appeared: Macrianus. Valens' brother Valentinian spent half a decade trying to curb his power, making a number of kidnap and murder attempts. But, unlike Chnodomarius, Macrianus never let his ambitions stray on to Roman territory, so that when trouble brewed on the Middle Danube Valentinian could invite him, without too much loss of face, to a shipborne summit on the Rhine of the kind at which Valens had entertained Athanaric on the Danube. There he gave Roman approval to Macrianus' pre-eminence, and Macrianus proved a reliable Roman ally as long as he lived. These client kingdoms also had

political agendas that didn't involve Rome. Political life among the
Alamanni had its own pattern, with kings regularly inviting each other
to feasts. We hear too of wars between Alamanni and Franks, and
between Alamanni and Burgundians, but nothing of their causes and
consequences.[39]

Overall, then, Rome's relations with its fourth-century European
frontier clients didn't fit entirely comfortably within the ideological
boundaries set by the traditional image of the barbarian. The two
parties now enjoyed reciprocal, if unequal, relations on every level.
The client kingdoms traded with the Empire, provided manpower
for its armies, and were regularly subject to both its diplomatic
interference and its cultural influence. In return, each year they
generally received aid; and, sometimes at least, were awarded a degree
of respect. One striking feature is that treaties were regularly formalized according to norms of the client kingdom as well as those of
the Roman state. The Germani had come a long way from the 'other'
of Roman imaginations, even if the Empire's political elite had to
pretend to Roman taxpayers that they hadn't. What has also become
clear in recent years, is that this new order in Roman–German
diplomatic relations was based on a series of profound transformations
in Germanic society.

The Transformation of Germanic Europe

THE WRITTEN EVIDENCE does contain some important clues that
fundamental changes had occurred in the three and a half centuries
separating Arminius from Athanaric. In the mid-third century, the west
Germanic tribal names famous from the works of Tacitus suddenly
disappear from our sources. Cherusci, Chatti and so forth were
replaced by four new ones: Franks and Alamanni on the Rhine frontier,
and Saxons and Burgundians further to the east (map 4). South-eastern
Europe north of the Black Sea also now saw major political changes.
By the fourth century, a huge swathe of territory from Rome's Danube
frontier to the River Don was dominated by Gothic and other
Germanic-speaking groups, making late Roman Germania even larger
than its first-century counterpart.

The new situation beyond the Black Sea was generated by the
migration of Germanic groups from the north-west, largely from what

is now central and northern Poland. In a series of independent, small-scale initiatives, between about AD 180 and 320, they had advanced around the outer fringes of the Carpathian Mountains. North of the Black Sea, the migrating groups were competing against each other, against indigenous populations such as the Dacian-speaking Carpi and Iranian-speaking Sarmatians, and against Roman garrison forces. The process was, not surprisingly, violent. The Empire decided to abandon its north Danubian province of Dacia in 275, and large numbers of Carpi were eventually resettled on Roman soil around the year 300. The violence spilled over on to Roman soil in regular raids, and it was during one of these that Ulfilas' parents were captured. The result was a series of largely Gothic-dominated political units, of which Athanaric's Tervingi were closest to the Danube. Beyond them, to the north and east, was an unknown number of others.[40] We have no idea of relative percentages, but the populations of these units were certainly mixed, with large numbers of Dacians and Sarmatians, not to mention Roman prisoners, living under the political umbrella of immigrant Goths and other Germani. The dominance of the Germanic immigrants is clear, however, from both Roman narrative sources and the linguistic evidence of Ulfilas' Bible.[41]

The significance of the name changes on the Rhine frontier and in its hinterland has been hotly disputed. Again, in all probability, immigration was involved. Burgundians do appear in Tacitus' account of first-century Germania, but significantly to the north-east of the region inhabited by their fourth-century namesakes. It is likely enough that some kind of migration was behind this shift of locale, but, as in the east, it probably did not take the form of a total replacement of the existing population.[42] Otherwise, we know that beneath the umbrella of the new names, some of the old groups continued to exist. Bructeri, Chatti, Ampsivarii and Cherusci are all reported in one source as belonging to the Frankish confederation of tribes, and detailed contemporary evidence shows that among the Alamanni several kings always ruled simultaneously, each with his own largely autonomous domain. At the battle of Strasbourg, for instance, Julian faced seven kings and ten princes.

At the same time, however, Alamannic society was by this date consistently throwing up an over-king: an individual in each generation who wielded more power than his peers. Chnodomarius, defeated by Julian at Strasbourg in 357, was one of these, as were Vadomarius at whose rising power Roman policy was next directed, and Macrianus whom Valentinian was eventually forced to recognize in 374. It was not a hereditary position, and it is not recorded either how you became an over-king, or what benefits it brought you. Our Roman sources weren't interested enough to tell us. The chances are, however, that it involved some financial and military support upon demand, a development of some importance suggesting that the name changes of the third century had a real political significance. In Alamannic territories, a new superstructure had invaded the world of small independent political units characteristic of the first century. It is perfectly possible, although there is no evidence either way, that contemporary Franks and Saxons had developed similarly unifying institutions and habits. Further east, on the Danube, the Gothic Tervingi certainly had. Athanaric ruled a confederation that contained an unknown number of other kings and princes.[43]

But it wasn't merely in political structure that fourth-century Germania differed from its first-century counterpart. A range of archaeological evidence has shed new light on the deeper social and economic transformations that brought the world of Athanaric into being. The story begins in the muddy fields just east of the northern sector of Rome's Rhine frontier. In the early 1960s two small rural sites – Wijster in the Netherlands and Feddersen Wierde in Germany – were excavated. The findings were revolutionary. Both turned out to be farming settlements whose occupants practised mixed arable and pastoral agriculture, and both originated in the first century AD. The revolutionary aspect was that, for most of their history, these had been village communities with large numbers of houses occupied simultaneously: more than fifty in the case of Wijster, thirty at Feddersen Wierde. Furthermore, the settlements were occupied until the fifth century. The importance of this lies in what it implies about agricultural practice.

In the last few centuries BC, an extensive (rather than *intensive*) type of arable agriculture had prevailed across Germanic Europe. It alternated short periods of cultivation with long periods of fallow, and required a relatively large area of land to support a given population. These early Iron Age peoples lacked techniques for maintaining the fertility of their arable fields for prolonged production, and could use them for only a few years before moving on. Ploughing generally took the form of narrow, criss-crossed scrapings, rather than the turning-over of a proper furrow so that weeds rot their nutrients back into the soil. Ash was the main fertilizer.

This is where the settlements of Feddersen Wierde and Wijster differ. For early in the Roman period, western Germani developed entirely new techniques, using the manure from their animals together, probably, with a more sophisticated kind of two-crop rotation scheme, both to increase yields and to keep the soil producing beyond the short term. For the first time in northern Europe, it thus became possible for human beings to live together in more or less permanent, clustered (or 'nucleated') settlements. Further north and east, the muck took longer to spread. In what is now Poland, the territories of the Wielbark and Przeworsk cultures, Germanic settlements remained small, short-lived and highly dispersed in the first two centuries AD. By the fourth, however, the new techniques had taken firm hold. Settlements north of the Black Sea, in areas dominated by the Goths, could be very substantial; the largest, Budesty, covered an area of thirty-five hectares. And enough pieces of ploughing equipment have been found to show that populations under Gothic control were now using iron coulters and ploughshares to turn the earth properly, if not to a great depth. Recent work has shown that villages had emerged in Scandinavia too. More intensive arable agriculture was on the march, and pollen diagrams confirm that between the birth of Christ and the fifth century, cereal pollens, at the expense of grass and tree pollens, reached an unprecedented high across wide areas of what is now Poland, the Czech Republic and Germany. Large tracts of new land were being brought into cultivation and worked with greater intensity.[44]

THE MAIN OUTCOME of all this was that the population of Germanic-dominated Europe increased massively over these Roman centuries. The basic constraint upon the size of any population is the availability of food. The Germanic agricultural revolution massively increased the amount available, and the increase in population shows up in the cemetery evidence. Cemeteries in continuous use throughout the Roman period all show dramatic rises in burial numbers from the later period.

Other sectors of the economy were also transformed. It is impossible to construct any kind of global overview, but iron production in Germania increased massively. In Poland, production at the two largest centres (in the Swietokrzyskie Mountains and in southern Mazovia) generated in the Roman period 8–9 million kilos of raw iron. This was much more than could have been consumed by local Przeworsk populations, and plenty of smaller extraction and smelting sites have also been recovered, such as the fifteen or so fourth-century smithies clustered on the bank of a river at Sinicy in the Gothic-dominated Ukraine. Similarly with pottery: at the start of the Roman period, the Germani made all of theirs by hand, and for the most part, apparently, on a local and ad hoc basis. By the fourth century, this kind of pottery was being replaced by wheel-made wares, fired at much higher temperatures and hence more durable and more sophisticated. These were the products of highly skilled craftsmen. Whether Germanic potters could make a living just from their pottery is unclear, but economic diversification was certainly under way. The change was most marked in areas of production geared to elite consumption. Grave goods show that glass was a treasured item among Germanic populations in the early centuries AD. Up to about the year 300, all glass found in Germanic contexts was imported from the Roman Empire. This is presumably why it was so valued – rather like Italian handbags are now. In the 1960s, however, at Komarov on the outer fringes of the Carpathians, excavators unearthed a fourth-century glass foundry. Such was the quality of its widely distributed products (all the way from Norway to the Crimea) that they had previously been thought to be Roman imports. The glass factory, complete with moulds, left no doubt that they were made in Germania.

A similar story can be told about precious metals. Up to the birth of Christ, very few indigenously produced items of precious metalwork have been identified in Germanic settings, and in the first two centuries AD the vast majority of decorative items were still being produced in bronze only. By the fourth century, intricate silver safety-pins (*fibulae*) of a number of types had become familiar items of Germanic dress; and a few examples survive of work on a grander scale, notably one of the silver dishes of the famous treasure unearthed at Pietroasa in Romania in the late nineteenth century. How some, at least, of this ware was produced is suggested by evidence from the village of Birlad-Valea Seaca (in modern Romania), which probably fell within the territory ruled by Athanaric of the Tervingi. A characteristic grave good of Gothic territories north of the Black Sea is a composite comb made from deer antler. Combs had great cultural importance. Hair-styles were used by some Germanic groups to express either group affiliations (as in the famous Suebian knot) or status (the long hair of the Merovingian rulers of the Franks). At Birlad-Valea Seaca, excavators unearthed nearly twenty huts containing combs and their constituent parts at different stages of production. Clearly, the entire village was devoted to manufacturing combs.[45]

There is much more that we'd like to know. Were these combs being produced commercially and exchanged, or was this some kind of subject village from which so many combs were demanded annually as tribute? Whatever the answer, there is no mistaking the extent and importance of the economic revolution that had transformed Germanic Europe by the fourth century. New skills were being developed, and goods were being distributed over far wider areas. Some of this production may have been non-commercial, goods being destined as gifts from one ruler to another, for example, but we know that the Tervingi traded extensively with the Roman world, as did peoples on the Rhine frontier. And although no coinage was produced in Germania, Roman coins were in plentiful circulation and could easily have provided a medium of exchange (already in the first century, Tacitus tells us, the Germani of the Rhine region were using good-quality Roman silver coins for this purpose).

ECONOMIC EXPANSION was accompanied by social revolution. Dominant social elites had not always existed in Germanic Europe, or, at least, their presence is not visible in the cemeteries which are the main source of our knowledge. For much of the first millennium BC, central and northern Europe was marked by a near-universal adherence to cremation as the main form of burial rite, and grave goods were pretty much the same everywhere: some tatty handmade pottery and the odd decorated pin. Only in the third century BC did richer burials (the grandest among them often referred to by their German term, *Fürstengraber*, 'princely graves') begin to appear, and they were few and far between. Once again it was first in the Roman imperial period that strikingly disparate quantities of goods began to be buried with different members of the same Germanic communities. In the west, rich graves cluster chronologically, with one group at the end of the first century AD and another at the end of the second. But it is extremely unlikely that 'princes' existed only at these isolated moments, so that there is no easy correlation between wealthy burials and social status. Further east, numbers of grave goods built up similarly over the Roman period, but other means, such as huge mounds of stones, for marking out special status were first explored by second-century Germani. Unusually rich or grand burials say most, of course, about the pretensions and claims of those doing the burying, and it has been suggested that rich burials mark moments of intense social competition rather than moments of particular wealth.[46]

Fortunately, we have some less ambiguous evidence, some of it written, to help us interpret their longer-term significance. Although there is little sign in the first century of the hereditary transmission of political pre-eminence, and leadership even within small groupings was often multiple rather than individual, in the fourth century leadership among the Tervingi was handed down across three generations of the same family: in reverse order, Athanaric, his father the hostage, and the leader of the Tervingi who negotiated with Constantine. The best-informed of our Greek and Latin sources consistently label these leaders 'judges', but we don't know what title 'judge' translates. There is every reason to suppose that the power of the second stratum of kings and princes, beneath these overall leaders, was also hereditary. A similar pattern prevailed among the Alamanni. The position of over-king was *not* hereditary, as we noted earlier, not least because the Romans tended to remove those who achieved that status; but the status of Alamannic sub-kings clearly was. Mederichus, the high-status Alamannic hostage who changed his son's name to Serapio in honour of the Egyptian god, was the brother of Chnodomarius who led the Alamanni to defeat at Strasbourg in 357. Serapio also ruled as a king, and commanded the army's right wing in the battle – a sign, perhaps, that he was not overly enamoured of his exotically Mediterranean name. Succession may not have passed straightforwardly from father to son, but Chnodomarius, Mederichus and Serapio represent a royal clan with the ability to pass its power across the generations. The same was probably true of other Alamannic kings. When the Romans eliminated the over-king Vadomarius, considering him to pose too great a threat, they also removed his son Vithicabius from the scene, suggesting that the father's power was at least potentially heritable.[47]

Archaeological evidence, too, has shed important light on the fourth-century Germanic elite. Archaeologists have managed to identify, dotted across Germania, some of the centres and dwellings from which it exercised dominion. On the fringes of the Rhine valley, in prime Alamannic country, excavations on the hill known as the

Runderberg at the town of Urach have revealed a massive fourth-century timber rampart surrounding an ovoid area of seventy by fifty metres. Inside, several buildings were constructed, including a large timber hall, and smaller buildings dotted the hillside below. The hall was very much the kind of place where Alamannic leaders would have hosted gatherings for each other, and no doubt also feasted their retainers. Whether the smaller dwellings were occupied by retainers, craftsmen or ordinary Alamanni is not yet clear (the excavation has not been fully published). Further east, in Gothic-dominated territories, a few fortified centres, such as Alexandrovka, have been identified and partially explored. On most sites north of the Black Sea, Roman pottery sherds account for between 15 and 40 per cent of the total findings. At Alexandrovka, Roman, largely wine, amphorae sherds amount to 72 per cent; clearly a lot of entertaining went on here. What would appear to be the villa of another Gothic leader has been found at Kamenka-Antechrak. Consisting of four stone buildings with annexes and a courtyard, it covered an area of 3,800 square metres. Its extensive storage facilities and its above-average quantity of Roman pottery (over 50 per cent, this time consisting of both wine amphorae sherds and fine table wares) indicate that it, too, was a major consumption centre. At Pietroasa in Romania, finds of pottery and storage facilities show that a fourth-century Gothic leader reused an old Roman fort for similar purposes. This kind of separate elite dwelling was a new phenomenon.[48]

Clearly, therefore, the new wealth generated by the Germanic economic revolution did not end up evenly distributed, but was dominated by particular groups. Any new flow of wealth – such as that generated by the Industrial Revolution, in more modern times, or globalization – will always spark off intense competition for its control; and, if the amount of new wealth is large enough, those who control it will erect entirely new authority structures. In Western Europe, for instance, the Industrial Revolution eventually destroyed the social and political dominance of the landowning class who had run things since the Middle Ages, because the size of the new industrial fortunes made the amount of money you could make from farming even large areas look silly. It is hardly surprising, therefore, that Germania's economic revolution triggered a sociopolitical one, and other archaeological finds have illuminated some of the processes involved.

In antiquity, much of the Jutland peninsula was dotted with pools and extensive peat bogs, now largely dried out by modern land reclamation projects. Recent excavations have shown that, because of their capacity to swallow even very large items, these and similar parts of the North Sea coastal hinterland have long been used by nearby populations as depositories for their sacrifical goods. Individual items – from chariots to gold dishes – datable to a variety of periods have been unearthed. In the Roman period, from the later second to the fourth century AD, a series of weapon sacrifices were made, many of which have emerged from bogs and pools across the area: Vimose, Thorsbjerg, Nydam near Ostersotrrup, and Ejsbøl Mose. Many comprised the arms and equipment of large retinues – even whole armies – which were ritually mutilated as part of the sacrificial act. The most astonishing set of finds of the third century, made at Ejsbøl Mose in southern Jutland, gives us the profile of the force to which the weapons originally belonged. In this excavation archaeologists found the weapons of a small army of two hundred men armed with spears, lances and shields (at least sixty also carried swords and knives); an unknown number of archers (675 arrowheads were excavated) and twelve to fifteen men, nine of them mounted, with more exclusive equipment. This was a highly organized force, with a clear hierarchy and a considerable degree of military specialization: a leader and his retinue, not a bunch of peasant soldiers.[49]

From this we can begin to see how leaders could so distance themselves from their peers as to make their power hereditary. In the Germanic world of the first century, power ebbed and flowed quickly. But if one generation of a family could use its new wealth to recruit an organized military force of the kind found at Ejsbøl Mose, and then pass on both wealth and retainers, its chances of replicating power over several generations were considerably increased. Organized military forces provided the enforcement by which the claims aired in rich burials were asserted in practice. By the fourth century, retinues were a crucial attribute of the powerful. Chnodomarius, the Alamannic leader defeated by Julian at Strasbourg, had a personal retinue of 200 warriors,[50] inviting comparison with the Ejsbøl Mose deposit.

Other sources emphasize that such retinues had plenty of uses outside of battle. The persecution of Christians which the Goth Athanaric launched after partially extracting the Tervingi from Roman domination in 369 generated a document of particular vividness, the *Passion of St Saba*, the story of the persecution and death of the Gothic martyr of that name. Saba was a 'proper' member of the Tervingi, not the descendant of Roman prisoners. The *Passion* was written on Roman territory, where the saint's body was found after his death. Among the many precious details we are given is that intermediate-level leaders among the Tervingi had their own retinues and used them to enforce their will. It was a pair of heavies sent by a certain Atharid who eventually did Saba to death by drowning.[51]

Retinues also help explain the nature of fourth-century seats of power. They were built and functioned, as we have seen, as centres of consumption (like the Runderberg, or Pietroasa in Romania). From the early medieval texts we learn that generous entertaining was the main virtue required of Germanic leaders in return for loyal service, and there is no reason to suppose this a new phenomenon. It required not only large halls, but also a regular flow of foodstuffs and the means to purchase items such as Roman wine, not produced by the local economy. As the existence of specialist craftworkers also emphasizes, Germania's economy had developed sufficiently beyond its old Jastorf norms to support a far larger number of non-agricultural producers.

The bog deposits make another crucial point. As sacrifices to the gods, they were probably thank offerings for victory: the Ejsbøl Mose deposit celebrates the *destruction* of the 200 men whose weapons were consigned to its depths. There's no way of knowing exactly who they were. Were they the army of one small Germanic group defeated by that of another? Tacitus offers a revealing commentary on some Chatti and those who defeated them, a group of Hermenduri, in a struggle over salt deposits: 'Both sides, in the event of victory, had vowed their enemies to Mars and Mercury. This vow implied the sacrifice of the entire beaten side with their horses and all their possessions.'[52] The ritual sacrifice of defeated enemies was clearly not new. Just one of these small first-century tribal groupings could have put more than a couple of hundred men in the field, so that the Ejsbøl Mose deposit may celebrate the destruction of a bunch of rootless warriors on the make – possibly defeated while raiding south Jutland for booty, or in order to establish the kind of dominance that would have allowed them to extract tribute and foodstuffs more regularly. Either way, the find shows that while new flows of wealth usually end up being distributed unequally, this never happens without conflict.

Another feature of much of Germania in the Roman period was a marked increase in the *number* of weapons burials. Military retinues were not only the result of sociopolitical revolution, but also the vehicle by which it was generated, and large-scale internal violence was probably a feature of the Germanic world from the second to fourth centuries. The hereditary dynasts who dominated the new Alamannic, Frankish and Saxon confederations probably established their power through aggressive competition. The same was true, in a slightly different context, of the Gothic world further east. There, a much larger element of migration was involved, but to create the confederations such as Athanaric's Tervingi, indigenous populations had to be subdued and new hereditary hierarchies established. In both east and west, the growing wealth of the region generated a fierce struggle for control, and allowed the emergence of specialist military forces as the means to win it. The outcome of these processes was the larger political confederation characteristic of Germania in the fourth century.

The Beginnings of Feudalism?

SOME SCHOLARS have concluded that, already in fourth-century Germanic society, it was only a small aristocratic class, well equipped with armed retainers, that mattered. There are, however, many third- and fourth-century burials, apart from the richest, that contain *some* grave goods: males with weapons and females with quite sophisticated arrays of personal jewellery. These burials are far too numerous to belong just to kings and a feudal nobility. Later, written evidence offers strong hints as to whose they might have been. In the late fifth and early sixth centuries, Germanic successor states to the western Roman Empire produced large numbers of legal texts. These consistently portray Germanic (and Germanic-dominated) societies at this later date as comprising essentially three castes: freemen, freedmen and slaves. Unlike its Roman counterpart, where the offspring of freedmen were completely free – and thus freemen – freedman status in the Germanic world was hereditary. Intermarriage between the three castes was banned, and a complicated public ceremony was required for an individual to jump across any of the divides. This mode of legal categorization is widely found – amongst Goths, Lombards, Franks and Anglo-Saxons, for instance. A relatively large freeman class, rather than a small feudal nobility, is also visible playing important political and military roles in the Ostrogothic Italian kingdom, and important political, military and landowning roles in the Frankish and Lombard. Freemen were probably also the subjects of the weapons burials of fifth- and sixth-century Anglo-Saxon England, which were clearly used to claim status rather than merely to signal that the individual had been a warrior.[53]

Given that much more wealth had flowed into Germanic society between the fourth and the sixth centuries, as various Germanic groups took over parts of the Roman Empire, I don't believe that political participation could have been any less in the fourth century than in the sixth. If anything, it ought to have been broader. So if a relatively numerous freeman class still existed in the sixth century, it surely did two hundred years before. In other words, a quasi feudal warrior aristocracy did not yet dominate Germania in the late Roman period. And Roman sources, despite their lack of interest in the inner working of Germanic societies, provide just enough evidence to confirm the point. Fourth-century Gothic kings couldn't just issue orders, for instance, but had to sell their policies to a relatively broad audience, and Gothic armies of about AD 400 contained large numbers of elite fighters – freemen, in other words – not just a few warrior aristocrats. These elite fighters had their own fighting dependants; the later law codes state that freedmen (but not slaves) fought, presumably alongside the freemen whose dependants they were.[54] This is not to say that all freemen were equal: some were much richer than others, especially if high in royal favour. But social power was not yet confined to a small nobility.

How kings and nobles, complete with their retinues, interacted with the rest of freeman society is not something that archaeology can shed much light upon. Nor are the Roman sources much help. But, to be able to feed and reward them, every figure with a substantial armed retinue – all the Alamannic kings, and the 'judges' and kings of the Tervingi – must have established some rights to economic support from freemen and their dependants. In fourth-century Germania there is no sign of the bureaucratic literacy necessary for large-scale taxation, but agricultural produce must have been regularly exacted. Again, therefore, the situation had clearly moved on from the first century, when contributions were occasionally made to distinguished chiefs on a voluntary basis (as Tacitus tells us in his *Germania*). Obviously, kings were responsible for representing their subjects in any negotiations with outside powers – such as the summit meeting between Athanaric and Valens – and for formulating 'foreign policy'. They must also have had the right to require military service of their subjects, as foreign policy often involved little more than deciding whom to make war upon. The job description also included some kind of legal function. At the very least, kings will have judged disputes between their grander subjects. Whether they had the right to make general laws, as opposed to decisions in specific cases, is more doubtful. Law-making in the Germanic kingdoms of the post-Roman west looks like a new function, and, even then, was exercised only in the context of consensus. When a law code was devised, it was at assemblies of the great and the good, and issued in the name of all.[55]

Fourth-century Roman sources shed little light on how precisely kings and their retinues intersected with this freeman caste, but the *Passion of St Saba* does get us a bit closer. The persecution of Christians among the Tervingi was a policy decision of the overall leadership, involving the sub-kings as well as Athanaric himself. Enforcement, however, was largely in the hands of local village communities, retainers unfamiliar with local circumstances being sent round from time to time to check on progress. In the case of Saba's village, this gave the locals every chance to frustrate a policy with which they were clearly out of sympathy. Faced with the order to persecute, they swore false oaths that there weren't any Christians amongst them. This village, at least, clearly wanted to protect its Christians from Athanaric's persecution, and there was nothing his retainers could do about it. They had no idea who might or might not be a Christian; it was because Saba wouldn't go along with the deception that he was martyred.[56]

Germanic society remained, then, a broadly based oligarchy with much power in the hands of a still numerous freeman elite. It had some way to go before it reached the feudal state of the Carolingian era.

Rome, Persia and the Germans

OUR EXPLORATION OF the changes that remade the Germanic world between the first and fourth centuries clearly shows why Roman attention remained so firmly fixed on Persia in the late imperial period.

The rise of that state to superpower status had caused the massive third-century crisis, and Persia remained the much more obvious threat, even after the eastern front had stabilized. Germania, by contrast, even in the fourth century, had come nowhere close to generating a common identity amongst its peoples, or unifying its political structures. Highly contingent alliances had given way to stronger groupings, or confederations, the latter representing a major shift from the kaleidoscopic first-century world of changing loyalties. Although royal status could now be inherited, not even the most successful fourth-century Germanic leaders had begun to echo the success of Ardashir in uniting the Near East against Roman power. To judge by the weapons deposits and our written sources, fourth-century Germani remained just as likely to fight each other as the Roman state.

That said, the massive population increase, economic development and political restructuring of the first three centuries AD could not fail to make fourth-century Germania much more of a potential threat to Roman strategic dominance in Europe than its first-century counterpart. It is important to remember, too, that Germanic society had not yet found its equilibrium. The belt of Germanic client kingdoms extended only about a hundred kilometres beyond the Rhine and Danube frontier lines: this left a lot of Germania excluded from the regular campaigning that kept frontier regions reasonably in line. The balance of power on the frontier was, therefore, vulnerable to something much more dangerous than the periodic over-ambition of client kings. One powerful exogenous shock had been delivered by Sasanian Persia in the previous century – did the Germanic world beyond the belt of closely controlled client kingdoms pose a similar threat?

Throughout the Roman imperial period, established Germanic client states periodically found themselves the targets of the predatory groups settled further away from the frontier. The explanation for this is straightforward. While the whole of Germania was undergoing economic revolution, frontier regions were disproportionately affected, their economies stimulated not least by the presence nearby of thousands of Roman soldiers with money to spend. The client states thus tended to become richer than outer Germania, and a target for aggression. The first known case occurred in the mid-first century AD, when a mixed force from the north invaded the client kingdom of one Vannius of the Marcomanni, to seize the vast wealth he had accumulated during his thirty-year reign.[57] And it was peripheral northern

groups in search of client-state wealth who also started the second-
century convulsion generally known as the Marcomannic War. The
same motivation underlay the arrival of the Goths beside the Black
Sea. Before the mid-third century, these lands were dominated by
Iranian-speaking Sarmatian groups who profited hugely from the close
relations they enjoyed with the Roman state (their wealth manifest in
a series of magnificently furnished burials dating from the first to third
centuries). The Goths and other Germanic groups moved into the
region to seize a share of this wealth.

The danger posed by the developing Germanic world, however,
was still only latent, because of its lack of overall unity. In practice, the
string of larger Germanic kingdoms and confederations – now stretching all the way from the mouth of the Rhine to the north Black Sea
coast – provided a range of junior partners within a dominant late
Roman system, rather than a real threat to Rome's imperial power.
The Empire did not always get what it wanted in this relationship, and
maintaining the system provoked a major confrontation between
senior and junior partners about once every generation. Nonetheless,
for the most part, the barbarians knew their place: none better than
Zizais, the leader who approached the emperor Constantius for assistance in 357:

> On seeing the emperor he threw aside his weapons and fell flat
> on his breast, as if lying lifeless. And since the use of his voice
> failed him from fear at the very time when he should have made
> his plea, he excited all the greater compassion; but after several
> attempts, interrupted by sobbing, he was able to set forth only a
> little of what he tried to ask.[58]

An inability, at first, to speak, then a little quiet sobbing and the
stuttering out of a few requests, did the trick. Constantius made Zizais
a Roman client king and granted him and his people imperial protection. Woe betide the barbarian who forgot the script.

The later Roman Empire was doing a pretty good job of keeping
the barbarians in check. It had had to dig deep to respond to the
Persian challenge, but it was still substantially in control of its European frontiers. It has long been traditional to argue, however, that
extracting the extra resources needed to maintain this control placed
too many strains on the system; that the effort involved was unsustainable. Stability did return to Rome's eastern and European frontiers in

the fourth century, but at too high a price, with the result that the Empire was destined to fall – or so the argument goes. Before exploring the later fourth and fifth centuries, it is important to examine the Empire of the mid-fourth more closely. *Was* it a structure predestined to collapse?

3

THE LIMITS OF EMPIRE

IN AD 373 OR THEREABOUTS, the commander of Roman military forces in North Africa (in Latin, *comes Africae*), one Romanus by name, was cashiered for provoking some of the Berber tribes settled on the fringes of the province to rebel. Theodosius, the field marshal (*magister militum*) sent to deal with the emergency, found amongst Romanus' papers a highly incriminating document. It was a letter to the commander from a third party, which included the following greeting from a certain Palladius, until recently a senior imperial bureaucrat: 'Palladius salutes you and says that he was dismissed from office for no other reason than that in the case of the people of Tripolis he spoke to the sacred ears [of the Emperor Valentinian I] what was not true.'[1] On the strength of this, Palladius was dragged out of retirement from his country estates and frogmarched back to Trier. Lying to the emperor was treason. Rather than face interrogation, which in such cases routinely involved torture, Palladius committed suicide en route. The full story slowly emerged.

The trail led back to 363, when Romanus had first been appointed. The countryside around the town of Lepcis Magna in the province of Tripolitania had just been looted by Berber tribesmen from the neighbouring desert hinterland, and its inhabitants wanted Romanus to retaliate. He duly gathered his forces at Lepcis, but demanded logistic support to the tune of 4,000 camels, which the citizens refused to provide. Romanus thereupon dispersed his soldiers, and no campaign was mounted. The outraged citizens used their next annual provincial assembly, probably that of 364, to send an embassy of complaint to the emperor Valentinian. Romanus tried to head things off at the pass, getting his version of the story to Valentinian first via a relative called Remigius who was currently *magister officiorum* (something like the head of the Civil Service, one of the top bureaucrats of the western Empire). Valentinian refused to believe either version at first telling, and ordered a commission of inquiry. But it was slow to get moving, and in the meantime further Berber attacks prompted the townsfolk of Lepcis to send a second embassy to complain about Romanus' continued inactivity. Hearing of yet more attacks, Valentinian lost his temper, and this is where Palladius enters the story. He was chosen to conduct a fact-finding mission, and was also given the job of taking with him gifts of cash for the African troops.[2]

Following the emperor's orders, Palladius travelled to Lepcis and discovered for himself the truth about what Romanus had – or rather, had not – been up to. At the same time, however, Palladius was doing deals with the commanders and paymasters of African army units, which allowed him to keep for himself some of the imperial cash in his care. Everything was set up for a meeting of minds. Palladius threatened Romanus with a damning indictment of his inactivity, while Romanus brought up the small matter of Palladius' embezzlement. In a devil's bargain, Palladius kept the cash, and, back in Trier, told Valentinian that the inhabitants of Lepcis had nothing to complain of. The emperor, believing his time had been wasted, unleashed the full apparatus of the law on the plaintiffs of Lepcis. Palladius was sent to Africa a second time, to preside over the trials. With so much at stake for the judge, there could be only one outcome for the defendants. So a few witnesses were bribed, and agreed that there had never been any attacks; the loose ends were neatly sewn up, probably in 368, and one governor and three ambassadors were executed for making false statements to the emperor. There the matter rested until Palladius' letter to Romanus came to light six years later. Two surviving ambassadors, who'd had the sense to go into hiding when sentenced to have their tongues cut out, then re-emerged from the woodwork to have their say. The affair duly claimed its final victims: Palladius, of course, and Romanus, not to mention the *magister officiorum* Remigius, and the false witnesses.

At first sight, there might seem nothing out of the ordinary here: negligence, embezzlement and a particularly nasty cover-up. What else would you expect of an imperial structure caught in a declining trajectory towards extinction? Ever since Gibbon, the corruption of public life has been part of the story of Roman imperial collapse. But while the fourth-century Empire had its fair share of corruption, it is important not to jump to conclusions. In sources of the time you can easily find examples of every kind of wrongdoing imaginable: from military commanders who artificially inflate manpower returns while keeping their units under strength so as to pocket the extra pay, to bureaucrats shuffling money around between different accounts until it becomes 'lost' in the paper trail and they can divert it to their own purposes.[3] But whether any of this played a substantial role in the collapse of the western Empire is much more doubtful.

Uncomfortable as the idea might be, power has, throughout history, had a long and distinguished association with money making: in states both big and small, both seemingly healthy and on their last legs. In most past societies and many present ones, the link between power and profit was not even remotely problematic, profit for oneself and one's friends being seen as the whole, and perfectly legitimate, point of making the effort to get power in the first place. When our old friend the philosopher Themistius started to attract the attention of the emperor Constantius in the early 350s, Libanius, a friend who taught rhetoric and was a great believer in the moral values of a classical education, wrote to him: 'Your presence at [the emperor's] table denotes a greater intimacy ... anyone you mention is immediately better off, and ... his pleasure in granting such favours exceeds yours in receiving them.' For Libanius, Themistius' new-found influence was not a problem: quite the reverse. In fact, the whole system of appointments to bureaucratic office within the Empire worked on personal recommendation. Since there were no competitive examinations, patronage and connection played a critical role. In more than one speech to different emperors, Themistius dwelt on the topic of 'friends', an emperor's immediate circle who were responsible for bringing to his attention the names of suitable appointees for office. Certainly, Themistius wanted these friends to have powers of discernment, so that they would make first-class recommendations; but he had no desire to change things in any structural way. Nepotism was systemic, office was generally accepted as an opportunity for feathering one's nest, and a moderate degree of peculation more or less expected.[4]

And this was nothing new. The early Roman Empire, even during its vigorous conquest period, was as much marked as were later eras by officials (friends of higher officials) misusing – or perhaps one should just say 'using' – power to profit themselves and their associates. According to the historian Sallust, writing in the mid-first century BC, Roman public life had been stripped of its moral fibre with the destruction of Carthage, its last major rival, in 146 BC. In fact, though, the great magnates of public life had always been preoccupied with self-advancement, and the early Empire had been no different. Much of what we might term 'corruption' in the Roman system merely reflects the normal relationship between power and profit. Some emperors, like Valentinian I, periodically made political capital out of cracking down on 'corruption', but even Valentinian made no attempt to change the system.[5] To my mind, it is important to be realistic about the way human beings use political power, and not to attach too much importance to particular instances of corruption. Since the power-profit factor had not impeded the rise of the Empire in the first place, there is no reason to suppose that it contributed fundamentally to its collapse. In the Lepcis scandal, Romanus, Palladius and Remigius overstepped the mark. Looked at more closely, Lepcisgate offers us something much more than a good cover-up.

The Limits of Government

IN THEORY, the emperor was the supreme authority when it came to issuing general legislation, and in individual cases he had the right to modify the law, or break it, as he chose. He could condemn to death, or pardon, with a single word. To all appearances, he was an absolute monarch. But appearances can be deceptive.

Valentinian, a long-time soldier before his accession, had first-hand experience of supervising the Rhine frontier; based at Trier, he was close enough to investigate promptly any untoward incident. But a problem arising in Africa was a very different matter. The first Valentinian knew of the Lepcis episode was the sudden arrival at his court of two diametrically opposed accounts of it, one brought by the first legation from the provincial assembly, the other from Romanus via the *magister officiorum*, Remigius. Trier placed Valentinian about 2,000 kilometres away from the scene of the action. As he couldn't leave the Rhine frontier to investigate one relatively minor incident in a rather obscure corner of North Africa, all he could do was send a representative to sort out the facts for him. If that person fed him misinformation, as was the case here, and ensured that no alternative account reached the imperial ears, the emperor was bound to act accordingly. The essential point that emerges from Lepcisgate is that, for all an emperor's power, in both theory and practice, Roman central government could only make effective decisions when it received accurate information from the localities. The regime of Valentinian liked to style itself as the protector of the taxpayer from the unfair demands of the military. But, thanks to Palladius' false report, the emperor's actions in the case of Lepcis Magna had entirely the opposite effect.

A leap of imagination is required to grasp the difficulty of gathering accurate information in the Roman world. As ruler of just half of it, Valentinian was controlling an area significantly larger than the current European Union. Effective central action is difficult enough today on such a geographical scale, but the communication problems that Valentinian faced made it almost inconceivably harder for him than for his counterparts in modern Brussels. The problem was twofold: not only the slowness of ancient communications, but also the minimal number of lines of contact. The Lepcis problem was exacerbated not only by the snail's pace of such communications as there were, but also by the sheer paucity of points of contact: two in the first instance (the ambassadors, plus Remigius representing Romanus' view), supplemented by a third when Valentinian sent his fact-finding mission in the person of Palladius. Once Palladius verified Romanus' view, that was two against one, and Valentinian had no additional sources of information. In the world of the telephone, the fax and the internet, the truth is much harder to hide. Beyond the immediate vicinity of his base on the Rhine frontier, Valentinian's contacts with the city communities that made up his Empire were sparse and infrequent.

Insight into the problem is provided by another extraordinary survival from the later Roman Empire: papyrus documents preserved through the centuries by the dry heat of the Egyptian desert. (As fate would have it, most of the archive ended up in the John Rylands Library in Manchester, a city famous for its rainfall.) These particular papyri, purchased by the great Victorian collector A. S. Hunt in 1896, come from Hermopolis on the west bank of the Nile at the boundary between Upper and Lower Egypt. One key letter got separated from the rest, ending up in Strasbourg. When identified as part of the same collection, it became clear that these were the papers of a certain Theophanes, a landowner from Hermopolis and a fairly high-level Roman bureaucrat of the early fourth century. In the late 310s he was legal adviser to Vitalis who, as *rationalis Aegypti*, was the finance officer in charge of the arms factories and other operations of the Roman state in the province. The bulk of the archive refers to a journey

Theophanes made from Egypt to Antioch (modern Antakya in southern Turkey, close to the Syrian border), a regional capital of the Roman east, on official business, sometime between 317 and 323. The papers don't provide a narrative of the journey – we can only guess what the aim of the mission may have been – but something in its own way more valuable: packing lists, financial accounts and dated itineraries which, between them, bring Roman official travel vividly to life.[6]

Being on official business, Theophanes was able to use the same public transport system that carried Symmachus to Trier, the *cursus publicus*, which comprised neatly spaced way-stations combining stables – where official travellers could obtain a change of animals – and (sometimes) travel lodges. The most immediately striking documents are those dealing with Theophanes' itineraries: daily listings of the distances he managed to cover. Having begun the journey to Antioch on 6 April at the town of Nikiu in Upper Egypt, he eventually rolled into the city three and a half weeks later on 2 May. His daily average had been about 40 kilometres: on the first part of the journey, through the Sinai desert, he made only about 24 kilometres a day, but speeded up to about 65 once he hit the Fertile Crescent. And on a breakneck final day into Antioch, scenting the finishing line, his party covered over a hundred. The return journey took a similar time. Bearing in mind that Theophanes' official status allowed him to change horses whenever necessary – so there was no need to conserve equine energy – this gives us a benchmark for the bureaucratic operations of the Roman Empire. We know that in emergencies, galloping messengers, with many changes of horse, might manage as much as 250 kilometres a day. But Theophanes' average on that journey of three and a half weeks was the norm: in other words, about 40, the speed of the oxcart. This was true of military as well as civilian operations, since all the army's heavy equipment and baggage moved by this means too.

The other striking feature of Theophanes' journey is its complexity. As might be expected, given such rates of travel, only the top echelons of the Roman bureaucracy tended to travel outside their immediate province – hence, lower-level officials wouldn't know their counterparts, even in adjacent regions. Egypt, for most purposes, ran itself, so Theophanes didn't usually need to know people in Antioch, and neither, for that matter, did he know people anywhere else en route. Vitalis armed him, accordingly, with letters of introduction to everyone who mattered on the way, some of which he didn't use (which is how they come to survive in the archive). Given contemporary rules of etiquette, you had to think ahead and take with you a range of appropriate offerings: courtesy demanded that an exchange of gifts – sometimes valuable ones – inaugurate any new relationship. The accounts record items destined for such a fate, such as *lungurion* (coagulated lynx musk), an ingredient of expensive perfumes.[7] Large amounts of cash also had to be carried, probably supplemented in Theophanes' case by letters of authorization allowing him, as an official traveller, to draw funds from official sources. Hence such travellers would often need protection, hiring armed escorts where necessary. Theophanes' accounts record food and drink bought for soldiers who accompanied them during the desert legs of the journey in Egypt.

The packing lists also make highly illuminating reading. Theophanes obviously needed a variety of attires: lighter and heavier clothing for variations in weather and conditions, his official uniform for the office, and a robe for the baths. The travel lodges of the *cursus publicus* were clearly very basic. The traveller brought along his own bedding – not just sheets, but even a mattress – and a complete kitchen to see to the food situation. As this suggests, Theophanes did not travel alone. We don't know how many went with him, but he was clearly accompanied by a party of slaves who dealt with all the household tasks. He generally spent on their daily sustenance just under half of what he spent on his own. This battered bundle of papyrus documents at Manchester is full of such gems of detail. Just before leaving civilization to cross the desert again, the party bought 160 litres of wine for the home journey. This cost less than the two litres of a much rarer vintage that Theophanes had with his lunch on the same day. At another point, the accounts record the purchase of snow, used to cool the wine for dinner. What emerges is an arresting vision of the complex and cumbersome nature of official travel.

In reality, then, places were much further away from one another in the fourth century than they are now. As I sit here writing, it's about 4,000 kilometres from Hadrian's Wall to the Euphrates, and so it was in Theophanes' day. But at Theophanes' rate of progress – even giving him a higher average daily rate of 50 kilometres (not counting the days spent crossing the desert) – a journey that overland would now take a maximum of two weeks would in the fourth century have taken something close to three months. Looking at the map with modern eyes, we perceive the Roman Empire as impressive enough; looked at in fourth-century terms, it is staggering. Furthermore, measuring it in the real currency of how long it took human beings to cover the distances involved, you could say it was five times larger than it appears on the map. To put it another way, running the Roman Empire with the communications then available was akin to running, in the modern day, an entity somewhere between five and ten times the size of the European Union. With places this far apart, and this far away from his capital, it is hardly surprising that an emperor would have few lines of contact with most of the localities that made up his Empire.

Moreover, even if his agents had somehow maintained a continuous flow of intelligence from every town of the Empire into the imperial centre, there is little that he could have done with it anyway. All this putative information would have had to remain on bits of papyrus, and headquarters would soon have been buried under a mountain of paperwork. Finding any particular piece of information when required would have been virtually impossible, especially since Roman archivists seem to have filed only by year.[8] Primitive communication links combined with an absence of sophisticated means of processing information explain the bureaucratic limitations within which Roman emperors of all eras had to make and enforce executive decisions.

The main consequence of all this was that the state was unable to interfere systematically in the day-to-day running of its constituent communities. Not surprisingly, the range of business handled by Roman government was only a fraction of that of a modern state. Even if there had been ideologies to encourage it, Roman government lacked the bureaucratic capacity to handle broad-reaching social agendas, such as a health service or a social security budget. Proactive governmental involvement was necessarily restricted to a much narrower range of operation: maintaining an effective army, and running the tax system. And, even in the matter of taxation, the state bureaucracy's role was limited to allocating overall sums to the cities of the Empire and monitoring the transfer of monies. The difficult work – the allocation of individual tax bills and the actual collection of money – was handled at the local level. Even here, so long as the agreed tax-take flowed out of the cities and into the central coffers, local communities were left – as the municipal laws we examined in Chapter 1 imply – to be autonomous, largely self-governing communities.[9] Keep Roman central government happy, and life could often be lived as the locals wanted.

This is a key to understanding much of the internal history of the Roman Empire. Lepcisgate illustrates not so much a particular problem of the later Empire, but the fundamental limitations affecting Roman central government of all eras. To comprehend the operation of government fully, the logistic impossibility of day-to-day interference from the centre must be considered alongside the imperial centre's absolute legal power and unchallenged ideological domination. It was the interaction of these two phenomena that created the distinctive dynamic of the Roman Empire's internal functioning. Given that it was administratively impossible for central government to control everything, anything to which it *did* add its stamp of authority carried an overwhelming legitimacy, if put to the test. What tended to happen, therefore, was that individuals and communities would invoke the authority of the centre for their own purposes. At first sight, this could suggest that the imperial finger was constantly being stuck into a whole host of local pies, but such an impression is misleading. Outside of taxation, emperors interfered in local affairs only when locals – or at least a faction of local opinion – saw an advantage to themselves in mobilizing imperial authority.

We have already seen this pattern at work in the early imperial period. As the Spanish inscriptions (pp. 38–9) show us, Roman-style towns existed right across the Empire as a consequence of local communities adopting municipal laws drawn up at the centre. In particular, the richer local landowners had quickly appreciated that securing a constitution with Latin rights was a path to Roman citizenship, which would qualify them to participate in the highly lucrative structures of Empire. The story had its shadier side, of course. A grant of Italian status was so valuable to the leaders of the community involved that they were willing to do whatever it took to win the privilege, often by courting patrons at the centre who would put in a good word for them with the emperor of the day. This kind of relationship between centre and locality was the bedrock on which the Empire was built.[10]

This relationship also applied to individuals who used the 'rescript' system. Rescripts allowed you to consult the emperor – in practice, his legal experts – on a matter of legal detail. Using the top half of a piece of papyrus, anyone could write to the emperor about an issue on which he wanted a decision. The emperor would then reply on the bottom half. You couldn't use the system to get him to settle an entire case – only to raise a technical point of law that might dictate its outcome. Again, we're indebted to a unique papyrus survival for an indication of how extensively the system was used. In the spring of AD 200, the emperors Severus and Caracalla were installed in the city of Alexandria in Egypt. A papyrus, now to be found at Columbia University, records that the emperors answered five rescripts (the replies were posted publicly) on 14 March, four on 15 March, and another four on the 20th.[11] So even if we allow emperors lots of annual holidays, at least a thousand people a year could cite an imperial opinion in their private legal disputes.

Equally important, once a rescript had been sent back to the provinces, the emperor lost control over it, so a piece of paper carrying his name and his authority was on the loose. Hardly surprising, then, that these imperial replies were used in all kinds of unintended ways. The fifth-century *Theodosian Code* (see pp. 124–5) cites a number of scams: cases where the imperial answer had been physically detached from the original question and then used to answer another, others where letters extracted for one case had been applied to another, and still others where letters had been extracted under false pretences.[12] Roman lawyers were as inventive as their modern counterparts, and subject to much less control. Not only does the rescript system show us an imperial authority that was essentially reactive, but abuses of it also make clear that distance could allow the suitor to make unintended use of the potent weapon represented by a legal ruling with the emperor's name on it.

In addition to the rescript system, emperors were also deluged with requests of a more general kind, which they might or might not respond to positively. They could either launch their own inevitably slow investigation, or accept the petitioner's inherently biased version of the truth. This usually meant the deployment of imperial power to more or less random effect: the emperor chose either to believe or not to believe the petitioner, and acted accordingly. The impact this had on day-to-day affairs depended upon the lengths that citizens in local communities would go to in order to exploit that power.

Any picture of Roman government, then, has to bear in mind that, for all their legal and ideological authority, emperors' control was limited. All the same, such was their monopoly of authority that their approval was constantly being solicited by the citizenry. Consequently, the imperial centre was both powerful and strictly constrained.

IN THE MIDDLE years of the third century, this inherently limited governmental machine was suddenly forced to confront an entirely new range of problems, all traceable to the rise of Sasanian Persia. As we have seen, the immediate problem was solved by the military, fiscal and political restructuring of the Empire. It has long been customary to argue, however, that, while rescuing the Empire from these difficulties, the changes it put in place doomed it to decline and collapse in the longer term. After Diocletian, according to this view, the Roman agricultural economy was substantially overtaxed. Peasants were forced to surrender so much of their produce that some of them died from starvation. The new tax levels, it is argued, also ruined the landowning classes who had built and run the towns of the Empire since its formation. In fact, the whole imperial edifice came to be dominated by constraint rather than consent, symbolized in a repressive, bureaucratic machine staffed, as one influential view put it, by many 'idle mouths', a further burden on the taxpayer. On the military side, the enlarged army may have done its job in the short term; but manpower shortages within the Empire forced fourth-century emperors to draw increasingly on 'barbarian' recruits from across the frontier. As a result, the Roman army declined in both loyalty and efficiency. All in all, this line of argument goes, while the initial Persian crisis was overcome, it had required such an effort that the financial, political and even military strength of the Empire was visibly draining away.[13]

These views remain deeply entrenched. The present generation of scholarship has demonstrated beyond reasonable doubt, however, that such a stance greatly underestimates the economic, political and ideological vitality of the late Roman world.

The Price of Survival

ANCIENT AGRICULTURE suffered from two limitations. First, before the invention of tractors, the productivity of any piece of land was hugely dependent on how much labour was available to work it. Second, ancient farmers, while employing their own sophisticated techniques for maintaining fertility, were unable greatly to increase their output of foodstuffs in anything like the way that the use of chemical fertilizers has made possible in the modern era. This in turn acted as a brake on population levels, since human numbers tend to increase up to a limit imposed by the availability of food. In addition, transport was hugely expensive; Diocletian's Prices Edict (see p. 65) records that a wagon of wheat doubled in price for every fifty miles it travelled. In these fundamental ways, the Roman economy was at every era trapped at not much above subsistence levels. Until very recently, scholars have been confident that the higher tax-take of the late Roman state aggravated these conditions to the extent that it became impossible for the Empire's peasant population to maintain itself even at existing low levels.

The evidence comes mostly from written sources. To start with, the annual volume of inscriptions known from Roman antiquity declined suddenly in the mid-third century to something like one-fifth of previous levels. Since chances of survival remained pretty constant, this massive fall-off was naturally taken as an indicator that landowners, the social group generally responsible for commissioning these largely private inscriptions, had suddenly found themselves short of funds. A study of the chronology also led the heavier tax burden imposed by the late Roman state to be seen as the primary cause, since the decline coincided with the tax hikes that were necessary to fight off the increased Persian threat. Such views were reinforced by other sources documenting another well known fourth-century phenomenon, commonly known as the 'flight of the curials'. Curials (or decurions) were the landowners of sufficient wealth to get a seat on their town councils (Latin, *curiae*). They were the descendants of the men who had built the Roman towns, bought into classical ideologies of self-government, learned Latin, and generally benefited from Latin rights and Roman citizenship in the early imperial period. In the fourth century, these descendants became increasingly unwilling to serve on the town councils their ancestors had established. Some of the sources preserve complaints about the costs involved in being a councillor, others about the administrative burden imposed upon the curials by the Roman state. It has long been part of the orthodoxy of Roman collapse, therefore, that the old landowning classes of the Empire were overburdened into oblivion.[14]

Other fourth-century legal texts refer to a previously unknown phenomenon, the 'deserted lands' (*agri deserti*). Most of these texts are very general, giving no indication of the amounts of land that might be involved, but one law, of AD 422, referring to North Africa, indicates that a staggering 3,000 square miles fell into this category in that region alone. A further run of late Roman legislation also attempted to tie certain categories of tenant farmers (*coloni*) to their existing estates, to prevent them moving. It was easy, in fact irresistible, to weave these separate phenomena into a narrative of cause and effect, whereby the late Empire's punitive tax regime made it uneconomic to farm all the land that had previously been under cultivation. This was said to have generated large-scale abandonment – hence the *agri deserti* – as well as governmental intervention to try to prevent this very abandoning of the lands that the new tax burden had made uneconomic. Stripped of a larger portion of their production, the peasantry could not maintain their numbers over the generations, which further lowered output.[15]

Into this happy consensus a large bomb was lobbed, towards the end of the 1950s, by a French archaeologist named Georges Tchalenko. As with many revolutionary moments, it took a long time for bystanders to realize that they had witnessed something earth-shattering, but this bomb set off a chain of detonations. Tchalenko had spent much of the 1940s and 1950s roaming the limestone hills in what is now a fairly obscure (and relatively peaceful) corner of the Middle East. In antiquity, these hills belonged to the rural hinterland of one of the great imperial capitals, Antioch: Antakya in modern Turkey. (The hills, by a quirk of fate, have ended up over the border in northern Syria.) In his explorations, Tchalenko came across the remains of a dense spread of villages, sturdily constructed from limestone blocks, which had been abandoned in the eighth to ninth centuries after the Arab conquest of the region.

The villages showed that these hills had once been the home of a flourishing rural population, which could afford not only to build excellent houses, but to endow their villages with sizeable public buildings. This ancient population was much denser than anything the region has supported at any point since, and it clearly made its living from agriculture; Tchalenko believed it produced olive oil commercially. The really revolutionary bit was Tchalenko's discovery that prosperity first hit the region in the later third and early fourth centuries, then continued into the fifth, sixth and seventh with no sign of decline. At the very moment when the generally accepted model suggested that the late Roman state was taxing the lifeblood out of its farmers, here was hard evidence of a farming region prospering.[16]

Further archaeological work, using field surveys, has made it possible to test levels of rural settlement and agricultural activity across a wide geographical spread and at different points in the Roman period. Broadly speaking, these surveys have confirmed that Tchalenko's Syrian villages were a far from unique example of late Roman rural prosperity. The central provinces of Roman North Africa (in particular Numidia, Byzacena and Proconsularis) saw a similar intensification of rural settlement and production at this time. This has been illuminated by separate surveys in Tunisia and southern Libya, where prosperity did not even begin to fall away until the fifth century. Surveys in Greece have produced a comparable picture. And elsewhere in the Near East, the fourth and fifth centuries have emerged as a period of *maximum* rural development – not minimum, as the orthodoxy would have led us to expect. Investigations in the Negev Desert region of modern Israel have shown that farming also flourished in this deeply marginal environment under the fourth-century Empire. The pattern is broadly similar in Spain and southern Gaul, while recent re-evaluations of rural settlement in Roman Britain have suggested that its fourth-century population reached levels that would only be seen again in the fourteenth. Argument continues as to what figure to put on this maximum, but that late Roman Britain was remarkably densely populated by ancient and medieval standards is now a given.[17] The only areas, in fact, where, in the fourth century, prosperity was not at or close to its maximum for the entire Roman period were Italy and some of the northern European provinces, particularly Gallia Belgica and Germania Inferior on the Rhine frontier. Even here, though, estimates of settlement density have been revised substantially upwards in recent years.

For the poverty of the latter two northern provinces, the explanation probably lies in third-century disruption. The Rhine frontier region was being heavily raided at the same time as so much energy was being poured into solving the Persian problem, and it may be that rural affluence in parts of the region never recovered. A methodological problem may also provide at least part of the explanation. Roman-period surveys rely on datable finds of commercially produced pottery to identify and date settlements. If a population ceased to import these wares, reverting to undatable locally made ceramics, especially if at the same time they were also building more in wood than in the traditional Roman stone, brick and tile – which surveys also find – then they would have become archaeologically invisible. This was happening in several areas of northern Europe by at least the mid-fifth century, so it is far from impossible that the seeming lack of fourth-century inhabitants in parts of the northern Rhine frontier region was caused not by substantial population decline, but by the first appearance of these new habits. The jury is still out.

The case of Italy is rather different. As befitted the heartland of a conquest state, Italy was thriving in the early imperial period. Not only did the spoils of conquest flood its territories, but its manufacturers of pottery, wine and other goods sold them throughout the western provinces and dominated the market. Also, Italian agricultural production was untaxed. As the economies of the conquered provinces developed, however, this early domination was curtailed by the development of rival enterprises closer to the centres of consumption and with much lower transport costs. By the fourth century, the process had pretty much run its course; and from Diocletian onwards, Italian agriculture had to pay the same taxes as the rest of the Empire. So the peninsula's economy was bound to have suffered relative decline in the fourth century, and it is not surprising to find more marginal lands there being taken out of production. But as we have seen, the relative decline of Italy and perhaps also of north-eastern Gaul was more than compensated for by economic success elsewhere. Despite the heavier tax burden, the late Roman countryside was generally booming.[18] The revolutionary nature of these findings cannot be overstated.

Looked at with this in mind, the literary evidence is far from incompatible with the archaeology. The laws forcing labour to stay in one place, for example, would only have been enforceable where rural population levels were relatively high. Otherwise, the general demand for labour would have seen landowners competing with one another for peasants, and being willing to take in each other's runaways and protect them from the law. More generally, the term 'deserted lands' (*agri deserti*) was coined in the fourth century to describe lands from which no tax was being collected. It carries no necessary implication that land so labelled had ever previously been cultivated, and certainly the large tract of North African territory referred to in the law of 422 consisted mostly of desert and semi-desert hinterland where normal agriculture had always been impossible. Nor is the late Empire's more demanding tax regime incompatible with a buzzing agricultural economy. Tenant subsistence farmers tend to produce only what they need: enough to provide for themselves and their dependants and to pay any essential additional dues such as rent. Within this context there will often be a certain amount of economic 'slack', consisting of extra foodstuffs they could produce but which they choose not to because they can neither store them, nor, thanks to high transport costs, sell them. In this kind of world, taxation – if not imposed at too high a level – can actually *increase* production: the tax imposed by the state is another due that has to be satisfied, and farmers do sufficient extra work to produce the additional output. Only if taxes are set so high that peasants starve, or the long-term fertility of their lands is impaired, will such dues have a damaging economic effect.

None of this means that it was fun to be a late Roman peasant. The state imposed heavier demands on him than it had on his ancestors, and he was prevented by law from moving around in search of the best tenancy terms. But there is nothing in the archaeological or written evidence to gainsay the general picture of a late Roman countryside at or near maximum levels of population, production and output.[19]

There is, however, no doubt that most cities of the Empire appear to have suffered in one respect. The decline in inscriptions from the mid-third century reflects a fall in the number of new public buildings being commissioned. The only cities that continued to see public building on a large scale were the central and regional capitals of the Roman state. And even here, instead of local grandees endowing their towns with another memorial toilet block (or some such structure) in their own memory, buildings were being erected by state officials using state funds.[20] The private funding of public building in one's hometown belonged to the very early imperial period, when this constituted the prime route to self-promotion. Putting up the right kinds of public building was part of persuading some high official to recommend your hometown to the emperor for the grant of a Roman constitution. Once your town had Latin rights, then financing buildings became a strategy for winning power and influence within it. The towns of the Empire quickly built up endowments of publicly owned land (often from wills), and also acquired the right to levy local taxes and tolls, in itself a substantial annual income whose expenditure was controlled by the town council and particularly by its leading magistrates. Magistrates were voted into office by a town's free citizens. Competitive local building in this context was all about winning elections and hence controlling the use of local funds.[21]

The confiscation by the state of local endowments and taxes in the third century removed most of the fun from local government. By the fourth, there was little point in spending freely to win power in your hometown, if all you then got to do was run errands for central government. By this time, retired members of the expanding class of imperial bureaucrats (honorati) were being given all the interesting and prestigious tasks in local government, including the detailed allocation of their town's tax burden. Nothing would be more guaranteed to generate invitations to dinner and other small marks of attention than the knowledge that, when the time came, you were going to be in charge of setting the new tax bills. Honorati also got to sit with the provincial governor when he was trying legal cases, and helped him arrive at verdicts. As the many surviving letters to local honorati make clear, this was another moment when great influence could be brought to bear, and, again, it tended to make the honoratus very popular in local society. What happened in the late Empire, in other words, was a major shift in local political power away from town councils to imperial bureaucrats. This did away with the whole point of the local displays of generosity recorded in the early imperial inscriptions.

The stock image of the late Roman bureaucracy also needs revising. Much of its characterization as an oppressive alien force of 'idle mouths' sucking the vitality out of local society can be traced back to a speech of the rhetor Libanius, which catalogued the dubious social origins of some of the leading bureaucrats and senators of mid-fourth-century Constantinople. Three Praetorian Prefects (chief civilian executive officers) of the 350s and early 360s – Domitianus, Helpidius and Taurus – had fathers, Libanius tells us, who personally engaged in manual labour; the father of a fourth, Philippus, made sausages, and the governor of the province of Asia, Dulcitius, was the son of a fuller.[22] The image conjured up of a bureaucracy dominated by new men from nowhere is very powerful, but in this speech Libanius had a very particular axe to grind. The Senate of Constantinople had just refused membership to one of his protégés, a certain Thalassius, on the grounds that Thalassius' father was a 'tradesman' (he had owned an arms factory). As a vast body of other evidence makes clear (including endless letters of reference written by Libanius himself), however, the vast majority of the new bureaucrats and senators of the fourth-century Empire were actually drawn from the curial classes, not from further down the social scale. The language of this bureaucracy was the 'correct' Latin and Greek espoused by the traditional educational curriculum. This tells us instantly that its members had benefited from a lengthy and expensive private education. The bureaucracy of the late Roman period did not consist of outsiders or parvenus, then, but of town councillors who had renegotiated their position within the changing structures of Empire. Only a small hard-headed inner elite – called *principales* in Latin – stayed on the councils in order to monopolize the few interesting jobs left.

Because bureaucratic positions were so attractive, emperors were flooded with requests for appointments. Many of these were granted. Emperors always liked to raise their popularity ratings by appearing generous, and these kinds of grants seemed, individually, pretty harmless. Despite the laws attempting to regulate bureaucratic expansion by forcing ex-town councillors back to their cities, by AD 400 large numbers of wealthy landowners were making the central imperial bureaucracy the main focus of their careers. At this date, the eastern financial office (the *largitionales*) had a staff of 224 officers, and a waiting list of 610 ready to take their places when they finished their stint. And, because of the delay involved in getting a post under these conditions, parents were appending their children's names to waiting lists at birth. Thus, far from showing the power of a newly oppressive central state, the rise of the imperial bureaucracy demonstrates the continuation of the same kind of political relationship between centre and locality that we have already observed. Here again, as in the rescript system and in the whole process of Romanization itself, the state certainly started the ball rolling by setting up a new rule book, as it were. But the process was taken over by locals responding to the rule changes and adapting them to their own interests.

Understanding bureaucratic expansion in this way makes it impossible to see the 'flight of the curials' as fundamentally an economic phenomenon, or, at least, as reflecting a decline in the private fortunes of the landowning class. It also takes much of the sting out of the argument that the bureaucracy were so many 'idle mouths'. It is hard to suppose that these bureaucrats' ancestors, as local landowners sitting on town councils, had been any less 'idle' – if one chooses to see them this way. They had always been essentially a rentier class, overseeing the labour of their peasants rather than engaging in the primary work of agricultural production. But whereas before they had been 'idling' on their town councils, now they were idling in the offices of the central Roman state. Their salaries, paid by the state, were also very low. Bureaucratic expansion needed little extra taxation to fund.[23] What made the jobs attractive, as we have seen, was the status that accompanied them and the chance to charge fees to those who needed your services.

While these changes in upper-class career patterns certainly had some economic effects, there is nothing to suggest that upper-class life changed in any fundamental way. Written sources and archaeological excavation both confirm that the late Roman landowning elite, like their forebears, would alternate between their urban houses and their country estates. Fourth-century Antioch, for instance, boasted the hugely wealthy suburb of Daphne, and extensive investigations at the city of Sardis in modern Turkey have uncovered numerous wealthy private houses of the fourth and fifth centuries. There is no reason to suppose, therefore, that luxury urban trades, which depended on landowners coming to 'town' from time to time to spend their wealth, will have suffered very much. What *may* have happened is that the reorientation away from town councils to an imperial bureaucracy meant that larger landowners maintained houses in regional and provincial imperial capitals rather than in their hometowns. This would have increased the tendency – already noticed in patterns of public spending – for capitals to prosper at the expense of lesser towns.[24]

What the new evidence and the consequent reinterpretations of the old evidence have demonstrated, then, is that although, in order to meet the strategic challenge posed by Persia, the state was taking a bigger share of agricultural output in tax and had confiscated local city funds, agriculture itself, the main engine of the economy, was not in crisis, nor was the fate of the landowning classes as bleak as tradition-ally supposed. The 'flight of the curials' was an adjustment, if a major one, in the location of political power. Old arguments that fifth-century political collapse was the result of fourth-century economic crisis cannot, therefore, be sustained.

There is also more than enough here to prompt a rethink about claims that, from the mid-third century, the army was so short of

Roman manpower that it jeopardized its efficiency by drawing ever increasingly on 'barbarians'. There is no doubt that the restructured Roman army did recruit such men in two main ways. First, self-contained contingents were recruited on a short-term basis for particular campaigns, returning home once they were over. Second, many individuals from across the frontier entered the Roman army and took up soldiering as a career, serving for a working lifetime in regular Roman units. Neither phenomenon was new. The auxiliary forces, both cavalry and infantry (*alae* and *cohortes*), of the early imperial army had always been composed of non-citizens, and amounted to something like 50 per cent of the military. It is impossible to know much about recruiting patterns among the rank and file, but nothing about the officer corps of the late Empire suggests that barbarian numbers had increased across the army as a whole. The main difference between early and late armies lay not in their numbers, but in the fact that barbarian recruits now sometimes served in the same units as citizens, rather than being segregated into auxiliary forces. Training in the fourth century remained pretty much as fierce as ever, producing bonded groups ready to obey orders. From Ammianus Marcellinus' picture of the army in action we find no evidence that its standards of discipline had fallen in any substantial way, or that the barbarians in its ranks were less inclined to obey orders or any more likely to make common cause with the enemy. He records one incident in which a recently retired barbarian let slip some important intelligence about Roman army dispositions, but none showed disloyalty in combat. There is no sign, in short, that the restructuring of the Empire had important knock-on effects in the military sphere.[25] It is entirely possible, nonetheless, that the extra costs incurred in the running of the fourth-century Empire could have alienated the loyalty of the provincial populations that had bought into the values of Romanness with such vigour under the early Empire.

Christianity and Consent

WITH THE EMPEROR Constantine's conversion to Christianity in 312, the old ideological structures of the Roman world also began to be dismantled, and for Edward Gibbon this was a key moment in the story of Roman collapse:

The clergy successfully preached the doctrines of patience and pusillanimity; the active virtues of society were discouraged; and the last remains of the military spirit were buried in the cloister; a large portion of public and private wealth was consecrated to the specious demands of charity and devotion; and the soldiers' pay was lavished on the useless multitudes of both sexes, who could only plead the merits of abstinence and chastity. Faith, zeal, curiosity, and the more earthly passions of malice and ambition kindled the flame of theological discord; the church, and even the state, were distracted by religious factions, whose conflicts were sometimes bloody, and always implacable; the attention of emperors was diverted from camps to synods; the Roman world was oppressed by a new species of tyranny; and the persecuted sects became the secret enemies of their country.[26]

Others have not been so strident. But the notion that Christianity broke up ideological unity and hindered the ability of the state effectively to win support has since been shared by others; so too the fear that the Church diverted financial and human resources from vital material ends. The issues of both taxation and the rise of Christianity thus raise the more general question of whether it was against a backdrop of local discontent that the reconstructed imperial authority struggled to maintain its legitimacy.

Fourth-century sources make occasional complaints about tax rates. There was also one major tax riot. In Antioch in 387, a crowd gathered to protest about the imposition of a supertax. The mood got ugly, and imperial statues were toppled. Imperial images, like everything else to do with emperors, were sacred, and assaults on them an act of treason. The local community was terrified that army units might be turned loose on the city in punishment, but the reigning emperor, Theodosius I, took a conciliatory line to resolve the crisis. And this is a fair enough indicator of the general climate.[27] Tax collection goes more smoothly, and rates can be increased more easily, if taxpayers understand and broadly accept the reasons for which they are being taxed. Fourth-century emperors perfectly understood the principle of consent, and never lost an opportunity to stress that taxation paid above all for the army – which was true – and that the army was necessary to defend Roman society from outside threats. Most of the ceremonial occasions of the imperial year involved a keynote speech lasting about an hour whose purpose was to celebrate the regime's recent successes. Hardly any of our surviving late imperial examples fail to make some reference to the army and its function of protector of the Roman world.

Different emperors sold their frontier policies in different ways, but there was no disagreement on this basic purpose of taxation. The population was daily reminded of the point on its coinage: one of the most common designs featured an enemy grovelling at the emperor's feet. On the down side, military failings might be criticized for wasting the taxpayers' contributions. In one famous incident, Ursulus, chief financial minister of the emperor Constantius II, complained sarcastically and publicly about the performance of the army on a visit to the ruins of Amida, shortly after the Persians sacked it in 359: 'Look at the courage with which the cities are defended by our soldiers, for whose huge salary bills the wealth of the Empire is already barely sufficient.' The generals didn't forget this. When Constantius died, part of the price paid by his successor for their support was the condemnation to death of Ursulus in the political trials that marked the change of regime. For the most part, however, the system worked tolerably well; the Antioch tax riot is an isolated example, which was caused, notice, not by the usual taxes but by an additional imposition. While, of course, many landowners sought to minimize their tax bills – the laws and letter collections are full of uncovered scams and requests for dispensations to this effect – fourth-century emperors did manage to sell to their population the idea that taxation was essential to civilized life, and generally collected the funds without ripping their society apart.[28]

On the religious front Constantine's conversion to Christianity certainly unleashed a cultural revolution. Physically, town landscapes were transformed as the practice of keeping the dead separate from the living, traditional in Graeco-Roman paganism, came to an end, and cemeteries sprang up within town walls. Churches replaced temples; as a consequence, from the 390s onwards there was so much cheap second-hand marble available that the new marble trade all but collapsed. The Church, as Gibbon claimed, attracted large donations both from the state and from individuals. Constantine himself started the process, the *Book of the Popes* lovingly recording his gifts of land to the churches of Rome, and, over time, churches throughout the Empire acquired substantial assets. Furthermore, Christianity was in some senses a democratizing and equalizing force. It insisted that everybody, no matter what his economic or social status, had a soul and an equal stake in the cosmic drama of salvation, and some Gospel stories even suggested that worldly wealth was a barrier to salvation. All this ran contrary to the aristocratic values of Graeco-Roman culture, with its claim that true civilization could only be attained by the man with enough wealth and leisure to afford many years of private education and active participation in municipal affairs. Take also, for instance, the grammarians' traditional use of the veil. In antiquity, a veil marked the entrance to higher places, as in the monumental audience halls where the imperial presence was normally veiled from the main body of the court. St Augustine dismissed with contempt in his *Confessions* the grammarians' use of veils to cover the entrances to their schools. For him and other late Roman Christians, the practice came to be dismissed as a false claim to wisdom.

Instead, fourth-century Christian intellectuals set up in their writings a deliberately non-classical anti-hero, the uneducated Christian Holy Man, who, despite not having passed through the hands of the grammarian, and despite characteristically abandoning the town for the desert, achieved heights of wisdom and virtue that went far beyond anything that could be learned from Homer or Vergil, or even from participating in self-government. The Holy Man was the best-case product of the monastery – as Gibbon pointed out, Christian monasticism attracted a substantial number of recruits at this time. The monastic lifestyle was extravagantly praised by highly educated Christians, who saw in its strictures a level of devotion equivalent to that of the Christian martyrs of old. Nor does it take much sifting through the sources to find examples of high-status Christians rejecting participation in the normal practices of Roman upper-class life. In Italy, around the turn of the fifth century, within a few years of one another, the moderately wealthy Paulinus of Nola and a staggeringly wealthy senatorial heiress, Melania the younger, both liquidated their fortunes and embraced lives of Christian devotion. Paulinus became a bishop, devoting himself to the cult of the martyr Felix, while Melania took herself off to the Holy Land. Thus Christianity asked awkward questions of, and forced some substantial revisions in, many of the attitudes and practices that Romans had long taken for granted.[29]

But while the rise of Christianity was certainly a cultural revolution, Gibbon and others are much less convincing in claiming that the new religion had a seriously deleterious effect upon the functioning of the Empire. Christian institutions did, as Gibbon asserts, acquire large financial endowments. On the other hand, the non-Christian religious institutions that they replaced had also been wealthy, and their wealth was being progressively confiscated at the same time as Christianity waxed strong. It is unclear whether endowing Christianity involved an overall transfer of assets from secular to religious coffers. Likewise, while some manpower was certainly lost to the cloister, this was no more than a few thousand individuals at most, hardly a significant figure in a world that was maintaining, even increasing, population levels. Similarly, the number of upper-class individuals who renounced their wealth and lifestyles for a life of Christian devotion pales into insignificance beside the 6,000 or so who by AD 400 were actively participating in the state as top bureaucrats. In legislation passed in the 390s, all of these people were required to be Christian. For every Paulinus of Pella, there were many more newly Christianized Roman landowners happy to hold major state office, and no sign of any crisis of conscience among them.

Nor was there any pressing reason why Christianity should have generated such a crisis, since religion and Empire rapidly reached an ideological rapprochement. Roman imperialism had claimed, since the time of Augustus, that the presiding divinities had destined Rome to conquer and civilize the world. The gods had supported the Empire in a mission to bring the whole of humankind to the best achievable state, and had intervened directly to choose and inspire Roman emperors. After Constantine's public adoption of Christianity, the long-standing claims about the relation of the state to the deity were quickly, and surprisingly easily, reworked. The presiding divinity was recast as the Christian God, and the highest possible state for human-kind was declared to be Christian conversion and salvation. Literary education and the focus on self-government were shifted for a while to the back burner, but by no means thrown out. And that was the sum total of the adjustment required. The claim that the Empire was God's vehicle, enacting His will in the world, changed little: only the nomenclature was different. Likewise, while emperors could no longer be deified, their divine status was retained in Christian-Roman propaganda's portrayal of God as hand-picking individual emperors to rule with Him, and partly in His place, over the human sphere of His cosmos. Thus, the emperor and everything about him, from his bedchamber to his treasury, could continue to be styled as 'sacred'.[30]

These were not claims asserted merely by a few loyalists in and around the imperial court. On Christmas Day 438, a new compendium of recent Roman law, the *Theodosian Code* (*Codex Theodosianus*), was presented to the assembled senators in the old imperial capital. All senatorial meetings were fully minuted and the minutes passed on to the emperor. Not surprisingly, these records have not survived; the piles of verbiage would not have made wildly exciting reading for medieval or even late Roman copyists. The minutes of the *Theodosian Code* meeting were, however, incorporated into the Preface to official copies of the *Code* made after 443. A single eleventh-century manuscript deriving from one such official copy is preserved in the Ambrosian Library at Milan. Such is the slender thread by which this unique text survived.[31] The Praetorian Prefect of Italy, Glabrio Faustus, who presided, and in whose palatial home the senators had gathered, opened the meeting by formally introducing the text to the assembly. After reminding his audience of the original edict that had established the law commission, he presented the *Code* to them. In response, the assembled senators let rip at the tops of their voices:

> 'Augustuses of Augustuses, the greatest of Augustuses!'[32] *(repeated 8 times)*
> 'God gave You to us! God save You for us!' *(27 times)*
> 'As Roman Emperors, pious and felicitous, may You rule for many years!' *(22 times)*
> 'For the good of the human race, for the good of the Senate, for the good of the State, for the good of all!' *(24 times)*
> 'Our hope is in You, You are our salvation!' *(26 times)*
> 'May it please our Augustuses to live forever!' *(22 times)*
> 'May You pacify the world and triumph here in person!' *(24 times)*

The repetition of these acclamations seems extraordinary to us, but the message conveyed by this ceremony is worth careful consideration.

Its most obvious message was Unity. The great and good of the Roman world were speaking with one voice in praise of their imperial rulers in the city that was still its symbolic capital. Only slightly less obvious, when you stop to think about it, is the second message: the confidence of the senators in the Perfection of the Social Order of which they and their emperors were symbiotic parts. You can't have complete Unity without an equally complete sense of Perfection. The normal state of human beings is disunity. The only things that people can be of one mind about are those that are self-evidently the best. And, as the opening acclamations make clear, the source of that Perfection was, straightforwardly, God, the Christian deity. By 438, the Senate of Rome was a thoroughly Christian body. At the top end of Roman society, the adoption of Christianity thus made no difference to the age-old contention that the Empire was God's vehicle in the world.

The same message was proclaimed at similar ceremonial moments all the way down the social scale, even within Church circles. Town council meetings always began with similar acclamations, as did formal gatherings of an entire urban populus to greet an emperor, an imperial official or even a new imperial image. (When a new emperor was elected, images of him were distributed to the cities of the Empire.) At all of these moments – and there were many in a calendar year – the same key idea predominated.[33] Many Christian bishops, as well as secular commentators, were happy to restate the old claim of Roman imperialism in its new clothing. Bishop Eusebius of Caesarea was already arguing, as early as the reign of Constantine, that it was no accident that Christ had been incarnated during the lifetime of Augustus, the first Roman emperor. Despite the earlier history of persecutions, went his argument, this showed that Christianity and the Empire were destined for each other, with God making Rome all-powerful so that, through it, all mankind might eventually be saved.

This ideological vision implied, of course, that the emperor, as God's chosen representative on earth, should wield great religious authority within Christianity. As early as the 310s, within a year of the declaration of his new Christian allegiance, bishops from North Africa appealed to Constantine to settle a dispute that was raging among them. This established a pattern for the rest of the century: emperors were now intimately involved in both the settlement of Church disputes and the much more mundane business of the new religion's adminstration. To settle disputes, emperors called councils, giving bishops the right to use the privileged travel system, the *cursus publicus*, in order to attend. Even more impressively, emperors helped set the agendas to be discussed, their officials orchestrated the proceedings, and state machinery was used to enforce the decisions reached. More generally, they made religious law for the Church – Book 16 of the *Theodosian Code* is entirely concerned with such matters – and influenced appointments to top ecclesiastical positions.

The Christian Church hierarchy also came to mirror the Empire's administrative and social structures. Episcopal dioceses reflected the boundaries of city territories (some even preserve them to this day, long after they have lost all other meaning). Further up the scale, the bishops of provincial capitals were turned into metropolitan arch-bishops, enjoying powers of intervention in the new, subordinate sees. Under Constantine's Christian successors, the previously obscure Bishop of Constantinople was elevated into a Patriarch on a par with the Bishop of Rome – because Constantinople was the 'new Rome'. Very quickly, too, local Christian communities lost the power to elect their own bishops. From the 370s onwards, bishops were increasingly drawn from the landowning classes, and controlled episcopal suc-cessions by discussions among themselves. With the Church now so much a part of the state – bishops had even been given administrative roles within it, such as running small-claims courts – to become a Christian bishop was not to drop out of public life but to find a new avenue into it. If the Christianization of Roman society is a massively important topic, an equally important, and somewhat less studied one, is the Romanization of Christianity. The adoption of the new religion was no one-way street, but a process of mutual adaptation that reinforced the ideological claims of emperor and state.[34]

None of this is to say, of course, that the Christianization of the Empire was achieved without conflict, or that Christianity and the Empire were perfectly suited to one another. Like Paulinus of Nola and Melania, some bishops and other Christian intellectuals, not to mention Holy Men, explicitly or implicitly rejected the claim that the Empire represented a perfect, God-sustained civilization. But rejection of the Empire was little more than an undertone among fourth-century Christian thinkers. The fourth century was also a crucial moment in the formation of Christian doctrine, a process that generated many inner Christian conflicts into which a succession of emperors was drawn to one side or the other. Conflict over doctrine was for the most part confined, however, to the bishops. There were a few moments when it spilled over into large-scale rioting, but it was never widespread or sustained enough to suggest that Christians' capacity to disagree with one another caused any serious damage to the function-ing of the Empire.[35]

What the rise of Christianity really demonstrates, like the creation of the newly enlarged bureaucracy, is that the imperial centre had lost none of its capacity to draw local elites into line. As much recent writing on Christianization has emphasized, religious revolution was achieved more by trickle-down effect than by outright confrontation. Until the end of the fourth century, seventy years after Constantine first declared his new religious allegiance, the perception that emperors might show more favour to Christians in promotions to office was what spread the new religion among the Roman upper classes. All Christian emperors faced intense lobbying from the bishops, and all made highly Christian noises from time to time. Also, from an early date they banned blood sacrifices, which were particular anathema to Christians. Other pagan cult practices were allowed, though, and there was no imperial mechanism to enforce Christianity at the local level. This meant that, as in everything except taxation, the preference of the citizens decided what actually happened on the ground. Where the bulk of critical opinion was, or became, Christian, pagan temples were closed and sometimes dismantled. Where it remained true to the old cults, religious life continued much as before, and Christian emperors were happy enough to allow the variety. It was only when a critical mass of important local decision-makers had already become Christian towards the end of the century, after three generations of imperial sponsorship, that emperors could safely enact more aggressively Christianizing measures.[36]

The imperial centre thus retained enough ideological force and practical power of patronage for a more or less uninterrupted run of Christian rulers over three or four generations to bring local opinion largely into line with the new ideology (Julian the Apostate ruled the whole Empire as a pagan for less than two years). To my mind, a similar dynamic was at work here as in the earlier process of Romanization. The state was unable simply to force its ideology on local elites, but if it was consistent in making conformity a condition for advancement, then landowners would respond. As the fourth century progressed, 'Christian and Roman' – rather than 'villa and town dwelling' – were increasingly the prerequisites of success, and the movers and shakers of Roman society, both local and central, gradually adapted themselves to the new reality. As with the expansion of the bureaucracy, the imperial centre had successfully deployed new mechanisms for keeping the energies and attentions of the landowning classes focused upon itself.

Taxes were paid, elites participated in public life, and the new religion was effectively enough subsumed into the structures of the late Empire. Far from being the harbingers of disaster, both Christianization and bureaucratic expansion show the imperial centre still able to exert a powerful pull on the allegiances and habits of the provinces. That pull had to be persuasive rather than coercive, but so it had always been. Renegotiated, the same kinds of bonds continued to hold centre and locality together.

The Roman Polity

THE FIRST IMPRESSION given by Roman state ceremonies such as the one held to introduce the *Theodosian Code* to the Roman Senate is one of overwhelming power. A state machine that could make an assemblage of its richest landowners engage in such a spectacle of synchronized acclamation is not to be trifled with. But there are other aspects of the *Theodosian Code* ceremony, as well as the law-book's reception, that give us a rather different insight – this time, into the political limitations, which, for all its continued strength, lay at the heart of the Roman imperial system.

After their rousing introduction, the assembled Roman fathers get down to the nitty-gritty:

'We give thanks for this regulation of Yours!' *(repeated 23 times)*
'You have removed the ambiguities of the imperial constitutions!'[37]
   (23 times)
'Pious emperors thus wisely plan!' *(26 times)*
'You wisely provide for lawsuits. You provide for the public peace!'
   (25 times)
'Let many copies of the Code be made to be kept in the
   governmental offices!' *(10 times)*
'Let them be kept under seal in the public bureaux!' *(20 times)*
'In order that the established laws may not be falsified, let many
   copies be made!' *(25 times)*
'In order that the established laws may not be falsified, let all copies
   be written out in letters!'[38] *(18 times)*
'To this copy which will be made by the constitutionaries, let no
   annotations upon the law be added!' *(12 times)*
'We request that copies to be kept in the imperial bureaux shall be
   made at public expense!' *(16 times)*

'We ask that no laws be promulgated in reply to supplications!'
    (21 times)
'All the rights of landowners are thrown into confusion by such
    surreptitious actions!' *(17 times)*

A ceremony introducing a new compendium of law was a highly
meaningful moment for the Roman state. We've already seen the role
that education and self-government played in the traditional Roman
self-image. For Roman society as a whole, written law possessed a
similarly loaded significance. Again in the Romans' own view of things,
its existence made Roman society the best of all possible means of
ordering humanity. Above all, written law freed men from the fear of
arbitrary action on the part of the powerful (the Latin word for
freedom – *libertas* – carried the technical meaning 'freedom under the
law'). Legal disputes were treated on their merits; the powerful could
not override the rest. And Christianization merely strengthened the
ideological importance ascribed to written law. For whereas Christian
intellectuals could criticize as elitist the moral education offered by the
grammarian, and hold up the uneducated Holy Man from the desert
as an alternative figure of virtue, the law was not open to the same
kind of criticism. It protected everyone in their designated social
positions. It also had a unifying cultural resonance, since God's law,
whether in the form of Moses and the Ten Commandments or Christ
as the new life-giving law, was central to Judaeo-Christian tradition. In
ideological terms, therefore, it became easy to portray all-encompassing
written Roman law – as opposed to elite literary culture – as the key
ingredient of the newly Christian Empire's claim to uphold a divinely
ordained social order.[39]

Reading between the lines, however, the *Theodosian Code*, in both
ceremony and content, can also take us to the heart of the political
limitations within the late Roman system. One such limitation is
implicit in the original Latin text of the acclamations, but hidden in
the English translation, English being unable to distinguish between
the singular and the plural 'you'. The acclamations were all addressed
to both the emperor Theodosius II, ruler of the east, and his younger
first cousin Valentinian III, ruler of the west. Both were members of
the Theodosian dynasty, and the original issuing of the *Code* in the east
in 437 was carefully timed to coincide with a marriage alliance between
the two branches, Valentinian marrying Theodosius' daughter Eudoxia.

Marriage and law code together highlighted unity in the Roman world, with eastern and western emperors functioning in perfect harmony. As its name implies, though, all the hard work behind the *Theodosian Code* had actually been done in Constantinople, by commissioners appointed by Theodosius.[40] And the fact that Theodosius was the dominant partner here underscores a fundamental problem in the structure of power within the late Empire. For the administrative and political reasons discussed in Chapter 1, the imperial office had to be divided. Harmony between co-rulers was possible if one was so predominant as to be unchallengeable. The relationship between Theodosius and Valentinian worked happily enough on this basis, as had that between Constantine and various of his sons between the 310s and the 330s. But to function properly, the Empire required more or less equal helmsmen. A sustained inferiority was likely to be based on an unequal distribution of the key assets – financial and military – and if one was too obviously subordinate, the politically important factions in his realm were likely to encourage him to redress the balance – or, worse, encourage a usurper. This pattern had, for example, marred Constantius II's attempts to share power with Gallus and Julian in the 350s.

Equal emperors functioning together harmoniously was extremely difficult to achieve, and happened only rarely. For a decade after 364, the brothers Valentinian I and Valens managed it, and so did Diocletian, first with one other emperor from 286, then with three from 293 to 305 (Diocletian's so-called Tetrarchy). But none of these partnerships produced lasting stability, and even power-sharing between brothers was no guarantee of success. When they succeeded to the throne, the sons of Constantine I proceeded to compete among themselves, to the point that Constantine II died invading the territory of his younger brother Constans. Diocletian's Tetrarchy, likewise, worked well enough during his political lifetime, but broke down after his abdication in 305 into nearly twenty years of dispute and civil war, which was ended only by Constantine's defeat of Licinius in 324.

In fact, the organization of central power posed an insoluble dilemma in the late Roman period. It was an administrative and political necessity to divide that power: if you didn't, usurpation, and often civil war, followed. Dividing it in such a way as not to generate war between rivals was, however, extremely difficult. And even if you solved the problem for one generation, it was pretty much impossible to pass on that harmony to your heirs, who would lack the habits of trust and respect that infused the original arrangement. Consequently, in each generation the division of power was improvised, even where the throne was passed on by dynastic succession. There was no 'system', and whether power was divided or not, periodic civil war was inescapable. This, it must be stressed, wasn't just a product of the personal failings of individual emperors – although the paranoia of Constantius II, for example, certainly contributed to the excitement. Essentially, it reflected the fact that there were so many political concerns to be accommodated, such a large spread of interested landowners within the much more inclusive late Empire, that stability was much harder to achieve than in the old Roman conquest state, when it had been only the Senate of Rome playing imperial politics.

In many ways, then, periodic conflict at the top was the price to be paid for the Empire's success in integrating elites across its vast domain. This is much better viewed, though, as a limitation than as a basic flaw: the Empire was not fundamentally undermined by it. It was a systemic fact of life that imparted something of a rhythm to imperial politics. Periods of political stability were likely to be punctuated by moments of conflict before a new regime, effectively recombining a sufficiently wide range of interests, managed to establish itself. Sometimes the conflict was brief, sometimes extended, as in the fall-out from the Tetrarchy, when it took two decades to narrow succession down to the line of Constantine. But the civil wars of the fourth century did not make the Empire vulnerable, for instance, to Persian conquest. Indeed, the propensity at that time to divide imperial authority achieved a better outcome than the refusal to do so had in the mid-third, when twenty legitimate emperors and a host of usurpers each averaged just two years in power.

A second major political limitation of the Roman world emerges from a closer look at the Senate's ceremonial greeting to the *Theodosian Code*. Even if the irregularity in the number of repetitions suggests that the senators' enthusiasm may have run away with them at times, the specificity of the comments relating to the *Code* itself indicates that the individual acclamations were carefully scripted. The closest modern analogy for such a prescriptive line in public ceremonial is provided by the proceedings of the old annual congress of the Communist Party of the Soviet Union in its pre-1989 days. Amongst other things, these involved stage-managed, mutually congratulatory, applause at the end of the Party Secretary's address. The audience roared its approval, and then the speaker stood up to applaud back: presumably congratulating the audience on its good sense in recognizing the terrific value of whatever he had just said. In the case of the *Theodosian Code*, the Roman Senate ran to a more ambitious script, but the underlying message was the same. Both were highly public celebrations of a proclaimed ideological unity, based on a claim to a perfection grounded in the structures – here, particularly the legal ones – of the state. Public life in the Roman Empire, I would argue, is best understood as working like that of a one-party state, in which loyalty to the system was drilled into you from birth and reinforced with regular opportunities to demonstrate it. A couple of important differences, however, are worth underlining. Unlike the Soviet state, which lasted only about seventy years and faced powerful ideological competition, totalitarian and non-totalitarian, the Roman state lasted for half a millennium and operated for the most part entirely unchallenged. The resonance of Roman superiority imbued every facet of public life throughout an individual's lifetime.

As with any one-party system, though, this one had its limitations too. Free speech, for instance, was to some extent restricted. Given that everyone was fully committed to the ideology of Unity in Perfection, it was only on the level of personality (rather than policy) that disagreement could be allowed.[41] Its unchallenged ideological monopoly made the Empire enormously successful at extracting conformity from its subjects, but it was hardly a process engaged in voluntarily. The spread of Roman culture and the adoption of Roman citizenship in its conquered lands resulted from the fact that the Empire was the only avenue open to individuals of ambition. You had to play by its rules, and acquire its citizenship, if you were to get anywhere.

The one-party state analogy points us to two further drawbacks of the system. First, active political participation was very narrowly based. To participate in the workings of the Roman Empire, you had to belong to the wealthier landholding classes. It's impossible to put an exact figure on this group, but its defining features are clear enough. In the early Empire, it required meeting the property qualification for membership of your town council by owning enough land in one city territory and being able to afford to educate your children with a grammarian. This required a substantial income. St Augustine, before he was a saint, belonged to a minor gentry landowning family from the small town of Thagaste in North Africa. His family had no problem affording the grammarian's fees, but he had an enforced gap year while his father got enough money together for him to be able to finish off his higher education with a rhetor in Carthage, so that his family's level of wealth provides us with a good indicator of the cut-off point.[42]

In the later Empire, political and civic participation could be expressed in a wider variety of ways than had been available earlier. Some local landowners still dominated the few worthwhile positions on their city councils, many more joined the central imperial bureaucracy, and still others, the lesser gentry, were happy to serve in its provincial offices. The latter were called *cohortales*, and some, according to inscriptions from the city of Aphrodisias, were even wealthy enough to act as city benefactors. The late Empire also had a more developed legal system. Since the early third century, Roman law had applied to every inhabitant of the Empire, and there were usually plenty of openings for trained lawyers. These again came from the old curial classes, young hopefuls moving on from the grammarian to study law as part of their higher education. By the third quarter of the fourth century, as Christianity spread and attracted imperial patronage, the landowning classes likewise began to move, as we have seen, into the Church and soon came to dominate the episcopate. The first grammarian-trained bishops I know of are Ambrose in the west and the Cappadocian Fathers (Basil of Caesarea, Gregory Nazianzus and Gregory of Nyssa) in the east, all ordained in about 370.[43] This opening-up of a wider range of professions did not bring with it any significant changes in the amount of wealth required. All these professions still needed a traditional grounding with a grammarian.

The politically active landowning class probably amounted, therefore, to less than 5 per cent of the population. To this we might add another percentage or so for a semi-educated professional class, found particularly in the towns. Especially in imperial capitals, a somewhat broader group, by belonging to circus factions and taking part in vociferous demonstrations in the theatre – a means of expressing discontent with particular officials – were able to voice their opinion. They could also exercise an occasional veto by rioting, if they were really upset, but this kind of action never amounted to more than a rather blunt weapon against particular individuals or policies.[44]

★

THE VAST MAJORITY of the population – whether free, tied or slave – worked the land, however, and were more or less excluded from political participation. For these groups, the state existed largely in the form of tax-collectors making unwelcome demands upon their limited resources. Again, it is impossible to estimate precisely, but the peasantry cannot have mustered less than 85 per cent of the population. So we have to reckon with a world in which over four-fifths had little or no stake in the political systems that governed them. Indifference may well have been the peasants' overriding attitude towards the imperial establishment. Across most of the Empire, habitation and population levels increased in the course of its history, as we have noted, and it is hard not to see this as an effect of the Pax Romana – the conditions of greater peace and stability that the Empire generated. On the other hand, patchy and sporadic peasant resistance, often to do with tax issues, certainly occurred, but manifested itself only in the form of a low-level, if endemic, banditry. Some areas did throw up the occasional bout of more sustained trouble. Isauria, the Cilician upland region of what is now south-western Turkey, was famous for its bandits, and one lot – the Maratacupreni – achieved particular fame in northern Syria by marauding the land in the guise of imperial tax-collectors and helping themselves to people's possessions. That they were plausible gives some idea of what it could feel like to be taxed by the Roman state, but they eventually attracted too much official attention and were wiped out to a man (and woman, and child). The exclusion from – or only very partial inclusion in – the benefits of the Roman system that the majority of the population experienced was one of its core limitations, then, but nothing new. The Empire had always been run for the benefit of an elite. And while this made for an exploited peasantry and a certain level of largely unfocused opposition, there is no sign in the fourth century that the situation had worsened.[45]

The second, rather less obvious, drawback was potentially more significant, given the peasantry's underlying inability to organize itself for sustained resistance. To understand it, we need to consider for a moment the lifestyles of the Roman rich. As we have seen, they spent some of their time on matters of state, whether as local councillors collecting tax, as relatively senior bureaucratic functionaries (*cohortales* or *palatini*), or as semi-retired imperial bureaucrats. But these activities occupied only a limited amount of their time. By the year 400, the average length of service in many of the central departments of state had declined to no more than ten years: hardly a lifetime, even when life expectancy was considerably lower than today. What they did the rest of the time, and what provided the underlying focus of their lives, emerges clearly, once again, from the correspondence of Symmachus. He belonged, of course, to the super-rich, so that the scale of his other activities is unrepresentative. The nature of these activities, though, is entirely typical.

There were other forms of wealth in the Roman world apart from landowning; money could be made from trade and manufacture, the law, influence-peddling and so on. But landowning was the supreme expression of wealth, and, as in pre-industrial England, those who made money elsewhere were quick to invest it in estates – because, above all, land was the only honourable form of wealth for a gentleman. This was as much practical as the product of snobbery. Land was an extremely secure investment, and in return for the original outlay estates offered a steady income in the form of annual agricultural production. In the absence of stock markets, and given the limited and more precarious investment opportunities offered by trade and manufacture, land was the gilt-edged stock of the ancient world (and indeed of all worlds, pretty much, prior to the Industrial Revolution). This dictated many of the concerns of upper-class Roman life.

First and foremost, landowners needed to keep the output of their estates up to scratch. A piece of land was in itself only a potential source of revenue; it needed to be worked, and worked efficiently, to produce a good annual income. The right crops had to be grown, for a start. Then, investment of time, effort and capital always offered the possibility of what in pre-Industrial England was termed 'improvement': a dramatic increase in production. Roman landowners spent much of their lives checking on the running of their estates, either directly or through agents. The first five letters of the Symmachus collection were written, for instance, while he was on an extended tour of his central and southern Italian holdings in 375, looking to maximize his income. As he wrote to his father, 'Our estates which are in disorder require to be looked into in all their particulars . . . In fact, it has now become customary to provide for a countryside which used to be a provider.' Later letters continue to refer periodically to revenue problems, and, in the case of someone as rich as Symmachus, distance added extra ones. Estates in Sicily and North Africa were always more problematic than those closer to home.[46] It was more efficient, likewise, to work one large rather than two small tracts, so that the canny landowner was always on the lookout for opportunities either to buy suitable extra land, or arrange mutually advantageous swaps. Again, Symmachus' letters in particular, but late Roman sources in general, show that much time and effort went into buying and selling suitable plots.[47]

There was also a host of legal problems. As in Dickens's England, wills were often disputed. Since land, unlike other forms of wealth, was not easily divisible into still profitable portions, parents often faced the choice of either handing over shares in the income of an intact estate, or of favouring one heir over the others by giving him the whole estate. Either way, things could get nasty, or complicated, especially when the heirs with shares came in turn to decide what to do with their stakes after their deaths. Much effort had to go into wills and codicils so as to define the exact solution that the testator was after, and to make sure that it couldn't be challenged. Not surprisingly, Symmachus followed changes in inheritance law closely, and wills are frequently mentioned in his letters.[48] Roman landowners played all the usual tricks. For instance, Symmachus' father transferred to him ownership of one estate on the River Tibur early, to avoid the creditors who might gather after his death.[49] Marriage was in this context much more than the romantic coupling of individuals in love. It involved the establishment of a new household requiring its own economic base. A suitable match had to be found, and a settlement made, with both parties usually contributing to the new couple's financial well-being. One letter refers to a certain Fulvius, 'for a long time of an age to marry', who had been lucky enough to nab the sister of a certain Pompeianus: 'she is not from a less good family than him, and has perhaps the greater wealth'.[50]

Marriage settlements, likewise, offered lawyers the opportunity to make fat fees. Symmachus' own marriage brought him property from his father-in-law's patrimony, which, because it had been transferred, was not confiscated by the state when the latter was prosecuted for fraud.[51] Further legal problems were thrown up by the tax system. One of the things that patrons were often approached for was a reduction in tax bills. There are no known examples of landowners, even with excellent connections, being let off tax entirely, but many won reductions. All reductions were, however, precarious in that if your patron lost power, then the benefits that accrued to you might also be lost. There was thus huge scope for landowners to quarrel with the staff of the Praetorian Prefect's office about what tax reductions might apply and for how long, and what liabilities had already been met. And despite all the care taken with wills and marriage settlements, the fall of a patron could lead to quarrels about rights of ownership. Symmachus' correspondence, not least his official letters as Urban Prefect of Rome, provide plentiful instances of this kind of dispute.[52]

But if being a landowner involved a host of responsibilities, it had its pleasures too. Burdensome though owning lots of houses might be administratively, as long as one had the income, there were endless opportunities for remodelling and redecorating. One letter from Symmachus to his father rattles on about the new marble revetments for his house – so cunningly done that you would have thought them made from a single piece. He was also very proud of some columns that looked like expensive Bithynian marble but had cost him virtually nothing. And on it goes. A new bath-house for his Sicilian estate is mentioned in many letters, and many others refer to odd bits of work being done here and there throughout his lifetime. One letter complains about the builders taking for ever in his house on the Tibur.[53] Some things never change.

After your house or houses had been made suitably comfortable and adorned with the latest fashions (not least, in fourth-century Britain, the installation of colour mosaics), there was all the pleasure of actually living in them. Symmachus particularly loved his villa at Baiae on the Bay of Naples, in many of his letters extolling the beauties of the scenery and food (especially in the autumn). In 396 he spent a particularly pleasant few months between April and December at one after another of his properties at Formia, Cumae, Pozzuoli, Baiae, Naples and Capri. Some of these are still favoured celebrity getaways. He and his wife also had a home on the Tibur just downriver from Rome, which they lived in when Symmachus needed to be in town on business. A favourite pastime of the Roman landed gentry, as of their peers at so many times and places, was hunting, for which a little place just on the edge of the hills or close to a forest was just the thing.[54] Thus, strategically located properties could offer the landowner all the pleasures of the different seasons.[55]

Your country house – or houses – also provided the backdrop for the other joys of upper-class life. Symmachus often extols the pleasures of working on ancient Latin texts in the seclusion of one or other of his retreats. In one letter, he declares, he has been much too busy with his studies to write; and he also sometimes wrote to friends for copies of works he couldn't find, while describing what he had been up to.[56] Sometimes we find him with good friends staying at their own retreats close by – less often, the friends staying with him – which permitted frequent exchanges of epistolary compliments, not to mention picnics and dinner parties.[57] The health of friends and relatives was a frequent topic, one minor illness requiring multiple missives of inquiry within the space of twenty-four hours. From his daughter, who was clearly a little delicate, he demanded at one point daily bulletins about her health, recommending in return various dietary cures.[58]

The lifestyle of Symmachus and his friends provides a blueprint for that of the European gentry and nobility over much of the next sixteen hundred years. Leisured, cultured and landed: some extremely rich, some with just enough to get by in the expected manner, and everyone perfectly well aware of who was who. And all engaged in an intricate, elegant dance around the hope and expectation of the great wealth that marriage settlement and inheritance would bring. Symmachus and his friends may have enjoyed editing Latin texts rather than painting watercolours and learning Italian, and their notions of such things as childhood and gender may have been rather different, but there is certainly a touch of Jane Austen in togas about the late Roman upper crust.

A FURTHER LIMITATION imposed by the Roman imperial system stems from this elegant, leisured and highly privileged lifestyle. It rested upon the massively unequal distribution of landed property: as noted earlier, less than 5 per cent of the population owned over 80 per cent, and perhaps substantially more. And at the heart of this inequality was the Roman state itself, in that its laws both defined and protected the ownership rights of the property-owning class to whose upper echelons Symmachus belonged. Its land registration systems were the ultimate arbiter of who owned – and hence who did not own – land, and its criminal legislation rigorously defended owners against the hostile attentions of those left out in the economic cold.[59] The fifth-century historian Priscus records a much quoted conversation with a Roman merchant who had fought for the barbarian Huns. The talk ebbed back and forth on what was good and bad about Roman and Hunnic societies, until Priscus hit the nail on the head:

> Amongst the Romans there are many ways of giving freedom. Not only the living but also the dead bestow it lavishly, arranging their estates as they wish; and whatever a man has willed for his possessions at his death is legally binding. My [Roman-turned-Hun] acquaintance wept and said that the laws were fair and the Roman polity was good . . .

Both parties eventually agreed on two points: first, that Roman law generated a superior society; and second, that its chief beneficial effect was to guarantee the rights of property-holders to dispose of their assets as they saw fit.[60] This wasn't an isolated opinion. Remember the acclamations of the Roman Senate – the senators, too, were pretty clear that the overall effect of the *Theodosian Code* had been to protect 'the rights of landowners' (see p. 128).

A huge amount of Roman law dealt precisely with property: basic ownership, modes of exploiting it (selling, leasing for longer or shorter terms, simple renting and sharecropping), and its transfer between generations through marriage settlements, inheritance and special bequests. The ferocity of Roman criminal law, likewise, protected ownership: death was the main punishment for theft – certainly, for anything beyond petty pilfering. Again, we can see a resemblance here to later 'genteel' societies based on similarly unequal distributions of landed wealth in an overwhelmingly agricultural economy. When Jane Austen was writing her elegant tales of love, marriage and property transfer, you could be whipped (for theft valued at up to 10d), branded (for theft up to 4s 10d) or hanged (theft over 5 shillings). In eighteenth-century London an average of twenty people were hanged each year.[61]

The Roman state had to advance and protect the interests of these landowning classes because they were, in large measure, the same people who participated in its political structures. This didn't mean that there weren't occasional conflicts between the state and individual landowners, or even whole groups of them. Landowning families sometimes lost their estates by confiscation if they ended up on the wrong side of a political dispute, for instance. (This didn't necessarily mean that they were ruined for ever: as in the medieval world, restoring confiscated lands was a favoured way for a subsequent ruler to win a family's loyalty.[62]) Nonetheless, as we have seen, the state relied on the administrative input of its provincial landowning classes at all levels of the governmental machine, and in particular to collect its taxes – the efficient collection of which hung on the willingness of these same landed classes to pay up.

This delicate balance manifested itself in two ways. First, and most obviously, taxes on agriculture could not rise so high that landowners would opt out of the state system en masse and attempt to frustrate its operation. As we have seen, there is plenty of evidence that emperors were aware that the way to a landowner's heart was to tax gently. In the mid-360s, the emperors Valentinian and Valens started their joint reign with a financial charm offensive. Taxes were held stable for three years, then cut in the fourth, because, as their spokesman put it, 'a light hand in taxation is a boon shared by all who are nurtured by the earth'. With a (very modern) flourish, they also promised, 'if revenues turned out as expected', to cut them again in the fifth.[63] Second, the landowners' elite status and lifestyles depended upon a property distribution so unequal that the have-nots had a massive numerical advantage – which should surely have led to a redistribution of wealth unless some other body prevented it. In the fourth century, this other body was, as it had been for centuries, the Roman state. Landowners could generally rely on its ability to counterbalance their numerical weakness by enforcing the laws in their favour. If the state ceased to be able to do this – should it, for instance, start to lack the brute power to enforce its property laws – then landowners would have no choice but to search for another agency that could perform the same role in its place.

We might understand the participation of the landowners in the Roman system, therefore, as a cost-benefit equation. What it cost them was the money they paid annually into the state coffers. What they got in return was protection for the wealth on which their status was based. In the fourth century, benefit hugely outweighed cost. But, as we shall see, should the taxman become too demanding, or the state incapable of providing protection, then the loyalty of the landowning class could be up for renegotiation.

The Balance Sheet

It has been a long journey of discovery, but the evolution of the Roman Empire up to about AD 300 is finally coming into focus. On the one hand, we are dealing with an historical phenomenon of extraordinary power. Built originally on military might, the Empire deployed, across the vastness separating Hadrian's Wall from the Euphrates, an all-encompassing ideology of superiority. By the fourth century, subjected peoples had so internalized the Roman way of life that the original conquest state had evolved into a commonwealth of thoroughly Roman provincial communities.

But this extraordinary state also had major drawbacks. Distance, primitive communications and a limited capacity to process data hamstrung the operation of its systems. Except in the field of taxation, the state was fundamentally reactive, generally drawn into situations by groups seeking to take advantage of its power. Its economy produced an output not much above subsistence. And in political terms, the number of people clearly benefiting from the Empire's existence was small. (We have just glimpsed the massively privileged lives led by the small Roman landowning class.)

For all this, there is no sign in the fourth century that the Empire was about to collapse. The adjustment called for after fifty years of turmoil caused by the rise of Sasanian Persia was neither straightforward nor easy, but a military, financial, political and bureaucratic transformation did at last, more or less organically, generate an enlarged state machine capable of dealing at one and the same time with Persia and with the consequences of 300 years of internal evolution. There was, of course, a price to be paid. The state confiscated local funds, breaking up the unity of the old self-governing towns. It also proved necessary to divide the ultimate power between two or more individuals, even though this could not but generate regular tension and periodic civil war.

Nonetheless, the late Empire was essentially a success story. The rural economy was mostly flourishing, and unprecedented numbers of landowners were keen to fill the offices of state. As the response to the Persians showed, the Roman imperial structure was inherently rigid, with only a limited and slow-moving bureaucratic, economic and political capacity to mobilize resources in the face of a new threat. But the Persian challenge had been successfully seen off, and the overwhelming impression the Roman state gave was one of continuing unmatchable power. It was not, however, destined to be left to its own devices. While fourth-century Romans continued to look on Persia as the traditional enemy, a second major strategic revolution was about to unfold to the north.

PART TWO

CRISIS

4

WAR ON THE DANUBE

IN THE WINTER OF 375/6, rumour reached Rome's Danube frontier that heavy fighting was under way in eastern Germania north of the Black Sea. Ammianus Marcellinus reports:[1] 'In the beginning the news was viewed with contempt by our people because wars in those districts were not ordinarily heard of by those living at a distance until they were either over, or had at least died down for a time.' You could hardly blame the imperial authorities for not taking the matter too seriously. The migration of the Goths and other Germani in the mid-third century had prompted a political reconfiguration that had led to a hundred years of relative stability in the region. Moreover, the trouble then had come from the north-west (present-day Poland and Byelorussia), not the north-east (modern Ukraine). The last time the north-east had posed a problem was when the Sarmatians had swept all before them in the fifty years either side of the birth of Christ, three centuries earlier. But the Romans quickly learned the error of their ways.

In the summer of 376, a vast throng of people – men, women and children – suddenly appeared on the north bank of the River Danube asking for safe haven in Roman territory. One source, not our best, reports that 200,000 refugees appeared beside the river; Ammianus, that there were too many to count. They came with innumerable wagons and the animals to pull them, presumably their plough-oxen, in the kind of huge procession that warfare has generated throughout history. There were certainly many individual refugees and small family groups, but the vast majority were Goths organized in two compact masses and with defined political leaderships. My own best guess is that each was composed of about 10,000 warriors. One group, the Greuthungi, had already moved a fair distance from lands east of the River Dniester, in the present-day Ukraine, hundreds of kilometres from the Danube. The other comprised the majority of Athanaric's Tervingi, now led by Alavivus and Fritigern, who had broken away from their former leader's control to come here to the river.[2]

If the size of the immediate problem for Roman frontier security was bad enough, the refugees' identity was even more ominous. Though the first reports had concerned fighting a long way from the frontier zone, the two large bodies of Gothic would-be immigrants camped beside the river were from much closer to home. The Tervingi, in particular, had been occupying lands immediately north of the Danube, in what is now Wallachia and Moldavia, since the 310s at the latest. Whatever was going on in the far north-east was no local skirmish; its effects were being felt throughout the region north of the Black Sea.

The Romans quickly learned what lay behind all the mayhem. Again in Ammianus' words: 'The seed-bed and origin of all this destruction and of the various calamities inflicted by the wrath of Mars, which raged everywhere with extraordinary fury, I find to be this: the people of the Huns.'

Ammianus was writing nearly twenty years later, by which time the Romans had a better understanding of what had brought the Goths to the Danube. Even in the 390s, though, the full effects of the arrival of the Huns were far from apparent. The appearance of the Goths beside the river in the summer of 376 was the first link in a chain of events that would lead directly from the rise of Hunnic power on the fringes of Europe to the deposition of the last western emperor, Romulus Augustulus, almost exactly one hundred years later. None of this was even remotely conceivable in 376, and there would be many twists and turns on the way. The arrival of Goths on the Danube marked the start of a reshuffling of Europe-wide balances of power, and it is to this story that the rest of the book is devoted. We must begin, like Ammianus, with the Huns.

From the 'Ice-Bound Ocean'

THE ORIGINS OF the Huns are mysterious and controversial. The one thing we know for certain is that they were nomads from the Great Eurasian Steppe.[3] The Eurasian Steppe is a huge expanse, stretching about 5,500 kilometres from the fringes of Europe to western China, with another 3,000 kilometres to its north and east. The north–south depth of the steppe ranges from only about 500 kilometres in the west to nearly 3,000 in the wide-open plains of Mongolia. Geography and climate dictate the nomadic lifestyle. Natural steppe grasslands are the product of poorish soils and limited rainfall, which make it impossible, in general terms, for trees and more luxurious vegetation to grow. The lack of rainfall also rules out arable farming of any sustained kind, so that the nomad makes a substantial part of his living from pastoral agriculture, herding a range of animals suited to the available grazing. Cattle can survive on worse pasture than horses, sheep on worse pasture than cattle, and goats on worse than sheep. Camels will eat anything left over.

Nomadism is essentially a means of assembling distinct blocks of pasture, which between them add up to a year-round grazing strategy. Typically, modern nomads will move between upland summer pasture (where there is no grass in the winter because of snow and cold) and lowland winter pasture (where the lack of rain in summer means, again, no grass). In this world, grazing rights are as important in terms of economic capital as the herds, and as jealously guarded. The distance between summer and winter pasture needs to be minimal, since all movement is hard both on the animals and on the weaker members of the human population. Before Stalin sedentarized them, the nomads of Kazakhstan tended to move about 75 kilometres each way between their pastures. Nomadic societies also form close economic ties with settled arable farmers in the region, from whom they obtain much of the grain they need, though some they produce themselves. While part of the population cycles the herds around the summer pastures, the rest engage in other types of food production. But all the historically observed nomad populations have needed to supplement their grain production by exchanging with arable populations the surplus generated from their herds (hides, cheese and yoghurt, actual animals and so on). Often, this exchange has been one-sided, with the arable population getting in return no more than exemption from being raided, but sometimes the exchange has been properly reciprocal.

Nomadism, or part-nomadism, has never been the preserve of any particular linguistic or cultural population group. Across the Great Eurasian Steppe many peoples have, at different times, adopted nomadic lifestyles. In the first three centuries AD the western end of the steppe – from the Caspian Sea to the Danube – was dominated by Iranian-speaking Sarmatian and Alan nomads. These had ousted Scythian nomads, also Iranian-speaking, in the last two or three centuries BC. By the sixth century AD at the latest, Turkic-speaking nomads were dominant from the Danube to China, and a Mongol-speaking nomad horde would cause untold devastation in the high Middle Ages. Other population groups, too, took to nomadism. The Magyars who arrived in central Europe at the end of the ninth century spoke – as their Hungarian descendants still do – a Finno-Ugrian language that suggests they may have come from the forest zone of north-eastern Europe, the only other region where such languages are spoken.

Where the Huns fit into this sea of cultural possibilities is unclear. Ammianus Marcellinus knew more about them than did our other Roman sources, but he didn't know much. His best shot is that they came from beyond the Black Sea 'near the ice-bound ocean'. They were not literate, so leave us no records of their own to go on, and even their language affiliation is mysterious. Failing all else, linguists can usually decode basic linguistic affiliations from personal names, but even this doesn't work with the Huns. They quickly got into the habit of using Germanic names (or perhaps our sources preserve the Germanicized versions or Germanic nicknames given them by their Germanic neighbours and subjects), so that the stock of properly Hunnic personal names is much too small to draw any convincing conclusions. They were probably not Iranian-speaking, but whether they were the first Turkic-speaking nomads to explode on to the European scene, as some have argued, remains unclear.[4] With such pathetic sources of information, Hunnic origins can only remain mysterious, but a little spice has been added by a famous controversy over whether the Huns were in fact the nomadic Hsiung-Nu, well known from imperial Chinese records.

In the centuries before and after the birth of Christ, the Hsiung-Nu – under the leadership of their Shan-Yu[5] – harassed the north-west frontiers of Han China, extracting from it huge quantities of tribute in silks, precious metals and grain. They also contested the control of some of its important western territories, particularly the Tarim Basin where the Silk Road (which started to operate in the last century BC) reaches China. Under pressure from Han armies, they split in AD 48 into northern and southern branches. The southern Hsiung-Nu were subsequently brought into the Chinese orbit, becoming an important force within the imperial system. The northerners remained external, independent and highly troublesome until AD 93, when the Chinese government paid another nomadic group, the Hsien-Pi, to launch a devastating attack upon their homelands. Many northern Hsiung-Nu (reportedly 100,000 households) were absorbed into the victorious Hsien-Pi confederation, but others fled 'to the west'. That's the last we ever hear of the northern Hsiung-Nu in the Chinese records.

The Huns we're concerned with appear suddenly in Roman records in the third quarter of the fourth century. The problem inherent in the superficially attractive equation of these people with the Hsiung-Nu is this: we have gaps between the Chinese and Roman records of nearly 300 years (AD 93 to about 370) and 3,500 kilometres to account for. Moreover, the Huns known to the Romans had a completely different form of political organization from the Hsiung-Nu's. After AD 48, both branches of the latter had their own Shan-Yu, but the Huns arrived in Europe with a multiplicity of ranked kings and no sign of one dominant figure. The surviving ethnographic descriptions – such as they are – also raise objections. The Hsiung-Nu customarily wore their hair in a long pony-tail; the Huns did not. The two groups used similar weaponry, and bronze kettles are customarily found among their archaeological remains. Given this, there may be some connection, but it clearly won't do just to say that the Hsiung-Nu had started running west in AD 93 and kept going until they hit Europe as the Huns. The Great Eurasian Steppe is a vast place, but it didn't, even then, take 300 years to cross. Equally, like most nomadic empires, that of the Hsiung-Nu was a confederation, comprising a smallish Hsiung-Nu core and many other subject groups. The ancestors of our Huns could even have been part of the confederation, therefore, without being 'real' Hsiung-Nu. Even if we do make some connection between fourth-century Huns and first-century Hsiung-Nu, therefore, an awful lot of water had passed under an awful lot of bridges during 300 years worth of lost history.[6]

Roman sources also give us only a very general idea of what brought the Huns to the fringes of Europe. For Ammianus, it was enough just to point out that they exceeded 'every measure of savagery' and 'were aflame with an inhuman desire for plundering others' property'. The most commonly repeated story in the Roman sources claimed their landing up at Europe's gates was partly an accident. Some Hunnic hunters, out after game one day, trailed a hind through a marsh into new lands of which they had previously been ignorant. This kind of tale rubbed off on early twentieth-century commentators, who tended to suppose that the Huns had for centuries been engaged in nomadic wanderings in different parts of the Eurasian

Steppe, and one year just happened to wander on to the fringes of Europe.[7] But this was before anthropologists understood quite so clearly that nomads do not wander around at random, but move cyclically between carefully designated pastures. Given that grazing rights are a key element in nomad subsistence, and guarded so jealously, shifting from one set of pastures to another could never be an accident.

Unfortunately, we can only guess at the motives behind the Huns' decision to shift their centre of operations westwards. The story of the hind concludes with the hunters telling the rest of the Huns of the wonders of the new land they'd found, and Ammianus, too, picked out the motive of economic gain. The idea that it was the wealth of the northern shores of the Black Sea that attracted Hunnic attentions is perfectly plausible. While less extensive, the grazing lands of the western steppe are rich, and have attracted many a nomad group over the years. The area north of the Black Sea was occupied by client groups of the Roman Empire, who benefited economically from different relationships with the Mediterranean world, and there is no reason to doubt that Huns also felt its call. At the same time, in the case of some later nomad groups for whom we have more infor-mation, a move on to the western edge of the steppe was often associated with the desire to escape a more powerful nomad confeder-ation operating towards China. The Avars, who would have much the same kind of impact on Europe as the Huns, but two centuries later, were looking for a safe haven beyond the reach of the western Turks, when they appeared north of the Black Sea. At the end of the ninth century, likewise, the nomadic Magyars would move into Hungary because another nomad group, the Pechenegs, was making life intol-erable for them further east. In the case of the Huns, we have no firm indication that a negative as well as a positive motivation was at work, but we can't rule it out. Further east, in the later fourth century, the Guptas were pushing on to the Silk Road from northern India, and by the early to mid-fifth century the Hephthalite Huns were ruling the roost somewhere between the Caspian and Aral Seas. As early as the 350s, this reconfiguration of the balance of power was reverberating further east on the steppe, causing the Chionitae to move into the fringes of the Persian Empire, east of the Caspian Sea.[8] It may also have played a role in the Huns' decision to shift their grazing lands westwards.

Mysterious as the Huns' origins and animating forces may remain, there is no doubt at all that they were behind the strategic revolution that brought the Goths to the Danube in the summer of 376. It is normally assumed that at that time they were fleeing from Huns who had suddenly exploded en masse on to the northern Black Sea littoral. It is further assumed that these Huns were virtually breathing down the Goths' necks as they scrambled for the Danube in the hope of securing asylum inside the Empire, and that, once the Goths had reached Roman territory, the Huns immediately became the dominant power in the lands adjacent to the river. This is what you will find stated more or less explicitly in most modern accounts: Huns arrive suddenly (375/6); Goths leave in panic for the Empire (376); Huns become dominant beside the Danube (from 376).

This pattern is based on the account given by Ammianus, who paints a highly convincing picture of Gothic panic: 'The report spread widely among the other Gothic peoples that a race of men hitherto unknown had now arisen from a hidden nook of the earth, like a tempest of snows from the high mountains, and was seizing or destroying everything in its way.' We need to look past the rhetoric, however, at what Ammianus is actually telling us. After first sub-jugating the Alans, the Huns then started attacking the Gothic Greu-thungi. The resistance of the Greuthungi was led by Ermenaric, who eventually gave up and seems to have allowed himself to be ritually sacrificed for the safety of his people.[9] Ammianus' wording is a little vague, but the reflex, documented among several ancient groups, to hold their political leadership responsible for the fate of the group, is an interesting one. When times got tough, it was seen as a sign from the gods that the old leader had offended them and needed to be sacrificed in propitiation of the offence. Ermenaric was succeeded by Vithimer, who carried on the fight but was eventually killed in battle.

At this point, control of the Greuthungi passed to two military leaders, Alatheus and Saphrax, who ruled in the name of Vithimer's son Vitheric. Having decided to retreat to the banks of the River Dniester, they were met there by a force of Tervingi under Athanaric. But Athanaric was now attacked from the rear by some Huns, who had found an alternative ford over the river, and retreated back to his heartlands closer to the Carpathian Mountains. There he attempted to stem the Hunnic tide by constructing a fortified line against them. In my view, this was probably the old Roman walls on the River Olt, the Limes Transalutanus.[10] But the plan came to naught. The Tervingi were harassed by more Hunnic attacks as they worked on the defences, which damaged their confidence in Athanaric's leadership. Most of the Tervingi broke with him at this point, and under new leaders, Alavivus and Fritigern, came to the Danube to request asylum inside the Roman Empire. The Greuthungi of Alatheus and Saphrax opted for a similar strategy, following the Tervingi to the river (map 5).[11]

Some of these events unfolded very quickly. From the death of Vithimer in battle, the action is pretty continuous down to the arrival of both Tervingi and Greuthungi on the banks of the Danube. Even in its entirety, this sequence needn't have occupied any great length of time. If, as seems likely, the Goths arrived sometime in late summer or early autumn 376, then Vithimer's death need be placed no more than a year before. In principle, even a few months would have been sufficient for the intervening events, which would place Vithimer's death between mid-375 and early 376. Given that a good time for agriculturalists to move on is after they've taken in the harvest, it was

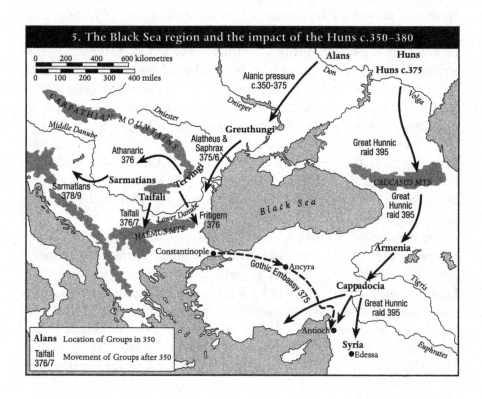

5. The Black Sea region and the impact of the Huns c.350–380

perhaps most likely late summer or early autumn 375 that the Greuthungi took to the road.[12]

This somewhat breathless last act, however, followed a more measured drama. It is impossible to date precisely, because Ammianus gives us only vague indications of time; but what he does tell us is suggestive. He states, first of all, that Ermenaric resisted the storm brewed up by the Huns 'for a long time' (diu). We also hear that Ermenaric's successor Vithimer fought 'many engagements' (multas . . . clades) against the Huns until he was killed in battle. There is obviously no way to be sure how long all this took, but the swift denouement which followed Vithimer's death clearly ended a longer struggle, and it was the Greuthungi's decision to move that precipitated the final crisis. How far back in time the preceding struggle might have gone on is a matter of judgement, but the nature of Hunnic operations does have a bearing on the argument.

To secure their entry to the Empire, first of all, Gothic embassies left the banks of the Danube to seek out the emperor Valens and put their case. Valens, however, was in Antioch – which meant a round trip of over 1,000 kilometres; even so the ambassadors were not deterred. Once they reached Antioch, the two parties had to confer and decisions had to be made, then communicated back to the Roman commanders on the Danube. All of this must have taken well over a month, during which time the mass of Goths continued to sit beside the river, more or less patiently, waiting for the green light to cross. There is no record of any Hunnic attacks upon them during this period. Furthermore, the Huns who attacked Athanaric came in small groups, sometimes weighed down by booty:[13] raiders, therefore, rather than conquerors. The Huns' political organization at this date didn't run to an overall leader but comprised a series of ranked kings with plenty of capacity for independent action. When he was trying to fend off the Greuthungi's Hun-generated military problems, for instance, Vithimer was able to recruit other Huns to fight on his side.[14] In 375/6, there was no massive horde of Huns hotly pursuing the fleeing Goths: rather, independent Hunnic warbands were pursuing a variety of strategies against a variety of opponents.

What was happening, then, was not that a force of Huns conquered the Goths in the sense we normally understand the word, but that some Goths decided to evacuate a world that was becoming ever more insecure. As late as 395, some twenty years later, the mass of Huns remained further east – much closer, in fact, to the northern exit of the Caucasus than to the mouth of the Danube.[15] And it was other Gothic groups, in fact, not the Tervingi or Greuthungi, who continued to provide Rome with its main opposition on the Lower Danube frontier for a decade or more after 376. The Romans had to deal with a heavy assault on the same front launched by a second force of Greuthungi under one Odotheus in 386; and still more Goths – perhaps the leftover Tervingi who hadn't followed Alavivus and Fritigern to the Danube – were operating somewhere in the Carpathian area at much the same time.

The Golden Bow

NONE OF THIS MAKES the arrival of the Huns any less revolutionary. While small-scale trouble was endemic to the Danube frontier, as every-where else, strategic revolution was rare. Roman imperial history had seen only two such moments in the northern Black Sea region. A varied climate and ecology is one of the area's chief peculiarities. Between the Carpathians and the Don there is enough water, particularly in the river valleys, to support arable agriculture, but east of the Don grain cannot be grown without irrigation. At the same time, the southern part between the Carpathians and the Don, just beyond the Black Sea coastal strip, is dry enough to generate steppe conditions. In this fringe of Europe, adjacent areas are ecologically suited, therefore, to nomads and agriculturalists and, in antiquity, the region was dominated by first one type of population group and then the other. Alongside the Scythian nomads, Germanic-speaking agriculturalists, Bastarnae and others, had thrived in the last few centuries BC. Their domination was broken by nomadic Iranian-speaking Sarmatians around the year zero. Two hundred years later agricultural Goths pushed south and east around the Carpathians, extending their domain as far east as the Don, subduing those Sarmatians who remained. What was it about the Huns, then, that allowed them in the later fourth century to redress the military balance in favour of the nomadic world?

The Romans quickly came to appreciate where the military strength of the Huns lay. Ammianus describes no Hunnic battle in detail, but leaves us this general description that gets straight to the point:

[The Huns] enter battle drawn up in wedge-shaped masses . . .
And as they are lightly equipped for swift motion, and unexpected
in action, they purposely divide suddenly into scattered bands and
attack, rushing about in disorder here and there, dealing terrific
slaughter . . . They fight from a distance with missiles having
sharp bone, instead of their usual points, joined to the shafts with
wonderful skill; then they gallop over the intervening spaces and
fight hand to hand with swords.

Zosimus, a sixth-century writer drawing on the account of the
fourth-century historian Eunapius, is equally vivid: '[The Huns] were
totally incapable and ignorant of conducting a battle on foot, but by
wheeling, charging, retreating in good time and shooting from their
horses, they wrought immense slaughter.'[16] These Roman commentators leave no room for doubt. The Huns were cavalry, and above
all horse archers, who were able to engage at a safe distance until
their opponents lost formation and cohesion. At this point, the Huns
would move in for the kill with either bow or sabre. The essential
ingredients in all this were skilled archery and horsemanship, the
capacity to work together in small groups, and ferocious courage.
As many have commented, and as was demonstrated repeatedly in
antiquity and in the Middle Ages, the Eurasian pastoralist's life was a
hard one, and the kinds of skills, not to mention the magnificent
horses, a nomad required for everyday existence set him up equally
well for battle.

But this was true of all Eurasian nomads, and doesn't really explain
why the Huns were particularly successful. As well as the Germanic
Goths, they were also able to defeat fellow nomads, such as the
Iranian-speaking Alans. What gave them the edge? Both were
renowned horsemen, but they fought in different ways. Whereas the
Huns, as relatively lightly equipped horse archers, set a high value on
manoeuvrability, the Alans, like the Sarmatians in general, specialized
in heavy cavalry – cataphracts, as the Romans called them. Both rider
and horse were protected; the rider's main weapon was the lance,
supplemented with a long cavalry sabre, and the lancers operated in
a compact mass. This narrows the question down further. For the
Scythians, whom the Sarmatians replaced as the dominant power north
of the Black Sea in the early imperial period, had been horse archers,
just like the Huns, and employed very similar tactics – but at that

point, lance had prevailed over bow. Why, three centuries later, did the balance tilt in favour of the bow?

The answer doesn't lie in the basic construction of the bow the Huns used. Both Huns and Scythians used the so-called 'wonder weapon of the steppe'. When we in the West think of bows, we usually have in mind 'self' bows, made of a single stave of wood and assuming a simple concave shape when put under tension. Steppe bows were completely different. To start with, they were composite. Separate sections of wood provided a frame for the other constituent parts: sinew on the outside that would stretch, and bone plates on the inside that would be compressed, when the bow was tensed. Unstrung, these bows also curved in the reverse direction: hence the weapon's other name, the recurve bow. Wood, sinew and bone were glued together with the most powerful adhesive that could be concocted from fishbone and animal hide, and when fully seasoned the bow's hitting power was tremendous. Remains of such bows (usually the bone plates) have been found in graves from the Lake Balkhash region dating back to the third millennium BC. So by the fourth AD, it was hardly a new weapon.

The key to Hunnic success seems to lie in one particular detail whose significance has not been fully recognized. Both the Huns and the Scythians used the composite bow, then, but whereas Scythian bows measured about 80 centimetres in length, the few Hunnic bows found in graves are much larger, measuring between 130 and 160 centimetres. The point here, of course, is that size generates power. However, the maximum size of bow that a cavalryman can comfortably use is only about 100 centimetres. The bow was held out, upright, directly in front of the rider, so that a longer bow would bang into the horse's neck or get caught up in the reins. But – and here is the answer to our question – Hunnic bows were asymmetric. The half below the handle was shorter than the half above, and it is this that allowed the longer bow to be used from horseback. It involved a trade-off, of course. The longer bow was clumsier and its asymmetry called for adjustments in aim on the part of the archer. But the Huns' asymmetric 130-centimetre bow generated considerably more hitting power than the Scythians' symmetrical 80-centimetre counterpart: unlike the Scythians', it could penetrate Sarmatian armour while keeping the archer at a safe distance and not impeding his horsemanship.

Some idea of what it was like to use the recurve, or reflex, bow can be derived from trials with composite 'Turkish' bows in the early modern and modern periods. These were generally about 110 centimetres in length, but symmetric, since they were made for infantry rather than cavalry. They were also the product, of course, of a further millennium of development, outperforming larger Chinese and Asian bows of the same basic design. Their performance certainly startled Europeans, used to 'self' bows. In 1753 the best shot before the modern era, Hassan Aga, launched an arrow a grand total of 584 yards and 1 foot (roughly 534 metres). He was a renowned champion, but distances of well over 400 metres were commonplace. This bow's power, too, is awesome. From just over 100 metres' distance, a Turkish bow will drive an arrow over 5 centimetres through a piece of wood 1.25 centimetres thick. Because of its asymmetry and the fact that infantry archers can plant their feet firmly, unlike their mounted counterparts, we need to knock something off these performance figures when thinking about what they tell us about the fourth century. The Huns didn't have stirrups, but used heavy wooden saddles which allowed the rider to grip with the leg muscles and thus create a firm firing platform. Nonetheless, Hunnic horse archers would probably have been effective against unarmoured opponents such as the Goths from distances of 150 to 200 metres, and against protected Alans from 75 to 100 metres. These distances were more than enough to give the Huns a huge tactical advantage, which, as Roman sources report, they exploited to the full.[17]

The bow wasn't the Huns' only weapon. Having destroyed the cohesion of an enemy's formation from a distance, their cavalry would then close in to engage with their swords, and they often used lassos, too, to disable individual opponents. There is also some evidence that high-status Huns wore coats of mail. But the reflex bow was their pièce de résistance. Carefully adapted, by the mid-fourth century it could face down the challenge of the Sarmatian cataphracts. The Huns, as you might expect, were well aware of their bows' uniqueness, as slightly later sources, dating to the fifth century, attest. The historian Olympiodorus of Thebes tells us that in about 410 Hunnic kings prided themselves on their archery skills,[18] and there is no reason to suppose that this was not already the case in 375. On the night that the greatest Hun of all – Attila – died, the Roman emperor Marcian dreamt that 'a divine figure stood by him and showed him the bow of Attila broken that night'.[19] And the archaeological record confirms, likewise, that the

Hunnic bow was a symbol of supreme authority. In four burial sites
the remains of bows entirely or partly encased in engraved gold sheet
have been found. One was entirely symbolic: only 80 centimetres long,
it was covered with so much gold that it could not have been flexed.
The other three were full length, and it's possible that here we are
looking at real weapons with gold casings.[20] Thus embellished, the
source of the Huns' military dominance became a potent image of
political power. It also allowed them to dominate the western edge
of the Great Eurasian Steppe.

Ammianus Marcellinus was right. It was the Huns who were
behind the military revolution that had brought the Tervingi and
Greuthungi to the Danube sometime in the late summer or early
autumn of 376. At this point, the rise of Hunnic power ceased to be a
problem for the peoples of the northern shores of the Black Sea
exclusively. It now presented the eastern emperor Valens with a huge
dilemma. Tens of thousands of displaced Goths had suddenly arrived
on his borders and were requesting asylum.

Asylum Seekers

WITH A RARE UNANIMITY, the vast majority of our sources report that
this sudden surge of would-be Gothic immigrants wasn't seen as a
problem at all. On the contrary, Valens happily admitted them because
he saw in this flood of displaced humanity a great opportunity. To
quote Ammianus again – but most other sources tell a similar story:

> The affair caused more joy than fear and educated flatterers
> immoderately praised the good fortune of the prince, which
> unexpectedly brought him so many young recruits from the ends
> of the earth, that by the union of his own and foreign forces he
> would have an invincible army. In addition, instead of the levy of
> soldiers, which was contributed annually by each province, there
> would accrue to the treasury a vast amount of gold.

Thus soldiers and gold both at the same time – usually you got one or
the other. No wonder Valens was pleased.

Most of the sources also give a broadly similar account of what
went wrong after the Goths crossed the river (probably at or around
the fortress of Durostorum (map 6). The blame for what happened

next is placed mostly on the dishonesty of the Roman officials on the spot. For once the immigrants started to run short of supplies, these officials exploited their increasing desperation to run a highly profitable black market, taking slaves from them in return for food. Unsurprisingly, this generated huge resentment, which the Roman military, especially one Lupicinus, commander of the field forces in Thrace (*comes Thraciae*), only exacerbated. Having first profited from the black market, then having made the Goths move on to a second camp outside his regional headquarters at Marcianople (map 6), he made a botched attack on their leadership, at a banquet supposedly given in their honour. This pushed the Goths from resentment to revolt.[21] So the story goes, and so it has often been repeated by historians. Blaming Valens for his stupidity in agreeing to admit the Goths, the local Roman military for their greed, and the Goths – just a bit – for resorting to violence makes for a perfectly coherent account. Considered in all its details, however, it is not the whole truth.

Take, to begin with, normal Roman policy towards asylum seekers. Immigrants, willing or otherwise, in 376 were a far from new phenomenon for the Roman Empire. Throughout its history, it had taken in outsiders: a constant stream of individuals looking to make their fortune (not least, as we have seen, in the Roman army), supplemented by occasional large-scale migrations. There was even a technical term for the latter: *receptio*. An inscription from the first century AD records that Nero's governor transported 100,000 people 'from across [north of] the Danube' (*transdanuviani*) into Thrace. As recently as AD 300, the tetrarchic emperors had resettled tens of thousands of Dacian Carpi inside the Empire, dispersing them in communities the length of the Danube, from Hungary to the Black Sea. There had been a number of similar influxes in between, and while there was no single blueprint for how immigrants were to be treated, clear patterns emerge. If relations between the Empire and the would-be asylum seekers were good, and the immigration happening by mutual consent, then some of the young adult males would be drafted into the Roman army, sometimes forming a single new unit, and the rest distributed fairly widely across the Empire as free peasant cultivators who would henceforth pay taxes. This was the kind of arrangement agreed between the emperor Constantius II and some Sarmatian Limigantes, for instance, in 359.[22] If relations between the Empire and migrants were not so good, and, in particular, if they'd been captured during military operations, treatment was much harsher. Some might still be drafted into the army, though often with greater safeguards imposed. An imperial edict dealing with a force of Sciri captured by the Romans in 409, for instance, records that twenty-five years – that is, a generation – should pass before any of them could be recruited. The rest, again, became peasant cultivators, but on less favourable terms. Many of the Sciri of 409 were sold into slavery, and the rest distributed as unfree peasants (*coloni*), with the stipulation that they had to be moved to points outside the Balkans, where they had been captured. All immigrants became soldiers or peasants, then, but there were more and less pleasant ways of effecting it.[23]

There is, however, another common denominator to all documented cases of licensed immigration into the Empire. Emperors *never* admitted immigrants on trust. They *always* made sure that they were militarily in control of proceedings, either through having defeated the would-be immigrants first, or by having sufficient force on hand to deal with any trouble. Constantius and the Limigantes provide a case in point. In 359, something went badly wrong. True to form, Ammianus puts it down to bad faith on the part of the Sarmatians, but the causes may have been more complex. Be that as it may, all hell broke loose at a crucial moment:

> When the emperor was seen on the high tribunal and was already preparing to deliver a most mild address, intending to speak to [the Sarmatians] as future obedient subjects, one of their number struck with savage madness, hurling his shoe at the tribunal, shouted 'Marha, marha' (which is their warcry), and the rude crowd following him suddenly raised a barbarian banner and with savage howls rushed upon the emperor himself.

What happened next is very revealing:

> Although the attack was so sudden that they were only partly armed, with a loud battlecry [the Roman forces] plunged into the bands of the savages . . . They butchered everything in their way, trampling under foot without mercy the living, as well as those dying or dead . . . The rebels were completely overthrown, some being slain, others fleeing in terror in all directions, and a part of them who hoped to save their lives by vain entreaties, were cut down by repeated strokes.

The Limigantes' acceptance on to Roman soil had been carefully negotiated before Constantius showed himself, so all should have been well. But when it wasn't, there were plenty of Roman troops to hand and it was the Limigantes who were wiped out.[24]

This highlights a key element in the generally accepted account of what happened in 376 that just doesn't ring true. Valens, we are told, was filled with joy at the Goths' arrival on the Danube. But in 376 the Roman army was demonstrably not in charge of the situation, and when things started to go wrong after the crossing, order could not be restored. Lupicinus, whatever his personal culpability for the Goths' revolt, simply didn't have enough troops on hand. After the banquet, he immediately rushed his available forces into battle against the rebellious Goths and was soundly defeated.[25] In the absence of total military superiority, which was central to normal Roman *receptiones*, it is just not credible that Valens was anything like as happy about the arrival of the Goths on the Danube as the sources claim.

The shortage of Roman troops in the Balkans had a simple enough cause. In the summer of 376, Valens was deeply embroiled on his eastern front, and had been for some time. As we saw in Chapter 3, he had ended his war against Athanaric in 369 with a compromise, because he was needed in the east to deal with Persian ambitions in Armenia and Iberia. After 371, taking advantage of Persia's difficulties in its own far eastern territories, Valens had made some important gains, managing to put Roman nominees in control of these Caucasian territories. By 375, though, Shapur, Persian King of Kings, was back. Determined to hold firm, Valens sent three aggressive embassies in the summer of 376, which told him to back off or expect a fight. Such diplomatic posturing required appropriate military preparations, so that not only had Valens made haste to Antioch, the regional headquarters for Persian campaigns, but the vast majority of his mobile striking forces was in the east as well. When the Goths arrived on the Danube, therefore, Valens was already fully committed to an aggressive policy in the east, and it was bound to take him at least a year to extract his forces diplomatically, or even just to turn them around logistically.[26]

For a while Valens probably still hoped that the Danube crisis could be managed in such a way as to allow him to pursue his Caucasian ambitions, perhaps even with the addition of some extra Gothic military manpower, as the sources report. Given how far the Danubian situation departed from normal Roman expectations of control, however, we might also expect him to have been treading very carefully, wary of potential problems. And the available evidence shows that he was. As we noted earlier, one thing is clear: of the two Gothic groups who arrived at the Danube, only the Tervingi were admitted.[27] The Greuthungi were refused permission to enter the Empire, and such troops and naval craft as were available in the Balkans were placed opposite them to keep them north of the river.[28] Valens did not, then, rush to accept every Goth he could find so as to build up his army and fill the treasury's coffers at one and the same time.

Let's also have a closer look at his relations with the Tervingi. No source describes the terms agreed with this group in any detail, and, thanks to the rebellion, they were never fully implemented. The new relationship was certainly presented to the Roman public as a Gothic surrender – *deditio* – but that in itself tells us little; both Constantine's and Valens' earlier treaties with the Tervingi were described as such when they involved quite different relationships (see pp. 72–6). Everything suggests that the agreement of 376 incorporated some unusual features, highly favourable to the Goths. To start with, they exercised an unusual degree of control over their place of settlement. In normal circumstances, the emperor decided where to place immigrants, tending to spread them out. In 376, it was agreed that the Tervingi should be settled only in Thrace, and this was their choice. The details of how the settlement was to be organized are unclear; in particular, we are left in the dark on the crucial issue of whether they were to be settled in clusters large enough to preserve their political and cultural identity. This would again have been highly unusual, but, given that they were able to choose their own settlement area, may well have been part of the agreement. Otherwise, we know only that hostages were taken, and an immediate draft of young men for the regular Roman army; and that the agreement envisaged the Goths possibly serving en masse as auxiliaries on particular campaigns, much as they had between 332 and 369. There were also some confidence-building measures. In particular, the Tervingi leadership declared itself willing to convert to Christianity.

The fact that the agreement was sold to its Roman audience as a surrender must not confuse the issue. In both its military and its diplomatic details it departed from Roman norms. The Tervingi extracted much better terms in 376 than those usually granted even to immigrants being treated as friends. Lacking sufficient military clout on the Danube, Valens was forced to depart from tried and trusted Roman methods. We might expect him to have been wary about admitting even the Tervingi, therefore, and there are, in fact, strong hints that he was.[29]

As we've seen, the main cause of the Tervingi's revolt was food shortages and black-marketeering beside the Danube. The Goths, it seems, spent autumn and part of winter 376/7 beside the river, and only moved on to Marcianople sometime in late winter or early spring. Even when the revolt got under way, they still had difficulty in finding food, because 'all the necessities of life had been taken to the strong cities, none of which the enemy even then attempted to besiege because of their complete ignorance of these and other operations of the kind'. This relates to the summer of 377, but long before that year's crops had ripened. The Romans, it would seem, had deliberately moved the harvest of 376 to fortified strongpoints which the Goths lacked the military technology to take. Feeding the hungry Tervingi was anyway a formidable task for the Roman state, given its bureaucratic limitations. It had to plan carefully enough for major military campaigns when its own troops needed feeding. The Goths, of course, had no means of growing their own food at this point, since the agreement hadn't yet got as far as land allocations. Once their stocks had been consumed, securing all other food supplies gave Valens a lever of control over them.

The emperor was also quick to negotiate military assistance from his western colleague, the emperor Gratian, son of his brother Valentinian I. Probably in 377 our old friend Themistius, orator, philosopher, senator of Constantinople and a close confidant of Valens, visited Rome. There he delivered his thirteenth oration. This speech, derivative and uninspired – perhaps delivered on the tenth anniversary of the emperor's accession, which fell in 377 – celebrated Gratian as the Platonic ideal of a ruler. Much more interesting than the speech is the fact that Themistius was present in the west at such an important moment. And, as he makes clear, his journey from Syria had been made at breakneck speed:

> ... my course was almost equal to the course of the sun, from the Tigris to Ocean [the Atlantic; i.e. the west]; it was an urgent journey, a flight over the surface of the earth, just as you

> [Socrates] say Eros once hurried, with sleepless days following the
> nights. I lived my life on the road and under the open skies,
> sleeping on the ground and out of doors, with no bed to lie on
> and no shoes to put on . . .[30]

The pace he described here is much faster than you'd think the rather
run-of-the-mill contents of the speech would demand, which suggests
that his embassy had another, more urgent aim. The presence of some
western troops, already available to the east for campaigning in the
Balkans in summer 377, gives the clue. Such campaigning would have
required prior negotiation sometime during winter 376/7, possibly
even before the revolt of the Tervingi had broken out. It was this
necessity that drove Themistius and his companions so relentlessly
across land and sea. The ambassadors were charged with negotiating a
joint imperial response to the Gothic problem that had suddenly
appeared on Valens' doorstep.

A note of caution on the eastern emperor's part too is suggested
by the most mysterious of all the events that were unfolding at this
time beside the Danube. As food shortages worsened, and the Goths'
hostility grew, Lupicinus moved the Tervingi on to his regional
headquarters at Marcianople, as we noted. But to supervise the process,
he was obliged to use the forces that had previously been keeping out
the Greuthungi. The Tervingi did eventually move, but the redeploy-
ment of the Roman forces allowed the Greuthungi to cross the river
on to imperial territory. Lupicinus, as commander, must have been
getting desperate – clearly, the situation was spiralling out of control.
Ammianus reports that, to cap it all, the Tervingi moved only slowly
towards Marcianople, so as to allow the Greuthungi to catch up with
them. (The Greuthungi may have crossed the Danube slightly more
to the east than the Tervingi, at Sacidava or Axiopolis (map 6).) When
the Tervingi were about 15 kilometres from their destination, Lupicinus invited their leaders to dinner. Ammianus describes the party:

> Having invited Alavivus and Fritigern to a dinner party, Lupicinus
> posted soldiers against the main body of the barbarians and kept
> them at a distance from the walls of the town . . . Great wrangling
> arose between the inhabitants and those who were shut out,
> which finally reached a point where fighting was inevitable.
> Whereupon the barbarians . . . killed and despoiled a great troop
> of soldiers. When Lupicinus learned by a secret message that this

had happened ... he put to death all the attendants of the two leaders, who as a guard of honour and to ensure their safety were waiting for them in front of the general's quarters. When the [Goths] who were besieging the walls heard this news, in their resentment they gradually increased their number to avenge their kings, who, as they thought, had been detained by force ... And since Fritigern was quickwitted and feared that he might be held with the rest as a hostage, he cried out that they [the Romans] would have to fight with heavy loss of life, unless he himself were allowed to go out with his companions to quiet the people ... And when this request was granted, they all departed.[31]

It is difficult to know precisely what happened. On the face of it, the botched attack was the result of misunderstanding and panic, but banquet hijacks were a standard tool of Roman frontier management.

Removing dangerous or potentially dangerous leaders was an excellent means of spreading confusion amongst opponents. Ammianus describes four other occasions over a span of just twenty-four years when Roman commanders made dinner invitations an opportunity for kidnap. One of these four was the unauthorized initiative of a local commander, but the other three resulted from direct imperial orders. In one case, a commander on the Rhine was given a sealed letter, which he was not to open unless he saw the Alamannic leader in question on the Roman side of the river. When this happened, and he did, he was instructed to shunt him off to Spain. Lupicinus, I suspect, was in receipt of similarly contingent orders. Valens, still at Antioch, could not be consulted at every turn – requests for orders from his Danubian commanders would have had a turn-around time of weeks. So Lupicinus' instructions with regard to the Tervingi must have left considerable room for personal initiative; all the same, I don't believe that he would have been let loose on the Gothic problem without careful guidance about what to do in a variety of foreseeable scenarios. The arrival of a huge number of unsubdued Goths in Roman territory at a point when the main Roman army was mobilized elsewhere, was much too potentially dangerous not to have been thought through. Lupicinus had been told, I suspect, that if things looked as if they might be getting out of hand, then he should do what he could to disrupt the Goths – and hijacking enemy leaders, as already mentioned, was a standard Roman reflex. But it was Lupicinus' call. In the event, he went for that worst of all possible worlds: first one thing, then the other, with neither stratagem whole-heartedly pursued. Instead of a continued if uneasy peace or a leaderless opposition, he found himself facing an organized revolt under an established leader.[32]

Both common sense – would *you* be pleased to see chaos descend on a second front while you are heavily engaged on a first? – and comparison with other cases of licensed migration into the Roman Empire make it clear that Valens could not have been nearly so pleased to see huge numbers of Goths arrive on the Danube as our sources, however unanimously, report. As we have seen, imperial ideology required all barbarians to be shown to be subservient, and whatever the panicking going on behind the scenes in 376, the emperor's policy had to be presented to his taxpayers as a freely chosen strategy that would benefit the Empire. Ammianus offers us a strong hint here. His account refers to the input of 'learned flatterers' (*eruditis adulatoribus*) into Valens' Gothic policy.[33] This immediately brings to mind Themistius, who did such a good job for Valens on the peace of 369. He was with the emperor in Syria in the summer of 376, before his sudden dash westwards, and I suspect that a speech such as that of 369 was one of the ways whereby he convinced the east Roman court that, contrary to all appearances, letting in a horde of untamed Goths was actually a jolly good idea. The unanimity of our sources, then, reflects the propaganda that the emperor used to justify his policy, not the real reasoning behind it.

The Huns had thrown the Roman Empire and a large number of Goths into a new and unprecedentedly close relationship. The emperor certainly didn't desire this relationship: not, at least, in the form it took. The Goths too had their doubts and hesitations. Their decision to seek asylum inside the Empire was not taken lightly. When the majority of the Tervingi broke with Athanaric, they had done so at a large gathering where the issues were debated at length.[34] You can understand their wavering. Moving into the territory of such a powerful neighbour was no easy decision. Given the efficiency of the cross-border telegraph, they probably knew that Valens was currently overstretched on the Danube because of the war with Persia. The emperor might be willing to grant concessions for the moment, but there could be no guarantee that his attitude might not harden later. It's hardly surprising, therefore, if the Goths were trying to think ahead: to prepare themselves to deal with the power of the Empire in the longer term as well as now.

Although the Romans treated them quite differently, the Tervingi and Greuthungi remained closely in touch. Hence, as already noted, when the Tervingi were forced by Lupicinus' troops to move on to Marcianople, they were already aware that the Greuthungi had crossed the river and so slowed their pace.[35] The Tervingi were entering the lion's den and, even if apparently receiving more favourable treatment than the Greuthungi, they had every interest in forming a united front with as many Goths as possible against the Empire's overwhelming superiority in both manpower and resources. By so doing, of course, they broke at least the spirit of their agreement with Valens. But if the emperor could find ways of rewriting the agreement of 376 for the longer term, then so could the Goths.[36]

And this, it seems to me, is the real story. Both the Goths and the Romans had been thrown by the Huns into a new and more intense relationship. Neither side trusted the other, and neither was totally committed to the agreement negotiated – when both were under duress – in 376. That this initial agreement failed to hold cannot really have surprised anyone. The way was now clear for a test of military strength, upon whose outcome would hang the nature of a more durable settlement between the immigrant Goths and the Roman state.

The Battle of Hadrianople

HOSTILITIES OPENED ON the morning after Lupicinus' fatal banquet. The return of Fritigern and the violence of the night before prompted a first round of pillaging in the immediate vicinity of Marcianople. In response, Lupicinus gathered what men he could and advanced to the Gothic camp, about 15 kilometres outside the city. His force was quickly overwhelmed – few, apart from Lupicinus himself, managed to escape. Sometime in late winter or spring of 377, war began in earnest and was to last no fewer than six campaigning seasons before peace was restored on 3 October 382.[37] The action of the first two years, up to the battle of Hadrianople, can be followed in considerable detail in the narrative of Ammianus Marcellinus (which is not to say that he tells us everything that we want to know). After the battle, the sources become thinner. What is very clear, however, is that the entire

war – all six seasons' worth – was confined to the Balkan provinces of
the Roman Empire. This is a landscape that has been fought over
many times in history, and its very particular geography has always
dictated the nature of the action.

The northern part of the peninsula is roughly rectangular, broader
to the north than the south, and to the west than the east (map 6),
its salient physical feature being its mountains. To the east, the Stara
Planina (or Haemus Mountains) rise to rounded summits averaging
750 metres; the highest peak reaches 2,376, while the more rugged
Rhodopes are a touch higher with many peaks at over 2,000 metres.
Further west, running north–south, are the Dinaric Alps. Over time,
their limestone has eroded into sharp crags and pockmarked hillsides,
often covered with prickly, unpleasant scrub: the characteristic Karst
landscape of the western Balkans. Alongside the mountains lie three
wide plains: the Danubian Plain to the north, the Thracian in the
south-east, and the Macedonian between the Rhodopes and the Dinarics. Another characteristic feature of the peninsula is its many alluvial
upland basins, where rainwater and snowmelt erosion have built up
layers of fertile soil in pockets between the mountain peaks.

The nature of this landscape has shaped the region's history. Most
obviously, the plains and upland basins define discrete sections of
cultivable land, where there are likely to be concentrations of population. Many of the mountain zones are extremely rugged, which,
especially combined with the region's harsh winters, has limited long-
distance communications to only two main routes. North–south, the
key highway runs through the Morava and Vardar river valleys
connecting the Danube via modern Skopje (the Roman Scupi) to the
Aegean at Thessalonica. North-west to south-east, a second important
route starts again at the Morava valley, but turns left at Niš (the
Roman Naissus) to work its way through fertile upland basins past the
Bulgarian capital Sofia (the Roman Serdica), then over the Succi Pass
to connect with the rich upland plain of the Sredna Gora and on to
the Thracian Plain. In the Roman period, this was a military trunk
road. Landscape also dictates communications more locally. The Rhodopes are extremely difficult to cross from north-east to south-west,
for instance, and movement north and south through the Haemus
mountains is channelled through just five major passes: the Iskar valley
in the west, the Trojan and Shipka Passes in the centre, and the Kotel
and Riski further east.

When the Goths crossed the Danube in AD 376, they entered a Roman world that had imposed itself on this landscape for over 300 years in the north, and nearer 500 in the south, where by 146 BC Macedonia had been conquered and turned into a Roman province. In large measure, the Romans worked with the landscape, rather

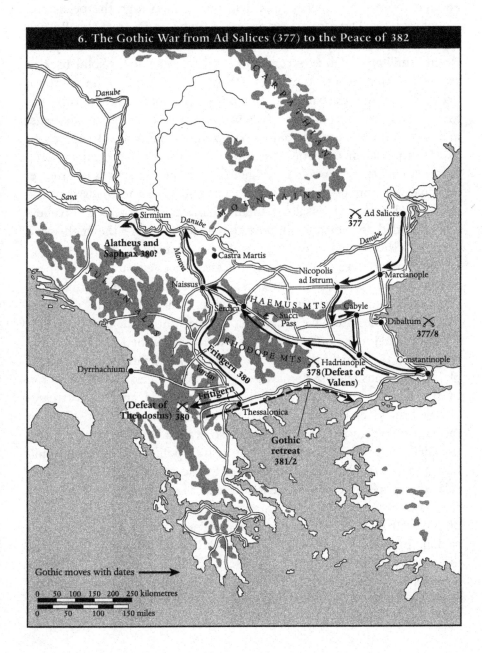

6. The Gothic War from Ad Salices (377) to the Peace of 382

than against it, but there was one main exception. Aside from the two natural axes of long-distance communication, they forced two additional east–west routes through the Balkans. In the south, and constructed as early as 130 BC, the famous Via Egnatia followed the Aegean coastline from Constantinople to Thessalonica – an easy enough route – but then struck determinedly through the peaks and troughs of the Dinarics to reach the Adriatic at Durres (the Roman Dyrrhachium). Further north, at the end of the first century AD, Roman military engineers carved a road through sheer solid rock at the Iron Gates, where the River Danube cuts through the southern extension of the Carpathian Mountains, to connect the Lower and Middle Danube regions. The Balkans was the junction between east and west, and the Empire didn't skimp on its highways. Even as late as 376, the Balkans' prime function, viewed from a central imperial perspective, was to provide a bridge between the two halves of Empire; and many resources were devoted to maintaining the roads, and the towns and way-stations along them. These both protected travellers and provided the logistic support that made possible the high-speed connections recorded in the papers of Theophanes (see pp. 104–7).

The imperatives of Empire also dictated that central funds be spent in two other areas of the Balkans. The Danube Plain north of the Haemus Mountains had been an imperial frontier for three centuries by the time the Huns were creating mayhem north of the Black Sea. Early on, major legionary bases had been established at Oescus and Novae. By the fourth century, the regional headquarters at Marcianople, whose walls enclosed an area of 70 hectares, oversaw the operation of the frontier zone, and a series of larger and smaller fortresses guarded the river line and studded the countryside behind it. Many of the larger civilian settlements were also walled by this date, and had subsidiary military functions. Further south, political rather than military imperatives dictated expenditure. In the south-east of the peninsula, the emperor Constantine refounded the ancient Greek *polis*, or city-state, of Byzantium as Constantinople, which, by the third quarter of the fourth century had become in every respect a new imperial capital. Endowed with mighty walls and beautiful public buildings, the city had also seen massive investment on infrastructure: harbour facilities and granaries that could deal with grain fleets from Egypt, and aqueducts that drained the hills over 100 kilometres away to service the burgeoning population of a naturally rather arid site. It was a huge centre of economic demand, and, in addition to all the imperial funds spent on it, had many inhabitants with money to burn. The rich needed both houses inside the city and cooler retreats in the country, as well as services of all kinds. In the fourth century, the south-eastern Balkans were booming as never before, and Constantinopolitan cash spilled over into the nearby communities of the Thracian Plain.

The Balkans were also host to other Roman communities, whose Romanness was the product of a more organic, long-term development. Some Roman cities sat on ancient foundations. Many of the communities of the Adriatic coast had a long pre-Roman past, and this was even more true of Macedonia and the Black Sea littoral, where cities like Thessalonica, Philippopolis, Anchialus and Odessus had classical Greek roots. These areas boasted both proper Roman cities complete with the standard repertoire of public buildings, and a flourishing countryside, cheerfully exploited to good effect by a landowning class living in luxurious villas. 'Proper' Roman life could also be found in other parts of the peninsula. In the fourth century, the Danubian Plain was still dotted with Roman towns and villas. In part, these communities can be viewed as a spin-off from Roman defence spending. Many of the town councils of the region were populated with the descendants of legionary veterans, and many villa estates had their origins in the land grants the state customarily made to retired soldiers. Many fortunes were made servicing the consumer demand triggered by soldiers' pay. But Roman life in the region had generated its own momentum, and its monuments are too substantial to be explained solely by state spending. The same was true of the central corridor from Philippopolis through the Sredna Gora and Serdica into the Morava valley. Here again, state spending had certainly kick-started things, but the Pax Romana had allowed an authentic Roman life to develop, and in most of the upland basins as well. The twin obstacles of mountain and climate that had resulted in far fewer cities and a correspondingly lower percentage of intensely worked land than in many other areas of the Empire, had not prevented the Balkans from developing into a properly Roman world.[38]

This was the panorama that faced the Goths at the outbreak of war. Everything suggests that the Greuthungi joined in the hostilities immediately.[39] Established at this point in the vicinity of Marcianople, they found themselves in the middle of the belt of Roman military installations that guarded the Danube line. Some layers showing damage, datable to the war years, have been found in the remains of smaller forts, but both written and archaeological evidence confirm that Ammianus was right to emphasize that the Gothic leader Fritigern 'kept peace with walls'.[40] It would have been suicide for the Goths to assault these Roman frontier forts, many of which had been re-equipped at the start of the fourth century with huge U-shaped bastions designed to carry the brutally effective Roman wall artillery. The garrisons were pretty numerous: twenty-three units in the province of Scythia and twenty-seven in Lower Moesia, with particular concentrations at Noviodunum, Axiopolis, Troesmis, Transmarisca, Durostorum and Novae (map 6). These garrison troops, however, were primarily trained to patrol and deal with small-scale raids, not to provide mobile forces for large-scale field operations, and Lupicinus had anyway drawn off much of their manpower to create his scratch force. In defeating Lupicinus, therefore, the Goths had already neutralized the only mobile Roman force in the region, and the remaining garrisons faced certain destruction if they ventured out piecemeal. These installations posed no immediate threat to the Goths and could be safely ignored.[41]

Besides, the Goths had more immediate concerns. They had, of course, plenty of scores to settle. As we noted earlier, a winter in the open on the Danubian Plain, where even average daytime temperatures do not climb above zero in January and February, combined with the Romans' black-marketeering, had infuriated them. There was also the pressing need to secure food supplies. The Goths may well have brought with them at least some of the harvest of 376, and the Romans had been supplying them with a certain amount of food in the meantime, but there was no possibility of planting crops for the current year. After plundering easy targets in the immediate vicinity of Marcianople, therefore, Gothic eyes turned to the great highways running from the Danube towards the metropolitan splendour and economic boom that was the south-east Roman Balkans.

Goths next appear in the vicinity of Hadrianople, already south of the Haemus Mountains, and some two hundred kilometres south of Marcianople. The total defeat of Lupicinus' force there had robbed the Romans of any chance, at this point, of holding the Haemus barrier against them. A much smaller force of Goths was stationed at Hadrianople. Led by Sueridas and Colias, it had long been part of the Roman army. When news of the revolt further north reached the city, trouble broke out between the citizens and these Goths, and they threw in their lot with Fritigern. It was at this moment, Ammianus records, that Fritigern 'advised them to attack and devastate the rich and fruitful parts of the country, which were still without protectors and could be pillaged without any danger'. The outcome, from the Roman point of view, was frightful:

[The Goths] advancing cautiously spread over every quarter of Thrace, while their prisoners or those who surrendered to them pointed out the rich villages, especially those in which it was said that abundant supplies of food were to be found . . . With such guides, nothing that was not inaccessible and out of the way remained untouched. For without distinction of age or sex, all places were ablaze with slaughter and great fires; babies were torn from the very breasts of their mothers and slain, matrons and widows whose husbands had been killed before their eyes were carried off, boys of tender or adult age were dragged away over the dead bodies of their parents. Many older men, lamenting that they had lived long enough after losing their possessions and their beautiful women, were led into exile with their arms pinioned behind their backs, weeping over the glowing ashes of their ancestral homes.[42]

The Goths were hungry and had many resentments to burn off; the people of the Thracian Plain suddenly found themselves in the front line, and paid the price for everything that had happened during that winter on the Danube. Note, too, the willingness of some of the Roman population to assist the Goths in their plundering. Some perhaps helped them out of fear, but there was many an oppressed peasant with his own scores to settle. The Pax Romana did not benefit all Romans equally.

The Roman response to these disasters came in the form of a first consignment of troops from the east. Valens sent one of his chief advisers, the general Victor, to sue for peace with Persia on whatever terms he could get; and in the meantime he detached some troops from Armenia under the generals Trajanus and Profuturus, who reached the Balkans in the summer of 377. Their impact was substantial. The Goths quickly withdrew north of the Haemus Mountains. At this point, too, the first fruits of Valens' hasty diplomacy materialized. A smallish force from the western Empire under the command of Richomeres hastened over the Succi Pass to join

Trajanus and Profuturus. Reinforced, the Romans advanced north of the Haemus range as far as the Gothic wagon laager, which, Ammianus tells us, was situated at a place called *Ad Salices*, 'town by the willows' (map 6).[43] The Romans decided to risk battle; and the Goths were up for a fight, once the last of their foraging parties returned. Only Ammianus describes the encounter, and his account is far from graphic. About half of it is devoted to a rhetorical description of the dead and dying, and he tells us nothing of the numbers or dispositions of the two sides. In overall terms, however, the battle was clearly a bloody draw. At one point, the Roman left wing gave way, but reserves rescued the situation and the fighting ended at nightfall. The Romans had suffered grievous losses, but so too had the Goths, and afterwards they stayed inside their wagon circle for an entire week. Summer was at this point giving way to autumn, so we are probably in September 377.[44]

The Romans made excellent use of the respite. The battle had cost them dear, but for the moment they had retaken the initiative, for the first time since Lupicinus' defeat. Heavily outnumbered as they were, the available forces had no prospect of defeating the Goths; so instead, quick to exploit one of the features of the Balkan landscape, they fortified the passes through the Haemus Mountains. Marcianople itself commanded the eastern end of the range, so presumably a substantial garrison was left there. The rest of the troops were dispersed to block the five main routes south. The plan was simple, as Ammianus explains: 'They doubtless hoped that the dangerous mass of enemies, crowded together between the Hister [Danube] and the waste places, and finding no way out, would perish from lack of food.' It was also well laid. Some of the passes through the Haemus Mountains are quite broad, but they are all high. Exactly 1,500 years later, in the Russo-Turkish war of 1877, the Russians sent a flying column south from the Danube to seize the Shipka Pass, which leads through the central Haemus range to Hadrianople and the main road to Constantinople/Istanbul. They successfully captured it, but weren't reinforced, and for five days (21–25 August) 4,400 Russians had to face the assault of 30–40,000 Turks under Suleiman Pasha. At the end of the battle there were three and a half thousand Russian casualties, but they had held the pass, and over 10,000 dead Turks littered the hillside. For two months after the encounter at 'the town by the willows', the Romans were as successful as the Russians would be:

Since everything that could serve as food throughout the lands of
Scythia and Moesia [the two Roman provinces north of the
Haemus] had been used up, the barbarians, driven alike by ferocity
and hunger, strove with all their might to break out . . . After
many attempts, they were overwhelmed by the vigour of our
men, who strongly opposed them amid the rugged heights.

The Romans were desperately trying to buy time, hoping that the
arrival of winter would bring the campaigning to an end and give
Valens and Gratian time to bring reinforcements to the Balkans by
springtime.

Their hopes, however, were misplaced. 'Just as autumn was
turning to winter',[45] intelligence reports came in that the Goths had
found new allies. A force of Huns and Alans had been recruited to the
Gothic cause by promises of booty. When he heard this, the Roman
commander decided that the passes could no longer be held. As soon
as one pass was forced, the soldiers holding the others would be cut
off and stand little chance against the numerically superior Goths. He
lost no time in pulling back his troops. For the most part the retreat
worked, but one Roman detachment was caught in the open at a
major crossroads near Dibaltum south of the Haemus Mountains, and
seems to have been exterminated.[46] The Goths, now with Hunnic
and Alan allies (who need not have been very numerous to swing
the delicate balance of power back in the Goths' favour), were free
again to rampage south of the Haemus Mountains. They did so, to
telling effect, in dispersed groups throughout the winter of 377/8,
'filling [as Ammianus tells us] the whole country as far as [the
province of] Rhodope and the strait which separates the two great
seas [the Hellespont] with a most foul confusion of robbery, murder,
bloodshed, fires, and shameful violation of the bodies of freemen.'

This time the raiding spread wider and lasted longer, but there was
plenty to occupy the Goths on the rich Thracian Plain, and the damage
extended no further west than the eastern slopes of the Rhodope
Mountains. Ammianus treats us to another lengthy account of Roman
misery rather than giving any precise details, but other sources tell us
that the Goths came close to the walls of Constantinople, where they
were finally driven off by Arab auxiliary forces in Roman service. The
Arabs' habit of drinking the blood from the slit throats of their dead
opponents discouraged the Goths from pursuing the argument further,

but there were not enough Roman troops or allies available to take broader countermeasures. Until reinforcements started to arrive from the east, the Goths had plenty of time for some productive looting. Some of the damage shows up in the archaeological record. All the main excavated late Roman villas of the region, north and south of the Haemus Mountains, were abandoned at this point, most of them showing an extensive destruction layer.[47]

Sometime early in 378, the bulk of Valens' field forces began to arrive from the east. The army gathered slowly in the vicinity of Constantinople, as its units arrived from Mesopotamia and the Caucasus. It is probably wrong to imagine this happening very early in the year, since a Roman field army, like its counterparts everywhere until recent times, could not begin operations until the grass was growing sufficiently to feed the animals pulling its baggage and heavy equipment. Valens himself didn't arrive in Constantinople until 30 May, and this was probably more or less the point at which large-scale operations first became feasible. He received from the capital's population a far from warm welcome, and there was some rioting. Constantinople had been a hotbed of resistance to Valens during an attempted usurpation at the start of his reign, and there were also religious issues afoot. In addition, of course, many of the richer citizens would have recently suffered financial and other losses in the Gothic raiding. Once assembled after the long march from the east, his army rested in preparation for battle. Valens was an emperor with a great deal to prove.

THE ROMAN PLANS for 378 were well laid. By granting major concessions in the Caucasus, Valens had bought peace from the Persians and could shift most of his mobile forces back to the Balkans. Negotiations had continued with Gratian: the western emperor had promised to come in person to Thrace, bringing with him the western field army. The best troops from both halves of the Empire were thus gathering in order to put the Goths in their place. No source defines the precise aim of the joint campaign, but it is pretty easy to guess. The emperors were assembling enough troops to win a resounding victory; then it would be business as usual. Imperial invincibility would be seen to be re-established, and of those Goths who remained on Roman territory some would die in amphitheatres across the Empire, some would be drafted into the army, and the majority widely distributed as unfree labour.

But in the fourth century, as in any other, 'no plan survives first contact with the enemy'. In this case, the enemy took an unexpected form. As Gratian was collecting his expeditionary army in the west, it became obvious, from the other side of the frontier, that gaps were appearing in the Roman defensive line-up on the Upper Rhine and Upper Danube. The news was confirmed by a Roman soldier of Germanic origin returning home to his people the Lentienses, a branch of the Alamanni, who inhabited the Alpine foothills on the frontiers of Roman Raetia (modern Switzerland). In February 378, when Gratian had already sent many troops east to Pannonia in the Middle Danube region for the upcoming campaign, the Lentienses crossed the upper reaches of the frozen Rhine. This initial assault was repulsed, but Gratian received intelligence that it was merely an opening gambit, and that much more substantial attacks, by many thousands of Alamanni, were being planned. The emperor and his advisers decided that the Goths would have to wait. Part of the expeditionary army was pulled back west from Pannonia and more troops drafted in from Gaul, enough to allow Gratian to launch a strong pre-emptive assault. He was determined to secure his rear before turning east, and pressed home the assault to the point of a lengthy siege against the chief group of suspects, who were holed up on a mountain top. Slowly but surely the campaign ground on until the Lentienses surrendered and the ex-Roman soldier was punished.[48]

All of this made perfect sense from Gratian's perspective, but placed Valens in an impossible situation. He had arrived in Constantinople on 30 May and left the city twelve days later, advancing to an imperial villa at Melanthias, 50 kilometres further into Thrace, where his troops were concentrating. Pay and supplies were distributed and attempts made to bolster the troops' morale in preparation for the campaign. But Gratian failed to appear. And while Valens waited, the Goths were far from idle. Their foraging parties continued to operate and their main forces were distributed between Nicopolis and Beroea, thus controlling both ends of the strategic Shipka Pass. The Goths, it would seem, were keeping their options open: they might move on north, or south through the Haemus Mountains. At this point, Valens' generals got wind of a detached Gothic raiding party in the vicinity of Hadrianople, and rushed a column forward to ambush it. The night attack was a success, and prompted Gothic countermeasures. Fritigern called in all his raiding parties and moved the entire main

body, wagons and all, south of the Haemus Mountains to Cabyle –
then further south still, on to the Thracian Plain proper, to avoid the
danger of further ambushes. The endgame was fast approaching. The
mass of Goths were now north of Hadrianople on the main road from
Cabyle. Valens was south of Hadrianople, with his army collected and
rested. Gratian, however, was still nowhere to be seen, and summer
was dragging on.

Valens joined his army outside Constantinople on 12 June. But
July came and went, and still no Gratian. The eastern army had been
sitting around for the best part of two months, and nothing had
happened except for the ambush of one Gothic raiding party. The
troops were becoming restive and morale was ebbing away. Then,
instead of Gratian's army, a letter arrived minutely detailing the
victories the western emperor had won over the Alamanni. He was,
he promised, still coming; but it was already August, late on in the
season, and Gratian's successes touched a nerve. Valens' patience
was fast approaching breaking-point. Then came news of the Goths'
advance south towards Hadrianople. Intelligence reports put the
Gothic numbers at only 10,000 fighting men, many fewer than Valens
was expecting. This figure was based, I believe, on the misconception
that only Fritigern's Tervingi, and not the Tervingi and Greuthungi
combined, were nearing Hadrianople at this point. Jealous of Gratian's
success, Valens was deeply tempted. Was this an opportunity to win a
morale- and esteem-boosting victory over a significant number of the
enemy? Opinion among his generals was divided. Some urged bold-
ness; others counselled waiting for Gratian. Provisionally, the hawks
won. Trumpets sounded the advance, and Valens' army moved in
battle order up to Hadrianople, then constructed a defended marching
camp (temporary earth ramparts) outside the city.

Now more letters arrived from Gratian. He was on the move, and
his advance guard had kept open the vital Succi Pass between the
Haemus and Rhodope Mountains, so that he could move straight
down the great military road to Hadrianople. Some of Valens' generals
continued to argue for delay, therefore, but as Ammianus reports, 'the
fatal insistence of the emperor prevailed, supported by the flattering
opinion of some of his courtiers, who urged him to make all haste so
that Gratian might not have a share in the victory which, as they
represented, was already all but won.'

On the night of 8/9 August, with the two sides now in close

proximity, Fritigern sent a Christian priest to Valens as a peace envoy, but the emperor would have none of it. At dawn, the Roman army hastened on to the north of Hadrianople, leaving its baggage and a suitable guard in the marching camp; the imperial treasury and other more valuable items were left inside the city walls. All morning the Romans marched north, until, at about two in the afternoon, the Gothic wagon circle ('as if turned by a lathe', as Ammianus puts it) came into view. As the Roman army deployed, two further sets of Gothic peace envoys arrived. Valens dithered. He was in the process of arranging an exchange of hostages when two regiments on the Roman right wing, without having been ordered to do so, surged forward to attack. After months of waiting, battle had finally begun in earnest.[49]

Accounts of ancient battles are never all you would like them to be. Ancient audiences wanted to hear about great deeds of derring-do, not military science. In the case of Hadrianople, in fact, Ammianus presents us with one of his best efforts at battle depiction. The Goths had drawn up their wagons in a circle to reinforce their battle line; the Romans deployed with a mixture of cavalry and infantry on each wing, and the bulk of the heavy infantry in the centre. Although the left wing had not fully formed when the battle began, it seemed, at first, to be making the most progress. It pushed the oncoming Goths right back to their wagon circle and was on the verge of carrying even that by storm, when disaster struck. As the Roman left wing surged forward, Gothic cavalry under Alatheus and Saphrax, combined with some Alans (presumably the ones with whom an alliance had been made the previous autumn), 'dashed out as a thunderbolt does near high mountains and threw into confusion all those whom they could find in the way of their sudden onslaught and quickly slew them'. With both Tervingi and Greuthungi confronting him on the battlefield, Valens was now exposed to a far larger enemy force than he had imagined. He had given battle on mistaken intelligence, and the Goths had achieved complete tactical surprise.

Ammianus is not absolutely clear about what happened next, but the Gothic cavalry seems to have smashed into the Roman left wing. It was certainly from the left wing that the disaster unfolded. First, its cavalry support was dispersed and then its main force was over-whelmed – caught, perhaps, between the defenders of the wagon circle and the onrushing Gothic cavalry. The destruction of the left wing in turn exposed the Roman centre to a massive flanking attack. Since the Romans were in their customary close order – in the fourth century they often still operated the *testudo* (tortoise) wall-of-shields formation – the effect was calamitous:

> The foot-soldiers thus stood unprotected, and their companies were so crowded together that hardly anyone could pull out his sword or draw back his arm . . . arrows, whirling death from every side, always found their mark with fatal effect since they could not be seen beforehand nor guarded against . . . and in the press of ranks no room for retreat could be gained anywhere, and the increased crowding left no opportunity for retreat.

Indeed, the heavy Roman infantry regiments of the centre were so closely pressed together that they had no hope of manoeuvring to bring the weight of their weaponry to bear. Their normal tactical advantages in arms, armour and training now counted for nothing.

The troops were also reaching exhaustion point. Valens had pushed them into battle, without rest or food, after an eight-hour march in the August sun; on the Thracian Plain, the average midday temperature at this time of year approaches 30 degrees Celsius. The Goths had turned the temperature up even further by taking advantage of a favourable wind to light huge fires, which were now pouring smoke and heat down on their opponents. After fierce fighting, the main Roman battle line eventually broke and fled. The result, as always in such circumstances, was a massacre. Army and emperor perished together. What exactly happened to Valens, nobody knew for sure. His body was never found. Some said that, wounded, he was taken to a farmhouse which the Goths surrounded and burned to the ground when arrows were fired at them from an upper window, and that one of his attendants escaped to tell the story. Ammianus doesn't seem to have believed this account, although it is widely reported. Perhaps the emperor was stranded and simply cut down in anonymous fashion somewhere on the battlefield.

Valens' gamble had failed. The emperor himself was dead, and the Goths, against all expectations, had won a stunning victory, destroying in the process the best army of the eastern Roman Empire. How many Roman troops died that day is hotly disputed. Ammianus tells us that thirty-five officers of tribune rank (approximately equal to regimental commander) died, along with two-thirds of the troops. From a complete listing of the eastern army dating from about 395, about twenty years after the event, we also know that sixteen elite regiments suffered such severe losses that they were never reconstituted. But none of this gives us a total figure, since we don't know the size of the original army and a number of the dead tribunes will have been staff officers rather than unit commanders. Some historians think that Valens brought with him upwards of 30,000 men – 20,000 dead at Hadrianople, then. Even given the peace deal with Persia, however, the emperor could not afford to denude the east of all its troops and we have to remember that he was expecting reinforcements from Gratian. My own opinion is that Valens brought more like fifteen thousand men to the Balkans in 378, and was looking for a similar number from Gratian. Between them, these forces would have enjoyed a 1.5:1–2:1 advantage over the Goths, which ought to have been more than enough. But because of the faulty intelligence report, Valens gave battle at Hadrianople, in my view, with perhaps a slight numerical disadvantage instead of, as he thought, a 1.5:1 advantage over just the Tervingi. His force was undone by the Goths' extra numbers, but above all by the huge tactical surprise they brought off. If I'm right, Roman losses on 9 August will have been more in the region of 10,000 men.[50]

But in an important sense, the quarrel over numbers is academic. The central point is that Valens' jealousy of Gratian, and his impatience, had undone the Empire. In Ammianus' view, the Romans had known no such defeat since the battle of Cannae in 216 BC, when Hannibal had annihilated a whole imperial army. Victory left the Goths masters not only of the battlefield, but of the entire Balkans. Roman military invincibility had been overturned in a single afternoon, and Gratian could only look on helplessly from the other side of the Succi Pass, about 300 kilometres distant, as the triumphant Goths rampaged through the southern Balkans. Against all the odds, and despite their opponents' advantages in equipment and training, the Goths had triumphed and the path to Constantinople lay open. As Ammianus reports, 'From [Hadrianople] they hastened in rapid march to Constantinople, greedy for its vast heaps of treasure, marching in square formations for fear of ambuscades, and intending to make many mighty efforts to destroy the famous city.'

Valens was dead, his army destroyed; the eastern Roman Empire was there for the taking.

'Peace in Our Time'

I'VE NEVER QUITE known whether to believe the vignette with which Ammianus, on almost the last page of his history, takes his leave of the Gothic war. Having shown us the victorious Goths preparing to besiege Constantinople, he then feeds us the following image:

> [The Goths'] courage was broken when they beheld the oblong circuit of the walls, the blocks of houses covering a vast space, the beauties of the city beyond their reach, the vast population inhabiting it, and the strait nearby that separates the Black Sea from the Aegean. So they destroyed the stores of military equipment they were preparing . . . and spread everywhere across the northern provinces.[51]

It is almost too good to be true: a perfect metaphor for the entire war. And you have to remember that, by the time he was writing, in the early 390s, Ammianus knew the outcome of the war even if he chose to end his account in 378. Victory over Valens at Hadrianople was just enough to give the Goths a glimpse of the prize that was Constantinople; but that in turn was enough to convince them that they hadn't the slightest chance of capturing it.

The Goths faced three overwhelming disadvantages that made it impossible for them to defeat the Roman Empire outright. First, even if, taking the maximum conceivable figure, we reckon that there were 200,000 of them in all, with the capacity to produce an army of 40–50,000 men – although I do think this figure too high – this would still have been rather paltry compared with the grand sum of imperial resources. The Empire's army totalled, as we've seen, 300–600,000, and its population was in excess of 70 million (a minimum figure). In a fight to the death, there could be only one winner, and the cannier Goths – some of whom among the Tervingi had travelled the breadth of Roman Asia Minor to fight in the Persian wars – were perfectly well aware of this. Fritigern's peace overtures to Valens before Hadrianople show that he, for one, never lost his sense of perspective. He told Valens that, if the imperial army put on a decent enough show of martial intimidation, he would be able to persuade his followers to reel in their military ardour and make a compromise peace.[52] The quid pro quo that Fritigern had in mind for himself, interestingly enough,

was that Valens should recognize him as king of all the now allied
Goths, thus cutting out Alatheus and Saphrax, not to mention all
his other would-be rivals among the Tervingi. As it turned out, the
imperial army failed to deliver its part of the deal, perishing virtually
to a man. But, a bit like Pearl Harbor, when there is a fundamental
mismatch in resources and capacity one shock victory at the beginning
of a struggle can't change its course.

To this fundamental problem we can add two more. First, there is
no record of the Goths taking any major fortified imperial centre
during the six years of war. Conditions clearly became fraught in the
Roman Danubian communities that were cut off from the centre for
extended periods; we don't know, for instance, if and when they were
able to plant crops. But no city was ever taken by siege.[53] This meant
that the Goths were unable to get their hands on stocks of weapons
and supplies, or to set themselves up in a defended stronghold of their
own. The second problem arrived on the back of the first. The Gothic
force at large south of the Danube between 377 and 382 wasn't just an
army, but an entire population group: men, women and children,
dragging themselves and their possessions around in a huge wagon
train. With no secure lands available to them for food production, and
unable to break into fortified storehouses, the Goths were forced to
pillage in order to eat, and, because so much food was required, it was
extremely difficult for them to stay in the one place. Already in
autumn 377, there was nothing left north of the Haemus Mountains,
and the pattern of the subsequent war years, in so far as we can
reconstruct it, saw them moving from one part of the Balkans to
another. Sometimes it was the Roman army that forced them on, but
this restlessness was largely attributable to their lack of secure food
supplies.

Victory at Hadrianople allowed the Goths to range as they wished
in Thrace during the rest of 378. The next year, however, even though
the Empire had no more than light skirmishing forces available in the
eastern Balkans, they shifted the centre of their operations further west
into Illyricum, the combined Gothic force advancing north-west over
the Succi Pass into Dacia and Upper Moesia (map 6). In 380, Tervingi
and Greuthungi then divided, perhaps because of the difficulty of
supplying their combined numbers. Alatheus and Saphrax moved
further north into Pannonia, where they were defeated, it seems,
by the forces of the western emperor Gratian. The Tervingi under

Fritigern moved south and east along the Morava–Vardar trunk road to Thessalonica and the provinces of Macedonia and Thessaly. They seem to have learned from previous experience, contenting themselves with exacting only a moderate tribute from the cities – repeatedly taking protection money – rather than trashing the place and moving on. Whether this would have continued we cannot know, because in 381 forces of the western Empire drove the Goths back into Thrace, perhaps this time along the Via Egnatia rather than through the heart of the Balkans. It was in Thrace again, finally, in 382 that peace was made.[54]

The Roman Empire, however, could not in the end, after six years of war, claim total victory, although the formal ceremony that inaugurated the peace treaty on 3 October 382 certainly took the form of a Gothic surrender. Themistius was again an eyewitness, and he leaves us in no doubt:

> We have seen their leaders and chiefs, not making a show of surrendering a tattered standard, but giving up the weapons and swords with which up to that day they had held power, and clinging to the king's [the emperor Theodosius'] knees more tightly than Thetis, according to Homer, clung to the knees of Zeus when she besought him on her son's behalf, until they won a kindly nod and a voice which did not rouse war but was full of kindness, full of peace, full of benevolence and the forgiveness of sins.[55]

But Themistius' vocabulary immediately signals that this was not the kind of peace deal that normally followed Roman victories over hostile would-be immigrants. The language of 'kindness', 'benevolence' and 'forgiveness' strikes a new note, and the difference is not merely rhetorical. For the surrender generated no theatrical bloodbaths, no mass selling of Goths into slavery, no large-scale distributions of Gothic captives as unfree farm labourers. When, in 383, an emperor wanted to reassure the population of Rome that the Empire was once more secure, it was Sarmatians who were slaughtered in the Colosseum, not Goths. But the Goths had killed a Roman emperor, destroyed a Roman army, and laid waste with fire and rapine large tracts of the Roman Balkans. In a world where a Roman emperor considered himself well within his rights to throw a fit if 'barbarian' ambassadors didn't grovel with sufficient conviction, the absence of revenge, punishment and example-setting in the peace settlement of 382 is extraordinary.

Once again, we don't know everything we'd like to know about the terms agreed. They clearly broke new ground in some important ways, but although they were strikingly generous to them, the Goths did not get everything they may have wanted. Before Hadrianople, Gothic peace offers tended towards the possibility of Thrace becoming an independent Gothic kingdom. Fritigern, as we've seen, was also angling to have Valens recognize him as new overall leader of all the Gothic immigrants. Neither of these things happened. Neither Fritigern nor Alatheus nor Saphrax survived to participate in the peace deal. They may have died in battle somewhere, but, if not, I have no problem in seeing their overthrow as part of the price the Goths had to pay for peace. The Empire needed tokens of victory to show off to its taxpayers, and the survival – indeed prosperity – of the victors of Hadrianople would have been completely unacceptable. Indeed, for the next decade or so, in a replay within the frontier of the policy commonly pursued towards the Alamanni beyond the Rhine (see Chapter 3), the Romans refused to recognize any overall Gothic leader, no doubt hoping to keep them politically divided. Nor did the Goths as a whole get Thrace as an independent fiefdom. The integrity of the diocese of Thrace as a centrally run unit of the Roman Empire was reasserted with vigour. Frontier fortifications were rebuilt and remanned where necessary; Roman law and tax-gathering resumed. In this sense, Gothic ambitions had been pruned right back.

At the same time, the Goths were given grants of land for themselves, not to farm for others as unfree tenant farmers. We don't know exactly where these were located. Some were north of the Haemus Mountains in Lower Moesia and Scythia close to the Danube, where the Carpi had lived around the turn of the fourth century, but there may also have been some settlements in Macedonia.[56] Much more important, wherever they were, they were clearly in sufficiently large clusters to allow the political and cultural life of the Goths to continue. This is explicitly acknowledged in Roman sources of the late 390s, and shows up implicitly in the narrative of intervening events. One of the things that the Empire got from the peace deal was a military alliance. Not only did it take the normal draft of Gothic recruits for its regular army, but the Goths also agreed to provide much larger forces, serving under their own leaders, for specific

campaigns. These times of special service required the emperor to
negotiate with leading Goths as a group. On the one occasion for
which we have details, we learn that the emperor Theodosius threw a
great feast for them.[57] If, in 382, the three leaders of the revolt were
sacrificed as part of the peace deal, a large number of their peers
clearly survived to sustain some sense of Gothic community. Under
the peace, despite losing the right to operate independently under the
leader of their choice, the Goths continued to enjoy the freedom to
negotiate and act as one, with or against the Roman state, as we shall
see in the next chapter.[58] The break with established ways of dealing
with immigrants could not be clearer.

According to Themistius, speaking to the Senate of Constantinople
in January 383, this transformation in imperial policy was the result of
some divinely inspired decision-making on the part of Valens' successor
Theodosius.[59]

> He was the first who dared entertain the notion that the power
> of the Romans did not now lie in weapons, nor in breastplates,
> spears and unnumbered manpower, but that there was need of
> some other power and provision, which, to those who rule in
> accordance with the will of God, comes silently from that source,
> which subdues all nations, turns all savagery to mildness and to
> which alone arms, bows, cavalry, the intransigence of the Scythi-
> ans, the boldness of the Alans, the madness of the Massagetai
> yield.

Taking his inspiration from God – and it was really to Him that he
owed his appointment as eastern emperor – Theodosius understood
that a better and more total victory could be won through forgiveness
than by arms. Consequently, his chief negotiator 'led the Goths [to the
emperor] docile and amenable, all but twisting their hands behind their
backs, so that it was a matter of doubt whether he had beaten the
men in war or won their friendship'. And the overall outcome, for
Romans and Goths, was better for both:

> If the Goths have not been utterly wiped out, no complaint
> should be raised . . . Was it then better to fill Thrace with corpses
> or with farmers? To make it full of tombs or living men? . . . I
> hear from those who have returned from there that they are now
> turning the metal of their swords and breastplates into hoes and
> pruning hooks, and that while paying distant respect to Ares [god

of war], they offer prayers to Demeter [goddess of corn and fruitfulness] and Dionysus [god of wine].

The Goths, Themistius told the Senate, have given up fighting for farming, and everyone has gained. Theodosius, Themistius' new employer, had come up with a brilliant solution – forgiveness for the Goths and a compromise peace that would subdue them more thoroughly than war ever could, while considerably benefiting the Empire. Once again, it's important to remember the tyranny of imperial ideology and the fact that Themistius was a remarkably adept propagandist (over a thirty-year period, he managed to create a niche for himself with no fewer than four imperial employers). As usual, he was being economical with the truth – before coming up with his peace deal, Theodosius had had a pretty good shot at winning the Gothic war by more conventional means.

The death of Valens had left a power vacuum which lasted until Gratian appointed Theodosius as his counterpart in the east in January 379. The new emperor had clearly been appointed to avenge Hadrianople. He came from a distinguished military family – his father was a five-star general under the emperor Valentinian I – and he had a good military record of his own. Immediately he was given temporary control of part of the prefecture of Illyricum – the dioceses of Dacia and Macedonia – which belonged to the western Empire, in order to exercise a unified control over the entire area vulnerable to the rampaging Goths. He spent his first year in office rebuilding the eastern field army: calling up veterans, recruiting new units, and drafting in more troops from Egypt and other parts of the east. Themistius' first speech for the new emperor, in spring 379, confirms the thrust of all of this activity: the emperor's initial self-presentation was as 'the man to win the Gothic war' –

It is because of ... you [Theodosius] that we have taken a stand ... and believe that you shall now check the impetus of success for the Scythians [the Goths] and quench the conflagration that devours all things ... Fighting spirit returns to the cavalry and returns to the infantry. Already you make even farmers a terror to the barbarian ... If you, though not yet in the field against the guilty ones [the Goths], have checked their wilfulness merely by pitching camp nearby and lying in blockade, what do we suppose those damned villains will suffer, when they see you readying

your spear and brandishing your shield, the lightning flash from
your helm gleaming close at hand?[60]

Unfortunately, things didn't work out as planned. Theodosius' new
model army fell apart when it tried to take on the Goths head to head
in Macedonia and Thessaly in the summer of 380. The circumstances
are mysterious – the sources hint at treachery and unreliability. It was
not another bloody catastrophe like Hadrianople, but there's no doubt
that Theodosius failed and that the Goths overcame a second Roman
army. In the autumn, Theodosius had to hand back control of the war
to Gratian's generals, and it was they who eventually drove the Goths
from Thessaly in summer 381, while he ran for cover in Constantinople
to secure his political position there in the aftermath of military
failure.[61]

Theodosius may have come up with a new plan, then, but not
without trying traditional means first. He turned to diplomatic innovation in 382 only because military incapacity – the defeat of *two*
Roman armies – required it. And this was the only time he resorted to
such a deal. If he had won the war, I have not the slightest doubt that
the normal terms would have been imposed upon any defeated Goths
left inside the Empire. When, four years after 382, another group of
Goths tried to force their way across the Danube, they were massacred
in large numbers. Some of the survivors were drafted into the army,
the rest distributed as unfree tenant farmers – both groups sent far
afield, to Asia Minor.[62]

The Goths might be hounded out of rich areas like Thessaly,
ground down by constant battering of their raiding parties, starved
into submission. But after the summer of 380 the Romans would not
risk another set-piece battle.

Given that it was impossible, as we've seen, to admit that a God-
appointed emperor had ever been forced into a course of action by
barbarians or even by circumstances beyond his control, Themistius
came remarkably close, in January 383, to telling the truth, making
little attempt to downplay Roman disarray at the time of Theodosius'
appointment:

> . . . after the indescribable Iliad of evils on the Ister and the onset
> of the monstrous flame [of war], when there was not yet a king
> set over the affairs of the Romans, with Thrace laid waste, with
> Illyria laid waste, when whole armies had vanished completely

like a shadow, when neither impassable mountains, unfordable rivers, nor trackless wastes stood in the way, but when finally nearly the whole of the earth and sea had united beside the barbarians.

Nor did he pretend that Theodosius could easily have chosen to press the war to a fully victorious conclusion:

> ... just suppose that this destruction was an easy matter and that we possessed the means to accomplish it without suffering any consequences, although from past experience this was neither a foregone nor likely conclusion, nevertheless just suppose, as I said, that this solution lay within our power ...

For the man who had felt constrained to claim, in 364, that the loss of provinces, cities and fortresses to Persia was actually a Roman victory, this is not so far removed from an admission that Theodosius had had no choice but to opt for a compromise peace with the Goths.

'This Is Not Yet the End'

THE TRADITIONAL INTEGRITY of the Roman state had been breached, but we mustn't get carried away. We are still a long way from imperial collapse. The war on the Danube had affected only the Empire's Balkan provinces, a relatively poor and isolated frontier zone, and even here some kind of Romanness survived. The late fourth- and early fifth-century layers of the recently excavated Roman city of Nicopolis ad Istrum are striking for the number of rich houses – 45 per cent of the urban area – that suddenly appeared inside the city walls.[63] It looks as though, since their country villas were now too vulnerable, the rich were running their estates from safe inside the city walls. At the end of the war, moreover, both eastern and western emperors remained in secure occupation of their thrones, with their great revenue-producing centres such as Asia Minor, Syria, Egypt and North Africa entirely untouched. And most parts of the Empire hadn't even seen a Goth.

In his final spin on the peace deal Themistius tried to reassure Roman taxpayers that the Goths would lose even their semi-autonomy in due course. He took, as a case in point, some Celtic-speaking barbarians who had crossed the Hellespont in 278 BC and carved out the territory of Galatia (named after themselves) in Asia Minor, but who over the next centuries became fully assimilated into Graeco-Roman culture.[64] Given the huge disparity in resources between themselves and the Roman Empire, it no doubt did seem that the Goths' present status must eventually be reversed, whether by long-term assimilation, as Themistius archly evokes, or, much more likely, by renewed conflict once the Roman army had been properly rebuilt. As events turned out, Themistius' confidence was misplaced. The descendants of the Tervingi and Greuthungi were destined not only to survive as Goths, but would eventually carve out on Roman soil the fully independent kingdom that they had originally sought. Writing soon after Hadrianople, Bishop Ambrose of Milan summarized the prevailing crisis with admirable economy: 'The Huns fell upon the Alans, the Alans upon the Goths and Taifali, the Goths and Taifali upon the Romans, and this is not yet the end.'[65] The bishop had in mind only the ongoing war with the Goths, but his words were prescient. The Empire would never get the chance to reopen the Gothic question on its own terms. Hadrianople was indeed not yet the end, and the Empire would have many more challenges to face before the full effects of the Hunnic revolution worked themselves out.

5

THE CITY OF GOD

ON A HOT AUGUST DAY IN 410, the unthinkable happened. A large force of Goths entered Rome by the Salarian Gate and for three days helped themselves to the city's wealth. The sources, without being specific, speak clearly of rape and pillage. There was, of course, much loot to be had, and the Goths had a field day. By the time they left, they had cleaned out many of the rich senatorial houses as well as all the temples, and had taken ancient Jewish treasures that had resided in Rome since the destruction of Solomon's temple in Jerusalem over three hundred years before. They also left with treasure of another sort: Galla Placidia, sister of the reigning western emperor Honorius. And arson too had been on the agenda – the area around the Salarian gate and the old Senate building had been among the casualties.

The Roman world was shaken to its foundations. After centuries as mistress of the known world, the great imperial capital had been subjected to a smash-and-grab raid of epic proportions. In the Holy Land, St Jerome, an émigré from Rome, put it succinctly: 'In one city, the whole world perished.' Pagan reactions were more pointed: 'If Rome hasn't been saved by its guardian deities, it's because they are no longer there; for as long as they were present, they preserved the City.'[1] The adoption of Christianity, in other words, had led to this devastation. But the immediate emotional reaction to any great event is rarely the best indicator of its real significance. Reconstructing the causes, and especially the true importance, of the sack of Rome is a detective story of great complexity. It will take us back in time over the best part of two decades before that fateful summer day, and forward again for another. Geographically, the story ranges from the Caucasus Mountains in the east to the Iberian Peninsula in the west. What emerges is that, while the sack of Rome might have seemed fatefully symbolic at the time, in itself it did no fundamental harm to the Empire's capacity to fight back.

All Chaos on the Western Front

NO SINGLE SOURCE lays out for us in one clear sequence everything leading up to this momentous event, let alone explores their underlying cause. In part, this is testimony to its complexity. The sack of Rome was the end product of an interaction between multiple protagonists that no contemporary historian – none, at least, whose work has survived – was able to understand in its entirety. There is also a more specific reason why the event presents us with so many difficulties. Much of the history of the period AD 407–25 was covered in a lengthy work by a well informed contemporary writer, Olympiodorus of Thebes, whose writings we briefly dipped into earlier. Originating in Egypt, and of impeccable classical education, he found employment in the Foreign Office of the eastern Empire, conducting a series of diplomatic missions, most notably to the Huns, accompanied for more than twenty years by his pet parrot who could 'dance, sing, call its owner's name, and do many other tricks'. Olympiodorus wrote in Greek, not Latin, and his style was less rhetorical and dramatic than was popular at the time – for which fault he apologized to his readers. This was a bonus for the modern reader, of course: his history is less overblown and more straightforwardly informative than, for instance, Ammianus Marcellinus' account of the Gothic war in the Balkans. Unfortunately, though, Olympiodorus' history does not survive in full. Some four hundred years later one Photius, a Byzantine bibliophile and (briefly) Patriarch of Constantinople, produced a long work – the *Bibliotheca* – which summarized the contents of his library; luckily for us, Olympiodorus' history was one of the volumes. From Photius' brief description, we can also tell that, much nearer to the time, the work was heavily drawn upon by two other writers, the Church historian Sozomen in the mid-fifth century and the pagan historian Zosimus in the early sixth. Both were interested in the sack of Rome and wrote out large, more or less intact chunks of the first part of Olympiodorus' history, down to the year 410. For our purposes, this is clearly a good thing, but both abridged and reworked the text for their own purposes, and in so doing introduced mistakes. In particular, Zosimus, trying to join as seamlessly as possible the work of his two main sources Olympiodorus and Eunapius, which slightly overlapped at the early fifth century, omitted some key events and garbled others.[2]

AFTER THE APPEARANCE of our Gothic asylum seekers on the Danube in 376, relative calm returned to Rome's European frontiers for the best part of a generation. The peace was shattered again, however, between 405 and 408, when four major incursions overturned frontier security all the way from the Rhine to the Carpathian Mountains. The Carpathians form the east wing of the central European mountain chain which also includes the Alps. They start and finish on the River Danube, running about 1,300 kilometres from the Slovak capital Bratislava in the west to Orsova in the east, describing a huge east-facing arc (map 7). They are generally lower than the Alps, with only a few summits over 2,500 metres, and no permanent glaciers or snowfields. Their width varies dramatically between about 10 and 350 kilometres, and their western, narrower end is penetrated by many

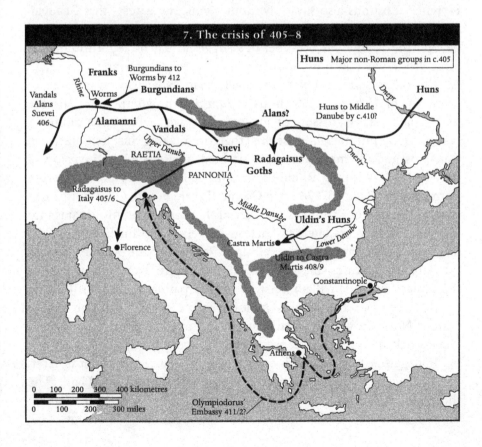

7. The crisis of 405–8

more passes than the eastern slopes facing out towards the Great Eurasian Steppe. The Carpathians have always functioned as a defining feature of European geography, separating eastern and central Europe on the one hand, and north and south on the other. Their significance is also historical, and the organization of the later Roman Empire reflected this. The Danube region east of Orsova, the Lower Danube, belonged to Thrace and was administered from the east, whereas the Middle Danube, west and south of the mountains, protected the passes into Italy and was always part of the west. To understand the various invasions of the early fifth century, we must situate the action against this Carpathian backdrop.

In 405/6, a pagan Gothic king by the name of Radagaisus led a large force across the Alps into Italy. Because of Zosimus' garbling of Olympiodorus' history, our knowledge of this attack is patchy. Most glaringly, Zosimus reports that Radagaisus was defeated beyond the frontier, when he was actually captured at Fiesole and executed outside Florence. Zosimus also says – without giving any dates – that Radagaisus gathered under him a mass of Celtic and Germanic peoples from beyond the Rhine and Danube; this suggests that he led a multiracial force from what is now southern Germany, Austria and Bohemia.[3] All the other sources insist, however, that Radagaisus was a leader primarily of Goths. As Zosimus' reworking nowhere mentions the slightly later Rhine crossing of 406, which, as we shall see in a moment, was indeed multiracial, it seems that, in making his join between Eunapius and Olympiodorus, he jumbled up Radagaisus' invasion of Italy in 405/6 with the Rhine crossing of 406.[4] One key point emerges immediately. Back in 376, the Gothic Tervingi and Greuthungi had crossed the Lower Danube from east of the Carpathian Mountains into Thrace. Thirty years later, the action moved a step further west. The fact that Radagaisus' invasion fell upon Italy, without passing through the Balkans, indicates that he invaded the Empire from somewhere on the Great Hungarian Plain west of the Carpathians (map 7). Judging by finds of coin hoards, his invasion route passed through south-eastern Noricum and western Pannonia; it also generated a stream of panic-stricken refugees who preceded him over the Alps.[5]

Radagaisus met his end on 23 August 406. Four months later, on 31 December, a mixed force crossed the Rhine into Gaul. The three largest groupings were Vandals, Alans and Suevi – the Vandals in two separate political units, the Hasdings and the Silings. Like that of Radagaisus, this second assault on the Empire also originated west of the Carpathian Mountains. In winter 401/2, the Vandals had raided the Roman province of Raetia, which places them, immediately before the Rhine crossing, somewhere in the Middle or Upper Danube region (map 7). For most of the fourth century they had lived further away from the Roman frontier, more to the north-east, but still west of the Carpathians, in what is now Slovakia and southern Poland.[6] The identity of the Suevi is more problematic. The term is often used of an old Germanic confederation of the early imperial period, but between about AD 150 and the Rhine crossing itself it is no longer found in the Roman sources. Its reappearance probably indicates that some of the Marcomanni and Quadi (and possibly also Alamanni), who had formed part of that early Roman confederation and had been settled in the Middle Danube region since that time, were participants in the attack. Quadi, at least, are specifically mentioned in one source as taking part in the crossing of 406, and in the fifth century 'Suevi' came back into use as a general term for Germanic people who continued to live around the Danube bend and the fringes of the Great Hungarian Plain – presumably the descendants of other Marcomanni and Quadi who had not participated in the Rhine crossing.[7] Both Vandals and Suevi, therefore, originated west of the Carpathians, as did other, smaller groups mentioned only by St Jerome: particularly Sarmatians and 'hostile Pannonians' (*hostes Pannonii*).[8] As with the events of 377–82, disaffected elements among the Roman population played some part in the action (see p. 173).

The history of the Alans, Iranian-speaking nomads exploiting the dry steppe lands east of the River Don, is more complicated. As late as roughly 370, they had lived over 3,500 kilometres away from the Rhine. The first population group to feel the force of the increasing power of the Huns, some Alans quickly fell under their domination. But the Alans were organized into numerous autonomous subgroups, of which several remained independent of the Huns after 376, and many moved long distances west (both under their own steam and in company with Huns) in the generation after the Tervingi and Greuthungi initially crossed the Danube. Already in 377, a mixed force of Huns and Alans joined the Goths south of the Danube, their arrival forcing the Romans to abandon their defence of the Haemus Mountains. In 378, the emperor Gratian had 'unexpectedly' encountered more Alans at Castra Martis in Dacia Ripensis, west of the Carpathians, which delayed still further his march to join Valens. In the early 380s, Zosimus records, the same emperor recruited a particularly large force of Alans into the *western* Roman army.[9] Thus, while the Alans originated east of the Don, many of them quickly moved west of the Carpathians under the impact of Hunnic power. While they proceeded in different directions, then, the attacks of Radagaisus in 405/6 and the Rhine crossing in 406 both originated in the same broad region of Germanic Europe.

The third major invasion of this decade involved a Hunnic leader by the name of Uldin, and happened further east. Previously a Roman ally, in 408 he changed allegiances. Crossing the Danube with a force of Huns and Sciri, he seized Castra Martis and, addressing some plainly confused Roman ambassadors, he made some extravagant claims: 'He [pointed] to the sun, and [declared] that it would be easy for him, if he so desired, to subjugate every region of the earth that is enlightened by that luminary.' Precisely where we should place Uldin before this invasion is unclear. In 400, he had defeated a Roman rebel, who then fled north of the Danube through Thrace, which might place him north of the lower Danube (map 7). In 406, however, he had provided military aid to the Romans, in Italy, then two years later seized a major Roman base in Dacia Ripensis, west of Orsova. These later glimpses of him suggest that we should actually place him just west of the Carpathians, perhaps in the Banat or Oltenia. The arrogance of Uldin's claims has led some to view him as the leader of a massive force. But what happened next tells us otherwise. Many of his followers were won over from their allegiance by east Roman diplomacy; the Roman army then killed or captured many of the others as they ran back hell for leather towards the Danube. Uldin is never heard of again, and his rhetoric sounds more like bluff than the arrogance of a major warlord. His gamble in seizing Castra Martis clearly backfired, and led directly to the destruction of his power base.[10]

The Burgundians, the fourth focus of our attention at this point, have gone down in history for their size, their taste in food and their hairdressing, thanks to the fifth-century Gallo-Roman poet and land-owner Sidonius, who at one point had to share his house with some of them:

Why . . . do you [an obscure senator by the name of Catullinus] bid me compose a song dedicated to Venus . . . placed as I am among long-haired hordes, having to endure Germanic speech, praising often with a wry face the song of the gluttonous Burgundian who spreads rancid butter on his hair? . . . You don't have a reek of garlic and foul onions discharged upon you at early morn from ten breakfasts, and you are not invaded even before dawn . . . by a crowd of giants.[11]

In the fourth century, the domain of the Burgundians lay to the east of the Alamanni, well outside Roman territory, between the Upper Rhine and the Upper Danube, just on the other side of an old Roman frontier line abandoned in the third century (map 7). By 411 they had moved about 250 kilometres to the north-west, and now straddled the Rhine in the region of Mainz and Coblenz, at points both inside and outside the Roman province of Lower Germania. This shifting of their centre of operations hardly compares with the wholesale incursions into Roman territory described above, but the Burgundians must nonetheless be considered alongside their more adventurous peers. Something was afoot at this time in Germania west of the Carpathians.[12] After an uneventful couple of decades, the barbarians were on the move again.

To grasp the significance of all this, we need some idea of the numbers involved. Sources for this period being what they are, we have no reliable figures, and some historians would argue that it is pointless even to raise the issue. In my view, however, there are a few pointers, direct and indirect, that between them suggest at least an order of magnitude. An important starting-point is the fact that both the attack of Radagaisus and the Rhine invasion involved mixed population groups: women, children and other noncombatants, as well as fighting men. The constituent elements of these migrant groups is not something that our Roman sources tend to dwell upon: their interest was always firmly focused on the men, those responsible for any military or political threat that a migrant force might pose to the Roman state. All the same, women and children are mentioned just about enough to confirm their presence in both groups. The wives and children of some of the followers of Radagaisus, who eventually found themselves drafted into the Roman army, were, we are told by Zosimus, quartered as hostages in a number of Italian cities.[13] For the Vandals, the Alans and the Suevi we have no evidence contemporary with their first moves across the Rhine; but another group of Alans, operating in Gaul with some Goths in the early 410s, certainly had their families in tow.[14] And when the main force of Vandals and Alans moved on to North Africa in the 420s (see Chapter 6), they certainly moved in large mixed groups of men, women and children. It is possible to argue that wives had been picked up en route, but I see no good reason to doubt that they had been present since 406. As in 376, whole communities were on the march.

As to the actual numbers, Uldin's force – to judge by the fact that they seized only the one town and were then easily dispersed – perhaps wasn't very large. Nonetheless, disposing of all the Sciri captured on his defeat posed the Constantinopolitan authorities a huge administrative headache, so that we must be talking of several thousand individuals.[15] Radagaisus' force of Goths, and the Vandals, Alans and Suevi, however, could each put much more substantial military forces into the field. To fight Radagaisus in 406, the western Empire was forced to mobilize thirty *numeri* (regiments) – on paper, at least 15,000 men[16] – as well as call upon allies such as the Alan auxiliaries under Sarus and the Huns of Uldin (making their last appearance in Roman colours before seizing Castra Martis in 408). On Radagaisus' defeat, 12,000 of his warriors were drafted into the Roman army, which still left enough over for the bottom to fall out of the slave market when the remaining prisoners were sold off. All of this suggests that Radagaisus' force originally consisted of 20,000-plus fighting men. The proportion of combatants to noncombatants is generally reckoned at something like 1:4–5, so that his total number of followers may have been heading towards the 100,000 mark.[17]

For the Vandals, Alans and Suevi who crossed the Rhine, the best indication comes from about two decades later, when the Vandals and Alans together are said to have numbered a maximum of 80,000, implying that they could field a military force of 15–20,000.[18] This followed very heavy losses inflicted especially on the Siling Vandals and Alans, and makes no allowance at all for the Suevi, so that the original force that crossed the Rhine probably numbered more like 30,000 warriors – again, therefore, around 100,000 people in total. For the Burgundians, two sources offer us the figure of 80,000, but Jerome thought it a total figure for the entire population (suggesting a military force of perhaps about 15,000), while the Spanish chronicler Orosius says this was the size of their army.[19] As with many of the figures for the groups involved in the invasions, none of this is very convincing, but they do suggest – in each case – military forces of at least 20,000-

plus, and total populations nearing 100,000. Such a scale is more than enough to explain how the immigrants were able to force their way across the Roman frontier in the first place. Late Roman military reorganization operated with substantial numbers of garrison troops stationed in a sequence of watch-towers and larger installations along the border: in the case of the Danube and Rhine, right on or adjacent to the river line. But these forces were designed to counter only endemic small-scale raiding; larger incursions, even of a few thousand warriors, were the job of the 'comitatensian' troops (see Glossary, *comitatenses*) stationed behind the frontier. Tens of thousands of barbarians, even if many were noncombatants, were well beyond the competence of border troops.

THESE VAST POPULATION displacements also show up in the archaeological evidence. Two geographically extensive material cultural systems dominated the southern regions of central and eastern Europe in the third and fourth centuries AD: the Cernjachov and Przeworsk (map 7). The Przeworsk was one of the old Germanic or Germanic-dominated cultures of central Europe, with a continuous history of development which, by about AD 400, stretched back well over half a millennium. In the fourth century, it covered what is now central and southern Poland, parts of Slovakia and the Czech Republic.

The Cernjachov system was a much more recent phenomenon, dating to the third century AD. By the later fourth, it had spread through what is now Wallachia, Moldavia and the southern Ukraine, from the Carpathians to the River Don. Old-style archaeology used to equate these kinds of culture with individual 'peoples', but they are much better understood as systems incorporating many separate population groups and political units. What created the boundaries of these cultural areas were not the political frontiers of a particular people, but the geographical limits within which population groups interacted with sufficient intensity to make some or all of the remains of their physical culture – pottery, metalwork, building styles, burial goods and so on – look very similar. The Cernjachov system was dominated by the military power of the Goths, but included other Germanic immigrants to the northern Black Sea region, together with indigenous Dacians of the Carpathian region and Iranian-speaking Sarmatians. The area it covered was subdivided into a number of separate kingdoms (see Chapter 3).

Given its much lengthier history, the Przeworsk area may have been culturally more unified, with a higher percentage of Germanic-speakers, but they were no more a political entity than were the Cernjachov areas. The Vandals were to be found within the Przeworsk confines, but also a number of other groups whose populations also interacted with those of the Cernjachov system, for many aspects of their material cultures, not least glass, were very similar. The main discernible difference between the two lay in the fact that Cernjachov populations rarely buried weapons with their dead, while Przeworsk populations did so regularly.

Both of these systems vanished in the late Roman period. A certain amount of controversy surrounds the date of the Cernjachov collapse, but all working on the problem agree that it had disappeared by about 450;[20] likewise, although it continued for longer in the north, the Przeworsk culture in southern Poland had disappeared by c.420. From the Ukraine in the east to Hungary in the west, traditional – in the Przeworsk case, very long-established – patterns of material remains thus disappeared between about AD 375 and 430.

When cultures were equated with peoples, it was natural to see 'culture collapse', as this phenomenon has come to be known, as reflecting mass migration: a given culture disappeared from an area with the people who generated it. And given that Vandals and Goths, traditionally equated with the Przeworsk and Cernjachov cultures, were appearing as immigrants in the Roman world at the same moment as the two cultures disappeared, this seemed logical enough. But since cultures actually reflect the interaction of mixed populations, culture collapse cannot be so easily explained. Iron Age Germanic cultures such as the Przeworsk and Cernjachov are identified on the basis of the continued development over time of particular items: especially pottery types – notably, fine wares – and metalwork of various kinds, such as weapons and personal ornaments. When we say that a culture has ended, what we mean is that a demonstrable continuity of development in these characteristic items ceases in the archaeological record. Whether the disappearance of these items means that an area's entire population had disappeared as well is debatable. Recently, some have argued that the characteristic items used to identify the Przeworsk and Cernjachov systems were all quite expensive, produced only for a relatively small military elite. Their disappearance need mean no more, theoretically, than that these consumers had moved on, leaving a substantial peasant population behind. Since this supposed peasantry used the kind of rough pottery that is impossible to date, and did not have metal ornaments, its persistence would be archaeologically invisible. The argument fits in with other attempts, the written and archaeological evidence notwithstanding, to argue that the migrations into the Roman Empire of the later fourth and early fifth centuries constituted a relatively small-scale phenomenon.

Even accepting that culture collapse doesn't have to mean the total disappearance of an existing population, I don't find this conclusion convincing. When you put Radagaisus, the Rhine crossing, Uldin and the Burgundians in their proper chronological and geographical relationship, it becomes clear that the years 405–10 saw a huge population displacement out of Germania west of the Carpathians. We are not able, and surely never will be, to put an absolute figure on the combined movements, or to reckon the migrants as a percentage of the total population of the areas affected. At the very least, though, culture collapse shows that these population movements were signifi- cant enough to transform the material culture of central Europe, where they originated. Written sources too, while far from complete, confirm that these migrations were not undertaken merely by a tiny social elite – unlike, for instance, the case of the Norman Conquest when, after 1066, only about 2,000 immigrant families moved in to take control of all the landed assets of the Anglo-Saxon kingdom. Radagaisus' force, for instance, included two categories of fighter, not just his elite warriors. This important piece of evidence is entirely consistent with more general indications that Gothic groups of the era were always composed of two grades of fighting men: the 'best' (the freemen) and the rest (the freed).[21] Moreover, as we saw in Chapter 3, fourth-century Germanic society, while certainly hierarchic, was not yet dominated by the kind of very small feudal elite that would dominate the post-Carolingian society.

Some thirty years after the Tervingi and Greuthungi crossed the Lower Danube, then, a second crisis unfolded. Roman frontier security, this time west rather than east of the Carpathians, was breached on no fewer than three occasions within a short time. The four main invasions – Radagaisus', the Rhine crossings, Uldin's, and the Burgun- dians' – hit the Roman frontier at different points. Radagaisus moved south and west into Italy; the Vandals, Alans and Suevi, as well as the Burgundians, slammed west into the Rhine frontier and across it, while

Uldin moved south. These movements, originating from broadly the same region, add up to a massive convulsion along Rome's European frontiers. Tens of thousands of warriors, which means well over a hundred thousand people all told – just possibly a few hundred thousand – were on the move.

Cometh the Hour, Cometh the Hun

IF THE SCALE AND geographical concentration of the crisis of 405–8 can't be picked up easily from the ancient sources, its causes are even harder to reconstruct. Fragmentary at best, at this point the written sources practically dry up. One, written over a hundred years later, records that it was food shortages that drove the Vandals out of central Europe, but this is unconvincing. They had lived there for hundreds of years, and the period around AD 400 was one of European climatic optimum, with sunny, warm summers. Uldin's boast (see p. 196) might indicate that his motive was conquest pure and simple; but, then again, the ease with which he was crushed suggests that he was not nearly powerful enough to make a conqueror.

In my view, the crisis of 405–8 must be seen as a rerun of 376, with the further movements of nomadic Huns as the trigger. This has been suggested many times before, but, in the absence of explicit confirmation, has never achieved consensus.[22] It is precisely at this point that it becomes important to realize that Huns in large numbers had not themselves been directly involved in the action of 376.[23] As late as 395, twenty years after the Goths crossed the Danube, most of the Huns were still well to the east. In that year they launched a massive raid into Roman territory, but via the Caucasus, not over the Danube (map 7). This has sometimes been explained as a cunning plan by Danube-based Hunnic groups to outflank the Roman defences, but both men and horses would have been exhausted by the inevitable 2,000-kilometre trek around the northern coast of the Black Sea before they could even launch their assault. The direction of the attack makes it clear that, as late as 395, the Huns were still centred much further to the east, perhaps on the Volga Steppe; and, in at least partial confirmation of the point, for a decade or more after 376 Goths continued to provide Rome's main opposition north of the Lower Danube, as we saw in Chapter 4.[24]

But by the 420s large numbers of Huns were established in central Europe, occupying the Great Hungarian Plain west of the Carpathian Mountains. This point is well documented. In 427, for instance, the Romans expelled them from Pannonia, the richest Roman province south of the Middle Danube (map 7).[25] And in 432, when a Roman general needed their help, he travelled 'through Pannonia' to reach them, his route showing that they had remained west of the Carpathians even after the expulsion.[26] By the early 440s, likewise, Hunnic royal tombs were to be found on the opposite bank of the Danube from the city of Margus – again, firmly west of the Carpathians, as was Attila's main base in the 440s.[27] Sometime between 395 and 425, then, the main body of the Huns made a 1,700-kilometre trek westwards from north of the Caucasus to the Great Hungarian Plain.

Whether it was precisely during 405–8 that the Huns made this move is less certain, but we do have a few tantalizing hints that this may have been the case. For example, in 412/13 Olympiodorus and his parrot visited them on an embassy. Part of the journey involved a horrendous sea voyage, during which their ship put in at Athens. Since Olympiodorus worked for the eastern Empire, he must have started from Constantinople. And since his route to the Huns passed via Athens, he was presumably looking to sail through the Aegean and up the Adriatic, probably to Aquileia at its head. This points to the Middle Danube Plain as the home of Olympiodorus' Huns by the early 410s, since the port of Aquileia had long existed to service this region (map 7).[28]

Confirmation that something very serious was afoot in central Europe round about the year 410 is provided by other, more indirect evidence. At this time the eastern imperial authorities in Constantinople perceived a substantial stepping-up of the threat facing their Balkan territories. In January 412, a programme was put in place to strengthen the Danubian fleets.[29] One year later, Constantinople, vulnerable to attack through the Balkans from the north, was provided with new defences. It was at this point that the city acquired its famous landwalls: the formidable triple belt of fortifications much of which still stands in modern Istanbul.[30] These walls were powerful enough to keep the city safe for a millennium, and no attacker managed to take it from its landward side until 1453, 1,040 years after their construction, when Turkish cannon blasted a hole through them, near the modern Topkapi coach station. Both of these defensive measures have sometimes been taken as a response to Uldin's attacks of 408/9, but in that case they would be strangely postdated, and Uldin had anyway suffered a crushing defeat. I find it very tempting, therefore, to associate them with the closer proximity of the main Hunnic threat.

The evidence is not all that we would like it to be. But, as already noted, it is certain that by 420, and quite probably by 410, the Huns had moved from the Caucasus, where they were in about 395, to the Great Hungarian Plain. Given that their arrival on the outer fringes of Europe in 376 had triggered the appearance of the Goths on the banks of the Danube, it is inevitable that a second Hunnic advance into the heart of Europe would have had similarly dramatic knock-on effects.[31] There is also the fact that we have no serious alternative to fall back on. General Roman policy towards immigrants had not changed. All the groups of 405–8 were resisted; none of them was licensed to enter imperial territory. Moreover, Roman frontier security had been reasserted successfully since 376 (and many of the immigrants of 405–8, as we shall see, were about to die). The Rhine crossing of December 406 occurred long enough after Radagaisus' catastrophic defeat – he had been executed in August that year – for us to suppose that news of it would have filtered back across the frontier, yet still the next wave of immigrants came. Again, all of this suggests that the events of 405–8 were motivated from the barbarian side of the frontier, and were not dependent upon changing perceptions of imperial policy or imperial strength.

The story takes some piecing together, but the pieces do fit. The key points are these. The intrusion of the Huns into Europe was a two-stage process, part one (the occupation of land north of the Black Sea) triggering the crisis of 376, part two (the occupation of the Great Hungarian Plain) causing, and being preceded by, the displacements from that plain into the Roman world of Radagaisus, the Vandals, Alans and Suevi, Uldin and the Burgundians. All these groups came from the region that was to be the heartland of Hunnic power for the next fifty years, just before Huns in large numbers are documented occupying it. This cannot be coincidence. Like the Goths in 376, many of the inhabitants of Germania west of the Carpathians voted with their feet between 405 and 408: the dangers inherent in trying to make a new life on Roman soil were less threatening than the notion of life under Hunnic domination. Where the crisis of 376 reflected the appearance of the Huns on the far eastern fringes of Europe, beyond the Carpathians, that of 405–8 was caused by their transfer to the very heart of Europe.

THE FIRST STEP, remote as it might seem, on the road to the sack of Rome in 410 was taken far off on the northern shores of the Black Sea. The further advances of the Huns threw Germania west of the Carpathians into crisis, and the major knock-on effect observed by the Romans was large-scale armed immigration into their Empire. For the eastern Empire, the new proximity of the Huns generated a heightened anxiety which betrayed itself in new and far-reaching defensive measures. But it was the western Empire that bore the brunt of the fall-out both immediately and in the longer term. The collision of the invaders with the central Roman authorities and local Roman elites would have momentous repercussions.

Pillage and Usurpation

THE IMMEDIATE EFFECTS of these population displacements were exactly what you would expect. None of the refugees entered the Empire by agreement; all behaved as enemies and were treated as such. The Goths of Radagaisus at first met little opposition, but when they reached Florence, matters came to a head. They had blockaded the city and reduced it virtually to the point of capitulation, when a huge Roman relief force, commanded by Stilicho, generalissimo of the western Empire, arrived just in the nick of time. Stilicho ruled the west at this point, in the name of the emperor Honorius, infant son of Theodosius I. He had mobilized for this counterattack an enormous force: thirty regiments from the field army of Italy, together with a contingent probably from the Rhine frontier,[32] supplemented by Alan and Hunnic auxiliaries.[33] The delay incurred in mobilizing so many men explains why Radagaisus had enjoyed a free hand in northern Italy for six months or more. But when the Roman response eventually came, it was brilliantly successful. Radagaisus was forced to retreat with his army up to the heights of Fiesole, and there blockaded. The Gothic king eventually abandoned the scene and tried to escape, but was captured and executed. Some of his followers were dispersed, many of them being sold into slavery, as mentioned earlier;[34] while at some point in the action his higher-status warriors were brought over by Stilicho into the Roman army. We hear about this only in a brief snippet from Olympiodorus' history as preserved by Photius, and it's not clear when it happened. It could have been part of the mopping-up operation, but – perhaps more likely – it may have represented a considerable diplomatic coup, drastically cutting away Radagaisus' support and ruining his chances of standing up to Stilicho's army. Either way, Stilicho had faced down the first of the challenges posed by the crisis of 405–8.

In dealing with the Vandals, Alans and Suevi, however, he was much less effective. If he had transferred part of the Gallic army to Italy to help defeat Radagaisus, this would help to explain why the attack on Gaul, from a non-Roman point of view, was that much more successful. As we know, trouble had been brewing for some time before December 406 in the nexus of lands between the Upper Rhine and Upper Danube. Fragments of a contemporary history written by one Renatus Profuturus Frigeridus, preserved in the sixth-century *History* of Gregory of Tours along with other texts, indicate that the Vandals had been stirring things up on the frontiers of the province of Raetia as early as the winter of 401/2; but if this took the form of an attempt to cross into the Empire, it was certainly repulsed. The Vandals are next encountered trying a quite different tack. By the summer or autumn of 406, the Hasding Vandals had moved some 250 kilometres further north, trying their luck against the Franks of the Middle Rhine. According to the Frigeridus fragments, they took a terrible beating until Alan reinforcements saved the day. This fighting is not dated, but it presumably took place just before the alliance of Hasding and Siling Vandals, together with Alans and Suevi, broke across the Rhine on 31 December 406. The fact that they crossed near Mainz (map 8) confirms that, having tried their luck in the south these groups then shifted their point of attack northwards, circling round, it would seem, the main territories of the Alamanni, and hence coming into conflict with Franks.

The Rhine invasion cannot be reconstructed in detail: all we have is an outline trail of destruction (map 8). It started where the invaders crossed the river, with the sacking of Mainz, then spread west and north to the large centres in the hinterland of the Rhine frontier – Triers and Rheims – before moving further afield to Tournai, Arras and Amiens. The invaders then turned south and east, drifting through the vicinity of Paris, Orléans and Tours to Bordeaux and the Narbonnaise. All of this took the best part of two years, and our most vivid evidence is provided by some Christian Gallic poets who drew a variety of moral lessons from the disaster and, while doing so, gave us a pretty good picture of the action. The most famous, Orientus, produced a terrific one-liner, quoted in all the best histories: 'All Gaul was filled with the smoke of a single funeral pyre.'[35] Writing to his wife, another poet, Prosper of Aquitaine, pondered on the idea that they were seeing the collapse of 'the frame of the fragile world' (laboured though this passage may be, it was following the norms of the genre in listing one by one the conventional categories of Roman society):

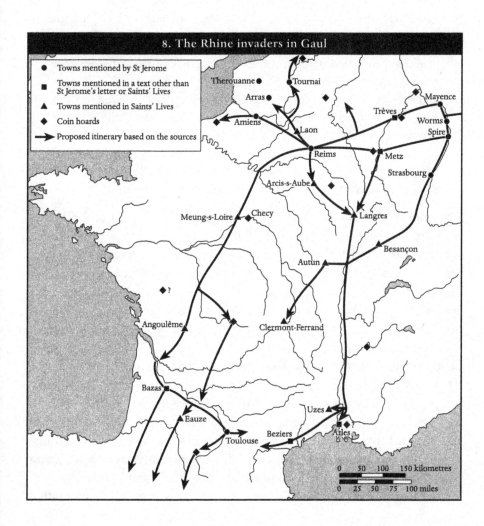

8. The Rhine invaders in Gaul

He who once turned the soil with a hundred ploughs, now labours to have just a pair of oxen; the man who often rode through splendid cities in his carriages now is sick and travels to the deserted countryside wearily and on foot. The merchant who used to cleave the seas with ten lofty ships now embarks on a tiny skiff, and is his own helmsman. Neither country nor city is as it was; everything rushes headlong to its end.

Then, rather more animatedly: 'With sword, plague, starvation, chains, cold and heat – in a thousand ways – a single death snatches off wretched humankind'.[36]

After ransacking Roman Gaul, in 409, this bunch of Vandals, Alans and Suevi forced their way over the Pyrenees into Spain, where they wreaked yet more damage. Such was their mastery of the peninsula by 411, the Spanish chronicler Hydatius tells us, that:

> [they] apportioned to themselves by lot areas of the provinces for settlement: the [Hasding] Vandals took possession of Gallaecia, and the Sueves that part of Gallaecia which [is] situated on the very western edge of the Ocean. The Alans were allotted the provinces of Lusitania and Carthaginensis, and the Siling Vandals Baetica [map 9]. The Spaniards in the cities and forts who had survived the disasters surrendered themselves to servitude under the barbarians, who held sway throughout the provinces.[37]

The trail of devastation was finally halted by the seizure and distribution among themselves of one of the most prosperous areas of the western Empire. On the basis of a mid-sixth-century Byzantine source, the historian Procopius, the settlement has sometimes been seen as organized by the central Roman authorities in Italy.[38] But Procopius was writing far from these events in both time and space, while the Spanish chronicler Orosius, writing within five years or so, is explicit that the settlement was completely unauthorized.[39] His account must be preferred. By 411, after four years of living hand to mouth, the Rhine invaders had had enough of their rootless existence. Rather than looting their way across Roman Europe for ever, they needed to find, and settle, revenue-producing territories that would support them in the longer term. Hydatius (who was also bishop of a small town just inside the borders of what is now Galicia in north-western Spain) isn't too clear on what exactly happened, but it's a fair guess that the Vandals, Alans and Suevi diverted the tax revenues of their allotted provinces, which normally went to the Roman state, to their own coffers.[40] Fire, rape and pillage in Gaul was thus followed by the forced annexation of Spain, but this is only the beginning of the catalogue of disasters that followed the breakdown of frontier security in the western Empire.

WHILE THE VANDALS, Alans and Suevi were rampaging through Gaul and Spain, the instability of the western Empire was exacerbated by a new problem. Just before the emperor Honorius' seventh consulship in 407:

> the troops in Britain mutinied and enthroned Marcus, obeying him as emperor there, but when he would not accede to their demands, they killed him and brought forward Gratian, to whom they gave a purple robe, a crown and a bodyguard, just like an emperor. Becoming displeased with him also, after four months they deposed and killed him, and made Constantine his successor.

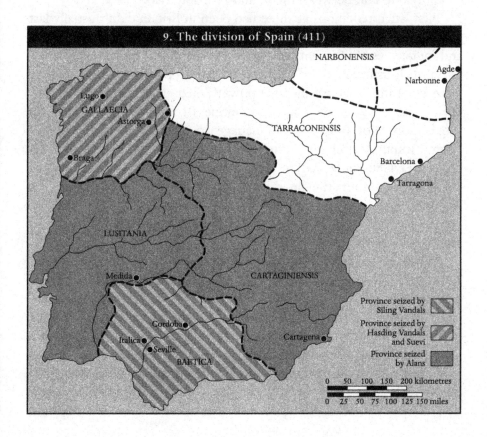

9. The division of Spain (411)

After appointing Justinianus and Nebiogastes as generals in Gaul, he left Britain and crossed to the continent. Arriving at Boulogne ... he stayed there a few days and, having won over all the troops of Gaul and Aquitaine to his side, became master of the whole of Gaul up to the Alps.[41]

Of all the Roman provinces, Britain, as we saw in Chapter 3, was the province most prone to revolts during the late Empire. Not that they had any particular separatist leanings, but the Roman civilian and military establishment there often felt left out of the loop in the distribution of favour and patronage, and occasionally rebelled in search of a better deal. So we are not necessarily looking for any specific motivation for this latest sequence of revolts, which apparently began in the autumn of 406 – a little *before* the Vandals, Alan and Suevi crossed the Rhine. On the other hand, the two phenomena share a suspicious chronological proximity, and I suspect that there was certainly one link between them, and probably two.

First, such rebellions as there had been in Britain didn't usually last long, rarely spreading across the Channel to the much larger political and military establishments on the Rhine frontier. The fate of the first two British usurpers in 406/7 was pretty much par for the course: they were nonentities whose bids for power failed at the first hurdle. The third – normally known as Constantine III – was a very different proposition. Not only did he manage to avoid being lynched just twenty minutes after his enthronement, but he quickly extended his sway over Gaul as far as the Alps, winning over the Roman army of the Rhine. By the time he shifted his power-base to Boulogne, the Vandals, Alans and Suevi were already across the frontier, and the central Roman authorities in Italy – Stilicho ruling in the name of Honorius – had so far failed to act.

What we see here is another instance of a classic Roman pattern. Thoroughly Italocentric as it was, Stilicho's regime failed to come quickly enough to the assistance of Gaul in its hour of need, and Constantine III, shifting his banner to Gaul in spring 407, offered the chance of an effective response to the impending disaster. Once Constantine had established himself south of the Channel, troops under his command fought a number of sharp engagements against the Vandals and their cronies.[42] This presumably explains the invaders' itinerary. As the Roman response to their incursions in the northern

Rhine region became more coherent, the invaders switched their attentions south towards Aquitaine and the Pyrenees. Orosius tells us that Constantine made treaties with some of the more stable Germanic clients of the Rhine frontier region – the Alamanni, Franks and Burgundians – both to secure his own position and to ensure that the Gallic provinces wouldn't be troubled by more invasions.[43] He won support in Gaul, therefore, by supplying a focus for Roman resistance to the barbarian invaders, which the central authorities in Italy were conspicuously failing to deliver. The need for such a response may even have been what triggered the British usurpations. Although the first revolt took place a little before the Vandals and their friends crossed the Rhine, trouble had been brewing for some time, as we've seen; even if the hammer blow didn't fall until 31 December 406, there can have been no doubt in Roman military circles on the Rhine that a major crisis was developing. This, I suspect, prompted the unrest against Stilicho's rule, of which Constantine III would be the prime beneficiary.

Alaric's Goths

TWO-THIRDS OF our cast have now assembled. To this already volatile mixture we need to add a third element: the Goths of Alaric, into whose hands Rome would eventually fall. To understand these Goths and their part in the action, we must cast our eyes back over the twenty-odd years that had passed since the emperor Theodosius I had finally returned peace to the Balkans, four years after the battle of Hadrianople.

Alaric's Goths were the direct descendants of the Tervingi and Greuthungi who had negotiated the compromise peace of 382 with Theodosius.[44] Their relations with the Roman state, as you might expect of such a shotgun wedding (see Chapter 4), were subject to periodic strains. Instances of partial and full-scale revolt reflected continuing distrust on both sides. The imperial authorities, for their part, did what they could – up to a point – to build trust. When a Gothic soldier was lynched by a mob in Constantinople, substantial financial penalties were imposed on the city. Likewise, when a Roman garrison stationed at Tomi, on the Lower Danube frontier, turned on a Gothic military contingent quartered alongside it, the Roman officer in charge was cashiered. Theodosius was clearly anxious not to allow moments of friction to spark off a major revolt, and we know too that he would from time to time entertain the Goths' leaders at lavish banquets.

Nonetheless, the Goths, or some of them, clearly suspected that the Roman state was still looking to dismantle the licensed semi-autonomy that they had extracted by force of arms between 376 and 382. In particular, the peace of 382 had stipulated that large Gothic contingents would be liable for military service when called upon by the Empire. Theodosius did this twice, when confronting western usurpers: first Magnus Maximus in 387/8, then Eugenius in 392/3. On each occasion, some of the Goths preferred to revolt, or at least desert, rather than fight in a Roman civil war. The reason for this was straightforward. The Roman state tolerated the Goths' semi-autonomy only because the prevailing military balance of power made it do so. Time-honoured policies had been suspended, but only in the case of these particular immigrants, and only because of their victories over Valens and Theodosius. Fighting in any Roman civil war would necessarily cost the Goths casualties, and should their military man-power be eroded too far, there would be nothing to prevent the Roman state from enforcing its usual asylum-seeker policy. In selling the peace treaty to the Senate of Constantinople in January 383, as we have seen, Themistius was already looking forward to the Goths losing their semi-independent status.

A large amount of fuel was heaped on the fires of Gothic suspicion during the second of these campaigns, against the usurper Eugenius. Theodosius had been trying to rule the entire Empire from Constantinople, with the predictable result that disaffected elements in the west threw up their own candidate for ruler. At the crucial battle of the River Frigidus, on the fringes of Italy, the Goths found themselves in the front line during the first, inconclusive, day of battle and suffered heavy casualties. One report, clearly exaggerating, says that 10,000 Goths died. Its author, the Christian Orosius, even said the battle produced two Roman victories: one over Eugenius, and a second over the Goths because they had suffered such heavy losses.[45] When the emperor Theodosius died in early 395, therefore, the Goths were ripe for revolt, ready to rewrite the terms of the agreement of 382 to secure a greater degree of security. And in raising the banner of rebellion they appointed for themselves an overall leader, for the first time since the suppression of Fritigern and Alatheus and Saphrax – in direct contravention of the treaty. Their choice fell upon Alaric, who had made a name for himself in an earlier, smaller revolt after the Maximus campaign. As to how, precisely, the Goths wished to rewrite the peace deal, our hostile Roman sources are not very informative. One thing the Goths wanted, in any new deal, was that the Romans recognize their right to a leader by granting him official status as a fully fledged Roman general (*magister militum*). Whether there were further conditions attached – in particular, that the office of general should come with full military salaries for his followers – is unclear but perfectly possible.[46] The Goths had had enough of their half-baked political autonomy within the Roman state, ground-breaking though it had been when instituted a quarter of a century earlier.

There's another crucial thing about Alaric's Goths. In 376, the Goths had come to the Danube in two separate groups, the Tervingi and Greuthungi, each with their own leaderships. They cooperated well enough during the subsequent war, but some jostling for position went on all the same. On the eve of Hadrianople, Fritigern tried to sell himself to Valens as the single recognized leader of all the Goths. Then, two years later, the two groups parted company again, moving off in different directions. What happened next is disputed. Some argue that the Tervingi and Greuthungi made separate treaties with Rome. My own view is that the treaty of 382 applied to both. Whichever option you go for doesn't change the bigger point – which follows. In the course of Alaric's reign the old distinction between Tervingi and Greuthungi disappeared for ever, and the two forces became one.[47] The process that we have observed in Germania beyond the Roman frontier between the first and the fourth centuries – the growth of larger and more coherent political groupings – had now spread to Roman territory, and was becoming a force to be reckoned with. The reasons behind the unification of the Goths were very simple, and explained why they were already cooperating during the war of 376–82. By operating as one much larger group, they acquired safety in numbers and the chance to negotiate a better deal, thus increasing their chances of a better future in a Roman world that was far from reconciled to their presence.

The revolt of Alaric's Goths in early 395 was thus a momentous event. A new force was on the loose, seeking to avenge their losses at the River Frigidus and to rewrite the peace treaty of thirteen years earlier. These issues did not prove easy to resolve. The united Goths were too powerful to be quickly despatched. In 395, and again in 397, they were confronted by a substantial Roman army, but actual fighting was limited, probably because the forces were too evenly matched for either side to risk engaging with the enemy.[48] At the same time, old attitudes died hard, and no Roman politician was about to rush into granting the Goths new terms. Frustrated in his desire for a political deal, Alaric set his men loose. Once more, it was the provincial population of the Balkans that suffered. The revolt first broke out in Thrace in the north-east, but between 395 and 397 the Goths worked their way all the way south to Athens, then west and north up the Adriatic coast as far as Epirus, cheerfully pillaging as they went, while all the time putting out feelers for a new political deal.

Court politics in Constantinople were highly volatile during these years. Theodosius' older son, the eastern emperor Arcadius, though twenty years old in 397 never actively ruled, but was always surrounded by a swarm of ambitious politicians seeking power through his favour. By 397, currently the most powerful of these courtiers, the eunuch Chamberlain Eutropius, was ready to negotiate. He made Alaric a Roman general and granted the Goths the better terms and extra guarantees they required. He allowed them to settle in Dacia and Macedonia, and probably arranged for local produce, levied as tax in kind, to be diverted to their subsistence. Eutropius' fate is highly instructive. Eunuchs were generally figures of ridicule in the Roman world, portrayed as immoral and greedy: just the sort to go soft on barbarians demanding money with menaces. As both a eunuch and a Goth appeaser, Eutropius' position was vulnerable, and was brilliantly exploited by his opponents. He was duly toppled in the summer of 399.[49] His successors tore up the agreement with Alaric and refused to negotiate further.

Over the next two years Constantinople saw frequent regime change, but no eastern politician was prepared to talk to Alaric; granting the Goths the kind of terms they might accept would be political suicide. In the year 400, a political coup was staged in Constantinople against Gainas, a Roman general of Gothic origins who was one of several contenders for power after Eutropius' fall. The prominence of Gainas – and other generals of non-Roman origin like him – follows on from the reorganization of the army in the late Roman period. Unlike the early Roman period when only Roman citizens were recruited into the legions, anyone could serve in the politically important field armies (*comitatenses*) of the later Empire. There was nothing to stop able individuals of non-Roman origin from rising through comitatensian ranks to acquire political prominence. As a result, from the early- to mid-fourth century onwards, a series of generals of barbarian origin figure in accounts of court politics. Occasionally, such men had, or were suspected of having, designs on the purple itself. Silvanus, of Frankish origins, was one case in point: one of our historians, Ammianus Marcellinus, participated in an assassination mission to remove him. Much more often, however, 'barbarian' generals jostled with civilian politicians to wield influence behind the throne. But, whatever hostile sources may say, there is no evidence that these generals were anything other than entirely loyal to the Empire. Some of those labelled 'barbarian' were classically educated second-generation immigrants – as fully Roman, in other words, as anybody else.

A dominant figure in Constantinople in autumn 399, Gainas was ousted by some of his erstwhile allies early in the next year. He was, it seems, a first-generation Gothic immigrant, and hence an easy target for anti-barbarian propaganda, but particularly so at a time when Alaric's Goths were rampaging through the Balkans. There is no evidence, however, that he had the slightest intention of making common cause with them. In the violent coup that broke his hold on power, Gainas managed to get out of Constantinople alive, but several thousand Goths, including many women and children who lived in the city as part of the east Roman military establishment, were massacred. In the aftermath, Alaric's Goths faced no direct military threat from the east Roman armies, but they were now excluded from Constantinopolitan politics, and soon lost all hope of obtaining a new agreement. To try to break the deadlock, in the autumn of 401 Alaric took his followers to Italy and attempted over the next twelve months to extract a deal from Stilicho, effective ruler of the western Empire, instead. Again, Alaric tried intimidation, but Stilicho was no more forthcoming than the successors of Eutropius had been in the east. Cut off from the established sources of supply available to them in the Balkans, the Goths could not maintain their Italian adventure indefinitely.[50] In the autumn/winter of 402/3, two drawn battles later, they retreated back over the Dinaric Alps to their old haunts in Dacia and Macedonia.

Alaric had had no choice. And he had now to think again about how to get one half or other of the Empire round the negotiating table. The Goths re-established themselves in the same areas of the Balkans they had occupied between 397 and 401 – reactivating, one presumes, the sources of supply that had sustained them then. And here they remained for over three years. Stuck in a political wasteland, they found themselves caught, literally and metaphorically, between the eastern and western halves of the Empire, waiting for someone to give them a call. Late in 406, an approach eventually came – much to Alaric's amazement, I suspect – from Stilicho in Italy. Just four years earlier, the western regent-ruler had moved might and main to keep Alaric and his Goths at arm's length. Now, here he was courting them for an alliance. Even more peculiar, Stilicho made his approach to Alaric after the defeat of Radagaisus, when, as we have seen, the Rhine frontier was already showing clear signs of the turmoil that would boil over on to Roman territory. But what Stilicho proposed was an alliance in which he and Alaric would both fight Constantinople, not deal with the problems on the Rhine. To understand Stilicho's seemingly bizarre behaviour, and how its unforeseen consequences led to the sack of Rome, we need to take a closer look at the western generalissimo and his position in the great scheme of things.

Stilicho and Alaric

FLAVIUS STILICHO is a figure about whom opinion – ancient and modern – is heavily divided. He was a particularly successful product of the late Roman career path that saw non-Romans – such as Gainas – rise through the military to political prominence. The son of a Roman cavalry officer of Vandal origins and a Roman mother, he enjoyed a distinguished military career at the court of Theodosius I in Constantinople, holding a series of prestigious staff appointments in the 380s and early 390s. In 393, he accompanied his emperor west on the campaign against the usurper Eugenius, and in its aftermath was appointed senior general (*comes et magister utriusque militiae praesentalis*) in command of the western Empire's armed forces. Early in 395, Theodosius died unexpectedly in Milan at the age of forty-nine, having apparently appointed Stilicho guardian to his younger son Honorius, who had also come west. At least, that's what Stilicho reported about a deathbed conversation he had had with the emperor, and there was no one there to deny it. Theodosius' older son, Arcadius, was left to govern the east from Constantinople. Born in September 384, Honorius was less than ten years old on his father's death, and so the reins of power fell naturally into Stilicho's hands.

The general's career had thus far been entirely eastern in focus, but now he found himself undisputed ruler of the west. A clear sign of his need to build bridges to every wielder of power and influence is his careful courting of the old Roman Senate. In May 395, he passed a law rehabilitating all those who had held office under the usurper Eugenius – a huge gesture in that direction.[51] Sometime after 395, our old friend Symmachus – enjoying an Indian summer, to judge from his correspondence – suddenly found himself amongst those being courted.[52] Perhaps two-thirds of his surviving letters were written between 395 and his death in 402, and these late letters show him as a man with considerable clout. For one thing, he was able to rescue his son-in-law Nicomachus Flavianus from the consequences of having served as Urban Prefect under Eugenius, securing a political rehabilitation which culminated in his becoming Urban Prefect once again in 399–400 under Honorius and Stilicho, and with his landed fortune protected.[53] While not holding formal office, Symmachus also operated in the public sphere, in 397 playing a material role, as we shall see, in getting the Senate to declare Gildo, the commander in North Africa who would revolt against Stilicho in favour of Constantinople, a public enemy.

For more than a decade, as a result of this careful political courting, Stilicho held on to power: no mean feat, given the vicissitudes that fortune put in his way. Some were self-generated. The real truth about Theodosius' deathbed wishes will never be known. But shortly after his death, Stilicho claimed that the dying emperor had ordered that he be guardian of *both* of his children. As the poet Claudian, Stilicho's resident spin-doctor in Rome, put it to the Senate: 'Then was the power of Rome entrusted to your care, Stilicho; in your hands was placed the governance of the world. The brothers' twin majesty and the armies of both royal courts were given into your charge.'[54] Everything suggests – at least as regards Arcadius – that this was a lie, conveniently authorizing Stilicho to seek power in his native east, in addition to the power he already held in the west, where he had only recently taken up residence. He proceeded to act on the claim. The underlying aim of his two interventions on eastern territory, in 395 and 397, against Alaric's revolting Goths was to establish his credentials as the saviour – and hence natural ruler – of the east. These ambitions were firmly resisted by his peers in Constantinople. As we have seen, they were busy fighting among themselves for control of the inactive Arcadius, and the last thing any of them wanted was to see Stilicho riding over the horizon to their rescue. Not surprisingly, they now kept him at bay by throwing as many grenades in his direction as they could lay their hands on.

The most dangerous of these detonated in autumn 397, when the aforementioned military commander in Africa, Gildo, was induced to transfer his allegiance to Constantinople. This was a huge threat to Stilicho, because African grain was used to feed the city of Rome. Any disruption to the supply would quickly undermine his political position. In the event, he dealt with the crisis brilliantly, sending Gildo's brother Mascezel to North Africa. Gildo had been responsible for the death of his children, so Mascezel had grudges to burn off. The revolt was over by July 398, and Africa had returned to its traditional western allegiance before that year's harvest was in. Stilicho also weathered Alaric's invasion of Italy in 401/2 – which, though the Constantinopolitan authorities probably didn't authorize it, as has sometimes been thought, they certainly did nothing to discourage. Then, just three years later, came Radagaisus and his Gothic horde. Yet again, Stilicho coped – comfortably enough, in the end. Throughout all this, there were many components to his power – central and regional military establishments, the Senate of Rome and the imperial bureaucracy, to mention just three. But one thing was key: his relationship with Theodosius' son Honorius. To keep a firm grip on the emperor, as Honorius grew into adolescence, in 398 Stilicho married him to his daughter Maria. This added some extra security to the general's position, but relations with Honorius were bound to need some finessing as the young emperor matured.

Up to August 406, Stilicho walked this tightrope pretty well. He had failed to unite east and west, but Honorius remained firmly under his thumb. Africa had been induced to resume its western allegiance, and two Gothic assaults on Italy had been dealt with successfully. Then, in the aftermath of the defeat of Radagaisus occurred the most mysterious episode in Stilicho's career. At this point, things were already going wrong in the north. The first of the British usurpations had broken out; there was fighting east of the Rhine, and every indication that it would spill over on to Roman territory (though no inkling in any quarter of the scale of the forthcoming Rhine crossing or the form it would take). However, as we have seen, instead of moving north with every trained soldier he could muster, Stilicho picked a new fight with his counterparts in Constantinople. His aim in reopening hostilities at the tail end of 406 was much more limited than in 395/6. He demanded the return of the dioceses of Dacia and Macedonia (the eastern half of the prefecture of Illyricum, which had been transferred to the administrative control of Constantinople in the reign of Theodosius. Then, threatening war if the east resisted, he sought a military alliance with Alaric's Goths.

It is possible, of course, that Stilicho simply suffered a catastrophic failure of judgement, obsessed on the one hand with his eastern ambitions and, on the other, underestimating the crisis in the north. But even though he probably did fail to grasp the speed with which crisis was about to become disaster, I don't believe he lost the plot so completely. And I am not alone in this. The critical point here is that Stilicho was no longer trying to win power in Constantinople. His much more restricted aim – regaining Dacia and Macedonia in east Illyricum – suggests that there was some more specific issue, rather than pure vainglory, at stake. The mountains and upland basins of east Illyricum were a traditional recruiting ground for the Roman military (a bit like the Scottish Highlands for the British army). It has been suggested, therefore, that his apparently bizarre ambition to control east Illyricum in late 406 was linked to the unfolding crisis on the Rhine. Stilicho desperately needed military manpower, so winning back east Illyricum might have been a cunning plan to secure a vital recruiting ground. But it takes time to turn recruits into soldiers, and time was something that Stilicho conspicuously lacked. There was, however, one fully trained and experienced – even battle-hardened – military force already available in east Illyricum: the Goths of Alaric.

To understand why fighting Constantinople over east Illyricum might have something to do with winning Alaric's support against the broader northern threat, we also need to take account of the Gothic agenda. As Alaric had shown repeatedly since 395, he was perfectly willing to forge a military alliance with the Roman state, but the price had to be right, and the perceived deficiencies of the peace of 382 substantially rectified. As we know, this meant full recognition for their overall leader and a designated revenue-producing district legitimately earmarked for their support. (This is what they had got from Eutropius in 397, and they would continue to want it in the later 400s.) The only problem for Stilicho and Alaric was deciding precisely where the Goths should be established. In 406, their brief Italian job aside, they had been occupying Dacia and Macedonia since 397. But east Illyricum, contrary to established tradition, was currently part of the eastern Empire. Stilicho thus faced a dilemma. He could move the Goths from the territories they had occupied for the best part of a decade into lands that *he* controlled. This would give him the right to grant them the fully legal settlement they required, but would necessarily involve huge disruption, both for the Goths, and – perhaps more importantly from Stilicho's point of view – for the Roman landowners of any western territory into which the Goths might move. Alternatively, he could legitimize their control of the territories they *already* held, which would involve browbeating Constantinople into transferring east Illyricum back into his hands. The latter was his eventual choice, and was, on reflection, the simplest means of getting the Goths on side. Seen in this light, Stilicho's policies look far from crazy.

An alliance with Alaric's supergroup would give him the military manpower he needed to deal with the mayhem that was about to unfold in the north, and with little disruption to western territories. If all this involved a spat with Constantinople, then so be it.[55]

The Fall of Stilicho and After

As PART OF Stilicho's deal with Alaric, it was agreed that, for the assault on the eastern Empire, the Goths would be reinforced by a substantial contingent from the Roman army of Italy. I imagine he supposed that a display of his military resources, rather than a set-piece assault on Constantinople, would be sufficient to make the east hand back the disputed dioceses. To this end, Alaric moved his forces into Epirus (modern Albania), within what was still the formally west Roman territory of west Illyricum, and waited for Stilicho's troops to arrive from across the Adriatic. Since it was impossible to mount large-scale campaigns in the Balkans in winter, the assault was presumably planned for the following summer, in 407. However, any plans were wrecked by the speed with which events unfolded in Britain and Gaul. By May/June 407, when a major Balkans campaign might again be contemplated, the Vandals, Alans and Suevi had crossed the Rhine and spread out through Gaul. Even worse, Constantine III was already across the Channel and had rallied to his banner much of the military establishment of Gaul. To move a large portion of the army of Italy across the Adriatic in these circumstances was impossible. Rather than reinforcing Alaric in Epirus, therefore, Stilicho's only move in 407 was to send one of his generals, a Goth by the name of Sarus, to Gaul to try and snuff out Constantine's usurpation before it gathered momentum. The attempt failed.

By the beginning of 408, Stilicho's position was precarious. Constantine and the barbarians were manoeuvring in different parts of Gaul, and that entire province, together with Britain, had fallen out of central control. North Africa and Spain were still on side, but Alaric was getting restive in Epirus. His Goths had now been sitting there for a year, waiting for the legions to arrive, and the Gallic situation was still much too critical for anything to be about to happen. There was also another factor at work. Alaric's hold over his own men was by no means unassailable, and the rank and file had to be kept happy. Was Stilicho really going to deliver on his promises?

By the spring of 408, Alaric was sufficiently concerned to demand reassurance. Reminding Stilicho, not unreasonably, that his forces had as yet received no financial, let alone military, support, he demanded four thousand pounds of gold. Threatening war if they were not paid, they now advanced north and west to the Roman province of Noricum (modern Austria) in the Alpine foothills, conveniently placed for a move into Italy should that prove necessary. This was not the most sympathetic response to Stilicho's predicament from a supposed ally, but Alaric had his own constituencies to satisfy – and Stilicho, remember, hadn't shed a tear when he forced the Goths out of Italy in 401/2. The emperor and the majority of the Senate, we're told, were ready for war with the Goths. But this would have added to the Rhine invaders and Constantine III a third formidable enemy, and Stilicho took a different view. The Senate gathered in Rome for a set-piece debate, and Stilicho argued his case. He got his way, and the Senate approved the payment of gold. Opposition wasn't stilled, however, and a certain Lampadius has gone down in history for his judgement: 'This isn't peace, but a pact of servitude' (*non est ista pax sed pactio servitutis*). By this stage, Stilicho had pretty much expended every last piece of his remaining political capital, but fate hadn't yet finished with him.

On 1 May 408, the eastern emperor Arcadius, the western emperor Honorius' elder brother, died, leaving a seven-year-old son, Theodosius II, as his heir. Again, emperor and general disagreed. Stilicho wanted to go to Constantinople to have his say in the arrangement of eastern affairs, but so did Honorius. As over the payment to Alaric, Stilicho got his way, suggesting also that Alaric should in the meantime be sent to Gaul. But the rift between emperor and general was only too apparent, and one high court bureaucrat, Olympius, originally an appointee of Stilicho, laboured to widen it. Stilicho's will had prevailed on every issue, but the western Empire was still in a dreadful state. Constantine III had now taken up residence at Arles in southern Gaul, and was hovering over the passes into Italy. There were barbarians all over Gaul, and Alaric, having received his money, was still sitting in Noricum eyeing the eastern Alpine passes. No wonder, as the sources report, Stilicho spent the summer of 408 formulating plans but not implementing them; the whole imperial edifice was coming down around his ears. At this point, Zosimus records, Olympius played his trump card:[56] 'Stilicho – he said – was planning the journey to the east in order to plot the overthrow of the young Theodosius and the transfer of the east to his own son Eucherius.'

This message was repeated at every opportunity, and carefully disseminated among the Roman troops of the army of Italy, gathered in their main headquarters at Pavia (Ticinum). When Honorius came to review them, before sending them off on 13 August to engage with Constantine III, the troops mutinied and killed many of Stilicho's main supporters in the upper echelons of the bureaucracy. On hearing the news:

[Stilicho] assembled the leaders of all the barbarian allied troops he had with him, to hold a council about what should be done. Everyone agreed that if the emperor had been killed, which was still in doubt, all the barbarian allies should fall on the Roman soldiers at once and teach all the others a lesson, but that if the emperor were safe, even though the bureaucratic officers had been killed, only the instigators of the mutiny should be punished ... When, however, they found that no insult had been offered to the emperor, Stilicho decided to proceed no further with punishing the soldiers but to return to Ravenna.

These barbarian troops were mainly the twelve thousand or so followers of the Gothic king Radagaisus, whom Stilicho had drafted after the former's defeat and who formed a distinct grouping within the Italian army. Nothing suggests that there was any kind of Roman/barbarian split in the other, regular regiments, and after Stilicho's fall many non-Romans, individuals recruited over the years, continued to serve in them. In Ravenna, Stilicho first sought sanctuary in a church; but then he surrendered himself to certain death, not allowing his personal retainers to intervene. He was decapitated on 22 August.

So perished, after thirteen years of power, the western generalissimo. Many of his chief appointees had been killed in the mutiny at Pavia, and others were now hunted down and killed. His son Eucherius was arrested and executed, and Honorius divorced his daughter. Regime change Roman-style was – like many politicians – nasty, brutish and thorough. Olympius' last throw against his former mentor took the form of a series of laws enacted between September and November 408, which confiscated all of Stilicho's property and punished anyone who tried to hold on to anything that had once belonged to this 'public brigand'.[57] To my mind, like the Thane of Cawdor, nothing in his life became him like the leaving of it. He preferred to die quietly, rather than convulse what remained of the Roman state in further civil war. What's left to us is the vignette of a loyal state servant of considerable stature; the best of our sources, Olympiodorus, for one, was highly sympathetic towards him. Although one anti-barbarian Greek historian, Eunapius, accuses him of colluding with Alaric from the early 390s onwards, there is not the slightest sign that having a Vandal father made him comport himself as anything other than a loyal Roman officer. Stilicho just had the misfortune to be in authority at the moment when the Huns overturned the balance of power on which the Empire had traditionally rested. There aren't many individuals in history who would have been able to deal successfully, and all at the same moment, with restive emperor, Vandals, Alans and Suevi, large-scale usurpation and Gothic supergroup.[58]

The wisdom behind Stilicho's policies shows up in the events that followed his death. The new regime headed by Olympius, who made himself Master of Offices (*magister officiorum*) – a senior bureaucratic position with wide-ranging responsibilities, not unlike head of the Civil Service – completely reversed Stilicho's policies. War, not peace, with the Goths became the order of the day, and Alaric's offer to exchange hostages, in return for payment and withdrawal from the fringes of Italy, was firmly rejected.

The Goths were now back in the political wilderness, worse off in some ways than before 406. At least then they had had a well established base. Now, they were in an unfamiliar territory and lacking ties to any local food-producing population. But in one important respect, Alaric's Goths were soon to be better off. Shortly after Stilicho's execution, the native Roman element in the army of Italy launched a series of pogroms against the families and property of the barbarian troops that he had recruited, many of them the former followers of Radagaisus. These families, who had been quartered in various Italian cities, were massacred wholesale. Outraged, the menfolk threw in their lot with Alaric, increasing his fighting force to perhaps around 30,000. Nor was this first reinforcement the end of the story. Later, when the Goths were encamped outside Rome in 409, they were joined by enough slaves to take Alaric's force to a total of 40,000 warriors. Again, I suspect that most of these slaves were the less fortunate followers of Radagaisus, rather than ex-Roman pastry-cooks. Just three years after hordes of them had been sold into slavery, Alaric had offered them a means of ending their servitude to the Romans.[59]

In the autumn of 408, now in command of a Gothic supergroup larger than any yet seen, Alaric made a bold play. Gathering all his men, including those stationed in Pannonia with his brother-in-law Athaulf, he marched across the Alps and into Italy, sowing destruction far and wide as he made a beeline for Rome. He arrived outside the city in November and quickly laid siege to it, thus preventing all food supplies from entering. It soon emerged, however, that Alaric had not the slightest intention of capturing the city. What he wanted – and what he got by the end of the year – was, most obviously, booty. The Roman Senate agreed to pay him a ransom of 5,000 pounds of gold and 30,000 of silver, together with huge quantities of silks, skins and spices – particularly handy at this moment when he had a newly recruited army whose loyalty he needed to court. But as he had since 395, the Goth also pressed on with his efforts to find a modus vivendi with the Roman state; and he wanted the Senate's help in achieving this, the main aim of his entire political career. A senatorial embassy duly approached Honorius as mediators, urging the case for a hostage swap and a military alliance. The emperor made assenting noises, so the Goths dropped the siege, withdrawing north into Tuscany.

But Honorius was either playing for time, or else unsure of what to do. Olympius' influence was still strong enough to prevent the agreement being ratified, and so, particularly incensed by the ambush of part of his force near Pisa, Alaric returned to Rome to ram his message home. Under Gothic pressure, another senatorial embassy, this time with an escort of Goths, trotted north to Ravenna – now the political heart of the Empire – where Honorius was based. It was time to talk, they declared. This was enough to destroy Olympius' credibility with the emperor. It simply was not possible to mobilize the Roman army in Italy and attack the Goths – the sides were too evenly matched for victory to be certain, and a head-on Roman–Gothic confrontation would have allowed Constantine III to advance over the Alps. The only alternative was to negotiate. By April 409, the man with most influence over the emperor was a former supporter of Stilicho, Jovius the Praetorian Prefect of Italy – he had previously been sent to liaise with the Goths as they waited in Epirus for the arrival of Stilicho before launching their projected joint campaign against the eastern Empire. Negotiations opened between Alaric and Jovius at Rimini, and the prospects for peace seemed good precisely because the imperial party had few bargaining chips. Constantine III was still in Arles, busy promoting his sons to the purple – a direct threat of impending dynasty change, if ever there was one. Honorius was now so scared of Constantine, indeed, that at some point early in 409, in an act of formal recognition, he sent him a purple robe. An attempt by some of Honorius' officers to infiltrate a garrison of 6,000 men into Rome also ended in disaster, with barely a hundred getting through. Meanwhile, the troops in Ravenna were becoming restive. For Honorius, therefore, fighting just wasn't an option. Alaric knew it, as his first demands reveal. Zosimus tells us:[60] 'Alaric demanded that a fixed amount of gold and corn be provided every year, and that he and all his followers should live in the two Venetias, Noricum and Dalmatia.' Jovius acquiesced, and also requested that Honorius formally appoint Alaric to a senior imperial generalship (*magister utriusque militiae*). The agreement would make the Goths rich and their leader a figure of great influence at court; it would also place a Gothic army astride the major eastern passes into Italy and close to Ravenna.

But there was a sticking-point. Honorius was ready to agree to the requests for corn and gold, but not to the generalship. He responded with an insulting letter that was read out during the negotiations. Alaric stormed out – but then, fascinatingly, changed his mind. This time he recruited some Roman bishops to serve as his ambassadors. The message they delivered was this:

> Alaric did not now want office or honour, nor did he now wish to settle in the provinces previously specified, but only the two Noricums, which are on the far reaches of the Danube, are subject to continual incursions, and pay little tax to the treasury. More-over he would be satisfied with as much corn each year as the emperor thought sufficient, and forget the gold ... When Alaric made these fair and prudent proposals, everyone marvelled at the man's moderation.

Gone was the putative Gothic protectorate; gone too were the payments in gold; the Goths would live quietly in a frontier province, well away from Ravenna. Alaric's moderation may astonish, but it reveals his vision of the big picture. Currently he had the military power to take pretty much whatever he wanted, but was willing to trade it in for a stable peace agreement with the Roman state. He must have had a powerful sense of a latent strength that the Empire might at some point reassert, and that demanded a safety-first approach.

Unrest still reigned, however, at Honorius' court. The historian Olympiodorus thought Alaric's revised terms supremely reasonable, but they were again rejected. So Alaric returned to Rome for a third time, set up his second siege, and decided to up the stakes. At the end of 409 he persuaded the Senate to elect its own emperor, Priscus Attalus, and for a time the west had a third Augustus alongside Honorius and Constantine III. From a leading senatorial family, Attalus had been prominent in public life for over a decade. Embassies were now sent to Honorius from the Senate, threatening him with mutila-tion and exile; Alaric himself – appointed Attalus' general-in-chief – proceeded to subdue most of the cities of northern Italy and to besiege Ravenna; and other forces were despatched to North Africa, which had remained loyal to Honorius. At one point Honorius was ready to flee, but in the nick of time 4,000 troops arrived from the east to make Ravenna safe, and enough money was sent from North Africa to secure the loyalty of the army of Italy. Attalus tried twice, if rather half-heartedly, to take North Africa, but he refused to employ any of Alaric's men. The Gothic leader had had enough. Perhaps his original notion had been to set up his own tame emperor, or perhaps Attalus' promotion had always been a bargaining counter. Be that as it may, in July 410 he deposed Attalus and reopened negotiations with Honorius, who – thanks to the influx of eastern troops and African funds – had recovered his confidence. A meeting was arranged, and Alaric moved to within 60 stadia (about 12 kilometres) of Ravenna. Rogue elements in Honorius' military, meanwhile, were against all negotiation. As Alaric awaited Honorius, he was attacked by a small Roman force led by Sarus. Later, in the mid-410s, Sarus' brother Sergeric was prominent enough among Alaric's Goths to make a bid for its leadership, which, taken with Sarus' documented hostility to Alaric and his brother-in-law Athaulf, suggests to me that he was a rival whom Alaric had defeated for the leadership of the Goths back in the 390s.[61]

Alaric was outraged, both at the attack, and – if I'm right – at the identity of his attacker. Giving up on the idea of negotiating with Ravenna, the Goths turned on their heels and returned to Rome a fourth time. There they mounted their third siege. No doubt by this time Rome's suburban landladies had their old rooms waiting for them. There was a brief halt outside the walls, but then the Salarian Gate opened.[62]

The Sack of Rome

BY ALL ACCOUNTS, there followed one of the most civilized sacks of a city ever witnessed. Alaric's Goths were Christian, and treated many of Rome's holiest places with great respect. The two main basilicas of St Peter and St Paul were nominated places of sanctuary. Those who fled there were left in peace, and refugees to Africa later reported with astonishment how the Goths had even conducted certain holy ladies there, particularly one Marcella, before methodically ransacking their houses. Not that everyone, not even all the city's nuns, fared so well, but the Christian Goths did keep their religious affiliation firmly in view. One huge silver ciborium, 2,025 pounds in weight and the gift of the emperor Constantine, was lifted from the Lateran Palace, but the liturgical vessels of St Peter's were left in situ. Structural damage, too, was largely limited to the area of the Salarian Gate and the old Senate house. All in all, even after three days of Gothic attentions, the vast majority of the city's monuments and buildings remained intact, even if stripped of their movable valuables.

The contrast with the last time the city had been sacked, by Celtic tribes in 390 BC, could not have been more marked. Then, as Livy tells it, the main Roman forces had found themselves tied up in a siege of the Etruscan city of Veii (modern Isola Farnese), so that a Celtic warband was able to walk straight into Rome. The few men of fighting age left there defended the capitol with the help of some geese, which provided early warning of surprise attacks, but they abandoned the rest of the town. Older patricians refused to leave, but sat outside their houses in full ceremonial robes. At first the Celts approached reverentially 'beings who . . . seemed in their majesty of countenance and in the gravity of their expression most like to gods'. Then:

> A Celt stroked the beard of one of them, Marcus Papirius, which he wore long as they all did then, at which point the Roman struck him over the head with his ivory mace, and, provoking his anger, was the first to be slain. After that, the rest were massacred where they sat and . . . there was no mercy then shown to anyone. The houses were ransacked, and after, being emptied, were set aflame.

In 390 BC, only the fortress on the Capitol survived the burning of the city; in AD 410 only the Senate house was set on fire.[63]

That Rome should have seen a highly civilized sack conducted by Christian Goths who respected the sanctity of St Peter's might seem a dreadful anticlimax compared with expectations of bloodthirsty barbarians running loose in the great imperial capital. It's much more exciting to think of the sack of Rome as the culmination of Germanic dreams of revenge – inspired by the slaughter of Varus' legions in AD 9 – against Roman imperialism. The inescapable conclusion to be drawn from a close exploration of the sequence of events between 408 and 410, however, is that Alaric did not want the sack to happen. His Goths had been outside the city on and off since late autumn 408, and, had they wanted to, could have taken it at any point in the twenty months since their arrival. Alaric could probably not have cared less about possible banner headlines in the historical press and a few dozen wagons' worth of booty. His concerns were of a different order altogether. Since 395, he had been struggling to force the Roman state to rewrite its relationship with the Goths as it had been defined in the treaty of 382. His bottom line, as we know, was the grant of recognized status by a legitimate Roman regime. Once he had given up on Constantinople in 400/1, this had to mean the regime of Honorius in Ravenna. Besieging Rome was simply a means of pressuring Honorius and his advisers to come to a deal. But the ploy never worked. Essentially, Alaric overestimated the significance of the city to an imperial authority based in Ravenna. Rome was a potent symbol of Empire, but no longer the political centre of the Roman world. Ultimately, therefore, Honorius could ignore its fate without the Empire suffering major damage. Alaric's letting his troops loose there for three days was an admission that his whole policy, since entering Italy in the autumn of 408, had been misconceived. It had not delivered the kind of deal with the Roman state that he was looking for. The sack of Rome was not so much a symbolic blow to the Roman Empire as an admission of Gothic failure.

But if its immediate importance was not at all what you might expect, Honorius and his advisers had not lightly abandoned Rome to the Goths, and the sack was part of a broad sequence of events of much greater historical significance. Ultimately, the events of late August 410 had their origin in the further advance of the Huns into the heart of Europe and the highly potent combination of invasion and usurpation that consequently convulsed the western Empire. For although the sack was historically insignificant, the events of which it was a part had massive significance for the stability of Roman Europe, their shock waves reverberating around the Roman world. From the Holy Land, as we've seen, Jerome lamented the fall of a city that for him still symbolized everything that was good and worthwhile. Elsewhere, the response was more strident. Educated non-Christians, for instance, argued that there could be no clearer sign of the illegitimacy of the new imperial religion: Rome had been sacked because its guardian gods, now rejected, had removed their protection. In North Africa, this line of thought was championed in particular by some of the upper-class refugees who fled there from Italy. And it was a challenge that St Augustine met with the full force of his intellect.

Many of his sermons can be quite closely dated, and those from

the later months of the year 410 show him grappling with a series of
related issues. He then took some of the most important of these ideas
and put them together – with much else besides – in what became his
magnum opus: *The City of God*. This grew into a work of twenty-two
books, and was not completed until 425. The first three books, though,
were published in 413, and contain Augustine's immediate responses
to the questions that the sack had led his congregation to pose, many
of them triggered by the taunts of pagan detractors of Christianity.

Augustine's immediate answer was of the straightforward yah-boo-
sucks variety. This bunch of vociferous pagans just hadn't read their
history. The Roman Empire had endured many a disaster long before
Christ had appeared on the earth, without blame having been laid at
the door of the divine powers:[64]

> Where were [the gods], when the consul Valerius was slain in
> defending the Capitol, which had been set on fire by exiles and
> slaves? . . . Where were they when Spurius Maelius, because he
> distributed free corn to the hungry people as the famine increased
> in severity, was accused of aiming at kingship and was slain? . . .
> Where were they when a fearful plague had broken out? . . .
> Where were they when the Roman army had for ten years fought
> without success and without intermission at Veii? . . . Where were
> they when the Gauls captured Rome, sacked it, burned it, and
> filled it with bodies of the slain?

A quick rereading of Livy's *History of the City of Rome* had furnished
Augustine with enough ammunition to make a decent counterblast to
the pagans' protests. But, possessed as he was of one of the finest
minds in antiquity, he was not content to limit his response to mere
on-the-spot retort. In the course of its fifteen-year gestation, *The City of
God* would deal with a multitude of issues and themes, but its first
three books already set out the central thrust of an entirely alternative
view of Roman history from that perpetuated by the ideology of the
Empire's one-party state.

Christians had long been familiar with the 'two-city' notion. This
developed out of the Book of Revelation's vision of a new Jerusalem
coming into being as the eternal dwelling-place of the righteous, after
the Last Judgement at the end of the world. This heavenly Jerusalem
was where the Christian really belonged, whatever city might claim
his or her affiliations in this world. In these early books of *The City of*

God, Augustine picked up this well established Christian concept and pursued it, with ruthless intellectual rigour, to some uncomfortable conclusions. Above all, Rome, whatever benefits it had to offer and despite its new Christian manifestation, was just like any other earthly city. Just because Rome's dominion was so wide and had lasted for so many centuries, there was no reason to confuse it with the heavenly Jerusalem. To make his argument stick, Augustine again raided the stock authors of Roman history, and to telling effect. In particular, he argued, the history of Rome, when closely studied, could sustain no claim that the Empire's unmatched success was due to any particular morality, and hence legitimacy, on its part. Borrowing from Sallust, one of the core authors of the Latin curriculum, he was able to claim that any real morality in the ancient Roman state had been attributable to the outside constraints imposed upon it by the war with Carthage, and that, when victory removed this balancing force, corruption set in.[65] The whole Empire was built on nothing more than the desire to dominate: 'This "lust for domination"[66] brings great evils to vex and exhaust the whole human race. Rome was conquered by this lust when [she] triumphed over the conquest of Alba [Rome's first victory], and to the popular acclaim of her crime she gave the name of glory.'

Augustine did not go on to claim that the entire imperial edifice was evil, or that earthly peace was a bad thing. But he urged his readers to understand that the Pax Romana was no more than an opportunity for Christians to come to God in the realization that their real loyalty was to the heavenly kingdom: 'The Heavenly City out-shines Rome beyond comparison. There, instead of victory, is truth; instead of high rank, holiness; instead of peace, felicity; instead of life, eternity.' In this world, citizens of the Heavenly City belong to different polities, so that even among the Goths sacking Rome there might be true friends, while some fellow Romans might be enemies.[67] The Heavenly City's citizens can owe no more than a passing loyalty to any earthly entity; they will be united in the next world:

> Christ with divine authority denounces and condemns the offences of men, and their perverted lusts, and he gradually withdraws his family from all parts of a world which is failing and declining through those evils, so that he may establish a city whose titles of 'eternal' and 'glorious' are not given by meaning-less flattery but by the judgement of truth.

In the sack of Rome, Augustine found the fundamental illegitimacy of all earthly cities, and raised a rallying cry to the citizens of the heavenly Jerusalem to look to the life to come.[68]

Sixteen hundred years on, it is easy to miss the revolutionary nature of Augustine's vision. Claims that the Roman Empire would last for ever – the image of *Roma aeterna* – have been shown to be hollow; the notion that its success was based upon a unique access to divine favour strikes us as ridiculous. In reading *The City of God*, however, we must forget all that we know from hindsight. When Augustine was writing, the Empire had lasted for centuries and had no serious rival. For as long as anyone could remember, its propaganda had been portraying it as the gods', now God's – the transition to Christianity had been surprisingly smooth – vehicle for civilizing humanity. Christian Bishops had been happy to propagate the idea that it was no accident that Christ and Augustus had lived at exactly the same moment. What better indicator that the Roman Empire was destined to conquer the world and bring the whole of humankind to Christianity? Everything from the emperor's bedchamber to his treasury was sacred, and the intensely orchestrated ceremonial life of the state was devoted to the idea that God ruled humanity through a divinely guided emperor.

Augustine's response to the sack of Rome put a huge black cross next to all of these comfortable ideas. The Empire was but one state among many in the course of world history; it was neither uniquely virtuous nor uniquely predestined to last.

The sequence of events surrounding the sack of Rome, and the response to its fall, offer us two contrasting interpretations, then, of the significance of those three days in August 410. On the one hand, both Jerome and Augustine in their different ways bear eloquent witness to a world turned upside down. On the other, we see that the city was sacked for the very prosaic reason that Alaric needed to compensate his followers for their loyalty, after his broader plans for Gothic prosperity had been thwarted. In *The City of God* Augustine was much too canny to commit himself on the point of whether the sack of the city, after the Goths' Roman holiday, meant the end of the Empire. This warns us not to jump to any conclusions without taking a much closer look at the Empire's strategic position.

Homecoming

IN OCTOBER AND November 417, Rutilius Claudius Namatianus made his way slowly back to Gaul. A native of Toulouse, he had been in Italy for several years: in 412 as Master of Offices at Honorius' court – the same position that had allowed Olympius to undermine Stilicho – then, briefly, as Urban Prefect of Rome in the summer of 414. On his return to Gaul he wrote an epic poem, *De Reditu Suo* (*On His Homecoming*), describing his journey. The first book comprised 644 lines of poetry, but the manuscripts break off after just sixty-eight lines of the second, at which point Rutilius was still only somewhere off the coast of north-west Italy. Although one more page – another forty-odd lines – turned up in the late 1960s (having been used to patch up a volume in the monastery of Bobbio in the sixteenth century), we are still not sure where exactly in Gaul the journey ended.[69] It was a sea voyage:

> For since the Tuscan fields, the Aurelian road,
> Have suffered Gothic raids with sword and fire,
> Since woods have lost their homes, their bridges streams,
> Better to trust with sails the uncertain sea.

The system of stables and guesthouses on the Via Aurelia, the main highway up the west coast of Italy, which had facilitated the comings and goings of official travellers such as Theophanes (see Chapter 2), had not been restored since the Goths occupied the region during 408–10. But Rutilius was far from downhearted. The poem opens with an evocation of the attractions of life in Rome undiminished by the sack:

> What tedium can there be though men devote
> The years of all their mortal life to Rome?
> Naught tedious is that which pleases without end.
> O, ten times happy – past all reckoning –
> Those whose desert it was to have been born
> On that propitious soil; the noble sons
> Of Roman chiefs, they crown their lofty birth
> With the proud name of citizens of Rome.

Nor has the sack raised in Rutilius' mind the slightest doubt about the Empire's destiny, its mission to civilize humankind:

> Thy gifts thou spreadest wide as the sun's rays,
> As far as earth-encircling ocean heaves.
> Phoebus,[70] embracing all things [,] rolls for thee;
> His steeds both rise and sink in thy domains . . .
> Far as the habitable climes extend
> Towards either pole thy valour finds its path.
> Thou hast made of alien realms one fatherland;
> The lawless found their gain beneath thy sway;
> Sharing thy laws with them thou hast subdued,
> Thou hast made a city of the once wide world.

Here are all the old ideas we met with at the height of imperial grandeur.

The poem is extraordinary. Here is Rutilius returning to Gaul a decade after the Vandals, Alans and Suevi had turned it into a single funeral pyre, and dwelling at length on the glories of Rome just seven years after the sack. But, having held high office at the court of the embattled Honorius, he could see as well as anyone the size of the task ahead. He returned to Gaul ready to roll up his sleeves:

> . . . the Gallic fields demand again
> Their countryman. Too sadly marred those fields
> By tedious wars; but the less fair they are
> The more to be compassioned. Lighter fault
> To slight one's countrymen in prosperous hours;
> The public loss claims each man's loyalty.

His faith in the Roman ideal rested on a determination to rebuild what the barbarians had laid waste, not a delusion that the history of the last decade hadn't happened:

> Let thy [Rome's] dire woe be blotted and forgot;
> Let thy contempt for suffering heal thy wounds . . .
> Things that refuse to sink, still stronger rise,
> And higher from the lowest depths rebound;
> And, as the torch reversed new strength attains,
> Thou, brighter from thy fall, to heaven aspirest!

Rome had taken much harder knocks from Carthage and the Celts. She would rise phoenix-like, strengthened and renewed by suffering.

Nor was Rutilius the only Gallo-Roman brimming with confidence in 417. His was a pagan take on history and fate, but his vision spanned the religious divide. The same year, in his *Carmen de Providentia Dei* (*Poem on the Providence of God*), a Gallic Christian poet reflected on the disasters that had afflicted Gaul in the last decade. This anonymous author stands in the same tradition as the Gallic poets we encountered earlier, and echoes many of the same themes. The passage of those few years, however, had given him a slightly different perspective:

> You, who weep over overgrown fields, deserted courtyards and the crumbling terraces of your burnt out villa, shouldn't you rather shed tears for your own losses, when you look at the desolate recesses of your heart, the beauty covered over with layers of grime, and the enemy rioting in the citadel of your imprisoned mind? If that citadel hadn't been surrendered . . . these beauties created by the hand would still remain to bear witness to the virtue of a holy people.

The message here is much more Old Testament: God's people were visited with destruction because they fell from righteousness. But this is a message with a flip side: 'If any mental energy remains, let us shake off the servile yoke of sin, break the chains, and return to freedom and the glory of our native land.' He closed with a call to arms: 'Let us not fear, because we have collapsed in flight in a first contest, to take a stand and embark on a second battle.'

The poet meant his message to be taken spiritually, but was also aware of its political dimension. Spiritual renewal would bring victory and prosperity on earth as well as in heaven. Worldly disaster wasn't a reminder of the essential division that must exist between the Heavenly City and any earthly state, but a call for moral reform. There is no rejection here of the Empire and its civilizing mission. The barbarians had done their worst, but this was only round one; round two would see the Empire triumph.[71] In this respect, Gallo-Roman pagans and Gallo-Roman Christians were of one mind. The message could not be more different from Augustine's.

Flavius Constantius

THE SOURCE OF this renewed confidence was an extraordinary change that had come over the western Empire in the ten years since Rome had been sacked. When we left the story at the end of August 410, prospects could hardly have looked worse. There was a Roman army in Italy, unable to move against Alaric's Goths for fear of leaving the back door open for Constantine III, still angling to overthrow Honorius. The Vandals, Alans and Suevi had turned their attention to Spain, and were on the point of dividing its territories between them. Constantine controlled not only the British provinces but the Gallic military too, and was pushing feelers into Spain and Italy. Control of the western state had thus fragmented into the hands of two bunches of barbarians and an unusually successful usurper. Now, seven years later, much of the imperial jigsaw had been put back together, and things were looking rosy again.

The chief architect of all this was an experienced military commander by the name of Flavius Constantius.[72] An Illyrian from Naissus (modern Niš) in the Balkans, the heart of one of Rome's recruiting grounds, he had originally joined the east Roman army and served in many of the campaigns of Theodosius I. He had presumably, like Stilicho, first come west in the campaign against the usurper Eugenius, probably when in his mid-thirties, and, again like Stilicho, had stayed on afterwards. As we shall see, there are good reasons for taking him to have been a supporter of the old generalissimo, although he was not senior enough to find any mention in the sources while Stilicho was alive.

> In public processions Constantius was downcast and sullen, a man with bulging eyes, a long neck and a broad head, who always slumped over the neck of the horse he was riding, darting glances here and there out of the corners of his eyes . . . But at banquets and parties he was so cheerful and affable that he even competed with the clowns who often played before his table.[73]

Hardly your charismatic hero, then. But his affability on more private occasions, Olympiodorus tells us, was a huge asset, and there is no doubting the energy with which he set about rebuilding the western Empire.

Flavius Constantius inherited Stilicho's position as senior western general (*magister militum*) in 410/11. His closeness to Stilicho is suggested by the fact that he took a leading role in the retribution dished out to the chief protagonist in the plot against him. Olympius met his grisly end – he was clubbed to death – at pretty much this time. With matters at court sorted out to his satisfaction, Flavius Constantius swiftly turned to more substantial problems. Having mobilized the Italian army for war, his first target was Constantine III.

By this stage, affairs in Gaul had taken an interesting turn, which aided our man in his endeavours. Constantine had fallen out with one of his generals, Gerontius, who had gone so far as to raise his own usurper, Maximus,[74] to the purple and advance on Constantine's headquarters at Arles. When Constantius' Italian army reached that city, therefore, it had first to defeat the forces of Gerontius. This was duly accomplished – it was enough to turn Gerontius' remaining troops against him, and he committed suicide. The next challenge came in the form of a relief force raised by Constantine's other leading general, Edobichus, who had recruited auxiliaries from the Franks and Alamanni to fight alongside whatever troops from the Roman army of Gaul remained under his command. Again, Constantius triumphed. To induce surrender, Constantine III was offered his life, but the promise was broken. On his way back to Honorius he was murdered, and on 18 September 411 it was only his head that arrived at Ravenna – at the top of a pole. One season's campaigning had been enough to wrap up a usurper who, only two years before, had had Honorius fearing for his life.

This wasn't quite the end of the usurper problem, though. In Roman politics, one usurpation tended to beget another, especially when the first had started to wobble. A mixture of ambition and fear of retribution prompted individuals who had taken part in the first revolt to try their hand at a second. In 411, it was not only Gerontius who smelt Constantine's blood in the water, but so did a Gallic aristocrat by the name of Jovinus. His centre of operations was further north. Proclaimed emperor perhaps at Mainz in the province of Upper Germania, his military power-base was provided by still dissident elements among the Gallo-Roman military, backed up by Burgundians and Alans.[75] He also gained the considerable fillip of support from Alaric's Goths, who were now in Gaul under the leadership of his brother-in-law Athaulf. This was a powerful combination, but an artificial one, and Constantius took time to consider the situation. Instead of rushing into battle, he used his diplomatic skills to work on the cracks in Jovinus' putative alliance and in 413 received his due reward. The Goths changed sides, and – a clear demonstration of the power of the supergroup Alaric had assembled – this left the usurper with no choice but to surrender. Executed en route to Honorius, he met the same fate as Constantine. His head duly arrived atop its pole on 30 August that year.

Concentrating so determinedly on defeating the usurpers before tackling the barbarians might seem the wrong order of priorities, and historians have often criticized it. But to combat the grave threats now facing the Empire, any leader needed to be able to deploy the full range of imperial resources: particularly, of course, on the military front. In the summer of 413, Constantius' defeat of the usurpers finally reunited, for the first time since the autumn of 406, the major armies of the western Empire, the different British, Gallic and Spanish elements of which had been won over by Constantine III, Gerontius and Jovinus. Having put the Roman house in order, and united the once disparate parts of the army under his command, Constantius was now ready to deal with the other problems. Very sensibly, before turning them loose on the various barbarian groups at large in the western Empire, he promised a pay rise to the troops who had only yesterday been fighting for the enemy.[76] Within the different regiments of Constantius' army were many individually recruited barbarians who were quite happy fighting under Roman colours. Individual barbarians were one thing, though; masses of independent Goths, Vandals, Alans and Suevi, quite another. This newly reunited army's first task was to bring the Goths to heel.

Athaulf's Goths

IN THE IMMEDIATE aftermath of the sack, the Goths headed south. Now that his attempt to stabilize their position within the Empire had failed, Alaric had in mind a complete change of strategy: he was now looking to relocate, lock, stock and both smoking barrels, in North Africa. But a well timed storm wrecked the fleet he was assembling, and he died shortly afterwards. In the course of 411 Athaulf moved the

Goths into Gaul, where we saw him first supporting, then abandoning, the usurper of Jovinus.

A mutually acceptable blueprint for Gotho-Roman relations was yet to be established. We know there was some fighting between the Goths and Constantius' forces around Marseille in late 413, and that the Goths afterwards established themselves at Narbonne. Here, as so often in this story, the loss of Olympiodorus' history is a considerable handicap, but everything suggests that Athaulf was continuing to demand a much higher price for an agreement than Constantius was willing to pay. The historian Orosius reports overhearing someone telling St Jerome that:

> He himself had been a very intimate friend of Athaulf at Narbonne, and . . . he had often heard what the latter, when in good spirits, health and temper [meaning after a few drinks], was accustomed to answer in reply to questions. It seems that at first he ardently desired to blot out the Roman name and make all the Roman territory a Gothic empire in fact as well as in name, so that, to use the popular expression, Gothia should take the place of Romania, and he, Athaulf, should become all that Caesar Augustus once had been. Having discovered from long experience that the Goths, because of their unbridled barbarism, were utterly incapable of obeying laws, and yet believing that the state ought not to be deprived of laws without which a state is not a state, he [Athaulf] chose to seek for himself at least the glory of restoring and increasing the renown of the Romans by the power of the Goths, wishing to be looked upon by posterity as the restorer of the Roman Empire.[77]

What precisely Athaulf meant by this emerges from his actions. In the train of booty that the Goths took from Rome were two human prizes: Priscus Attalus, whom Alaric had persuaded the Senate of Rome to raise to the purple and who had then been demoted again in 409/10; and the emperor Honorius' sister, Galla Placidia. In 414, after bringing down Jovinus, Athaulf proceeded to make strategic use of both of his hostages. Having been unceremoniously dumped by Alaric as part of a putative settlement with Honorius, Attalus was restored to the purple. It was then Placidia's turn to be exploited, in another effort at blackmail on Athaulf's part. In January 414, Olympiodorus tells us, the two were married, with the advice and encouragement of Candidianus ... at the house of Ingenuus, one of the leading citizens of [Narbonne]. There Placidia, dressed in royal raiment, sat in a hall decorated in the Roman manner, and by her side sat Athaulf, wearing a Roman general's cloak and other Roman clothing ... Along with other wedding gifts, Athaulf gave Placidia fifty handsome young men dressed in silk clothes, each bearing aloft two very large dishes, one full of gold, the other full of precious ... stones, which had been carried off by the Goths at the sack of Rome. Then nuptial hymns were sung, first by Attalus, then by Rusticius and Phoebadius.[78]

Clearly, Athaulf was pursuing here the more ambitious of Alaric's two peace plans – the one that included, for himself, a glittering career at the imperial court. Placidia duly fell pregnant and gave birth to a son, whom his proud parents named Theodosius. A momentous name-giving, indeed: the young Theodosius was grandson of one Roman emperor by that name, Theodosius I, and first cousin to another, the eastern emperor Theodosius II, son of Honorius' late brother Arcadius. When you also recall that Honorius had no children at this point, and in fact never did, this was a birth redolent with potential. A king of the Goths had fathered a child with an extremely good claim to be heir apparent to the western Empire.

But Athaulf had, in fact, overreached himself. Constantius and Honorius wanted Placidia back, but minus her Gothic husband. They refused to make a deal on Athaulf's terms. The Goths, anyway, had one huge strategic weakness. Since 408, when they moved on Italy, they had been operating without secure sources of supply. During the glory years culminating in the sack of Rome they had taken booty aplenty; now, with typical precision, Constantius identified their Achilles' heel. Rather than risking his army in battle, he blockaded the Goths by both land and sea. By early 415, food had run out in Narbonne and they had to retreat into Spain in search of supplies. Constantius' strategy was also materially aided by one of those stray accidents of history: the young Theodosius died soon after birth and was buried by his grieving parents in a silver coffin in a church at Barcelona. This took one of the trump cards out of Athaulf's hand. Constantius maintained the pressure, and in due course the Goths – or some of them – cracked. What was really standing in the way of a settlement – obviously in the air since Athaulf abandoned Jovinus in 413 – was Athaulf's determination to become an imperial bigwig.

In the summer of 415, enough resentment built up against his policies, and their cost to the Goths in general, to prompt an internal coup, during which Athaulf was mortally wounded. After his death (announced in Constantinople on 24 September), his brother and the children of his first marriage were all butchered by Sergeric, who belonged to a noble Gothic house that had earlier competed for the leadership of the Goths formerly united by Alaric. But after only seven days Sergeric too was ousted, and power passed to a certain Wallia. Neither of these successors was a blood relation of Alaric and Athaulf. Wallia gave in to Roman pressure, and returned Placidia, now widowed and childless. In return, Constantius handed over to the Goths six hundred thousand *modii* of wheat. The first two steps towards a different kind of peace deal had been taken – one that envisaged a much less important political role in the Empire for the Gothic leadership.[79]

A Phoenix Rising?

THE THIRD STEP, as well as cementing peace with the Goths, would deal with the burning issue that was Spain. For half a decade now, the Vandals, Alans and Suevi had been enjoying the revenues of the Spanish provinces that they had allotted themselves back in 411. But now a Gotho-Roman military alliance was about to take them on. In 416, operations began. Hydatius, in his *Chronicle*, tells us what happened:

> All of the Siling Vandals in Baetica were wiped out by King Wallia. The Alans, who were ruling over the Vandals and Sueves [Suevi], suffered such heavy losses at the hands of the Goths that, after the death of their king, Addax, the few survivors, with no thought for their own kingdom, placed themselves under the protection of Gunderic, the king of the [Hasding] Vandals, who had settled in Gallaecia.[80]

A succinct summary of three years' fighting (416–18) – its import could not be clearer. Having suppressed usurpers and subdued the Goths, Constantius now made use of these very people to tackle his other major problem. And how effective the campaigning was! The Silings ceased to exist, and the Alans – who, according to Hydatius, had previously been the dominant force among the Rhine invaders (a report in tune with their rescue of the Vandals from the hands of the Franks back in the autumn of 406) – suffered such heavy losses that the remnants attached themselves to the Hasding monarchy.

At this point Constantius recalled the Goths from Spain, and in 418 proceeded to settle them in Aquitaine, allotting them lands in the Garonne valley (south-west Gaul) between Toulouse and Bordeaux. Quantities of ink have been expended on the nature and purpose of this settlement. The one piece of hard information we have, which derives from Olympiodorus,[81] is that the Goths were given 'lands to farm'. I am happy to accept this. Certainly, there is no sign in subsequent years that the Roman state was directly supporting the Goths through its tax revenues; and, in fact, the previous decade had shown exactly how vulnerable, in strategic terms, they actually were without their own sources of supply. Athaulf's lofty ambitions had been brought low precisely because Constantius had been able to starve the Goths into insurrection against their own king. Handing them productive lands – much as under the 382 peace settlement – would have been an attractive option for both parties.

As to what happened on the ground, we can only guess. Much has been made of the fact that we hear of no complaints from dispossessed Roman landowners. One possible reason for this may be that it was public land (both imperial estates and lands belonging to public corporations such as city endowments) that was used for the Goths – hence no need for expropriation. As we shall see in the next chapter, this is the way the Roman state dealt with an analogous problem in North Africa. It is highly likely, too, that in many cases the peasants were left in situ, the Goths replacing existing landholders as recipients of rents. Whether this transfer endowed incoming Goths with full ownership rights – the right to sell on or bequeath an allotted piece of land – or only usufruct – the right to enjoy its revenues during one's lifetime – is a question we cannot answer.[82]

As to why Aquitaine was chosen, many different views have been aired: everything from the Goths' potential usefulness in dealing with separatists in north-western Gaul to countering the raids of Saxon pirates.[83] To my mind, Aquitaine was the logical intersection of two imperatives. First, the Goths needed to be put *somewhere*, and the key issue was how far the settlement area was going to be from the west's political centre. As we have seen, Alaric at the height of his power talked of settling them in and around Ravenna and either side of the Alpine passes. There they would have been in a position to intervene constantly at the imperial court. In his more realistic phase he was ready to surrender that vision – entirely unacceptable to the Romans – for some land 'near the frontier'. The Garonne valley, beside the Atlantic Ocean and 1,000 kilometres from Ravenna, fitted that bill perfectly. It also had the second virtue of putting them near routes through the Pyrenees into Spain. And the job in Spain, though well begun, was only half done. Some of the survivors of the Rhine invasion remained unsubdued, and by the early 420s the Goths were back in the peninsula operating jointly again with a Roman army against the Hasding Vandals. In my view, the land settlement was envisaged as no more than one stage in an ongoing process designed to resume with the Goths returning to Spain to finish off the Vandals, Alans and Suevi.

The scale of Constantius' achievement is breathtaking. Despite the fact that, in 410, the Goths were rampaging around Italy, Constantine III was in Arles threatening a total takeover of the west, and the Rhine invaders were dividing up Spain between themselves, enough of the major levers of power had remained intact for a leader of Constantius' ability to put things back together. The armies of Gaul and, especially, Italy – the force with which Stilicho had defeated Radagaisus – still constituted a formidable fighting machine, and the great revenue-producing reservoir of North Africa remained untouched. Between 408 and 410, successive chief ministers had been unable to use the Italian army against either the Goths or Constantine III, because it couldn't fight both enemies at once, and fighting one would have just left the door open for the other. The stalemate was broken, however, by the Goths' departure from Italy under Athaulf. The central authorities in Ravenna had hung on just long enough for the Goths to be starved into leaving, and this had handed freedom of manoeuvre back to Constantius. One, maybe two, outside sources of support also strengthened his hand. First, the eastern Empire sent considerable help to Honorius when Alaric was ravaging Italy in 410, and other moral and financial aid surely followed, even if our sources are too thin to report it.[84]

Paradoxically, given that they had caused the whole mess in the first place, Constantius may also have drawn upon Hunnic support. In

409, Honorius summoned 10,000 Hunnic auxiliaries to his assistance. Since they did not arrive in time to prevent the sack of Rome, some modern historians have concluded that they never appeared.[85] Whether they did or not, in the campaigning season of 411 Constantius, as we have seen, suddenly arose from his military paralysis and marched confidently into Gaul to overpower the usurpers. In part, this reflected his new-found freedom to deploy the powerful army of Italy, but an additional factor may have been the arrival, finally, of the Huns. Getting rid of the Goths from Italian soil, plus a little help from friends old and new, had been enough to tip the balance of power in Constantius' favour. No wonder, in 417, Rutilius and his anonymous Christian counterpart were facing the future with confidence.

It is important to examine more closely, however, Constantius' work of reconstruction. The western Empire, despite his many achievements, had not been returned to exactly pristine condition.

The Reckoning

IN ONE OBVIOUS SENSE, reconstruction wasn't complete in 418, nor would Constantius have claimed that it was. The Silings and Alans had been put through the mincer, but the Hasding Vandals, now reinforced, and the Suevi were still at large. Apart from the potential military dangers these groups posed, their continued presence also meant that the parts of Spain they occupied remained outside direct imperial control, and hence no longer contributed revenues to the state. In fact, the period 405–18 had seen a series of tax losses that Constantius had not yet been able to remedy. It's hard to believe, for instance, that the Garonne valley produced much tax revenue after the Goths were settled there in 418.[86]

It is extremely difficult to reconstruct events in Roman Britain during the 410s, or even the general status of the island, but what is clear is that it had fallen outside the imperial system. As we have seen, the usurpations of 406/7 began there, and the British provinces provided Constantine III with his first power-base. Then, from the moment he moved to the continent with – it has long been suspected – most of the island's remaining Roman military, Britain disappears from our sources, except for two brief notices in Zosimus. The first records that the British threw off Roman rule at a later point in

Constantine's usurpation but before the sack of Rome, 'expelling the Roman magistrates and establishing the government they wanted'.[87] The second states that Honorius, still before August 410, wrote to the cities of Britain 'urging them to fend for themselves'. What this means has been much argued about. Zosimus sees this further British revolt as a parting of the ways with Romanness and a return to native custom. I suspect that this is another of his sixth-century misunderstandings, and that in fact the British Romans, unhappy with Constantine's focus on Gaul and consequent inability to defend them, took matters into their own hands. Otherwise, it is hard to see why Honorius would have to write to them in 410 admitting that the state could not provide for their defence. It wasn't so much a question, then, of getting out the woad and relearning Celtic languages as of trying to defend themselves against seaborne attack, especially at the hands of Saxon pirates. This had been a problem for well over a hundred years, and had led the Roman state to construct a range of fortifications, some of which still stand today. The extent of Saxon inroads made between 410 and 420 is another hotly contested issue. Everything suggests that the real cataclysm came a bit later, but, for present purposes, the date doesn't really matter. Whether at the hands of Saxons or of local self-defence forces, Britain dropped out of the Roman radar from about 410, and was no longer supplying revenues to Ravenna.[88]

The same thing was happening at this time in Armorica (north-western Gaul). The chain of events here is harder to read, but Rutilius tells us that in 417, as he himself was journeying home, his relative Exuperantius was busy restoring order.[89] It would seem, then, that Constantius' regime hastened to reinstitute imperial order and imperial taxation in Armorica, if not in Britain. This was certainly the case in central and southern Gaul, most of which had probably paid its taxes to Constantine III throughout his usurpation. About the Rhine frontier area we have no firm information. The city of Trier lost its role as an administrative centre for the whole of Gaul at this time, when government was moved south to Arles instead. But there was no major break in Roman control of the Trier region, so that it too presumably continued to pay at least some tax to Ravenna.[90]

In addition to the territories lost outright to the Roman system, tax revenue was substantially down in those much larger parts of the west that had been affected by warfare or looting over the past decade. Much of Italy had been pillaged by the Goths, Spain by the survivors of the Rhine invasion, and Gaul by both. How much of these territories had been damaged is difficult to say, and agriculture could of course recover, but there is good evidence that warfare had caused serious medium-term damage. In 412, a law of the emperor Honorius instructed the Praetorian Prefect of Italy that for five years the provinces of Campania, Tuscany, Picenum, Samnium, Apulia, Calabria, Bruttium and Lucania should have their taxes reduced to one-fifth of their normal amount. The Roman state reckoned that these provinces merited such a reduction because it was from their lands that the Goths had mainly supported themselves when camping around Rome between 408 and 410. A second law, of 418, reduced Campania's assessment to one-ninth of its previous level, and that of the other provinces to one-seventh. Few other areas will have taken such sustained damage – the product of a two-year occupation, more or less. The Vandals, Alans and Suevi seem to have come to a more ordered arrangement with the local Hispano-Romans. Nonetheless, outright losses of tax base and damage to what remained must have substantially reduced the annual income of the western Empire between 405 and 418.[91]

We can also detect substantial damage to two other key pillars of state. Evidence of the first shows up in another of the extraordinary sources to survive from late antiquity (mentioned earlier), the *Notitia Dignitatum*. This is a listing of all the civilian and military officials of the later Roman Empire, divided into its eastern and western halves. The document was kept by one of the senior bureaucrats, the *primicerius notariorum* (Chief Notary), part of whose job it was to issue letters of appointment. As the bureaucratic or military structure of the Empire changed, so the document was amended. The eastern half of the text records the eastern Empire as it stood about 395, at or near the death of Theodosius I. The western half, on the other hand, was kept thoroughly up to date down to 408, then partially so down to the early 420s. In particular – and this is why it concerns us here – the *Notitia* contains two listings of the mobile field army units (the *comitatenses*) of the western Empire. The first names the regiments (*numeri*) under their overall commanders, the Masters of Infantry and Cavalry; the second (*distributio numerorum*) records their regional distribution.[92] Detailed analysis indicates that this second list gives us a snapshot of the western field armies as they stood at the end of the second decade of the fifth century.[93]

A close look at these lists, and a comparison with the eastern army lists of 395, is very revealing. First, and entirely unsurprisingly, it is clear that the western army suffered heavy losses in the wars of the early fifth century. The total number of eastern field army regiments in 395 was 157. About 420, the western army had 181, but of these as many as 97 had been raised since 395 and only 84 survived from the period before 395. During the fourth century, the field army units had been split between different emperors on a number of occasions, but everything suggests that they were of roughly the same order of magnitude in each half of the Empire. If, like the east, therefore, the western field army had numbered about 160 regiments in 395, then no fewer than 76 of them (47.5 per cent) had been destroyed in the twenty-five years between Honorius' accession and 420. This is a massive level of attrition, representing losses of upwards of 30,000 men.[94] The Roman army of the Rhine took the heaviest hit. In 420, it stood at 58 regiments; but of these only 21 were pre-395 units, the other 37 (or 64 per cent) having been created during the reign of Honorius. This makes perfect sense. The Gallic army had borne the brunt of the first Rhine crossing; then, under the control of Constantine III, it had continued the fight against the invaders down to the Pyrenees and beyond. It had also, subsequently, been caught on the wrong side of Constantius' counterattack. No wonder it emerged in tatters, with many of its old units shredded and disbanded.[95]

What the *Notitia* has to tell us about how the losses were made good is also extremely interesting. By about 420, the numbers of western comitatensian units had recovered substantially, thanks to the 97 new regiments created since 395. Indeed, if we are right in supposing that eastern and western field armies were roughly equal in size in 395, then its total establishment had even gone up by about 20 units (12.5 per cent). Of the 97 new units, however, 62 (64 per cent) were old frontier garrison regiments regraded to fill out field army numbers. Many of them still appear in their garrison positions in parts of the *Notitia* that had not been updated, and hence are easy to spot. All 28 of the *legiones pseudocomitatenses* were regraded garrison troops, as were another 14 of the supposedly more elite *legiones comitatenses*, and the same is true of another 20 cavalry units in North Africa and Tingitana. Apart from the North African force, Gaul again shows the most disruption. Twenty-one of the 58 regiments of the Gallic field army in 420 were regraded garrison troops. Most of the holes in the western field army created by sustained warfare from about 405 onwards had been filled not by recruiting new top-class forces, therefore, but by reclassifying old, lower-grade ones. And of the 35 new top-class units, about a third have regimental names (Attecotti, Marcomanni, Brisigavi and so on) that derive from the names of non-Roman tribal groupings and suggest that, originally at least, they were composed of non-Roman manpower.[96]

From the superficially dry-as-dust *Notitia Dignitatum* a fascinating picture emerges. On the face of it, the western field army was a larger force than it had been twenty-five years before. The increase in size, however, masks some fundamental problems, not the least of which was that half of its old regiments had been shredded in the intervening warfare. So while the field army was larger, the total military establishment was smaller, since there is no reason to suppose that the regraded garrison troops had been replaced by new forces on the frontier. Constantius achieved great things with this force between 411 and 420, but we can only conclude that, compared with its predecessor of 395, it was a sadly diminished one. An army thrives on continuity, and losses on this scale would have considerably reduced the overall efficiency of the entire western military establishment, and particularly its Gallic arm. Discounting the regraded garrison troops, 'real' comitatensian numbers had shrunk by about 25 per cent between 395 and 420 (about 160 units to 120). And here, I would suggest, we can see the financial losses of the period really beginning to bite. In 420, Constantius faced more, and more urgent, military problems than Stilicho had done in 395. Ideally, he could have used a larger army, but the financial constraints imposed by diminished revenues would not allow it.

Behind the façade of Constantius' very real successes, then, the longer-term effects of the crisis that toppled Stilicho can be clearly distinguished. And if a substantially reduced military force were not bad enough, one further problem had begun to emerge. We first get some inkling of it in Alaric's sieges of Rome, when he was able to extract a measure of cooperation from the Senate in his designs – a generalship for himself, gold for his supporters, greater political influence for the Goths overall – even though this was against the direct wishes of Honorius and the central authorities. Attalus was content to have himself made emperor by the Goths, although he drew the line at allowing Gothic troops to win over Africa to his cause – which really would have cut the last bit of ground from beneath an independent western Empire. The same phenomenon reappeared in Gaul after 414. When Athaulf, this time, restored Attalus to the purple, some of the Gallic landowning aristocracy were ready to rally to his support. The account of Athaulf's wedding is significant not only for where it took place, but also for the number of Gallic aristocrats willing to sing at it and to get into bed with the Gothic-based regime. Paulinus of Pella, who accepted the office of Count of the Sacred Largesse under Attalus, later put it on record that he had done so not because he had any real belief in the legitimacy or viability of the regime, but because it seemed the best path to peace.[97] This was probably the motivation of many of the senators who had cooperated with Alaric, but it was no less dangerous for that.

What we're seeing here is an early instance of the way in which outside military forces could open up pre-existing fault lines within the Roman political system. In the Hadrianople campaign (see Chapter 4), and again in the Rhine crossing at the end of 406, the Empire's lower social orders had been willing to help or even join in with the barbarian invaders. This is not so surprising, given how little such groups had invested in a system run by and for the landowning classes, as we saw in Chapter 3. The willingness of the landowning elite to do deals with barbarians was a very different phenomenon – and much more dangerous for the Empire – but it too had its origins in the nature of the system. Given its vast size and limited bureaucratic technology, the Roman Empire could not but be a world of self-governing localities held together by a mixture of force and the political bargain that paying tax to the centre would bring protection to local landowning elites. The appearance of armed outside forces in the heart of the Roman world put that bargain under great strain. The speed with which some landowners rushed to support barbarian-sponsored regimes is not, as has sometimes been argued, a sign of lack of moral fibre among late Romans, so much as an indicator of the peculiar character of wealth when it comes in the form of land. In historical analysis, not to mention old wills, landed wealth is usually categorized in opposition to moveable goods, and that captures the essence of the problem. You cannot simply pick it up and move, as you would a sack of gold or diamonds, should conditions in your area change. If you do move on, you leave the source of your wealth, and all of your elite status, behind. Landowners have little choice, therefore, but to try to come to terms with changing conditions, and this is what was beginning to happen around Rome in 408/10 and in southern Gaul in 414/15. In fact, it didn't get far, because Constantius reasserted central authority pretty quickly. He also seems to have been aware of the political problem, and acted swiftly to contain it.

In 418, to cap his other efforts at restoration, Constantius reconstituted an annual council of the Gallic provinces, to meet at Arles. Not only the provinces, but also individual cities in the regions close to Arles, were to send delegates selected from their upper classes to discuss matters of public and private concern, especially those pertaining to the interests of landowners (Latin, *possessores*). The timing is suggestively coincidental with the settlement of the Goths in the Garonne valley, and it is a fair bet that this was the main item on the agenda for the first year's meeting. The council was clearly designed – and did indeed function – as a forum at which local rich landowners, who would have the ear of their gentry neighbours as well, could talk regularly to imperial officials. It was a conscious effort to mend the tears, or perhaps just the frayed edges, that had shown up in relations between Gallic aristocrats and the imperial centre in the decade or so after 405. The appearance of outsiders had opened up a gap between the interests of landowners and those of the central administration, which it was the job of the council to close. And there was another coincidence, in the form of the arrival at Arles of Rutilius Namatianus (see p. 233), whose slow homeward journey in the autumn and winter of 417/18 was perfectly timed to bring him to Gaul for the council's first meeting. Well enough connected at Honorius' court to know what was in the wind, he was exactly the kind of ex-office-holder whose presence was required there. Perhaps the assembled bigwigs were treated over dinner to a stirring rendition by this Honorian loyalist of his poem anticipating the ascent from the ashes of Rome and Gaul. Sentiments in no way inappropriate: with the west rid of usurpers, the Goths quieted, the landowners of Gaul recalled into the imperial orbit, and half of the survivors of the Rhine invasion quashed, all was set fair for the rest to receive their just deserts.

6

OUT OF AFRICA

To the victor, the prizes: Constantius' achievements did not go unrewarded. From 411, he was supreme commander of the western army. Other honours swiftly followed as his successes multiplied. On 1 January 414 he received the supreme ceremonial honour of the Roman world, the award of a first consulship. In the old Republic, the two consuls annually elected had wielded real power, but the consulship had long ago ceased to incorporate any function. Since, though, all official documents were dated according to the names of consuls, it carried with it a promise of immortality, and, given that one of the two was often also an emperor, it retained all its cachet. The next year, *patricius* (Patrician) was added to Constantius' list of titles – this too meant nothing in practice, but the search was on for titles to express his special pre-eminence.

On 1 January 417 he became consul for the second time, and – even more significant – received in marriage the hand of Galla Placidia, the emperor Honorius' sister, whom he had forced the Visigoths to return. Their first child, the strong-minded princess Iusta Grata Honoria, was born about a year later. Shortly after, Placidia fell pregnant again, this time with a son, Valentinian, who was born in July 419. The emperor Honorius was still childless, and no one had any doubt by this date that he would remain so. Constantius, Placidia and their children were the first family of the western Empire. Still, however, Constantius wasn't finished. On 1 January 420, he became consul for the third time: then, on 8 February 421, inexorable political logic led to the final accolade. Married to the emperor's sister, father of the heir apparent and for the last decade effective ruler of the Empire, he was finally proclaimed co-Augustus by Honorius. A new golden age seemed to be unfolding. Fate, however, wasn't working to the same script. On 2 September, not quite seven months after his coronation, Constantius died.

Life – and Death – at the Top

To UNDERSTAND the catastrophic effects of Constantius' sudden removal, we need to consider how court politics worked in the later Roman Empire. Its public face was the ceremonial pomp appropriate for a ruler chosen by God to run an Empire destined by the same Divinity to bring Christian civilization to the entire world. All ceremonies were carefully orchestrated to express the unanimity of the participants in the belief that they formed part of a divinely ordained social order that could not be bettered.

Emperors were expected to conduct themselves accordingly. The pagan Ammianus Marcellinus criticized the pagan emperor Julian, in all other respects his hero, for breaking with these norms:

> One day, when [Julian] was sitting in judgement . . . it was announced that the philosopher Maximus had come from Asia, he started up in an undignified manner, so far forgetting himself that he ran at full speed . . . and . . . kissed the philosopher . . . This unseemly ostentation made him appear to be an excessive seeker for empty fame, and to have forgotten that splendid saying of Cicero's, which narrates the following in criticizing such people: 'those very same philosophers inscribe their names on the very books which they write on despising glory, so that even when they express scorn of honour and fame, they wish to be praised'.[1]

Departing from the formalities was deliberate affectation, in Ammianus' view. But Julian wasn't alone in finding the demands of imperial deportment onerous, as Olympiodorus records: 'Constantius . . . regretted his elevation because he no longer had the freedom to leave and go off wherever and in whatever manner he wished and could not, because he was emperor, enjoy the pastimes which he had been accustomed to.'[2] This no doubt included jesting with the clowns over dinner, as he had previously liked to do. Being emperor was not just about giving orders; it also involved satisfying expectations.

But if the public face of court life was a ceremonial swan gliding effortlessly over the waters of world affairs, inside it was a hotbed of rivalry. Given that the Empire was far too large for any one man to control unaided, there had to be subordinates to see to its actual running. At the height of their dominance over Honorius, first Stilicho and then Constantius controlled top appointments, both civilian and military. In making promotions, the need was to balance practicality with politics. A well judged distribution of favour would build up a body of grateful supporters that would insulate the top man from potential rivals. Not that rivals were always easy to spot. It was, as we saw, Stilicho who suggested the promotion of his own eventual nemesis Olympius.

The official arena where this struggle for office and influence was played out was the central council of the Empire: the imperial consistory. Here the emperor and his chief officials, military and civilian, gathered for regular sessions, and real politicking was some-times done. Ammianus records a general named Marcellus denouncing the Caesar Julian's pretensions to the full purple and crown of an Augustus, and an extremely brave Praetorian Prefect of Italy named Eupraxius telling Valentinian I, who had denied issuing an order allowing the judicial torture of senators accused in magic trials, that he had indeed just done so.[3] But business in the consistory was usually run on very formal lines. It was where all the court dignitaries lined up in order of precedence and in full ceremonial robes to receive foreign ambassadors. It was also where the ceremony of *adoratio* – kissing the imperial robe – was customarily performed. The full consistory was more often a place for announcing decisions than debating them.[4]

Much of the real business of political negotiation and policy-making took place at a further remove from the public gaze, at council sessions with a few trusted officials present or in private rooms out of sight of pretty much everybody. The decision to admit the Goths into the Empire in 376, for instance, emerged only after heated debate amongst Valens and his closest advisers, but the public face put on the decision when announced in the consistory was cheerful consensus. Likewise, Priscus tells us that when wanting to suborn a Hunnic ambassador to murder his ruler, an east Roman official invited him back to his private apartments after the formal ceremonies in the consistory were done.[5] The imperial court had to show complete unanimity in public, but knives were kept sharpened privately, and a constant flurry of rumours spread to advance friends and to destroy foes. Winning and exercis-ing influence backstairs was how the political game was played by everyone.

The rewards of success were enormous: staggering personal wealth and a luxurious lifestyle, together with both social and political power, as you helped shape the affairs of the day and those below you courted your favours. But the price of failure was correspondingly high; Roman politics was a zero-sum game. A top-level political career generated far too many enemies for the individual to be able to take his finger off the pulse for a moment. You don't hear of many retirements from the uppermost tiers of late Roman politics. The only exit for Stilicho, as we've seen, was in a marble sarcophagus, and the same was true for many other leading figures. Regime change, especially the death of an emperor, was the classic moment for the knives to come out. It was such a moment that claimed the life of Count Theodosius (father of the emperor Theodosius I) after the sudden death of Valentinian I, and later, of the faction behind the count's death. If you were lucky it was just you who snuffed it, but sometimes entire families were wiped out and their wealth confiscated – Stilicho's wife and son were killed shortly after him. Even if a fall from grace took the form of being retired from politics, you weren't necessarily safe. As with Palladius in the Lepcis affair (see pp. 100–101), sudden exclusion from central politics was the moment your enemies would start gathering evidence and whispering, so that you never knew when an official with a warrant might knock on your door. The pinnacle of late Roman politics was for high rollers only: if you failed to stay atop the greasy pole, you were likely to end up atop a bloody one. By the year 414, the heads of no fewer than six usurpers were to be seen displayed outside the city of Carthage: two old ones (Maximus and Eugenius from the time of Theodosius I), plus four more recent ones – Constantine III and his son, together with Jovinus and his.[6]

Ammianus gives us a brilliant pen portrait of one of these late Roman grandees, Petronius Probus, prominent under Valentinian I (364–75) and after, which beautifully captures the power and precariousness of life at the top.

> [Probus was] generous and ready to advance his friends, but sometimes a cruel schemer, working harm by his deadly jealousies. And although he had great power so long as he lived, because of the sums that he gave away and his constant resumption of offices, yet he was sometimes timid when boldly confronted, though arrogant against those who feared him . . . And as a fish, when removed from its own element, does not breathe very long

on dry land, so he pined away when not holding prefectures; these he was compelled to seek because of the constant lawlessness of certain families which, because of their boundless avarice, were never free from guilt, and in order to carry out their many evil designs with impunity, plunged their patron into affairs of state ... But he was suspicious ... and sometimes resorted to flattery in order to work harm ... At the very height of riches and honours he was worried and anxious, and hence always troubled with slight illnesses.[7]

Arrogant yet fawning, powerful yet plagued by anxiety and hypochondria: this seems like a perfectly reasonable reaction to the average career in late Roman politics. The other element here, which Ammianus picks out so well, is the extent to which top office-holders were subject to pressure from below. Above all, they were social fixers. Their power came from being seen to do a myriad small favours, from people knowing that so much influence was within their gift. Patrons were constantly harassed by petitioners, therefore, who would go elsewhere if the particular favour was not forthcoming.[8] Once you stepped on the up escalator, it was hard to get off.

Such is the backdrop to the unexpected death of Flavius Constantius, co-emperor and effective ruler of the west, in September 421. You could be excused for thinking that he had owed his promotion to the speed and efficiency with which, from roughly the year 410, he put the western Empire back on the road. In part, this is true. Without this success, marriage to Placidia and the imperial promotion of February 421 would never have come his way. But military success by itself was not enough. Constantius also used this success to cement his position at court. As his stock rose, he could dispose of his rivals and turn an averagely important position at court into an unassailable one.

Constantius can only have been a second-rank supporter of Stilicho at the time of the old generalissimo's death, since he survived the blood-letting. The early stages of his own rise were no less violent. The fall of Stilicho was followed by several swift changes of personnel as first one and then another politician rose and fell in Honorius' favour. The rising star of Olympius, organizer of the coup against Stilicho, faded when his policy of resisting Alaric got nowhere. He was followed by Jovius, who transferred his allegiance to Alaric and Attalus when Honorius torpedoed the diplomatic settlement he was trying to negotiate. Jovius' pre-eminence was followed by that of a eunuch official of the imperial household, the *praepositus sacri cubiculi* Eusebius; but he was soon ousted by the general Allobichus, who had Eusebius killed (along with two other senior military commanders) – clubbed to death in the emperor's presence.[9]

It was at this point that Constantius burst on the scene, benefiting hugely from all the blood-letting, which generated room at the top for someone bold enough to seize it. On the grounds of an alleged connection between Allobichus and Constantine III, Constantius was able to discredit the former and have him killed. It is sometimes thought that Allobichus was in the pay of Constantine, but it may well be that he was simply in favour of a negotiated peace – which would have clashed with Constantius' desire for violent confrontation. Constantius was then able to use the political capital gained from his early successes against Constantine and Gerontius to bring Stilicho's arch-enemy Olympius to 'justice': his ears were cut off and, like Eusebius, he was clubbed to death in front of the emperor.

Constantius' rise to power was equally based, then, on adroit political manoeuvring. By the end of the year 411, by dint of his execution of Allobichus and his military successes against the usurpers, he had stabilized the political situation around his own person. But one major rival remained: Heraclianus, military commander in North Africa. Heraclianus' loyalty had sustained the emperor Honorius in his darkest hours of 409/10, when he kept enough funds flowing in from Africa to keep the Italian army loyal. In 412 he was duly rewarded, being appointed consul designate for the next year: the supreme accolade, short of the imperial purple. But Heraclianus was an old associate of Olympius – it was said that he had personally executed Stilicho. This may have been the original bone of contention between the two remaining stars in the western military firmament, but Constantius' success was certainly another. Granting Heraclianus the consulship before Constantius, who had achieved so much more, suggests that the emperor was trying to reassure him that his position was safe. But the African commander was not reassured, and in spring 413, when Constantius was busy organizing the overthrow of the usurper Jovinus, he brought an army to Italy. The sources accuse Heraclianus of wanting the purple for himself, but he may just have wanted to destroy Constantius' influence over Honorius. Either way, he failed. His army was defeated by one of Constantius' lieutenants, and he himself was assassinated by two of Constantius' agents on his return to Carthage.[10]

Constantius' pre-eminence was based, then, on a mixture of outright victories, uninhibited back-stabbing and a little clubbing. With Heraclianus' defeat, he had now removed all his major rivals. Even so, the further stages of his ascent were to be far from smooth. Photius preserves for us this account of his marriage to Placidia:

> When Honorius was celebrating his eleventh consulship and Constantius his second [AD 417], they solemnized Placidia's marriage. Her frequent rejections of Constantius had made him angry at her attendants. Finally, the Emperor Honorius, her brother, on the day on which he entered his consulship [1 January], took her by the hand and, despite her protests, gave her over to Constantius, and the marriage was solemnized in the most dazzling fashion.[11]

Some have supposed that she still loved Athaulf, her dead Goth, but Placidia clearly wasn't keen on being used as a pawn in a strategy that closely imitated the one that had allowed Stilicho to marry his two daughters, in quick succession, to Honorius. While the emperor was clearly happy enough to hand over to Constantius the kind of power that Stilicho had enjoyed, his sister was much less keen.[12]

So nothing was easy for Constantius in his rise to pre-eminence. He had had to fight every inch of the way; even his promotion to the purple had been opposed by Constantinople, and the political establishment in the west had hardly rolled over in submission. Marriage to Placidia may have put Constantius beyond the reach of any rival, but his power had been built on a stack of bodies. On his death in 421, everyone in high office was a Constantian appointee, and all placed him at the centre of their political calculations (including those nursing plans for his removal). As in most one-party states, there was no successor-in-waiting – Constantius had seen to that. Honorius was incapable of politicking, so it remained for the leading subordinates that Constantius had left behind to devise amongst themselves a new pecking order. The result was more than a decade of political chaos, until a semblance of order finally re-emerged in the mid-430s.

After Constantius: The Struggle for Power

ROUND ONE of the struggle was quite short, lasting from the death of Constantius to the death of Honorius less than two years later, on 15 August 423. The game at this point still consisted of winning and retaining the confidence of the emperor. First off the blocks was his sister, who had the advantage of having been raised to the purple and having received the rank of Augusta when her husband became Augustus. As well as her own interests, she needed to safeguard those of her son by Constantius, Valentinian, potential heir to the throne. But there was nothing automatic in his progression to the purple. Succession, as we saw in Chapter 3, usually operated on a dynastic basis, but only if there was a plausible heir, one who could command general consent. Varronianus, infant son of the emperor Jovian, for instance, disappeared without trace after his father's death, because no one had any interest in backing his claims. Placidia thus cosied up to her brother – to the extent that Olympiodorus reports a whiff of scandal in the air:

> The affection of Honorius towards his sister grew so great after the death of her husband Constantius that their immoderate pleasure in each other and their constant kissing on the mouth caused many people to entertain shameful suspicions about them. But as a result of the efforts of Spadusa and of Placidia's nurse, Elpidia, and through the cooperation of Leontius, her steward, this affection was replaced by such a degree of hatred, that fighting often broke out in Ravenna and blows were delivered on both sides. For Placidia was surrounded by a host of barbarians because of her marriages to Athaulf and Constantius. Finally, as a result of this flare-up of enmity and the hatred as strong as their previous love, when Honorius proved the stronger, Placidia was exiled to Byzantium with her children.[13]

Unfortunately, at this point we are dependent on Photius' brief summary of Olympiodorus' account, so that it is not exactly clear who was on whose side. 'Spadusa' is possibly an error for 'Padusia', the wife of an army officer called Felix.[14] We know, too, that another senior military commander, Castinus, was involved. The fragment goes on to tell us that a third officer, Boniface, Heraclianus' successor in

Africa, stayed loyal to Placidia throughout her travails. The broad outlines, at least, are clear: Placidia tried to sustain her family's position by monopolizing her brother's affections, and attracted some support from among the military; but other interest groups prevailed, managing to prise brother and sister apart. The result was Placidia's exile to Constantinople late in the year 422.

The manoeuvring continued in her absence, but was brought to a halt with the death of Honorius a few days short of his thirty-ninth birthday. All bets were now off, and round two of the struggle for power in the west began.

Placidia having departed with Valentinian for the east, there was no obvious candidate for the throne. The many highly capable subordinates, whom Constantius had promoted, were jockeying for position. Power was eventually seized, after a few months, by the Chief Notary, John. Having lined up the necessary support in the top military and bureaucratic echelons, he was declared Augustus on 20 November. In Africa, Boniface kept himself aloof. John's most prominent backer was the general Castinus (whom we saw involved in palace plotting before Honorius' death). The regime had one other significant military supporter in the person of Aetius, who held the prominent court post of *cura palatii* (Curator of the Palace). Aetius had first achieved prominence while still an adolescent on being sent on two occasions either side of the year 410 as a hostage to barbarian allies. He spent three years with Alaric's Goths (405–8), followed by a stint with the Huns (perhaps in 411–14). The latter would have repercussions, as we shall see.

With the western military establishment divided, a key factor would clearly be the attitude of the eastern court of Theodosius II. John promptly sent an embassy requesting recognition, but the ambassadors were roughly received and sent into exile around the Black Sea. We don't know how much debate was involved, but Theodosius and his advisers, encouraged perhaps by the fact that Boniface had refused to throw North Africa into the ring on John's side, eventually decided to send an expeditionary force to Ravenna to uphold dynastic principle and the claims of his first cousin Valentinian. So Placidia and her son were despatched to Thessalonica, where Valentinian was proclaimed Caesar on 23 October 424 by Theodosius' representative, the Master of Offices Helion. A father-and-son team of generals – Ardaburius, recently victorious over the Persians, and Aspar – were sent with an

army, together with a third general by the name of Candidianus. At first, all went according to plan. Moving up the Adriatic coast of Dalmatia, they took the two important ports of Salona and Aquileia. But then disaster struck. A gale blew Ardaburius off course. He was captured and taken to Ravenna, where John tried to use him as a hostage. But the plan backfired because Ardaburius was able to sow dissent amongst John's supporters, probably by stressing the size of the expedition on its way from Constantinople. As Olympiodorus' history tells us:

> Aspar came quickly with the cavalry, and after a short struggle John was captured through the treachery of his own officials and sent to Aquileia to Placidia and Valentinian. There his hand was first cut off as a punishment, and then he was decapitated, having usurped power for a year and a half.[15]

Theodosius then had Valentinian sent on to Rome where, on 23 October 425, Helion proclaimed him Augustus – Valentinian III – and sole ruler of the west.

THE WHOLE EPISODE was a triumphant reaffirmation of the political unity of the two halves of the Empire. An eastern expeditionary force had put a legitimate scion of the house of Theodosius back on the western throne, and the alliance was secured by the betrothal of the young Valentinian III to Licinia Eudoxia, daughter of Theodosius II. Olympiodorus chose this moment to bring his work to a close, his history of disaster and reconstruction in the west climaxing with this greatest of recent triumphs.[16] But there was still a problem. Far from ending the political instability, the installation of Valentinian III merely redefined it. A six-year-old boy cannot rule an empire, even in the hands of so capable and experienced a mother as Galla Placidia. The race was now on among the grandees of the western court, and particularly the military, to see who could secure a pre-eminent influence over the boy emperor.

In the conflict that followed, his mother was a major protagonist. The fragmentary records indicate that she aimed to sustain a balance of power in which no one figure among the military or bureaucratic elite should become too dominant. The main contenders for power and influence in the years after 425 were the leaders of the three main western army groups: Felix, Aetius and Boniface. In Italy, the

main man was Felix, whose wife Padusia may have played a role in sowing dissent between Honorius and Placidia. He was senior central field army general (*magister militum praesentalis*). In Gaul, Aetius had replaced Castinus, who had been commanding general there under John's regime. The story of Aetius' survival in the new set-up is a significant one. When John had been faced with the overwhelming force of Theodosius' eastern expeditionary army, he sent Aetius, because of his old hostage connections, to the Huns to buy mercenary support. Aetius failed to arrive in time to save his master, but eventually turned up on the fringes of Italy with a huge force of Huns – sixty thousand, according to one source.[17] A deal was struck. For a moderate price, Aetius persuaded the Huns to go home, in return for which the new regime retained his services and sent him off to Gaul as military commander. Boniface, the third contender for power and loyal to Placidia throughout, remained commanding general in North Africa.

For a while, Placidia's strategy just about worked. The threatened dominance of first one figure, then another, was kept in check, if not entirely smoothly. Slowly, however, the situation fell out of the Augusta's control. Felix made the first move. Accusing Boniface of disloyalty, in 427 he ordered him to return to Italy. When he refused, Felix sent forces to North Africa, but they were defeated. Then Aetius stepped in. On the strength of some military successes in Gaul against Visigoths (426) and Franks (428) (to which we will return in a moment), he felt confident enough to move against Felix. Perhaps his successes had won him new favour with Placidia, or perhaps personal extinction was the price of Felix's failure against Boniface, but in 429 Aetius was transferred to Italy and to the post of junior central field army general. The sources don't permit us to be certain of what exactly happened next, but in May 430 Aetius had Felix and his wife arrested for plotting against him. They were executed at Ravenna. Three had become two, and high noon was fast approaching for Boniface.

Aetius seems to have lost a little ground at court after he got rid of Felix. Perhaps, once again, Placidia was fearful of the dominance of one unchallenged generalissimo. Boniface was therefore recalled to Italy, seemingly while Aetius was absent in Gaul again; and Boniface too was promoted to the post of central field army general. Aetius immediately marched to Italy with an army, and met Boniface in battle

near Rimini. Boniface was victorious, but also mortally wounded; he died soon afterwards. His political position, and the struggle with Aetius, were immediately taken up by his son-in-law Sebastianus. After the defeat, Aetius first retreated to his country estates, but after an attempt was made on his life, he turned to the Huns, as he had in 425. In 433, he returned to Italy with enough Hunnic reinforcements to make Sebastianus' position untenable. The latter fled to Constantinople, where he would remain for over a decade. Next, Aetius secured the post of senior central field army general – his position was now unchallenged. On 5 September 435 he adopted the title Patrician to express the pre-eminence that he had finally, and with so much difficulty, achieved.[18]

The Road to Morocco

TWELVE YEARS of political conflict, involving two major wars and a minor one, had finally produced a winner. By a combination of assassination, fair battle and good fortune, Aetius had emerged by the end of 433 as the de facto ruler of the western Empire. This kind of court drama was nothing new. It was, as we have seen, a structural limitation of the Roman world that every time a strong man bit the dust, be he emperor or power behind the throne, there was always a protracted struggle to determine his successor. Sometimes, the fall-out was far worse than that witnessed between 421 and 433. Diocletian's power-sharing Tetrarchy had brought internal peace to the Empire during 285–305, but the price was horrific: multiple, large-scale civil wars over the next nineteen years, until Constantine finally eclipsed the last of his rivals. This was a much longer and bloodier bout of mayhem than what took place in and around Italy between the death of Constantius and rise of Aetius.

There was nothing that unusual, then, in the jostling for power that took place during the 420s; but there was something deeply abnormal about its knock-on effects. While a new order was painfully emerging at the centre, the rest of the Roman world would usually just get on with being Roman. The landed elites carried on administering their estates and writing letters and poetry to one another, their children busied themselves with mastering the subjunctive, and the peasantry got on with tilling and harvesting. But by the second and

third decades of the fifth century there were untamed alien forces at large on Roman soil, and during the twelve years after the death of Constantius they were occupied with more than the business of being Roman. As a result, if the events of 421–33 were in themselves merely a retelling of an age-old Roman story, the same was not true of their consequences. Political paralysis at Ravenna gave the outside forces free rein to pursue their own agendas largely unhindered, and the overall effect was hugely detrimental to the Roman state. For one thing, the Visigothic supergroup settled so recently in Aquitaine got uppity again, aspiring to a more grandiose role in the running of the Empire than the peace of 418 had allowed them. There was also disquiet among some of the usual suspects on the Rhine frontier, particularly the Alamanni and the Franks.[19] Above all, the Rhine invaders of 406, the Vandals, Alans and Suevi, were on the move once again.

They were, as we saw in Chapter 5, in origin rather a mixed bunch. The Alans, Iranian-speaking nomads, as recently as AD 370 had been roaming the steppe east of the River Don and north of the Caspian Sea. Only under the impact of Hunnic attack had some of them started to move west, in a number of separate groups, while others were conquered. The two groups of Vandals, the Hasdings and the Silings – each under their own leaderships like the Gothic Tervingi and Greuthungi of 376 – were Germanic-speaking agriculturalists living, in the fourth century, in central-southern Poland and the northern fringes of the Carpathians. The Suevi consisted of several small groups from the upland fringes of the Great Hungarian Plain. This odd assortment of peoples may have made common cause in 406, but they were far from natural allies. First, the Hasdings and Silings and Suevi could certainly have understood each other, even if speaking slightly different Germanic dialects, but the Alans spoke another language entirely. Second, as far as we can tell, both Vandal groups and the Suevi are likely to have shared the tripartite oligarchic structure common to fourth-century Germanic Europe: a dominant, if quite numerous, minority free class, holding sway over freedmen and slaves. Tied to a nomadic pastoral economy, however, the Alans' social structure was completely different. The one comment about them of any substance comes from Ammianus, who notes that slavery was unknown amongst them, and that everyone shared the same 'noble' status.[20] Whatever the particular terms used to describe it, a more

egalitarian social structure is natural to nomadic economies, where wealth, measured in the ownership of animals, has a less stable basis than the ownership of land.[21]

Although rather odd bedfellows, then, the press of events prompted these groups to learn to work together, and this happened progressively over time. Even before crossing the Rhine, Gregory of Tours tells us in his *Histories*, the Alans under King Respendial rescued the Hasdings from a mauling at the hands of the Franks.[22] We have no idea how closely the groups cooperated in Gaul immediately after the crossing, but in 409, in the face of the counterattacks organized by Constantine III, they again moved en bloc into Spain. By 411, when the threat of any effective Roman counteraction had disappeared, the groups went their own separate ways once more, dividing up the Spanish provinces between them. As we saw, the Hasdings and Suevi shared Gallaecia, the Alans took Lusitania and Carthaginensis, and the Siling Vandals Baetica (map 8). The fact that they took two provinces indicates that the Alans were, at this point, the dominant force in the coalition, as their crucial role in the events of 406 might also suggest, and the Spanish chronicler Hydatius confirms.[23] These arrangements lasted for the first half of the 410s, when the coalition partners were left in peace: happy immigrants from the north soaking up the sun and wine of Spain.

It was, however, only the briefest of idylls. Constantius was tackling the western Empire's problems in order, and once usurpers and Visigoths had been dealt with in Gaul, the survivors of the Rhine invasion were next on the list. Between 416 and 418, the Silings in Baetica (part of modern Andalucía) were destroyed as an independent force, their king Fredibald ending up at Ravenna; and the Alans suffered such heavy casualties, Hydatius reports, that: 'After the death of their king, Addax, the few survivors, with no thought for their own kingdom, placed themselves under the protection of Gunderic, the king of the [Hasding] Vandals.'[24] These counterattacks not only returned three Hispanic provinces – Lusitania, Carthagena and Baetica – to central Roman control, but also reversed the balance of power within the Vandal–Alan–Suevi coalition. The previously dominant Alans suffered severely enough to be demoted to junior partners, and for three of the four groups a much tighter political relationship came into force. Hasding Vandals, surviving Siling Vandals and Alans were all now operating under the umbrella of the Hasding monarchy. In the

face of both the greater danger and the greater opportunity that being on Roman territory brought with it, much in the manner of Alaric's Gothic supergroup, by 418 the loose alliance of 406 had evolved into full political union. A second barbarian supergroup had been born.

How the difficulty posed by integrating Germanic-speaking Vandals with Iranian-speaking Alans was overcome is something we can only guess at, and the differences in social structure must also have posed problems. I suspect that the official title adopted by the Hasding monarchs from this point on – *reges Vandalorum et Alanorum*, 'kings of the Vandals and the Alans' – was much more than a polite sop to public opinion: more likely, it was a shorthand way of expressing a reality of only limited integration. The panic generated in these groups by Constantius produced a coalition of about 70–80,000, capable of putting an army of 15–20,000 into the field.[25]

After his initial successes against the Silings and Alans in Spain, Constantius had brought the action to a temporary halt, so as to settle the Visigoths in Aquitaine.[26] This brought a respite to the former Rhine invaders which Gunderic, head of the new Vandal-Alan supergroup, seems to have used in 419 to try to bring the Suevi, and their king Hermeric, under his control as well. The difficult mountainous territory of northern Gallaecia enabled the Suevi to resist, but they were struggling under a blockade. Then, imperial counteraction resumed in 420, when a Roman officer by the name of Asterius broke up the blockade, presumably not wanting Gunderic to increase his following still further. At this point, Constantius' death intervened. In 422, another joint Roman-Visigothic campaign began against the Vandals and Alans, who had now retreated into Baetica. Given the amount of time the Empire took to organize anything at all, the necessary arrangements may well have been put in place by Constantius before his death.

Two substantial Roman military contingents – one under Castinus, probably from the Gallic field army, the other under Boniface, possibly from North Africa – now combined with a large force of Visigoths to attack the Vandals. But if the political uncertainty at court hadn't prevented the campaign from starting, it certainly ruined its progress. Boniface broke with Castinus, presumably over the exile of Placidia, and retreated to Africa. The campaign continued, with Castinus at first seeming on the verge of another victory, conducting a successful blockade of his opponents which, according to Hydatius, had reduced them virtually to the point of surrender. But, again according to Hydatius, Castinus then 'recklessly' engaged in a set-piece battle, which, thanks to the 'treachery' of the Visigoths, he lost. Hydatius provides no details about this treachery, however, and for reasons of his own he hated the Visigoths, so I am uncertain about the reliability of his reporting here.[27] The loss of Boniface's contingent cannot have helped, but it's much more likely that what we are really seeing in Castinus' defeat is the overall effect of Vandal-Alan unification. Whereas, four years before, a combined Roman-Visigothic force had been able to defeat the two groups individually, the newly united force was much more able to resist. On his defeat, Castinus retreated north to Tarragona to think again. But before a further campaign could be launched or a new strategy formulated, Honorius was dead, and Castinus returned, as we noted, to become senior general in Italy under the usurper John. Political chaos at the centre had ruined any plans for exterminating the survivors of the Rhine invasion.

From 422, while the knives came out in Italy, the Vandals and the Alans were left in peace again. Not surprisingly, events in Spain attracted little attention from the chroniclers, given the star-studded mayhem going on at court, and we hear nothing at all about Vandals or Alans between 422 and 425. After this date, however, they were active for three years in rich districts of southern Spain: their capture of the cities of Cartagena and Seville are the two highlights mentioned by Hydatius. But from their experiences during Constantius' ascendancy in the later 410s, these people knew perfectly well that, when a new supremo eventually emerged at court, they would be public enemy number one. They were in Spain by force, and had never negotiated any treaty with the central imperial authorities. So, while presumably making the most of the extended interregnum, they also knew that they needed to be making longer-term plans for their future.

In 428, on Gunderic's death, leadership of the Vandals and Alans passed to his half-brother Geiseric. The sixth-century historian Jordanes, in his history of the Goths known as the *Getica*, gives us a pen portrait of the new king, who would go down in Roman circles as the epitome of barbarian cunning:[28] 'Geiseric . . . was a man of moderate height and lame in consequence of a fall from a horse. He was a man of deep thought and few words, holding luxury in disdain, furious in his anger, greedy for gain, shrewd in winning over the barbarians and skilled in sowing the seeds of dissension to arouse enmity.' Whether the new policy was entirely his own, or whether it had been slowly evolving in the second half of the 420s, is unclear, but Geiseric now had his sights set on Africa. The move was a logical solution to the Vandals' and Alans' problems. What they needed was a strategically safe area; in particular, somewhere as far away as possible from any more Roman-Goth campaigns. Africa fitted the bill perfectly – it was only a short hop from southern Spain, and much safer. Seaborne operations always pose many more difficulties than land-based ones, and the logic of this kind of move had presented itself to others before. In late 410, after the sack of Rome, Alaric had moved his forces south to Messina with their wholesale transfer to North Africa in mind. His successor Vallia contemplated the same move from Barcelona in 415. In both cases, storms had wrecked such shipping as the Visigoths had managed to muster, and the attempts were abandoned. The Vandals, though, had had much greater leisure to lay their plans. While in southern Spain, they had begun to establish relationships with local shipowners, which had allowed them, amongst other things, to raid the Balearic Islands. Such raids were just a warm-up for the main event, allowing the Vandals to orient themselves, formulate a plan, and get hold of the required shipping. In May 429 Geiseric concentrated his followers at the port of Tarifa, near modern Gibraltar, and the expedition to Africa began.

We have quite a lot of written source material generated in the heat of the subsequent conflict, but unfortunately it largely denounces rather than describes the activities of the Vandal-Alan supergroup. Amongst other things, we have some of the letters of St Augustine who was caught up in the action and eventually passed away when the Vandals were besieging his episcopal see of Hippo Regius, together with a set of contemporary sermons written for an audience in Carthage. Geiseric had recently declared his allegiance to the so-called Arian form of Christianity as espoused by Ulfilas (see Chapter 3), which may well have spread to the Vandals from the Visigoths in the early 410s. The Vandals not only did all the normal damage that an invading army does, but also targeted Catholic Christian institutions and expelled some Catholic bishops from their sees. What the sources transmit, therefore, is not detailed information, but the outrage of good Catholics in the face of persecuting heretics.

The big question left unanswered is: how, exactly, did Geiseric get his army across the sea? It used to be argued, for instance, that the

Vandals and Alans went a long way east from Tarifa by sea, landing close to Carthage itself. If so, where was the Roman army of North Africa? According to the listings of the *Notitia Dignitatum*, which records the state of the Roman field forces in or around the year 420, Boniface, the count of Africa, had at his disposal 31 regiments of field army troops (a minimum of 15,000 men), as well as another 22 units of garrison troops (at least 10,000 men) distributed from Tripolitania to Mauretania.[29] It is normally reckoned that, for a successful landing, a seaborne force needs five or six times more troops than land-based defenders. So if, as we think, the Vandal-Alans could put into the field at best maybe 20,000 warriors, they shouldn't have stood a chance, especially since they were also bringing with them large numbers of noncombatants.

The Constantinopolitan historian of the mid-sixth century, Procopius, tried to explain this conundrum by supposing that, faced with his own possible extinction in the three-way struggle for control of the young Valentinian III, the senior Roman commander in Africa, Count Boniface, invited the Vandals and Alans into his province – although even Procopius supposes that he later repented of the deed.[30] But there is no reference to any such treachery on Boniface's part in contemporary western sources (even after he was defeated by Aetius), and if you think about it, such an invitation would not make any sense: by 429, Boniface had made his peace with the imperial court, so he would have had no reason to invite them into Africa at this point.[31]

The real explanation for Geiseric's success is twofold. First, on simple logistic grounds, it is nigh inconceivable that he could have got together enough shipping to move his followers en masse across the sea. Roman ships were not that large. We know, for example, that in a later invasion of North Africa an east Roman expeditionary force averaged about seventy men (plus horses and supplies) per ship. If Geiseric's total strength was anywhere near 80,000, he would have needed over 1,000 ships to transport his people in one lift. But in the 460s the whole of the western Empire could raise no more than 300, and it took the combined resources of both Empires to assemble 1,000. In 429, Geiseric had nothing like this catchment area at his disposal, controlling only the coastal province of Baetica. It is overwhelmingly likely, therefore, that he would not have had enough ships to move all his followers in one go.

To move a hostile force piecemeal into the heart of defended

Roman North Africa would have been suicidal, offering the Romans the first contingent on a plate, while the ships went back for the second. So rather than trying to move his force a long distance by sea, Geiseric simply made the shortest hop across the Mediterranean, from modern-day Tarifa across the Straits of Gibraltar to Tangier (map 10): a distance of only 62 kilometres – even a Roman ship could normally make it there and back again inside twenty-four hours. For the next month or so, from May 429 onwards, the Straits of Gibraltar must have seen a motley assortment of vessels shunting Vandal-Alans across the Mediterranean. The intinerary is confirmed by the chronology of the subsequent campaign. It was not until June 430, a good twelve months later, that the Vandals and Alans finally appeared outside the walls of Augustine's town Hippo Regius, about 2,000 kilometres from Tangier, having travelled there by the main Roman roads (map 10). As the Allies found in late 1942 and early 1943, much of the area is far too rough and rugged for any straying off the beaten track, and

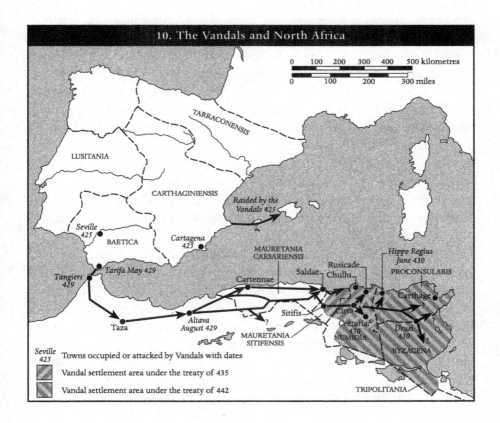

the Vandals were presumably hauling a wagon train to boot. French historians have busily calculated that, having finally assembled itself during the summer of 429, the force then moved east towards Hippo at a comfortable average of 5.75 kilometres a day.[32]

This also explains why the seaborne landing was successful. By choosing Tangier, Geiseric did not land his men in Roman North Africa proper. Tangier was the capital of Rome's westernmost possession in North Africa, the province of Mauretania Tingitana (modern Morocco). More than two thousand kilometres to the west and separated by the barren mountains of the Er Rif, it was in fact so far from the heart of Roman North Africa that, administratively, it was part of Spain (map 1). Its defence, correspondingly, was not the responsibility of the Count of Africa, but of the Count of Tingitana. He had under his command five field army regiments, which might be reinforced by a further eight units of garrison troops, giving a grand total of thirteen units, or maybe 5–7,000 men. However, the main job of the garrison troops had always been to police the comings and goings of nomads, and it must be extremely doubtful whether they were really up to set-piece confrontations with Geiseric's battle-hardened force. It had fought its way from the Rhine to Spain, and, at least from its unification in 418, had shown itself capable of standing up to major Roman field armies. The mismatch was even greater than first appears. As we saw in Chapter 5, Constantius responded to the huge losses suffered by western field armies after 405 by promoting garrison troops into mobile field army units. Of the force available to the Count of Tingitana, only two regiments were real field army units; the other three were promoted garrison troops.[33] So he had maybe 1,000, at best 1,500, decent-quality troops with which to frustrate Geiseric's designs. This despatches any idea of a contest, and with it, any mystery surrounding the Vandal-Alan coalition's ability to get ashore.

Once disembarked, the coalition headed slowly east. The one possible cross-check we have on their progress is an inscription from Altava, dated to August 429, which records that one of its leading inhabitants had been wounded by a 'barbarian', but whether of the Berber or Vandal-Alan variety we do not know. After Altava, 700 kilometres from Tangier, there was only another thousand or so to go before the invading force hit the richest provinces of North Africa: Numidia, Proconsularis and Byzacena. The sources give us no details of the march, but a great deal of vituperative rhetoric:

Finding a province which was at peace and enjoying quiet, the whole land beautiful and flowering on all sides, they set to work on it with their wicked forces, laying it waste by devastation and bringing everything to ruin with fire and murders. They did not even spare the fruit-bearing orchards, in case people who had hidden in the caves of the mountains ... would be able to eat the foods produced by them after they had passed. So it was that no place remained safe from being contaminated by them, as they raged with great cruelty, unchanging and relentless.

Stirring enough in its own way and probably fair historical colour, but not much help when it comes to historical reconstruction. Finally, on the borders of Numidia, the advancing horde was met by Boniface and his army. Boniface was defeated, and retreated to the city of Hippo Regius, where in June 430 a siege began that would last for fourteen months. While Geiseric's main army got on with the business of besieging, some of his outlying troops, lacking credible opposition, spread out across the landscape. Leaving devastation in their wake, looting the houses of the rich and torturing the odd Catholic bishop, they moved further west towards Carthage and the surrounding province of Proconsularis.[34]

Boniface's failure to hold the line was the result of the same financial stringencies that had hampered Constantius' reconstruction of Empire everywhere outside Italy. In the fourth century there had been no field army in North Africa, only garrison troops under a *dux* (duke), supplemented when necessary by expeditionary forces sent from Italy. By 420, and probably from rather earlier, Africa had acquired a field army commander (a count rather than a duke), and a substantial field force (see p. 268). Of the thirty-one regiments only four – maybe 2,000 men – were top-grade imperial field army units. Augustine, in a letter of 417, reports on the good job that Boniface, then a regimental commander, had done with just a small force of barbarian allies in securing the North African provinces against the new threats.[35] I take it that these allies will have been some or all of the four units. But the reinforcement was only small-scale: apart from these four, Carthage had to make do with the same old forces that the Empire had always maintained in Africa.

When Geiseric finally trudged into Numidia, therefore, it was the Tingitana story all over again, but on a larger scale. Boniface did what he could, but the Vandal-Alan coalition was much more awesome than the Berber nomads that most of his troops had been trained to deal with. The key North African provinces were now under direct threat, and the future of the western Empire lay in the balance. For while the province of Mauretania Tingitana in the far west was in no sense imperial heartland, Numidia and its two eastern neighbours, Proconsularis and Byzacena, clustered around their administrative capital Carthage, were a different matter. These provinces played such a critical role in the Empire's political economy that it is no exaggeration to state that, once the siege of Hippo had begun, Geiseric's forces were looming directly over the jugular vein of the western Empire.

Jewel in the Crown

TWO PICTORIAL representations of Roman North Africa survive in medieval copies of late Roman originals. Between them, they take us to the heart of the region's role in the western Empire. The first is the Peutinger Table, a copy of a fourth-century Roman world map made at Colmar in the Rhineland about the year 1200. It shows the inhabited world, stretching from Spain and Britain (all but fragments of which are missing) through the Mediterranean world, and on as far as India. The scroll is 6.82 metres long but only 34 centimetres deep: the world as you've never seen it before. Highly elongated, its proportions betray the place of its manufacture: about five-sixths of the total is devoted to the Mediterranean, and about a third just to Italy itself. North Africa appears as a line at the bottom, strung out below the west coast of Italy. Immediately below an elaborate Rome is a hardly less impressive representation of Ostia, Rome's great port. Through Ostia passed the tribute of Empire on its way to the capital. Clearly visible are its lighthouse, breakwater, quays and warehouses. Immediately below Ostia is a considerably more modest representation of Carthage, capital of Roman North Africa, given just a couple of towers. But for all its geographical oddity, the Table focuses our attention on a triangular relationship of key importance to the western Empire: Rome–Ostia–Carthage.

The nature of this relationship emerges clearly from the other late Roman image of North Africa: the *Notitia Dignitatum*, as well as its military lists, also gives us an illustrated list of the main civilian office-holders of the Empire, along with their staffs. The upper half of the picture accompanying the post of Proconsular Governor of Africa shows, between an inkstand and a desk (on which is pictured the official's letter of appointment), a female representation of the province holding out sheaves of corn.[36] Below, ships loaded with sacks of grain strike out across the sea. By the fourth century, Carthage was the port from which North African grain tributes flooded into Ostia, to be offloaded on to carts and smaller boats for the shorter trip inland and upstream to Rome. Carthage and its agricultural hinterland were responsible for feeding the bloated capital of Empire. But keeping the capital fed was no more than a specific application of a much more general point. By the fourth century AD, North Africa had become the economic powerhouse of the Roman west.

Given its ancient past, there is an irony here. The city of Carthage was founded in 814 BC, or thereabouts, as a Phoenician colony. And once it had come to dominate its hinterland, it spent a fair part of the next seven centuries vying, often violently, with Rome for mastery of the western Mediterranean. In 146 BC, when Carthage was captured after the three-year siege that ended the Third Punic War, the whole city was destroyed and its site symbolically ploughed with salt to prevent any resurrection of this great enemy of Rome. It seems odd, from the modern perspective, to think of North Africa, now very much on the periphery of the western European economy, as the powerhouse that it was back then. When the European colonial powers moved into the region in the nineteenth century, they were staggered by the wealth of its Roman remains – as tourists often are today – especially by the contrast between those remains and their barren and deserted surroundings.[37]

Most of the African continent north of the 15-degree parallel now consists of 10.25 million square kilometres of desert. Beneath it is a sunken water table, which, topped up by as little as 100 millimetres of rain each year, maintains a dispersed network of oases. In the very ancient past, the area was much more humid and the water table higher, and the nineteenth-century Europeans originally supposed that part of the answer to the prosperity of Roman North Africa lay in the fact that agricultural conditions had been considerably better then. But the land had dried up long before the rise of Rome, certainly by 2000 BC. The only holdover by Roman times of this different ecological era was the survival close to the Mediterranean of lions, elephants, giraffes and other animal species now confined to sub-Saharan Africa.[38] North African hillsides may also have been wooded, but otherwise, conditions were the same in the Roman period as they are today.

There are exceptions to the pattern of African aridness north of the 15-degree parallel: Egypt is watered by the Nile, for example. The Maghreb, heartland of Roman North Africa, receives rain from nearby uplands.[39] In the modern world, the Maghreb comprises Tunisia, Algeria and Morocco, an extensive landscape caught between the Atlas Mountains and the Mediterranean, varying between 300 and 500 kilometres from south to north over its 2,200-kilometre length from the Atlantic to the Gulf of Gabes. Hilly and interspersed with patches of desert, the region's agricultural possibilities are defined by the exact distribution of rainfall. Where the average is 400 millimetres per year or more, wheat can be grown straightforwardly. The broad river valleys of Tunisia and the great northern plains of Algeria, together with parts of Morocco in the west, fall into this category. Where precipitation is between 200 and 400 millimetres, some kind of irrigation is required, but Mediterranean dry farming can still be practised. Where rainfall is between 100 and 200 millimetres, olive trees will grow – olives requiring less water, even, than palm trees. The North African climate, then as now, was a constant, and had the potential for a wide range of produce.

The first Roman Africa, ruled directly from Rome after the destruction of Carthage in 146 BC, comprised only a small part of the Maghreb: about 13,000 square kilometres of northern and central Tunisia, bounded by the 'royal ditch' (fossa regia) which stretched from Thabraca to Hadrumetum (modern Souss). This territory was divided into 700 square-metre blocks. Apart from six small towns that had supported Rome in the war against Carthage, many of these blocks were kept as public property, rented out to settlers under long-term leases, while some were sold off to Roman magnates with money to invest. To this great sell-off is attributed the fact that in the fourth century AD many old Roman senatorial families (such as Symmachus') still possessed large estates in this territory – lands that had been passed down and shuffled around over the ages by inheritance and marriage. The rest of the Maghreb was still in the hands of local dynasts, but over the next century these individuals were increasingly sucked into the Roman orbit, while Roman settlers began to move beyond the confines of the royal ditch. As with so much of the Mediterranean, these developments paved the way for the extension of direct Roman rule: first into Numidia (modern eastern Algeria) in the time of Julius Caesar (46 BC), on the pretext that the last of the local kings had supported his great rival Pompey; then, under Claudius, when two provinces were created in Mauretania (western Algeria and Morocco). From that point on, all of the Maghreb was Roman, although for geographical reasons it came to be administered in two parts: western Mauretania Tingitana run from Spain, and Mauretania Sitifis, Numidia, Proconsularis and Byzacena run from Carthage.

From early on, the Roman authorities grasped the potential of the well watered coastal lands to provide grain for Rome. Caesar's expanded province of Africa – called 'New Africa' (*Africa Nova*) – was already shipping to the capital 50,000 tons of grain a year. One hundred years later, after the expansion of direct rule, the figure was 500,000 tons, and North Africa had replaced Egypt as the city's granary, supplying two-thirds of her needs. A substantial process of development was required to guarantee and facilitate this flow of grain.[40]

The first priority was security. In a view heavily coloured by nineteenth- and twentieth-century experience, French archaeologists, some of them military men, considered that 'civilized' Roman life in the region must have been under constant threat from indigenous Berbers pursuing a more pastoral lifestyle. Air surveys in the 1930s revealed two lines of fortification and a series of fortified houses and storage facilities in the pre-desert, which were taken as proof of habitual confrontation. No doubt, as on all Rome's frontiers, small-scale raiding was a constant irritant. It could also lead to larger-scale trouble. The Lepcis affair (see pp. 100–101) began, we noted, when a neighbouring tribal leader was burned alive in the city for unspecified crimes, then escalated into a more serious confrontation. But this clearly didn't happen often, and even the larger-scale conflicts were not that large. Throughout the first three centuries of its existence, Roman Africa required no more than one legion and a range of auxiliary forces (a maximum of 25,000 men) to guarantee peace and stability throughout its vast extent. Britain, by contrast, needed four legions.

More recent re-evaluations of Roman fortifications in North Africa have shown, from the distribution of men and installations, that their main job was actually to manage nomads, not to fight them. North African nomads go south into the pre-desert in winter, when there is enough water there to generate forage for their animals, and back north into the more agricultural regions in summer, when the pre-desert dries up. Roman soldiers and forts were there to make sure that the flocks didn't stray on to other people's crops. The Romans, in fact, seem to have got on reasonably well with the nomads: they were happy enough to buy their wares, even offering them substantial purchase-tax breaks, which doesn't really fit with a story of constant struggle.[41] Even in the fourth century, the main Roman force in Africa consisted of garrison cavalry, much more suited to patrolling and chasing the occasional raider than to heavy fighting.[42]

Once security issues had been sorted out, the region's infrastructure could be developed. Roman legionaries eventually constructed over 19,000 kilometres of roads in the Maghreb, both for their own military purposes and also to allow the easy movement of goods, such as the grain that arrived by cart at Carthage and the other ports. Carthage itself encompassed both beauty and functionality. It was in fact a double port, inherited by the Romans from the founding Phoenicians. A channel from the sea led into the outer, originally rectangular, har-bour. From here a further channel led into the inner, circular harbour, with the 'admiralty island' in the middle; ships were able to dock both against the outer walls and alongside the island. Taking this as their basis, the Romans increased the size of the outer, rectangular, harbour, and turned it, under either Trajan or Hadrian in the early second century AD, into a hexagon. The other hexagonal port known from antiquity, significantly enough, was that of Ostia (built by Trajan). At the end of the second century or the beginning of the third, the circular port was brought back into commission, a classical temple was constructed in the middle of the island, and a grand colonnaded boulevard led from there into the town centre. By about AD 200, the city was equipped to handle shipping on a massive scale. And Carthage was only one of a series of ports along the North African coast: Utica, for instance, could handle 600 ships.[43] The docks at Lepcis Magna in Tripolitania were also revamped in the early third century.

As we saw in Chapter 3, the governmental capacity of the Roman state was at all periods limited by its primitive bureaucratic technolo-gies. It tended to contract out, recruiting private parties to fulfil vital functions on its behalf. The African grain tax, or *annona*, was a classic case in point. Rather than finding and monitoring the thousands of labourers that would be required to operate the huge public estates that had come into its hands in North Africa, it leased land out to private individuals in return for a portion of the produce. Since the state wanted to lease out as much land as it could, the terms of these tenancies were made as attractive as possible. The emphyteutic lease allowed tenants heritable land more or less in perpetuity, plus the possibility of selling their leases on to a third party.

Shipping problems were similarly handled. By the fourth century the Empire had built up a powerful guild of shippers, the *navicularii*, who had to fulfil certain obligations to the state (though not every shipper was a member of the guild). The law codes make clear the broad principles on which the relationship between state and shippers was organized. The provision of shipping – operating not just out of Africa, but also in other parts of the Empire, particularly Egypt – was the first priority. With typical subtlety, therefore, the imperial authorities made membership of the guild an hereditary obligation, legislated against all possible means of exemption, and required that any land that had once been registered to a shipper should always be retained by a member of the guild, even if sold on, so that the guild's financial base could never be eroded. In return, the state then proceeded to buttress the shippers with financial and other privileges. They could not be liable to any additional tax or public service obligations, and were protected against any claims on their property by relatives. Guild members were eventually awarded equestrian rank (equivalent to the status of a medium-level civil servant); they were allowed tax reductions on their own transactions, and had up to two years to fulfil a state commission. Sometimes they also received state assistance in refurbishing their ships.[44] The state thus generated a powerful masonry of shipping magnates, with wide-ranging financial and legal privileges.

All of this, of course, the state set in motion for its own purposes. But such large-scale commerce stimulated the local economy too. If, in the first century and a half of Roman Africa (down to about AD 100), the focus was on grain production, during the next it was on olive oil and wine. Since both vines and olives require less water than grain, farmers were able to exploit the wider range of Mediterranean conditions available in the region. From about 150 to 400, with subsidized transport and land available on excellent terms, North Africa was booming.

The evidence is multi-faceted. It has long been realized that the buildings and inscriptions of North Africa indicate the flourishing here, after it had begun to decline elsewhere in the Empire, of a political culture typical of the high imperial period in which individuals competed for power on their town councils.[45] Recent rural surveys have confirmed that this local prosperity was based on agricultural expansion, with both numbers and prosperity of rural settlements increasing dramatically, as farmers pushed down from the north into the drier fringes where only the olive could flourish. By the fourth century, olive groves could be found 150 kilometres inland from the coast of Tripolitania, where there are none today. All of this confirms more anecdotal, but nonetheless suggestive, evidence, such as the inscription celebrating the octogenarian whose life's work it had been to plant 4,000 olive trees.[46]

Equally arresting is the huge amount of evidence demonstrating the ability of African goods to penetrate markets right around the Mediterranean. Our knowledge of this is based on archaeologists' newly developed skills in identifying olive oil and wine amphorae made in North Africa. Also very widely distributed were North African fine wares such as dinner services, especially of the red-slip variety. Given that transport costs were usually prohibitive except for high-value goods, the question arises as to how it could have been profitable to trade outside Africa in staples like wine and olive oil, grown everywhere around the Mediterranean, or in relatively cheap products such as dinner services. The answer lies in the state-subsidized transport system. This allowed shipping costs to be reduced through a little creative accounting, other goods to be sent piggy-back with state shipments, and African products to compete right across the Mediterranean. The state organized an economic infrastructure for its own purposes and the locals took advantage of it, so that private enterprise was able to operate within the state's version of a command economy.

And it wasn't just settlers from Italy who flourished. The kind of irrigation regimes being used in the late Roman period in North Africa were actually ancient and indigenous: everything from terraced hillsides – to catch water and prevent soil erosion – to cisterns, wells, dams, to full-blown and carefully negotiated water-sharing schemes such as that commemorated on an inscription from Lamasba (Ain Merwana).[47] These traditional means of conserving water were simply being applied more vigorously. The possibility of selling agricultural surpluses made it worth people's while to make the best use of every available drop of water and to increase production. This happened not just in settler communities but everywhere else as well, including such old tribal centres as Volubilis, Iol Caesarea and Utica. Demand hit the African countryside in a big way. Nor were nomads excluded from the action: not only did they provide crucial extra labour at harvest time, working the farms in travelling gangs, but their goods atttracted preferential tax treatment. The results could be spectacular. There is an inscription recording the success of one landless labourer turned harvest gang leader, who made enough money to buy a patch of land and a place of honour on the council of his hometown, Mactar.[48]

Over time, the flourishing provinces of Roman North Africa acquired a suitably impressive capital. Although played down pictorially in the Peutinger Table, fourth-century Carthage – or to give it its full Roman name, Colonia Iulia Concordia Carthago – was a teeming Roman metropolis. It is well known to us both from texts, not least the writings of St Augustine, and from recent excavations on the site. Abandoned soon after the Islamic conquest of North Africa at the end of the seventh century, it sat there like a fossil over the intervening centuries, waiting to be recovered. As a result, we can fill out in quite extraordinary detail the description of Carthage contained in a fourth-century survey, the *Expositio Totius Mundi* (*The Description of the Entire World*):

> Its [urban] plan is completely worthy of praise; in fact, the regularity of its streets is like that of a plantation. It has a Music Hall . . . and a port that is quite curious in appearance, which seems to provide, as far as one can see, a calm sea with nothing to fear for ships. You will find there an exceptional public amenity, the street of the silversmiths (*vicus argentariorum*). As for amusements, the inhabitants get excited about only one spectacle: the games of the amphitheatre.[49]

Not what you might find in a modern guidebook, but ancient urban life was all about imposing a rational, civilized order on a barbarian wilderness (see Chapter 1), and nothing symbolized this better than a nice, even street grid. As the *Expositio* implies, the city also had more than the standard stock of public buildings. Apart from the music hall and amphitheatre, it also boasted a theatre and, from the early third century, a 70,000-seater circus for chariot-racing. Down on the water-front was situated the large, second-century Antonine bath complex, and in the centre of the city around the Bursa Hill were the law courts, municipal buildings and the governor's palace. Here too was the domed Hall of Memory, where Boniface was assassinated.

Around the public buildings was a host of private dwellings. Some of the grander ones have been excavated, several producing extensive ground plans showing richly coloured mosaics: notably, the 'House of the Greek Charioteer' and the poetically named 'Villa with private bath'. But most of the area of the city where the majority of its population is likely to have lived has not yet been excavated, and we know of relatively few 'ordinary' dwellings. Everything suggests, however, that Carthage was home to about a hundred thousand people, a figure exceeded in the fourth century only by Rome and Constantinople, both of whose populations were artificially swollen by subsidized food supplies.

The public buildings hosted a wide range of cultural pursuits.[50] Religions of all kinds were practised, from Christianity in its various forms to the traditional pagan cults, with every kind of eastern mystery in between. And amidst all this, classical culture flourished too. Augustine, for example, was a first-rate Latinist who had completed his education in Carthage. He stayed on for a while to pursue his teaching career, at one point winning a Latin poetry competition. The prize was presented by the Proconsul of Africa, Vindicianus, himself a man of considerable learning and one of a succession of well connected Romans who spent short periods, usually a year at a time, as governor of the city. (Our old friend Symmachus held the job in 373.) Such events as poetry competitions offered ambitious young Romano-Africans opportunities to attract the attention of the governor, and to use their education and culture as a path to social advancement. When he left Carthage, Augustine headed for Rome, and from there for the court of Valentinian II at Milan, speeding on the wings of recommendations provided by a range of contacts such as Vindicianus and Symmachus.[51]

Fourth-century Carthage, then, was a cultural and, above all, an economic pillar of the western Empire. Huge and bustling, it was a city where the cramped houses of tens of thousands of ordinary citizens offered a sharp contrast to the lofty public buildings and the mansions of the rich. Above all: high on productivity and low on maintenance, North Africa was a massive net contributor to western imperial coffers.

'The Last True Roman of the West'

THE REVENUE SURPLUS from North Africa was essential for balancing the imperial books. Without it, the west could never have afforded armed forces large enough to defend its other, more exposed territories. Not only in Africa, but everywhere in the Roman west, predatory immigrants had been left to pursue their own agendas largely unhindered since the death of Constantius in 421. Along the Rhine frontier Franks, Burgundians and Alamanni, particularly the Iuthungi in the Alpine foothills to the south, had conducted raids over the frontier and were threatening further trouble. In southern France, the Visigoths had revolted and were making menacing noises in the direction of the main administrative capital of the region, Arles. In Spain, the Suevi were loose in the north-west and rampaging throughout the peninsula. With the arrival of the Vandal Geiseric on the fringes of Numidia in the year 430, the sword of Damocles was hanging over the entire western Empire.

Into the breach stepped the last great Roman hero of the fifth-century west, Flavius Aetius. As we have seen, he emerged in 433 as the eventual victor in the fierce disputes that followed the accession of Valentinian III. We also know that when young he had spent times as a hostage both with Alaric in the run-up to the siege of Rome and with the Huns in the 410s, a relationship which later allowed him to negotiate Hunnic help after the collapse of John's usurpation and then to defeat his rival Sebastianus. He would never have been chosen as a hostage, of course, had he not had high political connections. His father Gaudentius, like Flavius Constantius, came from a Roman military family of Balkan origin, in his case the province of Scythia Minor in the Dobrudja (modern Romania). In his early career, attached to the eastern court, Gaudentius held a succession of staff appointments. But in 399, during the supremacy of Stilicho, we find him commanding troops in Africa. Again like Constantius, he was probably a distinguished eastern soldier who threw in his lot with Stilicho on the death of Theodosius I. Gaudentius then married an Italian senatorial heiress of huge fortune and the high point of his career was his appointment as field army commander in Gaul (*magister militum per Gallias*) in the later 410s. He was killed there in an uprising, perhaps to do with the usurpation of John in the 420s.

Aetius' own career too followed a military trajectory, but rose to greater heights. Though never emperor himself, Aetius was the Octavian of his time. Once in power, he proved himself both a mighty politician and the restorer of Roman fortunes. The pen of a contemporary, one Renatus Frigiderus, in an extract preserved by Gregory of Tours in the later sixth century, draws this portrait of the man:

> Aetius was of medium height, manly in his habits and well-proportioned. He had no bodily infirmity and was spare in physique. His intelligence was keen; he was full of energy, a superb horseman, a fine shot with an arrow and tireless with the lance. He was extremely able as a soldier and he was skilled in the arts of peace. There was no avarice in him and even less cupidity. He was magnanimous in his behaviour and never swayed in his judgement by the advice of unworthy counsellors. He bore adversity with great patience, and was ready for any exacting enterprise; he scorned danger and was able to endure hunger, thirst and loss of sleep.[52]

His skill at horsemanship and archery was perhaps another legacy of his time among the Huns, and he certainly drew on both, as well as on the other qualities described above, in tackling the great project that was his life's work: trying to hold Octavian's Empire together for another generation.

When Aetius finally took control of the western Empire in 433, the consequences of nearly ten years of paralysis at the centre could be seen right across its territories. Each of the unsubdued immigrant groups within the frontiers of the west had taken the opportunity to improve its position, as had outsiders beyond. Also, as had happened in the aftermath of the Rhine crossing, the trouble generated by immigrants triggered the usurpation of imperial power by locals. In northern Gaul, in particular Brittany and round about, disruption had been caused by so-called Bagaudae. Zosimus mentions other groups labelled Bagaudae in the foothills of the western Alps in 407/8, and Hydatius tells us in his *Chronicle* that they had appeared in Spain by the early 440s.[53] Who these people were has long been a hot topic among historians. The term originated in the third century, when they were characterized as 'country folk and bandits'. For historians of a Marxist inclination it has been impossible not to view them as social revolutionaries who from time to time generated a groundswell of protest against the inequalities of the Roman world, and who appeared whenever central control faltered. Certainly, Bagaudae do consistently make an appearance where central control was disrupted by the hostile activities of barbarians, but the glimpses we get of their social composition don't always suggest revolutionaries. The smart money is on the term having become a catch-all for the perpetrators of any kind of dissident activity. Sometimes those labelled Bagaudae were bandits. Those of the Alps in 407/8, for instance, demanded money with menaces from a Roman general on the run. But self-help groups seeking to preserve the social order in their own localities when the long arm of the state no longer reached there, also seem to have been referred to as 'Bagaudae'. In the 410s Armorica had already asserted independence in an attempt to quell disorder; later, something similar was happening in Spain.[54]

Either way, Bagaudae plus barbarians spelt trouble. By the summer of 432, the threat was widespread and imminent: in north-west Gaul there were the Bagaudae; in south-west Gaul, Visigoths; on the Rhine frontier and in the Alpine foothills, Franks, Burgundians and Alamanni; in north-west Spain, Suevi; and in North Africa, the Vandals and Alans. In fact, much of Spain had not seen proper central control since the 410s. Given, too, that Britain had already dropped out of the western orbit, the only places in decent shape from an imperial viewpoint were Italy, Sicily and south-east Gaul.

To shed some light on Aetius' extraordinary achievement in dealing with this mess in the 430s, we have a few sparse entries in chronicles, which typically devote no more than two or three lines to an entire year's events. But we also have one extraordinary manuscript: the *Codex Sangallensis* 908, a rather tatty book from the ancient monastery of St Gall in Switzerland, just to the south of Lake Constanz. Dating from about AD 800, it contains an extensive Latin vocabulary list – just the sort of thing you'd expect to find in a good Carolingian monastery where the monks were being trained in classical Latin. But parts of the list were written on reused pages; and close inspection (in 1823) revealed that one of the palimpsest texts underneath consists of eight folios from a fifth- or sixth-century manuscript of a Latin rhetorician by the name of Merobaudes. Born in southern Spain, he was descended from an imperial general of Frankish origins who went by the same name in the 380s. His work, apart from one short religious poem, survives nowhere else, so we can thank a Carolingian monk who did a lousy job of rubbing out for the fact that any of Merobaudes' writings survive at all. Unfortunately, though, to make these few pages fit their new book, the monks trimmed them down from their original 260 by 160 millimetres to 200 by 135. All that scholars have managed to extract therefore is four short poems and the fragments of two longer panegyrics: about a hundred lines of one and two hundred of the other. (Contemporary examples of similar texts weigh in at around six hundred lines.)

As the virtuosity of his work shows,[55] our Merobaudes went through a full Latin education, then made his way to the western imperial court in Ravenna. Here another survival allows us to pick up his trail. Not only a scholar, he was also, like his ancestral namesake, a soldier, and became a devoted henchman to Aetius, serving him in his wars and afterwards singing his praises in public speeches. For all these services he was honoured, on 30 July 435, with a bronze statue at Rome, in the forum of Trajan no less.[56] That same year he was made a senator as a reward for an early panegyric to Aetius (one that hasn't survived), and fought with distinction in the Alps. He was subsequently awarded the epithet 'Patrician', and eventually became senior general (*magister militum*) commanding the Roman field forces in Spain. Not only does the case of Merobaudes show that *Romanitas*, the concept of Romanness, could still win over individual barbarians to the glories of Latin literature, but also his proximity to Aetius gives us privileged insight into how the latter wished his achievements to be viewed.[57]

The earliest of the surviving works, the hundred or so lines of the first panegyric, probably dates from the summer of 439. Not enough survives to recover anything much of its underlying argument, but its presentation of Aetius speaks for itself:[58]

Your bed is a barren rock or a thin covering on the ground; you spend your nights in watchfulness, your days in toil; furthermore, you undergo hardship willingly; your breastplate is not so much a defence as a garment . . . not a magnificent display but a way of life . . . Then if there is any respite from war, you survey either sites of cities, or mountain passes, or the broad expanse of fields, or river crossings, or distances on roads, and there you seek to discover what place is more suitable for infantry and cavalry, more suited for an attack, safer for a retreat, and richer in resources for a bivouac. Thus even the very interruption of war is advantageous for war.

The image of the breastplate as a way of life is magnificent PR, as is that of Aetius using any respite from war to extend his strategic and tactical grasp of potential battlefields. But it wasn't just spin – it was reality. The 430s saw Aetius conduct one campaign after another, many of them successful, and all directed towards putting the western Empire back on its feet again, very much as Constantius had done two decades before.

Many of these campaigns find brief mention in the chronicles, and Merobaudes' second panegyric, written in 443 to commemorate Aetius' second consulship, lists them in order. From Aetius' accession to power in 432 to the end of the decade, the record is impressive. The run of victories had started, in fact, well before the elimination of Felix and Boniface, and was one contributing factor to Aetius' success in the struggle for power. In Gaul, from 425 to 429, he was general commanding Roman field forces, and fought successful campaigns against the Visigoths in 425 or 426, driving them away from Arles, and regained some land from the Franks near the Rhine in 427. In 430 and 431, having succeeded Felix as commander in Italy, he defeated the Alamannic Iuthungi and extinguished some kind of rebellion in Noricum,[59] then wiped out a band of Visigothic freebooters near Arles; in 432 he again defeated the Franks.

From 433, his political dominance now secure, Aetius was in a position to take more comprehensive action to stabilize the Empire. Cold reason told him that the armies of the Roman west, while still powerful, were not up to tackling every problem at once. In particular, he was facing simultaneous conflict in two different theatres: on the one hand against the various parties inside Gaul and on its frontiers, and, on the other, against Geiseric and the Vandal-Alan coalition in North Africa. Rather than dividing his forces – always a dangerous move, and one that offered little hope of success – he extracted help from Constantinople. It came in the form of the general Aspar, one of the leaders of the army that had put Valentinian on the western throne in 425, at the head of a substantial force. Aetius had learned from Constantius' one mistake. Rather than making any move on the purple himself and incurring thereby the displeasure of the dynastically minded eastern emperor Theodosius, he contented himself with exercising power in fact, but not in name, thus retaining the favour and assistance of Constantinople. On what followed, we have practically no information. We do know that, basing himself in Carthage, Aspar launched a war of containment against the Vandals and Alans, which was successful enough to force Geiseric to negotiate. A treaty was declared on 11 February 435: the Vandal-Alans received parts of Mauretania and Numidia, including the cities of Calama and Sitifis (map 9); but Aspar had managed to protect most of Numidia by the terms of the treaty, together with the two richest North African provinces, Proconsularis and Byzacena.[60]

With one flank covered by Aspar, Aetius was free to take on the problems in Gaul. Such was their severity that he needed yet more help. Constantius had used the Visigoths to help bring other invaders back under control. But the Visigoths' ambitions were now running wild, and they were anyway a part of the overall problem: too many armed foreign groups on Roman soil. What Aetius needed was military aid from outside, at least until the Visigoths could be brought back into line. It couldn't come from Constantinople because the eastern Empire was already embroiled in North Africa. His only recourse was the Huns, a force that may also have been drawn upon by Constantius. The Huns had already played a crucial role in Aetius' career. Securing their departure from Italy in 425 had saved him from certain death for supporting the usurper John, and a Hunnic army had helped him regain power in 432 after his defeat by Boniface. So his first move, as the opening lines of the surviving section of Merobaudes' second panegyric tell us, was to do another deal with them: '[Aetius] has returned with the Danube at peace, and has stripped the Tanaïs [the River Don] of madness; he orders the lands, glowing hot with blackened upper air, to be free of their habitual warfare. The Caucasus has granted repose to the sword, and its savage kings renounce combat.'

Aetius' powers, of course, ran nothing like as far as Merobaudes' language might imply. What he was trying to evoke here was the notion that Aetius had established order within the land of Scythia, north of the Danube and east of Germania. This area, as we saw in Chapter 5, was dominated by the Huns from about 420 at the latest. What Merobaudes doesn't tell us is that they forced Aetius to pay a heavy price for their support. Previously they had served in Roman armies for cash. This time, it's possible that the west was simply skint – so many expensive wars had been fought and so much of its old territory was no longer producing revenue. Or perhaps the Huns now wanted something different. For whatever reason, Aetius was forced to cede to Hunnic control Roman territory along the River Save in Pannonia. Merobaudes never refers to this, although all of his listeners must have known what had happened. The best strategy for dealing with embarrassments is often not to mention them at all. Anyway, in return for the ceded territory, Aetius won sustained Hunnic military support, and this enabled him to do much good in Gaul.[61]

As Merobaudes tells us, the threats to the frontier regions of Gaul were duly nullified: 'The Rhine has bestowed pacts making the wintry world Rome's servant, and, content to be guided by western reins, rejoices that the Tiber's domain swells for it from either bank.'

In one case, Aetius took particularly drastic action. Fed up with the incursions of the Burgundians into Belgica in 436, he again negotiated Hunnic assistance. The next year, the Burgundian kingdom suffered a series of devastating attacks (one source, Hydatius, reports twenty thousand Burgundian dead), and Aetius resettled the survivors, now chastened Roman allies, in the vicinity of Lake Geneva. The frontier secure, he then turned his attention to the Gallic interior. Roman forces with Alanic allies did a similar job on the Bagaudae of Armorica, who had revolted under the leadership of a certain Tibatto in 435. Thus by 437 the integrity of Roman rule had been restored throughout the north-west. As Merobaudes commented: 'A native dweller, now more gentle, traverses the Armorican wilds. The land, accustomed to conceal with its forests plunder obtained by savage crime, has lost its old ways, and learns to entrust grain to its untried fields.' Aetius also took steps to ensure longer-term stability in the area, settling Alans across the region in a line from Orléans to the Seine basin.

The way was now open to bring the Visigoths to heel. While he was dealing with the Burgundians in 436 a second Visigothic rebellion broke out, more dangerous than their earlier move towards Arles of the mid-420s. Again they moved south, but this time besieging Narbonne. And again, Aetius was up to the challenge. Recruiting more Hunnic auxiliaries, he launched a massive counterattack which forced the Visigoths back to Bordeaux. The violence was brought to a halt in 439 – not without some significant Roman losses – but the treaty terms of 418 were reaffirmed. The relevant section of the second surviving panegyric of 443 is missing, but the defeat of the Visigoths was evidently a recent event when Merobaudes delivered the first in 439. Its surviving fragment details Aetius' defeat of the Visigoths at

Snake Mountain ('which the ancients as if by premonition called Snake Mountain, for here the poisons of the state have now been destroyed'), and the 'sudden horror' of the Visigothic king when he viewed 'the trampled bodies' of his dead followers.[62] This barbarian people hadn't been destroyed, but they had been checked, and with a bit of help from his Hunnic friends, Aetius had done wonders to stabilize the region after more than a decade of conflict.

Similar events were unfolding in Spain. The situation there had been significantly eased by the departure of the Vandals and Alans, which left only the Suevi at large in the north-west. Where before, Merobaudes tells us, 'there was no longer anything under our rule . . . the warlike avenger [Aetius] has opened up the captive road; driven out the marauder' – actually, they left for Africa of their own free will – 'and regained the obstructed highways; and returned the people to their abandoned cities.' Some of the locals, notably the chronicler-bishop Hydatius, wanted Aetius to come down over the Pyrenees with an army, but help seems to have mainly taken the form of diplomatic pressure. A political accommodation soon followed between the Suevi and the natives of Gallaecia, and the provinces abandoned by Geiseric were put back in some kind of order.

All in all, Aetius' achievement during the 430s was prodigious. Franks and Alamanni had been pushed back into their cantons beyond the Rhine, the Burgundians and Bagaudae had been thoroughly sub-dued, the Visigoths' pretensions had been reined in, and much of Spain returned to imperial control. Not for nothing did Constantinopolitan opinion consider Aetius the last true Roman of the west.[63]

BUT, JUST AS Merobaudes was putting the last full stop to his latest opus in Aetius' praise, and Aetius was contemplating sending his trusty breastplate to the cleaners, a new storm burst on the horizon. In October 439, after four and a half years of peace, Geiseric's forces broke out of their Mauretanian reservation and came thundering into the richer provinces of North Africa. But it was no walkover. They had to fight their way into Carthage, as a sermon given just after the action describes:

> Where is Africa, which was for the whole world like a garden of delights? . . . Has our city [Carthage] not been punished cruelly because she did not want to draw a lesson from the correction

1. A modern reconstruction of the city of Rome at the height of its imperial splendour. Note the great monumental centres, such as the circus and Colosseum, where the ceremonial life of the Empire declared its social order to be the divinely ordained summit of human ambition, and happily sacrificed barbarians to prove the point.

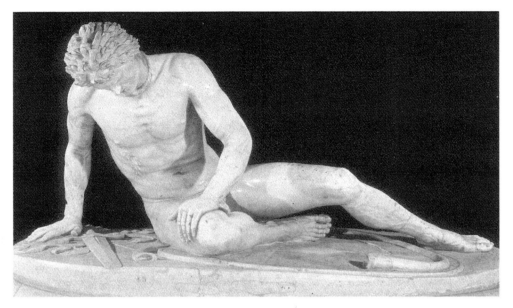

2. Whether idealized, as in this famous and beautiful statue of a dying Gaul, or treated more prosaically, dead, dying and submitting barbarians played a crucial role in all visual and some all too real representations of the Roman Empire's divinely ordained mission to overcome the forces of uncivilized chaos.

3. Britain was the one part of the Empire which occasionally showed separatist tendencies in the late period, but these were easily crushed. This coin was issued to commemorate its return to central rule in 296, showing the triumphal entry into London of the Emperor Constantius Chlorus, father of Constantine, after the defeat of the usurper Allectus.

4. An interior shot of the imperial audience hall at Trier where Symmachus presented
Crown Gold to Valentinian I in 369. The emperor sat in the apse at the far end of the photo,
with the grandees of state lined up in front of him in order of seniority. The hall itself
was richly decorated with marble, statues and luxury fabrics.

5. The Roman Emperor Valerian in chains kneeling before the Shapur I.
This great Sasanian rock relief encapsulates the strategic and ideological shock
administered to Rome's divinely protected self-image by the rise of Persia
to superpower status in the third century.

6. The Roman theatre at Lepcis Magna in North Africa. The standard stock of
public buildings which declared an attachment to Roman civilization was constructed
by participating locals everywhere from Hadrian's Wall to the Euphrates. It was general
Romanus's refusal to defend the olive groves which funded these buildings in Lepcis
that prompted the ten-year scandal under Valentinian I.

7. Constantine's victory arch in Rome, celebrating his defeat of Maxentius at the battle of the Milvian Bridge in 312. Constantine later attributed his victory to his adoption of Christianity, but the arch is famous for its continued use of straightforwardly pagan imagery and is an excellent symbol of the surprisingly unproblematic accommodation of Christianity into existing Roman ideologies of Empire.

8. Porphyry statue of the four emperors of the Tetrarchic system instituted by the Emperor Diocletian 284–305. Their embraces were meant to reassure late Romans that the emperors' concord would guarantee a peaceful sharing of power. But like all the different ways in which late emperors shared power with the colleagues they needed, the Tetrarchy was a short-term improvisation rather than a system.

9. This Pompeian fresco of a beautiful seaside villa illustrates the kind of delightful residence enjoyed by Symmachus and his peers among the richer landowners of central and southern Italy. They were a particularly privileged group, but the need to satisfy the aspirations of the land-owning class in general lay at the heart of the operations of the Roman state.

10. Roman imperial protagonists of the Gothic war:
Valens (top) whose body was never found after Hadrianople in 378;
Theodosius I (left) who was appointed to win the war, but failed badly
to do so in 380; and Gratian (right) whose troops at least managed
to force the Goths to negotiate.

11. The late Roman walls of Thessalonica, capital of the western Balkans and Theodosius' seat of power in 379–80 when he unsuccessfully tried to defeat the Goths. The city's walls were enough, nonetheless, like those of other centres of Balkans' Romanness, to protect local landowners from total disaster at the hands of the Goths, who twice marched past Thessalonica but had no mastery of siege technology.

12. An ivory diptych portrait of the western Emperor Honorius (395–423), younger son of Theodosius I. Never more than emperor in name, he survived the chaos generated by usurpers and invaders after 405 to die quietly in his bed. His one positive contribution to the historical narrative was a total refusal to grant the Gothic leader Alaric a major position at the imperial court.

13. The usurping Emperor Constantine III who led the Roman armies of the Rhine and Britain into battle against the Rhine invaders of 406. In 409/10 it looked as though his regime might totally replace that of Honorius, but he failed either to defeat the barbarians outright or to force his way into Italy, leaving him easy meat for Flavius Constantius.

14. The Patrician Stilicho with his wife Serena and son Eucherius. Labelled a barbarian by his enemies, he was a second-generation, thoroughly romanized, immigrant who manoeuvred with great skill for more than a decade at the head of the western Empire, before being overwhelmed by the combination of Rhine invaders, usurpers and Alaric's Goths which undermined western imperial stability after 405.

handed out to the other provinces? . . . There is no one to bury the bodies of the dead, but horrible death has soiled all the streets and all the buildings, the whole city indeed. And think on the evils we are talking about! Mothers of families dragged off into captivity; pregnant women slaughtered . . . babies taken from the arms of their nurse and thrown to die on the street . . . The impious power of the barbarians has even demanded that those women who were once mistresses of many servants, have suddenly become the vile servants of barbarians . . . Every day there comes to our ears the cries of those who have lost in this assault a husband or a father.[64]

MORALIZING RHETORIC rather than straightforward account, the passage nonetheless does justice to the picture of devastation reported in other Roman sources. No other single blow could have done the Empire so much harm. At a stroke, Geiseric had removed from Aetius' control the richest provinces of the Roman west, with the result that financial crisis loomed. How was it allowed to happen? Presumably, after four and a half years of relative peace, and thinking that Geiseric was going to keep to the treaty made in February 435, people took their eyes off the ball. There was, I suspect, simply too much instability in other parts of the Empire for troops to be left in Carthage on a 'what if?' basis. The Visigothic war in particular, brought to an end just before Geiseric made his move, had probably demanded every available man. So with the Carthage garrison at minimum strength, the cunning Vandal had taken full advantage.

But autumn 439 wasn't the time for recriminations, let alone commissions of inquiry. What was needed was decisive action to return Carthage and its provinces to Roman control. At around this time, in a short poem to commemorate the first birthday of Aetius' son Gaudentius, Merobaudes commented that Rome's 'fierce leader . . . was worthy of the staff of retirement' and might one day pass on the baton to Gaudentius.[65] But now was not the moment – and again, Aetius didn't shirk his duty. The logistic limitations characteristic of the Roman Empire ruled out all thoughts of an instant counterstrike, and for now the advantage lay with Geiseric. A series of laws issued in the name of Valentinian III in spring 440 testify to the impending sense of crisis. On 3 March, special license was granted to eastern traders in order to guarantee food supplies for the city of Rome: the cutting off

of the African bread dole to the capital was not the least of Aetius'
worries. The same law also put in place measures to rectify holes in
Rome's defences, and to ensure that everyone knew what their duty
was with regard to garrisoning the city. On 20 March, another law
summoned recruits to the colours, at the same time threatening
anyone who harboured deserters with the direst of punishments.[66] A
third law, of 24 June, authorized people to carry arms again 'because
it is not sufficiently certain, under summertime opportunities for
navigation, to what shore the ships of the enemy can come.'

These, however, were merely piecemeal defensive responses to
anticipated Vandal raiding, which duly followed when the sailing
season began. In particular, Geiseric launched a series of attacks upon
Sicily, including a siege of the island's main naval base, at Panormus,
which lasted most of the summer. Already, however, Aetius was
thinking along broader lines, and there are allusions to his plans for
restoring the situation in the law of 24 June: despite the immediate
problem, confidence was expressed that 'the army of the most invincible [eastern] Emperor Theodosius, our Father, will soon approach
and . . . We trust that the Most Excellent Patrician Aetius will soon be
here with a large force.'[67] Aetius had been out of Italy gathering all the
troops he could muster, but the key to success, given the diminution
in western resources since 406, was negotiating help from Constantinople. Again, Aetius' wisdom in not pushing for the purple is apparent.

Late in 440, after the onset of bad weather had forced the Vandals
back to Carthage, a joint imperial army began to assemble in Sicily:
1,100 ships to carry men, horses and supplies. Aetius' 'large force'
crossed to the island, and was joined there by a substantial expeditionary force from the east. No source puts a figure to the Roman forces
gathered there, but the shipping was enough to carry several tens of
thousands of men. The size of the eastern army is also indicated by
the fact that its leadership was shared between five commanders:
Areobindus, Ansilas, Inobindus, Arintheus and Germanus. Pentadius,
the lucky Constantinopolitan bureaucrat in charge of logistics, was
later promoted, his reward for dealing with the administrative night-
mare of despatching the expedition.[68] Everything was set for the
counterstroke that would return Carthage to Roman rule. Come the
end of March, when sailing to and from North Africa could resume
after the usual winter break, Aetius' greatest ever triumph would be
within sight. But the armada never sailed, the troops of both east and

west returned to their bases, and so much administrative effort came
to nothing.

Cause and Consequence

WHY DID THE joint expeditionary force never sail? Some further
fragments of Merobaudes' panegyric for Aetius' second consulship of
443 give us the clue. Having first enumerated his old victories of the
430s, then discussed his qualities as a peacetime leader, Merobaudes'
tone suddenly changed. He turned to an image of Bellona, the goddess
of war, complaining about the era of peace and plenty that Aetius had
brought into being:

> I am despised. Thus all respect for my kingdom has perished
> owing to one disaster after another [Aetius' victories and the
> Vandal peace]. I am driven from the waves and I cannot rule on
> land.[69]

But being a self-respecting goddess of war, she is not about to take this
lying down, and goes to find Enyo, her long-time ally:

> Sitting here under a jutting cliff, cruel Enyo had hidden a madness
> driven to flight beneath a long-lasting peace. She was distressed
> because the world was without distress. She groans in sadness at
> the rejoicing. Her ugly face is caked with hideous filth, and dried
> blood is still on her clothing. Her chariot is tilted back, and the
> harness hangs stiff. Her helmet's crest droops.

Bellona then goads Enyo to restore the 'madness' of war, and the
panegyric closes with everyone recalling Aetius to his customary
position at the head of Rome's armies:

> Let him [Aetius] not delegate, but wage war, and let him renew
> destiny with the triumphs of old; let not booty as his teacher and
> the mad desire for gold compel him to surrender his spirit to
> unceasing cares; instead, let a praiseworthy love of arms, and the
> sword, ignorant of Latium's blood but dripping with blood from
> enemy throats, show him unconquerable yet gentle.

The message is unmistakable. A new threat, well beyond anything the
Vandals might pose, had arisen, and Aetius was needed back in harness

to save the Roman world yet again. It was this threat that compelled the troops gathered in Sicily to return to their bases, thus leaving Carthage in the hands of the Vandals. And the western Empire would have to cope as best it could with the consequences of Geiseric's success.

Thus, in 442 a second treaty was made with the Vandals, this one licensing Geiseric's control of Proconsularis and Byzacena, together, it seems, with part of Numidia. The western Empire received back into its control the territories granted to him in 435; legal evidence confirms that it was subsequently administering the two Mauretanias (Sitifensis and Caesarensis) and the rest of Numidia.[70]

In return for peace, now that he had got what he wanted, Geiseric was willing to be generous. A grain tribute of some kind, although presumably rather diminished, continued to arrive in Rome from the Vandal provinces, and his eldest son Huneric was sent to the imperial court as a hostage. There is no doubting, though, the extent of Geiseric's success. From the status of 'enemy of Our Empire' in the law of 24 June 440, after 442 he was a formally recognized client king of the Empire, with the title *rex socius et amicus* ('allied king and friend'). Moreover, in a massive break with tradition the 'hostage' Huneric was betrothed to Eudocia, the daughter of the emperor Valentinian III. Thirty-odd years before, as we saw earlier, Alaric's brother-in-law the Visigothic king Athaulf had married Valentinian's mother Placidia, sister of the reigning emperor Honorius. But that was an unlicensed match. Now, for the first time, a legitimate marriage was being contemplated between barbarian royalty and the imperial family. The continuation of food supplies to the city of Rome probably seemed worth the humiliation.[71]

The fragments of Merobaudes' writings contain two pieces written after the conclusion of this peace. The panegyric of 443 comments:

The occupier of Libya [Geiseric] had dared to tear down by exceedingly fated arms the seat of Dido's kingdom [Carthage], and had filled the Carthaginian citadels with northern hordes. Since then he has taken off the garb of an enemy, and has desired ardently to bind fast the Roman faith by more personal agreements, to count the Romans as relatives for himself, and to join his and their offspring in matrimonial alliance. Thus, while the leader [Aetius] regains the peaceful rewards of the toga and orders the consular chair, now at peace, to abandon war trumpets, these very wars have given way everywhere in admiration of his triumphal attire.[72]

Merobaudes suggests that nothing could have been done about the seizure of North Africa, while stressing that Aetius has made the best of a difficult situation by coaxing a suppliant Geiseric towards a peaceful alliance with the Empire. A short poem about a mosaic continues the propaganda:

> The Emperor himself in full splendour occupies with his wife the centre of the ceiling [of an imperial dining room], as if they were the bright stars of the heavens on high; he is the salvation of the land, and worthy of veneration. In the presence of our protector a new exile suddenly weeps for his lost power. Victory has restored the world to the one who has received it from nature, and an illustrious court has furnished a bride from afar.[73]

The 'exile' is Huneric, whose presence at court is a sign of his people's subjugation to Rome but whose dignity will be in part restored by the gracious marriage alliance to follow. Just like Jovian's surrender of provinces and cities to the Persians in 363, so the loss of Carthage to the Vandals and Alans in 442 was presented as a Roman victory, and for the same reasons. A God-protected Empire simply could not admit to defeat: the image of control had to be maintained, come what may.

None of this meant, of course, that the consequences of the new peace treaty weren't disastrous. In Africa, Geiseric proceeded with the kind of pay-out that his followers were expecting, and that was essential to his own political survival. To provide the necessary wherewithal, he confiscated senatorial estates in Proconsularis such as those belonging to Symmachus' descendants, and reallocated them to his followers. These estates were called *sortes Vandalorum* ('allotments of the Vandals').[74] One influential line of argument holds that the Vandals were allocated portions of the state's land tax revenue rather than full ownership of actual pieces of real estate. But decisive contradictory evidence is provided by the fact that in 484 Victor of Vita refers to Huneric as launching a persecution of Catholic Christians in those 'allotments'.[75] Proof, surely that they came in the form of pieces of land. From much nearer to the early 440s, we have supporting evidence that this was the case. Legal texts refer to there having been a substantial number of senatorial exiles from North Africa at this time, and individual examples are met in other sources. In the correspondence of a certain Syrian bishop we find a dossier of no fewer than eight letters of recommendation written for one expelled North African landowner, Celestiacus, and the case of a woman called Maria who, having spent some time in the east, was eventually reunited with her father in the west.[76] The lands confiscated from these exiles provided the wherewithal to fund the settlement.

It is also important to consider the politics of settlement from a Vandal perspective. Here was a group of immigrants who, over a thirty-three-year period, had followed their leaders from central Europe, across France, Spain, and then on to North Africa. They had slogged over thousands of kilometres, and fought countless battles against Roman troops. Many of their campaigns were successful, but these Vandals and Alans had also suffered heavy casualties, particularly in Spain between 416 and 418 at the hands of Constantius' combined force of Visigoths and Romans. And now, or at least after the peace treaty of 442, they were in secure possession of the richest provinces of the Roman west. Hardly surprising, then, if they were looking foward to a mammoth reward for everything they had endured and for the loyalty they had shown since 406. Had Geiseric not satisfied their expectations, his head would have been likely to join those of the Roman usurpers still mouldering on poles somewhere on the outskirts of Carthage. I find it impossible to believe, in these circumstances, that the Vandals and Alans would have been content with taxation grants rather than full ownership of land. But neither do I believe that they had it in mind to do much farming. It was, after all, Roman landowners, not Roman peasant tenants, that had been expelled, so it's a fair bet that the same old peasantry continued to farm the same old bits of land. The difference was that the rent was now paid to new landowners.[77]

But this is what happened in Proconsularis. The rest of North Africa under Geiseric's control, Byzacena and part of Numidia, saw no further land confiscations. Proconsularis was the best choice for the settlement, for two reasons. First, many of its landowners, because of its particular past, were absentee Roman senators like the Symmachus family, so it was the province where dispossession would cause the fewest ructions. Second, it had the strategic advantage of facing towards Sicily and Italy, where any future Roman military threat was likely to originate.

Clearly, for many Roman landowners in Africa, the arrival of the Vandals and the subsequent peace treaty of 442 was a financial and personal disaster. The state did what it could to alleviate their situation. On the fourth anniversary to the day of Geiseric's seizure of Carthage, 19 October 443, Valentinian suspended the normal operation of financial laws in the case of Roman Africans 'who are despoiled, needy, and exiled from their country'. They could not be sued by moneylenders for monies borrowed since their exile 'until the recovery of their own property', unless they were 'rich elsewhere and financially responsible'. Likewise, they were not to be pressed on financial matters pertaining to the pre-exile period, and no one was to charge them interest on their borrowings. It may well be that quite a lot had been borrowed on the exiles' immediate arrival in Italy in 439/440, since, at that time, the reconquest of Carthage was confidently expected. Once the peace of 442 was made, these hopes evaporated and Valentinian acted to protect the exiles from the consequences of bad debt. About seven years later, presumably after a lot more lobbying, the state was even more magnanimous. On 13 July 451, Valentinian published another law:

> I decree that ... wise provision shall be made for the African dignitaries and landholders who have been despoiled by the devastation of the enemy, namely, that in so far as it is able, the august imperial generosity shall compensate for that which the violence of fortune has taken away.

In Numidia, part of which had been in Vandal hands for the seven years separating the two peace treaties, the emperor granted a five-year tax remission on 13,000 units of land, in the hope that this would enable them to be brought back into production. He also provided cash grants. In the two Mauretanian provinces of Sitifensis and Caesarensis, those who had lost their lands in Proconsularis or Byzacena were given priority in the leasing-out of public lands, and other, less afflicted landholders were expelled from their pre-existing leases.[78] Twelve years after the Vandal capture of Carthage, some of the dispossessed landowners of Proconsularis could look forward to at least a partial restitution of their fortunes by acquiring new lands in Mauretania: once again, we find the Roman state protecting its landowning classes.

The damage to the state itself could not be healed so easily. After

442, much of the revenue of North Africa, this crucial contributor to the western imperial budget, was lost outright, and the rest reduced by seven-eighths. Under the treaty, as we have seen, Byzacena and Proconsularis dropped out of central imperial control and, while some grain shipments did continue, most of their revenues were lost as well; the remaining provinces of North Africa either stayed under central control or were returned to it. On 21 June 445, Valentinian issued a tax edict covering these latter provinces, which reveals that Numidia and Mauretania Sitifensis were now producing only one-eighth of their previous land tax revenues.[79] In addition, some further tax had normally been raised from them in the form of subsistence allowances for soldiers, and here too the Africans benefited from reductions. These allowances were formally assessed in terms of food and fodder, but often commuted into a gold payment, the Africans being awarded a special commutation rate of four *solidi* (gold coins) per unit assessed instead of the usual five – effectively, a 20 per cent reduction.

The loss of its best North African provinces, combined with a massive seven-eighths reduction in revenue from the rest, was a fiscal disaster for the west Roman state. A series of regulations from the 440s show unmistakable signs of the financial difficulties that now followed. In 440 and 441, initial efforts had been made to maximize revenues from its surviving sources of cash. A law of 24 January 440 withdrew all existing special imperial grants of tax exemption or reduction.[80] In similar vein, a law of 4 June that year attempted to cut back on the practice of imperial officials – palatines – taking an extra percentage for themselves when out collecting taxes.[81] On 14 March 441, the screw was tightened further: lands that had been rented annually from the imperial fisc, with tax privileges attached, were now to be assessed at the normal rate, as was all Church land. In addition, the law cast its glance towards a whole range of smaller burdens from which the lands of higher dignitaries had previously been immune: 'the building and repair of military roads, the manufacture of arms, the restoration of walls, the provision of the *annona*, and the rest of the public works through which we achieve the splendour of public defence'. Now, for the first time, no one was to be exempt, and this was the justification offered:

> The Emperors of a former age ... bestowed such privileges on persons of illustrious rank in the opulence of an abundant era,

with less disaster to the other landowners ... However, in the difficulty of the present time this practice is obviously not only inequitable but also ... impossible.[82]

Thus the west Roman state, run by and for its landowners, in the early 440s was forced significantly to reduce the splendid range of tax benefits it had offered for so long to its most valued constituency. As the loss of tax base began to bite, the grandees at court were forced to cut down on the privileges and perquisites they had generally allowed themselves. Nothing could better illustrate the level of fiscal crisis.

Roman historians tend to consider that the late Empire spent about two-thirds of its revenues on the army, and this figure can't be far wrong. The army was bound to be the main loser, therefore, when imperial revenues declined drastically. There were no other major areas of spending to cut. And, as you might expect, the piecemeal measures of 440–1 were insufficient to compensate for the overall loss in African revenue. In the last quarter of 444, yet another imperial law admitted:

> We do not doubt that it occurs to the thoughts of all men, that nothing is so necessary as that the strength of a numerous army should be prepared for the ... afflicted condition of the state. But we have not been able because of various kinds of expenditures to effect the arrangement of a matter ... in which must be placed the foundations of full security for all ... [and] neither for those who are bound by new oaths of military service, nor even for the veteran army can those supplies seem to suffice that are delivered by the exhausted taxpayers with the greatest difficulty, and it seems that from that source the supplies that are necessary for food and clothing cannot be furnished.

Playing to taxpayers' sympathies in recognizing their 'exhaustion' was a softening-up exercise: the law's central provision was for a new sales tax of about 4 per cent, to be shared equally between buyer and seller. The law went on to state, quite straightforwardly, that the Empire could not afford, on its current tax revenues, the size of army that circumstances required. There is no reason to doubt that this was so.

How big a fiscal hole the loss of North Africa made in the western Empire's budget is impossible to say, but we can work out the reduction in the armed forces implied by the revenue lost from just

Numidia and Mauretania Sitifensis. From the figures given in the law of 445 it is possible to calculate that the total tax *lost* from these provinces, because of the new remissions, amounted to 106,200 *solidi* per annum.[83] A regular comitatensian infantryman cost approximately six *solidi* per annum, and a cavalry trooper 10.5.[84] This means that the reduced tax from Numidia and Mauretania alone implied a reduction in army size of about 18,000 infantrymen, or about 10,000 cavalry. This, of course, takes no account of the complete loss of revenue from the much richer provinces of Proconsularis and Byzacena, so that the total of lost revenues from all of North Africa must have implied a decline in military numbers of getting on for 40,000 infantry, or in excess of 20,000 cavalry. And these losses, of course, came on top of the earlier ones dating from the post-405 period. By 420, as we saw in Chapter 5, heavy losses in field army troops had already been papered over by upgrading garrison troops rather than by recruiting proper field army forces. We don't have an updated version of the *Notitia Dignitatum's* army lists (the *distributio numerorum*) for the early 440s, but if we did, they would certainly show a further substantial deterioration since 420. Only a massive new threat, therefore, could have made Aetius call off the joint east-west expedition and accept these disastrous consequences.

Where had this threat come from? Merobaudes, in the surviving fragments of the panegyric of 443 at least, is allusive rather than explicit. Bellona, goddess of war, comments:[85] 'I will call forth nations situated far away in the North, and the Phasian stranger will swim in the fearful Tiber. I will jumble peoples together, I will break the treaties of kingdoms, and the noble court will be thrown into confusion by my tempests.' Then she issues her orders to Enyo: 'Force savage crowds into war, and let the Tanaïs, raging in its unknown regions, bring forth Scythian quivers.'

Arrow-firing hordes from Scythia? In the middle of the fifth century, that could mean only one thing: Huns. And the Huns were, indeed, the new problem, the reason why the North African expedition never set sail from Sicily. Just as it was making final preparations to depart, the Huns launched an attack over the River Danube into the territory of the east Roman Balkans. Constantinople's contingent for Carthage, all taken from the Danube front, had to be recalled immediately, pulling the plug on any attempt to destroy Geiseric. Yet all through the 420s and 430s, as we have seen, the Huns had been a key ally, keeping Aetius in power and enabling him to crush the Burgundians and curb the Visigoths. Behind this change in attitude lay another central character in the story of Rome's destruction. It's time to meet Attila the Hun.

7

ATTILA THE HUN

FOR OVER A DECADE, from 441 to 453, the history of Europe was dominated by military campaigns on an unprecedented scale – the work of Attila, 'scourge of God'. Historians' opinions about him have ranged from one end of the spectrum to the other. After Gibbon, he tended to be viewed as a military and diplomatic genius. Edward Thompson, writing in the 1940s, sought to set the record straight by portraying him as a bungler. To Christian contemporaries, Attila's armies seemed like a whip wielded by the Almighty. His pagan forces ranged across Europe, sweeping those of God-chosen Roman emperors before them. Roman imperial ideology was good at explaining victory, but not so good at explaining defeat, especially at the hands of non-Christians. Why was God allowing the unbelievers to destroy His people? In the 440s, Attila the Hun, spreading devastation from Constantinople to the gates of Paris, prompted this question as it had never been prompted before. As one contemporary put it, 'Attila ground almost the whole of Europe into dust.'[1]

The Loss of Africa

ATTILA BURSTS into history as joint ruler of the Huns with his brother Bleda. The pair inherited power from an uncle, Rua (or Ruga; still alive in November 435).[2] The first recorded east Roman embassy to Attila and Bleda was sent sometime after 15 February 438, and it is likely that the brothers came to power only at the end of the 430s, possibly as late as 440. Their debut brought changes of policy, as new regimes usually do. Initial contacts with Constantinople led to a decision to renegotiate the existing relationship between the two parties. Their representatives met outside the city of Margus on the Danube in Upper Moesia (map 11). The fifth-century historian Priscus treats us to this detail:[3] 'the [Huns] do not think it proper to confer dismounted, so that the Romans, mindful of their own dignity, chose to meet [them] in the same fashion, lest one side speak from horseback, the other on foot.'

The salient feature of the new agreement was an increase in the amount of the annual subsidy paid to the Huns, from 350 pounds of gold to 700. The treaty also agreed the terms under which Roman prisoners might be returned and where and how markets would be conducted; also, that the Romans would receive no refugees from the Hunnic Empire. But the new terms, despite the increased payments, did not satisfy the Huns' new leaders. Shortly afterwards at a market, probably in winter 440/1, Hunnic 'traders' suddenly produced their weapons and seized the Roman fort in which the market was being held, killing the guards as well as some of the Roman merchants. According to Priscus, when a Roman embassy complained, the Huns retorted that 'the bishop of Margus had crossed over to their land, and searching out their royal tombs, had stolen the valuables stored there.' But our episcopal Indiana Jones was only a pretext. Taking the opportunity to raise the issue of refugees once again, Attila and Bleda threatened war if such Hunnic refugees as the Romans then held (and the bishop) were not immediately handed over. When they weren't, the Huns waited for the campaigning season, then crossed the Danube in force and took forts and cities along the frontier, including the major Roman military base at Viminacium.

At this point, the Bishop of Margus began to panic, and did a deal with the Huns to hand over his city if they would drop their accusations against him. Attila and his brother jumped at the chance to secure another strongpoint and to exploit the opportunities its capture presented. Margus was the key that opened up the great Roman military road across the Balkans, and the Huns were quick to besiege the next key point along it: the city of Naissus (modern Niš). At Naissus the road divides, one branch leading more or less due south to Thessalonica, the other running south-east via Serdica (Sofia) to Constantinople. This was a crossroads worth the taking, and, for once, we have a lengthy account (courtesy of Priscus) of the siege that followed:

> When ... a large number of [Hunnic siege] engines had been brought up to the wall ... the defenders on the battlements gave in because of the clouds of missiles and evacuated their positions;

the so-called rams were brought up also. This is a very large machine. A beam is suspended by slack chains from timbers which incline together, and it is provided with a sharp metal point and screens . . . for the safety of those working it. With short ropes attached to the rear, men vigorously swing the beam away from the target of the blow and then release it . . . From the walls the defenders tumbled down wagon-sized boulders . . . Some [rams] they crushed together with the men working them, but they could not hold out against the great number of machines. Then the enemy brought up scaling ladders . . . The barbarians entered through the part of the circuit wall broken by the blows of the rams and also over the scaling ladders . . . and the city was taken.

In the past, this passage aroused a great deal of suspicion. It contains obvious references to the most famous ancient siege account of them all: Thucydides' narrative of the siege of Plataea in 431 BC at the start of the Peloponnesian War. Traditionally, to draw such parallels would be taken as a sign that the whole story was fabricated. But ancient authors were expected to show off their learning, and audiences always enjoyed spotting the allusions. There is no need to dismiss the entire siege as fantasy, just because Priscus borrowed a few phrases from a well known historian.[4] We know, anyway, that Naissus was taken by the Huns in 442.

In their first campaign against the east Roman Empire, Attila and Bleda had shown that they had the military capacity to take fully defended front-rank Roman fortresses. They may have gained Margus by stratagem; but Viminacium and Naissus were both large and well fortified, and yet they had been able to force their way in. This represented a huge change in the balance of military power between the Roman and non-Roman worlds in the European theatre of war. As we have seen, the last serious attack on the Balkans had been by Goths between 376 and 382; and then, although they had been able to take smaller fortified posts or force their evacuation, large walled cities had been beyond them. Consequently, even though at times hard-pressed for food, the cities of the Roman Balkans had survived the war more or less intact (see Chapter 4). The same was true of western Germania. When Roman forces were distracted by civil wars, Rhine frontier groups had on occasion overrun large tracts of imperial territory: witness the Alamanni in the aftermath of the civil war between

Magnentius and Constantius II in the early 350s. All they had done then, though, was occupy the outskirts of the cities and destroy small watch-towers. They did not attempt to take on the major fortified centres such as Cologne, Strasbourg, Speyer, Worms or Mainz, all of which survived more or less intact.[5] Now, the Huns were able to mount successful sieges of such strongholds.

No source records the origins of this skill. Did they bring it with them from over the steppe, or was it a recent development? Siege techniques were hardly needed against the Goths and other groups north of the Black Sea – accounts of Hunnic fighting from the 370s concentrate on their skill in open combat as mounted archers. But if our Huns had been part of the old Hsiung-Nu confederation (see pp. 148–9), the latter had certainly needed to mount sieges in making war on the Chinese Empire. By the late antique period, in addition, even the more obscure steppe groups needed to take the rich fortified cities along the Silk Road, or at least apply pressure on them. So the capacity to mount a plausible siege would have been important in this context too.[6] On the other hand, by the 440s the Huns had been in the employ of Aetius certainly, and quite possibly of Constantius before him, so that close observation of the Roman army could easily have been the source of their knowledge – in other eras, Roman techniques and weaponry had quickly been adopted by non-Romans. As recently as 439, Hunnic auxiliaries had been part of the western Roman force that had besieged the Goths in Toulouse, and would have seen a siege at first hand. On balance, I think it slightly more likely that the Huns' capture of Viminacium and Naissus represented the deployment of a newly developed skill. And just as important for successful siege warfare was the availability of manpower. Men were needed to make and man machines, to dig trenches and to make the final assault. As we shall see later in this chapter, even if the designs for siege machinery did come from old knowledge, it was only recently that manpower on such a scale was available to the Huns.

Whatever its origins, the barbarians' capacity to take key fortified centres was a huge strategic shock for the Roman Empire. Impregnable fortified cities were central to the Empire's control of its territories. But, serious as the capture of Viminacium and Naissus was, what mattered most at this moment was that the Huns had picked their first fight with Constantinople at exactly the point when the joint east-west expedition force was gathering in Sicily to attempt to wrest Carthage from the Vandals. As we noted earlier, much of the eastern component for this expedition had been drawn from the field armies of the Balkans, and of this, no doubt, the Huns were well aware. Information passed too freely across the Roman frontier for it to be possible to hide the withdrawal of large numbers of troops from their normal stations.[7] I suspect that by raising the annual tribute so readily at the start of the reign of Attila and Bleda to 700 pounds of gold, the authorities in Constantinople were trying to buy a big enough breathing space for the African expedition to be launched. If so, they spectacularly failed. Instead of being bought off, the Huns decided to exploit the Romans' temporary weakness farther, and so, with havoc in mind, hurled their armies across the Danube. The authorities in Constantinople thus had no choice but to withdraw their troops from Sicily; and after the unprecedented loss of three major bases – Viminacium, Margus and Naissus (although the latter had probably not yet fallen when the orders were given) – it's hard to blame them. The Hunnic army was now poised astride the great military road through the Balkans and pointing straight at Constantinople. Without going anywhere near North Africa, Attila's first campaign had forced the two halves of the Empire to abandon a project of the utmost importance. The Huns had dealt a strategic blow to the Roman world whose consequences were every bit as wide-ranging as the one dealt by the Persians two centuries before. But the history of Attila the Hun doesn't end here, of course. He had a long agenda, and in the course of the next decade both halves of the Roman Empire were to feel its force.

Porphyrogenitus

THE INITIAL strategic effect upon the west of the increasing Hunnic aggression in the 440s is clear enough, but other aspects of the reign of Attila are less certain. Illiterate when they first hit the fringes of Europe in the 370s, the Huns remained so seventy years later, and there are no Hunnic accounts of even the greatest of their leaders. Our Roman sources, as always, are much more concerned with the political and military impact of alien groups upon the Empire than with chronicling their deeds, so there are always points of huge interest, particularly in the internal history of such groups, that receive little or no coverage. As in the case of Olympiodorus for the first two decades of the fifth century, we are left bemoaning the loss of the history of one particular Roman author: a man called Priscus (already quoted in this book), who came from the town of Panium in Thrace. Again, however, we have been lucky, because some substantial extracts from his history have been preserved in the works of an underemployed tenth-century Byzantine emperor by the name of Constantine VII Porphyrogenitus.

Porphyrogenitus, Greek for 'born in the purple', gives us a strong clue to this medieval emperor's predicament. He was born in 905, son of the emperor Leo VI 'the Wise', who died when Constantine was only seven. The tenth century was a time of imperial expansion, as the political unity of the Islamic world collapsed, leaving some easy pickings for Byzantine armies on its borders in Asia Minor and the Near East. Military success brought regular distributions of booty and estates, which in turn threw up a self-confident and ambitious officer class in Constantinople, who squabbled amongst themselves for political power. Constantine, however, had the useful quality of actually having been born into the purple. This made him an excellent vehicle for conferring legitimacy on the latest successful general, whether through marriage alliance or by elevating him to the position of co-emperor. But this was where the trouble lay. So powerful did his protégés become that it was only in the last fourteen years of his life, between 945 and 959, that Constantine was nominally in sole control of the Empire, and even then he was little more than a figurehead.[8] In its long stretches of political insignificance punctuated by occasional memorable moments, his reign resembled that of the emperor Honorius, whose travails concerned us in Chapters 5 and 6. But where Honorius, as far as we know, did little with his spare time apart from worrying about the next usurpation, Constantine VII devoted himself to culture with a capital C. In particular, he was concerned that Byzantium had lost touch with its classical heritage.

He conceived a maniacal project to preserve classical learning by assembling excerpts from all the great works of antiquity: 'Given the immensity of these writings which it is tiring even to think about and which seems generally overwhelming and heavy, [I] thought it a good idea to break it up and organize it in order to make more widely available everything it contains that is useful,' he tells us in the preface to one of his volumes. A grand total of fifty-three were planned, with titles as disparate as *Excerpts concerning Victories* and *Excerpts concerning*

Nations. We know the titles of twenty-three of the volumes, but all or parts of only four survive.[9] These alone fill six hefty tomes in the best modern edition, and it has been estimated that this is only one thirty-fifth of Constantine's original project. The only title to survive the Middle Ages in full was a single manuscript of number twenty-seven, *Excerpts concerning Embassies*. This was divided into *Embassies from the Romans to Foreigners* and *Embassies from Foreigners to the Romans*. And even this volume survived only by a whisker. The original manuscript was destroyed in a fire in the Escorial Palace library in Madrid in 1671, but not, thankfully, before it had been copied.[10] Both halves of volume twenty-seven contain extensive extracts from Priscus' history, leaving us for ever in Constantine's debt. Without them, our knowledge of Attila would be almost non-existent.

There is one more point to note. The titles of Constantine's volumes were accurate, if not pithy, and *Excerpts concerning Embassies* deals with precisely that. Military and other information may well be mentioned incidentally, but the main focus of the extracts is diplomacy. Consequently, while we are very well informed about negotiations between Attila and Constantinople, in which – as we shall see in a moment – Priscus himself played a major role, we are underinformed about the operations of the Hunnic war machine and the internal politics of the world that produced it. Much of this was presumably (and in part, demonstrably) well covered in Priscus' lost text. But what we need, and don't have, is Constantine's lost *Excerpts concerning Big Battles between the Romans and Foreigners*, should he have written such a volume. One of the lost volumes was entitled *Excerpts concerning Victories*, but, given that the Huns kept winning, this probably didn't contain much from Priscus. While we have much of his wonderful account of Romano-Hunnic diplomacy, then, we have to scrabble around in much lesser texts for details of Attila's campaigns and other aspects of his reign.

How Are the Mighty Fallen

ANCIENT LOGISTICS being what they were, the east Roman contingent to the expeditionary force bound for North Africa in 441, though withdrawn from Sicily in the same year, was not back in the Balkans in time to save Constantinople from the humiliation of having to make peace after the fall of Naissus in 442. We don't know the exact terms, as Constantine VII's flunkeys extracted no relevant fragment from Priscus' history, but its outlines are clear enough from references to it in later negotiations. As you might expect, the annual subsidy went up again: a plausible guess would be 1,400 pounds of gold per annum – in 447 it went up to 2,100 pounds, which would make 1,400 the halfway point (before the attacks of 441/2 it stood at 700). The figure also has to be high enough for arrears of 6,000 pounds to have built up by 447. Other than that, the Hunnic leadership continued to bang on about fugitives and Roman prisoners, and these issues were no doubt also settled to the Huns' advantage.[11]

The working methods of Constantine VII mean that Priscus' narrative outline of the 440s has been lost beyond recovery, so that the surviving fragments of diplomatic history have to be arranged chronologically according to information from other sources. In this case, reconstruction turns on the degree of credibility to be accorded the Byzantine chronicler Theophanes, who wrote in the ninth century. If you broadly accept his narrative construction, and the fragments of Priscus are arranged accordingly, you come to the conclusion that, after the engagements of 441/2, Attila mounted two further successful attacks upon east Roman forces in the Balkans: one in 443, when a Roman army was defeated in the Chersonesus, and a second in 447, when the Huns threatened the walls of Constantinople. Theophanes' credibility has been convincingly undermined, however, by Otto J. Maenchen-Helfen.[12] This extraordinary historian of the Huns spent many months in 1929 living with Turkish-speaking nomads in north-west Mongolia, and was equally at home in Greek and Latin, Russian, Persian and Chinese. Add to this a capacity for detailed observation and a logical mind. Maenchen-Helfen wasn't the first to assault Theophanes' credibility, but he did do the ultimate demolition job. He was able to show that Theophanes wrote one catch-all entry on the Huns in the era of Attila, placing everything that happened in the year 449/50, even though he was actually dealing with materials covering the whole of the 440s. Refracting the evidence through Maenchen-Helfen's lens, and comparing it with everything else we know, it becomes apparent that there were not two more wars between Attila and the east Romans after 442, but only one, in 447 (map 11).[13]

The road leading to that confrontation can be easily discerned. The east Romans had conceded the treaty of 442/3, with its increased annual gold subsidy, only in a moment of weakness when much of its Balkan army had been away in Sicily. As soon as the forces returned, attitudes hardened. At some point in 443 or soon afterwards, the authorities stopped paying the tribute. Hence the arrears of 6,000 pounds of gold that had built up by 447. So if the payments began in 442 when peace was negotiated, and the payment was indeed 1,400 pounds per annum, the east Romans paid only part of two years' instalments before calling a halt.[14] Other countermeasures followed. On 12 September 443, a new law was put in place to ensure military readiness: 'We command that each duke [dux, commander of limitanei garrisons] . . . shall restore the soldiers to the ancient number . . . and shall devote himself to their daily training. Furthermore, we entrust to such dukes also the care and repair of the fortified camps and the river patrol boats.'[15] Eastern field forces had also been strengthened by the recruitment of a large number of Isaurians – traditionally bandits – from the highlands of Cilicia in south-west Asia Minor.[16] Everything was now in place, and the east Romans were confident of being able to overturn the Huns' ascendancy.

They may also have been encouraged in this belief by a major ruction in the top Hunnic echelons. In 444 or 445, Attila had his brother Bleda murdered, and took unchallenged command of his people. Nothing survives from Priscus' account of this murder, so all we have is a date, no how or why. It coincided chronologically, though, with the east Roman countermeasures to overturn the peace of 442/3. Constantinople no doubt grasped the opportunity to cut off the annual payments without fear of immediate retribution, because the new sole ruler of the Huns was far too busy consolidating his authority to mount a major campaign. But both sides were gearing up for a test of strength, and it duly followed in 447.

Attila opened the exchanges, sending an embassy to Constantinople to complain about the arrears and the fact that fugitives had not been handed over. The east Romans replied that they were ready enough to talk, but nothing else. So Attila unleashed his armies, sweeping over the Danube and destroying the frontier forts in his way. So much for the poor old garrison troops, supposedly put on their mettle by the law of 443. The first big fortress Attila encountered was Ratiaria, an important base close to the river in the province of Dacia. It quickly fell. The Hunnic horde then advanced westwards along the Danube to the north of the Haemus Mountains. There they had their first confrontation with the Roman army. Arnegisclus, commander of imperial field forces in the eastern Balkans (*magister militum per Thraciam*), having advanced north-east from his headquarters at the city of Marcianople with every available man, gave battle on the river Utus. The Romans, we are told, fought bravely but were overwhelmed, and Arnegisclus himself fell, having carried on the fight after his horse was killed underneath him. Victory opened up the mountain passes to the Huns, who now swarmed south on to the Thracian Plain. Attila's first port of call was the eastern imperial capital.

On 27 January 447, during the second hour after midnight, an earthquake had struck Constantinople. The whole district around the Golden Gate was in ruins, and, even worse, part of the city's great landwalls had collapsed. Attila was on the point of invading anyway, but news of the earthquake may have altered his line of attack. By the time he got there, the crisis was over. The Praetorian Prefect of the east, Constantinus, had mobilized the circus factions to clear the moats of rubble and rebuild gates and towers. By the end of March the damage was repaired and, as a commemorative inscription put it, 'even Athene could not have built it quicker and better'.[17] Long before Attila's forces got anywhere near the city the opportunity to take it had gone, and the Huns' advance led not to a siege but to the second major confrontation of the year. Although the Thracian field army had been defeated and scattered, the east Romans still had central forces stationed around the capital on either side of the Bosporus. This second army was mobilized in the Chersonesus, where a second major battle, and a second huge defeat for the Romans, duly followed.

Attila had failed to force his way into Constantinople, but having reached the coast of both the Black Sea and the Dardanelles, at Sestus and Callipollis (modern-day Gallipoli) respectively (map 11), he had mastery of the Balkans in all other respects. And he proceeded to wield his domination to dire effect for the Roman provincial communities. In the aftermath of victory the Hunnic forces split up, raiding as far south as the pass of Thermopylae, site of Leonidas' famous defence of Greece against the Persians nearly a thousand years before. Accounts of the devastation are easy to come by, such as that recorded in the life of the more or less contemporary Thracian saint Hypatius:

> The barbarian people of the Huns . . . became so strong that they captured more than a hundred cities and almost brought Constan-

tinople into danger, and most men fled from it. Even the monks
wanted to run away to Jerusalem ... They so devastated Thrace
that it will never rise again and be as it was before.[18]

One hundred is a suspiciously round number, but there is no doubt
that many strongholds were captured and destroyed. Theophanes says
that everywhere except Hadrianople and Heracleia fell to the Huns,
and other sources give us some names of the victims: Ratiaria, where
it all began, Marcianople, Philippopolis (modern Plovdiv), Arcadiopolis
and Constantia. The list includes most of the major Roman towns of
the Balkans, though many of the other places destroyed were no doubt

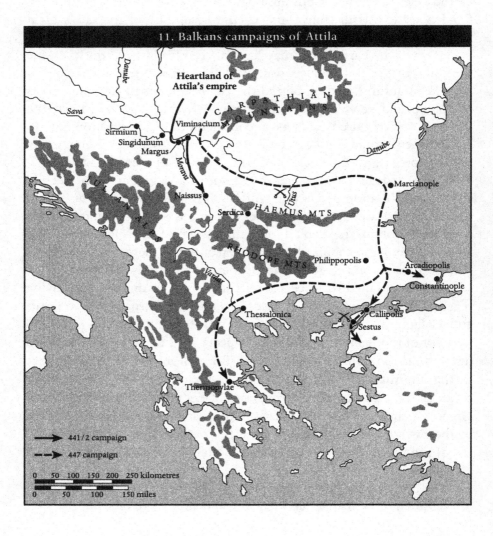

11. Balkans campaigns of Attila

quite small. We also have some specific evidence of what it meant for
such a city to be taken by Hunnic assault. As mentioned earlier, the
one major Roman city of the northern Balkans to have been excavated
more or less completely is Nicopolis ad Istrum, in the northern foothills
of the Haemus Mountains. Like Carthage, this site was abandoned in
the Middle Ages and has no modern town on top of it, so that it has
been possible, in a long-running excavation, to take a good look at a
lot of the city. In the Gothic war of 376 to 382, all the rich villas in the
countryside around Nicopolis had been destroyed and looted, presumably by Gothic marauders. These villas were never rebuilt, but from
the later 380s onwards a large number of rich houses were built in
the urban centre, by the first half of the fifth century occupying over
49 per cent of it. One reasonable guess would be that the local Roman
landowners responded to increased insecurity in the period after 376
by moving into houses in the walled city, while still continuing to farm
their estates as absentee landlords. The dig revealed that these houses,
as well as the city centre, terminated in a substantial destruction layer,
which the end of a more or less continuous coin sequence dates firmly
to the mid- to late-440s.

There is little doubt, therefore, that in the total destruction of the
old city we are looking at the effects of its sack at the hands of Attila's
Huns in 447. At a slightly later date part of the site was rebuilt, but
it covered a much smaller area and the place had changed out of
all recognition. Gone were all the opulent houses; in their place, the
excavators found only an episcopal complex, some poor housing and
some administrative buildings. Roman urban development north of
the Haemus Mountains, a phenomenon stretching back 300 years to
the Romanization of the Balkans in the first and second centuries AD,
was destroyed by the Huns, never to recover. This was evidently no
cosy little sack, like that of Rome in 410 when the Goths were paid
off, then went home. What we're looking at in Nicopolis is large-scale
destruction.[19]

Whether it was like this everywhere the Huns descended is
impossible to say. Of those places that managed to survive, the most
famous is the town of Asemus, perched on an impregnable hilltop.
Armed and organized, its citizens not only weathered Attila's storm
but emerged from the action with Hunnic prisoners. Their city would
survive further storms in the centuries to come.[20] But there can be no
doubt that the campaigns of 447 were an unprecedented disaster for

Roman life in the Balkans: two major field armies defeated, a host of defended strongholds captured and some destroyed. It's hardly surprising, then, that in the aftermath of their second defeat in the Chersonesus the east Romans were forced to sue for peace. An extract from Priscus' history gives us the terms:

> [Any] fugitives should be handed over to the Huns, and six thousand pounds of gold be paid to complete the outstanding instalments of tribute; the tribute henceforth be set at 2,100 pounds of gold per year; for each Roman prisoner of war [amongst the Huns] who escaped and reached his home territory without ransom, twelve *solidi* [one-sixth of a pound of gold] were to be paid . . . and . . . the Romans were to receive no barbarian who fled to them.

As Priscus went on to comment wryly:

> The Romans pretended that they had made these agreements voluntarily, but because of the overwhelming fear which gripped their commanders they were compelled to accept gladly every injunction, however harsh, in their eagerness for peace.

No doubt the propaganda machine was trundled out to explain the whys and wherefores of this latest Roman 'victory', but when the taxman came knocking no one could have been left in any doubt as to its true nature. Priscus went on to describe how hard it was to come up with the cash for the arrears payment: 'even members of the Senate contributed a fixed amount of gold according to their rank'. As with the west after the loss of Carthage, the terms of the 447 peace were sufficiently fierce for tax privileges to be at least partly rescinded. That the regime was willing to hit its chief political constituency in the pocket is a clear sign of the desperation to which Attila's campaigns had reduced the Constantinopolitan authorities.

The extent of Attila's success in the 440s emerges clearly, then, even from the truncated sources that have survived. What we're as yet no closer to understanding, though, is how he was so successful, or why, having been content hitherto with little more than a modest annual subsidy, he so fundamentally transformed the dynamic of the Huns' relationship with the Empire. We must begin with Attila himself, the man behind the reign of terror.

On the Trail of Attila

WE CAN GET closer to Attila than to most other 'barbarian' leaders of the late fourth and fifth centuries because the historian Priscus, following the path pioneered by Olympiodorus and his parrot forty years before, wrote a full account of the embassy that took him first into Hunnic territory and eventually into the presence of the great man himself. In 449 one of Priscus' friends, a distinguished staff officer by the name of Maximinus, having drawn the short straw became the latest in a long line of east Roman ambassadors to trudge north and attempt to placate Attila. Maximinus' brief was to tackle two outstanding issues: one was the perennial topic of Hunnic fugitives; the other concerned a strip of territory 'five days' journey wide' south of the Danube, which Attila was claiming as a result of his victories in 447. The Huns wanted this area evacuated, presumably to form some kind of buffer zone between Roman and Hunnic possessions – they complained that some of its native population were still farming there. The Romans' strategy was to try to get Attila's right-hand man Onegesius involved in the negotiations, in the hope that he had enough clout with his leader to persuade him to come to a settlement. They were well aware, though, that these two issues might yet provide Attila, should the mood take him, with the pretext for another war.

There were many preparations to make before the embassy could leave. We saw in Chapter 3, through the person of Theophanes, how cumbersome it was for a Roman official to get around even within the Empire, despite the logistic support provided by the public transport system, the *cursus publicus*. Moving outside the Empire was even more difficult. Theophanes had to take with him not only every conceivable item of household equipment and a gang of slaves to operate them, but also letters of introduction and gifts for anyone of substance he was likely to encounter. Going on a diplomatic embassy, especially such a sensitive one to a potential enemy whose hostility Maximinus and Priscus were anxious to head off, required a plentiful supply of rich and elegant presents. I count no fewer than five separate occasions when Priscus records gifts being handed over, and there may well have been others. Silks and pearls were delivered to the Hunnic ambassadors in whose company our heroes travelled. Bleda's wife, who gave the Romans hospitality, received unspecified 'gifts', as did Attila himself when the ambassadors were finally ushered into his presence. To solicit his good offices Onegesius was given gold, and there were yet more presents for Attila's wife Hereka. Gold, silks, pearls, perhaps also silver and gemstones, were clearly part of your average ambassador's luggage. Although, like the accompanying slaves, not explicitly mentioned by Priscus, an armed escort is likely to have been part of the delegation.

Ambassadors had also to be briefed on diplomatic niceties. Some potential banana skins were pretty obvious. If you were travelling on the same road as Attila you made sure that you were behind him, never in front. When camping near him, you made sure that your tents were not pitched on higher ground than his. (These were essential tips, in view of the fact that it was for Attila's camp they were heading.) Maximinus and Priscus got this last one wrong at one point, and had to move.[21] But it was also important for a Roman ambassador to maintain his dignity. He could not be seen hanging about Attila's headquarters trying to catch the eye of Hunnic bigwigs. That was Priscus' job, and the reason he went along. Their respective roles are nicely caught in his own words after the mission's first exchange with Onegesius: 'Having instructed that I should confer with him on questions we wished to ask of him – for continual visiting was not proper for Maximinus, a man in an official position – [Onegesius] went away'.[22] Priscus was, in short, Maximinus' go-between, there to lend dignity and grandeur to the Roman ambassador's presence; but he was also a significant player in the action, and had to be briefed accordingly. And all this placed him in an excellent position to make notes for his new bestseller.

We don't know how many Romans took to the road. Priscus' narrative concentrates on just three: Maximinus, himself and their interpreter Vigilas, who had participated in the peace delegation after the debacle of 447.[23] With them also travelled the two Hunnic ambassadors, Edeco and Orestes, the latter a Roman from Pannonia who had ended up in Attila's service after Aetius had handed over the province to the Huns. These two, and their large entourage, had come to Constantinople earlier in 449 to raise the issues to which it was now Maximinus' job to respond. Such was the pace of shuttle diplomacy in antiquity.

Setting off together from Constantinople in a northwesterly direction, the two parties followed the main military road through the

Balkans. After thirteen days travelling at breakneck speed, they reached the city of Serdica, 500 kilometres from the east Roman capital. There the Romans decided to break the ice by holding a dinner party, buying sheep and cattle for the purpose from the locals. Everything was going swimmingly until the toasts: 'When we were drinking, the barbarians toasted Attila and we Theodosius [the east Roman emperor]. But Vigilas said it was not proper to compare a god and a man, meaning Attila by a man and Theodosius by a god. This annoyed the Huns, and gradually they grew heated and angry.'

A bit of quick thinking saved the day: 'We turned the conversation to other things and by our friendly manner calmed their anger, and when we were leaving after dinner, Maximinus won over Edeco and Orestes with gifts of silk garments and pearls.'

All returned to sweetness and light, but there was one rather bizarre incident – or so it seemed at the time. As the Huns were waiting to return to their tents, Orestes remarked that he was very pleased that Maximinus and Priscus hadn't committed the same faux pas as the authorities in Constantinople: they had invited Edeco to dinner, but not himself. Neither Priscus nor Maximinus quite knew what Orestes was getting at, but the significance of the remark was to emerge later.[24]

Over the next few days, the caravan slowly wound its way north-west through the Balkans, crossing over the Succi Pass, to Naissus. There, the evidence of the city's capture by the Huns in 441/2 assailed the eye. The two parties had to search at length beside the river outside the city walls before they found a camping ground that wasn't still littered with the bones of the slaughtered. The next day, their numbers were increased by the arrival of five of the seventeen Hunnic fugitives that had been the subjects of Attila's complaints to Constantinople. They were handed over to Maximinus by Agintheus, commanding general of the Roman field forces in Illyricum. Everyone realized that these men were returning home to their deaths, so it must have been an emotionally charged occasion; Priscus notes that Agintheus treated them with great kindness. At Naissus, the road turned north and the cavalcade wound its way through woods and wasteland to the banks of the Danube. Here they found none of the proud cutters of the Roman navy that the law of September 443 had so recently commanded, but only 'barbarian ferrymen'. These conveyed the party across the river in canoes, each made from a single hollowed-out tree trunk. Now they were on the last lap of their journey. Another 70 stades (about 14 kilometres), plus another half-day's journey, and they finally arrived at the camp of Attila.

Here a second odd thing happened, this one rather more disturbing. Having finally reached their destination, after the best part of a month on the road, the ambassadors were ready to do their stuff. They had just pitched camp when a party of Huns rode up, including Edeco and Orestes, together with Scottas, another of Attila's inner circle. Onegesius, potential smoother of diplomatic channels, was not present, being away with one of Attila's sons. This was a setback in itself, but things went from bad to worse. The messengers demanded to know what the ambassadors wanted, and when the Romans replied that their message was for Attila's ears alone, went back to consult their leader. They then returned, and, Priscus reports, this time the Hunnic emissaries 'told us everything for which we had come on the embassy, ordering us to leave with all speed if we had nothing further to say'.

The Romans were dumbfounded. First, they had been greeted with unexpected hostility; then, the Huns knew everything that they'd come for anyway. The ambassadors could think of nothing to say, although Vigilas, the interpreter, later berated Maximinus for not making something up on the spot to keep the talks going. That would have been better than just turning for home, even if, whatever spin was put on their mission, the lie was exposed later. Months of preparation and journeying seemed down the drain. Then, when the slaves were loading up the animals and they were about to set off, even though darkness had fallen, another messenger from Attila arrived. He brought them an ox and some fish, and told them that Attila's instructions were that, because it was so late, they should have dinner and stay the night. So they duly ate their dinner and went to bed in more cheerful mood, certain that Attila must have decided to be more conciliatory.

When they woke up, their optimism evaporated. Attila's next message was unequivocal: unless they had something more to say, they were to leave. Dejectedly, they loaded up again. Maximinus, especially, was plunged in despair.

Priscus now made his first positive contribution. Seeking out Scottas, one of the messengers of the night before, he made a desperate play to keep the embassy afloat. Cunningly, he offered Scottas a reward if he could get the Romans in to see Attila, while presenting his proposition as a challenge: if Scottas was as important as he claimed to be, then certainly he could manage it. Scottas rose to the bait, and the Romans got their first audience. But having presented letters and gifts they soon found themselves faced with yet another obstacle: Attila refused to let the discussions get going along the lines the Romans desired, instead turning viciously on their interpreter. Vigilas knew full well that there were to be no more Roman embassies until all fugitives had been returned, he said. When Vigilas replied that they *had* been returned, Attila 'became even more angry and abused [Vigilas] violently, shouting that he would have impaled him and left him as food for the birds if he had not thought it infringed the rights of ambassadors to punish him . . . for . . . shamelessness and effrontery'.

Attila now ordered Maximinus to remain in attendance while he replied to the emperor's letters, but told Vigilas to hurry on home to pass on his demands about the fugitives. And that was the end of the audience.

Unnerved, the Romans returned to their tents, puzzled at what had made Attila so angry. Vigilas was particularly at a loss, because Attila had been extremely friendly towards him on the previous embassy. Then Edeco came to talk to Vigilas alone, emphasizing, or so the interpreter said afterwards, that Attila would indeed make war if the fugitives weren't returned. Neither Maximinus nor Priscus knew whether to believe this account of what had passed between the two men, but before they could press things further, more Hunnic messengers arrived. The Romans were to make no expensive purchases, or ransom any prisoners, they announced; until all disputes between the two camps were settled, they could only buy food. What were the Romans to make of it all? Before they had time to reflect, Vigilas had left.

For the next week or so, the Romans were reduced to trailing around after Attila as he made his way to the northerly parts of his kingdom. The journey was hardly comfortable. At one point they were caught in a downpour, from which they were rescued only by the intervention of one of Bleda's wives, who still ran her own fiefdom. Her hospitality included providing attractive women for the night, but after taking care to treat them with the greatest courtesy, the Romans sent them home.

Eventually they reached their destination: one of Attila's permanent palace compounds. Now diplomatic contact reopened, this time on a more friendly basis, and Priscus was afforded more leisure to observe this ruler and his world. From his observations, even as reflected through the distorting mirror of Roman cultural prejudice, there emerges a striking portrait of Attila, the court over which he presided and the means whereby he exercised power.

To Priscus' eyes, the settlement, consisting of a series of walled compounds, looked like no more than a 'very large village'. Attila's was the largest and most elaborate dwelling, embellished with towers where others had none. Leading figures such as Onegesius also had dwellings here, and each was surrounded by circuit walls 'made of timbers' – constructed with 'elegance' not 'security' in mind, Priscus emphasized:[25]

> Inside the wall there was a large cluster of buildings, some made of planks carved and fitted together for ornamental effect, others from timbers which had been debarked and planed straight. They were set on circular piles made of stones, which began from the ground and rose to a moderate height.

When the Roman ambassadors were invited to dinner, Priscus eventually gained entry to Attila's living quarters:

> All the seats were arranged around the walls of the building . . . In the very middle of the room Attila sat upon a couch. Behind him was another couch, and behind that steps led up to Attila's bed, which was screened by fine linens and multicoloured ornamental hangings like those which the Greeks and Romans prepare for weddings.

Attila's wife Hereka, mother of his eldest son, had her own dwelling, which, while not laid out for public entertaining, seems to have been similarly furnished:

> I . . . found her reclining on a soft couch. The floor was covered with woollen-felt rugs for walking upon. A group of servants stood around her in attendance, and servant girls sat facing her working coloured embroidery on fine linens to be worn as ornaments over the barbarian clothing.

The place looked not unlike a nomad's tented encampment, though constructed out of more permanent materials. Priscus implies that

Attila had several of these palace compounds dotted around his kingdom, but doesn't tell us how many.

The historian also gives us a sense of the public life that animated them. On their arrival, he witnessed the ceremonial greeting for Attila's return:

> As Attila was entering, young girls came to meet him and went before him in rows under narrow cloths of white linen, which were held up by the hands of women on either side. These cloths were stretched out to such a length that under each one seven or more girls walked. There were many such rows of women under the cloths and they sang Scythian songs.

At dinner, Priscus remarks, the seating was carefully arranged. Attila sat in the middle of a horseshoe arrangement of couches, in which it was more honourable to be seated on the right than on the left. Then the drinking began. A wine waiter brought Attila a cup, with which he greeted the first person on his right. That person stood up, and sipped or drained the cup in return, then sat down; every other guest, likewise, drank in honour of the first one greeted. Attila worked his way down the right-hand side of the horseshoe, then the left, greeting all his guests in turn. Nothing could have better illustrated the formal bond supposed to exist between all those gathered at his table, while at the same time making clear their positions in the pecking order.[26]

Priscus also introduces us to Attila himself. His account of the Hun's appearance does not survive at first hand in the fragments collected by Constantine VII Porphyrogenitus, but has been transmitted via an intermediary, the sixth-century historian Jordanes referred to earlier:[27]

> [Attila's] gait was haughty, and he cast his eyes hither and thither, so that the power of his pride was reflected in the movements of his body. Though a lover of war he was not prone to violence. He was a very wise counsellor, merciful to those who sought it and loyal to those whom he had accepted as friends. He was short, with a broad chest and large head; his eyes were small, his beard sparse and flecked with grey, his nose flat and his complexion dark.

Whether this is a direct translation of what Priscus said (he wrote in Greek, Jordanes in Latin) or a paraphrase is unclear, but in some ways a surprising picture of the great conqueror emerges from it. We would expect Attila not to shrink from conflict, but would we expect him to be described as wise and merciful? Both sides of his character emerge elsewhere in Priscus' account. On the one hand, we are told, he built a personality cult around his divine predestination to conquer; while in other respects he was unassuming. Priscus tells the story of a herdsman who followed the trail of blood left by a wounded heifer back to a buried sword on which he had trodden:

> He dug it up and took it straight to Attila. He was pleased by this gift and, since he was a high-spirited man, he concluded that he had been appointed ruler of the whole world and that through the sword of Mars he had been granted invincibility in war.

I don't doubt that the finding of the sword, if true, merely added to a conquest ideology that Attila was already fostering. At the same time, his habits and self-presentation were not what you might expect. Priscus reports on dining chez Attila:

> While for the other barbarians and for us there were lavishly prepared dishes served on silver platters, for Attila there was only meat on a wooden plate . . . Gold and silver goblets were handed to the men at the feast, whereas his cup was of wood. His clothing was plain and differed not at all from that of the rest, except that it was clean. Neither the sword that hung at his side nor the fastenings of his barbarian boots nor his horse's bridle was adorned, like those of the other Scythians, with gold or precious stones.

Archaeological finds, as we shall see later in this chapter, have demonstrated that Priscus was not exaggerating the richness of the utensils used by the Hunnic Empire's elite. But for the god-appointed conqueror, plain was good.

What all this tells us about the 'real' Attila is debatable. All we have is an exterior view, as it were, and nothing of his internal workings. But even this is enough to suggest that we are dealing with an intelligent man of some complexity who took considerable care over his public image. Totally confident in his own destiny, he had no need of the outward trappings of power. Rejecting rich dress and rich food showed that such worldly concerns were beneath one destined for greatness. This was one of the leadership secrets of Attila the Hun;

Priscus' history, supplemented by one or two other sources, lets us into one or two others. He was, as you might expect, ruthless when dealing with potential enemies. Priscus never tells us what happened to the five Hunnic fugitives the embassy had picked up at Naissus; but two who had been returned to Attila earlier, Mama and Atakam, described as 'children of the royal house', were impaled.[28] Impaling seems to have been the main method of dealing with most problems in the Hunnic world. Priscus later witnessed the impaling of a captured spy and the gibbeting of two slaves who had killed their Hunnic masters in the midst of battle.[29] And although they provide no details, our sources are unanimous that Attila was somehow responsible for the death of his brother Bleda.

At the same time, violence was tempered where it could be. Although Bleda himself was eliminated, one of his wives retained her fiefdom, receiving Maximinus and Priscus with great hospitality, it will be remembered, when they were caught in a rainstorm. That his brother's entire family was not wiped out compares favourably, perhaps, with the treatment meted out to the wives of Stilicho and Felix upon their political demise, as we saw in Chapter 5. Why this might have been so emerges from Attila's marriage policies. He took many wives, no doubt at least some for political reasons, using marriage alliances to bind important second-level leaders among the Huns to his support. Bleda had presumably done likewise, so the kings' wives are likely to have had important relations whom, even if one of the kings was to fall, it was sensible not to alienate. It also emerges from Priscus' account that Attila was careful to honour his chief supporters. The ceremonial drinking of toasts with which he began his formal dinners not only established hierarchies, but gave each man his due. Priscus witnessed a telling scene when, on the embassy, he arrived at the palace compound. The wife of Onegesius, Attila's right-hand man, came out to greet him 'carrying food and . . . wine (this is a very great honour among the Scythians), welcomed him and asked him to partake of what she had brought out of friendship. In order to please the wife of a close friend, he ate while sitting on his horse . . .' Good relations with key supporters no doubt required many such niceties of behaviour. (Attila could also behave with apparent unreasonableness, but this would often be when he wanted to pick a quarrel anyway.) More practically, good relations also demanded the regular sharing of the booty of war.[30]

None of this takes us far inside Attila's head, but it gives us some insight into his recipe for success: total self-confidence and the charisma that often flows from this; ruthlessness when called for, but also a capacity for moderation, married to shrewdness; and a respect for his subordinates, whose loyalty was so vital. The kind of hold that Attila had over his inner circle is well illustrated in the denouement of Priscus' embassy. On one level, it ended as a complete damp squib. The historian gives us this marvellous picture of Attila being chased around the Middle Danube Plain, lots of insights into how his Empire worked, and the battle even to gain admittance to the Hunnic court. Dramatic satisfaction then demands a verbal confrontation, in which Maximinus and Priscus somehow manage to win Attila over and return home heroes. Reality was more prosaic. Having secured access with so much difficulty, Maximinus and Priscus subsequently just had to hang around while Attila answered the emperor's letters, and their only triumph was to ransom one noble Roman lady, Sylla, for 500 *solidi*, with her children thrown in as a goodwill gesture. They were then sent packing with another of Attila's inner circle, Berichus, who started off friendly enough but, again inexplicably, became hostile en route, taking back a horse he had given them and refusing either to ride or eat with them. The embassy generated, therefore, neither peace nor war, and any contribution that Priscus and Maximinus may have made to Romano-Hunnic relations quietly fizzled out.

But the embassy did have another, more dramatic, climax, even if this didn't involve Priscus directly. Trudging home through the Balkans in the company of the grumpy Hun, Maximinus and Priscus were passed on the road by Vigilas, their interpreter, on his way back north, ostensibly with the emperor's answer on the fugitive issue. But as soon as Vigilas reached Attila's court, he was jumped by some of the Hun's men who found in his baggage the huge sum of fifty pounds of gold. Vigilas started to bluster, insisting that the money was for ransoming prisoners and buying better baggage animals, but as you will remember, Attila had ordered that the Roman ambassadors were to purchase nothing except food until a full peace was negotiated, and fifty pounds of gold would buy enough bread to feed a small army. When the Hun threatened to kill Vigilas' son, who was accompanying him on the trip, the interpreter confessed. What had happened was this. Back in Constantinople while the embassy of Maximinus and Priscus was being prepared, the current *éminence grise*, the eunuch Chrysaphius, had plotted with ambassador Edeco to assassinate Attila, and the money was Edeco's reward. The real job of Priscus and Maximinus, had they but known it, had been to provide a diplomatic front behind which the dirty-tricks brigade could do their stuff.

If this were not dangerous enough, the actual situation was even more convoluted. As soon as he was north of the Danube on that first journey, Edeco had told Attila everything. Writing in retrospect, Priscus could see that the plot explained all the odd incidents that he and Maximinus had noted in the course of their travels. It was the reason why Orestes, the other Hun ambassador, had not been invited to dinner with Edeco that time in Constantinople – that was the moment when the plot was first hatched. It also explained how the Huns knew all about the ostensible purpose of the embassy. Edeco had been let in on that as well, and had passed on the details to Attila. Hence, too, the private chat between Vigilas and Edeco, which Vigilas had tried to explain away in a fashion that Priscus had found unconvincing even at the time, Attila's hostility to Vigilas and, above all, the strange order that the Romans were not to buy anything except food. It was all a trap for Vigilas, who was left with no excuse when he turned up with the gold. Chrysaphius' plot was carefully laid, but doomed from the start; Attila's hold on Edeco, no doubt a mix of fear and admiration, was much too strong for him to act against his master.

Given the degree of intrigue, Priscus' narrative is surprisingly matter-of-fact. Attila could have had them all impaled at any moment, since the Romans had themselves broken all the normal rules protecting diplomats on their travels. Lucky for them that Attila was so calculating. Rather than gibbeting everyone in sight, he saw the plot as another opportunity to reinforce his psychological domination over the east Romans. Vigilas was allowed to ransom his son by payment of a further fifty pounds of gold, and two Hunnic ambassadors, Orestes again and Eslas, were sent to Constantinople:

[Attila] ordered Orestes to go before the emperor [Theodosius II] wearing around his neck the bag in which Vigilas had placed the gold to be given to Edeco. He was to show him and the eunuch [Chrysaphius] the bag and to ask if they recognized it. Eslas was to say directly that Theodosius was the son of a nobly born father, and Attila too was of noble descent ... But whereas Attila had preserved his noble lineage, Theodosius had fallen from his and was Attila's slave, bound to the payment of tribute. Therefore, in attacking him covertly like a worthless slave, he was acting unjustly towards his better, whom fortune had made his master.[31]

What a moment it must have been. Here was the full imperial court drawn up in their gorgeous robes and minutely defined order of precedence, the living representation of the divine favour that made the Roman Empire supreme, when in strode the two barbarian ambassadors to act out their pantomime. Priscus' description of the Roman reaction doesn't survive, but nothing better illustrates the confidence with which Attila trod his particular corner of the globe than this ceremonial humiliation of the ruler of the eastern Roman Empire.

An Empire of Many Colours

THERE WAS MUCH more to Attila's European reign of terror, however, than this personal charisma and his finely honed demonstrations of dominance. Such tours de force were as much effect as cause of the two transformations which, in just one generation, had turned the Huns from useful allies of Constantius and Aetius into world conquerors. Priscus' narrative, implicitly points us towards the causes of these changes, without which Attila's career of conquest could not have happened.

As we've seen, Priscus was not the first east Roman historian-cum-diplomat to visit the Huns. In 411/12, Olympiodorus had taken to sea with his parrot, braving fierce storms off Constantinople, then skirting Athens and up the Adriatic to Aquileia on its northern shore. Unfortunately, only a brief summary of this embassy survives, but it does contain one piece of crucial information:

> Olympiodorus discusses Donatus and the Huns and the natural talent of their kings for archery. The historian describes the embassy on which he went to them and to Donatus and . . . tells how Donatus was deceived by an oath and wickedly killed, how Charaton, the first of the kings, flared up with rage at the murder and how he was calmed down and pacified with regal gifts.[32]

The extract is not without mystery; not least concerning the identity of Donatus – opinions differ as to whether he was a Hun or not – and of his killers. Some have supposed that the arrival of Olympiodorus' embassy did not merely *coincide* with Donatus' death, but was an earlier and more successful enactment of the kind of plot that Priscus found himself embroiled in.[33] But the key point is that in 411/12 the Huns were ruled by a series of kings (how many is not specified), and that these kings operated according to a ranking system which clearly marked out Charaton as senior. It sounds highly reminiscent, in fact, of the hierarchical system of another nomadic group, the Akatziri, whose fate came to Priscus' attention during his own embassy. When the Romans arrived at the Huns' camp, Onegesius was away with Attila's eldest son subduing this group. The opportunity to do so had come about in an interesting fashion, as Priscus describes:

> The [Akatziri] had many rulers according to their tribes and clans, and the Emperor Theodosius sent gifts to them to the end that they might unanimously renounce their alliance with Attila and seek peace with the Romans. The envoy who conveyed the gifts did not deliver them to each of the kings by rank, with the result that Kouridachus, the senior in office, received his gifts second and, being thus overlooked and deprived of his due honours, called in Attila against his fellow kings.

Apart from allowing one the pleasure of imagining the report of the Roman ambassador who had managed to make such a mess of his mission,[34] the passage gives us some idea of the kind of political system operating among the Huns in the early 410s.[35]

The contrast with Attila's time, a generation or so later, could not be more marked. Priscus spent a great deal of time at the Hunnic court, and devoted many words to its structure and modes of operation. As we have seen, there was then an inner core of leading men – Onegesius first, then others such as Edeco, Scottas and Berichus – whom Attila treated with great respect; but none of them enjoyed any kind of royal dignity. In all of this information, there is not the slightest indication that the Huns had more than one ruler: Attila himself. The multiplicity of power-sharing kings of 411 had given way to a monarch in the literal sense of the word. Of the process that ended up with supreme power in one man's hands, no account survives. As you would expect, all the indications suggest, however, that it was not a peaceful evolution. The final act in the drama was Attila's murder of his brother Bleda. By that stage, power had anyway narrowed to just two members of the same family – which suggests that Rua (or Ruga), the uncle whom the brothers succeeded, must have played a major role in reducing the number of Hunnic royal lines.

The naked violence of Bleda's murder is probably a fair indication of how the other surplus kings had been removed. The first negotiations between Constantinople and Attila and Bleda, before they attacked Viminacium in 441, resulted in the return, as we have seen, of two fleeing Hunnic royals, Mama and Atakam, who were promptly impaled. They could have been cousins of Attila and Bleda, for Rua had at least two brothers, but might equally have been descended from royal lines suppressed earlier by Rua. The whole fugitive issue, which so bedevilled Hunno-Roman diplomacy in the 440s, was clearly concerned with Hunnic royals and ex-royals of one kind or another. Maximinus and Priscus had to listen to the names of seventeen fugitives being read out – a very small number, so we are clearly dealing here with individuals who posed some kind of threat at the highest level. It is also possible that some of the lesser kings had accepted demotion rather than face extinction. (When something similar was happening among Goths in the decade after Attila's death, though most of the minor royals died fighting or fled from the scene, at least one was willing to be demoted to leading-noble status.[36])

Set against what we know about nomad anthropology, political centralization – the first of the two transformations that concern us here – must also have been associated with a broader transformation among the Huns. Devolved power structures occur very naturally among nomadic groups, because their herds cannot be concentrated in large groupings, for fear of overgrazing. In the nomad world, the main purpose of any larger political structure is simply to provide a temporary forum where grazing rights can be negotiated, and a force put together, if necessary, to protect those rights against outsiders. This being the case, the permanent centralization of political power among the Huns strongly implies that they were no longer so economically dependent upon the produce of their flocks. Priscus provides a number of clues to the nature of these economic adjustments. As we saw in Chapter 4, nomads always need to form economic relationships with settled agricultural producers. This was clearly the case with the Huns, and commercial exchanges were still taking place in the 440s.[37] But by the time of Attila, the main form of exchange between Hunnic nomad and Roman agriculturalist was not grain in return for animal products, but cash in return for military aid of one kind or another. This form of exchange had its origins in previous generations, when Huns had performed mercenary service for the Roman state. Uldin and his followers were the first we know of to have fulfilled this role, in the early 400s, and larger Hunnic forces may have aided Constantius in the 410s, and certainly supported Aetius in the 420s and 430s.

Shortly after, military service for pay evolved into demands for money with menaces. Precisely when the line was crossed is impossible to say, but Attila's uncle Rua certainly launched one major assault on the east Roman Empire with cash in mind, even if he also provided mercenary service for the west. By the reign of Attila, targeted foreign aid had become tribute, and it clearly emerges from Priscus' record of Romano-Hunnic diplomacy that the main thing the Huns wanted from these exchanges, and from their periodic assaults across the frontier, was cash and yet more cash. As we saw earlier, the first treaty between Attila and Bleda and the east Romans fixed the size of this annual tribute at seven hundred pounds of gold – and from there the demands could only escalate. Hunnic warfare against the Romans also brought other one-sided economic exchanges in its wake: booty, slaves and ransoms such as the one Priscus and Maximinus negotiated.[38]

By the 440s, then, military predation upon the Roman Empire had become the source of an ever-expanding flow of funds into the Hunnic world. To overthrow a system of ranked but more or less equal kings, the king-who-would-be-preeminent needed to convince the followers of the other kings that they should transfer their loyalties to him. Cornering the market in the flow of funds from the Empire was the ideal means of putting sufficient powers of patronage into the hands of just one man, and rendering the old political structures redundant. Only by controlling the flow of new funds could one king outbid the others in the struggle for support. Already in the mid- to late-fourth century, Huns had presumably been raiding and intimidating both other nomads and Germanic agriculturalists north of the Black Sea, but real centralization only became possible once the main body of the Huns was operating close to the Roman world. Raid and intimidate the Goths and you might get some slaves, a bit of silver and some agricultural produce, but that was about it – not enough to fund full-scale political revolution. But do the same vis-à-vis the Roman Empire, and the gold would begin to roll in, first in hundreds of pounds annually, then thousands – enough to transform both economic and political systems.

While the argument is not susceptible to proof, we could understand these transformations as an adaptation away from nomadism, rather than a complete break with the past. As mentioned earlier, in normal circumstances nomads rear a range of animals to make full use of the varying qualities of available grazing. The horse figures primarily as an expensive, almost luxury animal, used for raiding, war, transport and trade; its meat and milk provide only a very inefficient return in terms of usable protein compared with the quality and quantity of grazing required. As a result, nomads generally keep relatively few horses. If, however, warfare becomes a financially attractive proposition, as it did when the Huns came within range of the Roman Empire, then nomads might well start to breed increasing numbers of horses for war – evolving, in the process, into a particular type of militarily predatory nomadic group. This could never have worked as a subsistence strategy out on the steppe, where the potential proceeds from warfare were so much less.

It is impossible to prove that this is what happened, but one relevant factor is the size of the fifth-century Hunnic homeland, the Hungarian Plain: while providing good-quality grazing, it was much smaller than the plains of the Great Eurasian Steppe the Huns had left behind. Its 42,400 square kilometres amount to less than 4 per cent of the grazing available, for instance, in the republic of Mongolia alone. And because the grazing was now so limited, some historians have wondered whether the Huns were evolving towards a fully sedentary existence in the fifth century. This is a possible argument, but not a necessary one. The Hungarian Plain notionally provides grazing for 320,000 horses, but this figure must be reduced so as to accommodate other animals, forest and so on; so it would be reasonable to suppose that it could support, maybe, 150,000. Given that each nomad warrior requires a string of ten horses to be able to rotate and not overtire them, the Hungarian Plain would thus provide sufficient space to support horses for up to 15,000 warriors. I would doubt that there were ever more Huns than this in total, so that, as late as the reign of Attila, there is in fact no firm indication that the Huns did not retain part of their nomad character.[39] Whatever the case, the real point is that, once they found themselves within hailing distance of the Roman Empire, the Huns perceived a new and better way to make a living, based on military predation upon the relatively rich economy of the Mediterranean world.

Priscus' evidence also implicitly documents the other fundamental change that made Attila's Empire possible. At his court, Maximinus and Priscus were interacting primarily with an inner core of second-rankers, rather than with Attila himself. Identifying the language group that ancient personal names belong to is fraught with danger, but the names of these men are extremely interesting. There is no doubt that Onegesius and Edeco possessed Germanic or Germanicized names, while Berichus and Scottas *probably* did. And both Attila ('Little Father') and Bleda are also Germanic. This doesn't mean that these individuals were necessarily of Germanic rather than Hunnic origin (though they may have been), because we know that by the mid-fifth century 'Gothic' – probably the collective term for a number of mutually comprehensible Germanic dialects spoken across central and eastern Europe – was one of the main languages of the Hunnic Empire, and was spoken at Attila's court. Hence, in addition to their original Hunnic names (and the argument continues over what type of language the Huns originally spoke), important figures in the Hunnic Empire seem to have had Germanic or Germanicized names as well.[40] Why had Germanic languages come to play a prominent role in the Hunnic Empire?

The explanation lies in the broader evolution of Attila's Empire. As far back as the 370s when they were attacking Goths beyond the Black Sea, Huns were forcing others they had already subdued to fight alongside them. When they first attacked the Greuthungi, starting the avalanche that ended at the battle of Hadrianople (see p. 167), they were operating in alliance with Iranian-speaking Alan nomads. And whenever we encounter them subsequently, we find that Hunnic forces always fought alongside non-Hunnic allies. Although Uldin, as we saw in Chapter 5, was not a conqueror on the scale of Attila, once the east Romans had dismantled his following, most of the force they were left with to resettle turned out to be Germanic-speaking Sciri.[41] Likewise, in the early 420s, east Roman forces intervening to curb Hunnic power west of the Carpathian Mountains found themselves left with a large number of Germanic Goths.[42]

In the years preceding the rise of Attila, the process of incorporation continued apace. By the 440s, an unprecedented number of Germanic groups found themselves within the orbit defined by the formidable power of Attila the Hun. For example, his Empire contained at least three separate clusters of Goths. One group, dominated by the Amal family and their rivals, would later become central to the creation of a second Gothic supergroup: the Ostrogoths. Another Gothic group was led in the mid-460s by a man called Bigelis, while a third remained under the tight control of Attila's sons until the later 460s. In addition, Germanic-speaking Gepids, Rugi, Suevi (left behind in 406), Sciri and Heruli were all by this point under direct Hunnic control, and a looser hegemony may also have been exercised over Lombards and Thuringians, as well as over at least some subgroups of the Alamanni and Franks.[43] We can't put figures on this vast body of Germanic-speaking humanity, but the Amal-led Goths alone could muster ten thousand-plus fighting men, and hence had maybe a total population of fifty thousand. And there is no reason to suppose that the other groups were much, if at all, smaller. Many tens of thousands, therefore, and probably several hundreds of thousands, of Germanic-speakers were caught up in the Hunnic Empire by the time of Attila. In fact, by the 440s there were probably many more Germanic-speakers than Huns, which explains why 'Gothic' should have become the Empire's lingua franca. Nor do these Germani exhaust the list of Attila's non-Hunnic subjects. Iranian-speaking Alanic and Sarmatian groups, as we saw earlier, had long been in alliance with the Huns, and Attila continued to grasp at opportunities to acquire new allies.

As this catalogue makes clear, the Hunnic Empire was all about incorporating people, not territory: hence Attila's virtual lack of interest in annexing substantial chunks of the Roman Empire. He took two Middle Danubian provinces from the western Empire as the price of his alliance with Aetius, as we saw in Chapter 6, but otherwise showed interest only in establishing a cordon sanitaire between himself and the east. Although there are many brief chronicle references to Attila's military forces as 'Huns' or (if they're archaizing) 'Scythians', from all the sources that go into any detail it is clear that his armies, like those of his less powerful predecessors, were always composites, consisting both of Huns and of contingents from the numerous other peoples incorporated into his Empire.[44]

Archaeological evidence confirms the point (map 12). Since 1945 a mass of material has been unearthed from cemetery excavations on the Great Hungarian Plain and its environs, dating to the period of Hunnic domination there. (Some treasure hoards have been discovered, but no one has ever found any of Attila's camps, since only post-holes would remain.) In this material, 'proper' Huns have proved extremely hard to find. In total – and this includes the Volga Steppe north of the Black Sea as well as the Hungarian Plain – archaeologists have identified no more than two hundred burials as plausibly Hunnic. These are distinguished by bows, non-standard European modes of dress,[45] cranial deformation (some Huns bound the heads of babies, which provoked a distinctive elongated skull), and the presence of so-called Hunnic cauldrons. So either the Huns generally disposed of their dead in ways that did not leave traces, or some other explanation is required for the scarcity of Hunnic material.[46] What these fifth-century Middle Danubian cemeteries have produced in large quantities, however, are the remains – or what *look* like the remains – of the Huns' Germanic subjects (unfortunately, it isn't possible to tell the latter apart from one another on the strength of archaeological finds alone).[47] These remains have close fourth-century antecedents in Gothic- and other Germanic-dominated areas east and north of the Carpathian Mountains. Those that interest us here – the fifth-century finds – mark

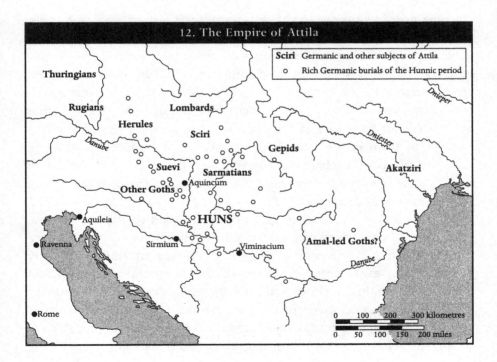

12. The Empire of Attila

the emergence of what has been christened the 'Danubian style' of Germanic burial.[48]

The Danubian style is characterized by inhumation rather than cremation,[49] with a large number of objects being deposited in a relatively small number of rich burials. (Many other individuals were buried with few or no grave goods at all.) These characteristic objects included items of personal adornment: particularly large semicircular brooches, plate buckles, earrings with polyhedric pendants, and gold necklaces. Weapons and military equipment have also been quite commonly found: saddles with metal appliqués, long straight swords suitable for cavalry use and arrows. The remains also show up some odd ritual quirks; it became quite usual, for instance, to bury broken metallic mirrors with the dead. The kinds of items found in the graves, the ways in which people were buried and, perhaps above all, the way women, in particular, wore their clothes – gathered with a safety-pin, or *fibula*, on each shoulder, with another closing the outer garment in front – all reflect the patterns observable in definitely Germanic remains of the fourth century. These habits and items were then pooled and developed further among the massed ranks of Attila's subjects on the Great Hungarian Plain in the fifth.

One possible answer to the question of the lack of Hunnic burials, then, is that, quite simply, they started to dress like their Germanic subject peoples, in just the same way that they learned the Gothic language. If so, it would be impossible to tell Hun from Goth – or anyone else – in the cemetery evidence. But even if our 'real Huns' are lying there in disguise, as it were, this doesn't alter the fact that there were an awful lot of Germani buried in and around the Great Hungarian Plain in the Hunnic period. What we're looking at in the richly furnished Danubian-style burials are the remains of many of Attila's elite Germanic followers. Date and geographical placement make this a dead certainty.[50]

Every time a new barbarian group was added to Attila's Empire, that group's manpower was mobilized for Hunnic campaigns. Hence the Huns' military machine increased, and increased very quickly, by incorporating ever larger numbers of the Germani of central and eastern Europe. In the short term, this benefited the embattled Roman west. The reason, as many historians have remarked, that the rush of Germanic immigration into the Roman Empire ceased after the crisis of 405–8 (see Chapter 5) was that those who had not crossed the frontier by about 410 found themselves incorporated instead into the Empire of the Huns; and there is an inverse relationship between the pace of migration into the Roman Empire and the rise of Hunnic power.[51]

In the longer term, however, the respite from assault was only illusory, and a succession of Hunnic leaders achieved something analogous to what the Sasanians had achieved in the Near East. For the first time in imperial Roman history, the Huns managed to unite a large number of Rome's European neighbours into something approaching a rival imperial superpower.

'The Whole North into Gaul'

THE FULL FEROCITY of this extraordinary new war machine was felt in the first instance by the east Roman Empire, whose Balkan communities suffered heavily in 441/2 and again in 447. After the two defeats of the 447 campaign, the east Romans had nothing left to throw in Attila's direction. Hence, in 449, their resorting to the assassination attempt in which Maximinus and Priscus found themselves unwittingly embroiled. Still Attila didn't let Constantinople off the hook. Having refused to settle the matter of the fugitives and repeated his demands for the establishment of a cordon sanitaire inside the Danube frontier, he now added another: that the east Romans should provide a nobly born wife (with an appropriate dowry) for his Roman-born secretary. These demands, if unsatisfied, were possible pretexts for war, and his constant agitating shows that Attila was still actively considering another major assault on the Balkans.

In 450, the diplomatic mood was to change abruptly. A new Roman embassy followed the same path north that Priscus and Maximinus had trodden the previous year. This one comprised Anatolius, one of the two most senior military commanders at the eastern court (*magister militum praesentalis*), and Nomus, the Master of Offices (*magister officiorum*). Anatolius was well known to Attila, having negotiated the interim peace deal that had followed the Hunnic victories of 447. It is hard to think of a grander ambassadorial duo – that he should treat only with the noblest had been one of Attila's stipulations. The Roman view of what happened next is recorded by Priscus: 'At first Attila negotiated arrogantly, but he was overwhelmed by the number

of their gifts and mollified by their words of appeasement . . .' In the
end:

> Attila swore that he would keep the peace on the same terms,
> that he would withdraw from the Roman territory bordering the
> Danube and that he would cease to press the matter of the
> fugitives . . . providing the Romans did not again receive other
> fugitives who fled from him. He also freed Vigilas . . . [and] a
> large number of prisoners without ransom, gratifying Anatolius
> and Nomus . . . [who were] given gifts of horses and skins of wild
> animals.[52]

Rarely can an international summit have had such a satisfactory
outcome. Back to Constantinople rode the jubilant ambassadors,
bringing with them Attila's secretary, who was to be found a suitable
wife.

What quickly emerged, however, was that Attila had settled with
Constantinople not because – as the stereotypical barbarian – he had
been blown away by the wisdom of his east Roman interlocutors, but
because he wanted a secure eastern front, having decided on a massive
invasion of the Roman west.

As Priscus tells it, in launching this new attack Attila was motivated by his hunger for further and greater conquests, thereby playing
out the destiny that the gods intended for him – as his finding of the
sword of Mars proclaimed – to conquer the entire world. On his
embassy to the Huns, Priscus had at some point in the summer of
449 witnessed Attila acting in what seemed to him an unreasonable
manner towards some ambassadors from the western Roman Empire.
Afterwards, the talk naturally turned to Attila's character, and Priscus
quotes with approval what one of the ambassadors had to say on the
matter:

> [Attila's] great good fortune and the power which it had given
> him had made him so arrogant that he would not entertain just
> proposals unless he thought that they were to his advantage. No
> previous ruler of Scythia . . . had ever achieved so much in so
> short a time. He ruled the islands of the Ocean [the Atlantic, or
> west] and, in addition to the whole of Scythia, forced the Romans
> to pay tribute . . . and, in order to increase his empire further, he
> now wanted to attack the Persians.[53]

Someone then asked how Attila proposed to get to Persia from central Europe, to which the reply was that the Huns remembered that, if you followed the north Black Sea coast all the way to the end, you could get there without having to cross Roman territory. True, of course, but going via the Caucasus would be an extremely long trek, and the last time the Huns had done this – in 395/6, as far as we know – they had been living north of the Black Sea, not on the Great Hungarian Plain so much further west. Ambitious plans of conquest, on the face of it, were being drawn up on the strength of half-remembered geography: here was pure lust for conquest aching to swallow up the known world.

But, as we know, Attila went west instead. The sources transmit a variety of reasons why he did so. According to one juicy piece of court gossip, he led his armies into the western Roman Empire because the sister of the western emperor Valentinian III, a high-spirited lady of considerable stamina by the name of Iusta Grata Honoria, offered him her hand in marriage with half the western Empire as her dowry. Supposedly, she sent him a brooch with her portrait on it, along with a letter, and this was enough to ensnare him. Honoria was the daughter of the formidable Galla Placidia who had a fondness for barbarians herself, as we learned in Chapter 6, having married and borne a son to Alaric's brother-in-law Athaulf in the 410s. Placidia, with her Gothic bodyguard, had had what it took to play a major political role, until Aetius took over.

Having fallen pregnant, her daughter Honoria was caught in an illicit love affair with her business manager, a certain Eugenius. Eugenius was executed, and Honoria removed from public life and betrothed to a dull senator by the name of Herculianus. It was in her distress and frustration that she had written to the lord of the Huns and asked him to rescue her. But the story gives one pause. Even after it was discovered that she had written to Attila she escaped death, and was handed over to the custody of her mother; but before, irritatingly, breaking off in mid-sentence, the pertinent Priscus fragment hints that further escapades followed. Honoria's antics are too well documented for there not to be some grain of truth in them,[54] but I don't believe that she was the reason why Attila eventually preferred the west Roman to the Persian option. Just consider the geography. As we will see in a moment, having decided to attack the west, Attila did not rush towards Italy, where Honoria was incarcerated, but first attacked Gaul.

While no doubt sketchy, Attila's knowledge of European geography was good enough for us to be sure he knew on which side of the Alps he was likely to find his putative bride. We don't know what ultimately happened to Honoria. Heading west out of Hungary, the Huns turned right towards Gaul rather than left into Italy, and that's enough in itself to relegate Honoria to a historical footnote.

The sources indicate that rescuing Honoria was only one of several reasons proposed for Attila's invasion of the west. Another was the issue that had prompted his tantrum before the conversation in the summer of 449 in which his possible ambitions concerning Persia had been raised. That particular western embassy had been sent to answer the charge that a Roman banker by the name of Silvanus was in possession of some gold plate that was Attila's by right of conquest. Trivial though the matter was, Attila was threatening war if it was not settled to his satisfaction. There are also vague, but quite convincing, hints of some kind of contact at this date between Attila and Geiseric, king of the Vandals, who is said to have bribed Attila to turn his armies westwards. Late in 450, Attila backed a different candidate for the recently vacant kingship of the Ripuarian Franks from the one Aetius had chosen to support. He had also recently given sanctuary to one of the leaders of a rebellion in north-west Gaul defeated by Aetius in 448. This suggests that Attila had in mind the possibility of using him to stir up trouble and to smooth the path of any Hunnic army operating in the west. Once his armies were on the move, in much the same vein the Hun sent out some mutually contradictory letters to different recipients, some of which claimed that the purpose of his campaign was to attack not the western Empire but the Visigoths of south-west Gaul, while others urged those same Visigoths to join him in attacking the Empire.[55]

What emerges, therefore, is that Attila was simultaneously juggling with several possible pretexts for an attack on the western Empire in the years 449 and 450, as he prepared his next move. Whether an attack on Persia was ever seriously contemplated I doubt, but in 449 he still hadn't decided whether to launch his next assault upon the eastern or the western half of the Empire; and he was not only stirring up trouble with the west, but also refusing to settle outstanding issues with Constantinople. The generous treaty he eventually granted Constantinople was the sign that he was ready to tie up loose ends in the east, having set his sights on the west.

In spring 451, Attila's massive army surged westwards out of the Middle Danube, probably following the route taken by the Rhine invaders of 406. 'It is said' that the army consisted of a staggering half-million men, reported Jordanes,[56] in his choice of words revealing that for once even he didn't believe the figure; but there is no doubting the huge size of the force, or that Attila was drawing on the full resources of the Hunnic war machine. As Sidonius Apollinaris, a more or less contemporary Gallic poet, put it:

> Suddenly the barbarian world, rent by a mighty upheaval, poured the whole north into Gaul. After the warlike Rugian comes the fierce Gepid, with the Gelonian close by; the Burgundian urges on the Scirian; forward rush the Hun, the Bellonotian, the Neurian, the Bastarnian, the Thuringian, the Bructeran, and the Frank.[57]

Sidonius was writing metred poetry, and required names of the right length and stress to make it work. What he gives us here is an interesting mixture of ancient groups who had nothing to do with the Hunnic Empire (Gelonian, Bellonotian, Neurian, Bastarnian, Bructeran) and real subjects of Attila (Rugian, Gepid, Burgundian, Scirian, Thuringian and Frank), not to mention, of course, the Huns themselves. But, in essence, Sidonius was spot on. And we know from other sources that large numbers of Goths were also present.[58]

No surviving source describes the campaign in detail, but we know roughly what happened. Having followed the Upper Danube north-westwards out of the Great Hungarian Plain, the horde crossed the Rhine in the region of Coblenz and continued west (map 13). According to some admittedly fairly dubious sources, the city of Metz fell on 7 April, shortly followed by the old imperial capital of Trier. The army then thrust into the heart of Roman Gaul. By June, it was outside the city of Orléans, where a considerable force of Alans in Roman service had their headquarters. The city was placed under heavy siege; there are hints that Attila was hoping to lure Sangibanus, king of some of the Alans based in the city, over to his side.[59] At the same time, according to another pretty dubious source, elements of the army had also reached the gates of Paris, where they were driven back by the miraculous intervention of the city's patron Saint Genevieve. It looks as if the Hunnic army was swarming far and wide over Roman Gaul, looting and ransacking as it went.

Aetius was still generalissimo of the west, and as we know from Merobaudes' second panegyric, he had been anticipating the possibility of a Hunnic assault on the west from at least 443. When it finally materialized, nearly a decade later, he sprang into action. Faced with this enormous threat, he strove to put together a coalition of forces that would stand some chance of success. Early summer 451 saw him advancing north through Gaul with contingents of the Roman armies of Italy and Gaul, plus forces from many allied groups, such as the Burgundians and the Aquitainian Visigoths under their king Theoderic. On 14 June, the approach of this motley force compelled Attila's withdrawal from Orléans. Later in the same month, Aetius' men caught up with the retreating horde somewhere in the vicinity of Troyes, another 150 kilometres or so to the east.

On a plain called by different sources the Catalaunian fields or *campus Mauriacus*, which has never been conclusively identified, a huge battle took place:

> The battlefield was a plain rising by a sharp slope to a ridge, which both armies sought to gain . . . The Huns with their forces seized the right side, the Romans, the Visigoths and their allies

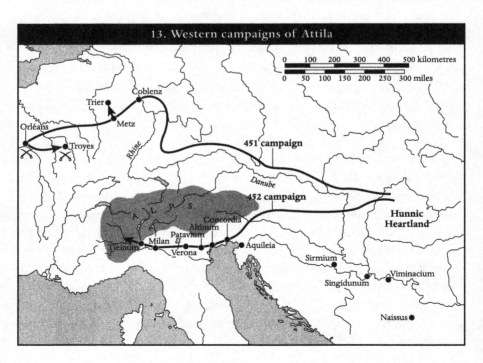

13. Western campaigns of Attila

the left . . . The battleline of the Huns was so arranged that Attila and his bravest followers were in the centre . . . The innumerable peoples of diverse tribes, which he had subjected to his sway, formed the wings.

The Romans and Visigoths reached the ridge first and thwarted every attempt to dislodge them – so our main source tells us, but then lapses into rhetoric (though pretty good rhetoric it is):

The fight grew fierce, confused, monstrous, unrelenting – a fight whose like no ancient time has ever recorded . . . A brook flowing between low banks . . . was swollen by a strange stream and turned into a torrent by the flow of blood. Those whose wounds drove them to slake their parching thirst drank water mingled with gore.

Theoderic was killed in the fighting, either struck by a spear or trampled to death when he fell from his horse, but the accounts of his death are confusing. Again according to our main source, a total of 165,000 men died, but this figure is nonsense. At the end of the day's fighting, Attila was distraught. Forced back inside a defensive wagon circle, for the first time ever his army had suffered a major defeat. His initial reaction was to heap up saddles to make his own funeral pyre.[60] But his lieutenants persuaded him that the battle was only a tactical check, and he relented. A stalemate followed, with the two armies facing each other, until the Huns began slowly to retreat. Aetius didn't press them too hard, and disbanded his coalition of forces as quickly as possible – a task made much easier by the fact that the Visigoths were keen to return to Toulouse to sort out the succession to their dead king. Attila consented to his army's continued withdrawal and, tails between their legs, the Huns returned to Hungary. Although the cost to the Roman communities in the Huns' line of march was enormous, Attila's first assault on the west had been repulsed. Yet again, Aetius had delivered at the moment of crisis. Despite the limited resources available, he had put together a coalition that had saved Gaul.

In his wrath, the Hun spent the winter of 451/2 limbering up for yet more violence. This time the blow fell on Italy. In the spring of 452, his force broke through the Alpine passes. The first obstacle in their path was Aquileia. Here they were held up by the city's massive defences – Attila even contemplated calling off the whole campaign.

On the point of bringing their long and frustrating siege to a halt, he saw a stork shipping its young out of the nest that it had built in one of the city's towers, carrying one by one those that couldn't yet fly. Seeing this, Priscus tells us, 'he ordered his army to remain still in the same place, saying that the bird would never have gone . . . unless it was foretelling that some disaster would strike the place very shortly.'[61] The stork, of course (not to mention Attila), was right. The Huns' precocious skill at taking fortified strongholds prevailed, and Aquileia fell to them in short order. Its capture opened up the main route into north-eastern Italy.

The horde then followed the ancient Roman roads west across the Po Plain. One of the political heartlands of the western Empire and agriculturally rich, this region was endowed with many prosperous cities. Now, as in the Balkans, one after the other these cities fell to the Huns, and they took in swift succession Padua, Mantua, Vicentia, Verona, Brescia and Bergamo (map 13). Now Attila was at the gates of Milan, a long-time imperial capital. The siege was protracted, but again Attila triumphed, and another centre of Empire was looted and sacked. A fragment of Priscus' history preserves a nice vignette:

> When [Attila] saw [in Milan] in a painting the Roman Emperors sitting upon golden thrones and Scythians lying dead before their feet, he sought out a painter and ordered him to paint Attila upon a throne and the Roman emperors heaving sacks upon their shoulders and pouring out gold before his feet.

But, as in Gaul the previous year, Attila's Italian campaign failed to go entirely to plan. Papal sources and Hollywood scriptwriters love to focus on one incident in particular when, after the capture of Milan, Pope Leo, as part of a peace embassy that included the Prefect Trygetius and ex-consul Avienus, met Attila to try to persuade him not to attack the city of Rome. In the end, the Huns did turn back, retreating to Hungary once again.

In some circles this went down as a great personal triumph for the Pope in face-to-face diplomacy. Reality was more prosaic. Other forces apart from the God-guided Leo were at work. Attila's Italian campaign, essentially a series of sieges, lacked substantial logistic support; and in their often cramped conditions the Hunnic army was vulnerable in more ways than one. The chronicler Hydatius put it succinctly: 'The Huns who had been plundering Italy and who had also stormed a number of cities, were victims of divine punishment, being visited with heaven-sent disasters: famine and some kind of disease.' By the time Milan was captured, disease was taking a heavy toll, and food running dangerously short. Also, Constantinople now had a new ruler, the emperor Marcian, and his forces, together with what Aetius could put together, were far from idle: 'In addition, [the Huns] were slaughtered by auxiliaries sent by the Emperor Marcian and led by Aetius, and at the same time they were crushed in their settlements by both heaven-sent disasters and the army of Marcian.'[62] It looks as though, while the Hunnic army in Italy was being harassed by Aetius leading a joint east-west force, other eastern forces were launching a raid north of the Danube, into Attila's heartland. The combination was deadly, and, as in the previous year, the Hun had no choice but to retreat. With some kind of peace or truce in operation, his army rolled back into central Europe.[63]

If 451 was itself no more than a tactical check, two major defeats in as many years put a substantial dent in the great conqueror's reputation. These western campaigns were much more difficult to mount, in fact, than Attila's Balkan adventures of the previous decade. The Hunnic Empire did not have the bureaucratic machinery of its Roman counterpart, however lumbering that might be. As far as we know, it ran to one Roman-supplied secretary at a time, and a prisoner called Rusticius who was kept for his skill at writing letters in Greek and Latin. Nothing suggests that the Huns had any equivalent, therefore, of the Romans' capacity for planning and putting in place the necessary logistic support, in terms of food and fodder, for major campaigns. No doubt, when the word went out to assemble for war, each warrior was expected to bring a certain amount of food along with him, but as the campaign dragged on, the Hunnic army was bound to be living mainly off the land. Hence, in campaigns over longer distances, the difficulties involved in maintaining the army as an effective fighting force increased exponentially. Fatigue as well as the likelihood of food shortages and disease increased with distance. There was also every chance that the army would spread so widely over an unfamiliar landscape in search of supplies that it would be difficult to concentrate for battle. In 447, during the widest-reaching of the Balkan campaigns, for their first major battle Attila's armies had marched west along the northern line of the Haemus Mountains, crossed them, then moved south towards Constantinople, then south-west to the Chersonesus for their second: a total distance of something like 500 kilometres. In 451, the army had to cover the distance from Hungary to Orléans, about 1,200 kilometres; and in 452 from Hungary to Milan, perhaps 800, but this time they were laying siege as they went, which made them yet more susceptible to disease.[64] As many historians have commented, in campaigns covering such vast distances into the western Empire, Attila and his forces were almost bound to experience serious setbacks.

But Attila didn't learn the lesson. Early in 453, he was on the eve of launching yet another destructive campaign across the European landscape, when finally the scourge of God went to meet his employer. He had just taken another wife (we don't know how many he had in total). On his wedding night he drank too much, burst a blood vessel and died. His bride was too scared to raise the alarm, and was found beside the corpse in the morning. The funeral was an orgy of mourning and glorification, as Jordanes describes:

> His body was placed ... in state in a silken tent ... The best horsemen of the entire tribe of the Huns rode around in circles ... and told of his deeds[:] 'The Chief of the Huns, King Attila, born of his father Mundiuch, lord of the bravest tribes, sole possessor of the Scythian and German realms – powers previously unknown – captured cities and terrified both empires of the Roman world and, appeased by their entreaties, took annual tribute to save the rest from plunder. And when he had accomplished all this ... he fell not by wound of the foe, nor by treachery of friends, but in the midst of his nation at peace, happy in his joy and without sense of pain.'

When the wake had finished:

> In the secrecy of the night they buried his body in the earth. They bound his coffins, the first with gold, the second with silver and the third with the strength of iron ... iron because he subdued the nations, gold and silver because he received the honours of both empires. They also added the arms of foemen won in the fight, trappings of rare worth, sparkling with various gems, and ornaments of all sorts ... then ... they slew those appointed to the work.[65]

The Huns and Rome

THE FULL EFFECT upon the Roman world of the rise of the Hunnic Empire can be broken down into three phases. The first, as we saw in Chapters 4 and 5, generated two great moments of crisis on the frontier for the Roman Empire, during 376–80 and 405–8, forcing it to accept upon its soil the establishment of enclaves of unsubdued barbarians. The existence of these enclaves in turn created new and, as we saw in Chapter 6, hugely damaging centrifugal forces within the Empire's body politic. In the second phase, in the generation before Attila, the Huns evolved from invaders into empire-builders in central Europe, and the flow of refugees into Roman territory ceased. The Huns wanted subjects to exploit, and strove to bring potential candidates under control. In this era, too, Constantius and Aetius were able to make use of Hunnic power to control the immigrant groups who had previously crossed the Empire's frontier to escape from the Huns. Since none of these groups was actually destroyed, however, the palliative effects of phase two of the Hunnic impact upon the Roman world by no means outweighed the damage done in phase one.

Attila's massive military campaigns of the 440s and early 450s mark the third phase in Hunnic-Roman relations. Their effects, as one might expect, were far-reaching. The east Roman Empire's Balkan provinces were devastated, with thousands killed as one stronghold after another was taken. As the remains of Nicopolis ad Istrum so graphically show, Roman administration might be restored but not so the Latin- and Greek-speaking landowning class that had grown up over the preceding four centuries. The Gallic campaign of 451, and particularly the assault upon Italy in 452, inflicted enormous damage upon those unfortunate enough to find themselves in the Huns' path.

But if we step back from the immediate drama and consider the Roman state in broader terms, Attila's campaigns, though serious, were not life-threatening. The eastern half of the Roman Empire depended on the tax it collected from a rich arc of provinces stretching from Asia Minor to Egypt, territories out of reach of the Huns. For all the latter's siege technology, the triple landwalls surrounding Constantinople made the eastern capital impregnable; and the Huns had no navy to take them across the narrow straits that separated the Balkans from the rich provinces of Asia. A similar situation prevailed in the west. By the time of Attila, it was already feeling a heavy financial strain, as we have seen, but given the logistic limitations of the Hunnic military machine, Attila came nowhere near to conquering it. In fact, far more serious damage was indirectly inflicted upon the structures of Empire by the influx of armed immigrants between 376 and 408. Moreover, it was again the *indirect* effects of the age of Attila that posed the real threat to the integrity of the west Roman state. Because he had to concentrate on dealing with Attila, Aetius had less time and fewer resources for tackling other threats to the Roman west in the 440s. And these other threats cost the western Empire much more dearly than the Hunnic invasions of 451 and 452. The first and most serious loss was the enforced abandonment of the reconquest of North Africa from the Vandals.

In such circumstances, most unfortunately, Aetius could give little help to the Iberian peninsula. There, the departure of the Vandals in 429 had seen some restoration of Roman order, and some reclamation of the revenues that had been lost in the 410s. The Hispanic provinces were rich and well developed, and, if no match for the abundance of North Africa, were still a valued contributor to western coffers. In the 410s, most of the peninsula had fallen out of direct Roman control except for Tarraconensis in the north-east, as the Vandals, Alans and Suevi shared out the rest. After 429, only the Suevi remained in large numbers, confined to the least prosperous north-western upland zone of Gallaecia. Aetius, like his predecessors, was happy to leave them there, seeing no need to risk valuable troops for its recovery.[66] Instead, he concentrated his efforts on restoring order and on maintaining the flow of funds from the richer provinces abandoned by the Vandals and Alans, until he was interrupted by Geiseric's seizure of Carthage.

Under their new king Rechila, who succeeded his father in 438, the Suevi took advantage of Aetius' preoccupation with North Africa to expand their dominion. In 439, they moved out of Gallaecia to take Merida, the main city of the neighbouring province of Lusitania. In 440, they captured Aetius' military commander and main representative in the peninsula, the *comes* (count) Censorius. In 441, they took Seville and extended their control over the whole of Baetica and Carthaginiensis. The lack of any concerted response from Aetius, who was now frantically gathering his forces in Sicily, gave local self-help groups, the Bagaudae, the chance to undermine central control in parts of Tarraconensis, the one province still in imperial hands. As had been the case in Gaul, these uprisings were probably assertions of local power at a time when the imperial grip was perceived to be slipping. At least one of the revolts, led by one Basilius in Tyriasso (Tirasona) in 449, seems to have favoured a Suevic takeover, perhaps because it seemed the best way to guarantee peace, just as Gallic landowners had supported Athaulf the Visigoth in the early 410s.

The situation in Spain went from bad to worse, then, between 439 and 441, and the flow of tax revenue dried up. Even after making peace with the Vandals, there was little Aetius could do. Large-scale intervention was out of the question. A series of commanders were sent to Spain: Asturius in 442, Merobaudes himself in 443, and Vitus in 446. Asturius and Merobaudes concentrated on defeating the Bagaudae, presumably so as to hold on at least to Tarraconensis. Vitus' brief was more ambitious. Repeating the strategy of the 410s, he led a combined Romano-Visigothic force into Carthaginiensis and Baetica. Our main informant, the bishop-chronicler Hydatius, complains about this army's 'plundering', but his attitude was perhaps shaped by the expedition's outcome. When Vitus' force met the Suevi in battle, it was routed. Aetius had, in fact, scraped together what Hydatius calls a 'not inconsiderable' body of troops for Vitus, in the circumstances a fair testimony to the importance he accorded to retrieving the Hispanic revenues. What he clearly could not do, however, was bring down on the Suevi the full weight of the remaining western field armies, since they had to be kept in reserve to defend the Empire against Attila. This defeat confirmed the Suevi in their possession of most of the peninsula; and once again the bulk of Hispanic revenues were lost.[67]

Roman Britain, too, was in its death throes. Although, despite the letter of Honorius in 410 'urging [the British] to fend for themselves' (p. 245), the Empire had no pretensions to direct control there, Roman life had survived in parts of the province, and there was a fair amount of informal contact between Romano-Britons and their continental counterparts. In 429, then again in the early 440s, Bishop Germanus of Auxerre made trips to the island to help native Christians combat the influence of Pelagian heretics.[68] But heresy wasn't the only problem facing this last generation of Romano-Britons: raiders from Ireland (the Scots) and Scotland (the Picts) were troubling the western and northern fringes of the province, and Saxons from across the North Sea also took advantage of Romano-British isolation to start helping themselves to its wealth. The latter had been a worry since at least the third century, and their incursions had prompted the construction of massive fortifications along the eastern and southern shores. Some of them still stand today, notably the forts of Portchester and Caerleon. We don't know who was exercising authority in the troubled world of sub-Roman Britain, but for a generation or so the cities continued to function, still producing at least some tax revenues in kind.[69]

A sixth-century British source, the monk Gildas, reports in his appropriately named *On the Ruin of Britain* that power eventually fell into the hands of an unnamed tyrant, whom Bede names as Vortigern. He and a 'council' (perhaps representatives from the surviving city councils) decided that employing Saxon mercenaries was the solution to the problems of the much threatened, much raided, Romano-British. The story of what happened next is told in outline by Gildas, who was writing a moral tale for his own times, but, as far as it goes, the account is credible enough:[70]

> The [Saxons] ... asked to be given supplies, falsely representing themselves as soldiers ready to undergo extreme dangers for their excellent hosts. The supplies were granted and for a long time 'shut the dog's mouth'. Then they again complained that their monthly allowance was insufficient ... and swore that they would break their agreement and plunder the whole island unless more lavish payment were heaped upon them. There was no delay: they put their threats into immediate effect.

And the result:

> All the major towns were laid low by the repeated battering of enemy rams; laid low, too, all the inhabitants – church leaders, priests and people alike, as the swords glinted all around and the flames crackled ... In the middle of the squares the foundation-stones of high walls and towers that had been torn from their lofty base, holy altars, fragments of corpses covered with a purple crust of congealed blood looked as though they had been mixed up in some dreadful wine-press.

Gildas does not date the revolt – actually, he doesn't explicitly date anything – but two chronicles written in Gaul, whose knowledge of events in Britain demonstrates the continued cross-Channel contact also evident in the *Life of St Germanus*, note that conditions turned seriously nasty in what remained of Roman Britain round about the year 440. Faced with an ever-worsening situation, the Romano-British made one final appeal to be taken back under the imperial wing, writing formally to Aetius. The date of the letter is controversial, but Gildas refers to Aetius at that point as 'three times consul'. Aetius became consul for the third time in 446, so if Gildas' usage is accurate, the appeal arrived just as he was anxiously scanning the Danube for early signs of the brewing Hunnic tempest. Even if Gildas is wrong, though, the general point holds. Aetius was facing too many threats

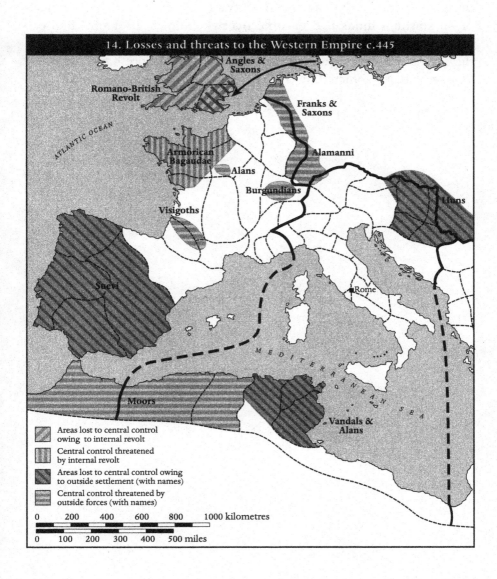

14. Losses and threats to the Western Empire c.445

Areas lost to central control owing to internal revolt

Central control threatened by internal revolt

Areas lost to central control owing to outside settlement (with names)

Central control threatened by outside forces (with names)

0   200   400   600   800   1000 kilometres

0   100   200   300   400   500 miles

elsewhere to be able to answer the last desperate call of Roman Britain.[71]

The picture was bleak. The western Empire had by 452 lost a substantial percentage of its provinces (map 14): the whole of Britain, most of Spain, the richest provinces of North Africa, those parts of south-western Gaul ceded to the Visigoths, plus south-eastern Gaul ceded to the Burgundians. Furthermore, much of the rest had also seen serious fighting in the last decade or so, and the revenues from these areas too would have been substantially reduced.[72] The problem of diminishing funds had become overwhelming. The Huns' indirect role in this process of attrition, in having originally pushed many of the armed immigrants across the frontier, did far more harm than any damage directly inflicted by Attila.

PART THREE

FALL OF EMPIRES

8

THE FALL OF THE HUNNIC EMPIRE

THE FALL OF ATTILA'S EMPIRE is an extraordinary story in its own right. Up to about AD 350, the Huns had figured not at all in European history. During 350–410, the only Huns most Romans had encountered were a few raiding parties. Ten years later, Huns in significant numbers had established themselves west of the Carpathian Mountains on the Great Hungarian Plain, but they still functioned mostly as useful allies to the Roman state. In 441, when Attila and Bleda launched their first attack across the Roman frontier, the ally revealed his new colours. In forty years, the Huns had risen from nowhere to European superpower. By anyone's standards, this was spectacular. But the collapse of Attila's Empire was more spectacular still. By 469, just sixteen years after his death, the last of the Huns were seeking asylum inside the eastern Roman Empire. Their extinction would cause deep reverberations in the Roman west.

Empire to Extinction

RECONSTRUCTING the collapse of Hunnic dominion in central Europe is a tricky proposition. Our old friend Priscus told the story in some detail, but since there was little diplomacy involved in the fall, his account hardly made it into Constantine VII's *Excerpts concerning Embassies* (see p. 306). For the most part we have to rely on one of the most intriguing historical works to survive from late antiquity: the *Gothic History*, or *Getica*, of Jordanes, whose voice we have already heard in earlier chapters. About ten pages of text (half of it notes) in the standard edition provide the only coherent existing account of the fall of Attila's Empire.[1]

Jordanes was a man of Gothic descent living in Constantinople around the year 550, so he was writing nearly a century after the events we're interested in. At this point he was a monk, but had previously served as a secretary to a Roman commander on the Danube, so was not without relevant experience. He tells us in the preface to the *Getica* that his history of the Goths is largely an abridgement of a lost history written by an Italo-Roman called Cassiodorus. Cassiodorus was adviser to Theoderic the Amal, Ostrogothic king of Italy, in the 520s. Jordanes says that he had access to Cassiodorus' history for just three days when compiling his own and that, as he puts it, 'the words I recall not, but the sense and deeds related I think I retain entire'. Some have sensed something a bit fishy in this, arguing either that Jordanes had much greater access to his model than he pretends, or that he had very little to do with him and was trying to use Cassiodorus' name for his own purposes. These hypotheses founder, however, on their proponents' failure to come up with a convincing reason for Jordanes to have lied.[2] I am confident that he is broadly telling the truth in claiming to have followed Cassiodorus' outline closely. The *Getica* corresponds well enough with the few things we know from elsewhere about Cassiodorus' history.[3]

But even if Jordanes' preface is not disguising some massive deception, this doesn't make the *Getica* a reliable source. Cassiodorus wrote his history of the Goths for the court of the Ostrogothic king, Theoderic the Amal, and this has a significant bearing on the narrative of Hunnic collapse that has come down to us in the *Getica*. Above all, and as you might expect, it is a thoroughly Gotho-centric account. Only the story of the Goths removing themselves from Hunnic overlordship is told in any detail in its pages, and even the Huns appear only incidentally. More specifically, Cassiodorus had to tell his Gothic history as his particular Gothic king wanted it told. As a result, it contains two historical distortions.

First, it claims that all the Goths who didn't flee from the Huns in AD 376 by crossing over into the Roman Empire immediately fell under Hunnic control. This is nonsense. We actually know of *seven* groups of Goths, other than the Greuthungi and Tervingi who sought asylum from the emperor Valens in 376 (and there is no reason to suppose that even this list is exhaustive):

1. The Amal-led Goths, who were under Hunnic control by the time of Attila and were presently ruled by Theoderic.
2. The Goths of Radagaisus who invaded Italy in 405/6 and

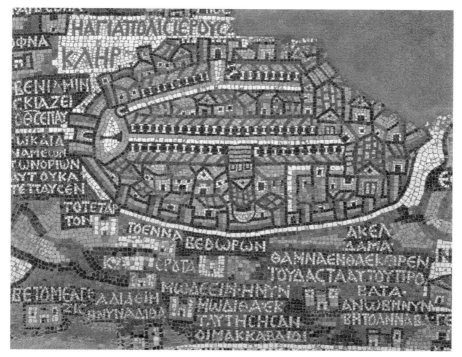

15. The sack of Rome caused some educated Romans to question the Empire's claim to be a unique, divinely supported state. Most, however, saw the crisis as another challenge to be overcome and retained faith in the empire's destiny – here symbolized pictorially in a mosaic representation of Jerusalem with Constantine's churches there at its heart – to Christianize the entire world.

16. The ruins of Portchester castle, one of the string of military installations, soldiers and fleets brought under unified command in the late Roman period to protect the Channel and North Sea coasts of Britain from Saxon attack. When the central state was no longer willing to subsidize British defence, the island quickly fell prey to Saxon predators.

17. Flavius Constantius, Patrician, general, and then briefly western emperor
in 421. He defeated political rivals, usurpers, Goths and Rhine invaders in that – highly
rational – order between 411 and 418 to bring the western Empire back from the brink of
total collapse and inspire renewed confidence among Christian and pagan landowners alike.

18. The eastern emperor Theodosius II (sole ruler 408–50). Largely a ceremonial ruler,
his lengthy reign saw, amongst other major events, the eastern Empire intervene in the
west to put Valentinian III on the throne in 425, the production of the Theodosian Code
in 438, and the east's desperate struggle for survival in the face of Attila's Hunnic
power in the 440s.

19. *Opposite*. The Mausoleum of Galla Placidia, sister of the emperor Honorius. Captured
by the Visigoths in the sack of Rome, she married Alaric's brother-in-law and bore him a
child with an excellent claim to be the next western emperor. After their deaths she then
married, against her will, Flavius Constantius, and spent the rest of her eventful life
trying to safeguard the political interests of their son, Valentinian III.

20. Some of the ruins of late Roman Carthage. By the late imperial period, Carthage had evolved from Roman public enemy number 1 into a great centre of Roman culture and the busy port from which North Africa's grain fleets left to feed the city of Rome.

21. The ruins of Bulla Regia against its typical North African backdrop. This was one of the province's string of agro-towns whose production of olive oil, wine and grain combined with the lack of any serious threat to its borders to make North Africa the jewel in the western imperial crown.

22. The great landwalls of Constantinople. As practical as they were beautiful, they were constructed in the early 410s to defend the eastern capital against the massive new threat posed by the Huns. Despite an earthquake, they were still enough to deter Attila in 447, and would not be breached until Ottoman cannon blew a hole in them in 1453.

23. The spread of such characteristic Hunnic cauldrons and associated remains westwards from the steppe onto the great Hungarian Plain, where these were found, gives us a physical manifestation of the Hunnic revolution which totally overturned the existing balance of power on Rome's European frontiers.

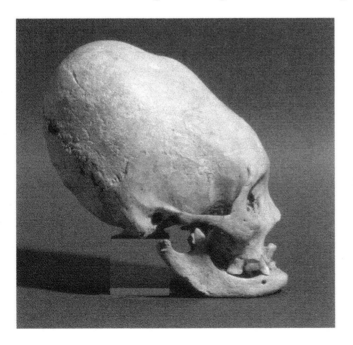

24. The Huns tightly bound the heads of infants to generate from their still-unfused skullbones the characteristic elongated shape demonstrated by this individual. The habit spread to some of their European neighbours for a brief period at the height of Hunnic power in the mid-fifth century.

25. The Emperor Valentinian III came to the throne as an infant and never managed to make himself a ruler in more than name, even after he personally (with just a little help) assassinated the general and Patrician Aetius who had dominated western imperial politics for most of his adult lifetime.

26. The interior of the great church of Hagia Sophia, constructed by eastern emperor Justinian I in Constantinople in the 530s. Long after the western Empire ceased to exist, its eastern counterpart flourished as a great imperial power, constructing monuments to match. This continued prosperity makes it difficult to argue that the western Empire was destined to collapse for reasons internal to the Roman imperial system itself.

27. A medieval portrait of the great Carolingian emperor Charlemagne.
His refounded Empire lasted for less than a hundred years as opposed to
Rome's half a millennium. The narrative of its collapse provides a tellingly
contrasting example of an Empire that really did fall apart for
internal reasons.

eventually became part of Alaric's new Visigothic group (see Chapter 5).

3. The Goths of Pannonia, detached by Roman military action from Hunnic hegemony in the 420s, and resettled by the Romans in Thrace; quite possibly the ancestors of group 6 below.

4. The Goths of a king called Bigelis, who unsuccessfully invaded the east Roman Empire sometime between 466 and 471.

5. The Goths operating in the train of Dengizich, son of Attila, when he invaded east Roman territory in the late 460s.

6. A large group of Goths already settled in Thrace as Roman allies in about 470.

7. Two other, smaller, Gothic groups established in enclaves around the Black Sea: the Tetraxitae of the Cimmerian Bosporus and the Goths of Dory in the south-western Crimea.[4]

In concentrating solely upon group 1, therefore, the *Getica*'s historical vision substantially simplifies Gothic history.

Second – and closely related to the first point – the *Getica* overstates the historical importance of the Amal dynasty from which Theoderic, Cassiodorus' employer, was descended. By dividing the Goths into those who were conquered by the Huns in 376 and those who fled, the *Getica* can maintain that the Amal family had long ruled *every* Goth who did not enter Roman territory during the reign of Valens. The Amals were later responsible for the creation of the Ostrogoths, as mentioned earlier, but this happened between about 460 and 490. Nothing suggests that the Amal dynasty had been anything like as prominent before it acquired this new power-base. Parvenu dynasts often pretend that they are not parvenus at all, and Theoderic was a case in point. Cassiodorus' letters consistently refer to Theoderic's family as a 'purple dynasty'; this perspective permeated Cassiodorus' history – hence its presence in the *Getica*. Furthermore, there is no reason to suppose that our list of seven groups is exhaustive: there were many Gothic 'royal' families competing at the heads of their individual warbands.[5] In reality the fall of the Hunnic Empire was rather more messy than Jordanes makes out.

As the *Getica* tells it, the origins of Hunnic collapse lay in a dispute over succession between Attila's sons soon after their father's sudden death. At least three of the sons figure in different sources as important leaders in their own right – Dengizich, Ellac and Hernac – but we have no idea of how many there were in total, or of whether all, or only some, were potential candidates for their father's position. The quarrel soon degenerated into civil war, which resulted in one Germanic subject group, the Gepids under their king Arderic, throwing off Hunnic domination. This presumably meant that the Gepids refused to pay any more tributes or to answer demands for military service. The rebellion was not taken lying down, the *Getica* tells us, and the outcome was a battle on an unidentified river in Pannonia called the Nedao:[6]

> There an encounter took place between the various nations Attila had held under his sway. Kingdoms with their peoples were divided, and out of one body were made many members not responding to a common impulse. Being deprived of their head, they madly strove against each other . . . And so the bravest nations tore themselves to pieces . . . One might see the Goths fighting with pikes, the Gepids raging with the sword, the Rugi breaking off the spears in their own wounds, the Sueves [Suevi] fighting on foot, the Huns with bows, the Alans drawing up a battle-line of heavy-armed and the Herules of light-armed warriors. Finally, after many bitter conflicts, victory fell unexpectedly to the Gepids.

This is good breastplate-ripping stuff, but not very informative even if the outline story is plausible enough. Clearly, dynastic strife was the norm within the royal family of the Huns, once power became more centralized in the fifth century. We saw in Chapter 7 that royal refugees from previous succession struggles had ended up inside the Roman Empire in the 440s, for instance, and some were returned for execution. Jordanes is also unlikely to have given the Gepids a starring role unless it was impossible not to, especially since there was no love lost between Goths and Gepids by the sixth century.[7]

What's not at all clear, though, is who was on whose side in the battle, and whether there was just one big battle or a series of smaller ones. Jordanes is also a bit vague on the outcome of all this violence. He baldly reports that 'by his revolt [Arderic] freed not only his own tribe, but all the others who were equally oppressed'. But how precisely this liberation happened is open to question. When, in the battle (or battles), Attila's son Ellac was killed, Jordanes reports, the others immediately abandoned their homes in the Middle Danube and made for lands east of the Carpathians and north of the Black Sea, handing out freedom to all the Huns' subjects, no matter whose side they had fought on.[8] By about the year 460, the position of the major powers in and around the Middle Danubian Plain, in so far as we can reconstruct it, was more or less as follows (map 15). The Amal-led Goths occupied an arc of territory south of the River Danube in former Roman Pannonia, stretching from Lake Balaton towards the city of Sirmium. The Gepids controlled the north-eastern stretch, including much of the old Roman province of Dacia abandoned in the third century. Between the two were the Suevi north of the Danube bend, plus the Sciri, Herules, Rugi and Sarmatians/Alans. According to a literal reading of Jordanes, thanks to the revolt of the Gepids all of these groups rapidly converted from Hunnic subjects into independent kingdoms. There are enough hints in fragments preserved elsewhere, however, and in odd details of Jordanes' account, to make it clear that, again, this is much too simple a picture.

The idea that the Huns suddenly disappeared from the Carpathian region in 453/4, for instance, is deeply misleading. In the later 450s and early 460s, they twice intervened west of the Carpathians against

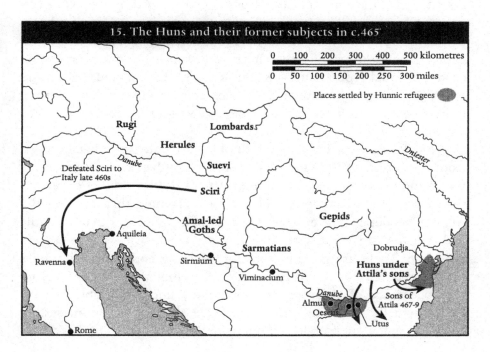

15. The Huns and their former subjects in c.465

the Amal-led Goths in Pannonia, as Jordanes himself tells us,[9] and in the later 460s Attila's remaining sons were still able to launch attacks into the Roman Empire across the Danube. If, as Jordanes reports, the Huns did leave the Middle Danube after the battle of the Nedao, they didn't go far. And while Nedao may have freed the Gepids, it clearly didn't free everyone. When the Huns, under Attila's son Dengizich, attacked the east Roman Empire for the last time in 467/8, there were still substantial numbers of Goths in his following, Priscus reports.[10] Jordanes also tells us that Dengizich had mobilized several groups – Ultzinzures, Angisciri, Bittugures and Bardores – for his second attack on the Amal-led Goths.[11] This doesn't mean that Nedao was not a significant turning-point, but it does demonstrate that Hunnic power over the other population groups of the Carpathian region wasn't suddenly extinguished.

The path to freedom of the Amal-led Goths, and most of the Huns' subjects, was not quite what Jordanes implies, either. No sudden moment of liberation freed everyone at the same time. As we have seen, there were at least three separate groups of Goths under Hunnic dominion at Attila's death, and there had earlier been a fourth (group 3/6, p. 353), detached from Hunnic control by east Roman action and resettled in Thrace in the 420s. Group 1 had escaped by the later 450s, group 4 by the mid-460s, while group 5 never escaped at all, participating in the Huns' final attack on the Empire in 467/8. We have no equivalent information for the Huns' other subject peoples, but behind each individual group name – Suevi, Rugi, Herules, Gepids, Alans and so on – there may likewise have been several independent political units who threw off Hunnic dominion at various points between 453 and 468.

Nor should we assume that each of the separate units that emerged from the wreck of the Hunnic Empire already had its own smoothly functioning leadership at the time of Attila's death. The *Getica* reports that this was true of the Amal-led Goths, claiming that Valamer the Amal, Theoderic's uncle, had been a trusted right-hand man of Attila and that the Amal dynasty's pre-eminence over Group 1 was beyond challenge. There are good reasons for doubting both claims. Jordanes himself reports that for forty years under Hunnic hegemony, before the appearance of Valamer, this supposedly unchallengeable dynasty hadn't actually ruled any Goths at all. He also tells some interesting stories about a supposedly Hunnic ruler by the name of Balamber, who defeated several Gothic rulers, in particular Vinitharius and Hunimund. Many chronological inconsistencies fizzle out once it is recognized that the accounts of Balamber's exploits probably describe how Valamer first consolidated his hold over the Amal-Goths. Balamber doesn't appear in any other sources; and in Greek, Valamer is written 'Balamer'. The stories tell of him defeating two rival Gothic ruling lines in the persons of Vinitharius and Hunimund, together with the latter's son Thorismund. Gesimund, the brother of Thorismund, accepted Valamer's overlordship rather than continuing the contest, while Thorismund's son Beremund fled west into the Roman Empire.

Instead of an Amal dynasty with a unique, long-established prestige at the time of Attila's death, then, we need to envisage several competing petty Gothic warlords, each with their own warbands. It was Valamer, it seems, who first united them, in some instances by direct military action (as in the killing of Hunimund); in others, as with Gesimund's surrender, by conciliation; and in yet others, by a mixture of the two – Valamer killed Vinitharius, then married his granddaughter.[12] My best guess is that all this political restructuring happened *after* the death of Attila. The process generated a much larger Gothic force, better able to resist Hunnic domination, and it is hard to think that Attila in his pomp would have tolerated it.[13]

Quite clearly, then, not all of the Huns' subjects came in neat units, with established leaderships ready and waiting to recapture their independence as soon as the great man died. The Gepids perhaps did, and this might explain why they were able to regain their independence so quickly. But other groups that we see asserting their autonomy after Attila's death had been generated only recently: on the hoof, as it were, around the leadership of new men. The emergence of the kingdom of the Sciri, for instance, was far from straightforward. In the 460s, they were ruled by the same Edeco whom we met in the last chapter as one of Attila's trusted inner circle, the man the east Romans had tried to bribe into assassinating the then Hunnic leader. Edeco was supported by two sons, Odovacar and Onoulph. As the Hunnic Empire collapsed, Edeco clearly managed to reinvent himself, turning from trusted Hunnic henchman into the king of the Sciri. Interestingly, he probably wasn't a Sciri by birth. His sons are described as having a Scirian mother, but he himself is labelled as either a Hun or a Thuringian. The latter – being more specific – is perhaps more likely to be correct. What qualified Edeco for leadership of the Sciri was not his origin, then, but a marriage alliance probably with the daughter of a Scirian bigwig, combined with his pre-eminence at Attila's court. For the other groups we have no information; but I suspect that plenty of this kind of political reordering went on in the mid- to late 450s before the successor kingdoms to the Hunnic Empire could emerge into the light of history.[14]

Putting all these fragments together suggests a rather different account of the collapse of the Hunnic Empire from that given by Jordanes. If the reassertion of independence on the part of at least some of the subject peoples had to be preceded by major political readjustments, this tells us that the Hunnic Empire eased towards extinction as the Huns gradually lost control of those peoples.

The emergence of the new independent groups then set in motion the final stage in the process of Hunnic extinction. The Huns had gathered most of them together on the Great Hungarian Plain, this unprecedented concentration of armed groups creating there a hugely powerful war machine.[15] In the Roman period, the area had been divided between just Sarmatians, Suevi and Vandals – Roman policy took great care to prevent overcrowding in the immediate frontier area, for fear that it would lead to violence. The removal of Hunnic domination created just the situation that these old Roman policies were designed to prevent: a concentration of competitive armed groups in a relatively small area. So battles for independence naturally evolved into a fight for regional hegemony in the 460s, as the new kingdoms took each other on in a struggle for mastery on the Danube.

Again, the only coherent narrative is to be found in the *Getica*, which of course presents it as a triumph for the Amal-led Goths.[16] As Jordanes tells it, these quickly came to blows with the Suevi, over whom they won a great victory. The Suevi then stirred up the other regional powers against the Goths, particularly the Sciri, who managed to kill Valamer in a first bout of fighting. The Goths, however, took a ferocious revenge, destroying the Sciri as an independent power. This led most of the rest – the Suevi, the remaining Sciri, Rugi, Gepids, Sarmatians 'and others' – to unite against the Goths. The result was a second great battle, on a second unidentified river in Pannonia, the Bolia, where, as Jordanes tells us:

> The party of the Goths was found to be so much the stronger
> that the plain was drenched in the blood of their fallen foes and

looked like a crimson sea. Weapons and corpses, piled up like hills, covered the plain for more than ten miles. When the Goths saw this, they rejoiced with joy unspeakable, because by this great slaughter of their foes they had avenged the blood of Valamer their king.[17]

Other sources provide just about enough information to confirm Jordanes' version. A fragment of Priscus' history records that, before the showdown, the Sciri and Amal-led Goths both sent embassies to Constantinople to try to procure east Roman assistance.[18] The destruction of the Sciri also figures in other sources. But whether and to what extent the Amal-led Goths were always victorious, we don't really know.

The violence and instability only began to ease off a little in the region as some of the competing groups were eliminated. The Scirian kingdom lost its independence in the late 460s, and in 473 the Amal-led Goths left the area to try their luck in the east Roman Empire. None of this came soon enough, however, to save the sons of Attila. As the events of the 450s and 460s unfolded, their position was fatally undermined. Each assertion of independence meant that another subject people had stopped paying their annual tributes. This was bad enough, but then the new kingdoms started to take the initiative, looking to maximize their positions at the expense both of each other and of the Huns. The transformation from victors to victims is well illustrated in the two wars that the sons of Attila fought, according to Jordanes, against the Amal-led Goths. In the first they attacked them as 'fugitive slaves', with the aim of reasserting their own hegemony and tribute rights. In the second, they were seeking to prevent some of the smaller groups settled in Pannonia from falling under Gothic dominion.[19] All the other major groups we hear about were doing much the same, so that the Huns' power-base was steadily eroded.

By the mid-460s the two surviving sons, Dengizich and Hernac, were desperate. The loss of subject peoples, combined with the increasing empowerment of groups like the Amal-led Goths, left their position north of the Danube untenable. The only option open to them was to seek an accommodation with the Roman Empire. But Dengizich got it wrong – perhaps he demanded too much. In 469 he was defeated by the Roman general Anagastes, and his head publicly displayed at Constantinople. Hernac and his followers, perhaps less greedy, were eventually resettled beside the Danube in northern Dobrudja (modern Romania), and some other Hunnic remnants settled in and around the fortresses of Oescus, Utus and Almus. Independent Hunnic power north of the Danube had ended. The demise of Attila's realm had been swift and total.

Riding the Tiger

DESPITE ITS MANY limitations, then, the *Getica*'s account allows us to reconstruct some of the key stages in the process of Hunnic collapse. Over the years, many explanations have been offered for this extra-ordinary phenomenon. Historians of earlier eras tended to argue that it was testament to the extraordinary personal capacities of Attila: the Empire could only exist with him at the helm. Edward Thompson, by contrast, rooted the Huns' demise in the divisive social effects of all the wealth they acquired from the Roman Empire.[20] There is some-thing in both of these theories. Attila the Hun, as we have seen, was an extraordinary operator, and no doubt the gold extracted from Rome was not distributed entirely evenly among his people. But a full understanding of the Hunnic Empire must turn on its relations with its largely Germanic subjects. As already suggested, it was the ability to suck in so many of these militarized groups that underlay the sudden explosion of Hunnic power in the 420s–40s. After Attila's death, likewise, it was his successors' increasing inability to maintain control over those same groups that spelled their own decline.

The key starting-point is that the Hunnic Empire was not generally enrolled voluntarily. All the evidence we have suggests that non-Hunnic groups became caught up in it through a combination of conquest and intimidation. In the time of Attila, the Akatziri were the latest to fall into the Empire's orbit. We took in the first half of the story in Chapter 7, when the east Roman ambassador gave the best gifts to the wrong king. Priscus tells us what happened next:

Kouridachus, the senior [king of the Akatziri] in office . . . called in Attila against his fellow kings. Attila without delay sent a large force, destroyed some, and forced the rest to submit. He then summoned Kouridachus to share in the prizes of victory. But he, suspecting a plot, declared that it was hard for a man to come into the sight of a god ... In this way Kouridachus remained amongst his own folk and saved his realm, while all the rest of the Akatzirian people submitted to Attila.[21]

Attila then sent his eldest son to rule over the conquered. The passage reveals that while Attila was capable of deft political manoeuvring when the occasion demanded, the basic tool of Hunnic imperial expansion was military conquest. It was, of course, to avoid Hunnic domination that the Tervingi and Greuthungi had come to the Danube in the summer of 376 in the first place. And it was after a savage mauling at the hands of the Huns in the 430s that the Burgundians also ended up in the Roman Empire. All this is consistent with the fact that there was, as we have seen, one way, and one way only, of quitting Attila's Empire: warfare.[22]

We don't have all the information we might like on relations between the Hunnic conquerors and their various subjects. Pride of place has tended to be given to a story told by Priscus, often seen as illustrating the ethnic and social mobility that was possible in the Hunnic Empire. While hanging around Attila's camp, Priscus ran into a well dressed Hun who greeted him in Greek. Upon inquiry, the 'Hun' turned out to be an ex-Roman prisoner, a former merchant captured at the fall of Viminacium in 441. In the share-out that followed he had been assigned to Onegesius and had fought in subsequent campaigns, against both the Romans and the Akatziri. He did well, won lots of booty, which he passed on to Onegesius, and was consequently freed. He'd then taken a Hunnic wife and was now a trusted companion of his former master, accustomed to dining with him. Thus a slave who did well in battle could win his freedom and be accepted in fairly exalted Hunnic circles. Not so commonly quoted is another story exposing the other side of master-slave relations under the Huns. Also during his stay at Attila's court, Priscus saw the gibbeting of two slaves who had taken the opportunity offered by the turmoil of battle to kill their master. And in fact, most of the Huns' subjects were exploited in a variety of ways and kept firmly in their place.[23]

A revealing fragment of Priscus' history records an incident in 467/8 during Dengizich's last attack on the east Roman Empire, when a mixed force of Goths and Huns was picked apart by Romans; they reminded the Gothic contingent of exactly how the Huns generally behaved towards them: 'These men have no concern for agriculture, but, like wolves, attack and steal the Goths' food supplies, with the result that the latter remain in the position of slaves and themselves suffer food shortages.'[24] Taking the subject peoples' supplies was, of course, only part of the story. They were also used, as we have seen, to fight the Huns' wars. Few civilian prisoners are likely to have been very good at fighting, and casualty numbers during Hunnic campaigns were probably enormous. Priscus' merchant-turned-Hun certainly prospered, but his was no doubt an unusual story.

Clearly, then, the Hunnic Empire was an inherently unstable political entity, riven with tensions between rulers and ruled. Tensions of a different kind also existed between the subject peoples themselves, who had a long history of mutual aggression even before the Huns appeared. This particular instability tends to receive little coverage from historians because most of our source material comes from a Roman, Priscus, and dates to the time when Attila's power was unchallengeable. Cast the net wider, though, and the evidence rapidly gathers itself. The greatest strength of the Hunnic Empire – the ability to increase its power by quickly consuming subject peoples – was also its greatest weakness. The Romans, for instance, were happy to exploit, whenever they could, the fact that these subject peoples were not there of their own free will. In the 420s, the east Roman counteraction against the rising Hunnic power in Pannonia was to remove from their control a large number of Goths whom they then settled in Thrace.[25] And an early fragment of Priscus tells us:[26] 'When Rua was king of the Huns, the Amilzuri, Itimari, Tounsoures, Boisci and other tribes who were living near to the Danube were fleeing to fight on the side of the Romans.' This dates to the late 430s, after Rua had achieved considerable success, indicating that even success wasn't enough to guarantee the quiescence of subject groups. The start of a new reign was a moment of particular stress. The first campaign of Rua's successors, Attila and Bleda, when they came to power in 440, was not against the Romans: 'When [at the start of their reign] they had made peace with the Romans, Attila, Bleda and their forces marched through Scythia subduing the tribes there and also made war on the Sorogsi.' Reasserting your overlordship over subject groups, once you had established your supremacy, was probably the first priority for any new ruler of the Hunnic Empire.

The conflicts that arose after Attila's death were not exceptional, then, but inherent in the relationship between the Huns and their subjects. When they could, Hunnic leaders tried to ensure that the Romans wouldn't stir up trouble for them in this quarter. In their first treaty with the east Romans, when the latter wanted peace on the Danube so as to be able to pursue their ambitions in North Africa, Attila and Bleda were able to ensure 'that the Romans should make no alliance with a barbarian people against the Huns when the latter were preparing for war against them'. Unlike the Roman Empire, which spent centuries dissipating the tensions of conquest turning their subjects – or, at least, the landowners among them – into full Romans, the Huns lacked the necessary stability and the bureaucratic capacity to run their subjects directly.[27] Instead of revolutionizing the sociopolitical structures of the conquered peoples or imposing their own, they had to rely on an indigenous leadership to continue the daily management of the subject groups. As a result, the Huns could exert only a moderate degree of dominion and interference, and even that varied from one subject people to another. The Gepids, as we have seen, had their own overall leader at the time of Attila's death, and so were quickly able to assert their independence. Other groups, like the Amal-led Goths, first had to produce a leader of their own before they could challenge Hunnic hegemony. Some, like the Goths in thrall to Dengizich when he invaded east Roman territory in the 460s, never managed to do so. But even these, still dominated by Dengizich in 468, had their own subchieftains.

If the sources were more numerous and more informative, I suspect that the narrative would show the Hunnic Empire peeling apart like an onion after 453, with different subject layers asserting independence at different times, in inverse relation to the degree of domination the Huns had previously exercised over their lives. The two key variables were, first, the extent to which the subjects' political structure had been left intact; and second – I strongly suspect but cannot prove – their distance from the heartland of the Empire where Attila had his camps. Some groups, settled close to the Huns' own territories, were kept on a very tight rein, with any propensity to unified leadership suppressed. Groups living further away preserved more of their own political structures and were less readily controlled. In the time of Attila, the Franks and the Akatziri defined the geographical limits of his marginal influence, while groups in between such as the Thuringians, Goths, Gepids, Suevi, Sciri, Herules, Sarmatians and Alans faced differing degrees of closer control.[28]

Archaeological evidence from Attila's Empire offers us a further perspective on relations between its subjects and rulers. As we saw in Chapter 7, this mainly takes the form of Germanic or seemingly Germanic cemeteries; a striking feature of the excavated material is the contrast between the large number of unfurnished burials and a smaller number of rich ones. These rich burials are not just *quite* rich: they are staggeringly so. They contain a huge array of gold fittings and ornamentation, the stars of the collections being the cloisonné gold and garnet jewellery in which the stones are mounted in their own gold cases to give an effect not unlike mosaic. This kind of work would later become the mark of elites everywhere in the late and post-Roman periods. For instance, the style of the cloisonné jewellery found in the Sutton Hoo ship burial of the early seventh century in East Anglia originally gained its hold on elite imaginations in Hunnic Europe.[29] One burial at Apahida (modern Transylvania) produced over sixty gold items, including a solid gold eagle that fitted on to its owner's saddle. Every other piece of this individual's horse equipment was likewise made of gold, and he himself was decked from head to foot in golden jewellery. There are other similarly wealthy burials, as well as others containing smaller numbers of gold items.[30]

The presence of so much gold in Germanic central and eastern Europe is highly significant. Up to the birth of Christ, social differentiation in the Germanic world manifested itself funerarily, if at all, only by the presence in certain graves of larger than usual numbers of handmade pots, or of slightly more decorative bronze and iron safety-pins. By the third and fourth centuries AD, some families were burying their dead with silver safety-pins, lots of beads, and perhaps some wheel-turned pottery; but gold was not being used to distinguish even elite burials at this point – the best they could manage was a little silver.[31] The Hunnic Empire changed this, and virtually overnight. The gold-rich burials of the 'Danubian style' mark a sudden explosion of gold grave goods into this part of Europe. There is no doubt where the gold came from: what we're looking at in the grave goods of fifth-century Hungary is the physical evidence of the transfer of wealth northwards from the Roman world that we read about in Priscus and the other written sources. The Huns, as we saw in the last chapter, were after gold and other moveable wealth from the Empire – whether in the form of mercenary payments, booty or, especially, annual tributes. Clearly, large amounts of gold were recycled into the jewellery and appliqués found in their graves. The fact that many of these were the rich burials of Germans indicates that the Huns did not just hang on to the gold themselves, but distributed quantities of it to the leaders of their Germanic subjects as well. These leaders, consequently, became very rich indeed.

The reasoning behind this strategy was that, if Germanic leaders could be given a stake in the successes of the Hunnic Empire, then dissent would be minimized and things would run relatively smoothly. Gifts of gold to the subject princes would help lubricate the politics of Empire and fend off thoughts of revolt. Since there are quite a few burials containing gold items, these princes must have passed on some of the gold to favoured supporters.[32] The gold thus reflects the politics of Attila's court. (It's nice to think that the prince buried at Apahida may have been one that Priscus encountered.) Equally important, the role of such gold distributions in countering the endemic internal instability, combined with what we know of the source of that gold, underlines the role of predatory warfare in keeping afloat the leaky bark that was the Hunnic ship of state.

First and foremost, success in warfare built up the reputation of the current leader as a figure of overwhelming power. Witness the case of Attila and the sword of Mars. But there is every reason to suppose that military success had been just as important for his predecessors. A reputation for power brought with it the capacity to intimidate subject peoples, and it was also military success, of course, that provided the gold and other booty that kept their leaders in line – although the speed with which subject groups opted out of the Empire after Attila's death suggests that the payments did not compensate for the burden of exploitation. In contrast to the Roman Empire, which, as we have seen, attempted to keep population levels low in frontier areas so as to minimize the potential for trouble, the Hunnic Empire sucked in subject peoples in huge numbers.[33] The concentration of such a great body of manpower generated a magnificent war machine, which had to be used – it contained far too many inner tensions to be allowed to lie idle. The number of Hunnic subject groups outnumbered the Huns proper, probably in a ratio of several to one. It was essential to keep the subject peoples occupied, or restless elements would be looking for outlets for their energy and the Empire's rickety structure might begin to crumble.

*

WE HAVE ARRIVED at a very different perspective on Attila the Hun. As is often the case, the factor that made him so powerful was at the same time his greatest liability. The military force that brushed aside the armies of the east Roman Empire in the 440s was itself highly unstable. The victories with which it provided him cemented Attila's control in the short term, but it was riven with internal tension: further victories were essential, to maintain his dominance. Should his reputation start to crack, then his subjects would desert into the welcoming arms of the Romans. Attila was the greatest barbarian conqueror in European history, but he was riding a tiger of unparalleled ferocity. Should his grip falter, he would be mauled to death.

To my mind, this in turn explains his otherwise mysterious turn to the west at the end of the 440s. Between 441 and 447, Attila's armies had ransacked the Balkans except for some small areas protected by two major obstacles: the Peloponnese because of its geographical isolation, and the city of Constantinople because of its stunning land defences. The eastern Empire was on its knees: the annual tribute it was having to pay out was the largest ever expended by a factor of ten. The Huns had squeezed out of Constantinople just about everything they were likely to get; at the very least, further campaigning against it was bound to run into the law of diminishing returns. But there on the Hungarian Plain Attila sat, still surrounded by a huge military machine that could not be left idle. With nothing to attack in the Balkans, another target had to be found. Attila turned to the west, in other words, because he'd exhausted the decent targets available in the east.

This suggests a final judgement on the Hunnic Empire. Politically dependent upon military victory and the flow of gold, it was bound to make war to the point of its own defeat, then be pushed by that defeat into internal crisis. The setbacks in Gaul and Italy in 451 and 452 must anyway have begun to puncture Attila's aura of invincibility. They certainly caused some diminution in the flow of gold, and some of the outlying subject peoples may already have been getting restive. Quite likely, Attila's death and the civil war between his sons provided just the opportunity they were looking for. Overall, there can be no more vivid testament to the unresolved tensions between dominant Hunnic rulers and exploited non-Hunnic subjects than the astonishing demise of Attila's Empire. The strange death of Hunnic Europe, however, was also integral to the collapse of the western Empire.

A New Balance of Power

INSTEAD OF ONE HUGE power centred on the Great Hungarian Plain, its tentacles reaching out towards the Rhine in one direction, the Black Sea in another, the Roman Empire both east and west now found itself facing a pack of successor states. Much of the time fighting amongst themselves, they also pressed periodically upon the Roman frontier. As the Empire became ever more deeply involved in the fall-out from the Hunnic collapse, the nature of Roman foreign policy on the Danube frontier began to change. In confronting their new situation, the Roman authorities had two priorities. They needed to prevent the squabbling north of the Danube from spilling over into their own territory in the form of invasions or incursions, while safeguarding that what emerged from the chaos should not be another monolithic empire.

The loss of the full text of Priscus' history prevents us from telling a continuous story from the Roman perspective, but the essence is easy enough to distil. The surviving sources refer to overflows of various kinds on to Roman territory, the result of the ferocious struggle for *Lebensraum* on the other side of the Danube. Into the western Empire large numbers of refugees now flooded, individuals and groups who had decided that life south of the river looked preferable to the continuing struggle north of it. The most famous of these refugees was Odovacar, son of Edeco and prince of the Sciri. After the Amal-led Goths destroyed the Scirian kingdom, he moved into Roman territory with a band of followers, heading first for Gaul and then for Italy, where he signed up with the Roman army. His lead was followed by many others of less distinguished origins. By the early 470s, the Roman army of Italy was dominated by central European refugees: Sciri are specifically mentioned, along with Herules, Alans and Torcilingi, who had all been recruited into its ranks.[34] The surviving sources give us no numbers and no precise dates for the population moves that had brought them to Italy. This perhaps suggests that we should think in terms of a steady flow of immigration and recruitment, rather than a single large-scale influx, although factors such as the destruction of Scirian independence presumably accelerated the process.

If some groups, displaced in dribs and drabs, were merely fleeing the carnage north of the Danube, others were seeking to create their own enclaves on Roman soil – perceiving this, it would seem, as an easier option than continuing to compete on the Hungarian Plain. By the mid-460s, a number of groups were finding the competition too hot to handle, and three separate incursions on to east Roman territory took place in quick succession. In 466 or just afterwards, the Gothic king Bigelis (of the fourth group mentioned on page 353) led his followers south of the Danube, where he was defeated, Jordanes tells us.[35] At more or less the same time a band of Huns led by a certain Hormidac raided Dacia, penetrating as far as the city of Serdica. There they were defeated by the east Roman general Anthemius.[36] It was at this point too that Attila's son Dengizich made his play for a piece of east Roman territory; as we have seen, he too failed to prosper. The arrival of these armed bands more or less coincides with the wars between the Amal-led Goths and their rivals on the Middle Danubian Plain, and, like the smaller flow of refugees into the western Empire, was perhaps caused by this new upsurge of violence.[37]

At the same time the new kingdoms were also, to an extent, carrying on from where the Huns had left off. Thanks to one of the two surviving fragments from Priscus' history that deal with the aftermath of the fall of Attila's Empire, we know that Valamer and his Goths invaded the east Roman Empire to extract an annual subsidy from it. By the early 460s, Priscus records, this amounted to 300 pounds of gold[38] – a much smaller amount than was extracted by Attila at the height of his power (2,100 pounds) and less than half that paid to the Hun at the start of his reign. But it was not an insignificant sum, and if Valamer were to succeed in expanding his power-base further, there was always the chance that he would up his demands, just as the Huns had done. Since the authorities in Constantinople were probably having to pay annual subsidies to some of the other successor kingdoms as well, they had to tread very carefully. The new kingdoms had the potential to amalgamate into something just as nasty as Attila's Empire. Some insight into Roman attitudes towards this potential problem is provided by the other relevant fragment to survive from Priscus' history.[39] During the interval between the first and second bouts of fighting between the Goths and the Sciri, both sides sent embassies to Constantinople asking for assistance. No one wanted to aid the Goths, but opinion was divided as to the best course to take. One counsel was that the Romans should keep out of the conflict entirely. Eventually, it was decided to give limited support to the Sciri. Jordanes ignores this dimension of the post-Attilan conflicts, but it's clear that all sides were not only manoeuvring with and against one another, but trying to secure Roman support as well. The fact that no one in Constantinople wanted to back them attests to the increasing power of the Amal-led Goths, who were the closest thing to a new superpower.

The Romans greeted the death of Attila as the dawn of a new era. On the night of the great Hun's death, the eastern emperor Marcian is said to have had a happy dream in which he saw Attila's bow broken in two.[40] However, the disappearance of a rival superpower proved not to be the end of all troubles, but a development that spawned a whole series of new problems. The prospect of a further clash of empires had vanished only to be replaced by many complicated regional conflicts with serious implications for both halves of the Roman world. And I strongly suspect that those we hear about in our motley collection of sources represent no more than the tip of the iceberg. Furthermore, the many and varied problems of refugees and invaders were as nothing compared with the broader consequences of the crash of Attila's Empire. Above all, it destroyed the balance of forces on which, by the mid-fifth century, the western Roman Empire had come to depend.

The Fall of Aetius

As we saw in Chapter 6, the emperor Valentinian III, son of Flavius Constantius and Galla Placidia, came to the throne in 425 at the age of six. He had been put there by the armies of the eastern Empire, and had never really held the reins of power. An eight-year domination by his mother, who eventually failed in her balancing act between the commanders of the several western army groups, had given way to that of Aetius. This man's extraordinary military acumen during the 430s would both keep the western Empire afloat and cement his own hold on power. At fourteen a Roman youth was notionally an adult and could make legally binding decisions about property, but at this age in 433 Valentinian was nowhere near ready to compete for power with a tough and experienced general, especially when the Empire faced so many military problems. And by the time he might have been able to exercise authority, five or six years later, Aetius' position was fully consolidated. By 440 it was the general, not the emperor, who was making the key decisions about policies and appointments – the very state of affairs that Placidia had laboured to avoid.

Thus, trapped within patterns of power over which he had no control, the notional emperor of the Roman west found himself a mere figurehead. The drudgery of such an existence is easy to underestimate. Never venturing out of Italy, Valentinian spent his time shuttling between Rome and Ravenna, his routine alternating between a private life replete with the trappings of almost limitless wealth, and state occasions. An emperor's job, as we have seen, was to embody the core ideologies of the Roman state. He was expected to encapsulate the superhuman, indeed God-ordained, nature of the Roman world order, displaying in his ceremonial self the divine support that had called the Roman Empire into being. As the star turn in the many ceremonies, processions, Christian masses and audiences, he could never let his halo slip. And what he had to officiate at, day in and day out, was supremely tedious in its repetitiveness. The Empire being the epitome of the one-party state in action, public disagreement was not tolerated. Unity was all. Ceremonies were relentlessly orchestrated to bring this point home. It was under Valentinian, it will be remembered, that the *Theodosian Code* was introduced to the Senate (see p. 124). Valentinian was spared this particular performance, but it was typical of what he had daily to endure. The acclamations that probably prefaced every major imperial ceremony involved 245 shouts of approval from the assembled senators. A brief experiment I have just run with my eleven-year-old son reveals that you can shout about eighteen such acclamations in a minute, so that the ceremony for the *Code* would have taken at least forty minutes – and that's not allowing for fatigue setting in and slowing things down towards the end.

Valentinian's predecessors had experienced the same daily grind, but they at least had the satisfaction of making policy decisions and appointments behind closed doors once the spectaculars were over. We have already witnessed the frustration that such a lifestyle engendered in Valentinian's sister Honoria: an affair with her estate manager, an unwanted pregnancy and a dangerous liaison with Attila the Hun (see Chapter 7). Nor was it easy for Valentinian to change things. Life is difficult for royal minors who reach adulthood only to find that they still remain marginal to the exercise of power. They may throw caution to the winds, like the seventeen-year-old Edward III, who at midnight on 19 October 1330 broke into Nottingham castle to remove his mother Queen Isabella, arrest her lover Mortimer, and seize the reins of power. But most royal minors are not so daring, and in the 440s Aetius was the young emperor's only bulwark against the Huns.

If there was nothing that Valentinian could do about his frustrations in the 430s and 440s, the collapse of the Hunnic Empire brought a wind of change blowing through western court circles. By 450 or so, two bones of contention had arisen between Aetius and his emperor. On 28 July that year the eastern emperor Theodosius II had died after a fall from his horse. Valentinian was of the Theodosian dynasty, married to one of Theodosius' daughters, Eudoxia, and it was Theodosius' forces who had put him on the western throne in a determined restatement of the unity of that dynasty (see Chapter 6). Theodosius had been its last male representative in the east, his only son Arcadius having predeceased him. Hearing of his cousin's death, Valentinian had the idea, so we are told, of going to Constantinople to assert his claim to rule the entire Roman world as sole emperor. Aetius set himself against the plan. It was certainly ill conceived. Valentinian had no contacts in Constantinople, and eastern political circles were not about to welcome him. Matters there were ordered by Theodosius' sister Pulcheria, who had been a strong voice throughout her brother's reign. Eventually she married a staff officer by the name of Marcian. On 25 August it was Marcian who became the new emperor of the east. Valentinian had missed his chance, such as it was, and Aetius' opposition to his plan continued to rankle.

The second disagreement between the two concerned marriage alliances. Valentinian's union with Eudoxia, produced only two daughters: Eudocia (born in 438 or 439) and Placidia (born between 439 and 443). By the early 450s, after fifteen years of marriage, it was unlikely that the imperial couple would have any more children. This meant that the succession to the western Empire was up for grabs, and the likeliest route to securing it would be marriage to one or other of Valentinian's daughters. As we saw in Chapter 6, Eudocia had been betrothed to Huneric, son of Geiseric king of the Vandals, as part of the peace deal of the 440s, and he was not a serious contender for the throne. It was thus Placidia who became the key to the future of the Roman west, and Aetius worked hard in the early 450s to persuade Valentinian to betroth her to his son Gaudentius. Such a marriage would have cemented Aetius in power, making it extremely likely that Gaudentius would succeed Valentinian. Given the lack of a male Theodosian heir, marriage into the dynasty would have been sufficient to confer legitimacy, especially as the same procedure had just been followed in Constantinople. Whether, in pushing for the marriage, Aetius was responding to a perception that the eastern succession issue had already weakened his hold over Valentinian, is unclear. But the proposal certainly increased the emperor's already festering resentment at the extent to which he was being marginalized within his own Empire.[41]

Moreover, with the death of Attila and the collapse of his Empire, Aetius now seemed much less critical to Valentinian's survival, and it was the emperor, not Aetius, after all, who embodied imperial continuity. For the first time since reaching adulthood, Valentinian could dare to contemplate life without his generalissimo. Aetius perhaps sensed the danger, which might be another reason why he risked adding the marriage issue to Valentinian's list of grievances. For all its emphasis on consensus, sharks always lurked in the deeper waters of Roman imperial politics; now, individuals in the emperor's entourage caught the first faint scent of blood. Of the plot that eventually brought Aetius down we are pretty well informed, thanks again to the labours of Constantine VII Porphyrogenitus. An account survives in another of his works: *Excerpts concerning Plots*. The fall of Aetius is preserved in a fragment from the history of a certain John of Antioch, but he was a late compiler and probably drew primarily on the history of Priscus. So it is again the Priscus–Constantine axis that tells us what we want to know.

There were two main conspirators. The first was a Roman senator of high birth named Petronius Maximus. He had begun his career before Aetius came to power, but was clearly considered an Aetian loyalist. Between 439 and 441 he held the important post of Praetorian Prefect of Italy, and was named consul for a second time in 443 – both appointments taking place during Aetius' pre-eminence.[42] The second was drawn from the A-list of likely suspects in any Roman palace plot: the eunuch head of the emperor's household Heraclius, the *primicerius sacri cubiculi* (Chief of the Sacred Bedroom). Armed with two issues with which to work on Valentinian, and aided by the fact that the Hunnic threat had receded, the plotters did their worst.[43]

As Aetius was explaining the finances and calculating the tax revenues, with a shout Valentinian suddenly leaped up from his throne and cried out that he would no longer be abused by such treacheries . . . While Aetius was stunned by this unexpected rage and was attempting to calm his irrational outburst, Valentinian drew his sword from his scabbard and, together with Heraclius, who was carrying a knife ready under his cloak . . . fell upon him.

Attacked simultaneously by emperor and eunuch, on 21 or 22 September 454 Aetius lay dead in the palace. His fall was followed by the usual round of bloodletting. Chief among the victims was Aetius' current Praetorian Prefect of Italy, a senator by the name of Boethius, grandfather of the famous philosopher.

Valentinian had waited until his thirties, but he had finally broken free. Unfortunately for him, he was not nearly as successful as the young Edward would be some 900 years later at rallying support afterwards. For one thing, the conspirators soon fell out among themselves:

After the murder of Aetius, Maximus paid court to Valentinian hoping that he would be made consul, and when he failed to achieve this, he wished to become Patrician. But Heraclius . . . acting from the same ambition and not wishing a counter-balance to his own power, thwarted Maximus' efforts by persuading Valentinian that, now he had freed himself from the oppression of Aetius, he should not transfer his power to others.

Old habits die hard, and even after Aetius' death Valentinian was not really in charge. The challenge was on to run him, especially as he had no male offspring, which meant that, in the longer term, the imperial succession remained an open race. Once it became clear that he was getting nowhere by persuasion, Maximus turned again to deadlier methods, this time suborning two guards officers, Optila and Thraustila, who had been close to Aetius. Priscus relates that, on 16 March 455:

Valentinian decided to go riding [in Rome] on the Campus Martius . . . When he dismounted from his horse and was walking off to practise archery, Optila and his followers . . . attacked him. Optila struck Valentinian across the side of the head and, when he turned to see who had struck him, felled him with a second blow to the face. Thraustila cut down Heraclius, and both of them took the emperor's diadem and horse and rode off to Maximus.

So perished Valentinian, less than six months after the murder of Aetius. This is the kind of political anarchy that always followed regime change in the Empire. After years of of autocratic rule, albeit in this case more a regency, there was no ready-made regime-in-waiting. As usual, a coalition had been hastily constructed by individuals who had no intention of sharing power with one another afterwards. But if the pattern of Aetius' fall was nothing out of the ordinary, and the fact that it failed to generate an immediate successor hardly surprising, other features were highly particular. Fascinating in this respect is the obituary for Aetius, originally appearing in Priscus' history immediately after the murder:

> Through his alliance with the barbarians, he had protected Placidia, Valentinian's mother, and her son while he was a child. When Boniface crossed from North Africa with a large army, he out-generalled him . . . Felix, who was his fellow general, he killed by cunning when he learned that he was preparing to destroy him at Placidia's suggestion. He crushed the [Visigoths] who were encroaching on Roman territory, and he brought to heel the [Bagaudae] . . . In short, he wielded enormous power, so that not only kings but neighbouring peoples came at his order.

As obituaries go, it's pretty succinct, and it captures the mix of plotting at court and campaigning in the field that was the reality of Aetius' political life. What is especially interesting is the mention in its opening words of Aetius' dependence on an alliance with 'barbarians'. Not just any barbarians, but one group in particular: the Huns. As the passage suggests, Aetius' career was founded upon his Hunnic alliance. It was the Huns who sustained him when he seemed about to lose civil wars – first in 425 as the usurpation of John unravelled, and again in 433 when Boniface defeated him at their first confrontation. And as we saw in Chapter 6, Hunnic troops played a central role in his restoration of order in Gaul in the 430s, particularly in his defeats of the Burgundians and Visigoths. Aetius' death was far more than one man's tragedy. It also marked the end of an era. The death of Attila and disappearance of the Hunnic Empire not only made it possible for

Valentinian to contemplate life without Aetius, it also undermined the delicate balance of powers by which Aetius had kept the western Empire in business. Aetius without the Huns had been surplus to requirements. His successors needed to find a new mechanism for sustaining the west.

Brave New World

THE KEY TO understanding the new political order brought on by the extinction of Hunnic power is provided by virtually the first act of the short-lived regime of Petronius Maximus.

Having murdered Valentinian III on 16 March 455, he was proclaimed emperor the following day. His hands had barely grasped the imperial sceptre when he sent an ambassador to solicit the support of the powerful Visigoths, who had been settled in south-western France since 418. The man he chose was one of his newly appointed military commanders, perhaps commanding general in Gaul (*magister militum per Gallias*), Eparchius Avitus. Avitus was a Gallic aristocrat of impeccable fortune and education. Descended from high office-holders, he was related to a network of important families, and his estates centred on Clermont-Ferrand in the Auvergne. He had served with distinction under Aetius in the campaigns against the Norici and Burgundians in the 430s, then followed this up with a spell as supreme civilian administrator in Gaul – Praetorian Prefect – between 439 and 441. At that point he left office, possibly through natural rotation or because he fell out with Aetius, to return to prominence about a decade later. He then played a major role in negotiating the Visigothic assistance that helped Aetius repel Attila's assault on Gaul in 451.[44] In every way, therefore, Avitus was an excellent choice. Close to Aetius, but not too close, he had a good track record and connections with both the Gallic aristocracy and the Goths.

From Avitus himself, no writings have survived. As more than partial compensation, however, we have a collection of poetry and letters from his son-in-law, a certain Gaius Sollius Modestus Apollinaris Sidonius (who has already been cited in this book). The name is generally shortened for sanity's sake to Sidonius. As his marriage alliance with the family of Avitus might suggest, Sidonius derived from Gallic landowning stock of similar standing – its main estates were situated around Lyon in the Rhône valley. His father had been Praetorian Prefect of Gaul himself about a decade after Avitus, holding the post in 448/9.[45] In the past, Sidonius' writings tended to get a rather bad press. At a time when any decent-thinking chap valued the standards of the classical Latin (first-century BC or AD) he was brought up on, the complexities and allusiveness of Sidonius' work could only aggravate, if not shock. Compared with the clarity and matter-of-factness of, say, Caesar, his love of showing off seemed the height of decadence. Writing at the end of the Victorian era, Sir Samuel Dill passed this judgement:

> [Sidonius] is essentially a literary man, of the stamp which this age of decadence [the fifth century] most admired. He is a stylist, not a thinker or inquirer. There is little doubt that he valued his own compositions not for their substance, but for those character-istics of style which we now think most worthless or even repulsive in them, the childish conceits, the meaningless anti-theses, the torture applied to language so as to give an air of interest and distinction to the trivial commonplace of a colourless and monotonous existence . . . .[46]

Even in translation, Sidonius can drive you crazy with his inability to call a spade a spade, and there's no doubt he spent a lot of time trying to say things in as complicated a way as possible. One of his later letters contains a nicely illuminating comment, delivered at a moment when he thought that the literary audience he had been educated to address had gone for ever: 'I am putting together the rest of my letters in more everyday language; it is not worth embellishing phrases which may never be published.'[47] But it is not fair to judge fifth-century style by first-century standards, and more recent commentators on late Roman Latin (not to mention late Roman Greek) have been less quick to condemn the stylistic complexities that were the height of artistic chic in the fourth and fifth centuries.[48] An age that can see chain-sawed cows in preservative as art is by definition unlikely to judge other artistic endeavours by rigid universal standards.

In any case, the issue of whether Sidonius wrote 'good' Latin or not is beside the point, since there is no doubting the historical importance of his oeuvre. The earliest of his extant writings date from the mid-450s, the latest to about 480, but the bulk fall into a twenty-year period after 455. He knew pretty much everyone who was anyone in southern, especially south-eastern, Gaul, and the great and the good figure prominently in his letters, which, unlike those of Symmachus, don't hesitate to discuss matters of political substance when appropriate. His poems, or some of them, are equally important. Sidonius was significant enough to be involved in politics, and for emperors to court him for his support, but he was not important enough to have to face execution when their regime collapsed. Recognized as one of the leading stylists of his age, he served a succession of emperors who drew on his talents as a writer of panegyrics – keynote speeches – in their praise. We have met such texts before, and while they certainly don't tell the truth as you or I might recognize it, they have the huge virtue of giving us access to the world as particular regimes wished it to be portrayed. Sidonius, like Themistius and Merobaudes before him, was a propagandist.

From Sidonius' account it emerges without a shadow of doubt that Petronius Maximus sent Avitus to the Visigoths to solicit their support for his regime. Sidonius, of course, dressed this bald fact up a little. As he portrays it, the Visigoths, after hearing of the murder of Valentinian III, were preparing to launch a hostile takeover bid for the entire Roman west, when news of the approach of Avitus filled them with sudden panic:[49]

> One of the Goths, who had reforged his pruning-hook and was shaping a sword with blows on the anvil and sharpening it with a stone, a man already prepared to rouse himself to fury at the sound of the trumpet and looking at any moment with manifold slaughter to bury the ground under unburied foes, cried out, as soon as the name of the approaching Avitus was clearly proclaimed: 'War is no more! Give me the plough again!'

You can see why those brought up on the tenets of classical Latin might find Sidonius' verbiage annoying, but the rhetoric is anything but pointless. It gives us a clear picture of his father-in-law as the one man able to dissuade the Visigoths from launching war. The same imaginary Goth goes on to declaim that, far from being mere onlookers, his people will now lend their military assistance to the new regime – and precisely because it is sponsored by Avitus: 'Nay, if I have gained a right knowledge of you [Avitus] in action before this, your auxiliary trooper will I be; thus at least I shall have permission to fight.' What strikes you here is the exaggerated presentation of Avitus' importance. Earlier in the poem, likewise, when talking of Aetius' successes of the 430s, Sidonius excels himself: 'He [Aetius], glorious in arms as he was, did no deed without you [Avitus], although you did many without him.' Avitus no doubt performed useful service to him, but Aetius managed perfectly well without him in the 440s, when the latter slipped out of office. There can be no disputing that Aetius was the dominant partner.

But irritation at Sidonius' hyperbole must not distract us from the historical significance of Petronius Maximus' first move as emperor. Both Flavius Constantius and Aetius had strained every political sinew to prevent the Visigoths from increasing their influence within western imperial politics. Alaric and his brother-in-law Athaulf had both had visions, if fleeting, of the Goths as protectors of the western Empire. Alaric had offered Honorius a deal whereby he would become senior general at court, and his Goths be settled not far from Ravenna. Athaulf married Honorius' sister and named his son Theodosius. But Constantius and Aetius, those guardians of the western Empire, had resisted such pretensions; they had been willing to employ the Goths as junior allies against the Vandals, Alans and Suevi, but that was as far as it went. Aetius had preferred to pay and deploy Huns to keep the Goths within this very real political boundary rather than grant them a broader role in the business of Empire. Avitus' embassy, which, as Sidonius makes clear, sought from the Visigoths not just peaceful acquiescence but a military alliance, reversed at a stroke a policy that had kept the Empire afloat for forty years.

The immediate aftermath only reinforces the point. While Avitus was still with the Visigoths, the Vandals under the leadership of Geiseric launched a naval expedition from North Africa which brought their forces to the outskirts of Rome. In part, its aim was fun and profit, but it also had more substantial motives. As part of the diplomatic horse-trading that had followed the frustration of Aetius' attempts to reconquer North Africa, Huneric, eldest son of the Vandal king Geiseric, had been betrothed to Eudocia, daughter of Valentinian III. On seizing power, however, in an attempt to add extra credibility to his usurping regime, Petronius Maximus married Eudocia to his own son Palladius. The Vandal attack on Rome was also made, then, in outrage at being cheated, as Geiseric saw it, of this chance to play the great game of imperial politics. Hearing of the Vandals' arrival, Maximus panicked, mounted a horse and fled. The imperial bodyguard and those free persons around him whom he particularly trusted deserted him, and those who saw him leaving abused him and reviled him for his cowardice. As he was about to leave the city, someone threw a rock, hitting him on the temple and killing him. The crowd fell upon his body, tore it to pieces and with shouts of triumph paraded the limbs about on a pole.[50]

So ended the reign of Petronius Maximus, on 31 May 455; he had been emperor for no more than two and a half months.

When the imperial capital was sacked for the second time, the damage sustained was more serious than in 410. Geiseric's Vandals looted and ransacked, taking much treasure and many prisoners back with them to Carthage, including the widow of Valentinian III, her two daughters, and Gaudentius, the surviving son of Aetius.[51] Upon hearing this news, Avitus immediately made his own bid for the throne, declaring himself emperor while still at the Visigothic court in Bordeaux. It was later, on 9 July that year, that his claim was ratified by a group of Gallic aristocrats at Arles, the regional capital. From Arles, not long afterwards, Avitus moved on triumphantly to Rome and began negotiations for recognition with Constantinople. The senior Roman army commanders in Italy – Majorian and Ricimer – were ready to accept him because they were afraid of the Visigothic military power at his disposal.[52]

A new order was thus born. Instead of western imperial regimes looking to keep the Visigoths and other immigrants at arm's length, the newcomers had established themselves as part of the western Empire's body politic. For the first time, a Visigothic king had played a key role in deciding the imperial succession.

The full significance of this revolution needs to be underlined. Without the Huns to keep the Goths and other immigrants into the Roman west in check, there was no choice but to embrace them. The western Empire's military reservoirs were no longer full enough for it to continue to exclude them from central politics. The ambition first shown by Alaric and Athaulf, and later by Geiseric in his desire to marry his son to an imperial princess, had come to fruition. Contemporaries were fully aware of the political turn-around represented by Avitus' elevation. Since time immemorial, the traditional education had portrayed barbarians – including Visigoths – as the 'other', the

irrational, the uneducated; the destructive force constantly threatening
the Roman Empire. In a sense, with the Visigoths now having served
for a generation as minor Roman allies in south-western France, the
ground had been well prepared. Nonetheless, Avitus' regime was only
too well aware that its Visigothic alliance was bound to be controversial. This is nowhere better demonstrated than in the writings of
Sidonius, in particular in a letter penned by him from the court of the
Visigothic king Theoderic II in the early months of Avitus' reign.
Sidonius' letters are in no sense private documents. He wrote them in
the expectation that their contents would be circulated. They were, in
short, an excellent mechanism for disseminating a point of view among
fellow Gallic landowners.[53]

Written to Avitus' son Agricola as a description of life at the
Visigothic court, it opens with a portrait of Theoderic: 'In his build the
will of God and Nature's plan have joined together to endow him with
a supreme perfection; and his character is such that even the jealousy
which hedges a sovereign has no power to rob it of its glories.' We
then hear about the king's day. Having started with a prayer or two,
he spends the morning receiving embassies and settling cases; then, in
the afternoon, perhaps a little hunting, at which, as in all else, he
excels. In the evening comes the main meal:

> When one joins him at dinner . . . there is no unpolished conglom-
> eration of discoloured old silver set by panting attendants on
> sagging tables; the weightiest thing on these occasions is the
> conversation. The viands attract by their skilful cookery, not by
> their costliness. Replenishment of goblets comes at such long
> intervals that there is more reason for the thirsty to complain
> than for the intoxicated to refrain. To sum up: you can find there
> Greek elegance, Gallic plenty, Italian briskness; the dignity of
> state, the attentiveness of a private home, the ordered discipline
> of royalty.[54]

The letter closes with a little joke at the king's expense. After dinner
Theoderic liked to play a game of dice, and would show the proper
spirit by protesting if he perceived that his rival was letting him win.
On the other hand, should you want a favour done, Sidonius notes,
the thing to do was to let the king win, but without his noticing what
you were up to. This bit of patronizing aside, Sidonius' message could
not be clearer. Theoderic II was not your run-of-the-mill barbarian,

driven by his senses, addicted to alcohol and the next adrenalin rush. He was, in fact, a 'Roman' in the proper sense, one who had learned reason and self-discipline, who ran his court, his life – indeed, himself – in the time-hallowed Roman manner. He was a man one could do business with. I have no idea what life was really like at the Visigothic court, but to justify Avitus' association with Theoderic, Theoderic had to be presented as possessing all the virtues, and Sidonius duly obliged. The revolution was gathering pace. Barbarians were being presented as Romans to justify the inescapable reality that, since they could no longer be excluded, they now had to be included in the construction of working political regimes in the west.

At first sight, this inclusion of the alien would not seem to be a mortal blow to the integrity of the Empire. Theoderic was Roman enough to be willing to play along; he saw the need to portray him as a good Roman in order to satisfy landowning opinion. There were, however, a couple of very big catches which made a Romano-Visigothic military alliance not quite the asset you might initially suppose. First, political support always came at a price. Theoderic was entirely happy to support Avitus' bid for power, but, not unreasonably, he expected something in return. In this instance, his desired reward was a free hand in Spain where, as we have seen, the Suevi had been running riot since Aetius' attention had been turned towards the Danube in the early 440s. Theoderic's request was granted, and he promptly sent a Visigothic army to Spain under the auspices of Avitus' regime, notionally to curb Suevic depredations. Hitherto, of course, when the Visigoths had been deployed in Spain, it was always in conjunction with Roman forces. This time, Theoderic was left to operate essentially on his own initiative, and we have a first-hand – Spanish – description of what happened. The Visigothic army defeated the Suevi, we are told, capturing and executing their king. They also took every opportunity, both during the assault and in the cleaning-up operations that followed, to gather as much booty as they could, sacking and pillaging, amongst others, the towns of Braga, Asturica and Palentia. Not only did the Goths destroy the kingdom of the Suevi, they also helped themselves uninhibitedly to the wealth of Spain.[55] Just like Attila, Theoderic had warriors to satisfy. His willingness to support Avitus was based on calculations of profits, and a lucrative Spanish spree was just the thing.

Second, the inclusion of barbarians into the political game of regime-building in the Roman west meant that there were now many more groups manoeuvring for position around the imperial court. Before 450, any functioning western regime had to incorporate and broadly satisfy three army groups – two main ones in Italy and Gaul, and a lesser one in Illyricum – plus the landed aristocracies of Italy and Gaul, who occupied the key posts in the imperial bureaucracy. The desires of Constantinople also had to be accommodated. As in the case of Valentinian III, should western forces be divided between different candidates, eastern emperors disposed of enough clout and brute force to impose their own candidate. Though too far away to rule the west directly, Constantinople could exercise a virtual veto over the choices of the other interested parties. Incorporating this many interests could make arriving at a stable outcome a long-drawn-out business.

AFTER THE COLLAPSE of the Hunnic Empire, the Burgundians and Vandals were the next to start jockeying for position and clamouring for rewards. The Burgundians had been settled by Aetius around Lake Geneva in the mid-430s. Twenty years later, they took advantage of the new balance of power in the west to acquire a number of other Roman cities and the revenues they brought with them from their territories in the Rhône valley: Besançon, le Valais, Grenoble, Autun, Chalon-sur-Saône and Lyon.[56] The Vandal–Alan coalition's sack of Rome in 455, as we have seen, betrayed a desire to participate in imperial politics. On the death of Valentinian, Victor of Vita tells us,[57] Geiseric too, expanding his powerbase, seized control of Tripolitania, Numidia and Mauretania, together with Sicily, Corsica and the Balearics. Allowing just some of the barbarian powers to participate in the Empire massively complicated western politics; and the greater the number, the harder it was to find sufficient rewards to generate long-term coalition.

A strong sense of the underlying tensions that made the regime of Avitus essentially unstable emerges from the second of Sidonius' poems to survive from this period. On 1 January 456, when the emperor assumed the consulship in Rome, his ever loyal son-in-law was called upon to make a speech on his behalf. It began, not surprisingly, by establishing the emperor's overwhelming suitability for office. In doing so, Sidonius took the opportunity to make some pointed comparisons. In particular, he dismissed Valentinian III as a 'mad eunuch' (*semivir amens*), and contrasted his style of leadership with the military and political skills that Avitus brought to the job. Turning to the key issue of Avitus' relationship with the king of the Visigoths, Sidonius handled this potentially explosive subject with subtlety, but his intent was clear enough. First, he argued with vigour that Avitus had never been one to cosy up to the Visigothic court. He had been there as a young man, as everyone knew, in the 420s, when '[the Visigothic king] desired exceedingly to have you [Avitus] as one of his own, but you scorned to act the friend rather than the Roman.'[58] Sidonius then focused on one small incident in the 430s when Avitus took a terrible revenge against a marauding Visigoth who had wounded one of his servants:

> When first they approached, breast to breast and face to face, the one [Avitus] shook with anger, the other [the Goth] with fear . . . But when the first bout, the second, the third have been fought, see! The upraised spear comes and pierces the man of blood; his breast was transfixed and his corselet twice split, giving way even where it covered the back; and as the blood came throbbing through the two gaps the separate wounds took away the life that each of them might claim.

Translated into English (or even into Latin), Sidonius is saying that Avitus found the Visigothic bastard who'd hurt his man, and ran him so far through with his spear that it came out the other side. Translated into politico-speak, the message is that Avitus was no Visigoth-loving traitor but a true Roman who had given the barbarians as hard a kicking as even the fiercest hawk could desire.

All of this was addressed to the suspicions of Sidonius' audience of Italo-Roman senators and generals, as was, above all, his account of the new emperor's elevation. On hearing of the deaths of Aetius and Valentinian, the Visigoths had begun to plan their own wars of conquest.[59] Then into the Visigothic camp strode Avitus, and everything changed. By his presence alone he spread panic among them, and such was their fear of him that the Visigoths' immediate impulse was to try to please him by engaging in a military alliance. But whether Avitus should declare himself emperor was his decision alone. As for the Visigothic king, Sidonius has him say:

> We do not force [the purple] on you, but we do beg you; with you as leader I am a friend of Rome, with you as emperor I am her soldier. You are not stealing the sovereignty from any man;

no Augustus holds the Latian hills, a palace without a master is
yours ... My part is only to serve you; but if Gaul should force
you, as she has the right to do, the world would love your
command for fear it would otherwise perish.

We see from this special pleading, and the allusion to the power
vacuum in Italy, exactly where the audience's political sensitivities lay.
To the Italians, the audience Sidonius was now addressing, Avitus
might appear no more than a creature of the Visigoths after the pattern
of Priscus Attalus under Alaric and Athaulf. The speech responded by
insisting that Avitus was his own man. You only had to look at his
long history of smacking the Visigoths around. He had also taken the
purple, if unwillingly, because he was the only man who could
command their obedience. In these straitened times, the barbarians'
military power was necessary to the safety of the Empire, but Avitus
remained a true Roman.

It was a good try. And so much for the claim that Sidonius lacked
ideas. But the Italian audience, particularly the army men amongst
them, were having none of it. The sources insist, as we have seen,
that the Roman army of Italy only ever tolerated Avitus because he
had the military backing of the Visigoths. When, in 456, the Visigoths
became too deeply embroiled in Spain to intervene any further in Italy,
the two main Roman commanders, Majorian and Ricimer, withdrew
their allegiance. On 17 October that year they gave battle to the few
forces Avitus could scrape together – presumably remnants of the
Roman field army of Gaul – outside the city of Placentia in northern
Italy. Avitus was beaten, forced to become the city's bishop, and died
shortly afterwards in mysterious circumstances.[60]

We see here, then, in a nutshell the problem now facing the west.
Avitus had the support of the Visigoths, the support of at least some
Gallic senators, and of some of the Roman army of Gaul. But faced
with the hostility of the Italian senators, and especially of the commanders of the Italian field army, the coalition didn't stand a chance.
By the early 460s, the extent of the crisis in the west generated by the
collapse of Attila's Empire was clear. There were too many interested
parties and not enough rewards to go round. Constantinople, however,
had decided on one last throw of the dice.

9

END OF EMPIRE

SOME HISTORIANS HAVE CRITICIZED Constantinople for not doing
more in the fifth century to save the embattled west. From the *Notitia
Dignitatum* (see p. 246) we know that the east's armies recovered from
Hadrianople to comprise, by the end of the fourth century, a field
army of 131 regiments distributed between four regional commands:
one on the Persian front, one in Thrace, and two central, 'praesental'
armies (from the Latin for 'stationed in the imperial presence'). Its
mobile forces, therefore, mustered between 65,000 and 100,000 men.[1]
Also, the east disposed of numerous units of frontier garrison troops
(*limitanei*). The archaeological field surveys of the last twenty years
have confirmed, furthermore, that the fourth-century agricultural prosperity of the east's key provinces – Asia Minor, the Middle East and
Egypt – showed no sign of slackening during the fifth. Some believe
that the eastern Empire thus had the wherewithal to intervene
effectively in the west, but chose not to. In the most radical statement
of the case, it has been argued that Constantinople was happy to see
barbarians settle on western territory for the disabling effect this had
on the west's military establishment because it removed any possibility
of an ambitious western pretender seeking to unseat his eastern
counterpart and unite the Empire. This had happened periodically in
the fourth century, when the emperors Constantine and Julian took
over the entire Empire from an originally western power-base.[2] But in
fact, bearing in mind the problems it had to deal with on its own
frontiers, Constantinople's record for supplying aid to the west in the
fifth century is perfectly respectable.

Constantinople and the West

THE EASTERN Empire's military establishment was very substantial,
but large numbers of troops had always to be committed to the two

key sectors of its eastern frontier in Armenia and Mesopotamia, where Rome confronted Persia. If you asked any fourth-century Roman where the main threat to imperial security lay, the answer would have been Persia under its new Sasanian rulers. And from the third century, when the Sasanian revolution worked its magic, Persia was indeed the second great superpower of the ancient world. As we saw earlier, the new military threat posed by the Sasanians plunged the Roman Empire into a military and fiscal crisis that lasted the best part of fifty years. By the time of Diocletian in the 280s, the Empire had mobilized the necessary funding and manpower, but the process of adjustment to the undisputed power of its eastern neighbour was long and painful. The rise of Persia also made it more or less unavoidable to have one emperor constantly in the east, and hence made power-sharing a feature of the imperial office in the late Roman period. As a result of these transformations, Rome began to hold its own again, and there were no fourth-century repeats of such third-century disasters as the Persian sack of Antioch.

When assessing the military contribution of the eastern Empire to the west in the fifth century, it is important to appreciate that, while broadly contained from about 300, the new Persian threat never disappeared. Even if there was less fighting – and what fighting there was largely confined itself to a wearying round of sieges and limited gains – the Sasanians maintained a constant presence in the strategic thinking of east Roman politicians and generals. Faced with the defeat of Julian's Persian expedition in 363, then the longer-term effects of the Hun-inspired mayhem on the Danube in the mid-370s, successive Roman emperors had been forced on two occasions to grant Sasanian rulers peace treaties they would normally only have dreamt about. Following Julian's defeat, the emperor Jovian made humiliating concessions of territory and bases in Mesopotamia. Valens made some preliminary noises, even moves, towards their recovery, but after his death at Hadrianople Theodosius not only confirmed Roman acceptance of these losses, but also did a deal over Armenia, the other great bone of contention – and again, massively in Persia's favour (map 3).[3]

These concessions ushered in a relatively peaceful phase in Roman-Persian relations, as Sasanian aspirations were, for the moment, largely satisfied. Anyway, Persia was facing nomad-inspired troubles of its own in two northern frontier sectors: to the east in Transoxania (modern Uzbekistan), and in the Caucasus, in which Constantinople, too, had an interest. Routes through the Caucasus led into Roman territory, if one turned right, and into Persian territory, if one carried straight on. The Huns had done both. The great Hunnic raid of 395 wreaked havoc not only in Rome's provinces south of the Black Sea but also over a surprisingly large area of the Persian Empire. So, in this new era of compromise when both Empires had Huns on their minds, they came to an unprecedented agreement for mutual defence. The Persians would fortify and garrison the key Darial Pass through the Caucasus, and the Romans would help defray the costs. So tranquil were Roman–Persian relations at this time, in fact, that the myth arose that the Persian Shah had adopted Theodosius II, at the request of his late father the emperor Arcadius, so as to smooth the boy's accession to the throne (he was only six when his father died).

None of this meant, however, that Constantinople could afford to lower its guard. Troop numbers were perhaps reduced in the fifth century, and less was spent on fortifications, but major forces still had to be kept on the eastern frontier. The *Notitia Dignitatum* – whose eastern sections date from about 395, after the Armenian accord – lists a field army of thirty-one regiments, roughly one-quarter of the whole, based in the east, together with 156 units of frontier garrison troops stationed in Armenia and the provinces comprising the Mesopotamian front, out of a total of 305 such units for the entire eastern Empire. And this in an era of relative stability. There were occasional quarrels with Persia, which sometimes came to blows, as in 421 and 441. The only reason the Persians didn't capitalize more on Constantinople's run-in with the Huns in the 440s seems to have been their own nomad problems.[4]

Just as, for Rome, Persia was the great enemy, so Rome was for Persia, and each particularly prized victories over the other. As we noted earlier, the provinces from Egypt to western Asia Minor were the eastern Empire's main source of revenue, and no emperor could afford to take chances with the region's security. As a result, Constantinople had to keep upwards of 40 per cent of its military committed to the Persian frontier, and another 92 units of garrison troops for the defence of Egypt and Libya. The only forces the eastern authorities could even think of using in the west were the one-sixth of its garrison troops stationed in the Balkans and the three-quarters of its field forces mustered in the Thracian and the two praesental armies.[5]

Up until 450, Constantinople's capacity to help the west was also deeply affected by the fact that it bore the brunt of Hunnic hostility. As early as 408 (see p. 196), Uldin had briefly seized the east Roman fortress of Castra Martis in Dacia Ripensis, and by 413 the eastern authorities felt threatened enough to initiate a programme for upgrading their riverine defences on the Danube[6] and to construct the triple landwalls around Constantinople (see p. 203). Then, just a few years later, eastern forces engaged directly in attempts to limit the growth of Hunnic power. Probably in 421, they mounted a major expedition into Pannonia which was already, if temporarily, in Hunnic hands, extracted a large group of Goths from the Huns' control and resettled them in east Roman territory, in Thrace. The next two decades were spent combating the ambitions of Attila and his uncle, and even after Attila's death it again fell to the east Roman authorities to clean up most of the fall-out from the wreck of the Hunnic Empire. As we saw in Chapter 8, it was the eastern Empire that the remaining sons of Attila chose to invade in the later 460s. Slightly earlier in the decade, east Roman forces had also been in action against armed fragments of Attila's disintegrating war machine, led by Hormidac and Bigelis. In 460, likewise, the Amal-led Goths in Pannonia had invaded the eastern Empire to extract their 300 pounds of gold (see p. 368).[7]

Judged against this strategic background, where military commitments could not be reduced on the Persian front, and where, thanks to the Huns, the Danube frontier required a greater share of resources than ever before, Constantinople's record in providing assistance to the west in the fifth century looks perfectly respectable. Although in the throes of fending off Uldin, Constantinople had sent troops to Honorius in 410, when Alaric had taken Rome and was threatening North Africa. Six units in all, numbering 4,000 men, arrived at a critical moment, putting new fight into Honorius when flight, or sharing power with usurpers, was on the cards. The force was enough to secure Ravenna, whose garrison was becoming mutinous, and bought enough time for the emperor to be rescued.[8] In 425, likewise, Constantinople had committed its praesental troops in large numbers to the task of establishing Valentinian III on the throne, and in the 430s Aspar the general had done enough in North Africa to prompt Geiseric to negotiate the first treaty, of 435, which denied him the conquest of Carthage and the richest provinces of the region. In 440/1, again, the east had committed so many of its Danubian and praesental troops to the projected east-west expedition to Africa, that the bureaucrat who organized it received a mention in despatches and Attila and Bleda were handed an unmissable opportunity to unleash their armies on to Roman soil.

Although, as we saw in Chapter 7, Attila granted the eastern Empire an extraordinarily generous treaty in 450, the east did not even then baulk at its duty to fellow Romans. Troops – we are not told how many – were sent to Aetius to assist him in harassing the Hunnic armies sweeping through northern Italy in 452, while other eastern forces achieved considerable success in attacking Hunnic homelands.[9] This is not the record of an eastern state that had no interest in sustaining the west. Nor is there the slightest sign that Constantinople had willed the barbarians to settle on western soil so as to weaken the power of the western emperors – not even, as used to be thought, to the extent of encouraging Alaric to transfer his Goths from the Balkans to Italy in 408. As Edward Thompson noted, choosing to fight and take what reprisals might come their way in 451/2, rather than grabbing Attila's generous peace and running, was a sign of real commitment on the part of Constantinople.[10]

Of course, in Constantinople emperors and – in particular – imperial advisers came and went, and policies towards the west varied. As mentioned earlier, up to the death of Theodosius II in July 450, commitment to the west derived partly from the fact that eastern and western emperors belonged to the same Theodosian house. In sustaining his cousin Valentinian, therefore, Theodosius was also stressing his own family's credentials for rule. And the largest single eastern expeditionary force of the period was sent west in 425 for a Roman civil war to put Valentinian III on the throne. But the catalogue of eastern assistance to the west cannot be reduced to mere dynastic self-interest. Help continued to be given after Theodosius' death, not least when Attila was attacking Italy in 452. Equally important, this aid list is compiled from a miscellany of sources and is unlikely to be exhaustive. In particular, I suspect that regular financial assistance was sent west during these years, in addition to the periodic offerings of military manpower. Thus, the decision of the authorities in Constantinople to mount a major rescue bid on the west's behalf in the 460s was no sudden aberration from the norm.

Regime Change, Anthemius and North Africa

THE MOST OBVIOUS problem facing the Roman west round about 460 was a crisis of succession; since the death of Attila in 453 there had been little continuity. Valentinian III had been cut down by Aetius' bodyguards, egged on by Petronius Maximus, who seized the throne but in no time at all was himself killed by the Roman mob. Soon afterwards, Avitus had appointed himself emperor in collusion with the Visigoths and elements of the Gallo-Roman landowning and military establishments. Then came his ousting in 456 by Ricimer and Majorian, commanders of the Italian field forces. This army was to be the single most powerful military-cum-political force in the Roman west, and the two commanders would play a central kingmaking role.

Of the two, Ricimer is a particularly fascinating character. His grandfather was the Visigothic king Vallia who had negotiated with Flavius Constantius in 416, and on his mother's side he was descended from a princess of the Suevi. His sister married into the Burgundian royal house. Thus, in his family connections Ricimer reflects the revolutions that had recently brought so many autonomous groups of outsiders on to Roman soil. His career, however, was purely Roman and purely military, first reaching prominence under Aetius. Some have sought anti-Roman, pro-barbarian leanings in his policies, but none is apparent. Like Aetius and Stilicho, he was ready, when necessary, to make alliances with the new barbarian powers established in the west, but there is no sign that his genetic inheritance predisposed him to favour them at the expense of the central Roman authorities – in fact, quite the opposite. He was very much the heir of Stilicho: a well-connected barbarian proud to follow a Roman career, and who showed impeccable loyalty to the imperial ideal. Majorian too had served under Aetius, but, unlike Ricimer, was of a solidly Roman military family. His paternal grandfather had been a senior general in the 370s, and his father an important bureaucrat under Aetius; Majorian himself had eventually fallen out with Aetius, but Valentinian III recalled him after the generalissimo's murder.[11]

Hostility to Avitus made allies out of Ricimer and Majorian but, having removed him, they weren't quite sure what to do next. The result was an interregnum of several months. Eventually, the two decided to make Majorian emperor, and his installation was celebrated on 1 April 457. Despite some initial successes, the new regime failed to find a definitive solution to the west's problems, and Ricimer and Majorian eventually quarrelled. On 2 August 461 Ricimer had his former partner in crime deposed, and executed five days later. He then turned to an elderly senator called Libius Severus to act as his new front man. On 19 November after another interregnum, Severus was raised to the purple. However, he was not well received elsewhere in the west. In particular, the commanders of what remained of the Gallic and Illyrian field armies, Aegidius and Marcellinus, were disgruntled enough to rebel.

The death of Valentinian III thus unleashed one of those bouts of protracted instability that were inherent to the Roman political system. Faced with nothing less than anarchy, Constantinople did what it could to promote stability. In the case of Avitus, the eastern emperor Marcian had refused to grant recognition, but negotiations with Constantinople over the accession of Majorian were eventually successful. After his initial installation, he was proclaimed emperor a second time on 28 December 457, quite probably on the receipt of recognition granted by Marcian's successor Leo I. That Majorian's regime had been recognized reflected the fact that it was much more broadly supported than that of Avitus. The same was not true, however, of Libius Severus – this time Leo would not play ball, and Severus remained resolutely unrecognized in Constantinople for the rest of his life.

As western regimes came and went, then, eastern emperors tried, it seems, to identify and support those with some real hope of generating stability. It was to preserve his position in Italy that Ricimer had appointed the harmless Severus. But as Aetius had shown, political longevity was inseparable from military success, and Ricimer also needed to defend Italy effectively, as well as the rest of the Roman west. For both of these objectives recognition and assistance from Constantinople were vital. Once it became clear that Severus was unacceptable to Leo – not least because of the opposition he had triggered in Aegidius and Marcellinus – he became an obstacle to Ricimer's policies. Severus eventually died at a suspiciously convenient moment, in November 465. One early sixth-century source suggests that he was poisoned, while Sidonius goes out of his way to stress that he had died by natural causes. The comment stands out so starkly in the middle of a passage devoted to other matters that it really does look like a case of protesting too much. Whatever the truth of the matter, with Severus dead, negotiations could begin again.[12]

But granting or withholding recognition did nothing to address the second and much more fundamental problem facing the Roman west. As we saw in Chapter 8, the disappearance of the Huns as an effective force left western imperial regimes with no choice but to buy support from at least some of the immigrant powers now established on its soil. Avitus won over the Visigoths by offering them a free hand – to their great profit, as it turned out – in Spain. Majorian had been forced to recognize the Burgundians' desire to expand, and had allowed them to take over some more new cities (*civitates*) in the Rhône valley; and he continued to allow the Visigoths to do pretty much as they wanted in Spain. To buy support for Libius Severus, similarly, Ricimer had handed over to the Visigoths the major Roman city of Narbonne with all its revenues.[13] But now, there were simply too many players in the field, and this, combined with rapid regime change, had created a situation in which even the already much reduced western tax revenues were being further expended in a desperate struggle for stability. Three things needed to happen in the west to prevent its annihilation. Legitimate authority had to be restored; the number of players needing to be conciliated by any incoming regime had to be reduced; and the Empire's revenues had to rise. Analysts in the eastern Empire came to precisely this conclusion, and in the mid-460s hatched a plan that had a very real chance of putting new life back into the ailing west.

THE DEATH OF Severus opened the path to renewed negotiations between Ricimer and Constantinople. They were long and tortuous. No source gives us details, but there was a seventeen-month interregnum – the longest yet – before the next western emperor was proclaimed, on 12 April 467. This gap, as much as the new emperor's identity, alerts us to the crooked diplomatic paths that must have been trodden in the interim. The choice fell on Anthemius, an eastern general of proven abilities and high pedigree, and the nominee of the eastern emperor Leo (although Ricimer certainly accepted the appointment). Anthemius' maternal grandfather – also called Anthemius – had been virtual ruler of the eastern Empire for the decade 405–14, acting as Praetorian Prefect in the east during the last years of the reign of the emperor Arcadius and the early years of his son Theodosius II. The new emperor's father, Procopius, was nearly as distinguished.

Descended from the usurper Procopius of the mid-360s, and hence distantly related to the house of Constantine, he had risen to supreme command of Roman forces on the Persian front (*magister militum per Orientem*) in the mid-420s. The younger Anthemius followed his father into the army, where he gained distinction, emerging in the mid-450s to play a leading role in containing the fall-out from the Hunnic Empire after Attila's death.[14] Immediately afterwards, he was named consul for 455, and Patrician, and promoted to commanding general of one of the central field armies (*magister militum praesentalis*). He also received the hand in marriage of the emperor Marcian's only daughter, Aelia Marcia Euphemia. Sidonius says that on Marcian's death back in 457 Anthemius had nearly become emperor, and for once this doesn't look like an exaggeration. The marriage suggests that Anthemius was Marcian's preferred successor. But the purple didn't come to him. Sidonius says that his own reluctance held him back (but that's another common trope of panegyric). Instead, Leo was promoted – he was a guards officer through whom the other *magister militum praesentalis*, Aspar, was looking to run the Empire. Anthemius cannot, however, have been too disaffected, because he continued to serve the new emperor as general.[15]

In short, Anthemius' imperial credentials were impeccable, and so equally applicable to the post of eastern emperor that Leo and Aspar may well have been scanning the 'Italian situations vacant' column in the *Constantinopolitan Times* for quite a while before Severus' convenient demise. Even if happy to be rid of him, it did not detract from the level of support they were willing to offer him. In the spring of 467 Anthemius arrived in Italy with a military force provided by the commanding general of Roman field forces in Illyricum (*magister militum per Illyricum*), Marcellinus.[16] Marcellinus was originally Aetius' appointee and had taken control of the area on his assassination. The emperor Majorian had reconfirmed his appointment, but after Majorian's death he applied to Constantinople rather than to Libius Severus, for authorization to continue in his post. It was through the eastern emperor Leo, therefore, that Marcellinus' support for Anthemius was channelled. Leo also secured Ricimer's consent to Anthemius' promotion, and the relationship was sealed by a marriage alliance: as soon as Anthemius arrived in Italy, his only daughter Alypia married Ricimer. Combining talent and pedigree with backing from both the west in the person of Ricimer, and Constantinople, Anthemius was the man to restore political stability, if anyone could, to the Roman west.

Anthemius went to Italy with a plan for dealing with the more fundamental problems facing his new Empire. First, he quickly restored a modicum of order north of the Alps in Gaul. It is difficult to estimate how much of Gaul was still functioning as part of the western Empire in 467. In the south the Visigoths, and certainly the Burgundians, accepted Anthemius' rule; both of their territories remained legally part of the Empire. We know that institutions like the *cursus publicus* were still functioning here. Further north, things are less clear. The Roman army of the Rhine, or what was left of it, had gone into revolt on the deposition of Majorian, and part of it still formed the core of a semi-independent command west of Paris. Refugees from battle-torn Roman Britain also seem to have contributed to the rise of a new power in Brittany, and for the first time Frankish warbands were flexing their muscles on Roman soil. In the fourth century, Franks had played the same kind of role on the northern Rhine frontier as the Alamanni played to their south. Semi-subdued clients, they both raided and traded with the Roman Empire, and contributed substantially to its military manpower; several leading recruits, such as Bauto and Arbogast, rose to senior Roman commands. Also like the Alamanni, the Franks were a coalition of smaller groups, each with their own leadership. By the 460s, as Roman control collapsed in the north, some of these warband leaders began for the first time to operate exclusively on the Roman side of the frontier, selling their services, it seems, to the highest bidder.[17]

None of these Gallic powers was strong enough directly to threaten what remained of the Roman west when it was buoyed up with eastern support, and Anthemius' arrival cowed all of them at least into acquiescence. Gaul, however, wasn't the fundamental problem. Even Majorian had done nearly as well there as Anthemius in attracting acceptance, even support, from the Gallo-Roman landowners. The Gallic Sidonius, for instance, had played a role in the Burgundians' seizure of Lyon, and for this Majorian initially punished him with a higher tax bill. In response, Sidonius wrote the emperor a poem, complaining in mannered and deliberately self-deprecating fashion: 'For now my talkative muse is silenced by the tax, and culls instead of Vergil's and Terence's lines the pence and halfpence owed to the Exchequer.'[18] So Majorian let him off and, along with many of his peers, Sidonius joined the ranks of the emperor's Gallic supporters. A letter of this era recalls a convivial evening when the emperor dined and swapped witticisms with Sidonius and his friends.[19]

The arrival in their midst of the engaging Anthemius led to queues of Gallo-Roman landowners anxious to court and be courted by the new emperor. We know that the *cursus publicus* was still working because Sidonius used it on his way to see Anthemius at the head of a Gallic deputation. Anthemius responded in kind. Sidonius wormed his way into the good graces of the two most important Italian senatorial power-brokers of the time, Gennadius Avienus and Flavius Caecina Decius Basilius, and with their help got the chance to deliver a panegyric to the emperor, on 1 January 468.[20] As a result, he was appointed by Anthemius to the high office of Urban Prefect of Rome. A time-honoured process was in operation: with self-advancement in mind, likely-looking landowners would turn up at the imperial court at the start of a new reign to offer support and receive gifts in return.[21] But fiddling with the balance of power in Gaul wasn't going to contribute anything much towards a restoration of the western Empire.

There was only one plan that stood any real chance of putting life back into the Roman west: reconquering North Africa. The Vandal–Alan coalition had never been accepted into the country club of allied immigrant powers that began to emerge in the mid-fifth century. The treaty of 442, which recognized its seizure of Carthage, was granted when Aetius was at the nadir of his fortunes; it was an exception to the Vandals' usual relationship with the Roman state, which was one of great hostility. The western Empire, as we have seen, from the 410s onwards had consistently allied with the Visigoths against the Vandals and Alans, and the latter's history after 450 was one of similar exclusion. Unlike the Visigoths or the Burgundians, the Vandals and Alans did not contribute to Aetius' military coalition that fought against Attila in Gaul in 451; nor were they subsequently courted or rewarded by the regimes of Avitus, Majorian or Libius Severus. Their leader Geiseric was certainly after membership of the club, as his sack of Rome at the time of Petronius Maximus paradoxically showed. This was partly motivated by the fact that Maximus had upset the marriage arrangements between his son Huneric and the elder daughter of Valentinian III. After they sacked Rome in 455, the Vandals continued to raid the coast of Sicily and various Mediterranean islands. This was an enterprise undertaken in large measure for profit, but Geiseric also had a more ambitious, political, agenda. Part of his booty from the sack of Rome had been Valentinian III's women: his wife Licinia Eudoxia, and his daughters Eudocia and Placidia. Eudocia was duly married to Geiseric's eldest son Huneric. Probably in 462, Eudoxia and Placidia were freed to go to Constantinople, where Placidia married a Roman senator called Anicius Olybrius, who had fled to the eastern capital to escape the sack. After 462, Geiseric was canvassing for Anicius Olybrius as heir to the western throne. From the Vandal point of view, this would have had the desirable outcome that the next western emperor would have the next king of the Vandals for a brother-in-law: another route to the political acceptance that Geiseric so obviously craved.[22]

The history that had brought the Vandals to North Africa was only marginally less respectable, from a Roman point of view, than that which had seen Visigoths and Burgundians installed in Gaul. All three had forced treaties out of the Roman state by military action, or the threat of it; given the choice, the west Roman imperial authorities would rather have had nothing to do with any of them. The real problem undermining Geiseric's bid to be admitted to the immigrant powers' club was not so much past indiscretions per se, but the fact that, while in flagrante, he had come into possession of the richest, most productive provinces of the western Empire. Since the 440s, in addition to the lands he already held in North Africa, he had seized Tripolitania and a number of Mediterranean islands. His annual raids were spreading fear and disorder up and down the Italian coastline. Destroying the Vandals would therefore achieve two highly desirable ends in one fell swoop. It would take out one of the three major barbarian powers established on western soil, and, more important, return an invaluable reservoir of wealth to the imperial treasury.

It is worth indulging here in a little counterfactual history. The knock-on effects of a decisive victory over Geiseric, itself far from inconceivable,[23] would have been far-reaching. With Italy and North Africa united, Spain could have been added to the new western power-base. Unlike the Vandal–Alan coalition, the Suevi who had stayed in Spain were no more than a relatively minor irritant. Their power ebbed and flowed according to the amount of Roman resources devoted to the peninsula at any one time, and there is no reason to think that they would have been able to hold out against a full-scale imperial counterattack. Then, once Hispanic revenues had begun to flow in again, much reconstruction would in turn have become possible in Gaul. At the very least, Visigoths and Burgundians could have been reduced to much smaller enclaves of influence, stripped of some of their more recent acquisitions such as Narbonne and the cities of the Rhône valley. The assertive Bagaudae of the north could likewise have been brought back into line.

Such a reborn west would still have looked more like a coalition, with substantially autonomous Gothic and Burgundian spheres of influence coexisting alongside the territories under direct Roman rule, than a single integrated state like the old fourth-century Empire. But the Roman centre would have become once again the dominant partner, with the strategic situation restored at least to a level comparable with that of the 410s, before the loss of North Africa – better, even, since there would be no Vandal–Alan coalition loose in Spain. Move on another twenty years, and even the Romano-Brits, struggling against the Saxon invaders, might have benefited. This is, of course, a best-case scenario. The Visigoths had proved impossible to destroy even during the eras of Theodosius I and Alaric when the Empire had disposed of much greater assets, so they were a problem that was unlikely to go away. Nonetheless, there were plenty of Rome-focused landowners still around in Gaul and Spain in the late 460s, as Sidonius' dash to Italy to seek out Anthemius shows, who would have welcomed the resurgence of a plausible western Empire. And, however you look at it, a reborn west based on the possession of Italy, North Africa, most of Spain and large chunks of Gaul was a formidable prospect. Even as late as the 460s, all was not lost: a successful campaign against the Vandals could have halted the vicious circle of decline and guaranteed the western Empire an active political life for the foreseeable future.

That eliminating the Vandals was the best available answer to the problems of the west had been appreciated for some time. The only other western regime to have shown much fight after the assassination of Aetius was that of Majorian, and he had adopted the same strategy. From early in his reign, we have a verse panegyric Sidonius gave in the emperor's honour during a stay at Lyon in 458. After the usual expression of superlatives designed to demonstrate that Majorian has been blessed with all the qualities of the perfect emperor, the scene then shifts to Rome, personified as an armed goddess surveying her territories. All is well, until:[24]

Of a sudden Africa flung herself down weeping, with her swarthy cheeks all torn. Bowing her forehead she broke the corn-ears that crowned her, ears whose fruitfulness was now her bane; and thus she began: I come, a third part of the world, unfortunate because one man is fortunate. This man [Geiseric], son of a slave-woman, hath long been a robber; he hath blotted out our rightful lords, and for many a day hath wielded his barbarian sceptre in my land, and having driven our nobility utterly away this stranger loves nothing that is not mad.

This opens a long appeal for Rome to awaken from her slumbers and right Africa's wrongs, into which Sidonius interweaves an account of Majorian's martial past, again so as to parade his credentials as the right man for the job. The goddess's speech comes to a close with a startling image of Geiseric:

he is sunk in indolence and, thanks to untold gold, no longer knows aught of steel. His cheeks are bloodless; a drunkard's heaviness afflicts him, pallid flabbiness possesses him, and his stomach, loaded with continual gluttony, cannot rid itself of the sour wind.

Nothing like a little fart joke to lighten the mood, even at an imperial celebration. But Sidonius also had a more serious point. The time was ripe for Majorian to avenge Africa 'so that Carthage may cease to war against Italy'.

This was a direct statement of intent. No imperial panegyrist was ever allowed to stand before an emperor and tell him to do some specific thing, unless that emperor already had every intention of so doing.[25] Sidonius had clearly been told that one of the aims of his panegyric was to prepare landowning opinion for an assault on the Vandals. This was early in the year 458. There was still much to do in preparation, as Sidonius makes clear. For a start, more order had to be restored in Gaul before they could concentrate on the North African adventure; and fleets had to be constructed.[26] But from its earliest days Majorian's regime committed itself to an assault on the Vandals.

In 461, it was ready to deliver. Majorian's plan was, with his main force, to follow the route taken by the Vandals themselves. By the spring, 300 ships were gathered in harbours along the coast of the Hispanic province of Carthaginensis, from Cartago Nova (Cartagena) to Illici (Elche) about a hundred kilometres further north. Majorian and his army duly arrived in Spain, from there to be transported, it seems, to Mauretania, with a view to marching in full battle order into the heartland of Vandal Africa.[27] At the same time, Marcellinus led elements of his Illyrican field army into battle in Sicily, expelling the Vandals from footholds they had established on the island. Securing Sicily was an end in itself, but may also have been designed to sow doubt in Geiseric's mind about the trajectory of the main attack. Feeling cornered, Geiseric made peace overtures, but Majorian was confident enough to reject them. More to the point, the emperor had staked too much in the expedition to contemplate compromise. But, informed of Majorian's plans, Geiseric struck first: his fleet raided the Spanish coast and destroyed Majorian's shipping. The emperor's army was left cooling its heels on the Spanish beaches; the campaign, heralded as the centrepiece of Majorian's policy as early as 458, had failed.

Majorian had lost his hold on power. He left Spain in high summer, travelling back overland to Italy. En route, he was arrested and deposed by Ricimer on 2 August, and executed five days later. For Majorian, the African gamble ended in disaster, but the reasoning behind it was sound. When Anthemius came west a few years later, it can have been no surprise to anyone that his eyes were fixed firmly on Carthage.

The Byzantine Armada

IF LEO WAS happy enough to remove so formidable a presence as Anthemius from Constantinople, the eastern emperor's contribution to his attempt to reconquer Vandal Africa was unstinting. This may well have been part of the deal between them. A number of sources give us a fair idea of the costs involved. The most detailed account is found in fragments from a work by another Constantinople-based historian. Penned by a certain Candidus in the late fifth century, the fragments are preserved in an encyclopaedic Byzantine work, the *Suda*, of the late tenth. Here we learn: 'The official in charge of [financial] matters revealed that 47,000 pounds of gold came through the Prefects, and through the Count of the Treasuries an additional 17,000 pounds of gold and 700,000 pounds of silver, as well as monies raised through confiscations and from the Emperor Anthemius.'[28] One pound of gold equated to more or less eighteen of silver, giving a total of about

103,000 pounds of gold, and it was called in from every available source: from general taxation (the purview of the Prefects), from the exploitation of imperial estates (that of the Count of the Treasuries), as well as confiscations and anything else that Anthemius could extract from the west. Of other sources, one gives more or less the same figure as Candidus, while two others put it higher: at 120,000 and 130,000 pounds of gold. The figures are roughly similar (Candidus' total does not include the monies he refers to as having been raised by Anthemius himself, from the west). The general level of magnitude is also perfectly plausible. The construction of Justinian's Church of Hagia Sophia in Constantinople in the 530s, for instance, cost the east Roman treasury 15–20,000 pounds of gold. The emperor Anastasius (reigned 491–517), whose financial prudence was legendary and whose reign had been blessed with relative peace, left, on his death, 320,000 pounds of gold for his successor. A hundred and three thousand pounds is forty-six tons: a huge figure, then, but plausible enough, and a good guide to Leo's commitment to the west.[29]

The military effort generated by all this cash was correspondingly massive. An armada of eleven hundred ships, nearly four times the size of the fleet assembled by Majorian, was assembled from across the eastern Empire. Again, the figure is plausible. If the much damaged western Empire could find 300 in 461,[30] 1,100 for such an ambitious project is entirely proportionate. No one gives tonnages for the 468 expedition, but the ships of an east Roman fleet of 532 varied between 20 and 330 tons. Most of the vessels were tiny by modern standards. The vast majority were merchant ships powered by sails alone, but there may have been some specialist warships, *dromons*, that would proceed as far as the action under sail, then join battle under oar power.[31] The military manpower committed was similarly to scale. Procopius puts the figure at 100,000, but that seems both high and suspiciously round. The later fleet of 500 ships in 532 carried an army of 16,000, so the 1,100 ships of 468 may have been conveying something over 30,000 soldiers (sailors are not included here). In addition, as in 461, Marcellinus and some of his Illyrian command also came west. This time they first drove the Vandals out of Sardinia, and then occupied Sicily in force. A third force, recruited from the army of Egypt and placed under the command of the general Heraclius, was put ashore simultaneously in Tripolitania, where it joined with the locals in throwing out the Vandals who had occupied their cities since

455. Adding together the sailors and all these subsidiary forces, then, the total committed to the expedition was certainly well over 50,000 men.[32]

Command of this huge expedition was allotted to Leo's brother-in-law, the general Basiliscus, who had recently enjoyed considerable military success in the Balkans fighting off the last attempts of Attila's sons to find sanctuary south of the Danube. By the beginning of 468 everyone knew what was coming, and there is a huge sense of expectation in the panegyric Sidonius gave in Rome on 1 January of that year in honour of Anthemius' accession to the consulship. One influential historian has claimed that there is little reflection of the Byzantine armada in western sources. For once, I disagree with him.[33] Imagery of the sea and sailing suffuse Sidonius' speech, beginning with his introduction of Anthemius:[34]

> This, my Lords, is the man for whom Rome's brave spirit and your love did yearn, the man to whom our commonwealth, like a ship overcome by tempest and without a pilot, hath committed her broken frame, to be more deftly guided by a worthy steersman that she may no more fear storm or pirate.

Marine metaphor then tacks in and out, with the speech concluding:

> But now too strong are the breezes that drive my sails before them. Check, O Muse, my humble measures, and as I seek the harbour let the anchor of my song settle at last in a calm resting-place. Yet of the fleet and forces that you, O prince [Anthemius], are handling and of the great deeds you will do in a short while, I, if God further my prayers, shall tell of in due course . . .

The sense of anticipation of a naval expedition in the offing is unmistakable. And Sidonius' speech captures the grand design: 'Anthemius came to us with a covenant made by the two realms; an empire's peace has sent him to conduct our wars.' He had come with the promise of military salvation for the west, and in 468 it arrived. Sidonius caught the moment perfectly. That such an armada could be assembled was in itself a tour de force. Now would come the true test. The storm of battle was about to detonate once more in the western Mediterranean. The fleet, the supreme symbol of imperial unity, was on its way.

The Roman plan was emphatically not to fight a fleet engagement.

As in 461, the Romans wanted to get their army to North Africa in one piece and then fight it out on land. The campaign proceeded accordingly. Basiliscus' fleet followed the main trade route south from Italy. It was a route dictated from time immemorial by the winds and currents of the central Mediterranean. In these waters the sailing season proper lasted from June to September, and it was probably in June that Basiliscus set out. With a decent following wind, it took no more than a day's sailing to reach North Africa from Sicily. The armada anchored in the shelter of Cape Bon – no more than 250 stades (about 60 kilometres), one source tells us, from Carthage. This places the fleet somewhere offshore between Ras el-Mar and Ras Addar in modern Tunisia, a good choice because the prevailing winds here in the summer months are easterly. (A fleet anchored on the other side of the peninsula would have been driven onshore.) What was meant to happen next, we're not certain. The armada was making for the army's designated embarkation point. The nearby harbour of Carthage was protected against enemy shipping by a chain, so perhaps Basiliscus' destination was the bay of Utica, a short march from Carthage.[35]

The Vandals, needless to say, were not prepared to follow a Roman script. In capturing Carthage in 439, they had taken possession of one of the busiest ports in the Roman Mediterranean, and had made full use of the shipping and maritime expertise they found there. Sea-raids had been their trademark since 439, and fighting at sea became something at which they excelled. We should not envisage here the sudden appearance from nowhere of hoary Vandal sea dogs. The nautical work was done by indigenous North Africans, as Sidonius conveys somewhat tortuously in a passage dramatizing their grievances in his panegyric to Majorian. As Africa herself complains: 'Now he arms mine own flesh against me for his own ends, and after all these years of captivity I am being cruelly torn under his authority by the prowess of mine own; fertile in afflictions I bring forth sons to bring me suffering.'[36] This is a phenomenon found elsewhere. In the third century, after taking possession of the northern shores of the Black Sea, Goths and other Germanic newcomers were able to persuade local sailors, in exchange for a share of the booty, to help them mount large-scale maritime raids on the Roman communities to the south. There's also a law in the *Theodosian Code* promising to burn alive anyone teaching barbarians the art of shipbuilding, but some clearly weren't put off.[37] Most of the Vandals' maritime manoeuvres took the form of hit-and-run attacks, forces being put ashore to raid and destroy. By 468, they and their naval aids could draw upon thirty years' experience in military operations at sea. With this powerful tool at his command, Geiseric proceeded to act, like any good commander, in the fashion least desired by his opponent.

With the east Roman armada riding at anchor, the Vandal fleet hove into view. Here we come face to face with the factor that has decided many a battle – the element of chance. Against normal expectations, the wind was blowing from the north-west. The Vandals, having put out from Carthage, held the wind gauge so could choose exactly when and where to engage, while the Romans, with the wind in their faces, could move only slowly and at an angle. The sources give no sense of one side or the other possessing the better ships; the unchanging wind kept the Roman fleet pinned against the western side of Cape Bon. Grasping at the opportunity, the Vandals did in 468 exactly what the English would do eleven hundred and twenty years later, in 1588, when they found the Spanish Armada similarly placed. They launched fireships. The annals of ancient sea warfare are not replete with references to fireships, but it was a stratagem employed from time to time in favourable circumstances, especially when an enemy fleet was at anchor or in harbour and unable to move with any speed. The earliest mention of fireships occurs in relation to an Athenian attack on Sicily in 413 BC, and the Romans and Carthaginians had for centuries used them against each other, the latter being particularly successful against a Roman fleet in the spring of 149 BC.[38]

To understand the threat posed by fireships, you need to think about the kind of vessels carrying the Roman army. The classic account of the Spanish Armada puts it simply: 'Of all the dangers to a fleet of wooden sailing-ships, fire was the gravest; their sails, their tarry cordage, their sun-dried decks and spars could catch fire in a minute, and there was almost nothing about them that would not burn.'[39] On the night of 7/8 August 1588, the English launched only eight fireships. No one tells us how many Geiseric had at his disposal, but Procopius, probably drawing on Priscus' history, gives us a vivid account of their effect:[40]

When [the Vandals] came near, they set fire to the boats which they were towing, and when their sails were bellied by the wind, they let them go against the Roman fleet. And since there were a

great number of ships there, these boats easily spread fire wherever they struck and were themselves readily destroyed together
with those with which they came in contact.

The sail-powered merchantmen of the Roman fleet were stuck
fast. All they could do was try to pull themselves out of danger by
attaching lines to all the rowboats they could muster – a slow process.
The oared warships of the fleet, the *dromons*, though in the minority,
were much better placed. The chief virtue of such vessels was that
they could move directly into the wind if necessary – at least, for as
long as the rowers could keep going. Procopius tells us what happened
next, off Cape Bon:

> As the fire advanced in this way the Roman fleet was filled with
> tumult, as was natural, and with a great din that rivalled the noise
> caused by the wind and the roaring of the flames, as the soldiers
> and the sailors together pushed with their poles the fire-boats and
> their ships as well, which were being destroyed by one another in
> complete disorder. And already the Vandals too were at hand
> ramming and sinking the ships and making booty of such of the
> soldiers as attempted to escape, and of their arms as well.

It sounds as though the Vandal fireships of 468 may have had a more
telling effect on the enemy fleet in terms of ships aflame than those of
the English in 1588. The classic counter to fireships was to put out
oared vessels to take them in tow and pull them away from your fleet.
In 1588 the Spanish dealt with two of the eight that way, but then lost
their nerve, and pretty much the whole Armada scattered pell-mell
into the night. Off Dunkirk, the Spanish did have sea room downwind,
and could at least put on sail to escape, so that the only immediate
casualty of the entire fireship episode was one already battered galleass
which ran aground trying to make it into the safety of Calais. However,
in escaping, the Spanish ships became so disordered that they lost all
ability to function as a coherent fleet, effectively handing victory to
the English.

In 468, the option of putting on more sail was not available to the
Roman merchantmen, since the contrary wind would have driven
them ashore, and ancient ships were not of strong enough construction
to stand being beached. And, perhaps, anyway, Geiseric had many
more fireships than eight. But if more direct damage was inflicted by

the fireships of 468, it is also clear that, as in 1588, the concomitant disorder was at least as disabling as the number of Roman ships sent up in flames. Ancient sea battles were all about getting behind your enemy by some means (either enveloping from a flank, or breaking through his line), then ramming him from behind. If you rammed head on, the force of the collision broke your ram off. Isolating and boarding enemy ships constituted a second line of attack. Although lacking detail, Procopius' account makes it clear that, following up the fireships, the Vandal fleet went quickly into action, making mayhem among the disordered Romans. The merchantmen, so busy avoiding the horror of fire, made easy prey.

The result was disaster. Some of the Byzantine armada stood and fought, though:

> Most of all John, who was a general under Basiliscus ... For a great throng having surrounded his ship, he stood on the deck, and turning from side to side kept killing very great numbers of the enemy from there, and when he perceived that the ship was being captured, he leaped with his whole equipment of arms from the decking to the sea ... uttering ... that John would never come under the hands of dogs.

Stirring stuff, and entirely typical of our ancient sources in concentrating on the actions of the few. It follows from this that we cannot assess the different elements of the action, such as how many ships were destroyed by fire, and how many subsequently by ramming and boarding. No one tells us, indeed, how many Roman ships were destroyed all told. This is where late Roman and Dark Age history ceases to be an unputdownable cryptic crossword puzzle and becomes merely annoying. What we do know is that the Vandals won a decisive victory – all the more decisive, of course, because every merchant ship they captured or sank meant the loss of Roman army units. Ancient warfare could be a bloody business, and the Romans could have lost here a hundred-plus ships and upwards of 10,000 men. My suspicion, however, would be that actual losses may have been smaller than Procopius' rhetoric would at first suggest, and that in its fundamentals the action was not dissimilar to 1588. The Roman survivors were much too scattered to pose any further threat; no possibility, then, of landing Basiliscus' expeditionary force as an effective army. Constantinople had stretched every sinew to reconquer the

Vandal kingdom, but the expedition had failed. When Leo died on 18 January 474, five years later, the treasuries of the eastern capital were still empty. He had mobilized all his reserves, leaving nothing for a second attempt.

According to Procopius, the failure of the Byzantine armada was due to treachery on the part of Basiliscus: he was handsomely paid by Geiseric to agree to a five-day truce, whose sole purpose was to allow time for the wind to change round to the right direction for the fireships. But in Roman historiography great disasters are often blamed on treachery – another instance of that tendency to look to the virtues and vices of individuals when seeking causes. Procopius similarly blamed the Vandals' arrival in North Africa in 429 on the treachery of Boniface, but this charge is certainly baseless. Basiliscus also, in January 475, seized the eastern Empire from Leo's successor Zeno, and hung on to it until summer 476, at which point Zeno regained his throne. This condemned Basiliscus to go down in history as a usurper, and blaming him for the debacle of 468 then became an easy option. The causes of Roman defeat were probably more prosaic: a mixture of bad luck with the wind, unimaginative tactics in trying to land so close to Carthage that there could be no element of surprise, and overambition.[41]

WHETHER THE PREDESTINED result of a flawed conception or the contingent outcome of bad luck with the weather, the failure of the Byzantine armada doomed one half of the Roman world to extinction. Not that everybody realized this instantly. When a state of affairs has prevailed for over five hundred years – the time separating us from Christopher Columbus – it is hard to believe that it can vanish overnight. The situation was, however, hopeless. Constantinople had no more money with which to mount a further rescue. The resources now controlled by Anthemius and Ricimer amounted to little more than the Italian peninsula and the island of Sicily – entirely insufficient, as a source of revenue, to support a military force powerful enough to keep in line Visigoths and Burgundians, Vandals and Suevi, not to mention assorted local Romans – all the centrifugal elements, in fact, now running riot within the western imperial borders. Basiliscus' defeat had destroyed the last chance of regenerating a dominant imperial force. In the decade after 468, despite the political and cultural inertia that made a world without Rome difficult to conceive, different people in different places gradually got to grips with the fact that the western Empire no longer existed.

The Unravelling of Empire 468–476: The Frontier

SOME OF THE first to realize the truth were Roman provincials living on the frontier. Historical and archaeological sources allow us to spotlight one particular group: the inhabitants of Noricum. This province comprised the foothill zone between the outer slopes of the Alps and the River Danube in what is now Lower Austria. Here the beautiful, fertile valleys of the Danube tributaries stretch towards Europe's highest mountains: a stunning landscape. Into this magical Sound of Music country sometime in the mid- to late 450s wandered a mysterious Holy Man by the name of Severinus (we met him fleetingly in Chapter 8). Severinus refused to say anything about his origins, except that he had trained as an ascetic far away in the eastern deserts; but we do know that he spoke beautiful Latin.[42] From the man himself no writings survive, but about a generation after his death one of his acolytes, a monk called Eugippius, wrote a memoir of the saint's life. Severinus died in January 482, and Eugippius was writing in 509/11. Eugippius hadn't been one of the saint's close companions, but he was present at his death and had access to stories told by those who knew him better. What Eugippius produced was a disjointed account of Severinus' life and miracles – hardly a biography, but it is packed with incidents that vividly evoke life in a frontier region as the tide of Empire ebbed away.

The old kingdom of Noricum had been founded about 400 BC when the Celtic-speaking Norici had established their dominance over a native population of Illyrian-speakers. In strategic terms, it was something of a backwater. It did control some routes over the Alps, but not the main ones running west and particularly east of it over the Julian Alps, whose lower slopes and wider passes offer much easier communications between Italy and the Middle Danube basin. Within its borders, though, were situated some important iron mines, and from the second century BC lively trade links had grown up between it and northern Italy, especially the city of Aquileia. This led to generally good relations between Noricum and the Roman Republic, evident not least in the permanent presence of large numbers of Roman traders at the royal residence from which the kingdom was run, the Magdalensburg.

Noricum was a Roman ally until the time of Augustus, when in 15 BC it was peacefully absorbed into the Empire. Since it was neither hostile to Rome nor sitting astride the major Alpine highways into Italy, Romanization took a different form here from that in Rome's other Danubian provinces. There was no major Roman army stationed here, for instance, and hence no hothouse economy driven by state spending on infrastructure and soldiers' pay packets. Nonetheless, roads were built and Roman-style towns sprang up in the same way we have observed everywhere else in the Empire: about one part central planning to eight parts local initiative. The province was badly hit during the Marcomannic War of the 160s and 170s AD (see pp. 97–8), and acquired a much more substantial garrison afterwards, but this did not affect the basic pattern of its development. By the late Roman period, Noricum was a province of smallish, moderately prosperous agricultural towns. Its landowning class spoke Latin, a reasonable elementary education could be got in the larger towns, and the region still swam in the mainstream of Empire. The best of the late Roman archaeological discoveries in the area is a Christian pilgrimage centre of the late fourth and fifth centuries, discovered on top of the Hemmaburg. Recent excavations have unearthed here three huge basilicas, and inscriptions commemorating the local donors responsible for their construction.[43]

For Noricum, as for so many other parts of the Roman west, the fifth century came as a nasty shock. It seems to have survived the major invasions in quite good shape. There was a moment in the late 400s when Alaric had his eye on the province as a suitable settlement zone for his Goths (see Chapter 5), but that never materialized and the Visigoths ended up in Aquitaine instead. Otherwise, precisely because there were better routes available on either side, the Noricans were able to be mere spectators as the waves of barbarians rolled past. The invaders of 406 moved north up the Danube valley and over the Rhine into Gaul, and Attila did the same in 451. Radagaisus, Alaric and their Gothic groups hurled themselves into northern Italy through Pannonia so as to take advantage of the passes through the Julian Alps, as did Attila in 452. Nonetheless, the first half of the fifth century witnessed a massive erosion in the general level of security enjoyed by the Norican provincials.

*

THE PATTERN OF settlement and order in Noricum – its spread of towns and agriculture – was the product of the military power of the Roman Empire. Round about the year 400, as recorded in the *Notitia Dignitatum*, the province was protected by a substantial garrison army (*limitanei*). Detachments of two legions provided the backbone of its defence: the Second Italica at Lauriacum (Lorsch) and Lentia (Linz), the First Noricorum at Adiuvense (Ybbs). Both legions included units of river police (*liburnarii*) stationed at three separate points on the river, and there were other fleet units. In addition, three infantry cohorts, four units of ordinary cavalry and two of mounted archers were stationed in the province, amounting, all told, to a force of close on 10,000 men, with a wide range of weaponry.[44]

In the *Life of Severinus*, beginning in the mid- to late 450s, there is not much evidence of this command. One unspecified military unit is mentioned at Faviana, modern Mautern (where the *Notitia Dignitatum* mentions river police belonging to the First Noricorum), and another stationed at Batavis (Passau), just beyond the border of Noricum in the province of Raetia (where the *Notitia* lists an infantry cohort). That's all: nowhere near 10,000 men, despite the fact that much of the *Life* is taken up with hostile contacts between Noricans and various barbarian outsiders. There's reason, in fact, to be just a little suspicious of this apparent absence of a decent-sized force. Since the whole point of the *Life* was to celebrate Severinus' ability to stop barbarians terrorizing the population of Noricum, the presence of a largish army in the province would tend to spoil that narrative line. And I strongly suspect that, at least at the start of Severinus' time in the province, there were a few more units around than the two that get a passing mention in the *Life*. Nonetheless, there is a broad range of evidence indicating that by the death of Attila, the Norican army was much reduced. It also makes clear how and why this had happened.

For one thing, archaeological evidence, particularly from the military installations, has shown that coin circulation collapsed in the province shortly after the year 400. The only partial exception to this was the old legionary base at Lauriacum. As we know, the Roman Empire produced coin above all for paying its army, so that a disturbance in the coin supply may well reflect disruption to military pay. The one exception suggests the same thing: since Lauriacum was the military command centre of the province, you would expect military units to

survive there if nowhere else. A reduced military presence is also suggested by clear archaeological signs of greater insecurity. Shortly after
400, all the villas in Noricum (those so far excavated, at least) were
abandoned or destroyed. Isolated, wealthy and undefended rural
manor houses, which is what villas essentially were, provided an obvious target for raiders, and could not survive without a certain level of
security. As we saw earlier, villas disappeared equally quickly in much
of the Balkans at the time of the Gothic war of 376–82.

This doesn't mean that all their former owners were necessarily
killed and the landowning class eliminated. Rural surveys in Noricum
have demonstrated, on the contrary, that building in the fifth century
switched to the construction of what Germanophone archaeologists
call *Fliehburgen*, 'refuge centres'. These are substantial walled settlements, sometimes built with permanent occupation in mind, placed in
highly defensible positions, usually on hill tops and frequently with a
church at their centre. There were a few *Fliehburgen* in favoured spots
to the north, close to the Danube, but most were further south,
nestling in the Alpine foothills south of the River Drava in East Tirol
and Carinthia. The largest of all was at Lavant-Kirchbichl, a settlement
that replaced the old Roman town of Aguntum, where powerful
defences surrounded an area of 2.7 hectares atop an almost inaccessible
crag, with houses, storehouses and an episcopal church 40 metres
long.[45] The *Life* has Severinus giving the following advice to inhabitants
of the countryside around Lauriacum in the 460s:[46]

> The man of God, by the divine inspiration of his prophetic mind,
> instructed them to bring all their modest belongings within the
> walls so that the enemy on their deadly expedition, finding no
> means of human support, would at once be compelled by famine
> to give up their cruel plans.

The evidence suggests that the Noricans didn't really need Severinus'
promptings, but had been busy constructing refuge centres since the
start of the century: an appropriate response to the inability of such
military garrisoning as there was in the province to protect Roman life
there.

Much of the action of the *Life of Severinus* takes place against a
backdrop in which small walled settlements, *castella* – the contemporary term for the archaeologists' *Fliehburgen* – provide the basic form of
settlement being used to protect Roman life. The *Life* also makes clear

that, by the 460s, the citizens of these small towns had become responsible for their own protection, putting together small forces to defend their walls – citizen militias, in fact. Walls and / or citizen guards are mentioned at Comagenis, Faviana, Lauriacum, Batavis and Quintanis. Another defensive option – paralleling that taken by Romano-Britons in similar circumstances – was for citizens to hire barbarian warbands to defend their town for them. This is mentioned only in the case of Comagenis on the Norican frontier, and, as in Britain too, led to trouble. The *Life* opens with the people of Comagenis depicted as sorely oppressed by their protectors' demands. They were lucky enough, with a bit of divine assistance mediated by the saint, to be able to drive the barbarians out.[47] (If the Romano-British had been able to do the same, then Welsh, rather than English, might now be the language of computers and world communication.)

In the early 460s, some Roman military survived in the province, but nothing like the substantial force listed in the *Notitia*. One factor in the decline of this Norican army shows up in that work itself. The field army of Illyricum in about 420, the time of Flavius Constantius, included among its pseudocomitatensian legions two regiments of *lanciarii* (lancers) who had previously been stationed at Lauriacum and Comagenis. Their withdrawal was part of Constantius' response to the heavy losses suffered by western field armies in the years after 406.[48] After 420, it is impossible to follow the history of the western army in detail, but the loss of North Africa certainly forced Aetius into another round of belt-tightening, which would have led the central authorities in Italy to withdraw yet more units from the Norican garrison. And this surely happened at other crisis moments too. Equally important was the effect – on Noricum as everywhere else – of declining revenues at the centre. The *Life* includes a much quoted but nonetheless fantastic vignette of the last moments of one particular unit of frontier garrison troops:

At the time when the Roman Empire was still in existence, the soldiers of many towns were supported by public money for their watch along the wall [the Danube frontier]. When this arrangement ceased, the military formations were dissolved and, at the same time, the wall was allowed to break down. The garrison of Batavis, however, still held out. Some of these had gone to Italy to fetch for their comrades the last payment, but on their way they had been routed by the barbarians, and nobody knew. One day when St Severinus was reading in his cell, he suddenly closed the book and began to sigh heavily and to shed tears. He told those who were present to go speedily to the river [the Inn], which, as he declared, was at that hour red with human blood. And at that moment, the news arrived that the bodies of the said soldiers had been washed ashore by the current of the river.

As with all the episodes in the *Life*, this is impossible to date precisely. But when central funds began to run out, the surviving garrison troops just disbanded themselves. As the flow of cash slowed to a trickle, soldiers were paid less and less frequently (prompting the ill-fated initiative of the Batavian garrison), and the supply of arms and other essentials declined too. We are told in another anecdote that the tribune in command of the surviving unit at Faviana hesitated to go after marauding barbarians because his men were few and had little weaponry. Severinus told them that all would be well, and that they would simply take the arms of the defeated barbarians.[49] This gives us a notion of what happened to those units of the frontier garrison force that were neither redeployed to field armies nor destroyed in encounters with the enemy. As the financial crisis worsened, deliveries of pay and equipment eventually dried up altogether.

In Noricum, it was sometime in the 460s that the troops disbanded, and my best guess would be that it happened shortly after the defeat of the Byzantine armada. But the garrison troops had wives and children living with them, so that even when they disbanded they stayed where they were. Old garrisons didn't die, but slowly faded away into the citizen militias who, as we've already seen, continued to protect their walled settlements once the formal Roman army in the province had ceased to exist. This is the situation that most of the anecdotes in the *Life of Severinus* presuppose. But because Noricum was a backwater, remote from the main action, provincial Roman life still went on there much as usual. We know from the *Life* that the roads were still in good repair, and that trading was maintained both with Italy and with near neighbours up and down the Danube. Roman landowners still worked their fields from their walled settlements. At the same time the new political powers dominating the north Alpine region after the collapse of the Hunnic and Roman Empires also figure in the text: the Herules, Alamanni, Ostrogoths and, above all, because they were the province's nearest neighbours, the Rugi.

The essential problem facing the Noricans at this point was how to continue living a provincial Roman life in the absence of the Empire within whose embrace it had evolved.

We learn from the *Life* that the Norican communities' efforts at self-defence were far from unsuccessful – particularly, Eugippius is at pains to convey, given the assistance of Severinus' powers of prophecy and mediation. Local communities had developed effective techniques for dealing with raiders, sending out scouts to provide advance warning of attacks so that everyone could hurry back inside the walls. Even full-scale assaults such as those carried out by the Alamanni on Quintanis and Batavis could be beaten off. And where raiders took provincials prisoner, they could sometimes be rescued or ransomed.[50] More generally, while other more peripheral powers, particularly the Alamanni but also the Herules and Ostrogoths, looked on the Noricans as a source of booty and slaves, their neighbours the Rugi were interested in a more ordered relationship. Some of the Norican towns began to pay tribute to them, in return for which the Rugi left them in peace. Their kings even paid court to Severinus and always listened to his advice, or so the *Life* tells us, and extensive trading was carried on back and forth across the river.

With the divine assistance to which the saint had access, says Eugippius, some of the towns of Noricum were able to maintain *for some time* a lifestyle that preserved much of its old Romanness. The emphasis has to be added. One theme of the *Life of St Severinus* is a kind of London-in-the-Blitz determination to carry on being more Roman than usual. Another is more pessimistic. A sense of danger and threat is felt everywhere. If you ventured out from your settlement even at midday to pick fruit, you might be dragged off into slavery. The citizens of Tiburnia were forced to buy off Valamer's Goths by handing them just about every item of moveable wealth they possessed, including old clothes and alms collected for the poor. More brutally, whole communities were picked off one by one by rampaging barbarian outsiders, who would carry off any survivors they chose to spare. Severinus tried to warn the inhabitants of Asturis of impending disaster when he left for Comagenis, but they wouldn't listen, and this town that was the site of his first monastery was duly destroyed, except for one refugee – the individual who brought the news of the disaster to Comagenis. Later on, sudden attacks by the Herules destroyed Ioviacum, and the Thuringi despatched the last inhabitants of Batavis.

Most of the Batavians had already left for Lauriacum, another surviving settlement, and retrenchment of this kind is a third theme of the *Life*. Outlying sites that were too isolated and dangerous were progressively abandoned. Thus the inhabitants of Quintanis moved to Batavis, and it was together that the two groups sought sanctuary in Lauriacum. Even here, though, they were not completely safe. For the Rugi, although interested in a long-term relationship, nonetheless viewed the Noricans as a resource to be exploited. Different princes of the Rugi, not content with merely extracting tribute from them, also sought on occasion to transplant large numbers north of the Danube, where they would be more fully under their thumb. Severinus fought off these attempts, but it was a losing battle.[51]

Up to about AD 400, the military power of the Roman Empire had protected the area between the Alps and the Danube, largely excluding from it other forces based north of the river. With the disappearance of that power, the region as it had so far evolved couldn't function as a self-sustaining unit. Its population became a valuable potential resource for a series of new powers. It was impossible for Norican settlements – even the *Fliehburgen* – to preserve their independence indefinitely; established patterns of Roman provincial life were bound to erode, whether through violent abduction or less aggressive resettlement.

All of this took some time to unfold. St Severinus died on 5 January 482, and at that point some of the towns even on the Danube line itself still existed. Many had already fallen by the wayside, however, and the new forces, which would eventually turn the region into a thoroughly non-Roman world, were irreversibly at work. As such, Noricum provides us with a case study, a model for what happened to provincial Roman life in areas where the Roman military presence withered away through lack of funds. The provincials were far from helpless, nor did their Romanness disappear overnight. But they and the pattern of their lives depended on the continued flow of imperial power into their locality, and when that ceased, the old way of life was doomed. Noricum also gives us a plausible model for the kind of thing that went on in post-Roman Britain, therefore, where another sub-Roman population struggled to preserve itself in the absence of central protection, first using immigrant Germanic warbands but then fighting against them. It didn't happen overnight, but Roman villas and towns were eventually destroyed, and the population made to serve the needs of new masters: no longer emperors in Italy but, in Noricum, the Rugi (if they avoided abduction) or, in Britain, various Anglo-Saxon kings.

Heartlands: Gaul and Spain

THE UNRAVELLING OF Empire in Noricum took a particular course, one that flowed from its role as a strategic backwater combined with its lack of a rich, well connected elite of Roman landowners to agitate for its protection by what remained of the state. As a result the Roman Empire, as far as this province was concerned, just faded away. In the old heartlands of the western Empire, Gaul and Spain, the end of the Roman imperial project was never going to be such a low-key affair. The defeat of the Byzantine armada pulled the plug on the expectations of revival aroused by the arrival of Anthemius, but the two regions were still home to rich and powerful Roman landowning families. In Italy and parts of Gaul some quite powerful imperial military formations remained, as well as the by now well established barbarian powers, particularly the Visigoths and Burgundians.[52] The fate of Gaul and Spain, therefore, could not be that of places like Noricum or Britain, where a relative power vacuum left provincials to struggle on as best they could. Gaul and Spain, by contrast, saw the intersection of, if anything, too many interested parties. A portrait of the end of Empire here must necessarily work, therefore, on the less intimate level of complicated manoeuvring at royal courts. But thanks to the surviving letter collection of Sidonius Apollinaris, it is no less vividly reflected than is the fate of Noricum in the *Life of Severinus*.

One of the first to grasp the significance of the defeat of the emperor Anthemius' North African expedition was the Visigothic king Euric. This younger brother of Theoderic II, who had thrown his weight behind the regime of the western emperor Avitus back in 454, perceived that the world had changed. Where Theoderic had been content to chart the Visigoths' future within a Roman world that seemed likely to continue and to seek power behind the imperial throne, Euric was made of different stuff. In 465 he had organized a coup in which Theoderic was murdered and he himself took power. Immediately, he sent ambassadors to the kings of the Vandals and Suevi, looking to reverse his brother's hostile stance towards them.[53] Theoderic had allied with the rump of Empire against these powers; now Euric aimed to ally with them against what remained of the Empire. The arrival of Anthemius with strong eastern reinforcements stopped these plans in their tracks, Euric immediately withdrawing his ambassadors so as to avoid finding himself in direct conflict with a newly rejuvenated western authority. With the defeat of the Byzantine armada, however, it became apparent that Anthemius would not become the power that Euric had feared. The *Getica* sums up succinctly: 'Becoming aware of the frequent changes of Roman emperor, Euric, king of the Visigoths, took the initiative to seize the Gallic provinces on his own authority.'[54] He understood that there was no longer any need to worry about the central Roman authorities. After their last defeat, they had lost all ability to intervene effectively north of the Alps. The way was open to him to pursue his own Visigothic agenda.

As soon as the dust had settled on the African fiasco, Euric set to work. In 469, he launched the first of a series of campaigns designed to carve out an independent Visigothic kingdom. In this year his forces went north, attacking the Bretons under King Riothamus, who were close allies of Anthemius. A Visigothic victory drove Riothamus into sanctuary in Burgundian territory, and gave Euric control of Tours and Bourges, thus extending his northern boundaries to the River Loire (map 16). Further advances in this direction were contained by what was left of the Roman army of the Rhine under its leader, a Count Paul, operating in conjunction with Salian Franks under their king Childeric. Gaul beyond the Loire, however, was of only peripheral interest to Euric. In 470/1, he turned his forces south-east towards the Rhône valley and Arles, the capital of Roman Gaul. There in 471 he administered the *coup de grâce* to Anthemius' dwindling hopes by defeating an Italian army led by his son Anthemiolus, who died in the fighting. But capturing walled Roman cities, it will be remembered, was not the Visigoths' forte. For instance, every summer for four years, 471–4, Visigothic would-be besiegers appeared outside the city of Clermont-Ferrand in the Auvergne without ever managing to force their way inside. It took Euric until 476, in fact, to gain possession of the region's two great prizes, Arles and Marseille – by which time he also controlled the Auvergne, ceded to him by the authorities in Italy in an abortive bid to halt his expansion towards Arles. At the same time, more dynamic campaigns had been taking place south of the Pyrenees. In 473, Euric's forces seized Tarragona and the cities of the Hispanic Mediterranean coast, and by 476 all of the Iberian peninsula was his, except for a small Suevic enclave in the north-west. The Visigothic settlement had finally become a kingdom, stretching from the Loire in the north, to the Alps in the east, to the straits of Gibraltar in the south.[55]

The Visigoths were not the only power interested in expansion during these years. Euric's campaigns ran up against the ambitions of the Burgundian kingdom, established in the upper Rhône valley. The Burgundians too had long had their eyes on Arles. Not powerful enough to defeat the Visigoths in the race southwards, they nonetheless had some success in moving the boundaries of their kingdom in that direction. By 476 they had taken a salient of cities and other

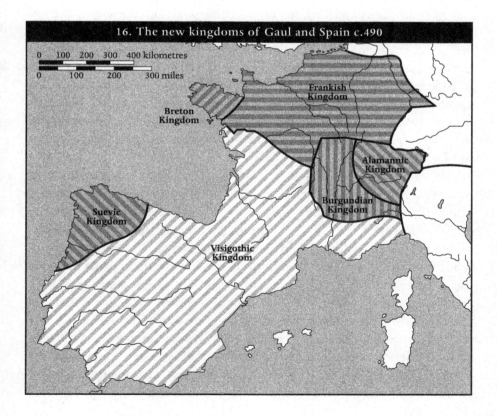

16. The new kingdoms of Gaul and Spain c.490

territory between the Alps and the Rhône, running as far south as Avignon and Cavaillon (map 16). Further north the Franks, too, were emerging for the first time as a major power on the Roman side of the Rhine. The full story is lost in myth and half-history, but roughly what happened is this. A Frankish world previously confined to the east of the Rhine and divided between a series of warband leaders both expanded its control west of the river and at the same time was slowly prompted to unite by the rise of more powerful warlords. Just as with the two Gothic supergroups unified by Alaric and Valamer, this created a force of unprecedented power, able to compete at an entirely new level and which rapidly acquired for itself new territories on former Roman soil. By the 470s, the process was far from complete, but Childeric was already prominent, and by the end of the decade, if not before, he and his Salian Franks had taken control of the old Roman province of Belgica Secunda with its capital at Tournai.[56] A whole series of powers, then, carved up between them the old imperial heartlands of Gaul and Spain. Some, like the Visigoths and Burgundians, were well established features of the strategic landscape; others, like the Franks and the Bretons, much more recent creations. South of the Loire, the lands they took were also home to powerful landowning families, used to holding high office within the Roman state. Thanks to Sidonius, who was one of them, we have an inside view of the significance of these upheavals for a select Gallo-Roman few. No source gives us access to the experiences of elite Hispano-Romans, but there is every reason to suppose that their reactions were pretty similar.

In the years between 468 and 476, some of these landowners were manoeuvring to remain part of a functioning western Empire, however much of a rump this might prove to be. This in itself is vivid testimony to how powerful the idea of Empire, despite all its recent setbacks, remained. Sidonius himself, in the time of Avitus, had been happy to work with Visigoths like Theoderic II who knew their place and saw the future in terms of a Visigothic sphere of influence *within* a continuing Roman world. When other Visigoths, like Euric, wanted their own entirely independent kingdom, however, Sidonius was ready to fight *not* to be a part of it. In the early 470s he and a group of like-minded friends, including his brother-in-law Ecdicius the son of the emperor Avitus (by birth from the Auvergne), did everything they could to keep Clermont-Ferrand Roman. For example they put money into raising a military force to fend off the annual summer siege of their city by Visigothic forces. The fighting that ensued was pretty desultory. Clermont-Ferrand was not the centrepiece of Euric's ambition, and Ecdicius once broke through Gothic lines with just eighteen men. The determination of these landowners to remain Roman, however, was deadly serious. They aimed to make enough of a show of armed loyalty to encourage first Anthemius, then his successors, to do their utmost to maintain the Auvergne within a minimal western Empire, rather than toss it away as a prize for Visigothic or Burgundian expansion.[57]

But while Sidonius and others like him were still labouring to remain Roman, others had already decided that the western Empire had no political future and that it was time to switch allegiance to one of the new powers in the land. The case of Arvandus provides a striking example. Though Praetorian Prefect of Gaul, he wrote to Euric immediately after the African defeat:[58]

> dissuading him from peace with the 'Greek Emperor' [Anthemius], insisting that the Bretons settled to the north of the Loire should be attacked, and declaring that the Gallic provinces ought according to the law of nations to be divided up with the Burgundians and a great deal more mad stuff in the same vein, fitted to rouse a warlike king to fury and a peaceful one to shame.

Arvandus, who cheerfully acknowledged authorship of this highly treasonable letter during his subsequent trial, clearly preferred the rule of Euric or the king of the Burgundians to that of Anthemius. Or perhaps, like some Gallic landowners in the 410s, he saw this kind of territorial division as the best path to peace and the maintenance of some kind of social order. Whatever his motivation, the episode demonstrates that opinion in Sidonius' circle of landowning peers was thoroughly divided. As we have seen, Sidonius took a very different view from Arvandus. But Arvandus was his friend and Sidonius did what he could to protect him when the former was indicted, even though the case had been brought to Italy by three other leading landowners who were also his friends (and one even a relative) – Tonantius Ferreolus, Praetorian Prefect of Gaul in 451; Thaumastius, Sidonius' paternal uncle; and a lawyer and high-ranking senator (*illustris*), Petronius of Arles. Arvandus was not, however, alone in his thinking. By 473, Euric's forces in eastern Spain were under the joint command (along with a Goth) of a certain Vincentius, who in a previous incarnation in the 460s had been commander of the last properly Roman forces in the region. Others of both greater and lesser standing in the Roman provincial hierarchy were making the same leap. One Victorius was commander of Euric's forces in Gaul in the early 470s. And a second celebrated treason trial centred on the deputy prefect of Gaul, Seronatus, who in 475 was accused of facilitating Euric's takeover of Gallic territories, and was eventually found guilty and executed.[59]

Further east, the rise of independent Burgundian power was having similar effects. Sidonius' collection includes a letter to a certain Syagrius, who wielded considerable influence at the Burgundian court, not least through speaking Burgundian better than the Burgundians:

> I am . . . inexpressibly amazed that you have quickly acquired a knowledge of the German tongue with such ease . . . You have no idea what amusement it gives me, and others too, when I hear that in your presence the barbarian is afraid to perpetrate a barbarism in his own language. The bent elders of the Germans are astounded at you when you translate letters, and they adopt you as umpire and arbitrator in their mutual dealings. A new Solon of the Burgundians in discussing the laws[60] . . . you are loved, your company is sought, you are much visited, you delight, you are picked out, you are invited, you decide issues and are listened to.

Sidonius was praising Syagrius for making himself part of a post-Roman world dominated by alien kings: precisely what he himself was striving to avoid.[61] There may even have been a generational element in the alertness of the younger men to the fact that the end of the old regime was nigh. Amongst Sidonius' supporters in the Auvergne was a certain Eucherius who seems to have put up cash for the city's defence, at the same time as his son Calminius could be spotted from the city walls lined up with the besieging Goths. Sidonius' son Apollinaris, too, embraced the new Gothic order with enthusiasm, eventually holding high military office under Euric's son.[62] Thus after 468 Gallo-Roman landowning opinion was split down the middle even within the same family. In the meantime, Euric played his hand with skill. The waning of central Roman imperial power was allowing him to use the military strength of his Visigothic followers to establish a large territorial power-base. But he had no model for governing this new domain other than that bequeathed to him by the dying Roman state.

The Visigothic kingdom that would emerge after 476 was thus thoroughly sub-Roman in character. It continued to operate, like its Roman predecessor, by means of an infrastructure of cities, provinces and governors. It had written law (very often a continuation of existing Roman regulations), and levied taxation on agricultural produce – a practice only possible given that the existing Roman social order of landowners and peasantry survived. Landowners needed to stay in business to extract the peasants' surplus, keeping part of it for themselves as rent while passing on the rest to the state as revenue. The operation of Roman law, together with the operation of the tax system, required the expertise of Roman functionaries to keep it going.

While he could use Visigothic arms to carve out a kingdom, then, Euric needed Romans to run it for him. The more members of the Roman aristocratic and administrative classes he could attract to his colours, the easier it would be to turn his conquests into a functioning kingdom. So he most graciously accepted all offers of service from Roman aristocrats, letting them praise him in iambic pentameters if they so chose. Euric was happy to perpetuate this practice begun in the reign of Theoderic, and showed the degree of respect for Roman cultural forms that was required to keep the flow of personnel coming. And he had his own Syagrius, a poet and lawyer from Narbonne called Leo, described by Sidonius in 476/7 as Euric's letter- and speech-writer:

> Through [Leo] the famous king himself [Euric] terrifies the hearts
> of nations far across the sea, or from his commanding eminence
> makes, after his victory, a complicated treaty with the barbarians
> trembling on the banks of the Waal, or having restrained people
> by arms now restrains arms by laws through the whole extent of
> his enlarged domains.

Having a deep need of them, Euric was willing to promote any Romans who would offer him service.[63]

He had, in fact, a mighty gift to offer in return. The disappearance of the Roman state put the Roman landowning class's position in doubt, since along with the state disappeared the legal system that had secured it against all comers. And although this privileged class survived, for instance, in the Visigothic and Burgundian kingdoms, it was not always the case elsewhere. Political revolution is often accompanied by social revolution, as it was in other parts of the Roman west. In post-Roman Britain, for instance, the old Roman landowning class disappeared completely. Even if they merely allowed their resident Roman landowners to continue living as before, therefore, new states such as the Burgundian and Gothic kingdoms were doing them a huge favour.

Historians have sometimes been taken aback by the seeming readiness of this class to throw off their allegiance to the Empire, and renegotiate a fallback position with the nearest barbarian power of significance. This, it has been argued, shows a fundamental lack of loyalty to the Roman state – an observation which then becomes part of a narrative of imperial collapse. Roman Europe disappeared, it is argued, because its elites didn't want to maintain it. In my view, such thoughts fail to do justice to the particularities of this group of people whose position was based almost exclusively on the ownership of land. Landed wealth is by definition immoveable. Unless you belonged to the super-rich of the Roman world, owning lands far to the east as well as in Gaul or Spain, then when the Roman state started to fail, you were left with little choice. You either had to mend fences with your nearest incoming barbarian king so as to secure the continuation of your property rights, or give up the elite status into which you had been born. If, as the Empire collapsed around them, Roman landowners perceived the slightest chance of holding on to their lands, they were bound to take it.

In his dealings with the provincial aristocracies of southern Gaul and Spain, then, Euric held the trump card. All he needed to do was steadily expand the area under his control – a relatively easy matter since the decline of its tax revenues meant that the Roman state could put few soldiers in the field – and the landowners would come running. Some required little prompting, others more persuasion, but most eventually came round. Even Sidonius himself crossed this Rubicon. Having led the resistance to Gothic expansion in Clermont-Ferrand, he could hardly expect Euric to smile upon him when the city finally fell into Gothic hands in 474/5. He was duly carted off to exile, first to a castle near Carcassonne, then to Bordeaux. There he tried to continue his literary studies, but 'my drooping eyelids scarcely got a wink of sleep; for a din would immediately arise from the two old Gothic women near the skylight of my bedroom, the most quarrelsome, drunken, vomiting creatures the world will ever see.' *Biberunt ut Gothi*

– 'drinking like Goths' – would be a proverbial expression in Italy by the sixth century. The letter from which this passage comes was written to Leo of Narbonne, poet, lawyer and Euric's chief adviser, accompanying a copy of a text called *The Life of Apollonius of Tyana*, which Leo had requested from Sidonius. Here, in fact, lay Sidonius' path to redemption. Euric was so busy that he could only see Sidonius briefly, at Bordeaux, twice in three months, but Sidonius had friends at court: Leo, and another literary acquaintance called Lampridius. By their intercession, he got off lightly in the end. His estates in Clermont, which could easily have been forfeit, were returned to him. He wrote an ingratiating little poem in return:

> Our lord and master [Euric], even he, has but little time to spare while a conquered world makes suit to him. Here in Bordeaux, we see the blue-eyed Saxon . . . Here your old Sygambrian,[64] who had shorn the back of your head after defeat . . . Here wanders the Herulian with his blue-grey eyes . . . Here the Burgundian seven-foot high oft begs for peace on bended knee . . . From this source the Roman seeks salvation, and against the hordes of the Scythian clime . . . it is your bands, Euric, that are called for.

Sidonius sent this first to Lampridius, hoping that he would show it to the king. He did. Euric, the beneficiary of so many conquests, accepted this literary flag of surrender and could afford to be generous.[65] Whether he let all his former opponents off so lightly is perhaps unlikely. And certainly in less successful kingdoms, where there were fewer resources to go round, Roman landowners found themselves having to accept harsher terms from their new masters than those meted out to Sidonius.

Compared with the Visigoths, for instance, the Burgundians managed to expand their domain only modestly between 468 and 476. Like Euric, the Burgundian monarchy needed to attract Roman supporters, but had its own armed men to reward as well; and all this from a much more restricted resource base. The result was a compromise, which we find reflected in one of the law-books of the new Burgundian kingdom, the *Book of Constitutions*:

> It was commanded at the time the order was issued whereby our people [the Burgundians] should receive one-third of the slaves, and two-thirds of the land, that whoever had received land

together with slaves either by the gift of our predecessors or of ourselves, should not require a third of the slaves nor two parts of the land from that place in which hospitality had been assigned him.[66]

There is much more that we would like to know, but the arrangement alluded to here gives us an insight into how Burgundian kings set about resolving the political balancing act that their situation required. About twenty years ago, the historian Walter Goffart argued that what was being referred to here was a division of the tax revenues from the Roman city territories (*civitates*) that had fallen into Burgundian hands, rather than actual real estate. This is a very forced reading and, as many have argued since, there is no doubt that what we're talking about here is the division of actual estates, parts of which were to be handed over to the Burgundian freemen.[67]

Within the Burgundian kingdom, then, occurred a root-and-branch recycling of landed assets. And as the law makes clear, it was again a process rather than an event. The order that they receive two-thirds of the estates and one-third of the tenants applied only to those Burgundians who had not already been granted land or slaves. We're also not told whether every Roman landowner was affected, or whether this was a matter in which the king exercised discretion. But the price of keeping some of your land was, on the face of it, relatively high for Roman estate owners. On the other hand, there is a singular lack of any mention of taxation in subsequent Burgundian legislation, which may also be significant. The total deal was perhaps that, in return for handing over two-thirds of your land, you not only got to keep the other third, but were also exempted from paying tax on it.[68] If so, the situation was not so harsh as it might at first seem. From the 470s, as the legal evidence makes clear, Euric and his son and successor, Alaric II, were also paying off their supporters in the Visigothic kingdom with grants of estates.[69] But that kingdom was much larger, and may not have required so much to be expropriated from its Roman landowners.

Either way, the final unravelling of the western Empire in its old heartlands of southern Gaul and Spain saw a great carve-up of the available assets. The interested military powers flexed their muscles, mounting the campaigns from which the new territorial boundaries emerged. The Visigoths came away with a huge kingdom, the Burgundians with just south-east Gaul. Further north, the situation remained in flux. In the north-east, the Salian Franks were the coming power, and in the north-west a Breton kingdom of some size was emerging. At the same time, the leadership of what remained of the Roman army of the Rhine seems to have established, for the moment at least, a power-base to the east of Paris. The defeat of Basiliscus' armada in 468 prompted Euric's wars of conquest, the campaigns of the Franks and Burgundians, and a consequent revolution in landownership. The overall result was a redrawing of mental as well as physical maps. Former barbarian settlements had become kingdoms, Roman landowners had been forced to make life-changing choices, and the central Roman state was in its last throes.

The Imperial Centre

WHILE WHAT REMAINED of the heartlands and outer reaches of the Empire in 468 was being annexed or just fading away, in the imperial centre – both in Italy and Constantinople – confusion and indecision reigned. In Italy, in the aftermath of the Byzantine armada's failure, Anthemius and Ricimer were evenly matched in their jostling for pre-eminence. Ricimer's acceptance of Anthemius' arrival on the scene had certainly reduced his own power. But hopes that the assistance Anthemius was bringing in from the east would kick-start the rebuilding of the west had come to nothing. Anthemius now had little to offer, serving merely as an obstacle to Ricimer's ambitions. A quarrel broke out between them in 470. Ricimer went as far as gathering an army of six thousand men and threatening war, but the two were reconciled early in 471. Then the defeat and death of Anthemiolus, the emperor's son, followed later that year by the loss of all the troops that Anthemius had sent with him against the Visigoths in Gaul, cut away the regime's last military prop, and Ricimer pounced. Anthemius holed up in Rome, and Ricimer besieged him there for several months before the city fell. The emperor was cornered and killed by Ricimer's nephew, the Burgundian prince Gundobad, on 11 July 472.

Olybrius, brother-in-law of the heir apparent to the Vandal kingdom, Huneric, had long been pushed by Geiseric as a candidate for the western throne. He was sent to Italy from Constantinople in 472 by the emperor Leo to act as mediator between Ricimer and Anthemius, but became instead Ricimer's next candidate for the purple. Having been made western emperor in April 472 (before the death of the present incumbent Anthemius), he died on 2 November of the same year, a short while after Ricimer himself, on 18 August. This left Gundobad as kingmaker-in-chief, and his choice fell upon a high-ranking guards officer, Glycerius, the Count of the Domestics (*comes domesticorum*). He was proclaimed emperor on 3 March 473. It was while all this fiddling was going on in Rome that the Visigoths, Burgundians and Vandals were busy expanding their realms. All that Glycerius ruled, therefore, as emperor of the west, was Italy and a tiny island of territory north of the Alps in south-eastern Gaul. The struggle for what was notionally the imperial throne had become a murderous competition for next to nothing. That, at least, seems to have been Gundobad's conclusion. Having briefly adopted his uncle's role as kingmaker, on the death of his father Gundioc king of the Burgundians in late 473 or early 474, he returned home. He must have decided that the struggle for power in Italy was a much less attractive proposition than claiming his share of the Burgundian kingdom alongside his brothers Chilperic, Godigisel and Godomar. What better measure of the erosion of the western Empire?

Gundobad's departure created a power vacuum into which stepped Julius Nepos, nephew and successor of Count Marcellinus, the ruler of Dalmatia since the 450s. After the murder of his uncle in Sicily in 468, Julius inherited Dalmatia and what remained of the Illyrian field army. With the eastern Empire's blessing but no actual assistance, he landed his forces at Portus, at the mouth of the Tibur just outside Rome, in early summer 474. Having overthrown Glycerius without a fight, he proclaimed himself western emperor on 19 or 24 June 474. But Nepos never reconciled the commanders of the army of Italy to his rule, which, as a result, lasted only just over a year. And it was one of his own appointees, the general Orestes, whom we met in Chapter 7 in the unlikely guise of ambassador of Attila the Hun, who eventually drove him out. Nepos' aim in appointing Orestes had been to clear up the mess in Italy, but Orestes turned his forces on Nepos instead. On 28 August 475, Nepos left Ravenna and sailed back to Dalmatia, abandoning the Roman west.[70]

WHILE ALL THIS was going on in Italy, the emperor Leo in Constantinople, rendered impotent by the fiasco of the 468 expedition, looked on with increasing despair. On his return to the east, the armada's commander Basiliscus fled for sanctuary to the Church of Hagia Sophia (not the current one, but its predecessor burned down in the Nika riot of 532), and refused to come out until Leo announced publicly that he was forgiven. The authorities in Constantinople had to decide what to do next. They did their best to stabilize the situation in Italy, wanting it to be ruled – naturally enough – by an ally. Although it should have been plain from the moment of the armada's defeat that the western Empire was doomed, it was only after the death of Anthemius that it became inescapably obvious in Constantinople that there was no further room for manoeuvre. Since they couldn't be defeated, and were already encroaching on the eastern Mediterranean, the Vandals needed to be conciliated. So negotiations began. The result was a treaty concluded between the emperor Leo and the Vandals in 474. Who could now doubt that Constantinople had given up all hope of reviving the Roman west?[71]

Fittingly, it was the army of Italy that was the last to give up on the idea of Empire. Having driven out Nepos, Orestes put his own son Romulus on the throne. Orestes had travelled twice on Hunnic missions to Constantinople. His father Tatulus and father-in-law Romulus were at this time, during the later 440s, close confidants of the Roman commander Aetius, and part of the embassy that arrived at Attila's court when Priscus was there. After the collapse of the Hunnic Empire, Orestes had found his way back to Italy, and rose through the imperial ranks until appointed to senior military command by Julius Nepos. Bearer of the same name as Rome's founder, Orestes' son Romulus was made emperor on 31 October 475, but Orestes and his brother Paul were the real *éminences grises*. No doubt whichever panegyrist it was who spoke at the coronation declared it the start of a new golden age ushered in by a second Romulus. Reality proved somewhat different, and Romulus, this last western emperor, has gone down in history as Augustulus – 'little Augustus'.

By this stage, no one could have thought that the ongoing struggle for power within Italy was likely to lead to the control of any assets outside the peninsula. With the rest of the west in the hands of other powers, and the remaining army of Italy more or less impotent, what further complications could there be?

As the Hunnic Empire collapsed in the mid-460s, many refugees of Germanic origin, particularly the Sciri but also the Rugi and others, had moved on to Italy and been recruited as allied soldiery by Ricimer.

During the first half of the 470s they had made themselves useful to the Italian military establishment, and their leader Odovacar, of the old Scirian royal family, had become an important voice in Italian politics. He'd played a key role in the civil war between Ricimer and Anthemius, and had become Count of the Domestics (*comes domesticorum*) under Nepos, evidently receiving from him the rank of Patrician.[72] On his way to Italy he had stopped off in Noricum to see Severinus: he was informed by the holy man that he would become famous.

> When he took his leave, Severinus again said to him: 'Go to Italy, go, now covered with mean hides; soon you will make rich gifts to many'[73]

By the early 470s, as we have seen, the Roman state's main problem was lack of money. Even into the 460s, the army of Italy had remained the single largest military formation in western Europe – considerably larger, I suspect, than the tax revenues of Italy alone could support. And, as pay started to dry up, the troops began to get restive, especially the Sciri. Odovacar had enough imagination and intelligence to grasp the point: with the army becoming increasingly difficult to manage, trying to set up yet another short-lived regime was a waste of time. In August 476 he had gathered enough support to act. He captured and killed first Orestes, near Placentia on 28 August, then his brother Paul in Ravenna, on 4 September. Now in control of the immediate situation, Procopius tells us, Odovacar set about addressing the underlying problem. Since there was no prospect of pay increases, another form of reward had to be found. Accordingly, Odovacar set about distributing to the soldiers some of the landed estates of Italy: 'By giving the third part of the land to the barbarians, and in this way gaining their allegiance most firmly, [Odovacar] held the supreme power securely.'[74] As so often, we know much less about what happened than we would like to. The distribution was organized by a Roman senator by the name of Liberius, but clearly not the whole of Italy was involved. The armed forces needed to be retained in the strategically important areas of the peninsula, particularly the north, to guard the Alpine passes, and probably also the Adriatic coast, since Nepos was still at large in Dalmatia.[75] Whether Odovacar needed, as had happened in Burgundy, to dispossess the Roman landowners of part of their estates, or whether sufficient land could be found by reallocating long-term leases on public ones, as Aetius had done for those senators driven out of Proconsularis by Geiseric (see Chapter 6), is also unclear. Certainly, unlike in the Burgundian kingdom, taxation remained a living feature of government in post-Roman Italy, so Odovacar, like Euric, perhaps had more freedom of manoeuvre and didn't need to resort to large-scale private confiscation. Either way, he found enough landed resources to satisfy the expectations of his men – he path to a secure hold on power in these changed times.

By early autumn 476, most loose ends had been tied up. The changes brought on by Odovacar's regime were pushing Italy towards a new political stability, even if no land distributions had yet taken place. One anomaly remained. At the moment, Italy still had an emperor in Romulus Augustulus, but Odovacar had no interest in preserving the position of this notional ruler who controlled nothing beyond the Italian peninsula. Consulting friends in the Senate, he came up with the solution. A senatorial embassy was sent to Constantinople, now presided over by Leo's successor the emperor Zeno,

> proposing that there was no need of a divided rule and that one, shared Emperor was sufficient for both territories. They said, moreover, that they had chosen Odovacar, a man of military and political experience, to safeguard their own affairs, and that Zeno should confer upon him the rank of Patrician and entrust him with the government of Italy.[76]

In the kind of language that accompanied the outbreak of the Falklands war in the 1980s, Zeno was to have sovereignty over Italy as Roman emperor, but Odovacar would control the administration. In practice, this meant merely that by promoting him to the rank of Patrician Zeno should legitimize Odovacar's seizure of power; it was the title that the effective rulers of Italy such as Stilicho and Aetius had been holding now for the best part of a century. Zeno hesitated for a moment – an embassy from Nepos had just arrived asking for his assistance in reclaiming the throne. Here was Zeno's chance to put the power of the east behind a last attempt to restore the western Empire. He weighed up the situation carefully, then wrote a sympathetic note to Nepos. The conclusion he had come to was what everyone else already knew. The western Empire was over. His letter to Odovacar expressed the pious hope that he would take Nepos back, but, more significantly, addressed him as Patrician, saying that he would have appointed him to this dignity but didn't need to since he had already received it under Nepos. The reply seemed ambiguous, but wasn't. The truth was that Zeno wasn't prepared to move a muscle on Nepos' behalf – he was writing to Odovacar formally, as ruler of Italy.

Odovacar took the hint. He deposed Romulus, pensioning him off with a charity rare in imperial politics to an estate in Campania. He then sent the western imperial vestments, including, of course, the diadem and cloak which only an emperor could wear, back to Constantinople. This momentous act brought half a millennium of empire to a close.

10

THE FALL OF ROME

IN 476 THE EASTERN Roman Empire survived the collapse of its western counterpart, and it continued to thrive, to all appearances, throughout the next century. Under the emperor Justinian I (527–65), it even mounted an expansionary programme of conquest in the western Mediterranean that destroyed the Vandal and Ostrogothic kingdoms of North Africa and Italy and captured part of southern Spain from the Visigoths. Gibbon concluded that the Roman Empire survived in the eastern Mediterranean for virtually a millennium, dating its fall to the Ottoman capture of Constantinople in 1453. To my mind, however, the rise of Islam in the seventh century caused a decisive break in east Mediterranean Romanness. It robbed Justinian's state of three-quarters of its revenues and prompted institutional and cultural restructuring on a massive scale. Even though the rulers of Constantinople continued to call themselves 'Emperors of the Romans' long after the year 700, they were actually ruling an entity best understood as another successor state rather than a proper continuation of the Roman Empire.[1] But even by my reckoning, a fully Roman state survived in the eastern Mediterranean for more than a century and a half after the deposition of Romulus Augustulus.

During the same period there were many living in western Europe and North Africa who continued to think of themselves, and were thought of by others, as Romans. In the 510s and 520s, Romans (*Romani*) were still referred to as a specific group in the official documents, not least the law codes, of the Visigothic, Ostrogothic, Burgundian and Frankish kingdoms. There have been attempts in recent years to argue that the designation lacked real meaning, but setting up independent kingdoms on former Roman soil involved substantial landed pay-offs to the non-Roman military followers of the new kings. This process turned these followers into a highly privileged group within the new kingdoms, giving new meaning to distinctions between these newcomers and less privileged Roman landowners.

Over time, the distinctions were eroded, but it took several generations.[2] After 476, then, we have 'proper' Romans still in both east and
west, so what was it exactly that fell?

The Destruction of Central Romanness

WHAT DID COME TO an end in 476 was any attempt to maintain the
western Roman Empire as an overarching, supra-regional political
structure. We have already discussed the important distinction between
'Roman' as applied to the central state, and 'Roman' as applied to the
characteristic patterns of provincial life lived within it. The Roman
state had consisted, at its simplest, of a decision-making centre –
emperor, court and bureaucracy – tax-raising mechanisms, and a
professional army whose military power defined and defended the area
of its dominion. Equally important were the centrally generated legal
structures that had defined and protected provincial Roman landowners. Within the social circle of these landowners operated most of the
cultural norms that made Romanness a distinctive phenomenon, and
their participation in the upper echelons of the bureaucracy, the court
and to some extent the army bound together the imperial centre and
its many local communities. After 476, all this came to an end. While
substantial numbers of the old Roman landowning class still survived
in the west with their distinctive culture more or less intact, the key
centralizing structures of Empire had gone. No single law-giving
authority was recognized, no centrally controlled tax structures
empowered a centrally controlled professional army, and political
participation in bureaucracies, armies and courts had all fragmented.
Surviving Roman landowners were busy advancing their interests at
the royal courts of the successor kingdoms, rather than looking
towards the central structures of one Empire. Provincial Romanness
survived in parts of the west after 476, but central Romanness was a
thing of the past.

The disappearance of the central structures of Empire was not felt
everywhere at exactly the same time. At one extreme, central Romanness disappeared, never to return, from the British provinces as early
as 410, though a degree of provincial Romanness survived there for
perhaps another generation, until the 440s. The North African provinces of Proconsularis, Byzacena and Numidia fell out of the system,

likewise, with the Vandal conquest of Carthage in 439. For most of the Roman west, however, the end was actually pretty quick. On the emperor Anthemius' arrival from Constantinople in 467, Italy, much of Gaul, a substantial part of Spain, Dalmatia and Noricum still owed political allegiance to the Italian centre. Some areas were more heedful of Italy than others, but Anthemius was taken seriously over a fair stretch of the old western Empire that had been much the same a hundred years earlier in the time of Valentinian I. Eight years later, the bonds had dissolved and the western Empire fragmented into a constellation of independent states. While I wouldn't want to play the old game of singling out a single date for unique significance, it is important to recognize the extraordinary rush of events that saw the Empire go from somewhere to nowhere in under a decade. There really was a historically significant process, in other words, that culminated in the deposition of the last Roman emperor of the west in September 476.

More than that, it is the fundamental thesis of this book that there is a coherence to the process of western imperial disintegration that unites this final collapse with the earlier losses of territory. This coherence stems from the intersection of three lines of argument.

First, the invasions of 376 and 405–8 were not random events, but two moments of crisis generated by the same strategic revolution: the rise of Hunnic power in central and eastern Europe. It is entirely uncontentious to state that the arrival of the Tervingi and Greuthungi on the banks of the Danube in the summer of 376 was caused by the Huns. That they were also responsible for a second cluster of invasions about a generation later – Radagaisus' attack on Italy in 405/6, the Rhine crossing of the Vandals, Alans and Suevi at the end of 406, and the westward advance of the Burgundians shortly after – has sometimes been asserted, but never won consensus. The fuller picture of the intrusion into Europe of Hunnic power depicted in Chapter 5 makes a powerful case for it. In 376, the Huns did not, as has usually been assumed, sweep in vast numbers as far west as the Danube frontier. For the next decade, it was Goths – not Huns – who were still providing the Romans' main opposition in this theatre; and as late as 395 most Huns was still located much closer to the Caucasus.[3] By about 420 at the latest, however, and perhaps the best part of a decade earlier, they had established themselves en masse at the heart of central Europe on the Great Hungarian Plain. No written source explicitly says that the Huns were making this move in 405–8 and that it caused the second wave of invasions. The fact, however, that they were still near the Caucasus in 395 and that they would somehow have to shift 1,500 kilometres further west by 420 makes it overwhelmingly likely that the 'blame' for 405–8 should be placed upon a second stage of Hunnic displacement. The growth of Hunnic power thus provides a unifying explanation for thirty-five years of periodic invasion along Rome's European frontiers.

Second, while some sixty-five years separate the deposition of Romulus Augustulus from the latest of these invasions, the two phenomena are causally connected. The various crises faced by the western Empire in the intervening years represented no more than the slow working-out of the political consequences of the earlier invasions. Damage inflicted upon west Roman provinces by protracted warfare with the invaders, combined with permanent losses of territory, generated massive losses of revenue for the central state, as we have seen. The Visigoths caused such damage to the areas around Rome between 408 and 410, for instance, that nearly a decade later these provinces were still contributing to state coffers only a seventh of their normal taxes. The Vandals, Alans and Suevi, likewise, cut a swathe of destruction through Gaul for five years after 406, before removing most of Spain from central imperial control for the best part of two decades. Worst of all, the Vandals and Alans then shifted their operations to North Africa, seizing the richest provinces of the Roman west in 439. Every temporary, as well as permanent, loss of territory brought a decline in imperial revenues, the lifeblood of the state, and reduced the western Empire's capacity to maintain its armed forces. From the *Notitia Dignitatum* we see that, already by 420, Flavius Constantius was making up for the field army losses incurred during the heavy fighting of the previous fifteen years by upgrading garrison troops, not by new recruitment. The loss of North African revenues threw the regime of Aetius further into crisis, generating a series of panic measures to try to keep the western army and Empire afloat.[4]

As the Roman state lost power, and was perceived to be doing so, provincial Roman landowning elites, at different times in different places, faced an uncomfortable new reality. The sapping of the state's vitality threatened everything that made them what they were. Defined by the land they stood on, even the dimmest, or most loyal, could not help but realize eventually that their interests would be best served by making an accommodation with the new dominant force in their locality. Given that the Empire had existed for four hundred and fifty years, and that the east continued to prop up the west, it is not surprising that such processes of erosion took time to work themselves out. Many in the old imperial heartlands, such as the Gallic supporters of Athaulf in the 410s or Sidonius in the 450s, quickly came to terms with Goths or Burgundians as autonomous elements within a central Roman state that still enjoyed a military power and political influence. But it took two or three generations for all to accept that this was only an intermediate position, and that the trajectory of the Roman west was set inescapably towards fully independent Gothic and Burgundian kingdoms.

The third line of argument concerns the paradoxical role played by the Huns in these revolutionary events. In the 440s, the era of Attila, the Hunnic armies surged across Europe from the Iron Gates of the Danube towards Constantinople, Paris and Rome itself. These exploits earned Attila undying fame, but his decade of glory was no more than a sideshow in the drama of western imperial collapse. Of much greater significance had been the Huns' indirect impact upon the Roman Empire in previous generations, when the insecurity they generated in central and eastern Europe forced various barbarian peoples across the Roman frontier. And while Attila inflicted huge individual defeats upon imperial armies, he never threatened the permanent alienation of a significant chunk of the western Empire's taxpayers. The groups who had fled across the frontier in the crises of 376–8 and 405–8, on the other hand, did precisely that. In the generation before Attila, the Huns had even sustained the western Empire by restricting further immigration into its territories after 410 and helping Aetius, particularly, to constrain the worst expansionary excesses of the Germanic groups already forced over the frontier. The Huns' second-greatest contribution to imperial collapse, in fact, was their sudden disappearing act after Attila's death in 453. This was the straw that broke the western Empire's back. Bereft of Hunnic military assistance, it had no choice but to build regimes that would include at least some of the immigrant powers. This started a bidding war in which the last of the west's disposable assets were expended in a futile effort to bring enough powerful supporters together to generate stability. But by the late 460s, the more ambitious leaders of these outside groups, particularly Euric, king of the Visigoths, could see that what purported to be the central western authority now controlled too little to prevent him from establishing an independent kingdom. It was this realization that led to the rapid unravelling of the last strands of Empire between 468 and 476.

In all this, it was armed outsiders warring on Roman territory who played the starring role. In successive stages, the different groups first forced their way across the frontier, then extracted treaties; then, in the end, detached so much territory from the Empire's control that its revenues dried up. Some of the first Goths of 376 were allowed across the Danube by agreement with the emperor Valens, but only because his army was already committed to battle on the Persian front. Otherwise, every stage of the process involved violence, even if it was followed by some kind of diplomatic agreement. But these agreements were no more than a recognition of the latest gains made by warfare, not the kind of diplomacy that moved events forward. I take an entirely different view, therefore, from one writer on fifth-century events who has commented: 'What we call the fall of the Roman Empire was an imaginative experiment that got a little out of hand.'[5] You can only argue this, it seems to me, if you don't let narrative history dirty your hands. Any attempt to reconstruct fifth-century events brings home just how violent the process was. In my view, it is impossible to escape the fact that the western Empire broke up because too many outside groups established themselves on its territories and expanded their holdings by warfare.

The process that brought down the western Empire was quite different, for instance, from the one that brought down the next major European empire, the Carolingian, in the late ninth century. Here the imperial centre, even after the great conquests of Charlemagne (768–813), controlled insufficient resources to maintain itself for more than two or three generations. In particular, it never developed the redistributive taxation powers that had kept the Roman state afloat for five centuries. The need to buy local political support, something it shared with its Roman predecessor, thus quickly bankrupted the Carolingian state. Within about a century of its creation, its local elites moved pretty quickly towards autonomy, sometimes without even having to assert themselves with any vehemence. In this the Carolingian collapse does slightly resemble the final unravelling of the west after the defeat of the Vandal expedition of 468. But, overall, the process was very different: no massive intrusions by outsiders; and the new rulers of the Carolingian successor states were mostly its indigenous nobility, not the leaders of intrusive military powers. In essence, the Carolingian state dissolved into bankruptcy because it controlled few assets to begin with, not because, as with the western Empire, outsiders stripped it of a centuries-old tax base.[6]

Local Romanness

WHILE CENTRAL Romanness was being destroyed, provincial Romanness met a variety of fates. As we have seen, the worst-case scenario – from a Roman perspective – unfolded to the north, in the British Isles. Here, it is impossible to offer any kind of connected narrative, but when history begins again about AD 600,[7] the Latin-speaking Christian Romanized landowning class, still dominant in central and southern Britain in about the year 400, had vanished. Along with it had gone the villas typical of its lifestyle, while economic production had both diminished in scale and regressed towards simplicity. Population had declined substantially, coins ceased to be used for exchange, towns no longer functioned as higher-order settlements, and most goods were produced at home rather than commercially. Late Roman pottery in Britain, for instance, was supplied by potters who distributed their wares over a radius of about forty kilometres from several centres of production such as Oxford and Ipswich. Soon after 400, pottery was being made for immediate consumption only. The old imperial provinces of Britain were likewise divided up into small kingdoms, at first maybe twenty or more, whose boundaries for the most part owed nothing to the political geography of Roman Britain. How this all came about is a matter of debate. The Victorians imagined Anglo-Saxon invaders chasing the entire Celtic sub-Romano-British population westwards into Wales and Cornwall, and across the sea into Brittany. More recent accounts have posited large numbers of indigenous British turning themselves into Anglo-Saxons in the same way that they had earlier become Romans. However you see it, characteristic Roman mores and lifestyles quickly disappeared from southern Britain after its ties with the rest of the Roman world were severed.[8]

British cataclysm was not typical, however. Parts of north-eastern Gaul aside, where the archaeological picture looks similar to that of southern Britain, the established forms of provincial life did not disappear so suddenly or so completely. South of the Loire in Gaul, whatever their initial misgivings, local Roman landowners reached a variety of accommodations with their new rulers. As we saw in Chapter 9, there was a price to be paid. Depending upon a variety of factors, not least the availability of assets within the new kingdoms, they had to give up more or less of their land. The smallish Burgundian kingdom seems to have enforced more large-scale confiscation than its better-endowed Visigothic peer, but sweetened the pill, perhaps, with tax reductions. But Roman landowners had much to offer the new barbarian rulers and, as a result, their regimes were willing broadly to uphold the unequal distribution of property that had brought the landowners into existence in the first place. We see remarkably little in terms of social upheaval, then, south of the Loire. Sidonius and his friends experienced difficult times, but emerged with enough of their property intact to retain their social positions. In Spain and Italy, too, the Roman landowning class generally survived the first shock of the end of Empire. Although in Vandal Africa Geiseric's seizure of Carthage was followed by large-scale property confiscations in Proconsularis, Roman landowners in the other two provinces that had fallen to him in 439 – Byzacena and Numidia – were left alone, and as other territories were added to the Vandal Empire, confiscation was not repeated.

In many places, then, local Romanness survived pretty well. Catholic Christianity, a Latin-literate laity, villas, towns and more complex forms of economic production and exchange all endured to some extent – except in Britain – on the back of the landowning class. Consequently, across most of the old Roman west, the destruction of the forms and structures of the state coexisted with a survival of Roman provincial life.[9]

Even under the southern Gallic model, however, local life in the post-Roman west did not just stay 'Roman'. The full story of what happened in these provinces after the fall of Rome is the subject of another book, but to bring the fall of the western Empire fully into perspective, it is important to make one major point. One of the many arguments surrounding the end of the Empire has focused on what significance to ascribe to the political changes that unfolded in the course of the fifth century. Was the end of the Roman state a major event in the history of western Eurasia, or merely a surface disturbance, much less important than deeper phenomena such as the rise of Christianity, which worked themselves out essentially unaffected by the processes of imperial collapse? Traditional historiography had no doubt that the year 476 marked, in western Europe at least, the divide between ancient and medieval history. More recently, the value-laden certainty that the end of the Roman Empire marked the start of a steep decline has given way to more nuanced views, which bear a closer relationship to historical reality. As we have seen, there was no sudden, total change, and this fact has laid a new emphasis on the notion of continuity, on the idea that the best way of understanding historical development in the late and post-Roman periods is to consider it in terms of organic evolution rather than cataclysm.[10]

I have no doubt that these new historiographical emphases are entirely necessary reactions to old historical orthodoxies, and I have no truck with the idea (originating with the Romans themselves of course) that the Roman Empire represented a higher order of society after whose demise the only possible way to go was downwards. But taking a minimalist view of the historical importance of the disappearance of the western Roman state is also, in my view, mistaken. It was certainly a ramshackle edifice. Running such a huge area on the basis of primitive communications and bureaucracy, it could hardly have been otherwise. Corruption was endemic, law enforcement sporadic, and much power retained in the localities. Nonetheless, because it was a long-established one-party state it managed to change the rules by which local life was conducted in some very profound ways. This manifests itself above all in the various processes that – slightly misleadingly – attract the label 'Romanization'. To participate in the benefits of Empire, provincial elites needed to gain Roman citizenship. The easiest way to do this was to set up your own town with Latin rights, and hold high office within it. A rush towards this kind of urbanization, therefore, followed the establishment of Roman dominance. You also needed to be able to speak 'proper' Latin, so that Latin literary education spread too, and to show that you had bought into the values of classical civilization. Public buildings in which such a civilized life might be lived with one's peers (meeting houses, baths and so on) and the villa style of domestic architecture were the concrete manifestations of that Roman vision. At the same time, the Pax Romana brought a massive peace dividend in its wake, creating regional interconnections that provided many new economic opportunities.

Most of what has been called Romanization was not a state-directed top-down activity. Rather, it was the outcome of the individual responses of conquered elites to the brute fact of Empire, as they adapted their society to the new conditions that Roman domination imposed upon them. An essential part of the deal, however, was that, while they transformed their lifestyles so as to participate in what the state had to offer, the Empire's armies protected them. Local Romanness was thus inseparable from the existence of Empire.

The symbiotic nature of this relationship shows up clearly. As we have seen, much of the burden resulting from the need of the third-century Roman state to extract a much higher level of tax from its provinces fell on the old town councils. It was largely in these councils that old forms of local Roman political life had been played out. You spent money to win office, making the friends and influencing the people whose support would in due course ensure that you rose to dominance and to the control of local funds. At a stroke, the confiscation of these revenues removed the whole point of the endeavour, and provincial elites weren't slow to notice: hence the almost immediate disappearance in the mid-third century of inscriptions recording the expensive acts of generosity by which people had previously gained advancement. By the fourth century, careers on town councils had been abandoned in favour of the imperial bureaucracy, which became the new path to local dominance. When the centre made changes to its modus operandi, then local Romanness would change in response – often, especially in the long term, in ways not anticipated

Too much of life in the provinces was dependent upon the political and cultural order of the state for its passing to go unnoticed. Take education, for instance. The literary education characteristic of late Roman elites – Latin in the west, Greek in the east – was not cheaply bought. It required the best part of a decade's intensive instruction with the grammarian, and only the landowning class could afford to invest so much in their children's education. As we noted earlier, they did so because speaking classical Latin (or Greek) instantly marked one out as 'civilized'. It was also necessary for most forms of advancement. The vast majority of the state's new bureaucrats came from the old town-council, or curial, classes, for whom a classical education continued to be de rigueur.[11]

In the post-Roman west, however, elite career patterns began to change. The new set-up saw military service for one's king, rather than a foot on the bureaucratic ladder, as the main path to advancement for most secular elites, even in areas where Roman landowners survived 476 and a southern Gallic model prevailed. As a result, an expensive literary education ceased to be a necessity. The descendants of both Roman and immigrant elites in fact continued to revere the old traditions. The odd Frankish and Visigothic king has gone down in the cultural annals for his Latin poetry. When a 'proper' Latin poet called Venantius Fortunatus turned up at court from Italy, he delighted equally both Roman- and Frankish-descended grandees present. This individual made a career out of singing for his supper, his party piece being elegant couplets in praise of the dessert. Despite this, neither kind of grandee bothered any more with a full Latin education. They did teach their children to read and write, but their aims were more limited. As a result, by about 600, writing was confined to clerics, while secular elites tended to be content just to be able to read, especially their Bibles; they no longer saw writing as an essential part of their identity. It was the Roman state which, again not very deliberately, had created and maintained the context in which widespread secular literacy was an essential component of eliteness, and with the passing of that state, new patterns of literacy evolved.[12]

A similar point can be made about Christianity. The Christianization of first the Mediterranean world, then of the broader reaches of central, eastern and northern Europe in the first millennium, is sometimes seen as a transformation entirely unaffected by the collapse of Rome. There is some truth to this notion, but it can also mislead. The Christian religion has always evolved, certainly institutionally, according to contemporary contexts. As we saw in Chapter 3, the Romanization of Christianity was as important an historical phenomenon as the Christianization of the Empire. Thanks to the emperor Constantine and his successors, imperially funded meetings of Christian leaders were able to define most of the religion's doctrines from the early fourth century onwards. The Church also developed a very particular hierarchy of bishops, archbishops and patriarchs whose geographical locations largely reflected the Empire's administrative structure of local and regional capitals. Nor did Christian Roman emperors step back one iota from the claim made by their pagan predecessors that they had been appointed by the Divinity – they simply re-identified that Divinity as the Christian God. So they had

every right, as they saw it, to involve themselves in the operation of
the Church at all levels. And they duly did so, calling councils, making
laws, and interfering in senior appointments.

Christianity as it evolved within the structures of the Empire was
thus very different from what it had been before Constantine's
conversion, and the disappearance of the Roman state profoundly
changed it yet again. For one thing, the boundaries of the new
kingdoms failed in some cases to respect the hierarchies of late Roman
administration. Bishops thus sometimes found themselves in one
kingdom, and their archbishops in another. Successive archbishops of
Arles, which was part of the Visigothic kingdom but whose metropolitan control extended into the Burgundian, fell foul of their kings who,
suspicious of their cross-border contacts, removed them from their
posts. There was change, too, of an intellectual kind. In the Roman
world, leading laymen – who were as well if not better educated than
the clergy – often contributed to religious debate. But with the
disappearance of widespread literacy, laymen soon ceased to be able to
do so, and the intellectual world of the early medieval Church became
a solidly clerical one. This would not have happened, had laymen
remained as educated as clerics. Equally important, post-Roman kings
inherited from their predecessors the claim to religious authority, and
took it upon themselves to appoint bishops and call councils. As a
result, Christianity operated at this time in what Peter Brown has
called 'Christian microcosms'. There was no single, unified Church;
rather, the boundaries of post-Roman kingdoms defined working
regional subgroupings, and these Church communities within the
different kingdoms had relatively little to do with one another.[13]

Above all, the rise of the medieval papacy as an overarching
authority for the whole of western Christendom is inconceivable
without the collapse of the Roman Empire. In the Middle Ages, popes
came to play many of the roles within the Church that Christian
Roman emperors had appropriated to themselves – making laws,
calling councils, making or influencing important appointments. Had
western emperors of the Roman type still existed, it is inconceivable
that popes would have been able to carve out for themselves a position
of such independence. In the east, where emperors still ruled, successive Patriarchs of Constantinople, whose legal and administrative
position was modelled on that of the Roman papacy, found it impossible to act other than as imperial yes-men. Appointed by the emperors

at will, they tended to be ex imperial bureaucrats highly receptive to imperial orders.[14]

The Components of Collapse

IN PRESENTING my own take on the reasons for the collapse of the west Roman Empire, I find myself lined up against one of the oldest historical traditions of all – in English writing, certainly. Famously, Edward Gibbon emphasized internal factors:

> The decline of Rome was the natural and inevitable effect of immoderate greatness. Prosperity ripened the principle of decay; the causes of destruction multiplied with the extent of conquest; and, as soon as time or accident had removed the artificial supports, the stupendous fabric yielded to the pressure of its own weight.

Gibbon's analysis picked up from where the Greek writer Polybius left off. Polybius, like most ancient historians, saw individual moral virtue or vice as the main moving force behind historical causation. The Roman Republic rose to greatness because of the self-discipline of its leaders, went his argument, and started to fall from grace when the excesses produced by success fed through to corrupt their descendants. Polybius was writing in the second century BC, long before the Empire reached its full extent, let alone started to shed territories. Picking up his general line of argument, Gibbon, addressing the subject of Christianity, saw it as contributing massively to the tale of woe. For him, the new religion sowed internal division within the Empire through its doctrinal disputes, encouraged social leaders to drop out of political participation by becoming monks, and, by advocating a 'turn-the-other-cheek' policy, helped undermine the Roman war machine.[15]

There may be something to be said for this way of thinking but there is one counter-argument that relegates it to no more than a footnote in the debate. Any account of the fall of the western Roman Empire in the fifth century must take full stock of the fact that the eastern Empire not only survived, but actually prospered in the sixth. All the evils identified in the western system applied equally, if not more, to the eastern. If anything, the Roman east was more Christian, and more given to doctrinal argument. Also, it operated the same kind of governmental system over the same kind of economy. Yet the east survived, when the west fell. This alone makes it difficult to argue that there was something so inherently wrong with the late imperial system that it was bound to collapse under its own weight. And if you start looking for differences between east and west that might explain their different fates, accidents of geography are what come most immediately to mind. The richest provinces of the east, the band stretching from Asia Minor to Egypt, were well protected by Constantinople against invaders from the north and east, whereas the western Empire had most of the Rhine and Danube frontier line to protect, and we have seen what hazards that threw up.

Both of these points were made by two earlier commentators, N. H. Baynes and A. H. M. Jones;[16] but since Jones was writing – forty years ago – it has become more necessary, I would argue, in any account of the collapse of the Roman west, to shine the spotlight on the barbarian-immigrant issue. This is for two reasons. First, the only factor that Jones saw as playing any real role in the different fates of east and west was their relative prosperity. In his view, overtaxation crippled the late Roman economy. Peasants were not being left with a large enough share of their yearly produce to feed themselves and their families, so that both population and output saw steady, if unspectacular, decline. This, he believed, was especially true in the west.[17] Jones's view of the late Roman economy was entirely based, however, on written, above all legal, sources. As he wrote, the French archaeologist Georges Tchalenko was publishing the account of his revolutionary trove of prosperous late Roman villages in the limestone hills behind Antioch (see pp. 112–13); and since Jones wrote, rural surveys, as we saw in Chapter 3, have completely recast our view of the late Roman economy. We know that in the fourth century, taxes were certainly not high enough to undermine peasant subsistence. In the west as well as the east, the late Empire was a period of agricultural boom, with no sign of an overall population decline. The east may still have been richer, of course, but there was no major internal economic crisis at play in the Roman world before the fifth century. Equally important, understanding that both moments of frontier crisis, 376–80 and 405–8, had the same non-Roman cause, and reconstructing the detailed narrative of subsequent imperial collapse from 405 to 476, underline the central role played by outside immigrants in the story of western collapse.

All this said, there is no serious historian who thinks that the western Empire fell entirely because of internal problems, or entirely because of exogenous shock. The emphasis of this book has been primarily on the latter, because in my view the growth of Hunnic power in Europe has been misunderstood and, with it, the intimate link between the arrival of the Huns and the deposition of Romulus Augustulus. To explore more fully the interaction of the Hun-generated invasions with the nature of the Roman imperial system, however, let's start by taking another look at the invaders.

THE INVADERS OF the late fourth and fifth centuries came in pretty large numbers. Ancient sources being what they are, the entire hundred years' worth of writings, from 376 to 476, offers us no precise figures for any of the barbarian groups involved in the action, let alone an appreciation of the global threat they posed. Some scholars would argue that the sources are so feeble on this front that it is pointless even trying to estimate their size. This is a justifiable stance, but some of the better sources do offer us plausible-looking figures, which suggest at least an order of magnitude for some of the invading groups and, occasionally, indirect ways of estimating their size. From these indications, my best guesses would be along the following lines.

The Tervingi and Greuthungi who appeared on the northern bank of the Danube in 376 could probably each put about 10,000 fighting men into the field. Radagaisus' force which invaded Italy in 405/6 was probably larger than these groups individually – maybe 20,000 fighting men. Taken together, these figures are broadly in line with other indications that, when he had united all three, Alaric could muster over 30,000 fighters.[18] When they crossed to North Africa, the military capacity of the united Vandals and Alans was seemingly in the region of 15–20,000, but that was after hard fighting and takes no account of the Suevi. In total, therefore, the Rhine invaders of 406 may, again, have numbered 30,000-plus fighting men. The Burgundians who converged on the Rhine in 410 are still harder to gauge. Compared with the Visigoths of the mid-450s, they only ever rated as a second-rank power, so their military capacity must have been lower, perhaps in the region of 15,000-plus fighters, but this was after their traumatic defeat at the hands of the Huns in the 430s.[19] Beyond this, we simply don't know how many Sciri, Rugi and Herules moved over with Odovacar to the Roman army of Italy as the Hunnic Empire collapsed in the

460s. They certainly numbered thousands, up to 10,000, perhaps. Roughly, therefore, the main invaders of the west might have amounted to 40,000 Goths (in the two waves of 376 and 405/6), 30,000 Rhine invaders, maybe 15,000 Burgundians, and another 10,000 refugees from Attila's collapsing empire. To this figure of 95,000 fighting men we would need to add whatever might be represented by various smaller groups, especially the Alans who didn't follow Geiseric to Africa, and, above all, the Frankish forces who from the mid-460s played an increasingly prominent role in Gallic politics. Although after 476 the Franks quickly became powerful enough to rival the Visigoths for dominance in Gaul, in the events leading up to the deposition of Romulus Augustulus, probably no more than 10–15,000 Franks were active. Overall, this suggests that around 110–120,000 armed outsiders played some part in bringing down the western Empire.[20]

On the one hand, narrative reconstruction leaves no room for doubt that the centrifugal forces generated by the intruders from outside fragmented the western Roman Empire into the new kingdoms of the late fifth century. On the other, these groups each weighed in at a few tens, not hundreds, of thousands of fighting men. This does not amount, at first sight, to an overwhelming level of force, especially when you remember that even the most conservative estimates would reckon the Roman army in AD 375 at 300,000 men, and some at double that figure. In a way, the narrative sequence confirms the point. The western Empire was not blown away in one moment of conquest, as for instance the Chinese Empire would be later at the hands of the Mongols. Initially, the immigrants had just enough military power to establish their enclaves, but the further expansion that created the independent kingdoms was a drawn-out process, taking two to three generations fully to erode the power of the Roman state. Another way of putting this is that, even in aggregate, the fifth-century invaders were not numerous enough to bring down just any Empire that we might imagine in control of the human and other resources of all the territory from Hadrian's Wall to the Atlas Mountains. They were able to push the western Empire from a state of relative health into non-existence only because they interacted in specific ways with the inherent military, economic and political limitations of the Roman system as it stood after half a millennium of evolution.

Considering the Empire's military capacity first of all, the invasions generated by the Huns have to be seen in relation to the rise of

Sasanian Persia to superpower status in the third century AD. As we saw in Chapter 2, Persia was eventually contained. However, containment did not remove the Persian Empire's power. Even after stability was restored to the eastern frontier by about the year 300, the military effort there could never be allowed to slacken, and upwards of 40 per cent of the eastern Empire's armies (20–25 per cent of the total east and west Roman military force) had always to be pointed at the Persians. The late fourth-century crisis on the Empire's European frontiers thus applied unwelcome pressure on a military structure that had already been subject to heavy strain.

A large proportion of the rest of the Roman army also consisted of garrison forces (*limitanei*), whose remit was essentially to deal with immediate, low-grade threats to frontier security. All had other duties and some may have lacked the training and equipment to make them of much use against the concentrated forces now generated by the Huns. Overall, then, the military capacity of the invaders needs to be measured not against the total armed forces of the Empire as a whole, for many units were fully committed to other tasks, but against the field armies of the west. These were grouped together largely in Gaul, Italy and western Illyricum, and amounted, in 420, to 181 units: on paper, upwards of 90,000 men. (At the onset of the crisis, the western field army probably numbered no more than 160 units, or 80,000-plus men.) Compared with this force, the number of intrusive barbarians starts to loom much larger, and it is easier to appreciate why they were eventually able to prevail. Far from being outnumbered, they probably enjoyed – between them – a not insignificant numerical advantage over imperial forces. This was hidden, initially, by the invaders' lack of unity, but numbers slowly told as the fifth century progressed.

If the incoming barbarians were sufficiently numerous eventually to overcome that section of the Roman army that could be pointed in their direction, why didn't the Empire simply raise more troops? The answer to this question lies in the limitations of its economy. As we have seen, late Roman agriculture was, if anything, booming in the fourth century, but there was no obvious means of quickly or substantially increasing output. In many provinces, the economy was operating at maximal levels of output. It is unlikely, therefore, that there was much extra slack left by the year 400 to fund still larger armies after the major increases in tax extracted a century earlier to fund the new armies required on the Persian front. The Empire's tax-take was also slightly limited by its bureaucratic capacity and the willingness of local elites to pay, but there is little sign that it was having much trouble with taxpayers before the 440s, when Aetius had to rein in tax privileges after the loss of North Africa. The most significant limitation on taxation would appear to be the buoyant but plateaued economy.

Political limitations, on the other hand, are directly relevant in another way to the story of western collapse. A relatively simple political deal, as we saw earlier, bound together Roman centre and locality. In return for tax payments, the machinery of the state, military and legal, protected a relatively small landowning class from both outside enemies and internal ones. Because their dominance was based on landowning, these people were vulnerable. They could not up sticks should the imperial centre cease to be able to guarantee their security, so it is hardly surprising that they tended to ingratiate themselves with the rising barbarian powers. This limitation within the system played a considerable role in shaping the nature of imperial collapse in the old Roman heartlands of central and southern Gaul and Spain.

Another political limitation relates to the operation of high politics. By virtue of the Empire's massive size and its previous success in Romanizing provincial elites, late Roman ruling regimes faced constant pressure from local interest groups, all pulling in different directions. By the fourth century power thus needed to be shared between more than one emperor, but there was no tried and trusted recipe for doing this successfully; all regimes were in this sense improvisations. At the centre, power could be distributed in various ways, such as between two emperors or more; or by means of puppet emperors whose strings were pulled by powerful men such as Aetius or Stilicho. Moments, even a decade or two, of political stability could ensue, but would tend to be punctuated by periods of brutal infighting, often ending in civil war. And instability at the centre gave the immigrants precious opportunities to advance their own interests.

Internal limitations must be given their due weight, then, but anyone who argues that they played a *primary* role in the Empire's collapse and that the barbarians were no more than an irritant hurrying the process along, has to explain exactly how the imperial edifice could have crumbled in the absence of massive military assault from outside.

And this, it seems to me, is very hard to do. It is not that the late Empire had a perfect political system. It encompassed many centrifugal tendencies, even before the advent of the barbarians, and some outlying areas were a lot less integrated into its structures than were the Mediterranean heartlands. Britain, in particular, showed a marked tendency to throw up dissident political movements, and to judge by the amount of banditry recorded there, north-western Gaul (Armorica) may have been similar. What happened with these revolts is instructive. First, they flared up only when there was instability at the centre; and all the Empire had to do was to send out a modest expeditionary force – in the case of Britain – to bring the province back into the fold. In 368, Count Theodosius, father of the first emperor by that name, managed the task with only four regiments.[21] For the Empire to have fallen apart on its own, therefore, a critical number of localities would have had to rebel simultaneously, each carrying with it enough of the Roman army to make it impossible for the centre to reconquer the rebels piecemeal.

Such a sequence of events, analogous to those which broke up the western half of the Carolingian world in the ninth century, is impossible to imagine in the fourth, precisely because the Roman Empire differed in some fundamental ways from the Carolingian. In the Carolingian Empire, the army consisted of local landowners leading armed contingents of their own retainers, whereas the Roman Empire operated with a professional army. When localities broke away from the Carolingian Empire, they already had their own ready-made armies. Roman landowners, by contrast, were civilian, and had to struggle to put together enough of a force in their locality to defend themselves from predation from the centre. Not only Britain, therefore, but northern Gaul, Spain and North Africa would have had to break away simultaneously to make internal collapse conceivable, and there is no sign of centrifugal pressure within the late Empire on anything like this scale. To my mind, rather than talking of internal Roman 'weaknesses' predestining the late imperial system to collapse, it makes more sense to talk of 'limitations' – military, economic and political – which made it impossible for the west to deal with the particular crisis it faced in the fifth century. These internal limitations were a necessary factor in, but not by themselves sufficient cause for, imperial collapse. Without the barbarians, there is not the slightest evidence that the western Empire would have ceased to exist in the fifth century.

Exogenous Shock

IN BRINGING this study of the destruction of the Roman west to a close, there is one final line of thought that I would like to explore. The exogenous shock, referred to earlier, had two components: the Huns who generated it, and the largely Germanic groups who caught its momentum and whose invasions fatally holed the west Roman ship of state. As far as we can tell, there is no deep-seated reason why the Huns should have moved into the lands north of the Black Sea at the precise moment they did. In the ancient and medieval periods, the Great Eurasian Steppe threw up from time to time militarily significant pulses of population. Sometimes these pressed eastwards towards China, sometimes westwards into Europe. The dynamics of this movement are still insufficiently understood for us to have a clear idea of any general underlying reasons that might explain why these pulses occurred when they did, or whether each had its own entirely individual explanation. In the case of the Huns, we can do no more than outline a few possibilities. These range from the environmental (the steppes becoming drier, and so less able to support livestock); to sociopolitical change; to military contingency (their having a more powerful bow). But as things stand, we have no more idea why the Huns moved west in the later fourth century than why the Sarmatians did the same around the birth of Christ.[22]

The Huns themselves, though, were only part of the problem. The more immediate and damaging component of the Hunnic crisis was the largely Germanic groups who forced their way across the imperial frontier in the two major waves of 376–80 and 405–8. If we can't get any further with the Huns, the interaction between steppe nomad and Germanic agriculturalist merits more attention, because its effects were, from a broader historical perspective, unique. In the first century AD, Sarmatian nomads similarly assaulted some Germanic-dominated agricultural societies at the eastern end of the Carpathians, and some of these Sarmatians eventually moved, like the Huns would, on to the Great Hungarian Plain. Despite these similarities, however, the arrival of the Sarmatians generated no knock-on effects remotely resembling the exodus of Goths, Vandals, Alans and others on to Roman soil some four hundred years later.[23] Why was this?

The likely explanation for this difference lies in the transformation of the Germanic world that had occurred between the first and the fourth centuries. As we saw in Chapter 2, first-century Germania was divided into many small, competitive political units, whose overall poverty was such that the Romans didn't think them worth conquering. At this time Germania could put together raiding parties and larger defensive alliances that might well successfully ambush a Roman army wandering in a forest, as Arminius did with Varus' legions in AD 9. But it possessed no political structure capable of standing up to Roman might and diplomatic manipulation in extended open conflict. By the time the Huns arrived, much had changed. An economic revolution, above all in agricultural production but also in certain manufactured goods, had generated both a much larger population and new wealth. Social stratification had increased, with a dominant free class, hereditary princes and armed retinues. This social change manifested itself at the top in the form of more robust political structures. By the fourth century, subsections of the Alamanni and Goths, amongst others, functioned as client states on the fringes of the Roman world. For the most part complaisant, they could nevertheless take action, when they thought it necessary, to limit the demands that the Empire made upon them.

As Germanic groups moved on to Roman territory to escape Hunnic aggression, this long-standing process of sociopolitical amalgamation acquired new momentum. One of the most important – and much discussed in this book – but least thought about phenomena of the fifth-century narrative is that all of the major successor states to the west Roman Empire were created around the military power of new barbarian supergroups, generated on the march. The Visigoths who settled in Aquitaine in the 410s were not an ancient subdivision of the Gothic world, but a new creation. Before the arrival of the Huns on the fringes of Europe, Visigoths – and don't let any old-style maps of the invasions convince you otherwise – did not exist. They were created by the unification of the Tervingi and Greuthungi, who had arrived at the Danube in 376, with the survivors of Radagaisus' force who attacked Italy in 405/6. Alaric's ambition brought the survivors of all three groups together, and created a new and much larger grouping than any previously seen in the Gothic world.[24] The Vandals who conquered Carthage in 439, likewise, were a new political entity. In this case, the new unit was generated out of just one pulse of migration, the invaders who crossed the Rhine at the end of 406.

These originally comprised a loose alliance of two separate groups of Vandals – Hasdings and Silings – an unknown number of Alanic groups (the largest force), and Suevi, who were probably the product of a renewed alliance among some of the Germani of the Middle Danube. Under Romano-Gothic military assault in the mid-410s, a new entity emerged; the Siling Vandals, and various Alans attached themselves to the Hasding Vandal ruling line.

At a later date, the emergence of a Frankish Gallic kingdom was made possible only by a similar realignment among the Franks. The Franks have not figured much in our narrative of Roman imperial collapse, essentially because they are an effect rather than a cause of the process. They start to feature as a significant force on Roman soil only from the mid-460s, by which time Roman power was already on the wane in northern Gaul. That their unification was intimately linked to Roman collapse isn't demonstrable, but it's highly likely. In the fourth century, Roman policy towards the Franks' southern neighbours in the Rhine frontier region, the Alamanni, was in part directed towards preventing the build-up of militarily dangerous political confederations. If the same was true of the Franks, it will have become significantly easier for political amalgamation to have occurred among the Franks as Roman power declined in the region. And certainly, the force of Frankish warriors that Clovis used after about AD 480 to bring about a united Gallic kingdom from the Garonne to the Channel, was created by the unification of at least six separate warbands. To that inherited from his father Childeric, Clovis added those of Sigibert (and his son Chloderic), Chararic, Ragnachar and Ricchar (brothers, but seemingly with their own followings) and Rignomer.[25] In the same way, the Ostrogoths, who deposed Odovacar in 492 to create the last of the successor states, were also a recent creation. Theoderic the Amal, first Ostrogothic king of Italy, completed the process begun by his uncle Valamer. In the 450s Valamer united some Gothic warbands, much as Clovis did among the Franks, to create one of the successor kingdoms to the Hunnic Empire in the Middle Danubian region. At this stage, the group numbered upwards of 10,000 or so. In the 480s, Theoderic united this force with another of more or less the same size: the Thracian Goths, previously settled in the eastern Balkans. It was this united force that then conquered Italy.[26]

It is worth taking a closer look at the process of reorganization into larger and more cohesive units from which the successor kingdoms sprang. In all cases, unification took place amidst a cacophony of dynastic rivalry. On the one hand, the process was fired by warband leaders readily killing each other off. Clovis, in particular, seems to have enjoyed the merry crack of axe on skull, and individual feuding was certainly rampant. On the other hand, although killing each other had always been popular with Germanic warband leaders, this had never before produced such major realignments in their society. Just as important as the leaders' individual ambitions, therefore, were the attitudes of the warriors witnessing the spectacle. Gregory of Tours' account of Clovis' unification of the Franks emphasizes that, with pretty much every assassination, the dead leader's followers declared themselves ready to ally with Clovis. And they did, of course, have a real choice. This applies equally to all the other unifications. The Visigoths were created not only by Alaric's ambition, but also by the willingness of most of the Tervingi and the Greuthungi, plus the defeated followers of Radagaisus, to attach themselves to his standard. The Vandal coalition, as we saw, came into existence when the Siling Vandals and the Alans decided to throw in their lot with the Hasdings and the Ostrogoths on the back of positive responses to the individual successes, over two generations, of Valamer and Theoderic. In some of these cases, we know of a few individuals who decided not to join the new alliances. Rather than focusing just on the leadership struggles, then, we need to think about the choices being made by the Germanic freemen, whose decisions turned the usual leadership rivalries into a process of political unification.[27]

We know from the available information that the Roman Empire played a critical role in this process on two levels. First, as the pre-eminent military power of the age, over the centuries it had developed tried and trusted methods for undermining the independence even of immigrants it welcomed. Faced with such power combined with the Empire's self-image as a society superior to all others, many of the immigrants newly arrived within the Empire became immediately aware of very good reasons, whatever their past divisions, to join forces. The Tervingi and Greuthungi were already cooperating as early as the summer of 376, when Valens tried to divide and rule them by allowing only the Tervingi into the Empire. Those in Radagaisus' following who were sold into slavery immediately after his defeat, or saw their wives and children massacred in Italian cities after the assassination of Stilicho, were quick to grasp the logic of attaching themselves to Alaric's following. And it was after major defeats that the Siling Vandals and Alans joined the Hasding Vandals, precisely to resist more effectively the campaigns being mounted against them by Constantius. The creation of the Ostrogoths, likewise, was marked by a thrilling moment in the summer of 478 when the emperor Zeno tried to make Theoderic the Amal fight the Thracian Goths. The emperor pretended that he would lend him a substantial force to help him defeat his rivals, while actually wanting the two Gothic forces to do each other serious damage, before sending in an imperial army to mop up. In the event, despite the two groups' leaders being at loggerheads, the rank and file refused to fight, well aware of the path to mutual destruction that Zeno had mapped out for them.[28]

Second, the Roman Empire operated a powerful redistributive tax machinery. This fact was exploited by Goths and others who made the Empire – more and less willingly – recognize them as allies, or picked off pieces of it in the form of revenue-generating city territories, to secure a level of income that was not available outside the Empire. For all its economic advances, the Germanic world of the fourth century remained relatively unproductive compared with the Empire. As we saw in Chapter 7, gold only appears in any abundance in Germanic burials from the time of Attila, who had exacted it in unprecedented amounts from the Roman state. For the adventurous, the Roman Empire, while being a threat to their existence, also presented an unprecedented opportunity to prosper. When it came to exacting riches by force, alien groups who could mobilize large armed forces again stood a better chance of achieving their aim. The precise admixture of fear and anticipated profit varied, but one way or another, a heady cocktail of the two fired all these migrants towards unification. There is a very real sense in which, once the Huns had pushed large numbers of them across the frontier, the Roman state became its own worst enemy. Its military power and financial sophistication both hastened the process whereby streams of incomers became coherent forces capable of carving out kingdoms from its own body politic.

This argument also, I think, can be taken one step further. If the Huns had arrived in the first century AD instead of the fourth, and had pushed Germanic groups of the kind that then existed across the Roman frontier, the result would have been very different. Because of the smaller size of their political units in the first century, too many of them would have had to be involved in too complicated a process of realignment to make the creation of large alliances at all likely. The three or four, maybe half a dozen, units that made up each fifth-century supergroup provided enough manpower to create a military force of 20–30,000 warriors – probably the minimum for long-term survival. To get that many Germanic warriors pointing in the same direction in the first century, you would have had to unite perhaps up to a dozen rival units, and the political problem involved would have been huge. This, I would argue, is why the Sarmatian movements in the first century created so much less of an impact than the Huns' did 300 years later.

The transformations separating fourth- from first-century Germanic society are thus a crucial factor in the story of western collapse. But what caused them? Why and how did this society change so radically?

Of the internal dynamics operating within Germanic society in these centuries, the sources – all Roman, of course – give no more than a hint. Tacitus in the first century and Ammianus Marcellinus in the fourth both mention violent struggles taking place between different groups of Germani, with no Roman involvement, and there is no reason to think this exceptional. Be that as it may, to my mind the key is the relations between Germania and the Roman Empire, on many levels, some of which we have touched on. With no judgement implied on their relative merits – let's not forget that the Roman Empire had central heating, but saw nothing amiss in feeding human beings to wild animals for the pleasure of the multitude – the Germanic world can be said to have been a relatively simple society located at the edge of a more complex one. The close geographical proximity of such disparate entities was bound to promote precisely the kind of changes that we have observed in the Germanic world.

The most obvious relationship, and one that has attracted plenty of attention from archaeologists, was economic, and the evidence for substantial economic exchange between Germanic societies and the Roman Empire is impressive. High-quality items of Roman manufacture became early on in the period a feature of rich burials in the far Germanic world beyond the frontier zone. Within the frontier zone, about two hundred kilometres wide, more ordinary Roman products were part and parcel of everyday life. In return, the written evidence suggests, the Roman Empire consumed large quantities of raw materials from across the frontier. At one point in the fourth century the emperor Julian used punitive diplomatic treaties to extract from various Alamannic groups wood, foodstuffs and manpower (both slaves and recruits for his army), on other occasions, such goods and services were paid for. Roman frontier garrisons had for centuries served as centres of demand for nearby German economies. The perishable exports produced by the Germanic world are not archaeologically visible, but they certainly generated enough wealth to matter. A major slave trade, for instance, operated out of Germania. As early as the first century AD, Rome's neighbours on the Rhine were using Roman silver coins as means of exchange, and even when 300 years later relations between the Empire and the Tervingi were more distant, trading stations remained open. We know, too, that it was common for individuals from beyond the frontier to sign up with the Roman army and then return home with their retirement bonuses.[29]

The Germanic world at the time of Christ operated largely as a subsistence economy. The effect of the subsequent four hundred years of trading was broadly twofold. First, wealth in new forms and unprecedented quantities entered Germania from across the Roman frontier. Economic ties with Rome offered unheard-of profits for everyone from slave-traders to agriculturalists selling foodstuffs to Roman garrison troops. For the first time, consequently, there was enough money around to generate real differences in wealth. Second – and more important than the mere fact of wealth – the new economic exchanges led to sociopolitical change, as particular groups jostled for control of the new riches flowing across the frontier. In AD 50, King Vannius of the Marcomanni, whose kingdom was situated beside the Danube in what is now the Czech Republic, was driven out by an enterprising group of adventurers from central and northern Poland. As Tacitus tells us,[30] they came south to claim a share in the trade-generated wealth he had amassed in the course of a thirty-year reign. Just as with the Mafia and Prohibition, a new flow of wealth was there to be fought over, until arguments were settled and all parties accepted that the current distribution of percentages reflected the prevailing balance of power. We generally hear nothing, of course, about the organization of trade links and who was gaining what, from Germania, because no one there was literate. In recent years, however, Polish archaeologists investigating the northern reaches of the Amber Route, which during the Roman period brought this semi-precious stone from the shores of the Baltic to Mediterranean workshops, have uncovered a series of causeways and bridges. Carbon and tree-ring dates identify these as of the early centuries AD, and show that they were maintained for over 200 years. Someone in northern Poland was making enough money on their percentage of the amber trade, therefore, to go to a great deal of trouble. It's also a pretty fair guess that most of the money was not being made by those who were cutting down trees and sinking logs into bogs. Organizing and controlling trade exchanges led naturally to greater social differentiation, as particular groups in Germanic society tried to grab the profits.[31]

Military and diplomatic relations pushed Germanic society in the same direction. For the first twenty years of the first century AD Rome's legions attempted to conquer its new eastern and northern neighbours. The Empire's attitude at this point was straightforwardly predatory, the Germani responding as you might expect. The first significant political coalition we know about in the Rhine region was put together by Arminius to fight off Roman intrusion. It achieved one great victory over Varus' legions, but then failed to hold together. As we saw in Chapter 2, over the next three centuries Roman policy towards those of its Germanic neighbours living within a hundred kilometres or so of the frontier involved punitive campaigns, perhaps one every generation, which formed the basis for interim peace settlements. In other words, four times a century the Roman legions invaded this hinterland, destroying everything and everyone that did not submit to them. Hardly surprising, then, if we find there a current of resistance. For a start, the Gothic Tervingi did not want to take on board the Christian religion of the emperor Constantius II, and for three years under Athanaric fought a successful holding action to avoid providing military contingents for Rome's wars against Persia. There is every reason to suppose that the desire to fend off the worst excesses of Roman imperialism had a lot to do with the evolution of the larger social structures that characterized the fourth century, which in turn made the new barbarian coalitions which formed in the fifth century on Roman soil possible.

Not, of course, that the violence was all one-sided. Rich pickings were available to those who could organize successful raids across the border (the frontier provinces were even quicker to develop economically than their Germanic neighbours). This provided yet another stimulus to political amalgamation since, generally speaking, the larger the group doing the raiding, the greater its chances of success. And border raiding was endemic, as we know, to Romano-German relations throughout the imperial period. Of the twenty-four years (354–78) covered by Ammianus Marcellinus, the Rhine frontier was disturbed by the Alamanni during no fewer than fourteen of them. Nor, I think, is it an accident that Alamannic over-kings of the fourth century, like Chnodomarius whom the emperor Julian defeated at Strasbourg in 357, tended to go in for predatory warfare across the frontier. The prestige and wealth gained from this kind of activity were part and parcel of sustaining their position. Whether with a view to fighting off Roman aggression, therefore, or to profiting from Roman wealth, coalition was the likely route to success. The internal adjustments set in motion by both the positive and the negative aspects of the Romano-German relationship pushed Germanic society towards larger size and greater cohesion. Whether the new coalitions that appeared in west Germania in the early third century were motivated primarily by fear or by the anticipation of profit, it is evident the power and wealth of the Roman Empire were in everyone's sights.

Once these more powerful coalitions had come into existence, Roman diplomatic practice tended to further the process. A tried and trusted tactic was to alight on a leader who was willing to help keep the peace, then seek to promote his hold over his subjects by targeted foreign aid, combined, very often, with trading privileges. Annual gifts were a feature of Roman foreign policy from the early centuries AD. But there was always some ambiguity in these relationships; favoured kings had to respond to the demands of their own followers, as well as those of their new imperial sponsors. More than one king of the Alamanni found himself forced by his followers to join in Chnodomarius' rebellion or face demotion.[32] Inevitably, leaders who could attract Roman largesse were likely to attract the largest number of followers.

Roman weaponry also played its part. It is unclear how the arms trade was carried on, but more Roman weapons have been found in Danish bog deposits than anywhere else in Europe.[33] The conclusion can only be that this particular type of Roman hardware was used in local conflict well beyond the frontier. Having gained control of new sources of wealth and success in organized raids, having received legitimation and other support from the Empire and having acquired decent Roman weaponry, the emergent Germanic dynast was now in a position to extend his power by less peaceful means than hitherto. His energies were partly directed towards Rome, but that fierce inter-Germanic rivalry must also have played its part in building up the larger power blocks in the Germanic world. Ammianus mentions that Burgundians were willing to be paid to attack Alamanni for a price, for instance, and that one pre-eminent king of the Alamanni, Macrianus, met his end in Frankish territory when a bout of local expansionary warfare went wrong.[34] Over the centuries, there must have been a myriad such wars. We should think of the Roman Empire, then, as having a host of unanticipated effects on the other side of the frontier, as local societies reacted in their own fashion to the dangers and opportunities thrown up by its overwhelming presence. When the amalgamation of groups and subgroups that had been going on for so long beyond Rome's borders interacted with the exogenous shock that was the arrival of the Huns, the supergroups that would tear the western Empire apart came into being.

There is, I suspect, an inbuilt tendency for the kind of dominance exercised by empires to generate an inverse reaction whereby the dominated, in the end, are able to throw off their chains.[35] The Roman Empire had sown the seeds of its own destruction, therefore, not because of internal weaknesses that had evolved over the centuries, nor because of new ones evolved, but as a consequence of its relationship with the Germanic world. Just as the Sasanians were able to reorganize Near Eastern society so as to throw off Roman domination, Germanic society achieved the same in the west, when its collision with Hunnic power precipitated the process much more quickly than would otherwise have been the case. The west Roman state fell not because of the weight of its own 'stupendous fabric', but because its Germanic neighbours had responded to its power in ways that the Romans could never have foreseen. There is in all this a pleasing denouement. By virtue of its unbounded aggression, Roman imperialism was ultimately responsible for its own destruction.

DRAMATIS PERSONAE

Aegidius – Commanding general of the Roman forces in Gaul under the emperor Majorian in the early 460s. Revolted on his murder, at which point Aegidius's command became the basis of an independent fiefdom on and behind the Rhine frontier, which preserved its independence until it was conquered by the Frankish king Clovis in the mid 480s.

Aetius – Commanding general, Patrician, and eminence grise in control of the western Empire between 433 and his assassination by Valentinian III in 454. Saw the need to draw on outside, Hunnic, power to control the immigrant groups who had forced their way into the western Empire in the period 405–8. Enjoyed considerable short-term military success, but his strategy was undermined by Attila's aggression in the 440s and his political position by the collapse of the Hunnic Empire subsequent to Attila's death.

Akatziri – Nomadic group occupying land north of the Black Sea and brought under Attila's hegemony in the later 440s. Their political structure consisted of a series of ranked kings and was probably similar to that of the Huns prior to the revolution which produced the dynasty of Rua and Attila.

Alamanni – Confederation of Germanic-speaking groups occupying land opposite the upper Rhine frontier region of the Roman Empire in the fourth century. Several kings always ruled simultaneously among them, each with their own cantons, and passed on their power by hereditary succession, but each political generation also threw up a non-hereditary, pre-eminent over-king.

Alans – Collective name for groups of Iranian-speaking nomads occupying land north of the Black Sea and east of the River Don in the fourth century. In the crisis generated by the Huns, some were quickly conquered and remained part of the Hunnic Empire until after the death of Attila. Others fled west into Roman territory and became part of the western Empire's military establishment. One large group participated in the Rhine crossing of 406, and, after heavy defeats in the late 410s, attached themselves to the Vandal–Alan confederation, which moved to North Africa and seized Carthage in 439.

Alaric – (Visi-)Gothic king (395–411). Leader, in 395, of a revolt of the Gothic Tervingi and Greuthungi who had crossed into the Empire in 376 and made the treaty of 382 with the emperor Theodosius I. Created a new Visigothic supergroup by definitively uniting these groups with a third, the survivors of Radagaisus' attack on Italy in 405/6. Also brought his Goths out of the Balkans and into the west in search of a political accommodation with the Roman state. Died after sacking Rome in 410, but before a lasting settlement was reached.

Alatheus – Leader, along with Saphrax, of the Gothic Greuthungi who crossed the Danube in 376. Disappeared, probably dead, by the time the treaty of 382 was made.

Ammianus Marcellinus – Late Roman historian, the surviving portion of whose work covers the period 354–78. Key source for the workings of the later Roman Empire and the onset of the Hunnic crisis up to the battle of Hadrianople in 378.

Anthemius – East Roman general who dealt with the fallout from the collapse of Attila's empire and then western emperor (467–72). Under his auspices the last attempt to retake North Africa from the Vandals and put new life into the western Empire was launched in 468. When it failed, the last threads of Empire quickly unravelled.

Arcadius – East Roman emperor (395–408). Son of Theodosius I who reigned rather than ruled. Alaric eventually failed to come to an accommodation with those running the eastern Empire on his behalf, and moved on to Italy.

Arminius (Hermann the German) – Chieftain of the Germanic-speaking Cherusci of the northern Rhine frontier region, who organized the temporary confederation which destroyed Varus' Roman army at the battle of the Teutoburg Forest in AD 9. Mistakenly seen as an early German nationalist.

Aspar – East Roman general responsible for putting Valentinian III on the western throne and for forcing Geiseric to make a first treaty with the west Roman state in 437. From 457, he became a considerable power behind the throne in Constantinople after the death of the eastern emperor Marcian.

Athanaric – Leader ('judge') of the Gothic Tervingi occupying land in Moldavia and Wallachia in the mid-fourth century. Successfully fended off the eastern emperor Valens' attempt (367–9) to assert total domination over his territory, negotiating a less burdensome treaty than that imposed by Constantine in 332. Lost the confidence of his followers in 376, when they refused to implement the measures he advised for dealing with the crisis generated by the Huns (*see also* Fritigern).

Athaulf – Visigothic ruler (411–15). Brother-in-law and heir of Alaric. Moved the Visigoths on from Italy to southern Gaul, where he adopted various stratagems, including marriage to Galla Placidia, sister of the western emperor Honorius, to force the Empire into a political settlement advantageous to his Goths. Over-ambitious in his assessment of what he could extract, and hence eventually assassinated when resentment built up at food shortages generated by Roman blockade.

Attalus, Priscus – Roman senator and usurper of the western Empire set up twice by Visigothic leaders: Alaric in Italy in 409/10 and Athaulf in Gaul in 413/14.

Attila – Ruler of the Huns (c.440–53). Inheriting pre-eminent power over the Huns and their subject peoples from his uncle Rua, he at first ruled with his brother Bleda. Responsible for switching the Huns to a policy of outright aggression towards the Roman Empire, launching massive attacks on the east in 441/2 and 447 and on the west in 451 and 452. Eliminated his brother in 445, and received the east Roman embassy which included the historian Priscus in 448/9. Hunnic Empire collapsed after his death (*see* Dengizich).

Augustus – First Roman emperor (27BC–AD14). Granted his title by senatorial decree in 27BC, he was Julius Caesar's heir who, on the latter's murder in 44BC, quickly gathered the reins of power into his hands (between 44 and 27BC he is conventionally known by his own name: Octavian).

Ausonius – Teacher of rhetoric at the university of Bordeaux, who became tutor to the young emperor Gratian in the 360s, and then, particularly under Gratian's rule from 375, rose to political pre-eminence at court. A correspondent of Symmachus and author of the *Mosella*, which was in part an answer to the attitude the latter had adopted to the Rhine frontier region during the period he spent there in 369/70.

Bigelis – Gothic leader of one group of former Hunnic subjects who invaded the east Roman Balkans in the mid-460s as the Hunnic Empire collapsed to extinction.

Bleda – *see* Attila.

Boniface – Commanding general in charge of Roman forces in North Africa at the time of Geiseric's invasion. Mistakenly accused in later sources of inviting the Vandals across the Mediterranean from Spain. He competed also with Aetius for control of the young western emperor Valentinian III after 425. Killed in battle against Aetius in Italy in 433.

Burgundians – Germanic-speaking group occupying lands east of the Alamanni in the fourth century. In the aftermath of the Rhine crossing of 406, moved west into territories right on the Rhine around Mainz, Speyer and Worms (by 411). Mauled by the Huns, on Aetius' orders, in the mid-430s and immediately resettled around lake Geneva. After the death of Aetius, they expanded the region under their control south into the Rhone valley, creating one of the successor kingdoms to the western Roman Empire. A second-rank power compared with the Visigoths, Franks and Ostrogoths.

Carpi – Dacian-speaking group beyond Roman control occupying land around the Carpathian Mountains in the third century. Many displaced into the Roman Empire and others conquered by the rise of Gothic power in the region in the later third and early fourth centuries.

Cassiodorus – Roman senator and highly ranked administrator of Ostrogothic kings of Italy between 522/3 and 540. Wrote a Gothic history, which is indirectly our major source on the collapse of the Hunnic Empire (*see also* Jordanes).

Celti, Celts – Collective name for a series of groups speaking related languages who in the last centuries BC dominated northern Italy, Gaul and the British Isles, together with much of the Iberian Peninsula and central Europe. Many were incorporated into the expanding Roman Empire, not least because the relatively developed economy of such groups offered a reasonable return on the costs of conquest.

Childeric – Leader of one group of Salian Franks as the western Empire unravelled to extinction. Operated west of the Rhine as well as in traditional Frankish territories east of the river and, by his death in 482, was in control of the old Roman province of Belgica II centred on Tournai. Possibly pre-eminent over other Frankish leaders, but Frankish unification was really achieved by his son (*see* Clovis).

Chnodomarius – Pre-eminent over-king of the Alamanni in the 350s, with a personal retinue of 300 warriors. His power was extinguished in the defeat he suffered at the hands of the emperor Julian at the battle of Strasbourg in 357.

Clovis – King of the Salian Franks (482–511). Created the Frankish kingdom in the aftermath of Roman collapse. At his death, it covered all of what is now France except its Mediterranean coast, together with Belgium and substantial territories east of the Rhine. The new kingdom was created by victories over the remnants of the Roman army of the Rhine (*see* Aegidius), Bretons, Alamanni, Thuringians and Visigoths, and by a process of centralization which saw Clovis eliminate a series of other Frankish warband leaders, uniting their followers in each case to his own.

Constantine I – Roman emperor (306–37). Emerged victorious from the wars which destroyed the Tetrarchy (*see* Diocletian) to rule the entire Empire from 324, though he shared power with his sons. Pacified the Rhine and Danube frontier regions, imposed considerable Roman domination on groups such as the Tervingi (*see* Athanaric). Brought to completion many of the military and administrative reforms which allowed the Empire to cope with the rise of Persia to superpower status, and started the process which saw Christianity become a key cultural component of the late Roman world.

Constantine III – Usurper (406–11), who quickly spread his power from Britain throughout Gaul and even into the fringes of Spain and Italy. Attracted support by offering a coherent response to the Rhine invaders of 406, and even threatened to supplant the emperor Honorius, before falling victim to the imperial recovery generated by Flavius Constantius.

Constantine VII Porphyryogenitus – Byzantine emperor (911–57). A figure-head who used his spare time to bring to fruition a project to save Byzantium's classical heritage by excerpting, in over fifty volumes, the works of ancient authors under a variety of headings. Few survive, but his *Excerpts concerning Embassies* took many extracts from the history of Priscus; these are crucial to our knowledge of Attila and the Huns.

Constantius II – Roman emperor (337–61). Considered by Ammianus Marcellinus the perfect ceremonial emperor, he struggled to find ways to share power even though his reign showed that one man could not deal with everything from the Rhine to Mesopotamia. Moved Christianization substantially forward.

Constantius, Flavius – West Roman general who reconstructed the western Empire in the chaos generated by the crisis of 405–8. Defeated usurpers in 411 and 413, brought the Visigoths to heel (by 416), and then campaigned effectively with them against the Rhine invaders in Spain (416–18). Made himself dominant at court, marrying Galla Placidia, sister of the emperor Honorius. Briefly emperor himself in 421, he died the same year without winning recognition from Constantinople.

Dengizich – Son of Attila and ruler of part of the Huns between 453 and his own death in 469. Presided over the collapse of his father's empire as the subject peoples threw off Hunnic domination, and eventually tried to carve out a new fiefdom for himself south of the Danube on east Roman soil. He was defeated and killed.

Diocletian – Roman emperor (285–307). Responsible for many of the reforms, especially financial, which allowed the Empire to sustain the larger army it required to reassert parity against Sasanian Persia. Also experimented with a power-sharing arrangement of two senior and two junior emperors: the Tetrarchy. This worked in his own lifetime but generated nearly 20 years of civil war afterwards.

Edeco – Leading henchman of Attila, who reinvented himself to become king of the Sciri when the latter reasserted their independence after the Hun's death. He became king through marriage and was either of Thuringian or Hunnic ancestry (or both). He was killed when the Ostrogoths destroyed Scirian independence in the 460s. Earlier, and unknown to Priscus in whose company he travelled home, the east Romans had attempted to suborn him, while on an embassy to Constantinople, to assassinate Attila.

Ellac – Son of Attila and ruler of part of the Huns after his father's death in 453, he was killed at the battle of the Nedao (454?), after which his father's largely Germanic subject peoples started to reassert their independence.

Eudocia – Elder daughter of the emperor Valentinian III. Betrothed to Huneric, eldest son of the Vandal king Geiseric, as part of the latter's treaty with Aetius in 442. She was eventually married to him after 455, when she was taken to Carthage on the Vandal sack of Rome.

Eunapius – Late Roman historian of the fourth and early fifth centuries, whose text survives partly in fragments and partly through its re-use by the sixth-century historian Zosimus.

Euric – King of the Visigoths (466–84). He murdered his brother Theoderic II to seize power, adopting the new policy of seeking to establish a Visigothic kingdom entirely independent of any surviving western Roman Empire. After the defeat of the 468 Vandal expedition, he launched wide-ranging campaigns which, by 476, had extended his realm as far as the Loire and Arles, in Gaul, and to the southern coast of the Iberian peninsula.

Franks – Collective name for Germanic-speaking groups occupying land opposite the lower Rhine frontier region of the Roman Empire in the fourth century. Clearly composed of several smaller groups, some of whom (such as the Bructeri) seem to have had a continuous history running back to the first century. The Franks figure little in the history of Ammianus, so it is unclear whether they had a confederative political structure like the contemporary Alamanni. Real political unity was generated among them only in the late fifth century after the collapse of the Roman Empire (*see* Clovis).

Fritigern – Ruler of those Tervingi who came to the Danube in 376 requesting asylum from the Huns within the Roman Empire. Later tried to win recognition as ruler of all the Goths – Tervingi and Greuthungi – who had entered the Empire in 376, but, although victorious at Hadrianople, did not survive the war to participate in the peacemaking of 382.

Galla Placidia – Sister of the emperor Honorius, she was captured by Alaric in the Gothic sack of Rome in 410. She later married Alaric's successor Athaulf, the marriage being part of his strategy for inserting himself (and his Gothic followers) into the heart of the Empire. She was eventually returned to her brother after her husband's and a son's deaths, marrying Flavius Constantius in turn. After his death, her energies focused on safeguarding the interests of their son, Valentinian III. She played a key role in persuading Theodosius II to put the young Valentinian on the western throne in 425 and then attempted to balance the influence at court of her competing generals. This eventually failed when Aetius made himself pre-eminent in the west from 433.

Geiseric – King of the Vandal–Alan coalition (428–79). Came to power in Spain, but quickly decided that North Africa offered his followers greater security. Crossing to Tangier in May 429, he led his followers west. After much fighting, a first treaty settled them in Mauretania and Numidia in 437. In September 439, he stormed Carthage and eventually extracted recognition of his conquest of the richest North African provinces in a second treaty of 442. Sacked Rome in 455 after the usurpation of Petronius Maximus threatened the proposed marriage between his son Huneric and Eudocia. Survived two major expeditions to reconquer his kingdom for the western Empire in 461 and 468, and able subsequently to negotiate a definitive peace settlement with Constantinople in 473.

Gepids – Germanic-speaking subject people of Attila's Hunnic empire. Initiated by their revolt and victory at the battle of the Nedao the process which led to Hunnic collapse. Emerged from the wars of the 450s and 460s with a kingdom in Transylvania and the eastern, especially north-eastern part of the Great Hungarian Plain.

Germani – Collective name for a series of groups speaking related languages who in the last centuries BC dominated much of north-central Europe between the Rhine and the Vistula, and the Carpathians and the Baltic. Largely not incorporated into the expanding Roman Empire around the birth of Christ because of the relatively undeveloped economy prevalent among them. First four centuries AD saw profound transformations in their socio-economic and political structures, together with a massive expansion in population numbers.

Goths – Germanic-speaking group first encountered in northern Poland in the first century AD. In the later second and third centuries, any original political unity fragmented, and Goths in a number of separate groups were involved in migratory activity towards the north Black Sea region (modern Ukraine and Moldavia). There, they built a number of new kingdoms (see Tervingi *and* Greuthungi), which were themselves destroyed in the turmoil generated by the rise of Hunnic power at the end of the fourth century. Various previously separate Gothic groups then came together to create two new and much larger supergroups in the fifth century (see Ostrogoths *and* Visigoths).

Gratian – West Roman emperor (375–83). Son of the emperor Valentinian I, he became responsible for the overall direction of the campaign against the Goths after the death of his uncle Valens at Hadrianople in 378. This included raising Theodosius I to the purple, and subduing the Goths after the latter's defeat in the summer of 380.

Gregory, bishop of Tours – Late-sixth-century historian of the Frankish kingdom. His work contains unique information about the reign of Clovis and important extracts from the lost work of a fifth-century Roman historian, Renatus Frigiderus, who was well informed about the era of Aetius.

Greuthungi – Either (in my view more likely) a collective name for a series of independent Gothic kingdoms established in what is now the Ukraine, east of the river Dniester, before 375, or the name of one huge Gothic Empire stretching from the Dniester to the Don which fragmented in the face of Hunnic aggression. One group of Greuthungi came to the Danube in 376 under the leadership of Alatheus and Saphrax. They participated in the battle of Hadrianople and probably also in the peace treaty of 382. Eventually they formed part of Alaric's new Gothic supergroup, the Visigoths. A further group of Greuthungi came to the Danube in 386, but were heavily defeated, the survivors being resettled in Asia Minor. It is unclear whether or not both these groups of Greuthungi had formed part of the same political unit before the arrival of the Huns.

Gundobad – King of the Burgundians (473/4–516). Pursued a Roman military career under Ricimer in Italy, before returning to the Rhone valley to claim a share (along with three brothers) of the emerging Burgundian successor kingdom as the western Empire finally unravelled.

Hasding Vandals – One of two Vandal groups who, to escape the insecurity generated in central Europe by the rise of Hunnic power, forced their way over the Rhine at the end of 406. The ruling Hasding dynasty then provided leadership for a new coalition comprising these Vandals and survivors of the Siling Vandals and Alans mauled by Visigothic–Roman forces in Spain between 416 and 418. Before the Hunnic crisis they had inhabited territories north of the Carpathian mountains, but had moved to the Upper Danube region opposite Roman possessions in Raetia (modern Switzerland) by 402.

Heraclianus – General commanding Roman forces in North Africa in c.410. Opponent of Stilicho, but loyal to Honorius. Provided funds to sustain the emperor in his darkest hours, then invaded Italy in 413, either to seize imperial power himself or to check the growing influence of Flavius Constantius. Defeated, and then assassinated on his return to Carthage.

Hernac – Son of Attila and ruler of part of the Huns after 453. Presided over the collapse of his father's empire as the subject peoples threw off Hunnic domination, and eventually tried to obtain a new fiefdom for himself south of the Danube on east-Roman soil. Unlike his brother Dengizich, he eventually came to terms and he and his followers were settled in the Dobrudja.

Heruli – Germanic-speaking group originally from north central Europe, some of whom migrated to regions north of the Black Sea in company with Goths and others in the third century. They became Hunnic subjects and moved west of the Carpathians to the Great Hungarian Plain under Attila's auspices. Re-established an independent kingdom in the wars of the 450s and 460s.

Honoria, Iulia Grata – Daughter of Galla Placidia and Flavius Constantius. Famous for offering herself in marriage to Attila the Hun as an escape route from a messy affair.

Honorius – Western Roman emperor (395–423). Came to the throne as a six-year-old boy and never managed to grasp the reins of power personally. His reign was dominated by two strong men – Stilicho (395–408) and Flavius Constantius (411–21) – whose eras were interspersed with and followed by some very bloody manoeuvring at court. The great crisis of 405–8 unfolded in his reign and generated a series of usurpations, notably that of Constantine III, which in c.409/10 threatened to overthrow him entirely. He had no children.

Huneric – Son of Geiseric and king of the Vandal–Alan coalition (474–84). Betrothed to Valentinian's daughter Eudocia under the treaty of 442, he lived as a hostage at Valentinian's court for a period in the 440s.

Huns – Nomadic steppe group, whose linguistic and cultural affiliations remain unclear. Power grew from c.350 in the region north-east of the Black Sea, generating an initial crisis in the largely Gothic-dominated world of the Ukraine in 375/6. Most Huns remained north of the Black Sea, however, until c.410 when they shifted westwards again to the Great Hungarian Plain. Here they built an Empire: first, on the basis of conquering subject groups, second, on extracting and recycling wealth from the Roman world and, third, by centralizing the workings of political power among themselves. After the death of Attila in 453, the process went into reverse and independent Hunnic power was extinguished within twenty years as subject peoples reasserted their independence.

Hydatius – Spanish bishop and chronicler. Our main source for events in the peninsula from the arrival of the Rhine invaders down to the 460s.

Jordanes – Historian of the Goths working in Constantinople in c.550. Claims to have followed closely the lost Gothic history of Cassiodorus, which I broadly believe but which has generated great historiographical argument. Main historical value lies in his account of events in Attila's time and afterwards, for some of which he drew on the history of Priscus.

Jovian – Roman emperor (363–4). Succeeded Julian and forced to surrender large tracts of strategic territory to rescue Julian's trapped army. Died of carbon monoxide poisoning.

Jovinus – Usurper in Gaul (411–13). Regime generated in the Rhine region originally with Burgundian and Visigothic support. Fatally undermined when Flavius Constantius attracted away the Visigoths.

Julian – Roman emperor (355–63), at first subordinate Caesar to the Augustus, his cousin Constantius II, then sole Augustus from 361. Highly successful at the battle of Strasbourg and afterwards in reining in the power of the Alamannic confederation under Chnodomarius. Declared his previously hidden pagan affiliations on seizing power, then launched a massive invasion of Persia which ended with his own death and strategic defeat (*see* Jovian).

Justinian I – East Roman emperor (527–68). Famous for launching wars of conquest in the western Mediterranean which destroyed the Vandal and Ostrogothic kingdoms in North Africa and Italy respectively, and seized a stretch of territory along the southern Hispanic coastline. Constructed many buildings, notably the church of Hagia Sophia which still stands in Istanbul.

Leo I – East Roman emperor (457–74). Tried to sustain the western Empire by identifying plausible regimes in the chaos which followed the murders of Aetius and Valentinian III, and above all by negotiating with Ricimer on behalf of Anthemius and providing a huge armada for the expedition against the Vandals of 468.

Libanius – Greek Rhetor established at Antioch, and associate of Themistius. His huge letter collection provides great insight into the values and inner workings of the late Roman elite.

Libius Severus – Italian senator and western emperor (462–6). Puppet eventually installed by Ricimer after his execution of Majorian. Never recognized in Constantinople and died at a suspiciously convenient moment allowing the negotiations which brought Anthemius to the west.

Lombards – Germanic-speaking group of the Middle Elbe region. May have acknowledged the power of Attila in his pomp, but did not form part of the Huns' core of conquered subject peoples.

Macrianus – Pre-eminent over-king of the Alamanni in the late 360s and early 370s. Valentinian I tried to eliminate him but eventually legitimized his position in 374, when he needed to be absent from the Rhine to deal with trouble in the Middle Danube region.

Majorian – West Roman emperor (458–61). Commander, with Ricimer, of the Roman army of Italy after the death of Aetius. Helped destroy the regime of Avitus in 457 and then, after an interregnum, was elected emperor. Eventually recognized in Constantinople, Majorian pulled much of the surviving western Empire back together and, anticipating Anthemius' strategy, tried to revive it by reconquering North Africa from the Vandal–Alan coalition. When the expedition failed, Ricimer removed and executed him.

Marcellinus, count – Commander of (west) Roman field forces in Illyricum from the mid-450s, effectively just Dalmatia since Pannonia to the north had been annexed by the Huns. Originally appointed by Majorian, he switched his allegiance to Constantinople on the latter's execution. Later backed the regime of Anthemius and provided forces for the 468 expedition to North Africa. He was assassinated in Sicily in the aftermath of its failure, but his fiefdom passed to his nephew Julius Nepos.

Marcian – East Roman emperor (450–7). High-ranking soldier who came to power after the death of Theodosius II by marrying Theodosius' sister Pulcheria. Provided substantial assistance to Aetius in 451 as he tried to fend off Attila's attack on Italy.

Merobaudes – Poet and soldier of the mid-fifth century. Born in Spain and classically educated, though descended from a Frank who had risen through the ranks in the late-fourth century to become a Roman general. A close associate of Aetius, the surviving fragments of his poetry offer valuable insight into the policies and self-presentation of the regime of Aetius, for whom Merobaudes worked as a spin-doctor as well as an active soldier.

Nepos, Julius – West Roman emperor (474–5). Nephew and successor of count Marcellinus, his power was likewise based on the surviving Roman armed forces of Dalmatia. Briefly west Roman emperor, he was driven out by Orestes. Returned to Dalmatia where he was eventually assassinated in 480.

Octavian – *see* Augustus.

Odovacar – 'King' in Italy (476–93). Son of Attila's henchman Edeco, he was a prince of the Sciri forced into exile after the Ostrogoths destroyed his father's Middle Danubian kingdom in the wars which followed the death of Attila. Eventually came to Italy, where he organized a coup d'etat using the last Roman army of Italy, itself substantially composed of refugees from the post-Attilan conflicts. He won their support by distributing landed assets to them in lieu of back pay. Deposed but didn't kill the last western emperor, Romulus, and reigned as 'king' afterwards, formally acknowledging the sovereignty of the eastern emperor in Constantinople. Eventually deposed and killed himself by Theoderic the Amal.

Olympiodorus of Thebes – East Roman historian and diplomat of the early-fifth century. Photius preserves only a brief summary of his work, but Zosimus copied out large portions of it dealing with events from c.405–10. A well-informed and intelligent contemporary, Olympiodorus is the source of most of what we know of the diplomatic and military tangles which generated Alaric's sack of Rome in 410.

Olympius – Senior western politician who organized the coup d'etat which ousted Stilicho in 408. Advocated a policy of hostility towards Alaric, but lacked the military power to make it work. Ousted himself when his policies failed, he was eventually clubbed to death in the emperor Honorius' presence.

Onegesius – Most senior of the notables at the court of Attila the Hun, whose good offices the east Roman embassy, which included Priscus, was ostensibly seeking to use to secure their ends.

Orestes – Originally a Pannonian landowner, he was employed by Attila the Hun as an ambassador to Constantinople. After the collapse of the Hunnic Empire he made his way to Italy, becoming, with his brother Paul, highly influential after the death of Ricimer and return to Burgundy of Gundobad. They organized the opposition which led Nepos to retreat to Dalmatia in 475 and proclaimed Orestes' son Romulus emperor. Both were executed by Odovacar in late summer 476.

Ostrogoths – A second Gothic supergroup created in the fifth century around the Amal dynasty, particularly the persons of Valamer and his nephew Theoderic the Amal. Valamer united a series of independent Gothic warbands probably after Attila's death in the 450s; his nephew added to this initial powerbase (probably itself numbering c.10,000 warriors), another force of similar size in the Roman Balkans in c.484. It was this combined force Theoderic led to Italy in 489, and which had put him in power there by 493. Like the Visigoths, it has been traditional to suppose that the Ostrogoths – equated with the fourth-century Greuthungi – already existed as a political unit before the arrival of the Huns north of the Black Sea in the fourth century, but this is mistaken.

Petronius Maximus – Italian senator and usurper (455). Prompted Valentinian III to assassinate Aetius in 454 and then plotted to kill the emperor and seize the purple. Killed in Vandal sack of Rome.

Photius – Ninth-century Byzantine bibliophile and (briefly) Patriarch of Constantinople. His extensive description of his massive library (the *Bibliotheca*) is an important source of information about many of the texts on which our knowledge of the late-Roman world is based.

Priscus – East Roman historian of the mid-fifth century. Famous for his account of an embassy to Attila the Hun, most of which survives in the *Excerpta* of Constantine VII Porphyryogenitus, and source of much of what we know about mid-fifth-century events.

Quadi – Germanic-speaking tribe occupying land on the north-western fringes of the Great Hungarian Plain in the Roman period. Contributed manpower to the Suevi who crossed the Rhine in company with the Vandals and Alans in 406.

Radagaisus – Gothic king. Invaded Italy with a huge force in 405/6. Zosimus' account would suggest that he led an entirely multiracial force, but all the other sources call him a Goth and Zosimus otherwise lacks an account of the thoroughly multiracial Rhine crossing of 406, which suggests that he has confused two separate invasions. Stilicho eventually defeated him, drafting many of his better troops into the Roman army. Radagaisus was executed outside Florence.

Renatus Frigiderus – *see in* Gregory, bishop of Tours.

Ricimer – Patrician and Roman general of mixed, and very grand, barbarian ancestry (he was, among other things, the grandson of the Visigothic king Vallia). Rose to high military command in Italy after Aetius' death, and then to pre-eminent political authority as kingmaker from the early 460s after his execution of Majorian. He has sometimes been accused of adopting policies harmful to the interests of the west Roman state, but, as well as certainly looking after his own interests, he also put his weight behind the regime of Anthemius with its project of reconquering North Africa. Everything suggests he was a later fifth-century version of Stilicho, desperately trying to keep the western Empire afloat in a situation which demanded political compromise with at least some of the new immigrant powers occupying its territories. Died in 473.

Romulus 'Augustulus' – Last Roman emperor of the west (475–6). *See* Orestes *and* Odovacar.

Rua (or Ruga) – Hunnic king of the 420s(?) and the 430s. Probably a key figure in the creation of the new system of centralized monarchical power among the Huns, which replaced an older one of multiple, ranked kings. This had still existed in 411, but had disappeared entirely by c.440, when he passed on power to his nephews Attila and Bleda. Rua also mounted at least one punishing raid on the eastern Empire to extract booty and tribute: monies which may have been what enabled him to centralize authority around himself.

Rugi – Germanic-speaking group to be found in the first century by the shores of the Baltic. Some at least participated in the expansion towards the Black Sea associated with the Goths in the third century. Their descendants were then caught up in the Hunnic Empire which shifted them west to the Middle Danube region. After Attila's death, they re-established an independent kingdom north of the Danube on the fringes of Noricum, where they are encountered in the *Life of Severinus*.

Saphrax – *see* Alatheus.

Sarmatians – Iranian-speaking, originally nomadic group, who conquered territories north of the Black Sea around the birth of Christ. Some stayed east of the Carpathians, others eventually moved west of it to the Great Hungarian Plain where they became long-standing Roman clients into the fourth century, before being conquered in turn by the Huns.

Sarus – Roman general and Gothic noble. Sarus' brother Sergeric organized the coup d'etat which led to the Visigothic king Athaulf's assassination, and then briefly became king before himself being killed. Sarus is found in the service of Stilicho and Honorius either side of 410 AD, and is noted for his implacable hostility to Alaric and his brother-in-law Athaulf. My suspicion is that Sarus, like a number of other Gothic nobles turned Roman generals, was a possible candidate for the leadership of the new Visigothic supergroup whom Alaric defeated, and who subsequently pursued a career in Roman service instead.

Saxons – A collective name for a number of Germanic-speaking groups occupying land to the east of the Franks in the fourth century. Whether the

Saxons had any functioning confederative political identity, like the Alamanni, or whether the collective was merely a term of convenience is unknown.

Sciri – Germanic-speaking group who probably emerged in some way from the Germanic expansion to the Black Sea region associated with the Goths in the third century. At least two separate groups of Sciri were then conquered by the Huns. One formed part of Uldin's following in 408/9, before being settled on Roman soil after his defeat, a second briefly re-established an independent kingdom in the Middle Danube from the wreck of the Hunnic Empire under Edeco, before being destroyed by the Ostrogoths in the 460s. Edeco's son Odovacar and other refugees then fled to still-Roman Italy.

Sergeric – *see* Sarus.

Severinus – Saint in Noricum c.460–80. Mysterious holy man from the east whose *Life*, penned by Eugippius, provides a series of fascinating vignettes of the end of Empire in an out-of-the-way Roman frontier province as its central authorities ran out of cash.

Shapur I – Sasanian ruler of Persia (240–72). Continued the work of his father Ardashir in turning the Near East into a superpower capable of rivalling Roman imperial power. This allowed him to win decisive victories over three Roman emperors, not least Valerian whom he captured and then later had skinned. The Sasanian revolution generated a huge strategic crisis for the Roman state which it took two political generations to overcome (*see* Diocletian).

Sidonius Apollinaris – Gallic landowner, poet and letter writer whose works document the last generation of the western Roman Empire in southern Gaul. His letters show his peers reacting variously to imperial collapse, and his panegyrics for a series of emperors (Avitus, Majorian and Anthemius) give us precious insight into the policies and self-presentation of these regimes.

Siling Vandals – One of two Vandal groups who, to escape the insecurity generated in central Europe by the rise of Hunnic power, forced their way over the Rhine at the end of 406. Before the Hunnic crisis they had inhabited territories north of the Carpathian mountains, but had moved to the Upper Danube region opposite Roman possessions in what is now Switzerland by 402. The Silings suffered heavily in the joint Romano-Visigothic campaigns organized by Flavius Constantius after 416, which led to the capture of their king Fredibald. The survivors threw in their lot with the Hasding dynasty.

Stilicho – General in charge of the western Empire between 395 and 408. The second-generation offspring of a Roman general of Vandal origins, he rose at court in the east and took control of the west on the sudden death of the emperor Theodosius I, ruling in the name of his young son Honorius. He first attempted to unite east and west, but had abandoned that ambition by c.400, after which he had to concentrate on holding on to power in the face of two separate Gothic attacks on Italy: Alaric in 401/2 and Radagaisus in 405/6. He weathered these storms, but could find no answer to the disruption caused by the Rhine crossing of 406 and the usurpations it generated in response in Britain and Gaul (*see* Constantine III). Lost the confidence of Honorius, when Alaric returned to the fringes of Italy in 407/8, and was overthrown by a coup d'etat organized by Olympius. Preferred to accept deposition and death rather than fight for his survival.

Suevi – Collective term for Germanic-speaking groups of north-west corner of the Great Hungarian Plain. Long-standing Roman clients, some participated in the Rhine crossing of 406 and eventually established themselves in north-western Spain. The remainder stayed in their old haunts and were conquered by the Huns, briefly re-establishing their independence in the late 450s. They were composed of a number of smaller entities such as the Quadi who, before 406, do not seem to have functioned as a confederative group. Both those who left, and those who remained, erected more unified political structures in the fifth century.

Symmachus, Quintus Aurelius – Roman senator and author of an extensive collection of extant letters, together with a number of much less well-preserved speeches. His life and writings offer us huge insight into the attitudes and lifestyles of the late Romans of Rome.

Tervingi – Name of the fourth-century Gothic grouping settled closest to Rome's Lower Danube frontier in Moldavia and Wallachia. One of the entities which emerged from third-century Gothic expansion into the Black Sea region, it was a confederation of kings ruled by a 'judge', whose power seems to have been passed by hereditary right through one family. As Roman clients, they sought as best they could to alleviate the terms the Empire imposed upon them (*see* Athanaric). The confederation splintered in the face of Hunnic pressure, and the majority eventually became part of the new Visigothic supergroup (*see* Fritigern *and* Alaric).

Themistius – East Roman philosopher and spin-doctor. Served a succession of east Roman emperors from the mid-350s to the mid-380s. His speeches were designed to sell imperial policy, particularly to the Senate of Constantinople, and contain a huge amount of information illustrating the evolution of policies towards the Goths in the reigns of the emperors Valens and Theodosius I.

Theoderic the Amal – Completed the work of his uncle Valamer, uniting the force of Goths he inherited from him to another of approximately the same size to create the new Ostrogothic supergroup. He led this force to Italy in 489, defeated Odovacar and established himself as king in Italy, reigning there from 493 to 526.

Theoderic I – King of the Visigoths (418–51). Succeeded Vallia; eventually killed in the battle of the Catalaunian Plains against Attila's Hunnic hordes.

Theoderic II – King of the Visigoths (453–66). Sponsored the regime of Avitus, and was generally happy to expand Visigothic interests while supporting the continued existence of a west Roman state. Murdered and supplanted by his brother Euric, who envisaged a Visigothic future independent of any lingering Roman state.

Theodosius I – Roman emperor (379–95). Selected originally by Gratian as a non-dynastic successor for the emperor Valens in the east to take charge of the war against the Goths after Hadrianople. Failed in that charge, but successfully established himself in Constantinople and spread his control over the entire Empire, defeating two would-be western usurpers, Maximus and Eugenius. Used the Goths settled under the treaty of 382 in these wars and spent much of his reign managing the relationship between them and the Roman state. Also associated with the final moves of the Roman state towards Christianization, spawning aggressively anti-pagan legislation and the destruction of temples.

Theodosius II – Roman emperor (408–50). Grandson of Theodosius I, he inherited power from his father Arcadius as a minor and never personally wielded the reins of power. Considerable aid was lent to the west in his reign, particularly to Honorius in c.410, in putting Valentinian III on the throne in 425 and in sending Aspar to Africa in the 430s. His later years were caught up in dealing with the menace of Attila. During his reign *The Theodosian Code* was also brought to completion (438).

Theophanes – Bureaucrat in Egypt in c.320. *The Theophanes Archive* offers huge insight into the cumbersome operations of late-Roman governmental technology.

Thuringians – Germanic-speaking group of the late-Roman period who gave their name to modern German Thuringia. May have come partly under the sway of Attila, and were one of the groups defeated by Clovis as he created the Frankish kingdom.

Treveri – Germanic-speaking group conquered originally by Caesar and source of the revolt which destroyed the force of Cotta in 54 BC. Later followed an archetypal path towards Romanization which saw Treveran grandees turned

Roman citizens competing with each other to endow their new capital city – Trier – with Roman public buildings and to construct Roman-style country residences (villas).

Uldin – Hunnic leader of the first decade of the fifth century. Shadowy figure who built up his power north of the Danube by incorporating subject groups such as the Sciri, while operating as a Roman ally, lending aid to Stilicho in his defeat of Radagaisus. Then invaded east-Roman territory where he suffered total defeat. Its ease suggests that he was not a precursor of Attila in terms of controlling a large body of united Huns; most Huns were still established much further to the east at this point.

Ulfilas – Apostle of the Goths. Born to a community of Roman prisoners among the Gothic Tervingi in the early-fourth century. When Christianity became a factor in Gotho–Roman diplomacy, he was first ordained bishop to, but shortly after expelled from, the territory of the Tervingi. Creating a written form of the Gothic language, he continued to translate the Bible after his expulsion, and played an influential role in Christian doctrinal disputes of the mid-fourth century.

Valamer – Ostrogothic leader. Began the process which generated a second Gothic supergroup, the Ostrogoths, by uniting a series of Gothic warbands who had been incorporated into Attila's Hunnic Empire. This created a powerbase of sufficient size for him to establish an independent Gothic kingdom as that Empire collapsed, and to extract moderate subsidies from the east-Roman state. Killed in the Middle Danubian wars of the 460s, after which his nephew Theoderic the Amal continued to increase the military power of the new group.

Valens – East Roman emperor (364–78). Chosen by his brother Valentinian I, his reign was marked by struggles against usurpers, the Gothic Tervingi under Athanaric and the Persians. Its greatest crisis unfolded in 376 when, under the impact of Hunnic aggression, Gothic Tervingi and Greuthungi came to the Danube. Valens died in battle against them two years later at Hadrianople.

Valentinian I – West Roman emperor (364–75). Received the senatorial embassy led by Symmachus which brought crown gold north to Trier in 369. Also struggled to uncover the truth about complaints of misgovernment in North Africa, involving the city of Lepcis Magna. Famous for being tough on barbarians, and even died of apoplexy brought on by Sarmatian and Quadi ambassadors who didn't show sufficient humility. This didn't stop him from reaching a compromise accommodation with the Alamannic over-king Macrianus, when the situation required it.

Valentinian III – West Roman emperor (425–55). Son of Galla Placidia and Flavius Constantius, he became emperor at the age of six thanks to an east Roman expeditionary force sent by Theodosius II. Remained a largely ceremonial emperor, who never wielded effective power; for most of his reign, this was in the hands of Aetius. Valentinian did rouse himself to assassinate Aetius in 454, when the latter had become disposable thanks to the death of Attila, but even then he did not really run the Empire. He was assassinated himself the next year.

Vallia – Visigothic king (415–18). Power eventually passed to him in the political chaos generated by the defeat of Athaulf's overly ambitious vision of the Visigoths' role in the western Empire. He negotiated the deal with Flavius Constantius, whereby the Visigoths would be settled in Aquitaine in return for fighting with the Romans against the Vandals, Alans and Suevi who had crossed the Rhine in 406 and were now established in Spain. Its full implementation, after his death, was left to the unrelated Theoderic I. Through a daughter, he was the grandfather of Ricimer.

Varus, P. Quinctilius – Roman general and politician. Famous for the total defeat of his army (three legions plus auxiliaries, maybe 20,000 men altogether) at the hands of the coalition created by Arminius in AD 9 at the battle of the Teutoburg Forest. Varus himself committed suicide.

Venantius Fortunatus – Latin poet. Classically trained in Italy, he found great favour among both Frankish and Roman aristocrats at the courts of a series of late-sixth-century Frankish kings in Gaul. His success shows that respect for classical literary values survived in Gaul, even though the classical education system had disappeared.

Visigoths – First of the new Gothic supergroups of the fifth century. Created by Alaric (395) during whose reign was achieved the definitive unification, among others, of the Tervingi and Greuthungi of 376 and the survivors of Radagaisus' attack on Italy (405/6). Under a succession of leaders, the new supergroup was eventually settled in the Garonne valley in Aquitaine in 418, from which core it expanded its power, particularly under Theoderic II and Euric after 450, to evolve from allied settlement to independent kingdom, as the central structures of the west Roman state ran out of tax revenues.

Zeno – East Roman emperor (474–91). An Isaurian general, he rose to power through marriage into the imperial family. Defeated the usurper Basiliscus (474–6) after a long struggle, and presided over the eastern response to the embassies sent by Odovacar which marked the death knell of the western empire. His later years saw Theoderic the Amal unite the new Ostrogothic supergroup on east Roman territory, and he negotiated its departure for Italy in 488/9.

Zosimus – Sixth-century east-Roman historian. Important source for the fourth and early fifth centuries because he made extensive use of the contemporary histories of Eunapius and Olympiodorus.

Timeline

LEADERS*

West Roman Emperors	East Roman Emperors	Non-Romans
Valentinian I (364–75)	Valens (364–78)	Athanaric, *iudex* of the Gothic Tervingi (c. 360–75, d. c. 381)
Gratian (375–83)	Theodosius I (379–95)	
Maximus (383–8)		
Valentinian II (383–92)		
Eugenius (392–4)		
Honorius (395–423)	Arcadius (395–408)	Alaric, creator and leader of the Visigoths (c. 395–411)
Constantine III (c. 406–11)	Theodosius II (408–50)	
Flavius Constantius (421)		
John (423–5)		
Valentinian III (425–55)		Geiseric, leader of the Vandal-Alan coalition (427–77)
Petronius Maximus (455)	Marcian (451–7)	Attila the Hun (c. 440–53)
Avitus (455–6)		
Majorian (457–61)	Leo I (457–74)	Valamer, leader of the Pannonian Goths (c. 455–67)
Libius Severus (461–5)		

* Italics = usurpers (emperors unrecognized in the other half of the Empire). Some minor western usurpers who never extended their power beyond one immediate locality are not included.

Anthemius (467–72)   Euric, creator of the
                                                            Visigothic kingdom
                                                            (467–83)

Olybrius (472)   Zeno (473–91)   Gundobad, king of the
                                                            Burgundians (474–?)

Glycerius (473–4)   *Basiliscus (474–6)*
Julius Nepos (474–5)

                                                            Theoderic, leader and
                                                            creator of the
                                                            Ostrogoths (474–526)

Romulus Augustulus   Odovacar, king in Italy
(475–6)   (476–93)

EVENTS

c.350   Hunnic attacks on Alans east of River Don and Gothic
         Greuthungi west of Don destabilize area north and east of
         Black Sea

375   autumn(?) – After death in battle of a second leader, one
         major group of Greuthungi moves west into territory of
         neighbouring Gothic Tervingi

**376   late(?) summer – Greuthungi and 'larger part' of Tervingi
         arrive on Danube requesting asylum inside Roman Empire**

377–82   Gothic war south of Danube

377   late winter/early spring – Initial revolt of Tervingi;
         Greuthungi force their way across Danube

377/8   1st phase of Gothic war, confined to eastern Balkans

378   24 Aug. – Battle of Hadrianople; death of Valens

379/81   2nd phase of Gothic war spreads to western Balkans

382   3 Oct. – Peace treaty ends the war; Tervingi and Greuthungi
         settled in Balkans on relatively generous terms

386   More Greuthungi try to cross Danube; defeated by
         Theodosius and settled on harsh terms in Asia Minor

387/8   Theodosius I defeats Maximus; Balkan Goths involved in war
         and some revolt

392/3   Theodosius I defeats Eugenius; Balkan Goths again involved in
         war and further revolt

c.395–411	**Alaric reigns over Tervingi and those Greuthungi encompassed by 382 treaty**
395/6	First major Hunnic attack on Roman Empire, via Caucasus (Persian Empire also heavily affected)
395–7	Alaric's 1st revolt
397	Treaty between Alaric and Eutropius; Alaric becomes Roman general commanding in Illyricum
399	Fall of Eutropius; end of treaty
401/2	Alaric's 1st invasion of Italy; battles of Pollentia and Verona
c.405–8	**2nd wave of Hun-inspired invasions of Roman Empire, affecting areas west of the Carpathians**
405/6	Treaty between Alaric and Stilicho
	Radagaisus invades Italy through Austrian passes, is defeated and killed; many followers sold into slavery, elite warriors drafted into Roman army
406	31 Dec. (?) – Rhine invaders – Vandals, Alans, Suevi and smaller groups – break over Rome's Upper Rhine frontier
407	Constantine III leads Roman forces stationed in Britain and Gaul against Rhine invaders
407–9	Rhine invaders ravage Gaul, then cross Pyrenees into Spain
408(?)	Minor Hunnic leader Uldin invades eastern Empire
408–11	Alaric's 2nd invasion of Italy; creation of Visigoths by addition of Radagaisus' followers to Tervingi and Greuthungi encompassed by 382 treaty
410	20 Aug. Alaric sacks Rome
c.410/11(?)	British provinces revolt against Constantine III (?)
411–21	**Flavius Constantius dominates western Empire**
411	Alaric dies, is succeeded by Athaulf; Olympiodorus goes on embassy to main body of Huns now established in central Europe(?)
	Fl. Constantius suppresses Constantine III and related usurpers
412	Rhine invaders divide Spanish provinces between them
412/13	Honorius sends letter to British provincials telling them that central Roman forces can no longer defend them

413–16   Fl. Constantius undermines Athaulf (killed in coup in 415) to force Visigoths into renewed alliance with western Empire; Visigothic settlement begins in Aquitaine

416–18   Combined Visigothic-Roman campaigns destroy independence of Alans and Siling Vandals in Spain; survivors unite behind Hasding Vandals to create new Vandal-Alan supergroup

421   Promotion to the purple, then death, of Fl. Constantius

423   Death of Honorius; usurpation of John

422–9   Free hand for Vandal-Alans in Spain culminates in their transfer to Morocco; from 427 led by Geiseric. Suevi establish control in north-western Spain (Galicia)

425   East Roman army puts Valentinian III, aged 6, on western throne

425–33   Struggle for domination at court of Valentinian III, ending with Aetius' defeat of rival generals Felix and Boniface; partial eclipse of influence of emperor's mother Galla Placidia

433–54 Aetius dominates western Empire

435   Vandal-Alans granted land in Numidia and Mauretania

436   Aetius' forces suppress Bagaudae in north-west Gaul

436/7   Destruction of Burgundian kingdom on both sides of Upper Rhine by Huns; Aetius' resettlement of survivors on Roman territory around Lake Geneva

436–9   Aetius' war with Visigoths in south-west Gaul ends in renewed treaty

438–41   Suevi under King Rechila seize provinces of Baetica and Carthaginiensis

439   Sept. Vandal-Alans seize Carthage, capital of Roman North Africa, and provinces of Proconsularis and Byzacena

c.440–53 Attila becomes supreme leader of Huns

441/2   Attila's 1st invasion of east Roman Balkans leads to recall of eastern army sent to participate in Sicilian expedition to recapture lost North African provinces

444   Treaty between Geiseric and western Empire recognizes his control of Proconsularis, Byzacena and Numidia

445(?)   Attila murders brother Bleda to take sole control of Huns

446(?)   Final appeal of British provincials for central Roman assistance against Saxon and other invaders

447 Attila's 2nd invasion of east Roman Balkans; heavy Roman defeats on River Utus and in the Chersonesus

448 Priscus participates in embassy to assassinate Attila

450 Attila grants Constantinople a generous treaty

451 Attila invades Gaul; defeated by Aetius' coalition force of Romans, Burgundians, Visigoths and Franks at the Catalaunian fields c. end June(?)

452 Attila invades Italy, sacks cities including Milan; retreats as disease and Roman harassment weaken army

453–69 Attila's Hunnic Empire collapses

453 Attila dies

454 summer(?) – Battle of Nedao; Gepids first subject group to reassert independence from Hunnic domination

21 or 22 Sept. – Murder of Aetius by Valentinian III

455 16 Mar. – Murder of Valentinian III by Petronius Maximus, declared Augustus next day

late May – Geiseric's forces sack Rome, Petronius Maximus killed fleeing city (31 May); Geiseric adds Tripolitania, Sardinia and Balearics to his kingdom

9 July – Avitus declared western emperor by Gallo-Roman senators with support of Visigothic king Theoderic II

late 450s(?) St Severinus starts work in Noricum

456 17 Oct. – Battle of Placentia and deposition of Avitus

457 1 Apr. – Majorian becomes emperor of west

459 Pannonian Goths of Valamer, now united and independent of Hunnic control, invade east Roman territory to extract annual subsidy of 300 lbs of gold

461–72 Ricimer dominates central imperial politics in west

461 summer – Defeat of Majorian's North African expeditionary force in Spain, followed on 2 Aug. by his deposition and on 7 Aug. by execution; Ricimer's domination of Italy uncontested

19 Nov. – Nominated by Ricimer, Libius Severus becomes western emperor

465 14 Nov. – Libius Severus dies

466 Euric kills and deposes Theoderic II to become king of Visigoths

467 Dengizich, son of Attila, makes war on eastern Empire

12 Apr. – After long negotiations between Ricimer and Constantinople, Anthemius declared western emperor

468–76 Western Empire unravels

468 June(?) – Defeat of final joint east-west Roman expedition against Vandal kingdom

469 Dengizich's head publicly displayed in Constantinople; Hernac, Attila's last surviving son, finds asylum in east Roman territory south of Danube

Euric's forces advance boundary of Visigothic kingdom northwards to Loire

472 Apr. – Olybrius declared western emperor by Ricimer

11 July – Murder of Anthemius by Gundobad, Ricimer's ally, after civil war

18 Aug. – Ricimer dies

2 Nov. – Olybrius dies

473–5 Sidonius and friends try to preserve Auvergne against Visigothic annexation within a rump western empire

473–89 Campaigns of Theoderic the Amal, nephew of Valamer, in east Roman Balkans, lead to creation of Ostrogothic supergroup

473 3 Mar. – Glycerius declared western emperor
Euric's forces seize Tarragona in Spain

474 pre-June – Gundobad abandons imperial politics to become joint king of Burgundians

19 or 24 June – Glycerius deposed by Julius Nepos and made Bishop of Salona; Nepos declares himself western emperor

475 28 Aug. – Attacked by Orestes, Nepos retreats to Dalmatia

31 Oct. – Orestes declares his son Romulus Augustulus western emperor

476 After executions of his father Orestes (28 Aug.) and uncle Paul (4 Sept.), **Romulus Augustulus, last western Roman emperor, is deposed.** Odovacar returns imperial vestments to Constantinople, telling emperor Zeno that no emperor is any longer required in the west

Euric's Visigothic kingdom now controls entire Hispanic peninsula except for north-west corner, and annexes Arles and the rest of Provence

481/2–507   Campaigns of Clovis bring both Frankish unification and extension of Frankish control over all of former Roman Gaul

482   Jan. – St Severinus dies

489–93   Theoderic the Amal conquers Italy, defeating and deposing Odovacar

GLOSSARY

adoratio – Imperial ceremony of kissing the emperor's purple robe: reserved for higher and more favoured dignitaries.

agri deserti – 'deserted lands'. Used to be interpreted as land that once was cultivated, but which had fallen out of use in the late imperial period. Now seen as a tax category for land that produced no income for the imperial fisc, and might never have done.

alae – Roman auxiliary cavalry, composed of non-citizens in the early imperial period.

annona militaris – A new tax on economic production, regularized under Diocletian at the end of the third century, often taken in kind, although it could be commuted into a gold payment.

aurum coronarium – 'crown gold'. A theoretically voluntary gold payment shaped into a crown made by individual cities; paid on an emperor's accession and every fifth anniversary subsequently.

Baiae – Watering hole of the Roman rich and famous on the Bay of Naples; much beloved of Symmachus.

barbaricum – 'land of the barbarians'. A collective term for everywhere not within the Roman Empire.

Černjachov culture – A zone of material remains extending over Wallachia, Moldavia and the southern Ukraine, from the Carpathian Mountains to the River Don, in the later third and fourth centuries. Built around the power of Goths and other immigrants from the north, but including a large indigenous population as well:

civitas (pl. *civitates*) – City territory; the basic administrative unit, consisting of urban core and rural hinterland, characteristic of the late Empire.

clarissimus (pl. *clarissimi*) – 'most distinguished'. A title originally reserved to senators of Rome and which became the honorific to which all professionals – civil and military – aspired under the status reforms of the emperors

Valentinian and Valens in 367. Designated, despite its literal meaning, the most junior of the three senatorial ranks that emerged in the later fourth century (see *illustris* and *spectabilis*).

clarissimate – The collective term for the *clarissimi*.

Codex Argenteus – A luxury sixth-century copy of Ulfilas' translation of the four Gospels into Gothic; now housed in the Uppsala University Library in Stockholm.

Codex Theodosianus – Theodosian Code. A collection of imperial legislation issued by the Emperor Theodosius II, covering new rulings of the period c. AD 300–440.

cohortales – Imperial functionaries, sometimes wealthy, of the provincial bureaucracy.

cohortes – Roman auxiliary infantry, composed of non-citizens, in the early imperial period.

coloni – Roman tenant farmers, increasingly tied to their lands in the late Roman period.

comes rei militaris – A senior but not most senior, military commander of the Roman field army (see *comitatenses, magister militum*). Some had regional responsibilities, such as *comes Africae* or *comes Thraciae*; some commanded sections of the central field army.

comes domesticorum – 'Count of the Domestics'. Commander of the field army's elite guard regiments.

comes ordinis tertii – 'count third class'. The counts (pl. *comites*) were an order of imperial companions created by the emperor Constantine, with three grades.

comitatenses (adj. comitatensian) – Mobile Roman field army forces, some placed centrally, some on the major frontiers (Rhine, Danube and eastern). Paid more than garrison forces (see *limitanei*).

consul – Originally chief executive officer of the Roman Republic, elected annually. In the late Empire, still elected annually, but nominated by the emperor; no longer an executive office, it was the supreme honour in public life short of the imperial title.

contubernium – The basic unit of the Roman army in the early imperial period, a section of eight men sharing a tent.

cura palatii – 'Curator of the Palace'. High Roman palace dignitary in the fourth/fifth centuries.

curia – The city council of Roman landowners who administered the *civitas*; its individual members were known as decurions or *curiales*.

cursus honorem – Roman senatorial career ladder.

cursus publicus – A transportation system with way- and supply-stations for state officals to use when travelling within the Roman Empire.

deditio – The 'surrender' of barbarians into Roman power; the terms enforced after the surrender could vary substantially.

denarius (pl. *denarii*) – Basic Roman silver coin used until the late third century, when it became worthless.

distributio numerorum – A section of the western *Notitia Dignitatum* (see below) recording the distribution of western Roman field army units in c. AD 420.

dromons – Specialist, oar-driven, decked warships of the east Roman navy.

duumviri – 'two men', a 'duo'. The standard executive officers of a *curia*.

dux – 'duke'. A regional commander of *limitanei*.

emphyteutic lease – A favourable grant allowing tenants a more or less permanent, heritable possession of land, which could be sold to a third party.

fibula (pl. *fibulae*) – A decorative safety-pin used to fasten cloaks.

Fliehburgen – 'refuge centres'. A German archaeological term for walled settlements built in many exposed areas of the Empire in the fifth century.

foedus – 'treaty'. Hence *foederati*, 'foreign group under treaty'. Often used by modern historians as a technical term with one clear meaning, but in my view it was more complex.

Fürstengraber – 'princely graves'. A German archaeological term for burials of such wealth that they seem to belong to royalty or those pretending to such a status.

Germania, Germani – Roman terms for area between the Rhine and the Vistula, and its inhabitants; the region was largely dominated by Germanic-speaking groups, but they never came close to forming one unified force in the Roman period.

gladius – Roman legionaries' characteristic short sword.

honoratus (pl. *honorati*) – A retired imperial bureaucrat of high rank; belonging increasingly to the clarissimate as the fourth century progressed, *honorati* largely replaced *curiales* as the dominant force in local Roman society.

illustres (pl. *illustres*) – Most senior of the three senatorial ranks of the later fourth century (see *clarissimus* and *spectabilis*).

imperator – 'emperor'. Deriving from the title of an army commander of the Roman republican period.

iudex – 'judge'. The title affected by the overall ruler of the kings who made up the coalition of the Gothic Tervingi in the fourth century, before the arrival of the Huns.

iugum (pl. *iugera*) – A unit of value, not geographical area, into which the assets of the Empire were divided under Diocletian; the basis for calculating the *annona militaris*.

Jastorf culture – A zone of relatively simple material remains dating to the last centuries BC, largely coincident with the spread of the Germani at that date.

jurisconsult – A first- to third-century AD specialist Roman academic lawyer who could make legal innovations via case law.

largitionales – The staff of the emperor's financial office, the Sacred Largesse.

La Tène culture – A zone of relatively developed material remains dating to the last centuries BC, largely coincident with the spread of Celtic-speakers at that date.

legiones comitatenses – Infantry unit assigned to field forces in the late imperial army.

legiones pseudocomitatenses – *limitanei*, regraded as field army troops in the early fifth century.

Lex Irnitanum – The constitution of the Roman town of Irni, characteristic of the so-called Flavian municipal constitution which defined the workings of most Roman towns in the early imperial period.

libertas – 'freedom'. Carried the technical meaning 'freedom under the law'.

limitanei – Frontier garrison troops in permanent stations, less well-paid than *comitatenses*.

magister (pl. *magistri*) *militum* – In full, *comes et magister utriusque militiae*. Highest-ranking field army commander. *Magistri militum praesentalis* commanded central field armies, and *magistri militum per Gallias, per Thraciam, per*

Orientem and *per Illyricum* commanded armies on the main frontiers (Gaul, Thrace, the east, Illyricum, respectively).

magister officiorum – 'Master of Offices'. Something like the head of the Civil Service, one of the top imperial bureaucrats.

navicularii – The state-subsidized guild of shippers, charged with transporting revenue in kind around the Empire (see *annona militaris*).

Notitia Dignitatum – A listing of all the military and civilian dignitaries and their office staffs of the later Empire, dating largely to c. AD 395, but its western section partly kept up to date to c. 420 (see *distributio numerorum*).

numeri – 'regiments'. Basic term for unit of the late Roman army.

Ostrogoths – A new and much larger Gothic force created by Valamer (c. 455–67) and his nephew Theoderic the Amal (474–526) out of several pre-existing independent groups. Sometimes equated with the Greuthungi (previously led by Ermenaric) who arrived at the Danube in 376, but this is mistaken.

palatini – Imperial Roman bureaucrats of the late period (from *palatium*, palace).

pars melior humani generis – 'The better part of humankind', Symmachus' term for the senatorial aristocracy of Rome.

pars rustica, urbana – The 'country' (working farm) and 'urban' (for 'civilized' entertaining) parts of a standard Roman villa.

patricius – 'Patrician'. Honorific title distinguishing the senior military commander or bureaucrat exercising the real power behind the throne in the fifth century.

Pax Romana – The 'Roman Peace': applied to the high imperial period after the conquests, but before the third century crisis; roughly, the later first to earlier third centuries AD.

possessores – The landowning class by whom and for whom the Empire was run.

praepositus sacri cubiculi – A eunuch official of the imperial household.

praesental armies, *praesentalis* – see *magister militum*.

primicerius notariorum – 'Chief Notary'. A senior bureaucratic functionary.

primicerius sacri cubiculi – A senior eunuch functionary in the imperial household.

principales – A small inner elite of the late Roman *curia*, who used the city council as a vehicle for self-advancement and profit.

proskynesis – The ceremonial act of throwing yourself to the ground when being introduced into the sacred imperial presence.

Przeworsk culture – A zone of remains extending over much of central and southern Poland between the fourth centuries BC and AD.

quaestor – A senior bureaucratic functionary, increasingly specializing in legal matters.

quinquennalia – An anniversary celebrated every five years of an imperial reign (see *aurum coronarium*).

rationalis Aegypti – The financial officer in charge of arms factories and other operations of the state in the Roman province of Egypt.

receptio (pl. *receptiones*) – The authorized large-scale migration of outsiders on to Roman soil.

Relationes (sing. *Relatio*) – Symmachus' official letters to the emperor as Urban Prefect of the city of Rome.

rescript – The emperor's answers on the bottom half of a piece of papyrus to legal questions put to him in the top half. Several hundred queries were answered every year.

Res Gestae Divi Saporis – The Acts of the Divine Shapur, king of Persia, recording his victories over third-century Roman emperors, inscribed at Naqs-i Rustam, seven kilometres north of Persepolis.

Romanitas – Latin term for cultural patterns characteristic of the Roman Empire; 'Romanness'.

Sasanians – A Near Eastern dynasty who united Iran and Iraq in the third century AD to create a superpower rivalling the Roman Empire.

solidus (pl. *solidi*) – From Constantine onwards the standard Roman gold coin, minted at seventy-two to the pound; half- and third-*solidi* were also minted.

sortes Vandalorum – 'allotments of the Vandals'. Grants of landed estates in the province of Proconsularis made by Geiseric to his followers after the capture of Carthage in 439, and subsequent confiscations of Roman senator-landowners' assets.

spectabilis (pl. *spectabiles*) – Intermediate senatorial rank of the later fourth century (see *clarissimus* and *illustris*).

testudo – 'tortoise'. The classic Roman wall-of-shields infantry formation, designed to give all-round and overhead protection.

Teutobergiensis Saltus – The Teutoburg Forest, where Arminius ambushed and destroyed Varus' three legions.

Visigoths – A new and much larger Gothic group created by Alaric I (king 385–410) out of parts of the Tervingi and Greuthungi who arrived at the Danube requesting asylum in 376, and the Goths of Radagaisus who invaded Italy in 405/6. The term has often been used as a synonym for the Tervingi before 376 (when they were led by Athanaric), but this is mistaken.

Wielbark culture – A zone of remains extending over much of northern Poland in the first and second centuries AD, then spreading eastwards and southwards in the third and fourth.

NOTES

ABBREVIATIONS

AM – anno mundi, year of the world

BC – *Book of Constitutions*: ed. Von Salis (1892); trans. Drew (1972)

CAH 1. 12 – *Cambridge Ancient History*, 1st edn, vol. 12: *The Imperial Crisis and Recovery AD 193–324*, ed. S. A. Cook et al. (Cambridge, 1939)

CAH 2. 7. 2 – *Cambridge Ancient History*, 2nd edn, vol. 7.2: *The Rise of Rome to 220 BC*, ed. F. W. Walbank et al. (Cambridge, 1989)

CAH 2. 8 – *Cambridge Ancient History*, 2nd edn, vol. 8: *Rome and the Mediterranean to 133 BC*, ed. A. E. Astin et al. (Cambridge, 1989)

CAH 2. 9 – *Cambridge Ancient History*, 2nd edn, vol. 9: *The Last Age of the Roman Republic 146–43 BC*, ed. J. A. Crook et al. (Cambridge, 1994)

CAH 2. 10 – *Cambridge Ancient History*, 2nd edn, vol. 10: *The Augustan Empire 43 BC–AD 69*, ed. A. K. Bowman et al. (Cambridge, 1996)

CAH 2. 11 – *Cambridge Ancient History*, 2nd edn, vol. 11: *The High Empire 70–192 AD*, ed. A. K. Bowman et al. (Cambridge, 2000)

CE – *Code of Euric*: in Zeumer, ed. (1902)

Chron. Gall. 452 – *Gallic Chronicle of 452*: in Mommsen, ed. (1892)

Chron. Gall. 511 – *Gallic Chronicle of 511*: in Mommsen, ed. (1892)

CIL – corpus inscriptionum latinarum

CJ – *Codex Justinianus*: in Kreuger, ed. (1877)

CM 1, 2 – *Chronica Minora*, vols 1 and 2: ed. Mommsen (1892; 1894)

CMH 1. 1 – *Cambridge Medieval History*, 1st edn, vol. 1: *The Christian Empire*, ed. J. B. Bury et al. (Cambridge, 1911)

CTh – *Codex Theodosianus* (*Theodosian Code*): ed. Mommsen and Kreuger (1905); trans. Pharr (1952)

fr., frr. – fragment(s)

HE – *Ecclesiastical History* (*Historia Ecclesiastica*)

ILT – P. Gauckler (ed.), *Rapport sur des inscriptions latines découvertes en Tunisie de 1900 à 1905* (Paris, 1907)

MGH – Monumenta Germaniae Historica

Not. Dig. Occ. – *Notitia Dignitatum*, western Empire: in Seeck, ed. (1876)

Not. Dig. Or. – *Notitia Dignitatum*, eastern Empire: in Seeck, ed. (1876)

Nov. Theod. – *Novels of the Emperor Theodosius II*: in Mommsen and Kreuger, eds (1905); trans. Pharr (1952)

Nov. Val. – *Novels of the Emperor Valentinian III*: in Mommsen and Kreuger, eds (1905); trans. Pharr (1952)

Or. – *Oration, Orationes*

P. Columbia 123 – Papyri from the Columbia University collection no. 123: ed. W. L. Westermann and A. A. Schiller, *Apokrimata: Decisions of Septimius Severus on Legal Matters* (New York, 1954)

P. Ital. – J.-O. Tjader (ed.), *Die nichtliterarischen lateinischen Papyri Italiens aus der Zeit 445–700*, 3 vols (Lund, 1954–82)

Pan. Lat. – *Latin Prose Panegyrics*: ed. and trans. Nixon and Rogers (1994)

PLRE 1 – A. H. M. Jones et al. (eds), *The Prosopography of the Later Roman Empire*, vol. 1, AD 260–395 (Cambridge, 1971)

PLRE 2 – J. R. Martindale (ed.), *The Prosopography of the Later Roman Empire*, vol. 2, AD 395–527 (Cambridge, 1980)

ref., refs – reference(s)

s.a. – *sub anno*, under the year

INTRODUCTION

1 *Fibulae*, as they're known in the scholarly literature.
2 The volumes generated by the European Science Foundation project can perhaps stand as a metaphor for the general state of scholarship: they encompass a multiplicity of stimulating essays, but no general overview (although, of course, that was not their point).
3 The truth of this is immediately apparent in the chapters devoted to the fourth and fifth centuries in the last volume of the old *Cambridge Ancient History* and the first volume of the old *Cambridge Medieval History*, both published in the 1910s, which project the same orthodoxies about inevitable Roman decline and collapse. They remained essentially unchallenged until the 1960s.
4 In saying this, I make not the slightest criticism of projects like 'The Transformation of the Roman World'. The aim there was to advance participants' knowledge and understanding by exposing them to the specialized work of others and, in doing so, to enable them to do their own work better. It is that drive which its volumes reflect, and I can gratefully testify to having learned a huge amount during five happy years of participation.

1. ROMANS

1   Caesar *Gallic War*, 6. 1.

2   *Gallic War* 3. 37.

3   St Bernard Pass: *Gallic War* 3. 1–6 Alesia: *Gallic War* 7. 75ff. Uxellodunum: *Gallic War* 8. 33ff. For further reading on the Roman army and its training methods, see *CAH* 2. 10, Ch. 11; *CAH* 2. 11, Ch. 9.

4   There were some additions. Areas between the Upper Rhine and Upper Danube – the Taunus/Wetterau salient and the Neckar region – were annexed before the end of the century. A much larger extension came under Trajan. At the start of the second century, he launched a series of campaigns (101–2, 105–6) which eventually added the whole of Transylvanian Dacia to the Empire. This territory was abandoned by the emperor Aurelian (before AD 275). Good general accounts of Rome's rise can be found in *CAH* 2. 7. 2, Chs 8–10.

5   Acco: *Gallic War* 6. 44. Avaricum: *Gallic War* 7. 27–8.

6   Indutiomarus: *Gallic War* 5. 58. 4–6. Catuvoleus: *Gallic War* 6. 31. Ambiorix: *Gallic War* 8. 25. 1.

7   Gibbon (1897), 160ff. Jones (1964), Ch. 25. Several studies have surveyed the many different explanations for the end of the Empire offered over the years: e.g. Demandt (1984); Kagan (1992).

8   On Rome, see, amongst many possibilities, Krautheimer (1980) with refs. Ostia: Meiggs (1973). Carthage is discussed in more detail in Ch. 6 below. An excellent introduction to the Empire is Cornell and Matthews (1982).

9   The Roman Republic is generally held to have lasted down to the reign of Augustus, the first Roman emperor, although he retained many republican constitutional trappings. Even before his reign, Rome had already acquired overseas territories by conquest, and must therefore be reckoned an imperial power.

10 On Symmachus in particular, see Matthews (1974); for detailed annotations, see the new French translation of his works (Callu (1972–2002)) and the ongoing volumes of the Italian commentary project. Good introductions to the senators of Rome in the late antique period are Matthews (1975); Arnheim (1972); Chastagnol (1960).

11 *Letters* 1. 52. 1.

12 E.g. 'A is – always – followed by B', or 'A will – in the future – be followed by B', or 'A would – if certain conditions apply – be followed by B'.

13 Palladius: Symmachus *Letters* 1.15. On this education more generally, see the excellent study of Kaster (1988).

14 *Letters* 1.1.

15 His speeches won less favour after his death than his letters: the seven we have survive only in one damaged manuscript, which would originally have contained many more.

16 Sometimes, what were originally a grandee's marginalia eventually became incorporated by mistake into the text proper, giving modern editors the

occasionally tricky job of separating original text from subsequent commentary. After Symmachus' death, the *Saturnalia* of Macrobius recalled the literary and philosophical ideals of Symmachus and his friends in fictional dialogue form, so as to transmit a potted version of the classical heritage to his son. On the ancient roots of the ongoing scholarly tradition that saved many classical texts, see Matthews (1975), Ch. 1.

17 Homes Dudden (1935), 39. In the view of Boissier (1891), vol. 2, 183, they are 'the dullest epistles in the Latin language'.

18 Excuses: Symmachus *Letters* 3. 4. Much of the prevailing etiquette is sorted out in Matthews (1974), (1986); Bruggisser (1993).

19 Caesar: Adcock (1956). The bibliography on Cicero is enormous, but see e.g. Rawson (1975) and, most recently on his oratory, Fantham (2004).

20 Food: Ammianus 27. 3. 8–9. Wine: Ammianus 27. 3. 4.

21 Symmachus *Letters* 5. 62.

22 Symmachus *Letters* 6. 33, 6. 42.

23 Symmachus *Letters* 4. 58–62, 5. 56.

24 Symmachus *Letters* 6. 43.

25 Ideology: Dvornik (1966). For an introduction to the ceremonial life of the Empire, see Matthews (1989), Chs 11–12; MacCormack (1981). The quotation is from Ammianus 16. 10. 10.

26 Development of Roman law: Robinson (1997); Honoré (1994); Millar (1992), Chs 7–8. Taxation: Millar (1992), Ch. 4; Jones (1964), Ch. 13.

27 The two most important imperial titles in the late period were Augustus and Caesar, both originally deriving from personal names (Julius Caesar and his nephew Augustus). In the fourth century, Augustus became the title adopted by senior emperors, while Caesar was reserved for junior colleagues.

28 Matthews (1989), 235 with refs.

29 Themistius *Or.* 6. 83 c–d.

30 General development of the imperial office: Millar (1992), esp. Chs 2 and 5; Matthews (1989), Ch. 11.

31 *Pan. Lat.* 6. 22. 6.

32 Introductions to the late Roman army: Jones (1964); Elton (1996b); Whitby (2002).

33 Growth of bureaucracy: e.g. Matthews (1975), Chs 2–4; Heather (1994b).

34 The Theodorus incident is recounted widely in the sources: Ammianus 29. 1, with full list at *PLRE*, 1, 898.

35 The deeper history of this development is well explored in *CAH*, 2. 11, Ch. 4.

36 A contemporary of Symmachus who figures in the letter collection, Petronius Probus, was, for instance, Praetorian Prefect (roughly the equivalent of first minister) for Italy, Africa and the western Balkans for about eight years altogether, in two separate stints.

37 For an introduction to these developments, see Jones (1964), Ch. 18; Dagron (1974); Heather (1994b).

38 General development of Trier: Wightman (1967).

39 Those for the presentation of crown gold were shorter than normal imperial

speeches, presumably because there were so many of them – one from each city of the Empire – that the imperial personage might be driven out of his imperial mind if they went on too long.

40 The bibliography on towns in the Roman Empire is enormous, but for introductions to their importance – physical, administrative and political – see Jones (1964), Ch. 19.

41 On Konz and the Moselle villas, see Wightmann (1967), Ch. 4. The literature on the villa as a cultural phenomenon is as profuse as that on towns, but see e.g. Percival (1976).

42 *Letters* 9. 88; the letter was first identified by Roda (1981).

43 On Ausonius' Latinity, see Green (1991). Ausonius' maternal grandfather was a major landowner among the Aedui of central Gaul. His mother's brother was a successful rhetorician who became court tutor to one of the emperor Constantine's family in Constantinople. Ausonius tells us less about his paternal ancestry, thereby generating suspicions that it may not have been so respectable, but his father was a doctor who owned property in south-western Gaul and his uncle made a mercantile fortune.

44 For Aristotle, this constituted the only good life, and someone living isolated on his estates was bound to be less rational. Our word 'idiot' comes from the Greek (*idiotes*) for someone shunning participation in this kind of local community.

45 Gonzalez (1986); trans. M. H. Crawford.

46 Villas were always divided into the *pars rustica* ('country part', the working farm) and the *pars urbana* ('urban part', for civilized living). The *pars urbana* incorporated substantial public rooms for entertaining peers, as well as baths, so that life in the villa was anything but idiotic. There are many good studies on the ideological adjustments involved in becoming Roman. See e.g. Woolf (1998); Keay and Terrenato (2001); D. J. Mattingly (2002).

47 Symmachus *Letters* 1. 14.

48 The next three quotations are from *Mosella* ll. 161–7, 335–48, 399–404.

49 Quintilian's contribution to the Latin tradition is examined in e.g. Leeman (1963).

50 Using the concordance to Symmachus' works (Lomanto (1983)), I count getting on for twenty mentions of Baiae and its pleasures in his correspondence.

51 *Letters* 1. 14.

52 According to the expert on the subject, Jones (1964), 528, by c. 370 'The third class of the *comitiva* [countship] was still conferred, but on persons of very humble degree, decurions who had completed their obligations to their cities, and the patrons of the guilds of bakers and butchers at Rome.'

53 On Ausonius' extraordinary rise to prominence, see Matthews (1975), Ch. 3.

2. Barbarians

1 Tacitus *Annals* 1. 61. 1–6.

2 Wells (2003), esp. Chs 2–3 and appendices, is a good introduction to the myth

of Arminius and the recent archaeological finds. Its account of the battle, however, is very odd, envisaging a massacre that was all over in an hour while making no comment on the fact that the best source describes a drawn-out four-day struggle fought out over a considerable distance (Cassius Dio 56. 19–22 (no other source contradicts Dio)).

3 Dahn ((1861–1909), (1877).

4 An excellent survey, bringing out the strategic differences between the various frontiers, is Whittaker (1994).

5 As Kossinna put it in the 1926 version of *The Origin of the Germani*, 'clearly defined, sharply distinctive, bounded archaeological provinces correspond unquestionably to the territories of particular peoples and tribes'. Kossinna's ideas were disseminated most influentially in the Anglophone world through the works of V. Gordon Childe (1926), (1927). For an introduction to recent reinterpretations of the meaning of archaeological cultural areas, see Renfrew and Bahn (1991).

6 Ariovistus: Caesar *Gallic War* 1. 31–53; Veleda: Tacitus *Histories* 4. 61, 65; 5. 22, 24. Useful introductions to early Germanic society are Todd (1975); (1992); Hachmann (1971).

7 Bructeri: Tacitus *Germania* 33; Ampsivarii: *Annals* 13. 56.

8 *Annals* 1. 68.

9 Elton (1996b), 66–9.

10 Strabo 4. 5. 3.

11 On Chinese expansion, see e.g. Lattimore (1940). For an introduction to the Oppida culture: Cunliffe and Rowley (1976); Cunliffe (1997). On the Jastorf culture, Schutz (1983), Ch. 6. For the Germani adopting La Tène cultural forms, see Hachmann et al. (1962). Much has been written on the dynamics of Roman imperial expansion, but for an introduction see *CAH* 2. 9 esp. Ch. 8a; *CAH* 2. 10 esp. Chs 4, 15; Isaac (1992), esp. Ch. 9; Whittaker (1994), Chs 2–3. Modern studies have shown that the process was much more anarchic than old views of planned conquests implied.

12 Trans. Dodgeon and Lieu (1991), 43–6, 50, 57.

13 For an introduction to Near Eastern history in the early Roman imperial period, see Millar (1993).

14 *Chronicon Paschale*, 510.

15 On the Sasanian revolution, see Christiansen (1944); Howard Johnson (1995); McAdams (1965); Dodgeon and Lieu (1991).

16 Global figures: Agathias *History* 5. 13; John Lydus *On the Months* (*de Mensibus*) 1. 27. General discussions: Jones (1964), 679–86 (inclined to accept an increase up to 600,000 after Diocletian); Hoffmann (1969); Elton (1996a); Whitby (2002). The widely disseminated arguments of MacMullen (1963) on the military ineffectiveness of *limitanei* have been overturned.

17 On the confiscations of city funds, see Crawford (1975), which remains controversial. Constantius returned one-quarter to the cities of Africa, Valentinian and Valens one-third to all cities; cf. Jones (1964), Ch. 19.

18 On these measures, see Jones (1964), esp. Ch. 13 and 623–30.

19 The one exception, a heavy Roman defeat in 363, was caused by the overambi-
    tion of the emperor Julian, to which we will return in a moment. For relations
    between Rome and Persia in the fourth century see e.g. Dodgeon and Lieu
    (1991); Matthews (1989), Chs 4 and 7.

20 For an introduction to these third-century events, see Jones (1964), Ch. 1;
    Drinkwater (1987).

21 This quotation is from Ammianus 28. 5. 4, and the next two from 28. 5. 7.

22 It was mentioned by two contemporary spin-doctors (*Pan. Lat.* 7. 10ff.; 10. 16.
    5–6), and made it into one of the main fourth-century annalistic histories:
    Eutropius 10. 3. 2.

23 *Relatio* 47.

24 Themistius *Or.* 10. 131b–c. On Themistius and his career, see Heather and
    Moncur (2001), esp. Ch. 1.

25 Roman ideological constructions of the barbarian were directly descended from
    those of the Greeks. See e.g. Dauge (1981); Ferris (2002).

26 Calo Levi (1952) and McCormick (1986) amongst many others underline the
    importance of victory.

27 Themistius *Or.* 5. 66a–c with Matthews (1989), Ch. 7, and Smith (1999) on the
    campaign.

28 Themistius *Or.* 6. 73c–75a.

29 The next two quotations are from Themistius *Or.* 10. 205a–b and 10. 202d–203a.

30 For full analysis of the different circumstances of Constantine's peace with the
    Goths in 332 and Valens' in 369, see Heather (1991), Ch. 3, with full refs.
    Themistius *Or.* 8. 116, delivered in March 368, refers to the arrival of the Iberian
    prince Bacurius at Valens' headquarters and dates the start of Chosroes'
    manoeuvres to the middle of the Gothic war. The story of the other waterborne
    fourth-century summit is told at Ammianus 30.3.

31 The 369 treaty is reported as a reasonable outcome to the war at Ammianus 27.
    5. 9; Zosimus 4. 11. 4. Even after defeating the Alamanni in the 350s, the
    emperor Julian still made annual gifts part of the peace treaties he negotiated
    with their various kings: Heather (2001); cf. Klöse (1934) for many earlier
    examples. A Gothic force of perhaps 3,000 (no small number when expedition-
    ary armies probably numbered about 20–30,000) had been provided on four
    occasions since Constantine's victory over the Goths in 332: in 348 (Libanius *Or.*
    59. 89), 360 (Ammianus 20. 8. 1), 363 (Ammianus 23. 2. 7) and 365 (Ammianus
    26. 10. 3).

32 Statue: Themistius *Or.* 15. 191a. Oath: Ammianus 27. 5. 9. On the use of
    hostages: Braund (1984). Cultural influence did not always have the desired
    effect. Arminius, three and a half centuries before, had served as a Roman officer
    in the auxiliaries before plotting Varus' destruction.

33 On these two MSS, see respectively Tjäder (1972); Gryson (1980).

34 The two main sources for Ulfilas – the letter of Auxentius and fr. 2. 5 of the
    Church history of Philostorgius – pose a problem over the dates of his ordination
    and his time in Gothia. See Heather and Matthews (1991), Ch. 5, with refs and
    translations for the reasoning behind my preferred solution. For a similar

community of Roman prisoners among the seventh-century Avars, see *Miracles of St Demetrius* 285–6.

35 The Gospel text of the *Codex Argenteus* preserves Ulfilas' work more or less untouched, whereas others worked after his death on the Epistle text: Friedrichsen (1926), (1939). Before Ulfilas, the Goths used runes for divinatory and other limited purposes, but, as mentioned elsewhere, Gothic did not exist as a written language. Ulfilas had first to devise an alphabet for it, which he did working largely from Greek with a few additions for particular Gothic sounds, and then render the Bible into the language he had created.

36 For an introduction to these theological debates and the manoeuvres, see Hanson (1988); Kopecek (1979).

37 Ammianus 16. 12. 26 and 63 for the numbers; 16. 12 generally for the battle.

38 For the theory and practice of these treaties, see Heather (2001).

39 Chnodomarius: Ammianus 16. 12. Macrianus: Ammianus 29. 4. 2. Alamannic, Burgundian and Frankish wars: Ammianus 28. 5. 9–10, 30. 3. 7.

40 It is traditional to envisage only two, the Visigoths and Ostrogoths, but this is an anachronism. As we shall see in Ch. 5, the traditional equation between the Tervingi and the Visigoths cannot stand; the latter were created on Roman soil in the reign of Alaric in the 390s.

41 The evidence is an amalgam of written and archaeological materials (Heather (1996), Ch. 3).

42 There is a little archaeological evidence, but linguistic evidence is very much stronger. The fifth- and early sixth-century Burgundian language is distinctly east rather than west Germanic, despite the fact that they were then living in the west (Haubrichs (forthcoming)).

43 Frankish subgroups: Gregory of Tours *Histories* 2. 9. Strasbourg: Ammianus 16. 12. Chnodomarius and Macrianus: n. 39 above. Vadomarius: Ammianus 21. 3–4. One source refers to Athanaric as the 'Judge of Kings' (Ambrose *On the Holy Spirit* prologue 17), and the confederation of the Tervingi contained a number of subservient 'kings' (the Greek and Latin terms probably translate the Germanic *reiks*, which may have meant 'noble' rather than 'monarch').

44 On Wijster and Feddersen Wierde, see Van Es (1967); Haarnagel (1979). For a broader run of evidence with refs: Heather (1996), Ch. 3.

45 Poland: Urbancyzk (1997), 40. Gothic pottery and combs: Heather and Matthews (1991), Ch. 3 with refs. Glass: Rau (1972); cf. Hedeager (1987) and Heather (1996), Ch. 3, for broader discussion.

46 Heather (1996), 65–75 with refs.

47 Tervingi: Wolfram (1988), 62ff.

48 Heather (1996), 66, 70–2 with full refs.

49 Ørsnes (1968); cf. Hedeager (1987) with refs.

50 Ammianus 16. 12. 60.

51 *Passion of St Saba* 4. 4, 7. 1–5.

52 *Annals* 13. 57.

53 Continental evidence: Heather (2000); Wickham (1992). Anglo-Saxons: Harke

(1990); a number of those buried with weapons couldn't possibly have fought, including one individual with spina bifida who couldn't even have walked.

54   Militarized freedmen among the Germani appear in sixth- and seventh-century Visigothic and Frankish law codes and also in fifth- and sixth-century literary evidence: Heather (1996), App. 2; Heather (2000).

55   Wormald (1999), Ch. 2.

56   *Passion of St Saba* passim.

57   Tacitus *Annals* 12. 25.

58   Ammianus 17. 12. 9.

3. THE LIMITS OF EMPIRE

1   Ammianus 28. 6. 26.

2   Probably those due from Valentinian's accession in 364. Offerings of crown gold, such as that taken by Symmachus to Valentinian in 369 (Ch. 1), were used to finance these payments.

3   Army returns: Jones (1964), Ch. 19. Lost cash: Symmachus *Relationes* 23. Mac-Mullen (1988) lovingly catalogues many of the documented scams.

4   Libanius *Letters*. 66.2 trans. in Norman (1992) as *Letter* 52. Themistius on an emperor's friends: e.g. *Or.* 1. 10c ff. Connection and position: Matthews (1975), esp. Chs 1–2.

5   The creation of the Roman Empire had been driven by the link between revenues from overseas and political influence (Ch. 2). The same was true of the British Empire: Ferguson (2001). Valentinian and corruption: Ammianus 30. 9.

6   The Theophanes archive is edited and discussed in Roberts and Turner (1952), 104–56.

7   Including Chanel No. 5, I am reliably informed.

8   Many letter collections – including that of Symmachus – betray signs of having been put together from originals stored in such a fashion, and the archives of the early papacy (usually taken to reflect late Roman governmental practice) certainly operated in this way (Noble (1990); Markus (1997), App.). To find anything, therefore, you'd have to know which year it belonged to; there is no sign of any attempt to cross-reference by subject or place. Kelly (1994) explores what is known about the imperial archives in Constantinople.

9   To decide a city's tax bill, the landed resources of each *civitas* were divided into units called *iugera* (sing., *iugum*). The *iugum* was a unit of value, not size, so a *iugum* of better-quality land would be smaller than a *iugum* of poorer quality. Each *iugum* was ascribed the same value of annual output, and had the same amount of tax levied on it. Deciding the total number of *iugera* for each city was the work of central government and required a thorough survey of agricultural assets (much complained about in our sources). Even this was not carried out uniformly throughout the Empire. In Syria, the assessors distinguished between three qualities of arable land and two types of olive grove. Elsewhere, a much simpler distinction between arable and pastoral was applied; while in Egypt and

North Africa, existing land measures were approximated to the new tax units and no reassessment took place, presumably in part because it was too difficult and in part because it might have aroused resistance. The poll tax, similarly, was not applied equally throughout the Empire, sometimes applying to urban and rural plebeians, sometimes just the latter. On the details of Roman taxation, see Jones (1964), Ch. 13.

10 Local communities are known to have got into debt, for instance, in their determination to build the kind of buildings that would secure the necessary constitutional grant. In this context, the case of Irni in Spain is very interesting. Archaeologists have so far failed to identify its site, so unimpressive are the remains in the vicinity, and despite its wonderful constitution you begin to wonder whether it was ever much more than a notional or legal town.

11 P. Columbia 123; cf. Millar (1992), 245; Honoré (1994).

12 CTh 1. 2.

13 Jones (1964), Ch. 25, is the most considered and coherent statement of this kind of analysis. The orthodoxy is expressed in more strident terms in some of the older literature: Rostovtzeff (1957); CAH 1. 12, esp. Ch. 7; CMH 1. 1. esp. Ch. 19.

14 For the standard vision of 'curial flight', see Jones (1964), 737–63, commenting above all on the massive run of legislation collected at CTh 12. 1.

15 Agri deserti: Jones (1964), 812–23. Tying of peasantry to their land: Jones (1964), 795–812.

16 His findings were published most fully in Tchalenko (1953–8). More recent work has suggested that some of his conclusions as to the source of these villages' prosperity need revision, but not the basic fact of it (e.g. Tate (1989)).

17 I have seen figures between 5 and 8 million bandied about.

18 Recent summaries and discussions of the survey evidence are: Lewitt (1991); Whittaker and Garnsey (1998); Ward Perkins (2000); Duncan Jones (2003).

19 In medieval England (up to c. 1300), bonds of serfdom tightened as the population grew and the peasants' need for land increased, but loosened after the Black Death, when landowners needed labour, rather than land. Revised view of agri deserti: Whittaker (1976). Tax and subsistence agriculture: Hopkins (1980).

20 In imperial capital cities like Trier, Antioch and Constantinople at the highest level, and lesser regional ones such as Aphrodisias in south-west Asia Minor. On this development, see e.g. Jones (1964), Ch. 19; Roueché (1989).

21 Some ancient historians use the Greek-derived term 'euergetism', 'good works', to describe the local competitive display of the early Roman period commemorated in the thousands upon thousands of inscriptions surviving from the first two and a half centuries AD. This is at least in part euphemistic.

22 Libanius Or. 42. 24–5.

23 Waiting lists: CTh 6. 30. 16; cf. Libanius Letters 358–9, 365–6, 362, 875–6. General reassessment of the problem: Heather (1994b) with full refs.

24 Among the main losers were builders and inscription-cutters in the small towns of the Empire.

25 Efficiency: Elton (1996a); Whitby (2002). Amongst the outside groups providing contingents for campaigns were the Gothic Tervingi (see Ch. 2). The really damaging sea-change came, after 382, when large contingents were recruited from barbarian groups who had established themselves on Roman soil and began to act as centrifugal political forces (see Chs 4 and 5). Much of the traditional argument has focused on the behaviour and loyalty of generals-cum-politicians of non-Roman origin who rose to positions of great influence. Although called 'barbarians', many of these, like Stilicho, were second-generation immigrants and hence Roman; and anyway, the behaviour of such men betrays no sign of disloyalty. On Stilicho in particular, see in more detail p. 216ff.

26 Gibbon (1897), vol. 4, 162–3 (from *General Observations on the Fall of the Roman Empire in the West*).

27 Liebeschuetz (1972), 37–8, 104–5.

28 Coinage: Calo Levi (1952). Ursulus: Ammianus 20. 11. 5 and 22. 3. 7–8. Tax minimization: Jones (1964), 462ff., who, in my view, is inclined to make too much of what is highly normal human behaviour.

29 Grammarians: Augustine *Confessions*, esp. books 2–4 passim. This cultural revolution, and the cases of Melania and Paulinus of Nola in particular, have been much explored in recent years. For an introduction, see the many works of P. R. L. Brown, esp. (1981), (1995); Markus (1990); Trout (1999).

30 *CTh* 16. 5. 42 of the year 408 debarred pagans from imperial service. On the ideologies of the Christian Empire, see Dvornik (1966).

31 The story of this remarkable MS is told in Matthews (2000), Ch. 3.

32 There were currently two emperors, Valentinian III in the west and Theodosius II in the east.

33 The Egyptian papyri preserve some nice acclamation evidence: Jones (1964), 722ff.

34 Scholarship has concentrated on the Christianization of the Empire, so that the full story of the other side of the coin has yet to be told. For an introduction, see Jones (1964), Ch. 22; Markus (1990).

35 Gibbon's case is actually much easier to make in relation to the Arab takeover of the eastern half of the Empire in the seventh century, where hostility between Greek and Syrian Orthodox (the latter often wrongly called monophysites) played a role in the process. On the contrary, religious disaffection played no substantial part in the Germanic takeover of the west in the fifth century.

36 On this softly-softly approach of fourth-century emperors to Christianizing their upper classes, see (most recently) Brown (1995); Bradbury (1994); Barnes (1995); Heather and Moncur (2001), esp. Ch. 1.

37 'Constitution' is the official term for a formal imperial edict.

38 Rather than in shorthand. Late Roman bureaucratese had many ways of speeding up the laborious process of writing out, but shorthand involved some risk that a word might then be read wrongly.

39 Dvornik (1966); Barnish (1992), introduction; Heather (1993).

40 The full story is told in Matthews (2000), esp. Chs 4–5.

41 Matthews (1986) is a fascinating exploration of how Symmachus found ways to

express criticism and conflict within the massive constraints imposed by the etiquette of Roman public life.

42 For Augustine's education, see Brown (1967), esp. Chs 3–4.

43 *Cohortales* of Aphrodisias and Egypt: Roueché (1989), 73–5. Legal profession: Jones (1964), Ch. 14. McLynn (1994) and Van Dam (2003) are recent studies of the first generation of upper-class bishops; cf. Brown (1967), esp. Chs 17–19, on the stir created by the highly educated Augustine among the backwoods bishops of North Africa.

44 In large cities, chariot-racing was conducted through four teams, or factions: greens, blues, reds and whites. These were highly organized and could occasionally be mobilized – not least through rioting – to exert political pressure or to fulfil civic functions.

45 Maratacupreni: Ammianus 28. 2.

46 *Letters* 1. 1–5 (quotation above from 1. 5. 2). Further estate management letters: 2. 30–1; 5. 81, 6. 66, 6. 81, 7. 126. Another good example of late Roman 'improvement' is Paulinus of Pella *Eucharisticon* 187–97.

47 E.g. *Letters* 2. 87, 6. 11.

48 *Letter* 2. 13 (refers to *CTh* 4. 4. 2 of 389); cf. more generally 6. 2, 11, 27; 7. 12.

49 *Letter* 1. 6.

50 *Letter* 6. 3; cf. other references to marriage at 4. 14, 4. 55, 9. 83, 106, 107.

51 On the 'Orfitus affair', see Symmachus *Relationes* 34.

52 'Normal' letters: *Letters* 1. 74; 3. 4; 4. 68; 5. 18; 6. 9 and the pair 5. 54 and 66. 'Official' letters: *Relationes* 16, 19, 28, 33, 38, 39, 41.

53 *Letter* 1. 12 (to his father). Sicilian baths: 1. 10, 2. 26, 2. 60, 5. 93; 6. 70, 7. 7, 7. 18, 8. 42. Builders: 6. 70. Cf., more generally, 1. 10, 2. 2, 6. 11, 6. 49, 7. 32.

54 Baiae in autumn: *Letter* 1. 7 (cf. 1. 3). The 396 'trip': 5. 21, 93; 7. 24, 31, 69; 8. 2, 23, 27, 61; 9. 111 and 125. Other estate refs: 1. 5, 2. 59, 3. 23, 3. 50, 7. 35, 7. 59, 9. 83.

55 Though Symmachus could be dismissive of hunting as an immature pastime: *Letter* 4. 18.

56 Too busy: *Letter* 1. 35. Cf. *Letters* 1. 24 (included with it, a gift of Pliny's *Natural History*), 3. 11 (on a Latin translation of Aristotle's *Constitutions*), 4. 20 (on learning Greek with his son).

57 *Letters* 2. 47, 48; 3. 4; 3. 23.

58 Daily health letters: *Letter* 6. 32, with 6. 4 and 6. 29 on diet. More generally: 1. 48, 2. 22, 2. 55, 5. 25, 6.20.

59 *P. Ital.* 10–11 is a superb illustration of the complexities of Roman property transfer, showing that legal exchange was finalized only when the new owner was inscribed as such in the relevant town's property register.

60 Priscus fr. 11. 2, pp. 267–73.

61 The headings of the *Theodosian Code* are deeply revealing – e.g. Purchase Contracts, Dowries, Inheritance – as are the curricula laid out for teaching Roman law: see Honoré (1978), Ch. 6, on both the new curriculum introduction in the sixth century by Justinian and the one it superseded. Eighteenth-century England: Linebaugh (1991), esp. Ch. 3.

62 The emperor Theodosius' propaganda, for instance, made a great deal of the fact that he'd restored the position of a senatorial family that had been ruined by his predecessor Valens (Themistius *Or.* 16. 212d; 34. 18).

63 Themistius *Or.* 8. 114d.

4. WAR ON THE DANUBE

1   Except where otherwise indicated, the quotations in this chapter are from Ammianus book 31, this one from 31. 4. 3.

2   Two hundred thousand: Eunapius fr. 42; cf. Lenski (2002), 354–5. In the 470s a force of something like 10,000 Gothic warriors dragged their families and possessions around with them in a train of at least 2,000 wagons (Malchus fr. 20). My own thoughts on numbers are based on the fact that Valens attacked the Goths at Hadrianople thinking that he was currently facing only about 10,000 Goths (Ammianus 31. 12. 3), at a point when he seems to have thought that he was facing only the Tervingi. Combatants to noncombatants has usually been estimated at 1:4 or 1:5, suggesting total numbers for the Tervingi of perhaps 50,000. The evidence suggests that the Greuthungi were similar in numbers to the Tervingi.

3   Ammianus 31. 2.

4   See Maenchen-Helfen (1973), Chs 8–9.

5   A title rather than – as per Walt Disney – a personal name.

6   Many studies have tackled this thorny question, but for an introduction see Maenchen-Helfen, (1945) and Twitchett and Loewe (1986), esp. 383–405.

7   Jordanes *Getica* 24. 123–6; cf. Vasiliev (1936), on the story. Twentieth-century commentary: Bury (1928).

8   For an introduction to the Chionitae and the Guptas, see *Encyclopaedia Iranica*: Yarshater (1985–2004, ongoing).

9   Ammianus 31. 3. 2: 'he found release from his fears by taking his own life'.

10 Ammianus 31. 3. 7 describes these walls as extending 'from the river Gerasus [the modern Pruth] to the Danube and skirting the lands of the Taifali [Oltenia]'. I argue my view in Heather (1996), 100, with refs to alternatives.

11 Ammianus 31. 4. 12.

12 This is the traditional chronology. Wanke (1990) has argued instead for the spring of 376 on no very good grounds, and Lenski (2002), 182ff., 325f., for the early summer on the grounds that it was the Goths' arrival that encouraged Valens to make aggressive noises towards the Persians in the summer of 376. I find it it inconceivable, however, that an emperor who had wrapped up the Balkan front before confronting Persia in the late 360s (see Ch. 2) would have deliberately stirred up conflict in Armenia after hearing that the Danube was again in turmoil; so for me this confirms that the Goths arrived on the Danube only after Valens had made his moves in the east, hence in late summer 376 at the earliest.

13 Ammianus 31. 3. 8.

14 Ammianus 31. 3. 3.
15 As emerges from a huge Hunnic attack of that year, which went through the Caucasus rather than over the Danube (see further p. 202ff.).
16 Ammianus 31. 2. 8–9. Zosimus 4. 20. 4–5.
17 The archaeological evidence for the Huns' bow is collected and discussed in Harmatta (1951); Laszlo (1951); Bona (1991), 167–74. The history of the recurve bow and information on best recorded shots are from Klopsteg (1927). Klopsteg's attempts to model firepower have been superseded by the mathematically based work of Kooi; for an introduction, see Kooi (1991), (1994). These and his other studies can be read online at his website www.bio.vu.nl/thb/users/kooi. Key variables affecting the performance of a bow include length of limbs, shape of cross-section, elastic properties of the material used, draw length, arrow weight, weight and elastic properties of the string.
18 Olympiodorus fr. 19.
19 Jordanes Getica 49. 254: attributed to Priscus.
20 Laszlo (1951); Harmatta (1951).
21 Sources: Ammianus 31. 4. 4; Eunapius fr. 42; Socrates HE 4. 34; Sozomen HE 6. 37. Most tell a broadly similar story, but Ammianus is much more detailed, and Eunapius places more emphasis on Gothic treachery.
22 Ammianus records a justification for the admission of the Limigantes that strongly recalls that given in relation to the Goths of 376: '[By accepting the Limigantes] Constantius would gain more child-producing subjects and be able to muster a strong force of recruits' (19. 11. 7).
23 St Croix (1981), App. III, gives an exhaustive list of known moments of immigration. The story of the Sciri is in Sozomen HE 9.3 and CTh 5. 6. 3. For full discussion of Roman policy and literature, see Heather (1991), 123–30.
24 The quotations are from Ammianus 10. 11. 10–15.
25 Ammianus 31. 5. 9.
26 Valens' aggressive moves against the Persians in summer 376 are well constructed in Lenski (2002), 180–5. Cf. n. 12 above: in my opinion (not Lenski's) all this must place the arrival of the Goths on the Danube after Valens' aggression – i.e., late summer at the earliest.
27 If Sozomen HE 6. 37. 6 can be given any credence, Ulfilas may have taken part in the diplomatic process; cf. Heather and Matthews (1991), 104–6.
28 Ammianus 31. 4. 12.
29 For detailed discussion of the treaty's terms, see Heather (1991), 122–8. There are two points of controversy. On the basis of Socrates HE 4. 33, some date the conversion of the Tervingi before 376; cf. Lenski (1995). This, however, contradicts Ammianus' detailed contemporary account of events. Socrates, later and much less well informed, is very unlikely to be correct. I hold, therefore, to the conclusion first reached in Heather (1986). The other controversy, from the same source, centres on the report of Eunapius fr. 42 that the Goths were meant to surrender their weapons on crossing into the Empire, but didn't. This source also claims that the Goths swore a secret oath never to stop until they destroyed the Empire. But neither the secret oath nor the illegal smuggling of weapons are

reported anywhere else, particularly not in Ammianus, and were clearly used by Eunapius as devices to explain the Goths' later victory at Hadrianople. Neither is convincing, in my view, since Valens was hoping to use Gothic auxiliaries alongside his regular troops, and the Goths, as we shall see in a moment, were much too wary of the Empire to have entered it unarmed. Most scholars who accept the disarming story reject the secret oath (e.g. Lenski (2002), 343ff.), a solution which seems to me arbitrary.

30 Themistius Or. 13. 163c after Socrates Symposium 203d.

31 Ammianus 31. 5. 5–8.

32 Other Roman kidnaps: Ammianus 21. 4. 1–5; 27. 10. 3; 29. 4. 2ff.; 29. 6. 5; 30. 1. 18–21. Many other scholars see malice aforethought in Lupicinus' banquet (e.g. Lenski (2002), 328) without drawing conclusions about what this suggests about the orders he had received from Valens.

33 Ammianus 31. 4.

34 Diuque deliberans: Ammianus 31. 3. 8.

35 Ammianus 31. 5.

36 It is not fanciful to suppose that the Goths were aware of the Persian situation. Barbarians watched troop movements on the other side of the frontier closely (Ammianus 31. 10. 3–5), and contacts were close enough for information to pass. The continued contact between the Tervingi and Greuthungi is powerful evidence of the Goths' suspicions.

37 Valens could still contemplate hiring Gothic auxiliaries for his Persian war sometime in winter 376/7 (Ammianus 30. 2. 6), which must have been before the outbreak of war.

38 There is an immense bibliography on the development of different parts of the Roman Balkans, but no overview. The preceding paragraphs are a synthesis based on such major studies as Mocsy (1974); Lengyel and Radan (1980); Wilkes (1960); and Hoddinott (1975), with monographs such as Poulter (1995), and Mango (1985) on Constantinople.

39 In Germanophone historiography, it has been traditional since Várady (1969) to argue that the Greuthungi of Alatheus and Saphrax were composed of three equal ethnic contingents: Goths, Alans and Huns (the so-called Drei Völker group). Part of this scholarly fantasy is the argument that Ammianus' report of Huns and Alans joining the revolt in autumn 377 (see below) depicts the moment when Alatheus and Saphrax joined the Tervingi in revolt. This is nonsense. The Huns and Alans of autumn 377 (Ammianus mentions no Goths) were entirely separate from Alatheus and Saphrax, who were already south of the Danube and probably joined in the revolt immediately after the revolt of Lupicinus. For full refs and further discussion, see Heather (1991), App. B; cf. Lenski (2002), 330–1.

40 Ammianus 31. 6. 4.

41 On the forts, see Scorpan (1980); Petrovic (1996); their garrisons are listed at Not. Dig. Or. 39.

42 Ammianus 31. 6. 5–8.

43 According to Roman itineraries, a road station called Ad Salices ('By the Willows') was located in the far north of the Dobrudja, but Ammianus says this confron-

tation took place near Marcianople, 150 kilometres further south. At the start of the revolt proper, the Gothic wagon train had already wound its way to within 15 kilometres of Marcianople, and it's hard to see why the Goths would have retreated again so far north. So perhaps *oppidum Salices* should not be identified with *Ad Salices*.

44 Summer to autumn: Ammianus 31. 8. 2. The 377 campaign is recounted at Ammianus 31. 7.

45 Ammianus 31. 10. 1: so early November, perhaps.

46 New alliance and collapse of blockade: Ammianus 31. 8.4. Cf. n. 39 above: some argue that this was the moment when Alatheus and Saphrax joined Fritigern in revolt. Note, however, that Ammianus makes no mention of Greuthungi in this context.

47 On the Arabs, see Lenski (2002), 335f. with refs. Destruction of villas: Poulter (1999).

48 Ammianus 31. 11.

49 The story of these months is told in Ammianus 31. 10–11.

50 Ammianus' account of the battle can be found at 31. 12. Larger estimates of Gothic losses: Hoffmann (1969), 444 n. 138, 450–8; cf. e.g. Lenski (2002), 339 with refs. But if Valens had really had 30,000-plus troops to deploy against the Goths, I doubt that he would have needed to wait for Gratian, nor had to worry about whether the Goths were all there or not, because I don't believe that even the combined Goths could put many more than 20,000 men in the field (see n. 2 above).

51 Ammianus 31. 16. 7.

52 Ammianus 31. 12.

53 Eunapius frr. 47–8, survive from what was originally seemingly a lengthy account of these cities' tribulations.

54 This reconstruction results from the realization that Zosimus 4. 24–33, based on Eunapius' history, is actually a coherent account of events between 378 and 382, which has been ruined only by Zosimus importing into his text a second account of the war at 4. 34. Most scholars think that the Greuthungi made a separate peace with Gratian and were settled in Pannonia in 380, but I remain unconvinced; see Heather (1991), 147ff. and App. B, for further argument and full refs.

55 Themistius *Or.* 16. 210b–c.

56 There is literally a hole at the crucial point in the manuscript at Themistius *Or.* 34. 24, which makes it unclear whether he's referring to Goths being settled in Macedonia post-382, or only to their attack on the province before the peace agreement.

57 These leaders are presumably those who would have held semi-autonomous *reiks* status beneath Athanaric the *iudex* (Judge) in the old days of the Tervingi confederation north of the Danube (Ch. 2), and from among whom Fritigern and Alatheus and Saphrax had emerged in 376.

58 The significance of this treaty has long been recognized: e.g. Mommsen (1910), Stallknecht (1969). For more detailed discussion and full refs, see Heather (1991), 158ff.

59 To the end of the chapter, unless otherwise indicated, the quotations are from Themistius *Or.* 16.

60 Themistius *Or.* 14. 181b–c.

61 Zosimus 4. 32–3, with Heather (1991), 152–5; Heather and Moncur (2001), Ch. 4; cf. n. 54 above.

62 These Goths were more Greuthungi led by a certain Odotheus: Zosimus 4. 35. 1, 38–9; Claudian *On the Fourth Consulate of the Emperor Honorius*, 626ff.

63 Poulter (1995), (1999).

64 'These men crossed over into Asia under the law of war, and, having depopulated [vast tracts] . . . settled in this territory which they now inhabit. And neither Pompey nor Lucullus destroyed them, although this was perfectly possible, nor Augustus, nor the emperors after him; rather, they remitted their sins and assimilated them into the empire. And now no one would ever refer to the Galatians as barbarian but as thoroughly Roman. For while their ancestral name has endured, their way of life is now the same as our own. They pay the same taxes as we do, they enlist in the same ranks as we do, they accept governors on the same terms as the rest and abide by the same laws. So will we see the Scythians [Goths] do likewise within a short time' (*Or.* 16. 211c–d).

65 Ambrose *Commentary on the Gospel According to Luke 10: 10*: trans. Maenchen-Helfen (1973), 20.

5. THE CITY OF GOD

1 Jerome *Commentary on Ezekiel*, Preface to book 1. Pagan comment: Augustine *Sermon* 296; for a full survey of the reactions, see Courcelle (1964), 58ff.

2 On Olympiodorus and his parrot, and subsequent uses of the text, see Matthews (1970); Zosimus made the join between Eunapius and Olympiodorus at 5. 26. 1.

3 Zosimus 5. 26. 3–5.

4 Radagaisus as Goth: sources as *PLRE* 2, 934.

5 These refugees included inhabitants of Scarbantia who took with them the body of St Quirinus. *CTh* 10. 10. 25 and 5. 7. 2 also refer to them: Alföldy (1974), 213ff.

6 Claudian *Gothic War* ll. 363ff. (cf. 414–15); cf. Courtois (1955), 38ff.

7 Alamanni and Quadi are mentioned by Jerome as participating in the Rhine crossing (*Letter* 123. 15). Wolfram (1988), 387 n. 55, takes a similar view, but Thompson (1982b), 152–3, disagrees. Fifth-century Suevi: Pohl (1980), 274–6.

8 Jerome *Letter* 123. 15. Fourth-century Sarmatians: Ammianus 17. 12–13 (Sarmatians who did not participate in 406 continued to live on the Danube (Pohl (1980), 276–7)).

9 March to join Valens: Ammianus 31. 11. 6. Western Roman army: Zosimus 4. 35. 2.

10 Sozomen *HE* 9. 25. 1–7; cf. *CTh* 5. 6. 2. Thompson (1996), 63–4, is clear that Uldin was a relatively minor figure. For an alternative view, to my mind mistaken, see Maenchen-Helfen (1973), 59–72, esp. 71.

11 Sidonius *Poems* 12.

12 Fourth-century Burgundians: e.g. Matthews (1989), 306ff.; on their subsequent movements: e.g. Demougeot (1979), 432, 491–3.

13 Zosimus 5. 35. 5–6.

14 Paulinus of Pella *Eucharisticon* 377–98.

15 *CTh* 5. 6. 2.

16 Perhaps more, since we are not entirely sure of late Roman unit sizes.

17 Radagaisus' warriors: Olympiodorus fr. 9: Photius' summary says '12,000 nobles', but this is usually taken as a confused total figure: e.g. Wolfram (1988), 169–70; Heather (1991), 213–14. According to Augustine, Radagaisus had 'more than' 100,000 followers (*City of God* 5. 23); according to Orosius (7. 33. 4), 200,000; and according to Zosimus, 400,000 (5. 26). None of these command much authority.

18 Procopius *Wars* 3. 5. 18–19 says that 80,000 was the number of warriors, but more contemporary and better-informed Victor of Vita (*History of the Persecution* 1. 2) gives this as a total figure, reporting that the king divided his followers into 80 groups of notionally 1,000 apiece, their real size being somewhat smaller. Eighty thousand warriors is unbelievable, making the new group twice as powerful in military terms as the largest possible estimate for Alaric's Goths. Victor lived among the Vandals and there is a good chance that he generally knew what he was talking about, even though his work is highly polemical. Goffart (1980), 231–4, takes a dismissive view even of Victor's evidence (Victor notes, incidentally, that others had even in his day confused the total figure for the number of warriors), but on p. 33 is happy enough on a priori grounds to suppose that Vandal–Alan forces must have numbered tens of thousands.

19 Jerome *Chronicle* 2389. Orosius 7. 32. 11.

20 Some would place it much closer to, or even before, the year 400 (Heather (1996), 117ff., for a summary with full refs).

21 Radagaisus: Olympiodorus fr. 9 distinguishes *optimatoi* ('the best') from the rest; cf. Heather (1996), App. 1, more generally.

22 For: e.g. Lot (1939), 78–9; Courtois (1955), 39–40; Musset (1965), 103–4; Demougeot (1979), 415. Against: Goffart (1980), 2ff., esp. 16–17; cf. Maenchen-Helfen (1973), 60–1, 71–2.

23 Some Hunnic raiding parties got as far as the Danube in 376 (Ch. 4), but they were operating from a power-base much further to the east.

24 Claudian *Against Rufinus* 2. 26ff. records two threats to the eastern Empire in 395, one through the Caucasus, one on the Danube; 36ff. makes clear that Alaric's Goths are the Danubian threat – not, as has sometimes been supposed, a second group of Huns settled much further west.

25 Marcellinus Comes s.a. 427; cf. Jordanes *Getica* 32. 166.

26 The general was Aetius, of whom we will have much to say in the next two chapters; the Hunnic help he had recruited seven years earlier presumably came from the same region (refs as *PLRE* 2, 22–4).

27 Royal tombs: Priscus fr. 6. 1. On Attila's camp: Browning (1953), 143–5.

28 On Olympiodorus' affiliations, Matthews (1970). The sea journey: Olympiodorus frr. 19 and 28, both surely referring to the same crossing; cf. Croke (1977), 353. Others have envisaged Olympiodorus visiting the Pontus – e.g. Demougeot

(1970), 391–2 – but we also know that in 409 Honorius was expecting the imminent arrival of ten thousand Huns (Zosimus 5. 50. 1). This was after the defeat of Uldin, implying that contact must have been made in the meantime with other Huns. It is tempting to associate this new alliance with general Aetius' period as hostage among the Huns in c. 410 (refs as *PLRE* 2, 22).

29 *CTh* 7. 17. 1, 28 January 412: 'We decree that there shall be assigned to the Moesian border ninety patrol craft of recent construction and that ten more shall be added to these by the repair of old craft; and on the Scythian border, which is rather widespread and extensive there shall be assigned one hundred and ten such new craft, with fifteen added by the restoration of antiquated ones ... These shall be equipped with all their weapons and supplies at the instance of the duke and shall be constructed on the responsibility of his office staff.'

30 Mango (1985), 46ff.

31 It doesn't matter that much to the argument whether the mass of the Huns arrived west of the Carpathians during the crisis of 405–8 or in the course of the next decade or so. After 376, when the Tervingi and Greuthungi abandoned their homes north of the Black Sea, it took some years for the Huns to reach the Lower Danube frontier. Given that their arrival north of the Black Sea had been preceded by a huge demographic convulsion east of the Carpathians, the Huns' intrusion on to the Hungarian Plain in 410–20 would certainly have been preceded by similar upheavals to the west.

32 In dealing with an attack on Italy in 401/2, Stilicho had drawn off forces from Gaul and Britain, and there's every reason to suppose he did the same this time.

33 The Alans were perhaps recruited from north of the province of Raetia (Claudian *Gothic War*, 400–3); the Huns were sent by the – at this point – still biddable Uldin.

34 Orosius 7. 37. 37ff.

35 *Commonitorium* 2. 184.

36 The last two quotations are from Prosper of Aquitaine *Epigramma* 17–22; 25–6. A good introduction to these poems is Roberts (1992); see also Courcelle (1964), 79ff.

37 Hydatius *Chronicle* 49.

38 *Wars* 3. 33.

39 Orosius 7. 43. 14.

40 The Goths of Fritigern did much the same thing in Macedonia in c. 380 after three years of looting (see Ch. 4).

41 Zosimus 6. 1. 2 slightly conflated with Olympiodorus fr. 13, on the original of which Zosimus directly drew. The Olympiodorus fragment makes clear that the British usurpations began before 1 January 407 (the seventh consulship of Honorius), whereas Zosimus misunderstood his source to say that they began *in* the seventh consulship.

42 This emerges, despite some garbling, from Zosimus 6. 3.

43 Orosius 7. 40. 4.

44 This, the consensus view, has been argued against by Liebeschuetz (1990), 48–85, but I remain content with the counter-arguments offered in Heather (1991), 193–9.

45 Orosius 7. 35. 19.

46 This was later the case with Attila, who was made a notional imperial general in order to facilitate the pretence that the cash subsidy paid to him was salary for his troops, rather than a subsidy. I suspect that the dodge was first hatched in the case of Alaric, fifty or so years before. On the background to Alaric's revolt, see in more detail, Heather (1991), 181–92, 199ff.

47 In my view, this had happened as early as 395, when the revolt broke out. Others argue that it didn't happen until 408/9 when Alaric's brother-in-law Athaulf joined him in Italy with a force of Huns and Goths from Pannonia. The date, however, is really a matter of detail. The fundamental point is that old distinctions had been put aside. This was presumably made much easier by the suppression of the two groups' former leaders (Fritigern, Alatheus and Saphrax, under the treaty of 382), who might have had an interest in preserving the difference. For full details and refs to alternative views, see Heather (1991), 213–14, App. B.

48 Cameron (1970), 159ff.; cf. 474ff. for a convincing unravelling of the two main sources' confusion regarding the two campaigns.

49 On the fall of Eutropius: Cameron (1970), Ch. 6; Heather (1988).

50 On Gainas and Constantinopolitan politics: Cameron and Long (1993), Chs 5–6 and 8. The Silvanus episode: Ammianus 15.5. The literature on Alaric's first Italian adventure is enormous, but for an introduction, see Heather (1991), 207ff.

51 CTh 15. 14. 11.

52 He had last held office in 383, and had made a number of bad decisions in between, including backing the usurper Maximus (Matthews (1974)).

53 Letters 5. 51; 6. 2 and 27.

54 In Rufinem (Against Rufinus) 2. 4–6.

55 On Stilicho in general, see Cameron (1970), esp. Chs 2–3, and Matthews (1975), Ch. 10. This view of Stilicho's manoeuvres with Alaric is argued in more detail with full refs in Heather (1991), 211–13.

56 The next two quotations are from Zosimus 5. 32. 1; 5. 33. 1–2.

57 CTh 9. 42. 20–2.

58 The fall of Stilicho and Olympiodorus: Matthews (1970); (1975), 270–83.

59 According to Zosimus, 30,000 fighters joined Alaric after the pogrom, but that is impossibly high. I suspect that he again misunderstood Olympiodorus, who was certainly his source here, thinking that 30,000 was the number of recruits when it was actually the total for Alaric's force including the recruits. Thirty thousand would be my guess for the approximate size of Alaric's force after the reinforcements arrived; i.e. 10,000 each from the Greuthungi and Tervingi of 376, combined with the 10,000-plus former followers of Radagaisus that Stilicho had drafted into the Roman army.

60 The next two quotations are from Zosimus 5. 48. 3 and 5. 50. 3–51. 1.

61 Sarus and Alaric had quarrelled at some point before the latter came to Italy

(Zosimus 6. 13.2). Sarus met his death at the hands of Athaulf (Olympiodorus fr. 18), and Sergeric benefited from the assassination of Athaulf and his family (Olympiodorus fr. 26. 1).

62 For more detailed accounts of the events leading to the sack, see e.g., with full refs, Matthews (1975), Ch. 11; Heather (1991), 213–18.

63 Livy 5. 41. 8–9. The sources for Alaric's sack are gathered in Courcelle (1964), 45–55.

64 The quotations in the rest of this passage, unless otherwise stated, are from St Augustine *City of God*, here 3. 17.

65 *City of God*, 2. 19–20.

66 The 'lust for domination' follows Sallust *Catiline War* 2. 2; the quotation is from *City of God* 3. 14.

67 The quotation is from *City of God* 2. 29. Augustine continues: 'Among these very enemies are hidden [the Heavenly City's] future citizens; and when confronted with them she must not think it a fruitless task to bear with their hostility until she finds them confessing the faith. In the same way, while the City of God is on pilgrimage in this world, she has in her midst some who are united with her in participation of the sacraments, but who will not join with her in the eternal glory of the saints' (*City of God* 2. 34–5).

68 The quotation is from *City of God* 2.18. For introductions to *The City of God* and the full range of response to the sack, see Courcelle (1964), 67–77; Brown (1967), Chs 25–7.

69 The next five quotations are from Rutilius *De Reditu Suo*. The poem is translated in Keene and Savage-Armstrong (1907). On the journey and its circumstances, see Cameron (1967); Matthews (1975), 325–8.

70 The sun god, pulled in a chariot, by horses, across the sky.

71 The *Carmen de Providentia Dei* is partly translated and fully analysed in Roberts (1992).

72 Usually known by his full name – although the Flavius would normally be dropped – to prevent possible confusions with the usurper Constantine III. Full refs to the sources for his career can be found at *PLRE* 2, 321–5. The best account of his career is Matthews (1975), Chs 12–14.

73 Olympiodorus fr. 23.

74 This usurper is not the Magnus Maximus defeated by Theodosius I in 387, but a much more obscure claimant of the same name.

75 Matthews (1975), 313–15 (there is a slight question mark over the geography).

76 On the pay rise, see Sivan (1985) who dates it to 416; but it was much more likely to have been an earlier measure to stimulate loyalty among troops who had followed the usurpers and were now to fight barbarians.

77 Orosius 7. 43. 2–3.

78 Fr. 24.

79 Sergeric: see n. 61 above. For more detailed discussion of Constantius and the Goths, with full refs, see Heather (1991), 219–24. One *modius* is approximately one-quarter of a bushel.

80 *Chronicle* 24.

81 If by an indirect route: via Photius' ninth-century summary of the church historian Philostorgius, who used Olympiodorus' work. The key passage can be found at Philostorgius *HE* 12. 4–5, or Olympiodorus fr. 26. 2.

82 North Africa in the 440s, see p. 292–3. On the larger historiographical issue which has surrounded the economic form of barbarian settlement inside the Empire, see p. 423–4ff. with refs.

83 Two distinguished historians of a previous generation, Professors Thompson (1956) (revolting peasants) and Wallace-Hadrill (1961) (possibly Saxon pirates), virtually came to blows over this. I would particularly recommend to readers the appendix to Thompson (1982c), whose substantive discussion begins 'Unfortunately, in 1961 discussion of the matter was thrown into confusion by some ill-judged pages of J. M. Wallace-Hadrill . . .'

84 The authorities in Constantinople have sometimes been criticized for not doing more, but that's not very realistic: Demougeot (1951), esp. pt III, places a complete split between east and west far too early. More balanced are Kaegi (1968), Ch. 1, and Thompson (1950). For fuller discussion of Constantinople and the west, see Ch. 9.

85 Maenchen-Helfen (1973), 69, doubted that these Huns ever arrived, although most scholars have thought the auxiliaries did eventually turn up. As part of this agreement, a young man by the name of Aetius, of whom we shall see a great deal more in subsequent chapters, spent time as a hostage among the Huns, which does suggest that the negotiated relationship had a real point.

86 The agricultural surplus of the Empire can be thought of as being divided between the landowning classes (who received their share in the form of rent) and the imperial authorities (who received theirs in the form of tax). In the interests of satisfying the Goths within a fairly restricted area, Constantius was perhaps willing to forgo the Empire's share of the Garonne surplus, so that the area's tax revenues – as well as rents on public lands – could be allocated to the Goths' support. Again, something similar happened in North Africa.

87 This quotation and the next one are from Zosimus 6. 5. 2–3; 6. 10. 2.

88 On the Saxon shore defences, see Pearson (2002). For introductions to the range of opinion generated by these (and a few other references), see e.g. Campbell (1982), Ch. 1; Higham (1992), esp. Chs 3–4; Salway (1981), Ch. 15.

89 *De Reditu Suo* 1. 208–13.

90 Taking a slightly more optimistic view than Matthews (1975), 336–8, on the basis of much the same evidence. Cologne and Trier did not fall into Frankish hands until 457 (*Book of the History of the Franks* 8).

91 *CTh* 11. 28. 7 and 12.

92 *Not. Dig. Occ.* 5 and 6; 7.

93 You can tell the date because, within each category of unit, regiments are arranged in the chronological order of their creation, and there are just a handful named after Valentinian, the son born to Constantius and Placidia in July 419. On all this and what follows, see above all, Jones (1964), App. II.

94 Uncertainty over late Roman unit sizes (p. 62) prevents greater precision, but 500 men per regiment is the minimum figure.

95 As with the losses after Hadrianople, we don't know what percentage of a unit had to die before the decision was taken not to re-form it (cf. p. 181).

96 For the *Notitia* and the western army, see Jones (1964), App. III, and the various papers in Bartholomew (1976).

97 *Eucharisticon* 302–10.

6. OUT OF AFRICA

1 Ammianus 22. 7. 3–4.

2 Fr. 33.

3 Ammianus 28. 1. 24–5.

4 On imperial ceremonial in general and Julian's impropriety, see Matthews (1989), Chs 11–12; MacCormack (1981). On patterns of appointment, a good introduction is Matthews (1975), passim, with many of the essays collected in Matthews (1985), esp. Matthews (1971) and (1974).

5 Fr. 11.1.

6 For an introduction to regime change Roman-style, see Matthews (1975), e.g. 64ff. on the aftermath of the death of Valentinian I.

7 Ammianus 27. 22. 2–6.

8 Many of Libanius' letters, for instance, are surprisingly aggressive to potential patrons, demanding that they show what they are made of: see e.g. Bradbury (2004), *Letters* 2, 5, 8, 9 etc.

9 The two commanders were first sentenced to exile but killed on the journey.

10 *The Annals of Ravenna* date the assassination to 7 March 413, but this seems too early in the year. Ships did not normally pass between Carthage and Italy between November and March, and we need time for Heraclianus first to land, be defeated and return to Africa. Perhaps he landed in Italy on 7 March. See generally Orosius 7. 42. 12–14; other sources as *PLRE* 2, 540.

11 Olympiodorus fr. 33.1.

12 On Galla Placidia, see Oost (1968).

13 Fr. 38.

14 *PLRE* 2, 1024.

15 Olympiodorus fr. 43.2.

16 See Matthews (1970) on Olympiodorus, with Matthews (1975), Ch. 15, on the history.

17 Prosper Tiro s.a. 425; *Chron. Gall.* 452 no. 102; the figure of 60,000 is impossibly large.

18 For Aetius, Felix and Boniface, refs as *PLRE* 2, 23–4, 238–40, 463–4. The main secondary accounts I have drawn upon in this and subsequent discussions of Aetius' activities are: Mommsen (1901); Stein (1959), Ch. 9; Zecchini (1983); Stickler (2002).

19 Refs. as *PLRE* 2, 22–3.

20 Ammianus 31. 2. 25.

21 No law codes survive from the Vandal kingdom, but Procopius' narrative of the

Byzantine conquest notes in passing the pattern observed among other Germanic groups of this period of having two distinct military castes, which I take to be those of the 'free' and the 'freed' (see Ch. 2). The remains of the Przeworsk culture, from which the Vandals derived, also suggest no obvious difference in social structure compared with other better-documented Germani. For an introduction to the fragile and relatively egalitarian social structures of nomads, see Cribb (1991) with full refs.

22 Gregory of Tours *Histories* 2. 9.

23 *Chronicle* 42, 49, 67–8, esp. 68: *Alani qui Vandalis et Sueuis potentabantur*: 'the Alans who were ruling over the Vandals and Sueves'.

24 Hydatius *Chronicle* 68.

25 Depending on the extent of the exaggeration reported by Victor of Vita, see p. 198–9. On the official titulature of the kings, see Wolfram (1967).

26 All narrative accounts of the Vandals and Alans in Spain are largely based on the *Chronicle* of Hydatius. Dating is affected by the controversy over how extant versions of the text should be edited: see e.g. Burgess (1993), 27ff., for an introduction to the dispute. My notes here follow the referencing system used in Mommsen (1894); for our purposes, these arguments fortunately affect details rather than overview.

27 Hydatius was writing when Visigoths were pillaging widely in Spain, and he is always critical of them. Given how readily they had helped defeat Vandals and Alans in the later 410s, it is unclear why they should have had such a change of heart in 422.

28 Jordanes *Getica* 33: 168.

29 *Not. Dig. Occ.* 25.

30 *Wars* 3. 3. 22f.

31 The peace was negotiated by the senator Darius, with whom Augustine exchanged pleasantries (Augustine *Letters* 229–31).

32 The historical reconstruction offered in the rest of this section depends upon Courtois (1955), 155ff. (with refs).

33 *Not. Dig. Occ.* 26.

34 The quotation above is from Victor of Vita 1. 3. Amongst the bishops tortured Victor names Pampinianus of Vita and Mansuetus of Urusi.

35 *Letter* 220. Olympiodorus fr. 42.

36 The illustrator of one of the later copies of this manuscript mistook these for upside-down ducks, presumably with rigor mortis having already set in, since Africa is holding them by the necks and the bodies are sticking up in the air.

37 As a politically incorrect and chronologically befuddled sergeant of the British Eighth Army put it in late 1941, after a lecture from the enthusiastic Director of Army Education in Tripoli on the wonders of Roman North Africa: 'We now know all about this place; it is full of the ruins of buildings put up by the Eyeties before the war, but as far as I can see, it is now just full of camels and Western Oriental Gentlemen' (quoted in Manton (1988), 139).

38 Even these were tending to dwarf: a sure sign that they had been cut off from the mainstream for some time.

39 Tripolitania was also administered from Carthage in the Roman period.

40 Historians of Roman Africa writing in the nineteenth and early twentieth centuries supposed that large-scale immigration from Italy was an important contributory factor. There certainly was some immigration. When Carthage was refounded as a Roman colony in 29 BC, for instance, 30,000 Italian settlers crossed the sea. Also, the third legion was stationed in North Africa from 23 BC, generating a steady trickle of veteran settlers who bought farms and established townships such as Diana Veteranorum, Timgad, Thurburbo Maius and Djemila. But by the third century AD the vast majority of the 600 Roman towns in North Africa were inhabited by indigenous Romano-Africans, so that the role of immigrants must not be overstated.

41 A famous inscription from Ain Zraia (ancient Zarai) in Algeria records that whereas most goods were taxed at 2–2.5 per cent, animals and their products (textiles, hides etc.) were rated at only one-fifth to one-third of 1 per cent.

42 The 'colonial' view of North Africa can be found in Baradez (1949). See also the more recent revisions of Whittaker (1994), 145–51, and the collected essays of Shaw (1995a), nos 1, 3, 5, 6, and (1995b), no. 7. Readily accessible general accounts of Roman North Africa are: Raven (1993); Manton (1988).

43 Carthage: Ennabli (1992), 76–86. Utica: Procopius *Wars* 3. 11. 13–15.

44 *CTh* 13.5 and 6 contain a long run of relevant imperial pronouncements.

45 Lepelley (1979–81). Even elsewhere, as we saw in Ch. 3, this change had more to do with the restructuring of city finance in the third-century crisis and its political repercussions than with economic decline.

46 *ILT* 243.

47 CIL 8, 18587. Again, the French colonial view held that it was European settlers who brought with them new water technologies, such as the 50-kilometre aqueduct which serviced Carthage in the late antique period, required to make North Africa bloom. But that massive construction brought water to the city for luxury, not agricultural, purposes, particularly to service its massive Antonine baths.

48 Mactar inscription, olives and rural expansion: Raven (1993), 84–6, 92–6. A good general account of the rural survey findings is Mattingly and Hitchner (1995).

49 *Expositio Totius Mundi* 61.

50 The amusements of the amphitheatre included everything from wild beast hunts, in which two hunters might be pitted against nine bears in a battle to the death, to risqué representations of the loves of Jupiter, to novelty acts such as acrobats acting out dramas on tightropes. At the circus, you could find the ever-popular chariot-racing, but the young Augustine particularly loved the theatre. At the age of sixteen he had come to Carthage, where 'a cauldron of illicit loves leapt and boiled about' him; and in response to the stage: 'In my wretchedness, I loved to be made sad and sought for things to be sad about: and in the misery of others – though fictitious and only on the stage – the more my tears were set to flowing, the more pleasure did I get from the drama and the more powerfully did it hold me' (*Confessions* 3. 2).

51 For an introduction to the findings of the UNESCO excavations, see Ennabli (1992).

52 Gregory of Tours 2. 8, after Renatus Frigeridus. On the background of Aetius, see most recently Stickler (2002), 20–5, with refs.

53 Zosimus 6. 2. 4–5; Hydatius *Chronicle*, 125, 128.

54 For revisionary views of the Bagaudae, see Drinkwater (1993); Halsall (1993); arguing against an older, more Marxist strand of interpretation, e.g. Thompson (1956).

55 They vary in form from Latin prose, to hexameters, to elegiac couplets, to Phalacean metre.

56 The base and commemorative inscription still survive (CIL 6. 1724).

57 On Merobaudes, see generally Clover (1971), who discusses the manuscript as well as editing and translating the poems; with further discussion in *PLRE* 2, 756–8.

58 The quotations in the next few pages, unless otherwise indicated, are from Merobaudes' *Panegyrics* 1 and 2.

59 The insurgents are called 'Nori', but this pre-Roman conquest tribe hadn't existed for centuries, so they may well have been another quasi-Bagaudic group.

60 Sources as *PLRE* 2, 166; cf. Courtois (1955), 155–71; Stickler (2002), 232–47.

61 Priscus fr. 11. 1, p. 243; the date and extent of the concession has occasioned much debate: for an introduction, see Maenchen-Helfen (1973), 87ff.

62 Merobaudes *Panegyric* 1 fr. IIB.

63 Refs as *PLRE* 2, pp. 24–5; most recent commentary, with full refs: Stickler (2002), 48ff. Procopius *Wars* 3. 3. 15 refers to Aetius (and Boniface) as the last of the Romans.

64 Quodvultdeus *In Barbarian Times* 2. 5.

65 Merobaudes *Carmen* IV.

66 *Nov. Val.* 5. 1, 6. 1.

67 *Nov. Val.* 9.

68 Force from the east: Theophanes AM 5941, with *CJ* 12. 8. 2 on Pentadius. Secondary commentary: Courtois (1955), 171–5.

69 *Panegyric* 2. 51–3. The next two quotations are from *Panegyric* 2. 61–7, 2. 98–104.

70 *Nov. Val.* 34: 13 July 451.

71 Basic terms of the 442 treaty: Procopius *Wars* 3. 14. 13, with Clover (1971).

72 *Panegyric* 2. 25–33.

73 *Carmen* 1. 5–10.

74 'Allotment' may conjure up visions of Vandals and Alans on the outskirts of Carthage tending their vegetable patches, putting up sheds and comparing the sizes of their marrows. And, in fact, that connotation is not entirely inappropriate: see next note.

75 Victor of Vita 2. 39. I owe this point to Moderan (forthcoming), whose discussion renders redundant the suggestion of Goffart (1980), 67–8 n., that the Vandal settlement after 439 merely reallocated provincial tax revenues. Goffart's suggestion was based on an argument by analogy rather than detailed consideration of the North African evidence. On this historiographical issue, see further pp. 423–4ff.

76 Celestiacus: Theodoret of Cyrrhus *Letters* 29–36; Maria: 70.

77 This is where the allotment image breaks down, and, in any case, any residual agricultural expertise among the north-central European Vandals would have been inappropriate for the Mediterranean littoral.

78 This wasn't as good as outright ownership, but the new tenants were given emphyteutic leases with full inheritance rights, so that they had some security (*Nov. Val.* 34).

79 *Nov. Val.* 13. This degree of remission is comparable with that granted to areas around Rome affected by Alaric's Visigoths between 408 and 410 (see p. 245–6).

80 These were the kinds of things that emperors often gave as favours, and when the tax-base was large they could be easily absorbed. Now, however, as the law put it: 'the weight of the tribute which is withdrawn from certain persons individually falls back on the others' (*Nov. Val.* 4).

81 *Nov. Val.* 7. 1; slightly modified in 7.2 of 27 September 442.

82 *Nov. Val.* 10.

83 Four thousand two hundred *solidi* (one-eighth of the old total) were now to be paid by Numidia under the general tax account, together with 1,200 military subsistence allowances and 200 units of animal fodder. Five thousand *solidi* (again, one-eighth of the previous figure) and 50 units of animal fodder were demanded from Mauretania Sitifensis. Each military subsistence allowance and fodder unit had also been reduced by one *solidus* (*Nov. Val.* 13).

84 Following the calculations of Elton (1996a), 120–5, which must be approximately correct, even if detailed points are arguable.

85 The next two quotations are from *Panegyric* 2. 55–8, 75–6.

7. ATTILA THE HUN

1 Opinions on Attila: Thompson (1996), 226–31; Maenchen-Helfen (1973), 94ff. Thompson and Maenchen-Helfen are the two main accounts available in English. The quotation is from Marcellinus Comes, *Chronicle* s.a. 447.2. A few years ago, I was asked to revise the old article on Attila in *The Oxford Dictionary of the Christian Church*. They said change whatever you like, but keep 'scourge of God'.

2 One source dates Rua's death to 434, but is demonstrably wrong (Maenchen-Helfen (1973), 91–4).

3 The next three quotations are from Priscus frr. 2, 6.1, 6.2.

4 Compare the approaches of Thompson (1945) and Blockley (1972).

5 Julian, *Letter to the Athenians* 279A–B; Ammianus 16. 2ff.; cf. Matthews (1989), Ch. 6.

6 For an introduction to the development of the Silk Road cities, see Boulnois (1966).

7 Ammianus 31. 10. 3–5 gives an excellent example of cross-border intelligence from winter 377/8. The Alamanni learned about Roman troop movements from a retired guardsman, but also observed them for themselves.

8   On the context of his life, see Toynbee (1973); Runciman (1929).

9   That we have part of volume 50 suggests that most of them did once exist; the quotation is from the Preface to Constantine's *Excerpts concerning Virtues and Vices*.

10 For an introduction to Constantine's project, see Lemerle (1971), 280–8.

11 I here broadly follow Maenchen-Helfen (1973), 116–17.

12 Working with his book is a bit like working with Priscus. As its editor's introductory note explains, the author brought a 'beautifully typed' manuscript into the offices of California University Press in early January 1969, but then died just a few days later. The manuscript turned out not to be a completed book, but only some chapters, and despite much editing the book as finally published remains highly episodic, missing a great number of connecting passages. But none of this detracts, again like the fragments of Priscus, from the quality of what is there.

13 Maenchen-Helfen (1973), 86–103, discussing Theophanes AM 5942.

14 Given that 442–7 is six years, 8,400 pounds should have been paid in this period, but that the arrears were 6,000 suggests that only 2,400 were ever handed over.

15 *Nov. Theod.* 24.

16 On the recruitment of Isaurians, see Thompson (1946).

17 Quoted in Maenchen-Helfen (1973), 121.

18 *Life of Hypatius* 104.

19 Poulter (1995), (1999).

20 Priscus fr. 9. 3, p. 238; cf. its survival of Avar attacks, too, 150 years later: Theophylact Simocatta *History* 7.3. The next two quotations are from Priscus fr. 9. 3.

21 Road: fr. 11. 2, p. 263. Tents: fr. 11. 2, p. 251.

22 Priscus fr. 11. 2, p. 275.

23 We have virtually the whole of Priscus' account transmitted in a number of different fragments. They are arranged in chronological order and translated in Gordon (1960), Ch. 3 (with commentary), and Blockley (1983), frr. ll. 1–15. 2, whose translation is quoted in what follows. Except where otherwise indicated, the quotations in the rest of this chapter are from Priscus.

24 Fr. 11. 2, pp. 247–9.

25 Circuit walls: Priscus fr. 11. 2, p. 265; buildings: fr. 11. 2, p. 275; seating arrangements: fr. 13. 1, p. 285; furnishings: fr. 11. 2, p. 275; greeting: fr. 11. 2, p. 265.

26 Rather as in the old game of Kremlin-watching, this ceremonial life made it abundantly clear when someone had been promoted or demoted.

27 The next two quotations are from *Getica* 34: 182; 35: 183 (= Priscus fr. 12. 2).

28 Fr. 2, p. 227.

29 Fr. 14, p. 293.

30 Priscus fr. 11. 2, p. 267. The sharing of booty is, as we shall see in a moment, fully reflected in the archaeological evidence, but also referred to in passing in the literary evidence: e.g. Priscus fr. 11. 2 p. 263f.

31 Priscus fr. 15.2, p. 297.

32 Olympiodorus fr. 19.

33 Some commentators have taken Matthews (1970) to task for simply assuming this to have been the case (see Matthews (1985), additional note), but the text is ambiguous and his original thought could easily be correct.

34 'Er, yes – I'm afraid I gave the best gifts to the wrong king and the Akatziri are now our mortal enemies. Sorry, Sir.' Nearly as good a diplomatic foul-up as the occasion when the Queen referred to the battle of Waterloo as an excellent example of Anglo-German cooperation, much to the chagrin of the French.

35 It also puts a further nail in the coffin of any idea that Uldin, prominent before 411, possessed anything like the power of Attila. There are other reasons, as we have seen, for rejecting this idea (p. 198), but, just as important, it is clear that no Hun king was so dominant at such an early date.

36 Heather (1996), 113–17, on the rise of Valamer among the Pannonian Goths: he killed Vinitharius, the head of one line (but also married his granddaughter), and forced Beremud, from another, to flee; but Gensemund, Beremud's uncle, accepted his overlordship. See further Ch. 8.

37 Part of the manoeuvre to catch Vigilas involved banning the Romans from making further purchases of Hunnic horses, and the first trouble with Attila and Bleda involved a surprise attack on market day (Priscus fr. 6. 1).

38 Itself worth the far from negligible sum of nearly seven pounds of gold.

39 The figures are those of Lindner (1981) who, in a famous article, concluded that, since Hunnic armies in the time of Attila certainly numbered tens of thousands, the Huns could no longer have been nomads, since there wasn't enough space in Hungary for so many horses. He missed the important point that most of the manpower for Attila's armies was provided by his Germanic subjects, not by the Huns themselves, so we don't need to postulate so many horses anyway. The military manpower point is fully explored later in this chapter.

40 Languages: Priscus fr. 11. 2, p. 267: 'Being a mixture of peoples, in addition to their own languages they cultivate Hunnic or Gothic or, in the case of those who have dealings with the Romans, Latin.' Names: Maenchen-Helfen (1973), 386ff.; cf. Jordanes Getica 9:58 on the adoption of names between different language groups.

41 Sozomen HE 9.5; CTh 5. 6. 3.

42 Theophanes AM 5931; cf. Procopius Wars 3. 2. 39–40, with Croke (1977). The date could be either 421 or 427.

43 Gepids, Rugi, Suevi, Sciri and Herules are all named in the post-Attilan narrative of events on the Great Hungarian Plain (see Ch. 8), while Attila intervened in the internal politics of the Franks (Priscus fr. 20. 3), which makes it very likely that he exercised some kind of hegemony over Lombards and Thuringians, and possibly Alamanni too, all of whom lived closer to the Hunnic heartland.

44 I find Priscus perfectly comprehensible, unlike Baldwin (1980), who argues that these terms were all used in a confused and confusing fashion.

45 You can tell how people were dressed by where they wore their safety-pins – all that tends to survive of clothing in most graves.

46 Reasons for archaeological invisibility can range from the dramatic, where bodies are left exposed to the elements and wild animals, to the prosaic: cremation

followed by the scattering of ashes, or bodies being buried without any chronologically indentifiable grave goods – which often makes medieval northern European cemeteries undatable once populations convert to Christianity.

47   Although written sources occasionally provide information, which can be used in conjunction with archaeological evidence to identify particular groups.

48   The archaeological 'horizons' are differentiated from one another by discernible variations in the manner in which broadly similar sets of grave goods were decorated. In chronological order – and there are overlaps – the sequence starts with the Villafontana horizon, followed by those of Untersiebenbrunn and Domolospuszta/Bacsordas (names not for the faint of heart!).

49   Many of the Germanic groups of central Europe in the first to third centuries had practised cremation, but inhumation was already spreading more widely before the arrival of the Huns.

50   For introductions to these finds, see Bierbrauer (1980), (1989); Kazanski (1991); Tejral (1999). Wolfram (1985) has some excellent illustrations.

51   The point was first emphasized by Bury (1928).

52   Priscus fr. 15. 4, p. 299.

53   Priscus fr. 11. 2, p. 277.

54   Sources as *PLRE* 2, 568–9. Besides, this kind of thing is typical of the rich and underemployed – especially those of energy and determination – caught up in the empty ceremonies of a highly orchestrated court life. In Nepal in 2001 a drunken prince went berserk and shot ten of his relatives, including the reigning monarch, before killing himself; readers with slightly longer memories will recall the much covered-up death of a Saudi princess who strayed from the expected paths of inaction.

55   Plate: Priscus fr. 11. 2, pp. 263, 265, 277. Frankish succession: Priscus fr. 20. 3. On contacts with Geiseric and the general diplomatic context: Clover (1972).

56   *Getica* 33: 182.

57   *Poem* 7. 319ff.

58   My account of Attila's two western campaigns draws heavily on Thompson (1996), Ch. 6; Maenchen-Helfen (1973), 129ff. The latter deals only with the Italian campaign: an account of the attack on Gaul was not found among the extant fragments (see n. 12 above).

59   Jordanes *Getica* 195.

60   The battle narrative is from Jordanes *Getica* 38:197–41:218.

61   Fr. 22. 2, p. 313 = Procopius *Wars* 3. 4. 33–4.

62   Hydatius *Chronicle* 154.

63   The fact that Aetius was either unable or unwilling to confront Attila head-on with another confederation, as in Gaul, has often aroused comment. Prosper Tiro s.a. 451 says that Aetius was caught unprepared, and some have believed this to be so. Maenchen-Helfen (1973), 135ff., convincingly reconstructs Aetius' countermeasures and sets them in the context of other contemporary Roman defences of the Po valley. I also follow Maenchen-Helfen in understanding Hydatius *Chronicle* 154 to mean that Aetius received eastern military help in Italy, as well as benefiting from a campaign by eastern troops on the Danube.

64 Even in more modern eras, armies campaigning over these kinds of distances have come unstuck. In the summer of 1914, German armies reached the gates of Paris, before rolling back again (there's no record that St Genevieve had anything to do with this). They were brought to a halt by a bold tactical manoeuvre on the part of the French army on the River Marne, but also by exhaustion, which gave the French their opportunity. A British trooper, falling back before the German advance, reported: 'The greatest strain . . . was . . . fatigue . . . I fell off my horse more than once, and watched others do the same, slowly slumping forward, grabbing for their horse's neck, in a dazed, barely conscious way. At any halt men fell asleep instantaneously' (quoted in Keegan (1988), 107). There were, of course, a number of differences between 451 and 1914. In 1914, the distance from Belgium to Paris was covered at speed in about two weeks, the men marching 40 kilometres a day, day after day. The Hunnic advance was a much more leisurely affair. In 1914 the Germans had travelled to the German-Belgian border by train, leaving only about 500 kilometres to cover on foot and on horseback, and they did have supplies and wagon trains.

65 *Getica* 49: 256–8.

66 Although they did attempt to broker a peace between the Suevi and the Gallaecian provincials.

67 Any account of Spain in the 430s and 440s has to be built up from Hydatius 91–142.

68 The Pelagian heresy is named after the Romano-British theologian Pelagius, who argued, not least against Augustine, that salvation required not just Divine Grace, upon which others put the emphasis, but also great individual effort to live a virtuous life.

69 Though not any more in cash, as the non-subsistence elements of the local economy, such as its pottery industries, seem to have collapsed by c. 420.

70 The three quotations that follow are from Gildas *On the Ruin of Britain* 23. 5, 24. 3 and 20. 1.

71 On the crisis of the 440s and the end of Roman Britain, see e.g. Campbell (1982), Ch. 1; Higham (1992), Chs 5–8; Salway (1981), Ch. 16; Esmonde Cleary (2000).

72 The rest of North Africa, southern Gaul as far east as Arles, north-western Gaul affected by the Bagaudae, central Gaul and northern Italy affected by Attila's campaigns.

8. THE FALL OF THE HUNNIC EMPIRE

1 Jordanes *Getica* 48: 246–55: 282.

2 Momigliano (1955) and Goffart (1988) come to opposite conclusions about the Cassiodorus–Jordanes relationship from more or less the same set of observations. Suggestions as to why Jordanes should have lied mostly turn on the fact that he was writing on the eve of an east Roman campaign which destroyed the Ostrogothic Italian kingdom. It has been argued that the *Getica* contains an important political message (from Cassiodorus, or pretending to be from

Cassiodorus), urging people not to resist the east Roman forces. These hypotheses conveniently ignore the problem of how the *Getica's* supposed political message was to be disseminated. The only way of turning a literary history into political propaganda is to suppose that landowners were assembled and exposed to the *Getica* in the way that people had been exposed to the speeches of a Themistius, a Merobaudes or a Sidonius Apollinaris. This is highly unlikely. For more technical argument, see Heather (1991), Ch. 2.

3   Cassiodorus concentrates on the royal dynasty from which Theoderic (Cassiodorus' master) came – the Amal family – and organized Gothic history by geography, dividing it up according to the different abodes inhabited by Goths at different times. Both of these points are evident in Jordanes' history. See further Heather (1993).

4   Group 1: first known from Jordanes' account of the collapse of the Hunnic Empire, then from many sources subsequently (see further Heather (1996), 111–17). Group 2: see p. 193–4. Groups 3/6: best evidence from Malchus of Philadelphia in the 470s, origins perhaps documented in Theophanes AM 5931 (see further Heather (1996), 152ff.); cf. above Ch. 7 n. 42. Group 4: Jordanes *Romana* 336. Group 5: Priscus fr. 49. Group 7: Procopius *Wars* 8. 4. 9ff. ('not numerous'), *Buildings* 3. 7. 13 (3,000 warriors strong).

5   Valamer and his nephew Theoderic united at least groups 1 and 6, but possibly also 3 and 4; see Heather (1991), Ch. 1, with full refs.

6   This reference and the next quotation are from *Getica* 50: 261–2, 50: 260.

7   Theoderic the Amal, the Ostrogothic king of Italy, fought against the Gepids, for instance, in 488/9 and again in the early 500s.

8   *Getica* 50: 262–4.

9   *Getica* 268–9, 272–3.

10   Priscus fr. 49.

11   *Getica* 272–3.

12   *Getica* 248–52.

13   The crucial passage is *Getica* 248–52 plus the discussion of Heather (1989), with full refs to previous attempts to resolve its obvious difficulties.

14   Refs as *PLRE* 2, 385f. Maenchen-Helfen (1973), 388 and n. 104, denies the identity of the two Edecos, but it is generally accepted; cf. (and more generally on the emergence of the kingdoms that would succeed the Huns') Pohl (1980).

15   Except possibly the Amal-led Goths. Jordanes says that they came west of the Carpathians after the Huns fled east after following the battle of the Nedao (*Getica* 50: 263–4). This seems unlikely, and I suspect that they were settled in Pannonia by the Huns and not on their own initiative, but there is no way to be certain.

16   *Getica* 53: 272–55: 282.

17   *Getica* 54: 279.

18   Fr. 45.

19   *Getica* 52: 268 vs. 53: 273.

20   Thompson (1996), esp. Ch. 7; cf. Maenchen-Helfen (1973), 95ff.

21   Priscus fr. 11. 2, p. 259.

22 Tervingi and Greuthungi: p. 145. Burgundians: p. 198. Of various Goths, group 3 above, perhaps identical with the later Thracian Goths (n. 4 above), were detached from Hunnic overlordship by Roman military intervention, and the Amal-led Pannonian Goths (group 1) were very clear that they had been made part of the Hunnic Empire by force, even if the 'Balamber stories' of the *Getica* are confused (n. 13 above).

23 Merchant: Priscus fr. 11. 2, p. 269 l.419–p. 272 l.510. Gibbeting: Priscus fr. 14 p. 293 ll. 60–5.

24 Fr. 49.

25 Theophanes AM 5931 (group 3): the point obviously holds, whether or not group 3 can be identified with group 6 (see n. 4 above).

26 The next three quotations are from Priscus fr. 2, p. 225; p. 227; p. 227.

27 The Romans provided Attila with a succession of secretaries, including the prisoner Rusticius who wrote the odd letter (Priscus fr. 14, p. 289). This governmental machine made lists of renegade princes who had fled to the Romans and possibly kept track of the supplies required from subject groups.

28 Most dominated: the Goths who appear in Priscus fr. 49, part of which is quoted above. Least dominated: the Gepids who led the revolt against Attila's sons (Jordanes *Getica* 50: 260–2). In between, the Pannonian Goths of Valamer (Jordanes *Getica* 48: 246–53, 52: 268ff.), with commentary by Heather (1996), 113–17, 125–6.

29 Each of the Hunnic-period 'horizons' is named after one of these rich burials.

30 An excellent introduction to Apahida and the other rich burials of the period is provided by the catalogue volume Menghin et al. (1987).

31 Gold certainly existed in fourth-century Germania and was being worked into plate. The famous fifth-century treasure from Romania, the Pietroasa horde (Harhoiu (1977), contains one or two items which were clearly antiques at the time of deposition and must have been made in the mid-fourth century. Roman gold coins were also far from unusual.

32 After Bierbrauer (1980).

33 E.g. Ammianus 17. 12–13, 19. 11, on Constantius' settlement in the Middle Danube in the late 350s, with further commentary by Heather (2001).

34 Odovacar in Gaul: Gregory of Tours *Histories* 2.18 (sometime between 463 and 469); cf. *PLRE* 2, 791–3. Herules, Alans and Torcilingi: Procopius *Wars* 3. 1. 6: Ennodius *Life of St Epiphanius* 95–100.

35 *Romana* 336.

36 Sidonius *Poems* 2. 239ff.

37 The other possibly complicating factor was the arrival of a new nomad power north of the Black Sea. By the early 480s, for instance, Bulgars had established themselves close to the Empire's Danube frontier (John of Antioch fr. 211. 4).

38 Fr. 37.

39 Fr. 45.

40 Jordanes *Getica* 49: 255, probably originating in Priscus and translated therefore by Blockley as Priscus fr. 24. 1.

41 Best general accounts of Aetius' fall: Stein (1959), 347ff.; Stickler (2002), 150ff.

42 For Petronius' career, with full refs, see *PLRE* 2, 749–51.

43 The next few quotations are from Priscus fr. 30.

44 On Avitus' early career, with full refs, see *PLRE* 2, 196–8.

45 For a recent study of Sidonius and his life and times, see Harries (1994); Stevens (1933) remains valuable.

46 Dill (1899), 324; for a collection of similar judgements, see Harries (1994), 1–2.

47 *Letter* 4. 10. 2, quoted in Harries (1994), 3.

48 Many have contributed to this revolution in appreciation, and an excellent introduction is Roberts (1989) with references to other relevant studies.

49 The next few quotations are from Sidonius *Poem* 7.

50 Priscus fr. 30. 2.

51 Full reconstruction: Courtois (1955), 185–6.

52 Priscus fr. 32 = John of Antioch fr. 202.

53 On this Gallic literary context, see e.g. Harries (1994), Chs 1–2.

54 Sidonius *Letters* 1. 2.

55 The story of the campaign is told in Hydatius *Chronicle* 173–86. On the previous joint Romano-Gothic campaigns in Spain, see Chs 5 and 6 above.

56 It is impossible to reconstruct Burgundian history in detail, but for fuller discussion and refs, see Favrod (1997).

57 *History of the Persecution* 1. 13.

58 This quotation and the next are from Sidonius *Poem* 7. 233–6, 286–94.

59 Sidonius *Poem* 361ff. Next quotation: 510–18.

60 Refs as *PLRE* 2, 198.

9. THE END OF EMPIRE

1 Depending on the balance between 500- and 1,000-man units: Jones (1964), vol. 3, 364 and 379; see further p. 63. The eastern section of the *Notitia* dates only to the mid-390s, but eastern armies suffered no massive losses after this. In 395, the east also controlled the entire field army of Illyricum (another 26 regiments), but thereafter west Illyricum and its forces were returned to western control.

2 The argument of Goffart (1981). Constantine defeated a series of rivals between 306 and 324 to unite the Empire, having started by controlling just Britain and Gaul. Julian had been appointed Caesar in the west by his cousin Constantius in 355, but revolted in 360, uniting the whole Empire under his control on Constantius' sudden death in 361.

3 Theodosius accepted that Persia should exercise hegemony over two-thirds of Armenia, taking just one-third for himself.

4 A fair summary of Roman–Persian relations can be found in Blockley (1992). Rubin (1986) brings out the extremely peaceful nature (in relative terms) of Roman–Persian relations in the fifth century as opposed to the sixth or fourth.

5 *Not. Dig. Or.* 5, 6, 8.

6 *CTh* 7. 17. 1 of 412.

7 421: Theophanes AM 5931 (cf. Ch. 8). Ruga: Maenchen-Helfen (1973), 81–94.

8 Zosimus 6. 8. 2–3.

9 Thus Hydatius *Chronicle* 154 reports: 'The Huns ... were slaughtered by auxiliaries sent by the Emperor Marcian and led by Aetius, and at the same time they were crushed in their settlements both by heaven-sent disasters and the army of Marcian.' See further Ch. 7 above.

10 Cameron (1970), 176ff. disposed of the old argument that Alaric was encouraged to move into Italy by Constantinople. Edward Thompson's judgement can be found at Thompson (1996), 161ff.; he was particularly exercised by the revenge Attila would have wreaked on the east in 453 had his own death not brought a halt to campaigning. I therefore find nothing in the detailed narrative to support the argument of Goffart (1979) (see n. 2 above).

11 Scholarly opinion on Ricimer's policies has ebbed and flowed, with some regarding his barbarian origins as having undermined his loyalty to Rome. But the Visigothic succession was actually in the hands of another line, descended from Vallia's successor Theoderic I, so that Ricimer would probably not have been very popular had he turned up in Visigothic Aquitaine; and Ricimer's policies, while certainly self-interested, show no general pro-barbarian bias. O'Flynn (1983), Ch. 8, provides a general survey. On Majorian, see *PLRE* 2, 702–3, with refs.

12 *Poems*, 2, 317–18. Best narrative account: Stein (1959); 380ff.; cf. O'Flynn (1983), 111–17. For the Gallic perspective on these manoeuvres, see Harries (1994), Chs 6–7.

13 Hydatius *Chronicle* 217.

14 As Sidonius put it: 'Receiving a count's authority, he traversed the Danube bank and the whole length of the great frontier lines, exhorting, arranging, examining, equipping' (*Poems* 2, 199–201). As *comes rei militaris* (second-grade field army general), he sorted out the mess on the Danube in 453/4, as the civil war between Attila's sons progressed and the successor kingdoms to the Hunnic Empire emerged.

15 He continued to deal with the longer-term fall-out from the Hunnic collapse, confronting Valamer when he invaded Illyricum in search of a subsidy in c. 460, and fighting off the Hunnic fragment led by Hormidac which invaded the Empire in the 460s.

16 In the 390s, as recorded at *Not. Dig. Or.* 19, the field army of Illyricum comprised 26 units, something over 10,000 men. Illyricum was then divided between the east and west on Stilicho's accession in 395, and its western army was already down to 22 units by 420 (*Not. Dig. Occ.* 7. 40–62). Subsequently, the region took a heavy pounding, including the loss of Pannonia to the Huns, so that by the 460s the command was largely confined to Dalmatia and its military establishment probably much smaller, although Marcellinus supplemented his regular troops with barbarian auxiliaries (Priscus frr. 29, 30). On Marcellinus in general, see MacGeorge (2002), pt 1.

17 Visigoths and Burgundians: Harries (1994), Ch. 6. Roman army of the Rhine: MacGeorge (2002), pt 2. Brittany: Galliou and Jones (1991), Chs 1–2. Franks: James (1988), Chs 2–3; Wood (1994), Ch. 3.

18 *Poems*, 13. 35–6.

19 *Letters* 1. 11.

20 *Letters* 1. 9.

21 Majorian had forced the Burgundians to give up some of the cities (*civitates*) of the Rhône valley and their revenues; most significantly Lyon, which they had seized during Avitus' reign; and he had browbeaten the Visigoths into acknowledging his power, as well as attracting Gallic landowners. On Anthemius and the Gallo-Romans, see Harries (1994), Ch. 7.

22 The sources variously report that the marriage occurred both before the Vandal sack and upon Placidia's arrival in Constantinople. They were perhaps betrothed in 454/5, therefore, and actually married in 462 (*PLRE* 2, 796–8, with Clover (1978) generally on Olybrius). Vandal sack of Rome: p. 378 above.

23 Justinian's general Belisarius managed to conquer North Africa in 532/3.

24 The next three quotations are from Sidonius *Poems* 5. 53–60, 338–41, 349–50.

25 I would assert this principle with the greatest insistence, although some don't seem to realize how much the public life of the late Empire resembled that of a one-party state: see further Heather and Moncur (2001), esp. Ch. 1.

26 Sidonius *Poems* 349–69, 441–69.

27 This raises the same issue faced with Geiseric in Ch. 5, as to whether Majorian's forces were to be transported in one lift or several. Belisarius required 500 ships to move 16,000 troops (see p. 400), so Majorian's 300 could have moved about 9,600 in one go, and I doubt that he was planning to go into battle with so few. So I suspect he was planning for at least two movements of troops, and hence would not have wanted to place his advance guard too close to Carthage. On Majorian's campaign, see further Courtois (1955), 199–200.

28 Candidus fr. 2 = *Suda* X 245.

29 Respectively John Lydus *On the Magistrates* 3. 43; Procopius *Wars* 3. 6. 1; cf. Courtois (1955), 201; Stein (1959), 389–91.

30 Eleven hundred ships: Priscus fr. 53 = Theophanes AM 5961; the MS reads '100,000 ships', 1,100 being an emendation based on the figure of 1,113 supplied by Cedrenus, p. 613. The amended figure would make the 468 armada the same size as that assembled for the putative 441 expedition which never sailed: see p. 290. In 532, when the emperor Justinian mounted a more exploratory expedition towards Vandal Africa, the eastern Empire assembled 500 ordinary ships, together with 92 specialist warships (*dromons*), which again makes 1,100 seem proportionate for an all-out effort.

31 On the fleet of 532, see Casson (1982) with refs to ancient shipping in general. To put the east Roman effort into broader perspective, the 'invincible Armada' which set sail from Spain in the late spring of 1588 comprised 90 great ships of 300 tons' displacement or more, and another 40 auxiliary craft. This, however, was merely a covering force for the army of the Duke of Parma, who was meant to provide additional barges to get his men across the Channel.

32 Manpower: Procopius *Wars* 3. 6. 1. Marcellinus: sources as *PLRE* 2, 710. Heraclius: Theophanes AM 5963.

33 In contradiction of Courtois (1955), 201, who is generally an excellent guide, but wished to downplay the scale of the effort made in 468.

34 The next three quotations are from *Poems* 2. 14–17, 537–43 and 315–16.

35 Belisarius' later fleet sailed from Italy for Africa on 21 June 532 and eventually put in to the Bay of Utica, close to Carthage, which was large enough to accommodate its 600 ships.

36 *Poems* 5. 332–5.

37 CTh 9. 40. 24; Zosimus 1. 31–3, with commentary by Heather (1996), 38–43, on the third century. Zosimus explicitly notes that ships and sailors were provided by settlements north of the Black Sea.

38 Viereck (1975), 165–6, gathers the references.

39 Mattingly (2002), 313.

40 The next three quotations are from Procopius *Wars* 3. 6. 18–19, 20–1 and 22–4.

41 Procopius *Wars* 1. 6. 10–16. It is worth comparing Basiliscus' failure in 468 with Belisarius' success in 532. Belisarius sailed with a smaller force, landed safely, and wrapped up the Vandal kingdom in under a year via two decisive land battles. He landed at Caputvada, south of Cape Bon, clearly much further away from Carthage than Basiliscus' target, whatever it was. Belisarius also achieved complete strategic surprise. The North African expedition was an unexpected gamble on the part of his master the emperor Justinian, prompted by a succession dispute in the Vandal kingdom which divided the Vandal forces. Hence, when Belisarius turned up, 120 ships and 5,000 of the Vandals' best fighters were away squashing a revolt in Sardinia, and he was able to land his men without a battle at sea. In amphibious landings, among the most difficult of military operations, the attackers should have at least a 6:1 advantage over the defenders according to modern doctrines. Basiliscus may well have been trying to land too close to Carthage, which would have brought him right into the middle of the Vandal fleet. But he may have been on a hiding to nothing anyway. News of his fleet, anticipated with so much excitement by Sidonius in January 468, could hardly be suppressed. Geiseric was bound to know of its arrival, so it is doubtful, huge as it was, that it had enough of an advantage to pull off victory in the face of forewarned and mobilized opponents. In 1588, likewise, the Spanish design was flawed: Medina Sidonia didn't have a powerful enough fleet to hold off the English, and the Duke of Parma had nowhere near enough transports and smaller escorts to get past a Dutch inshore fleet and make it to England. Parma knew this perfectly well, and didn't even try to get his men ready, even though he had plenty of advance warning of the Armada's arrival.

42 His reticence has prompted a wave of inconclusive speculation on the part of excitable modern historians. The most dramatic hypothesis about Severinus is that of Lotter (1976), who argues that the *Life* really begins after c. 460 and not c. 453 (the death of Attila), and that Severinus was in fact the consul of 461, with a long administrative career behind him. I don't subscribe to this (see the response in Thompson (1982)), but I do think that the events begin closer to 460 than 453, since, rather than the Huns themselves, they feature the successor states to the Hunnic Empire (such as the Rugi and the Goths of Valamer), which took some time to form.

43 On provincial development in Noricum, see Alföldi (1974), passim.

44 *Not. Dig. Occ.* 39: river police at Boiodurum (Passau Instadt), Asturis (Zeisel-mauer) and Cannabiaca; normal cavalry units at Comagena (Tulln), Augustiana (Tralsmauer), Arelape (Pochlarn) and Ad Mauros (Eferding); mounted archers at Lentia and Lacufelix.

45 For a survey of the evidence: Alföldi (1974), Ch. 12.

46 This quotation and the next are from the *Life of Severinus* 30. 1 and 20. 1–2.

47 Walls and militias: Comagenis *Life of Severinus* 2. 1; Faviana 22. 4; Lauriacum 30. 2; Batavis 22. 1; Quintanis 15. 1; barbarians 2. 1.

48 *Not. Dig. Occ.* 7. 40–62. The evolution of the Illyrican field army can be followed because we can compare the listing for it from AD 395, or just before, in the eastern *Notitia*, with the western listing from c.420 in the *distributio numerorum*. These *lanciarii* had clearly been drafted into the field army sometime between 395 and 420.

49 *Life of Severinus* 4. 1–4.

50 Advance warning: *Life of Severinus* 30; defeating assaults: 25, 27; rescuing prisoners: 4, 31.

51 Capture by slavers: *Life of Severinus* 10; Tiburnia: 17; Herules' destruction: 24, 27; Rugi and attempted transplants: 8, 31.

52 If increasingly manned by barbarians fleeing the fall-out from Hunnic collapse, the Roman army of Italy continued to exist under Ricimer; so too to some extent the army of Gaul, parts of which had gone into revolt under Aegidius in 462 (MacGeorge (2002), Ch. 6).

53 Hydatius *Chronicle* 238–40.

54 *Getica* 45: 237.

55 For further details and full refs, see Wolfram (1988), 181ff.

56 Burgundians: Favrod (1997). Franks: James (1988), 72ff.; Wood (1994), 38ff.

57 Harries (1994), 222ff.; cf. Sidonius, *Letters* 3. 3, on Ecdicius.

58 The next five quotations are from Sidonius *Letters* 1. 7. 5; 5. 5; 8. 3; 8. 9.

59 Arvandus: Sidonius *Letters* 1.7. Vincentius: *Chron. Gall.* 511, s.a. 473; cf. *PLRE* 2, 1168; Sidonius' description of the trial of Arvandus was also penned for a Vincentius, but it is unknown whether it was the same man. Victorius: *PLRE* 2, 1162–3; Seronatus: Sidonius *Letters* 2.1; 4. 13; 7. 2. Unlike Arvandus, Seronatus was not Sidonius' friend, so he was unmoved by the former's fate. As early as the 410s, some Gallo-Roman landowners had been attracted to Athaulf's standard as the best path to peace.

60 Solon was the legendary law-giver of Athens, who gave them their first written code. Written law had an important cultural significance for Romans.

61 But Sidonius was ever the Nimby.

62 Eucherius: Sidonius *Letters* 3. 8. Calminius: *Letters* 5. 12 (claiming that Calminius hadn't wanted to be there). On Sidonius' son, see *PLRE* 2, 114.

63 For an introduction to the Visigothic kingdom: Heather (1996), Ch. 7, with refs.

64 A common poetic designation for the Franks.

65 On Sidonius' imprisonment and release, see most recently Harries (1994), 238ff.

66 *Book of Constitutions* 54. 1.

67 Goffart (1980), supported esp. by Durliat (1988); (1990). For counter-argument specifically with regard to the Burgundian kingdom: Heather (forthcoming a); Innes (forthcoming). See more generally Wickham (1993); Liebeschuetz (1997), Barnish (1986) and n. 75 to Ch. 6 above on the Vandal kingdom. The Burgundian freemen had their own dependants – freedmen and slaves – which was why they received a smaller fraction of the labour force. Subsequent Burgundian legislation dealt with matters that changed the value of one of the partners' share in the joint estate (assarting by forest clearance, or the planting of vineyards – more valuable per hectare than arable fields), and with the pre-emption rights of the original Roman owner should his Burgundian partner decide to sell up. All of these regulations, like the original order, make much more sense in relation to actual landed property than to taxation deriving from it (BC 31, 55. 1–2, 67, 84).

68 This is an extremely unlikely omission if the collection and distribution of taxation played the key political role in the structure of the kingdom that Goffart's argument would suggest.

69 CE frr. 276, 277; cf. Liebeschuetz (1997).

70 Best narrative account: Stein (1959), 393ff. Gundobad's 'sudden' departure from Italy: Malalas 375.

71 Details: Courtois (1955), 209.

72 Count of the Domestics: Procopius Wars 5. 1. 6. Patrician: Malchus fr. 14 (not noted in PLRE 2, 791–3).

73 Life 7. 1.

74 Wars 5. 1. 8.

75 This was the distribution of forces used by Theoderic the Ostrogoth, who next ruled Italy after Odovacar (Heather (1996), Ch. 7 with refs). Goffart (1980), Ch. 3, again argued that, in both cases, rewards took the form of tax rather than land, but this doesn't make sense. The whole point of the revolt was that Italy wasn't generating enough tax revenue. After defeating Odovacar, Theoderic certainly allocated land, while maintaining part of the tax system (Barnish (1986)).

76 Malchus fr. 2.

10. THE FALL OF ROME

1 Tax reductions: Hendy (1985), 613–69; cf. more generally on seventh-century transformation, Whittow (1996), Haldon (1990).

2 The most extravagant of recent attempts to minimize the importance of group identities is Amory (1997); cf. Amory (1993). But see, for instance, the responses of Heather (2003) or Innes (forthcoming). Romani are mentioned in law codes from the Visigothic, Burgundian and Frankish kingdoms and, in Cassiodorus' Variae, from the Ostrogothic.

3 In that year, the Huns launched a huge attack on the Roman Empire, but to the east rather than the west of the Black Sea (p. 154).

4 Roman army of c. 420: p. 247. Tax crisis and loss of Africa: p. 296.

5 Goffart (1980), 35.

6 Carolingian collapse: Reuter (1985), (1990); cf. various essays in Gibson and
   Nelson (1981). For a more general overview, see Dunbabin (1985), and regional
   surveys in Hallam (1980). Goffart started life as a Carolingianist and I have often
   wondered if the processes of Carolingian collapse have not too much influenced
   his vision of Rome's fall. The one exception to the 'internalist' rule was the
   Duchy of Normandy, founded by the Viking Rollo, but here the key grant of
   territory was not made until 911, after the main process of Carolingian collapse
   had already worked itself out.

7 The arrival of the Christian mission sent to Canterbury by Pope Gregory I in
   597 pretty much defines the lower chronological limit of Bede's detailed
   knowledge of the Anglo-Saxon past.

8 General surveys: Campbell (1982), Ch. 2; Esmonde Cleary (2002); Higham (1992).
   The kingdom of Kent perhaps preserved the boundaries of the old Roman *civitas*
   of the Cantii, and the same may be true of Lincoln and Anglo-Saxon Lindsey.
   But most early Anglo-Saxon kingdoms were much smaller than the old Roman
   civitates and were clearly carved out from them piecemeal: cf. the essays in
   Bassett (1989).

9 Historians have sometimes fought over whether the end of the Empire should
   be thought of as destruction or evolution. As so often, the answer to this
   seeming question-cum-contradiction is to be clear as to what exactly one is
   talking about in any particular case.

10 Typical of the traditional approach was the title of Frank Walbank's study of
   1969: *The Awful Revolution*. The wind of change shows up nicely in the title
   given to the European Science Foundation project on the same subject, *The
   Transformation of the Roman World*.

11 In the high Empire, this form of education was geared to producing expert
   public speakers who would excel on the town council. In the late Empire,
   classical Latin (and to some extent Greek) became the language of the imperial
   bureaucracy, the new career structure that replaced the town councils.

12 General pattern: Heather (1994). On Venantius, see George (1992). The relevant
   evidence from across former Roman Europe is surveyed in Riché (1976).

13 Brown (1996) explores many of the changes.

14 The eastern Church: Hussey (1990); cf. revealing particular studies such as
   Alexander (1958).

15 Gibbon (1897), 160ff. (quotation from p. 161).

16 Baynes (1943); Jones (1964), Ch. 25.

17 Overtaxation, in Jones's view, was largely attributable to the need to support a
   large enough army to confront the barbarians and Persia; so even this, if
   indirectly, was due to the barbarians – although he did also identify 'idle mouths'
   in the new imperial bureaucracy (rather than, as Gibbon, in the Church) as a
   further source of trouble (Jones, 1964, Ch. 25).

18 Tervingi and Greuthungi: p. 145. Radagaisus: p. 198. Alaric: p. 224.

19 Rhine invaders: p. 198. Burgundians: p. 198.

20 I have not included anything for Anglo-Saxon immigrants into Britain because

they did not directly cause the British provinces to drop out of the imperial system.

21 Ammianus 27. 8.

22 The cases of some later nomads, such as the sixth-century Avars, are better documented; they were on the run from the western Turks (see e.g. Pohl (1988)). For an introduction to the Eurasian Steppe nomads, see Sinor (1977); Khazanov (1984).

23 Written and archaeological evidence both suggest that the Germanic-dominated groups affected, such as the Bastarnae, were conquered or fragmented (Shchukin (1989), pt 1, Chs 7–9; pt 2, Chs 7–8).

24 The figures, as we have seen, are little better than guesses, but the Tervingi and Greuthungi may have numbered c. 10,000 warriors apiece, and Radagaisus' force perhaps double that. The new group weighed in at more like 30,000 combatants. For detail see Heather (1991), pt 2.

25 Roman policy towards the Alamanni (p. 83–4) looks similar to the kind of pre-emptive action recorded against Frankish groups at Gregory of Tours Histories 2. 9. Subsequent unification under Clovis is recounted by Gregory of Tours at 2. 40–2. He dates it by implication after 507, but there is good reason to think that processes of conquest and unification had gone hand in hand between 482 and 507.

26 See, in more detail, Heather (1991), pt 3. The only new kingdom which we don't know to have been the product of a major political realignment is that of the Burgundians. This was a second-rank power, which preserved its independence only when it could play off the Franks against the Ostrogoths, and fell to the Franks when Justinian's conquest of Italy eliminated the latter. Two possibilities present themselves (both feasible, given the sparseness of information available). Either there was no significant fifth-century political realignment behind the creation of Burgundy, which might explain its relative lack of military power; or any alignment was not on the same scale as that which produced the other kingdoms.

27 On the freeman class, see p. 94. Many of the individuals who are known to have separated themselves from the uniting groups were defeated candidates for leadership, such as the Visigoths Modares, Fravittas and Sarus. Some Thracian Goths who stayed in the east rather than follow Theoderic the Ostrogoth to Italy were Bessas and Godisdiclus (Procopius Wars 1. 8. 3).

28 Radagaisus followers: Orosius 7. 37. 13ff. (slavery); Zosimus 5. 35. 5–6 (pogrom). Vandals and Alans: Hydatius Chronicle 67–8. Ostrogoths: Malchus frr. 15 and 18. 1–4 with Heather (1991), Ch. 8.

29 Julian's treaties: Ammianus 17. 1. 12–13; 17. 10. 3–4, 8–9; 18. 2. 5–6, 19. The evidence for economic contact is collected and analysed by e.g. Hedeager (1978). On the Tervingi, see p. 72ff.

30 Annals 12. 25.

31 Northern Amber Route: Urbanczyk (1997).

32 E.g. Ammianus 16. 12. 17; cf. generally Klöse (1934) on gifts.

33 Ørsnes (1968).

34 Ammianus 30. 3. 7.

35 What I'm offering very briefly here and will develop further in another study (Heather (forthcoming b)) is a centre/periphery model for developments around the fringes of the Roman world. For an introduction to this kind of vision, see Rowlands et al. (1987); Chamption (1989). To my mind, it is crucial to add to such analyses a powerful element of agency: (cf. e.g. Prakash et al. (1994)). Rome's neighbours were not passive recipients of Roman action and stimuli, but responded dynamically according to their own agendas.

BIBLIOGRAPHY

PRIMARY SOURCES

Following the usual conventions, editions of standard classical works are not cited in the bibliography; most are found in translation in either or both of the Loeb and Penguin Classics series. All Christian authors are available, if sometimes in outdated form, in Patrologia Latina or Patrologia Graeca editions. More recent (sometimes competing) editions of most of the texts cited in the Introduction and notes can be found in GCS (Die Griechischen Christlichen Schriftsteller der ersten Jahrhunderte), CSEL (Corpus Scriptorum Ecclesiasticorum Latinorum), CC (Corpus Christianorum), and SC (Sources Chrétiennes). Many are translated in the Nicene and Post-Nicene Fathers, and Library of the Fathers collections. Otherwise, the following editions and translations of late Roman sources have been used; where no translation is cited, the translation in the text is my own

Agathias *History*: ed. Keydell (1967); trans. Frendo (1975)
Ammianus Marcellinus *Res Gestae*: in Rolfe, ed. and trans. (1935–9)
The Annals of Ravenna: ed. Bischoff and Koehler (1952)
Book of the History of the Franks: ed. Krusch (1888)
Cedrenus: ed. Bekker (1838–9)
Chron. Gall. 452: in Mommsen, ed. (1892)
Chron. Gall. 511: in Mommsen, ed. (1892)
Chronicon Paschale: ed. Dindorf (1832); trans. Whitby and Whitby (1989)
Claudian *Works*: ed. and trans. Platnauer (1922)
Codex Justinianus: in Kreuger, ed. (1877)
Eunapius *History*: ed. and trans. Blockley (1982)
Eutropius: ed. Santini (1979); trans. Bird (1993)
Gregory of Tours *Histories*: ed. Krusch and Levison (1951); trans. Thorpe (1974)
Hydatius *Chronicle*: in Mommsen, ed. (1894); trans. Burgess (1993)
John of Antioch: in Mueller, ed. (1851–70); trans. Gordon (1966)
John Lydus *On the Months*: ed. Wuensch (1898)
John Lydus *On the Magistrates*: ed. and trans. Bandy (1983)
Jordanes *Getica*: ed. Mommsen (1882); trans. Mierow (1915)
Jordanes *Romana*: ed. Mommsen (1882)
Julian *Works*: ed. and trans. Wright (1913)
Letter of Auxentius: in Gryson, ed. (1980); trans. Heather and Matthews (1991)

Libanius *Works*: ed. Foerster (1903–27); *Letters*: partial trans. Bradbury (2004)

Life of St Epiphanius: in Vogel, ed. (1885)

Life of Severinus: ed. Noll and Vetter (1963); trans. Bieler (1965)

Malalas: ed. Dindorf (1831); trans. Jeffreys et al. (1986)

Malchus: ed. and trans. Blockley (1982)

Marcellinus Comes: in Mommsen, ed. (1894)

Miracles of St Demetrius: ed. Lemerle (1979–81)

Olympiodorus of Thebes: ed. and trans. Blockley (1982)

Passion of St Saba: in Delehaye, ed. (1912); trans. Heather and Matthews (1991)

Paulinus of Pella *Eucharisticon*: in Evelyn White, ed. and trans. (1961)

Priscus: ed. and trans. Blockley (1982)

Procopius *Works*: ed. and trans. Dewing (1914–40)

Prosper Tiro *Chronicle*: in Mommsen, ed. (1892)

Sidonius *Poems and Letters*: ed. and trans. Anderson (1936–65)

Symmachus *Works*: ed. Seeck (1883); *Relationes*: trans. Barrow (1973)

Synesius of Cyrene: ed. Garzya (1989)

Themistius *Orationes*: ed. Schenkl et al. (1965–74); partial trans. Heather and Moncur (2001)

Theophanes *Chronographia*: ed. Niebuhr (1839–41); trans. Mango and Scott (1997)

Theophylact Simocatta *History*: ed. De Boor and Wirth (1972); trans. Whitby and Whitby (1986)

Victor of Vita *History of the Persecution in Africa*: ed. Kalm (1879); trans. Moorhead (1992)

Zosimus *History*: ed. Paschoud (1971–81); trans. Ridley (1982)

General

Adcock, F. E. (1956). *Caesar as Man of Letters* (Cambridge)

Alexander, P. J. (1958). *The Patriarch Nicephorus of Constantinople: Ecclesiastical Policy and Image Worship in the Byzantine State* (Oxford)

Amory, P. (1993). 'The Meaning and Purpose of Ethnic Terminology in the Burgundian Laws', *Early Medieval Europe* 2.1, 1–21

—————— (1997). *People and Identity in Ostrogothic Italy 489–554* (Cambridge)

Alfoldy, G. (1974). *Noricum* (London)

Anderson, W. B. (ed. and trans.) (1936–65). *Sidonius Apollinaris Poems and Letters* (London)

Arnheim, M. T. W. (1972). *The Senatorial Aristocracy in the Later Roman Empire* (Oxford)

Ausenda, G. (forthcoming a). *The Burgundians: An Ethnographic Perspective* (London)

—————— (forthcoming b). *The Vandals: An Ethnographic Perspective* (London)

Bachrach, B. S. (1973). *The Alans in the West* (Minneapolis)

Baldwin, B. (1980). 'Priscus of Panium', *Byzantion* 50, 18–61

Bandy, A. C. (ed. and trans.) (1983). *John Lydus de Magistratibus Populi Romani* (Philadelphia)

Baradez, J. (1949). *Fossatum Africae: recherches aériennes sur l'organisation des confins sahariens à l'époque romaine* (Paris)

Barnes, T. D. (1995). 'Statistics and the Conversion of the Roman Aristocracy', *Journal of Roman Studies* 85, 135–47

Barnish, S. J. B. (1986). 'Taxation, Land and Barbarian Settlement in the Western Empire', *Papers of the British School at Rome* 54 (1986), 170–95

Barrow, R. H. (ed. and trans.) (1973). *Prefect and Emperor: The Relationes of Symmachus, AD 384* (Oxford)

Bartholomew, P. (1976). *Aspects of the Notitia Dignitatum* (Oxford)

Bassett, S. (1989). *The Origins of Anglo-Saxon Kingdoms* (Leicester)

Baynes, N. H. (1943). 'The Decline of the Roman Empire in Western Europe: Some Modern Explanations', *Journal of Roman Studies* 33, 29–35

Bekker, I. (1838–9). *Georgius Cedrenus Ioannis Scylitzæ*, 2 vols (Bonn)

Bieler, L. (1965). *Eugippius: The Life of Saint Severin* (Washington DC)

Bierbrauer, V. (1980). 'Zur chronologischen, soziologischen und regionalen Gliederung des ostgermanischen Fundstoffs des 5. Jahrhunderts in Sudosteuropa', in Wolfram and Daim (1980), 131–42

—— (1989). 'Ostgermanische Oberschichtsgräber der römischen Kaiserzeit und des frühen Mittelalters', in *Peregrinatio Gothica* 2, Archaeologia Baltica VIII (Lodz), 40–106

Bird, H. W. (trans.) (1993). *Eutropius Breviarium* (Liverpool)

Bischoff, B., and Koehler, W. (1952). 'The Annals of Ravenna', *Studi Romagnoli* iii, 1–17

Blockley, R. C. (1972). 'Dexippus and Priscus and the Thucydidean Account of the Siege of Plataea', *Phoenix* 26, 18–27

—— (1982). (ed. and trans.) *The Fragmentary Classicising Historians of the Later Roman Empire: Eunapius, Olympiodorus, Priscus and Malchus*, vol. 2 (Liverpool)

—— (1992). *East Roman Foreign Policy: Formation and Conduct from Diocletian to Anastasius* (Leeds)

Boissier, G. (1891). *La Fin du paganisme*, vol. 2 (Paris)

Bona, I. (1991). *Das Hunnenreich* (Stuttgart)

Boulnois, L. (1966). *The Silk Road*, trans. D. Chamberlin (London)

Bowman, A., and Woolf, G. (eds) (1994). *Literacy and Power in the Ancient World* (Cambridge)

Bradbury, S. A. (1994). 'Constantine and Anti-pagan Legislation in the Fourth Century', *Classical Philology* 89, 120–39

—— (trans.) (2004). *Selected Letters of Libanius from the Age of Constantius and Julian* (Liverpool)

Braund, D. C. (1984). *Rome and the Friendly King: The Character of Client Kingship* (London)

Brown, P. R. L. (1967). *Augustine of Hippo: A Biography* (London)

—— (1981). *The Cult of the Saints: Its Rise and Function in Latin Christianity* (London)

—— (1995). *Authority and the Sacred: Aspects of the Christianisation of the Roman World* (Cambridge)

———— (1996). *The Rise of Western Christendom: Triumph and Diversity*, AD 200–1000 (Oxford)

Browning, R. (1953), 'Where Was Attila's Camp?', *Journal of Hellenic Studies*, 143–5

Bruggisser, P. (1993). *Symmaque, ou, Le rituel épistolaire de l'amité littéraire: recherches sur le premier livre de la correspondance* (Fribourg)

Burgess, R. (trans.) (1993). *The Chronicle of Hydatius and the Consularia Constantinopolitana* (Oxford)

Bury, J. B. (1928). *The Invasion of Europe by the Barbarians* (London)

Callu, J. P. (1972–2002). *Symmaque Lettres: texte établi, traduit et commenté* (Paris)

Calo Levi, A. (1952). *Barbarians on Roman Imperial Coinage and Sculpture*, Numismatic Notes and Monographs 123 (New York)

Cameron, A. D. E. (1967). 'Rutilius Namatianus, St Augustine, and the Date of the *De Reditu*', *Journal of Roman Studies* 57, 31–9

———— (1970). *Claudian: Poetry and Propaganda at the Court of Honorius* (Oxford)

———— and Long, J. (1993). *Barbarians and Politics at the Court of Arcadius* (Berkeley)

Cameron, Averil, et al. (eds) (2000). *The Cambridge Ancient History* 2nd edn, vol. 14 (Cambridge)

Campbell, J. (1982). *The Anglo-Saxons* (London)

Casson, L. (1982). 'Belisarius' Expedition Against Carthage', in J. H. Humphrey (ed.), *Carthage VII: Excavations at Carthage 1978 Conducted by the University of Michigan* (Ann Arbor), 23–8

Champion, T. C. (1989). *Centre and Periphery: Comparative Studies in Archaeology* (London)

Chastagnol, A. (1960). *La Préfecture urbaine sous le bas-empire* (Paris)

Childe, V. G. (1926). *The Aryans: A Study of Indo-European Origins* (London)

———— (1927). *The Dawn of European Civilization* (London)

Christiansen, A. (1944). *L'Iran sous les Sassanides* 2nd edn (Copenhagen)

Clover, F. M. (1971). 'Flavius Merobaudes. A Translation and Historical Commentary', *Transactions of the American Philological Society* 61, 1–78

———— (1972). 'Geiseric and Attila', *Historia* 22, 104–17

———— (1978). 'The Family and Early Career of Anicius Olybrius', *Historia* 27, 169–96

Cornell, T., and Matthews, J. F. (1982). *Atlas of the Roman World* (London)

Courcelle, P. (1964). *Histoire littéraire des grandes invasions germaniques* (Paris)

Courtois, C. (1955). *Les Vandales et l'Afrique* (Paris)

Crawford, M. (1975). 'Finance, Coinage and Money from the Severans to Constantine', *Aufsteig und Niedergang der antiken Welt* 2. 2, 572–5

Cribb, R. J. (1991). *Nomads in Archaeology* (London)

Croke, B. (1977). 'Evidence for the Hun Invasion of Thrace in AD 422', *Greek, Roman and Byzantine Studies* xviii, 347–67

Cunliffe, B. (1997). *The Ancient Celts* (Oxford)

———— and Rowley, T. (eds) (1976). *Oppida, the Beginnings of Urbanisation in Barbarian Europe: Papers Presented to a Conference at Oxford, October 1975* (Oxford)

Dagron, G. (1974). *Naissance d'une capitale: Constantinople et ses institutions de 330 à 451* (Paris)

Dahn, F. (1861–99). *Die König der Germanen: Das Wesen des ältesten Königthums der germanischen Stämme und seine Geschichte bis auf die Feudalzeit* (Munich)

———— (1877). *Ein Kampf um Rom* (Leipzig)

Dauge, Y. A. (1981). *Le Barbare: recherches sur la conception romaine du barbare et de la civilisation*, Collection Latomus 176 (Brussels)

De Boor, C., and Wirth, P. (eds) (1972). *The History of Theophylact Simocatta* (Stuttgart)

Delehaye, H. (1912). 'Saints de Thrace et de Mésie', *Analecta Bollandia* 31, 161–300

Demandt, A. (1984). *Der Fall Roms: die Auflösung des römischen Reiches im Urteil der Nachwelt* (Munich)

Demougeot, E. (1951). *De l'Unité à la division de l'Empire romain 395–410: Essai sur le gouvernement impérial* (Paris)

———— (1979). *La Formation de l'Europe et les invasions barbares: II. De l'avènement de Dioclétien (284) à l'occupation germanique de l'Empire romain d'Occident (début du VIe siècle)* (Paris)

Dewing, H. B. (ed. and trans.) (1914–40). *The Works of Procopius* (London)

Diesner, H.-J. (1976). *Die Völkerwanderung* (Leipzig)

Dill, S. (1899). *Roman Society in the Last Age of the Western Empire* (London)

Dindorf, L., (ed.) (1831). *Malalas Chronographia* (Bonn)

———— (ed.) (1832). *Chronicon Paschale* (Bonn)

Dodgeon, M. H., and Lieu, S. N. C. (1991). *The Roman Eastern Frontier and the Persian Wars (AD 226–363): A Documentary History* (London)

Drew, K. Fischer (trans.) (1972). *The Burgundian Code: Book of Constitutions or Law of Gundobad* (Philadelphia)

Drinkwater, J. F. (1987). *The Gallic Empire: Separatism and Continuity in the North-western Provinces of the Roman Empire, AD 260–274* (Stuttgart)

———— (1992). 'The Bacaudae of Fifth-century Gaul', in Drinkwater and Elton (1992), 208–17

———— and Elton, H. (eds) (1992). *Fifth-century Gaul: A Crisis of Identity?* (Cambridge)

Dunbabin, J. (1985). *France in the Making, 843–1180* (Oxford)

Duncan-Jones, R. (2003). 'Economic Change and the Transition to Late Antiquity', in S. Swain and M. Edwards (eds), *Approaching Late Antiquity: The Transformation from Early to Late Empire* (Oxford), 20–52

Durliat, J. (1988). 'Le salaire de la paix sociale dans les royaumes barbares (Ve-VIe siècles)', in H. Wolfram and A. Schwarcz (eds), *Anerkennung und Integration: Zu den wirtschaftlichen Grundlagen der Völkerwanderungszeit (400–600)*, Denkschriften der Österreichischen Akademie der Wissenschaften, Phil.–Hist. Kl. 193 (Vienna), 21–72

———— (1990). *Les finances publiques de Dioclétien aux Carolingiens (284–889)* (Sigmaringen)

Dvornik, H. (1966). *Early Christian and Byzantine Political Philosophy: Origins and Background*, Dumbarton Oaks Center for Byzantine Studies (Washington DC)

Elton, H. (1996a). *Warfare in Roman Europe, AD 350–425* (Oxford)

———— (1996b). *Frontiers of the Roman Empire* (London)

Ennabli, E. A. (1992). *Pour Sauver Carthage: Exploration et conservation de la cité punique, romaine et byzantine* (Tunis)

Esmonde Cleary, A. S. (2000). *The Ending of Roman Britain* (London)

Evelyn White, H. (1961). *The Works of Ausonius*, vol. 2 (London)

Fantham, E. (2004). *The Roman World of Cicero's De Oratore* (Oxford)

Favrod, J. (1997). *Histoire politique du royaume burgonde (443–534)* (Lausanne)

Ferguson, N. (2001). *The Cash Nexus: Money and Power in the Modern World, 1700–2000* (London)

Ferris, I. M. (2000). *Enemies of Rome: Barbarians through Roman Eyes* (Stroud)

Foerster, R. (ed.) (1903–27). *Libanii opera* (Leipzig)

Frendo, J. D. (trans.) (1975). *Agathias: History* (Berlin)

Friedrichsen, G. W. S. (1926). *The Gothic Version of the Gospels: A Study of Its Style and Textual History* (Oxford)

—————— (1939). *The Gothic Version of the Epistles: A Study of Its Style and Textual History* (Oxford)

Galliou, P., and Jones, M. (1991). *The Bretons* (Oxford)

Garzya, A. (ed. and Italian trans.) (1989). *Opere di Sinesio di Cirene: epistole, operette, inni* (Turin)

George, J. W. (1992). *Venantius Fortunatus: A Latin Poet in Merovingian Gaul* (Oxford)

Gibbon, E. (1897). *The Decline and Fall of the Roman Empire*, ed. J. B. Bury, vol. 4 (London)

Gibson, M., and Nelson, J. (1981). *Charles the Bald: Court and Kingdom* (Oxford)

Goffart, W. (1980). *Barbarians and Romans AD 418–584: The Techniques of Accommodation* (Princeton)

—————— (1981). 'Rome, Constantinople, and the Barbarians in Late Antiquity', *American Historical Review* 76, 275–306

—————— (1988). *The Narrators of Barbarian History (AD 550–800): Jordanes, Gregory of Tours, Bede, and Paul the Deacon* (Princeton)

Gonzalez, J. (1986). 'The *Lex Irnitana*: A New Copy of the Flavian Municipal Law', *Journal of Roman Studies* 76, 147–243

Gordon, D. C. (trans.) (1966). *The Age of Attila* (Ann Arbor)

Green, R. P. H. (1991). *The Works of Ausonius* (Oxford)

Gryson, R. (ed.) (1980). *Littérature Arienne Latine* (Louvain)

Haarnagel, W. (1979). *Die Grabung Feddersen Wierde: Methode, Hausbau, Siedlungs- und Wirtschaftsformen sowie Sozialstruktur* (Wiesbaden)

Hachmann, R. (1971). *The Germanic Peoples* (London)

—————— et al. (1962). *Völker zwischen Germanen und Kelten: Schriftquellen, Bodenfunde und Namengut zur Geschichte des nördlichen Westdeutschlands um Christi Geburt* (Neumünster)

Haldon, J. F. (1990). *Byzantium in the Seventh Century: The Transformation of a Culture* (Cambridge)

Hallam, E. M. (1980). *Capetian France, 987–1328* (London)

Halm, C. (1879). MGH, auctores antiquissimi 2 (Berlin)

—————— (1879). *Victoris Vitensis Historia persecutionis africanae provinciae sub Geiserico et Hunrico regibus Wandalorum*, MGH, auctores antiquissimi 2 (Berlin)

Halsall, G. (1993). 'The Origins of the *Reihengraberzivilisation*: Forty Years On', in Drinkwater and Elton (1992), 196–207

Hanson, R. P. C. (1988). *The Search for the Christian Doctrine of God* (Edinburgh)

Harhoiu, R. (1977). *The Treasure from Pietroasa, Romania* (Oxford)

Härke, H. (1990). '"Warrior Graves?" The Background of the Anglo-Saxon Weapon Burial Rite', *Past and Present* 126, 22–43

Harmatta, J. (1951). 'The Golden Bow of the Huns', *Acta Archaeologica Hungaricae* 1, 114–49

Harries, J. (1994). *Sidonius Apollinaris and the Fall of Rome* (Oxford)

Haubrichs, W. (forthcoming). 'Burgundian Names – Burgundian Language', in Ausenda (forthcoming b)

Heather, P. J. (1986). 'The Crossing of the Danube and the Gothic Conversion', *Greek, Roman and Byzantine Studies* 27, 289–318

———— (1988). 'The Anti-Scythian Tirade of Synesius' *De Regno*', *Phoenix* 42, 152–72

———— (1989). 'Cassiodorus and the Rise of the Amals: Genealogy and the Goths under Hun Domination', *Journal of Roman Studies* 79, 103–28

———— (1991). *Goths and Romans 332–489* (Oxford)

———— (1993). 'The Historical Culture of Ostrogothic Italy', in *Teoderico il grande e i Goti d'Italia*, Atti del XIII Congresso internazionale di studi sull'Alto Medioevo (Spoleto, 1993), 317–53

———— (1994a). 'Literacy and Power in the Migration Period', in Bowman and Woolf (1994), 177–97

———— (1994b). 'New Men for New Constantines? Creating an Imperial Elite in the Eastern Mediterranean', in P. Magdalino (ed.), *New Constantines: The Rhythm of Imperial Renewal in Byzantium, 4th–13th Centuries* (London), 11–33

———— (1995). 'The Huns and the End of the Roman Empire in Western Europe', *English Historical Review* 110, 4–41

———— (1996). *The Goths* (Oxford)

———— (2000). 'State, Lordship and Community in the West (c. AD 400–600)', in Averil Cameron et al. (2000), 437–68

———— (2001). 'The Late Roman Art of Client Management and the Grand Strategy Debate', in W. Pohl and I. N. Wood (eds), *The Transformation of Frontiers from Late Antiquity to the Carolingians*, Proceedings of the Second Plenary Conference, European Science Foundation Transformation of the Roman World Project (Brill), 15–68

———— (forthcoming a). 'Law and Identity in the Burgundian Kingdom', in Ausenda (forthcoming b)

———— (forthcoming b). *Emperors and Barbarians: Migration and State Formation in First-millennium Europe*.

———— and Matthews, J. F. (1991). *The Goths in the Fourth Century*, Translated Texts for Historians (Liverpool)

———— and Moncur, D. (trans.) (2001). *Politics, Philosophy and Empire in the Fourth Century: Select Orations of Themistius*, Translated Texts for Historians (Liverpool)

Hedeager, L. (1978). 'A Quantitative Analysis of Roman Imports in Europe North of the Limes (0–400 AD), and the Question of Roman-Germanic Exchange', *New*

Directions in Scandinavian Archaeology, ed. K. Kristiansen and C. Paludan-Muller (Copenhagen), 191–216

———— (1987). 'Empire, Frontier and the Barbarian Hinterland. Rome and Northern Europe from AD 1 to 400', in Rowlands et al. (1987), 125–40

Hendy, M. F. (1985). *Studies in the Byzantine Monetary Economy, c. 300–1450* (Cambridge)

Higham, N. (1992). *Rome, Britain and the Anglo-Saxons* (London)

Hoddinott, R. F. (1975). *Bulgaria in Antiquity: An Archaeological Introduction* (London)

Hoffmann, D. (1969). *Das spätrömische Bewegungsheer und die Notitia Dignitatum* (Düsseldorf)

Homes Dudden, F. (1935). *The Life and Times of St Ambrose* (Oxford)

Honoré, A. M. (1978). *Tribonian* (London)

———— (1994). *Emperors and Lawyers*, 2nd rev. edn (Oxford)

Hopkins, K. (1980). 'Taxes and Trade in the Roman Empire', *Journal of Roman Studies* 70, 101–25

Howard Johnson, J. D. (1995). 'The Two Great Powers of Late Antiquity: A Comparison', in Averil Cameron (ed.), *The Byzantine and Early Islamic Near East* vol. 3: *States, Resources and Armies* (Princeton), 123–78

Hussey, J. M. (1990). *The Orthodox Church in the Byzantine Empire* (Oxford)

Innes, M. (forthcoming). 'On the Social Dynamics of Barbarian Settlement: Land, Law, and Property in the Burgundian Kingdom', in Ausenda (forthcoming b)

Isaac, B. (1992). *The Limits of Empire: The Roman Army in the East* (Oxford)

James, E. (1988). *The Franks* (Oxford)

Jeffreys, E., et al. (trans.) (1986). *The Chronicle of John Malalas* (Melbourne)

Jones, A. H. M. (1964). *The Later Roman Empire: A Social, Economic and Administrative Survey*, 3 vols (Oxford)

Kagan, D. (1992). *The End of the Roman Empire*, 3rd edn (Lexington, Mass.)

Kaegi, W. (1968). *Byzantium and the Decline of Rome* (Princeton)

Kaster, R. A. (1988). *Guardians of Language: The Grammarian and Society in Late Antiquity* (Berkeley)

Kazanski, M. (1991). *Les Goths (Ier–VIIe siècles après J.-C.)* (Paris)

Keay, S., and Terrenato, N. (eds) (2001). *Italy and the West: Comparative Issues in Romanization* (Oxford)

Keegan, J. (1988), *The First World War* (London)

Keene, C. H., and Savage-Armstrong, G. F. (1907). *The Home-coming of Rutilius Claudius Namatianus from Rome to Gaul in the Year 416 AD* (London)

Kelly, C. M. (1994). 'Later Roman Bureaucracy: Going through the Files', in Bowman and Woolf (1994), 161–76

Keydell, R. (ed.) (1967). *Agathias Historiae*, Corpus Fontium Historiae Byzantinae (Berlin)

Klopsteg, P. E. (1927). *Turkish Archery and the Composite Bow* (Evanston, Ill.)

Klöse, J. (1934). *Roms Klientel-Randstaaten am Rhein und an der Donau: Beiträge zu ihrer Geschichte und rechtlichen Stellung im 1. und 2. Jhdt n. Chr.* (Breslau)

Kooi, B. W. (1991). 'On the Mechanics of the Modern Working-recurve Bow', *Computational Mechanics* 8, 291–304

———— (1994). 'The Design of the Bow', *Proceedings Koninklijke Nederlandse Akademie van Wetenschappen* 97(3), 283–309

Kopecek, T. A. (1979). *A History of Neo-Arianism* (Philadelphia)

Kossinna, G. (1928). *Ursprung und Verbreitung der Germanen in vor- und frühgeschichtlicher Zeit* (*The Origin of the Germani*) (Leipzig)

Krautheimer, R. (1980). *Rome: Profile of a City, 312–1308* (Princeton)

Kreuger, P. (ed.) (1877). *Corpus Iuris Civilis* (Berlin)

Krusch, B. (ed.) (1888). *Liber Historiae Francorum*, MGH, scriptores rerum merovingicarum 2 (Berlin)

———— and Levison, W. (eds) (1951). *Gregory of Tours Historiae*, MGH, scriptores rerum merovingicarum 1. 1 (Berlin)

Laszlo, Gy (1951). 'The Golden Bow of the Huns', *Acta Archaeologica Hungaricae* 1, 91–106

Lattimore, O. (1940). *Inner Asian Frontiers of China* (Oxford)

Leeman, A. D. (1963). *Orationis Ratio: The Stylistic Theories and Practice of the Roman Orators, Historians and Philosophers* (Amsterdam)

Lemerle, P. (1971). *Le premier humanisme byzantin* (Paris)

———— (ed. and French trans.) (1979–81). *Les plus anciens recueils des miracles de Saint Démétrius* (Paris)

Lengyel, A., and Radan, G. T. B. (eds) (1980). *The Archaeology of Roman Pannonia* (Budapest)

Lenski, N. (1995). 'The Gothic Civil War and the Date of the Gothic Conversion', *Greek, Roman and Byzantine Studies* 36, 51–87

———— (2002). *Failure of Empire: Valens and the Roman State in the Fourth Century* AD (Berkeley)

Lepelley, C. (1979–81). *Les Cités de l'Afrique romaine au Bas-Empire* (Paris)

Lewitt, T. (1991). *Agricultural Production in the Roman Economy* AD 200–400 (Oxford)

Liebeschuetz, J. H. W. G. (1972). *Antioch: City and Imperial Administration in the Later Roman Empire* (Oxford)

———— (1990). *Barbarians and Bishops: Army, Church and State in the Age of Arcadius and John Chrysostom* (Oxford)

———— (1997). 'Cities, Taxes and the Accommodation of the Barbarians: The Theories of Durliat and Goffart', in W. Pohl (ed.), *Kingdoms of the Empire: The Integration of Barbarians in Late Antiquity* (Leiden), 135–52

Lindner, R. (1981). 'Nomadism, Huns and Horses', *Past and Present* 92, 1–19

Linebaugh, P. (1991). *The London Hanged: Crime and Civil Society in the Eighteenth Century* (London)

Lomanto, V. (1983). *A Concordance to Symmachus* (Hildesheim)

Lot, F. (1939). *Les invasions germaniques: La pénétration mutuelle du monde barbare et du monde romain* (Paris)

Lotter, F. (1976). *Severinus von Noricum, Legende und historische Wirklichkeit: Unters. zur Phase d. Übergangs von spätantiken zu mittelalterl. Denk-u. Lebensformen* (Stuttgart)

McAdams, R. (1965). *Land behind Baghdad: A History of Settlement on the Diyala Plains* (Chicago)

MacCormack, S. A. (1981). *Art and Ceremony in Late Antiquity* (Los Angeles and Berkeley)

McCormick, M. (1986). *Eternal Victory: Triumphal Rulership in Late Antiquity, Byzantium and the Early Medieval West* (Cambridge)

MacGeorge, P. (2002). *Late Roman Warlords* (Oxford)

McLynn, N. (1994). *Ambrose of Milan* (Berkeley)

MacMullen, R. (1963). *Soldier and Civilian in the Later Roman Empire* (Cambridge, Mass.)

—————— (1988). *Corruption and the Decline of Rome* (New Haven, Conn.)

Maenchen-Helfen, O. J. (1945). 'Huns and Hsiung-Nu', *Byzantion* 17, 222–43

—————— (1973). *The World of the Huns* (Berkeley)

Mango, C. (1985). *Le Développement urbain de Constantinople (IVe–VIIe siècles)*, Travaux et Mémoires, Monographies 2 (Paris)

—————— and Scott, R. (trans.) (1997). *Chronographia, The Chronicle of Theophanes Confessor* (Oxford)

Manton, E. L. (1988). *Roman North Africa* (London)

Markus, R. A. (1990). *The End of Ancient Christianity* (Cambridge)

—————— (1997). *Gregory the Great and his World* (Cambridge)

Matthews, J. F. (1970). 'Olympiodorus of Thebes and the History of the West (AD 407–425)', *Journal of Roman Studies* 60, 79–97 (Matthews (1985), no. III)

—————— (1971). 'Gallic Supporters of Theodosius', *Latomus* 30, 1073–99 (= Matthews (1985), no. IX)

—————— (1974). 'The Letters of Symmachus', in J. W. Binns (ed.), *Latin Literature of the Fourth Century* (London), 58–99 (= Matthews (1985), no. IV)

—————— (1975). *Western Aristocracies and the Imperial Court AD 364–425* (Oxford)

—————— (1985). *Political Life and Culture in Late Roman Society* (London)

—————— (1986). 'Symmachus and His Enemies' in F. Paschoud et al. (eds), *Colloque genevois sur Symmaque: à l'occasion du mille-six-centième anniversaire du conflit de l'autel de la Victoire* (Paris), 160–75

—————— (1989). *The Roman Empire of Ammianus* (London)

—————— (2000). *Laying Down the Law: A Study of the Theodosian Code* (New Haven, Conn.)

Mattingly, D. J. (2002). 'Vulgar and weak "Romanization", or Time for a Paradigm Shift?', *Journal of Roman Archaeology* 15, 163–7

—————— and Hitchner, R. B. (1995). 'Roman Africa: An Archaeological Review', *Journal of Roman Studies* 85, 165–213

Mattingly, G. (2002). *The Defeat of the Spanish Armada* (London)

Meiggs, R. (1973). *Roman Ostia* (Oxford)

Menghin, W. et al. (1987). *Germanen, Hunnen und Awaren: Schätze der Völkerwanderungszeit* (Nuremberg)

Mierow, C. C. (trans.) (1915). *Jordanes Getica* (New York)

Millar, F. (1992). *The Emperor in the Roman World*, 2nd edn (London)

—————— (1993). *The Roman Near East 31 BC–AD 337* (Harvard)

Mocsy, A. (1974). *Pannonia and Upper Moesia* (London)

Moderan, Y. (forthcoming). 'The *Notitia* of the Province of Africa 484 and Huneric's Persecution', in Ausenda (forthcoming a)

Momigliano, A. (1955). 'Cassiodorus and the Italian Culture of His Time', *Proceedings of the British Academy* 41, 215–48

Mommsen, Th. (ed.) (1882). *Jordanes Romana et Getica*, MGH, auctores antiquissimi 5. 1 (1882)

————— (ed.) (1892). *Chronica Minora 1*, MGH, auctores antiquissimi 9 (Berlin)

————— (ed.) (1894). *Chronica Minora 2*, MGH, auctores antiquissimi 11 (Berlin)

————— (1901). 'Aetius', *Hermes* lxxvi, 516–47

————— (1910). 'Das römische Militarwesen seit Diocletian', in *Gesammelte Schriften*, vol. 6 (Berlin), 206–83

————— and Kreuger, P. (eds) (1905). *Codex Theodosianus* (Berlin)

Moorhead, J. (trans.) (1992). *Victor of Vita: History of the Persecution in Africa* (Liverpool)

Mueller, K. (ed.) (1851–70). *Fragmenta Historicorum Graecorum*, vols 4–5 (Paris)

Musset, L. (1965). *Les invasions: Les vagues germaniques* (Paris)

Niebuhr, B. G. (ed.) (1839–41). *Theophanes Chronographia* (Bonn)

Nixon, C. E. V., and Rogers, B. S. (ed. and trans.) (1994). *In Praise of Later Roman Emperors: The Panegyrici Latini* (Berkeley)

Noble, T. F. X. (1990). 'Literacy and the Papal Government', in R. McKitterick (ed.), *The Uses of Literacy in Early Mediaeval Europe* (Cambridge), 82–108

Noll, R., and Vetter, E. (eds) (1963). *Eugippius Vita Sancti Severini*, Schriften und Quellen der Alten Welt 11 (Berlin)

Norman, A. F. (trans.) (1992). *Libanius: Autobiography and Select Letters*, 2 vols, Loeb (Cambridge, Mass.)

O'Flynn, J. M. (1983). *Generalissimos of the Western Roman Empire* (Edmonton, Alta)

Oost, S. (1968). *Galla Placidia Augusta: A Biographical Essay* (Chicago)

Ørsnes, M. (1968). *Der Moorfund von Ejsbøl bei Hadersleben. Deutungsprobleme der grossen nordgermanischen Waffenopferfunde*, Abhandlung der Akademie der Wissenschaft in Göttingen (Göttingen)

Paschoud, F. (ed. and French trans.) (1971–81). *Zosimus Historia Nova* (Paris)

Pearson, A. (2002). *The Roman Shore Forts: Coastal Defences of Southern Britain* (Stroud)

Percival, J. (1976). *The Roman Villa* (London)

Petrovic, P. (ed.) (1996). *Roman Limes on the Middle and Lower Danube* (Belgrade)

Pharr, C. (1952). *The Theodosian Code and Novels, and the Sirmondian Constitutions* (New York)

Platnauer, M. (ed. and trans.) (1922). *The Works of Claudian* (London)

Pohl, W. (1980). 'Die Gepiden und die *Gentes* an der mittleren Donau nach dem Zerfall des Attilareiches', in Wolfram and Daim (1980), 239–305

————— (1988). *Die Awaren: Ein Steppenvolk im Mitteleuropa, 567–822 n. Chr.* (Beck)

Poulter, A. G. (1995). *Nicopolis ad Istrum: A Roman, Late Roman, and Early Byzantine City: Excavations 1985–1992* (London)

————— (1999). 'The Transition to Late Antiquity on the Lower Danube: An Interim Report (1996–8)', *Antiquaries Journal* 79, 145–85

Prakash, G., et al. (1994). 'American Historical Review Forum: Subaltern Studies as Postcolonial Criticism', *American Historical Review* 99, 5

Ramsay, A. M. (1925). 'The Speed of the Imperial Post', *Journal of Roman Studies* 15, 60–74

Rau, G. (1972). 'Körpergraber mit Glasbeigaben des 4. nachschristlichen Jahrhunderts im Oder-Wechsel-Raum', *Acta praehistorica et archaeologica* 3, 109–214

Raven, S. (1993) *Rome in Africa*, 3rd edn (London)

Rawson E. (1975). *Cicero: A Portrait* (London)

Renfrew, C., and Bahn, P. (1991). *Archaeology: Theories, Methods and Practice* (London)

Reuter, T. (1985). 'Plunder and Tribute in the Carolingian Empire', *Transactions of the Royal Historical Society*, 5th ser. 35, 75–94

————— (1990). 'The End of Carolingian Military Expansion', in P. Godman and R. Collins (eds), *Charlemagne's Heir: New Perspectives on the Reign of Louis the Pious* (Oxford), 391–405

Riché, P. (1976). *Education and Culture in the Barbarian West, Sixth through Eighth Centuries*, trans. J. J. Contreni (Columbia)

Ridley R. T. (trans.) (1982). *Zosimus New History* (Canberra)

Roberts, C. H., and Turner, E. G. (eds) (1952). *Catalogue of the Greek and Latin Papyri in the John Rylands Library, Manchester*, vol. 4 (Manchester)

Roberts, M. (1989). *The Jeweled Style: Poetry and Poetics in Late Antiquity* (Ithaca)

————— (1992), 'Barbarians in Gaul: The Response of the Poets', in Drinkwater and Elton (1992), 97–106

Robinson, O. F. (1992). *The Sources of Roman Law* (London)

Roda, S. (1981). 'Una nuova lettera di Simmaco ad Ausonio? (a proposito di Symm. Ep. IX, 88)', *Revue des Études Anciennes* 83, 273–80

Rolfe, J. C. (ed.) (1935–9). Ammianus Marcellinus, Loeb (London)

Rostovtzeff, M. (1957) *The Social and Economic History of the Roman Empire*, 2nd edn, rev. P. Fraser (Oxford)

Roueché, C. (1989). *Aphrodisias in Late Antiquity: The Late Roman and Byzantine Inscriptions* (London)

Rowlands, M., et al. (eds) (1987). *Centre and Periphery in the Ancient World* (Cambridge)

Rubin, Z. (1986). 'The Mediterranean and the Dilemma of the Roman Empire in Late Antiquity', *Mediterranean Historical Review* 1, 13–62

Runciman, S. (1929). *The Emperor Romanus Lecapenus and His Reign: A Study of Tenth-century Byzantium* (Cambridge)

St Croix, G. de (1981). *The Class Struggle in the Ancient Greek World* (London)

Salway, P. (1981). *Roman Britain* (Oxford)

Santini, C. (ed.) (1979). *Eutropius Breviarium ab urbe condita* (Stuttgart)

Schenkl, H., et al. (eds) (1965–74). *Themistii Orationes* (Leipzig)

Schutz, H. (1983). *The Prehistory of Germanic Europe* (New Haven, Conn.)

Scorpan, C. (1980). *Limes Scythiae: Topographical and Stratigraphical Research on the Late Roman Fortifications on the Lower Danube* (Oxford)

Shaw, B. (1995a). *Environment and Society in North Africa: Studies in History and Archaeology* (Aldershot)

BIBLIOGRAPHY 549

———— (1995b). *Rulers, Nomads and Christians in North Africa* (Aldershot)

Shchukin, M. B. (1989). *Rome and the Barbarians in Central and Eastern Europe: 1st Century BC–1st Century AD* (Oxford)

Seeck, O. (ed.) (1876). *Notitia Dignitatum omnium tam civilum quam militarum* (Berlin)

———— (ed.) (1883). *Symmachus quae supersunt* (Berlin)

Sinor, D. (1977). *Inner Asia and Its Contacts with Medieval Europe* (London)

Sivan, H. (1985). 'An Unedited Letter of the Emperor Honorius to the Spanish Soldiers', *Zeitschrift für Papyrologie und Epigraphik* lxi, 273–87

Smith, R. (1999). 'Telling Tales: Ammianus' Narrative of the Persian Expedition', in J. W. Drijvers and D. Hunt (eds), *The Late Roman World and Its Historian: Interpreting Ammianus Marcellinus* (London), 89–104

Stallknecht, B. (1969). *Untersuchungen zur römischen Aussenpolitik in der Spätantike* (Bonn)

Stein, E. (1959). *Histoire du Bas Empire*, trans. J. R. Palanque (Paris)

Stevens, C. E. (1933). *Sidonius Apollinaris and His Age* (Oxford)

Stickler, T. (2002). *Aetius: Gestaltungsspielraume eines Heermeisters im ausgehenden Weströmischen Reich*, Vestigia 54 (Beck)

Tate, G. (1989). 'Les campagnes de la Syrie du Nord a l'époque proto-Byzantine', in C. Morrisson and J. Lefort (eds), *Hommes et richesses dans l'antiquité byzantine* (Paris), 63–77

Tchalenko, G. (1953–8). *Villages antiques de la Syrie du Nord* (Paris)

Tejral, J., et al. (eds) (1999). *L'Occident romain et l'Europe centrale au début de l'époque des Grandes Migrations* (Brno)

Thompson, E. A. (1945). 'Priscus of Panium, Fragment 1b', *Classical Quarterly* 39, 92–4

———— (1946). 'The Isaurians under Theodosius II', *Hermathena* 48, 18–31

———— (1950). 'The Foreign Policy of Theodosius II and Marcian', *Hermathena* 76, 58–78

———— (1956). 'The Settlement of the Barbarians in Southern Gaul', *Journal of Roman Studies* 46, 65–75

———— (1982a). 'The End of Noricum', in Thompson (1982c), 113–35

———— (1982b). 'Hydatius and the Invasion of Spain', in Thompson (1982c), 137–60

———— (1982c). *Romans and Barbarians: The Decline of the Western Empire* (Wisconsin)

———— (1996). *The Huns* (Oxford)

Thorpe, L. (trans.) (1974), *Gregory of Tours: The History of the Franks* (London)

Tjäder, J.-O. (1972). 'Der Codex argenteus in Uppsala und der Buchmeister Viliaric in Ravenna', in U. E. Hagberg (ed.), *Studia Gotica* (Stockholm), 144–64

Todd, M. (1975). *The Northern Barbarians 100 BC–AD 300* (London)

———— (1992). *The Early Germans* (Oxford)

Toynbee, A. (1973). *Constantine Porphyrogenitus and His World* (London)

Trout, D. E. (1999). *Paulinus of Nola: Life, Letters, and Poems* (Berkeley)

Twitchett, D., and Loewe, M. (1986). *Cambridge History of China*, vol. 1 (Cambridge)

Urbancyzk, P. (1997). 'Changes of Power Structure During the 1st Millennium AD in the Northern Part of Central Poland', in P. Urbancyzk (ed.), *Origins of Central Europe* (Warsaw), 39–44

Van Dam, R. (2003). *Becoming Christian: The Conversion of Roman Cappadocia* (Philadelphia)

Van Es, W. A. (1967). *Wijster: A Native Village beyond the Imperial Frontier 150–425 AD* (Gröningen)

Várady, L. (1969). *Das Letzte Jahrhundert Pannoniens: 376–476* (Amsterdam)

Vasiliev, A. A. (1936). *The Goths in the Crimea* (Cambridge)

Viereck, H. D. L. (1975). *Die Römische Flotte* (Herford)

Vogel, F. (ed.) (1885). *Ennodius Opera*, MGH, auctores antiquissimi 7 (Berlin)

Von Salis, L. R. (ed.) (1892). *Liber Constitutionum*, MGH, leges nationum germanicarum 2.1 (Hanover)

Walbank, F. W. (1969). *The Awful Revolution: The Decline of the Roman Empire in the West* (Liverpool)

Wallace-Hadrill, J. M. (1961). 'Gothia and Romania', *Bulletin of the John Rylands Library, Manchester* 44/1

Wanke, U. (1990). *Die Gotenkriege des Valens: Studien zu Topographie und Chronologie im unteren Donauraum von 366 bis 378 n. Chr.* (Frankfurt am Main)

Ward Perkins, B. (2000). 'Land, Labour and Settlement', in Averil Cameron et al. (eds) (2000), 315–45

Wells, P. S. (2003). *The Battle That Stopped Rome* (New York)

Whitby, L. M. (2002). *Rome at War AD 229–696* (Oxford)

——— and Whitby, J. M. (trans.) (1986). *The History of Theophylact Simocatta* (Oxford)

——— and Whitby, J. M. (trans.) (1989). *The Chronicon Paschale* (Liverpool)

Whittaker, C. R. (1976). 'Agri Deserti', in M. I. Finley (ed.), *Studies in Roman Property*, 137–65, 193–200

——— (1994). *Frontiers of the Roman Empire: A Social and Economic Study* (Baltimore)

——— and Garnsey, P. (1998). 'Rural Life in the Later Roman Empire', in Averil Cameron and P. Garnsey (eds), *The Cambridge Ancient History*, 2nd edn, vol. 13 (Cambridge), 277–311

Whittow, M. (1996). *The Making of Orthodox Byzantium, 600–1025* (London)

Wickham, C. (1992). 'Problems of Comparing Rural Societies in Early Medieval Western Europe', *Transactions of the Royal Historical Society*, 6th ser. 2, 221–46

——— (1993). 'La chute de Rome n'aura pas lieu. À propos d'un livre récent', *Le Moyen Age* 99, 107–26

Wightman, E. M. (1967). *Roman Trier and the Treveri* (London)

Wilkes, J. J. (1969). *Dalmatia* (London)

Wolfram, H. (1967). *Intitulatio 1: Lateinische Königs- und Fürstentitel bis zum Ende des 8. Jahrhunderts*, Mitteilungen des Instituts für österreichische Geschichtsforschung, Ergangzungsband 21 (Vienna)

——— (1985). *Treasures on the Danube: Barbarian Invaders and Their Roman Inheritance* (Vienna)

——— (1988). *History of the Goths*, trans. T. J. Dunlap (Berkeley)

———— and Daim, F. (eds) (1980). *Die Völker an der mittleren und unteren Donau im fünften und sechsten Jahrhundert*, Denkschriften der Österreichischen Akademie der Wissenschaften, Phil.-Hist. Kl. 145 (Vienna)

Wood, I. N. (1994). *The Merovingian Kingdoms* (London)

Woolf, G. (1998). *Becoming Roman: The Origins of Provincial Civilization in Gaul* (Cambridge)

Wormald, P. (1999). *The Making of English Law: King Alfred to the Twelfth Century*, vol. 1 (Oxford)

Wright, W. C. (1913). *The Works of the Emperor Julian*, 3 vols (London)

Wuensch, R. (ed.) (1898). *Ioannis Laurentii Lydi Liber de mensibus* (Leipzig)

Yarshater, E. (ed.) (1984–2004, ongoing). *Encyclopaedia Iranica* (London)

Zecchini, G. (1983). *Aezio: l'ultima difesa dell'Occidente romano* (Rome)

Zeumer, K. (ed.) (1902). *Leges Visigothorum* (Hanover)

INDEX